Recent Trends in Social and Behavior Science

Recent Trends in Social and Behavior Science

Edited by Chayma Hamdani

Clanrye International
www.clanryeinternational.com

Clanrye International,
750 Third Avenue, 9th Floor,
New York, NY 10017, USA

ISBN: 978-1-63240-732-0

Cataloging-in-Publication Data

Recent trends in social and behavior science / edited by Chayma Hamdani.
p. cm.
Includes bibliographical references and index.
ISBN 978-1-63240-732-0
1. Social Sciences. 2. Psychology. 3. Behavioral assessment. 4. Social psychology.
I. Hamdani, Chayma.
H61 .R43 2018
300.1--dc23

For information on all Clanrye International publications
visit our website at www.clanryeinternational.com

CLANRYE INTERNATIONAL

Printed in China.

Contents

Preface

It is often said that books are a boon to mankind. They document every progress and pass on the knowledge from one generation to the other. They play a crucial role in our lives. Thus I was both excited and nervous while editing this book. I was pleased by the thought of being able to make a mark but I was also nervous to do it right because the future of students depends upon it. Hence, I took a few months to research further into the discipline, revise my knowledge and also explore some more aspects. Post this process, I begun with the editing of this book.

Social science is an umbrella discipline integrating principles from political science, psychology, economics, sociology, anthropology, etc. to study in detail the dynamics of the society. Behavioral science is an allied field of social science which is concerned with understanding the behavior of humans. The integration of social and behavioral sciences helps in analyzing the relationships between individuals and also their relationship with their environment. This book is a compilation of chapters that discuss the most vital concepts and emerging trends in this field. Scientists and students actively engaged in this field will benefit from this book.

I thank my publisher with all my heart for considering me worthy of this unparalleled opportunity and for showing unwavering faith in my skills. I would also like to thank the editorial team who worked closely with me at every step and contributed immensely towards the successful completion of this book. Last but not the least, I wish to thank my friends and colleagues for their support.

Editor

Social versus Spatial Mobility? Mongolia's Pastoralists in the Educational Development Discourse

Ines Stolpe

Mongolian Studies, Bonn University, 53113 Bonn, Germany; E-Mail: istolpe@uni-bonn.de

Abstract

When it comes to education for mobile pastoralists, Mongolia is an exceptional case. Until fifty years ago, herders comprised the majority of the Mongolian population. Although a satellite of the Soviet Union, the Mongolian People's Republic was a state in which mobile pastoralism was not challenged, and herders were not constructed as social outcasts. Equally exceptional was the country's modernisation, witnessed in its decided alignment with equal opportunities. In Mongolia, it was not 'nomadism' that was associated with backwardness, but illiteracy. Policy-makers aimed to combine spatial with social mobility by building schools further and further out in the grasslands, employing locals as teachers, and fostering interplay between modern formal education and extensive animal husbandry. Yet after 1990, when development discourse pigeon-holed post-socialist Mongolia as a Third World country, the so-called shock therapy led to severe cuts in education. Herders were essentialised as 'nomads', which caused donor-driven policies of educational planning to construe pastoralists as challenges. Ironically, during the initial decade of *Education for All,* the younger generation had—for the first time in Mongolia's history—less educational opportunities than their parents. This article discusses narratives of inclusion and the political consequences of ascribed social identities.

Keywords

development discourse; essentialism; inclusion; nomads; postsocialism; social and spatial mobility

Issue

This article is part of the issue "Educating Nomadic People", edited by Caroline Dyer (University of Leeds, UK).

---

1. Introduction

Mongolia[1] is the least densely populated state in the world (1.8 people per square km), and has the largest contiguous common grasslands. Mongolia's herders have experienced drastic changes over the last twenty-five years during the so-called "transition".[2] Today, half of Mongolia's three million inhabitants cluster in the capital Ulaanbaatar; around 30% live in rural areas. Rural-urban migration was prompted largely by the neglect of rural areas, consecutive economic crises, and environmental degradation, but also by climate change and the mining boom. Although the country maintained high levels of education, the demographic changes caused by massive rural-to-urban migration led to alarming disparities between Mongolia's few urban centres and its rural areas. 47.8% of the rural population are now considered below the poverty line, and poor households show a high rate (20.5%) of having either no education or only a primary education. Agriculture, including herding, accounts for 18.1–23% of

[1] This article focuses on the Mongolian state (self-designated as *Mongol Uls*), the former Mongolian Peoples' Republic (1924–92), which is also known as Outer Mongolia. For studies on minority education in the Inner Mongolia Autonomous Region in PR China, see Leibold and Yangbin (2014).

[2] Former socialist countries, which used to belong to the so-called 'Second World', were classified as 'transition countries' in 1990 under the assumption that they would perform their "transition to a new order" (Innes-Brown, 2001, p. 77) by following Western ideas. The "prescribed pillars of transition" (Kerven, 2003, p. 16) were privatisation, deregulation, and withdrawal of the state.

Mongolia's GDP and provides work for 34–38.5% of the country's labour force. 92% of countryside inhabitants own livestock, as do 54% of county-centre residents and 17% of province-centre dwellers. The number of livestock, which had remained relatively stable between 22-25 million animals for fifty years, has nearly doubled since 1990—the number of cashmere goats has even quadrupled—at the cost of pasture degradation (United Nations Development Programme & Government of Mongolia, 2011, pp. 33-47).

Before the political changes of 1990, mobile herders were not characterized as 'nomads', and they were neither marginalised, nor educationally deprived. This article shows how the recent discursive 'nomadisation' of herders contributed to a dispossession of their previously well-respected status. In Mongolia, narratives of 'inclusion' are inseparably linked to constructions of social stratification, which in turn have been constituted by development discourses (Stolpe, 2008).

Hardly any state is so heavily associated with nomadism as Mongolia. Mongolians are portrayed as 'nomads' par excellence—whether in movies, picture books, photo exhibitions or at the International Tourism Fair, where Mongolia was featured as the official partner country with the slogan *Nomadic by Nature* in spring 2015. Yet those who live as mobile pastoralists have never labelled themselves 'nomads'. Until the mid-twentieth century, the majority of the Mongolian population was engaged in extensive pastoralism. Thus, as the norm, the mobile way of life did not require any contrastive terminology. Nowadays, the academic world widely agrees that "Nomadism is a category imagined by outsiders" (Humphrey & Sneath, 1999, p. 1), an external ascription of difference. Mongolian academics have criticised the emerging boom of a discursive 'nomadisation' as ingratiation with external perceptions. Dorjgotov (2002, p. 109) pointed out, "If we call ourselves *nomadic people* it will mean that we are simply a homeless tribe or people having no permanent abode. What kind of people will we be after all?" The quote indicates that the new nomad-image appears alien because it is implicitly associated with backwardness. Moreover, as Myadar (2011, p. 335) noted, the image serves "the habit of outsiders to construct an imagined Other and the need of Mongolians for cultural demarcation".

When today's urban Mongolians present their state as a 'country of nomads', they take up a common—and profitable—stereotype. Whether in tourism, research environments, development policy, or with regard to postmodern lifestyles, fascination with 'nomadism' is undiminished. More often than not, the ascription of this collective identity is associated with quite abstruse "myths of the nomad" (Khazanov, 1984/1994, p. 1), which derive their attraction from the binary opposition nomadic-sedentary. Not without reason, Chakrabarty (2000, p. 6) stated that European categories are "both indispensible and inadequate". In Mongolia, the stylisation as a 'country of nomads' is exclusively present in cosmopolitan settings, which indicates the political dimensions of cultural representation. Clammer (2003, p. 21) characterised the process of "mapping the Self with the categories of the Other" as "intellectual colonialism." When examining terminological change, I follow Clammer's suggestion to use a methodology "that might move beyond the temptations of either Orientalism or Occidentalism", particularly with regard to two aspects:

> First, recognition of the extent to which local readings of Asian societies using the disciplinary frameworks of Western academic subjects with their built-in epistemological biases is at the basis of self-misrepresentations, as much as it is the source of Orientalist misrepresentations. Second, paying serious attention to indigenous social theory and refusing the temptation to dismiss it as 'nativist'. (2003, pp. 28-29)

The Mongolian case features an additional dimension: before and after the Cold War, two contrary development paradigms determined the designation of herders, which reflected a change in the political frame of reference and entailed a shift in the external audience addressed. Mongolian categories remained largely untouched by these changes (but also largely ignored). Today's one-sided adaptation to hegemonic categories of the West may be motivated by strategic and/or pragmatic reasons; however, its associated homogenisation inevitably obscures distinctive cultural features. In order to shed light on the interplay of self-perception and ascribed attributes as well as their implications for the development discourse, let me start by giving a brief historical account of canonised narratives on Mongolian herders.[3]

2. Shifting Paradigms—Inclusive and Exclusive Terms of Reference

Those who engage in extensive animal husbandry have never called themselves 'nomads'; instead, their endonym has always been *malchid*, [4] a de-nominal derivation from *mal* (i.e. Mongolian livestock: horses, sheep, cattle, goats, and camels). The oldest surviving literary historiography, the *Secret History of the Mongols*, provides information on a self-designation as "people with

[3] For a complementary analysis of Mongolian educational terms, see Stolpe (2010).

[4] The spelling of modern Mongolian words follows the established convention widely accepted in English-language literature. Terms in quotations and names in references remain in their original form. Unless otherwise indicated, all materials appear in the author's translation.

felt-wall dwellings" (Taube, 2005, p. 139)—a medieval version of defining an ethnoscape (Appadurai, 1996) via this particular kind of mobile housing (commonly *yurt*, in Mongolian *ger*).

Since the 1990s, Mongolia-related English publications have used the term 'nomads' only reluctantly; instead, they have preferred 'herders', 'pastoralists' or 'herdsmen' (Fernández-Giménez & Huntsinger, 1999; Ginsburg, 1997; Mearns, 1993a, 1993b; Schmidt, 1995; Sneath, 1996, 1999, 2000; Szynkiewicz, 1998). This reluctance to use the term 'nomadism' mirrors an awareness that has arisen from the orientalism debates. While we hardly find 'nomadism' in the writings themselves, the term features prominently in book titles (Ginat & Khazanov, 1998; Humphrey & Sneath, 1999; Krätli, 2000 Stolpe, 2008; Tavakolian, 2003). Publications that have been translated from Mongolian into English also use the terms 'herders' or 'breeders', as they come closest to the original *malchid* (cf. Gundsambuu, 2002; Namkhainyambuu, 2000; Natsagdorj, 1967). In contrast to *malchid*, which dominates Mongolian discourses, *nüüdelchid*—the equivalent for 'nomads'—has been used primarily in historical accounts that deal with the emergence of human life in Central Asia (Ganbaatar, 2001; Lkhagva, 2003; Tömörjav, 1989; Tsanjid, 2005). Exceptions are publications by the *International Institute for the Study of Nomadic Civilisations,* where Mongolian authors have adapted their wording to fit the 'nomadism' programme (cf. Avdai et al., 2003; Enebish, 2002; Sum'yaa, 2005; Tömörjav, 2002). This terminological change towards 'nomads' and 'nomadism' applies all the more for English publications by Mongolian scholars (Enebish, 2004; Enkhtuvshin, 2002, 2004; Enkhtuvshin & Tumurjav, 2001). Although such terms were hardly used by Mongolian scholars prior to the end of the 1990s, they are currently booming. Apart from obvious pragmatic reasons, including a seemingly convenient translatability, the term 'nomad' provides considerable advantages in the struggle to gain attention—whether in tourism, pop culture, research proposals, or development projects. In this way, Mongolian 'nomads' are an invention of post-socialism.

During socialism, in all texts that were directed at an external audience, the discursive space that is today occupied by 'nomad' was the domain of *arat*. Within the socialist camp, this conception had evolved to become *the* established term for designating Mongolian herders, while it remained largely unknown on the other side of the Iron Curtain. Before the Mongolian revolution, *arat* was used to describe a certain group of herders through reference to property and ownership relations (cf. Natsagdorj, 1967). Sneath (2003) noted that, when the Mongolian Peoples' Republic was founded in 1924, no equivalent for the term 'people' existed. Since *arat* (correct in Mongolian: *arad/ard*) means 'common people/commoner', it came closest to the understanding of 'people' as intended in accordance with Marxist class theory. Given that Mongolia had neither a proletariat nor peasants, *arat* became their functional equivalent. Accordingly, the constitution of 1940 stated that the Mongolian Peoples' Republic was an independent state of working people, *arat*-herders, workers, and intelligentsia. Soon after, the notion of *arat* underwent another transformation: from class categorization to professional designation. Regardless of whether they had a formal education, herders were ascribed the status of well-respected professionals, and their societal acknowledgment was undoubted.

When comparing the disparate impact of the two terms used to address a foreign audience (the self-designation *malchid* has remained), the term *arat* has clearly created a positive collective identity. Ideologically-ridden or not, associating herders with 'the people' and equating their work with every other profession enabled *arats* to actively take part in modernization. Consequently, they were considered mainstream, and hence portrayed neither as exceptional nor as marginalised. In addition to its professional status, pastoralism was esteemed as a primary source of valuable indigenous knowledge—including on the philosophy of education—in countless Mongolian publications issued during socialism (Dash, 1966; Shagdarsüren, 1969; Sükhee, 1988; Tömörjav, 1989; retrospective: Chagdaa, 2002; Shagdar, 2000). In contrast, the post-socialist construction of the term 'nomad' came as an act of othering and caused pastoralists to be characterized as a challenge by donor-driven development policies. As will be shown below, the political dimension of social identities strongly influenced how "societies stratify and divide...and how the processes that include and exclude are talked about, described, understood, and experienced" (Allman, 2013, p. 6).

Pastoralism and education policy in the Mongolian People's Republic were once closely interconnected, aiming at combining spatial with social mobility. Yet, donor agencies, which dominated the formulation of Mongolian education policies after the end of socialism, denied this unique combination when they equated Mongolia with 'developing countries'. The term *arat* was replaced by 'nomad' at the same time Mongolia was downgraded from a Second World to a Third World country. These changing representations did not remain at a discursive level, but structured political action guided by a development paradigm, which did not favour social inclusion. Furthermore, there was a widespread tendency to condemn everything associated with socialism for ideological reasons and to simply equate Mongolia with the Soviet Union; in an orthodox narrative, nomadism and socialism are considered antipodes with the latter attempting to abolish the first by means of settlement. Such black-and-white thinking usually ignores two aspects: first, nomadism had been considered an outdated, inefficient way of life and an obstacle to modernization on *either* side of the Iron Curtain (cf. Dyer, 2001; Fratkin, 1997; Galaty & Johnson, 1990; Krätli, 2000). Second, forced settlement is, more often than not (especially under post-socialist conditions), connected to privatisation, poverty, and land grabbing. Throughout post-socialist Central Asia, pastoralists' mobility decreased after 1990 (cf. Kerven, 2003), and Mongolia is no exception to this trend.

However, the country used to be exceptional: although the Mongolian Peoples' Republic was strongly influenced by its 'elder brother to the North' (*khoid akh*), nomadism policy was one of the spheres in which the satellite kept a considerable distance from its leading star. Unlike pastoralists in Soviet Central Asia, herders in the MPR were spared settlement programmes since pastoralism was acknowledged as the key branch of Mongolia's agriculture. Another area in which the MPR kept its distance from Soviet policy was collectivisation. While it was pushed through violently in the Soviet Republics, the first attempt in the MPR was cancelled because of uprisings. The second attempt was not made until thirty years later and resulted in the desired success due to incentive-based procedures and improvements in overall conditions (cf. Finke, 2000, 2004; Humphrey & Sneath, 1999; Szynkiewicz, 1998; Tömörjav, 2002). Consequently, "Pastoralism did not experience any economic, political or ideological marginalisation in Mongolia because its importance in economic respects and its being a fundamental feature of traditional Mongolian culture was generally acknowledged" (Finke, 2004, p. 398).

The collectivisation of livestock was complemented by services provided through modern institutions like schools, hospitals, post-offices, veterinary stations, shops, cultural centres, and libraries. The presence of rural centres is sometimes interpreted as an indicator of settlement policy, although, as comparative studies have shown, the mere existence of immobile infrastructures does not imply decreasing spatial mobility (Humphrey & Sneath, 1999). There is a broad consensus that the successful combination of mobile and sedentary lifestyles in the course of modernisation led to mutual integration, which Mongolian scholars capture in a nutshell with the phrase *neg uls, khoyor irgenshil*—"one state, two civilisations" (Bira, 1998/1999; Chagdaa, 2002; Chuluunbaatar, 2002; Gundsambuu, 2002). This wording is by no means coincidental since civilisation is associated with modernity and progress. Both are unthinkable without social mobility. It is fair to say that the Mongolian Peoples' Republic was probably the only state with a "nomad-mainstreaming" (Stolpe, 2015, p. 28) strategy, since MPR state policy—as well as institutions—aimed to promote equal opportunities. By the end of the 1960s, the MPR was the first state in Asia to achieve general literacy through universal basic education; for its success, the MPR was awarded a UNESCO medal in 1970 (Dorzhsuren, 1981, p. 109; Sandhaasüren & Shernossek, 1981, p. 12). In discussing equal opportunities, another unique feature should be mentioned: the inverse gender gap. Since gender balance was reached in the 1970s, Mongolian educational institutions have had a higher proportion of female graduates. By the end of socialism, Mongolia had a literacy rate of 96.5% (Mongol Ulsyn Zasgyn Gazar & UNDP, 1997, p. 7). Thus, a country shaped by mobile animal husbandry had "a higher literacy rate than the United Kingdom or the United States, and a higher tertiary education rate than most countries in the developed world" ("Call for increased focus on education", 1997, p. 7).

All this could be achieved because of the close connection between education policy and animal husbandry—particularly witnessed in school organisation—and because of the permeability of Mongolia's educational system, which encouraged upward mobility for pastoralists. In brief, the following factors contributed to the mutual integration of education and nomadism. The universal right to free education was part of the first constitution of the MPR, issued in 1924. Consequently, secular primary schools implemented the modern and socially inclusive principal of co-education. Mobile teachers offered literacy training for youth and adults. The first boarding schools in the grassland appeared during the 1930s, and were—at first—mostly situated in *gers*. Unlike the USA (Child, 1998; Connell Szasz, 1974/1999) and the USSR (Bloch, 2003), Mongolia's boarding schools did not encourage assimilation to a sedentary lifestyle, de-skilling (Dyer, 2001; Krätli, 2000), or cultural alienation. In fact, they continued a pre-socialist model of access to formal education for children from herder families. Prior to the revolution, monastic schools throughout the country had offered formal education for boys. From the 1930s, anti-religious laws prohibited enrollment in monastic schools; yet by the time the first state-run boarding schools were established, the model of lodging in the nearest educational institution had already been mainstream in the steppe for a long time. They attempted to provide a family-oriented atmosphere, allowing siblings and/or neighbours (boys and girls alike) to share a *ger*, or, later, a room (Steiner-Khamsi & Stolpe, 2006). In 1943, schools for young herders were established in the countryside, and women were particularly encouraged to gain formal education. Nearly all teachers had a background in pastoralism, and most of them were locals. By the end of the 1940s, all provinces (*aimag*) and a few counties (*sum*)[5] had a secondary school. In Mongolia, it was not 'nomadism' that was associated with backwardness, but illiteracy, which the official historiographical narrative represented as the heritage of feudalism

[5] There were several administrative reforms during socialism. While the number of *aimag* (18) was stable for decades, the number of *sum* fluctuated around 300. Today, Mongolia is divided into 21 *aimag*, 331 *sum*, and 1,550 *bag*.

(Dorzhsuren, 1981, p. 109; Sanzhasuren, 1981, p. 89).

Compulsory school attendance for all children was fully implemented only in the school year 1955/56, when the herder collectives (*negdel*) helped build schools with dormitories further and further out in the steppe. With collectivisation came social security for herders and a reduction in workload due to specialisation. Nevertheless, labour was always scarce, which informed the annual school schedule's coordination around peak-periods in animal husbandry. Together with late school entry (at age 8) and long vacations, this coordination ensured that schoolchildren were continuously socialised into pastoralism, which encouraged situated learning (Lave & Wenger, 1991) in mobile animal husbandry. Moreover, polytechnical classes were now and again held by members of herder collectives, and university students were periodically sent to the countryside to help during labour peaks. Most Mongolian state institutions, including educational institutions, had their own herds. [6] Those who tended the school herds (*surguuliin malchid*) were members of the school collective; they appeared beside teachers, nurses, cooks, and janitors in wall newspapers or booklets that introduced school staff. The most considerable expansion and internal differentiation of the educational system began after 1962, when the MPR became a full member of the Council for Mutual Economic Assistance (COMECON/CMEA) and began receiving a higher amount of external funding to extend and maintain its boarding school system. By the 1970s, almost every county (*sum*) had a secondary school with a dormitory. Further, many herder collectives built primary schools in even the smallest administrative subunits (*bag*) that were closest to the pastures.

Most teachers shared their students' background, which explains why, to this very day, Mongolian schools are very flexible in adjusting to the needs of those who practice animal husbandry. For example, if weather conditions require herders to graze their animals on remote pastures, teachers tolerate students' late appearance at the beginning of the new school year. During times of hardship like *zud*,[7] rural schools still organise help for herders, as they did during socialism. Under socialism, schools introduced the so-called 'summer task' (*zuny daalgavar*), which required students to explore features of the local geography and prepare concentrated forage (i.e. allium pellets) as part of *zud*-prevention. During the post-socialist crisis of the 1990s, the summer task was distorted: since rural schools suffered from a lack of state support, children were expected to collect dried dung for heating, as well as bring meat and dried curd as contributions to the suddenly scarce food provisions in dormitories. With the recent commercialisation of horseracing, it has become customary for schools to allow students to take extra vacations to train racehorses in the steppe; nowadays, poor families who live in urban areas (especially in the highly polluted capital Ulaanbaatar) consider racehorse training a welcome opportunity to send their children to the countryside for healthier food and fresh air.[8] These examples may illustrate against what background Krätli, who did a comparative study on education provision to nomadic pastoralists, identified as a remarkable "non antagonistic culture towards nomadism" (Krätli, 2000, p. 48) during his on-site research in Mongolia. All schools were part of the same education system, and pastoralists were not segregated. Namkhainyambuu remembered:

> In 1971, I was a youth representative in Ulaanbaatar, and I participated in the Fourth Mongolian-Soviet Games. At that time I understood that there is nothing a young man can't do and can't learn. I also discovered how the young boast of their vigour and hard work, as well as realising that the profession of herder was well respected. In 1972, the labour youth representatives from one hundred and twenty nations held a meeting in Moscow....Thus because of my herds, I was able to travel abroad and see the world. (Namkhainyambuu, 2000, p. 53)

An even more prominent example of (even extraterrestrial) upward mobility is Mongolia's one and only cosmonaut J. Gurragchaa, likely the only spaceman worldwide who comes from a pastoralist family. Gurragchaa's parents followed their son's 1981 space flight by listening to a live broadcast from a battery radio in their *ger,* out in the steppe (Ontsgoi tomilolt, 2001).

Against this backdrop, it is evident why the post-socialist downgrade from the Second to the Third World was shocking, even more so since the *Human Development Index* data did not correspond to this category. But in the face of the severe economic crisis that followed the collapse of the COMECON, Mongolia's government had to make concessions to international donors to receive loans. While most accounts written by foreigners tend to praise the initial years of democratisation as liberation, paving the way to free-

[6] For rural schools, it is still an advantage to own a herd and thus be able to provide dormitory students and teachers with meat supplies.

[7] *Zud*: times of hardship during the winter/spring season. From the perspective of Mongolian herders, *zud* is the effect, not the cause, contrary to the widespread Eurocentric representation of *zud* as a 'high snow' or 'cold spell', neither of which necessarily leads to a disastrous mass mortality of livestock. The Mongolian standard idiom *gan zud* shows that drought (*gan*) usually precedes *zud*. The complexity of causes and effects is reflected in sub-categories of *zud*. Political and structural conditions significantly influence whether or not weather conditions result in a disastrous loss of herds (Stolpe, 2011).

[8] Personal communication and exchange of letters with teachers of rural and urban schools, as well as with students and parents (2003–2015).

dom, Mongolian citizens (even in retrospect) hardly describe the early years of post-socialism as times of upswing. Especially in rural areas, the so-called transition was perceived as a regression, as "having lost decades of improvement with conditions beginning to resemble those of the 1940s!" (Sneath, 2002, p. 196). What had happened? Reforms in the agricultural sector started in 1991–93 with de-collectivisation, which was generally well-received. Many herder families took their children, especially boys, out of school in order to cope with the workload that came with multi-species herds, and the inverse gender gap widened in the 1990s: by 1997, 16.7% more girls had entered secondary school in rural areas than boys (Yembuu, 2008, p. 28). After the privatisation of 26 million heads of livestock, animal husbandry was the only economic sector with good growth rates. But the withdrawal of the state resulted in the collapse of rural infrastructure, including essential social services. This led, in combination with unemployment and the disastrous supply situation, to a retreat into rural subsistence economy. The 95,000 so-called new nomads (Mongol Ulsyn Zasgyn Gazar & UNDP, 1997, p. 17) were mostly former state employees who tried to make ends meet with "pre-modern means of subsistence" (Bruun, 1996, p. 65). By the end of the 1990s, this apparent conversion to 'nomadism' had shifted into a massive rural-to-urban migration of more than half a million people, thus turning the so-called nomads into a minority.

Rural areas have been disadvantaged since 1990, especially in service provision. At present, 68% of Mongolia's three million people live in urban areas, most of which have settled in Ulaanbaatar (United Nations Development Programme in Mongolia, 2014). In the coldest capital of the world, which has recently gained sad notoriety for peak amounts of air pollution, two thirds of the population live in *ger* districts with insufficient infrastructure. Reasons for rural-to-urban migration are manifold, but the hope for social mobility—i.e. for better educational opportunities—ranks, after economic reasons, second. This is due to the fact that, after the political changes, the younger generation who lived in the countryside had poorer educational opportunities than their parents' generation had had. In contrast to other parts of the world (for Tibet see Postiglione, Jiao, Xiaoliang, & Tsamla, 2014), where pastoralists never had proper access to formal education, there was no need to popularise formal education in Mongolia. On the contrary, herders actively defended their right to equal educational access in order to remain an integral part of modern society.

2.1. Herders in the Blind Spot of Educational Development

The present unequal access to quality education in Mongolia is, for the most part, a result of the educational reform undertaken in the 1990s. The first Masterplan, prepared in 1993, proposed for rural areas low-budget schools with multi-class teaching, mobile teachers, and even *ger* schools. Under Qing rule, *ger* schools (*geriin surguul'*) were established to qualify clerks (*khia*) for menial tasks (Baasanjav, 1999, p. 325; Rinchen, 1964, pp. 30-33; Shagdar, 2000, p. 70; Shagdarsüren, 1976, p. 26). In the earliest years of socialism, *ger* schools were considered a makeshift solution because, in contrast to modern school buildings, they could not provide facilities for modern, science-oriented teaching. Hence, the rural population, including herders, who had been used to equal opportunities, did not approve of these discriminatory suggestions made by the Master Plan. While some foreign consultants considered it a good idea to link the present with pre-socialist times, even after more than seventy years, herders resisted school models, which they considered relics of a bygone past. Yet, the new dominant ideology implied that schools would be an "instrument of sedentarization", that "boarding schools introduce children to the sedentary lifestyle" (Postiglione et al., 2014, p. 108), and that "modern school education is not embraced by local people" (Postiglione et al., 2014, p. 118). In Mongolia, the opposite had been the case. Yet even the most successful features of the educational system had to give way to a neoliberal ideology that treated history as reversible, as though socialism "only existed outside the 'correct flow of history'", and as if countries could return to a "*status quo ante*" (Giordano & Kostova, 2002, p. 78), which was imagined as their 'true' self. Disillusioned statements like the following have been heard in Mongolia ever since: "Foreign consultants tend to come in with answers before they know the questions—these are answers they have produced in other countries and they don't really have the time to develop the true needs for Mongolia" ("Call for increased focus on education", 1997, p. 7).

In this context, Mongolian pastoralists were suddenly ascribed all kinds of vaguely 'nomadic' interests that, more often than not, ignored the target group's views. Herders saw mobile teachers,[9] *ger* schools, and multi-class instruction as second-class education that provided students with poor qualifications. Reducing people to being 'nomads' proved to be an essentialisiation of spatial mobility and demonstrated ignorance of the fact that modern social mobility is based, worldwide, on the social capital of formal education: as Dyer and Choksi found during their fieldwork among Indian pastoralists in Gujarat, the Rabari expected formal education to provide added value, and considered it an important means of emancipation (Dyer & Choksi, 1998).

Some proposals of the first Masterplan were a con-

[9] A much promoted mobile teacher project initiated by UNICEF was terminated in 1998; no replacement was provided.

sequence of downgrading Mongolia to the so-called Third World. As a result, the country was subjected to neoliberal education policies in a similar manner as sub-Saharan Africa (UNESCO, 1993), which had even been dealt with as a single entity (Samoff, 1999). The "discursive homogenization" (Escobar, 1997, p. 92) of the so-called developing world allowed 'developing' countries hardly any control, let alone ownership. They lost control to foreign consultants who displayed a been-there-done-that attitude and came up with a prefabricated canon of recommendations. Accordingly, former Education Secretary Tsanjid criticised the rigid policies of international donor agencies as "Westernising" (*örnödchlökh*) or "Americanising" (*amerikchlakh*) approaches, which seemed all the more bitter to Mongolians in light of their hope that ideological constraints would disappear with the end of socialism (Tsanjid, 2005). Regarding education for pastoralists, the status loss from Second to Third World became a self-fulfilling prophecy: simultaneously with what is usually called 'transition to democracy', children from nomadic families encountered significant structural discrimination for the first time in Mongolian history. Decreasing school attendance in the 1990s led to a statistically relevant recurrence of illiteracy—ironically synchronous with the first *Education for All* decade.[10]

Boarding schools, although undoubtedly key to ensuring universal access to education in Mongolia, turned into the most contested subject of educational reforms. Under the structural adjustment programme, the Mongolian government was pressured to reduce public spending on education and forced to cut its budget in half (World Bank, 2002). Small and boarding schools were now considered not cost-effective; some were shut down. Since the early 1990s, Mongolian government representatives desperately tried to garner support to save dormitories, but their requests fell on deaf ears. Even a specially prepared application for the 2001 donor conference in Paris was rejected. Since no Western models could have been imported into the Mongolian education system, boarding schools fell from grace for obviously ideological reasons: donors refused to retain a model that was associated with the socialist past, no matter its inclusivity. Thus, the main vehicle for education fell victim to a transfer vacuum. One noteworthy exception to this ideologically biased neoliberal policy was the Rural School Development Project, funded by DANIDA[11] and managed jointly by the Mongolian Association of Primary and Secondary School Development (MAPSSD) and the Mongolian State University of Education. The Rural School Development Project operated from 2000–2010, and engaged 80 remote boarding schools across Mongolia by using a community-based approach to enhance the quality of and access to education. At a time when rural Mongolia had been widely ignored by all major donors, the project helped communities improve boarding school facilities and develop strategies to foster social inclusion of children from herder and poor families.

The post-socialist crisis of Mongolia's educational system found its most spectacular expression in soaring drop-out rates, which reached a peak in 1992/93, when 48,446 students left school (Mongol Ulsyn Zasgyn Gazar & UNDP, 1997, p. 25). Most dramatic was the situation in rural areas, where nine out of one hundred children between ages 8 and 10 did not attend school. For youth between ages 11 and 17, drop-out rates reached 50% in 1996 (Batjargal, 1997, pp. 43-44). These unintended side-effects of the 'transition' became a hot issue of public debates. A much noted article was published in the national newspaper *Zuuny Medee* under the headline, "Among us are 200,000 adolescents who are illiterate" (Düger, 1999, p. 3). Sociologist Gundsambuu also expressed his concern about an emerging social inequality, and called the rising numbers of "uneducated or sub-educated youth and children" among herders "the main cattle-breeding feature of Mongolia" (Gundsambuu, 2002, p. 22). The 1997-Mongolian edition of the Human Development Report predicted that the low educational standard would be felt for the next 70 years (Mongol Ulsyn Zasgyn Gazar & UNDP, 1997, pp. 25-26). "70 years" clearly alludes to the success of accomplished literacy during the socialist era.

Interestingly, many studies located the problem's origin exclusively outside educational policy. The official *Education for All* report—which was published under the promising title *Mongolian National Report on Education for All Assessment—2000*, but was oddly based on a case study from 1996—provides the most striking example. The gross enrolment ratio showed a difference of more than 20% between enrolment in rural and urban areas, yet the report provided no analysis of this phenomenon, nor of the decrease in students who lived in dormitories, which dropped from 14.5% in 1990 to 4.1% in 1996. The study was compiled under the aegis of the government that was responsible for introducing the requirement that herder families provide foodstuffs in order to have their children accommodated in dormitories from 1996.[12] Through this requirement, mobile pastoralists became the only social group in Mongolia to pay for access to primary and secondary education, a payment that contravened article 16 of the 1992 Constitution, which declares the

[10] In 1990, Mongolia subscribed to the World Declaration on Education for All.

[11] DANIDA is the term used for Denmark's development cooperation, which falls under the Ministry of Foreign Affairs of Denmark.

[12] The policy requested 70 kg of meat per child each school year. Poor families, especially those with more than one child in school, could not afford to slaughter animals.

right to basic education free of charge.[13] After 1996, poorer herder households could not afford to send their children to boarding schools until 2000, when these hidden fees were cancelled by decree of the new government, and forbidden by educational law in 2002. Most startling for a study called an "assessment" and done under the auspices of UNDP, UNESCO, UNICEF, UNFPA, and World Bank is, in addition to being based on outdated data from 1996, the reliance on a sample of merely 108 interviewees, only four of which were in Ulaanbaatar. Among the five reasons the report listed for dropping out of school, all but one located the problem on the side of the students and their families. Particularly striking is the report's use of the blaming category "lack of interest in learning" (Munkhjargal, 1999, p. 43), which was introduced in Mongolian discourses in the 1990s, and still persists in modern statistics despite the fact that the category has never been explained.[14]

Finally, the decentralization policy had unintended consequences for the access to and quality of education. The policy was based on the unproven assumption that decentralised decision making would automatically lead to better management. Alas, quite the contrary occurred: responsibilities were ill-defined, there was a lack of communication, planning did not have much effect in an environment of uncertainties, and school principals were expected to raise funds at a time when there was hardly any cash available in rural areas.[15] Paradoxically, since only larger schools in *aimag* centres received support from the Asian Development Bank, Mongolia's once-decentralised net of boarding schools became more centralized. Consequently, education-minded pastoralists were forced to either settle in provincial centres or separate their families (Steiner-Khamsi, Stolpe, & Tümendelger, 2003; Stolpe, 2008).

3. Discussion

In 2013, Mongolia ranked 103rd in the inequality-adjusted Human Development Index (a fall from its 2010 rank of 100) with Turkmenistan and the Maldives, following after the Dominican Republic (102), and Samoa and Palestine.[16] Not without reason does the latest Human Development Report highlight Mongolia's issues with sustainability and recommend that citizens be given opportunities to exercise freedom of participation, including the freedom to learn (United Nations Development Programme & Government of Mongolia, 2011, pp. 13, 35). Low turnouts in the last parliamentary election give cause for concern, particularly as processes of social exclusion are driving forces of post-democratic tendencies. Without doubt, poverty is the main contributor to social exclusion. Many children in Mongolia grow up under precarious circumstances and experience marginalisation on a daily basis. Comparative studies (Solga, 2014) suggest that investment in education be combined with high standards of social protection in order to enable as many people as possible to achieve the highest possible level of education. Although Mongolia's education policy makers are busy overcoming negative consequences of the so-called shock therapy that led to a disadvantage of pastoralists, the country's new urban-centrism is a strong counterforce. Even stronger is middle class centrism, which creates a lack of solidarity. Before I briefly return to this aspect, let me give some examples of the struggle to compensate for the shortcomings of non-inclusive policies.

It took more than a decade and a half to rehabilitate school dormitories. The current Education Masterplan (2006–2015), in accordance with the *Dakar framework for action: Education for all,* aims at "reduction of social inequality and disparities through undertaking strategic actions to make educational services accessible and inclusive at all territorial levels", and aims "to expand further opportunities of rural people and social [sic] vulnerable groups to obtain education" (Government of Mongolia, 2006, p. ix). Herder's children's access is to be improved by increasing accommodation in dormitories by 40.5%, and is designed to finally reach 75%. Drop-outs are to be returned to schools, or provided with non-formal education (Government of Mongolia, 2006, p. xiii). In order to get an impression of recent developments, it may be useful to review some statistical figures. In 2008/2009, a total of 492 boarding schools hosted about 8.4% of the overall student population. Out of the 42,064 students enrolled, 36,786 came from herder families. In 2009, 57% of all countryside schools[17] were located in *sum* centres, and 6% in *bag*-centres. *Sum* schools accommodated 20% of their students in dormitories; *bag*-schools accommodated more than 50% (UNESCO, 2011; Asian Development Bank, 2013, pp. 10ff). According to current statistics provided by the Mongolian Ministry of Education, out of the 762 schools in Mongolia, 552 are rural schools. At present (school year 2014/15), there are 486 dormitories, 12 of them privately owned. Of the 505,816 students enrolled in school, 109,599 are children from herder families (*malchdyn khüükhed*), 32,858 (30%) of which live in dormitories (Ministry of Education, Culture and Science,

[13] Since the amount of meat had to be delivered before one's child could be enrolled, this was considered a hidden fee (*dald tölbör*) by herder families who depended on the boarding school system.

[14] For a recent example, see: http://www.meds.gov.mn/data/1503/BDB14-15.pdf. The habit of collecting data without properly analysing them has been criticised by Mongolian educationalists since the late 1990s (cf. Monkhor & Damdinsüren, 1998).

[15] For comparable experiences in other parts of the world in the 1990s, cf. McGinn and Borden (1995) and Tatto (1999).

[16] http://hdr.undp.org/en/search/node/hdi%20mongolia

[17] Mongolian education statistics usually count provincial (*aimag*) centres under the category "countryside".

2015). These figures make the Masterplan's ambitious goal to house 75% of herder children by the end of 2015 decidedly unlikely.

While the current Masterplan acknowledges the significance of dormitories, some ADB consultants still fail to recognize their importance, as the following example shows. As part of the Asian Development Bank's *Financial Crisis Response Project*, studies were completed under the headline "Education for the Poor" in 2013 (ADB, 2013). The suggestions put forward for revision concern per student financing, school uniform cost reduction, and the kindergarten free meal programme. Per student financing, introduced in 1998, contributed to a chronic underfunding of rural schools, who received less and less funding as a result of rural-to-urban migration. Representatives and advocates of remote schools objected to this funding scheme, which led to countless corrections of the funding formula. Yet, with the suggestions made in the ADB-paper, dormitories fell into disgrace once more: "This is an added cost, unrelated to a school's primary purpose—student learning" (ADB, 2013, p. 18). The paper suggested that funding for dormitories be slashed by 90%; ironically, a footnote indicates that the authors of the study did not know the amount then spent on dormitories.[18] Interestingly, the Mongolian version of the study does not read "Education for the Poor", but instead reads, "Making education accessible for citizens of socially vulnerable groups" (*Niigmiin emzeg bülgiin irgeded bolovsrolyn ülchilgeeg khürgekh ni*), thereby using more politically correct language.

Since 1997, "*Gegeerel* (Enlightenment) Centres" existed in every district and *sum,* and were expected to provide literacy programmes for out-of-school children and youth. In 2001, the Ministry of Education started equivalency programmes, which complied with 75% of formal education standards (Yembuu, 2008). The programmes were meant to provide equivalent knowledge for all levels of education and "eradicate illiteracy" (Yembuu, 2008, p. 10). The newly amended Education Law of 2006 aimed to serve people outside the formal education system. However, non-formal education often deprives children of quality teaching. Those in charge tend to offer short-term courses on what is called 'livelihood training'—a potpourri of 'life skills' that are often not in demand by the target group. At present (school year 2014/15), 10,067 students—of which 6,895 are boys—participate in the programme (*düitsen khötölbör*) (Ministry of Education, Culture and Science, 2015). The higher percentage of boys in the programme reflects the aftermath of the privatisation of livestock in the 1990s, when many herder families took boys out of school. Since a great number of pastoralists lost their herds during the consecutive *zud* disasters around the turn of the century, many of their now grown-up boys, lacking formal education, struggle to find a job.[19]

Statistical figures on drop-outs and out-of-school children are usually rather whitewashed, as they exclude those who participated in short-term courses of non-formal education. Figures currently report 94 drop-out/out-of-school children in Ulaanbaatar, and 1075 in the countryside. Of these children, 367 state poverty (*amidralyn gachigdal*) as the reason for their absence from school, but most (527) are reportedly out of school for health reasons. Figures are proportionally higher in the countryside, and the same applies for children not-yet enrolled (669 out of 726) (Ministry of Education, Culture and Science, 2015). Hence, it is difficult to avoid the impression that this disproportionality was caused by the lowering of admission age from eight to seven in 2005 and from seven to six in 2008. Pastoralist families are clearly disadvantaged by these measures, which favour urbanites who live close to schools. As a consequence, children who live in the countryside drop out more often, or enroll later, two patterns that may bar the children from formal schooling if the family migrates to Ulaanbaatar, where formal schools refuse to accept overage children.

After a decade of neglect, several programmes fostered the resurrection of the rural infrastructure in hopes of reducing rural-urban migration. The three-phase, World Bank-financed *Sustainable Livelihoods Programme*, launched in 2002, established community development funds. By 2013, before it entered its 3rd phase in 2014, these funds had financed 6,000 subprojects. Among the activities, endeavors on education, health, and pasture management featured prominently. The current phase intends to bolster the *Sum* Programme[20] and focus on capacity building for local governments.[21] However, all social sectors—including education—are negatively affected by the extreme politicization of administration: after each election, most people in leading positions (including school directors) are replaced according to party affiliation. This highly controversial rotation of public positions (*khalgaa selgee*) jeopardises any successes in capacity building. To make matters worse, each election is preceded by an aura of paralysis and followed by haggling over positions; during each period, crucial decisions are suspended. Needless to say, this procedure, which has been widely criticised as a "political disease" (*uls töriin övchin*), contributes to a loss of popular trust in public institutions and administrative services.

18 Peter R. Moock and Batchimeg Namsraidorj (2013).

19 Personal communication with teachers and parents at the nonformal education center *Childrens' Ger* in the period from 2003 to 2015.

20 The *Sum* Programme (*Shine Sum Tösöl* or *Sumyn Töviin Shinechlel*) was established in 2013.

21 http://www.worldbank.org/en/news/feature/2015/05/07/providing-mongolias-rural-communities-with-sustainable-livelihoods

4. Epilogue

As one of the ten richest countries in raw materials, "Minegolia" or "Moncoalia" is at the focus of transnational business interests. Environmental problems are as virulent as controversies over who should profit from the country's wealth. While rich elites seclude themselves in gated communities, one third of Mongolia's population is poor. Throughout the country, conflicts arise over land grabbing and the destruction of pasture land by mining. Herders engage in resistance movements to defend their pastoral livelihoods (Upton, 2012), and demand stricter enforcement of the so-called "law with the long name" (*urt nertei khuul'*), which prohibits mineral exploration and extraction near water sources, protected areas, and forests.[22] Yet, unlike under socialism, herders (i.e. former *arats* now referred to as 'nomads') lack a positive collective identity. I agree with Dan Allman, who noted that, "just naming who is at risk of social exclusion, based on identity, vulnerability, membership, or biology will not suffice without some reflection as to who is naming the excluded, where those who label or define the excluded stand ontologically relative to their own or others' exclusion, and what if any the influences of personal, political, stereotypical, or xenophobic biases may be" (Allman, 2013, p. 9).

Mainstream educational thinking in today's Mongolia is founded on an urban, upper-middle class centrism. The government campaign, *Zöv mongol khüükhed ündesnii khötölbör* (right/correct/good Mongolian child national programme), launched in 2013, is an illustrative example. The campaign's stated intent is to foster creativity, self-confidence, decisiveness, lifelong learning, acquisition of the Mongolian language, culture, and customs in order to make proper citizens out of Mongolian children, a goal that is supposed to be reached through families, education and the social environment.[23] The government and the Ministry of Education produced an official 5:07-minute video clip that shows the underlying value concepts.[24] It starts with the sun rising over the steppe blended into Ulaanbaatar's main square, where boys in uniforms parade and salute in front of the government building and the national flag. Next, we see children and young people—partly dressed in national costumes—singing, waving, and presenting their talents and hobbies to friendly teachers who support them in and outside school. From 1:39–2:03, a girl and a boy are shown translating the song into sign language. This is the only part that demonstrates any kind of social inclusion. The video clip is shot entirely in the flawless urban settings of Ulaanbaatar's city centre. Only three extremely short, inserted sequences show rural children—two small boys holding kids (1:06–08; 2:32–33; 4:51–52). These sequences account for less than 5 seconds in a 5:07 minute video clip. Rural life appears twee; the image of children and youths holding kids has become iconic and features prominently on postcards, coffee-table books, and the latest *Mongolia Human Development Report* (2011). While the video clip cast are happy urbanites, socially deprived groups are clearly outcast. Strikingly, not a single *ger*[25] appears in the whole video clip, let alone a *ger* district that is home to two thirds of the capital's residents. Of course, middle-class centrism in education is rather the rule worldwide. Yet, from a government that takes pleasure in promoting Mongolia as a "land of nomads" (Myadar, 2011), and from elites who usually associate true Mongolian culture with the countryside (*khödöö*), one would expect a different and more inclusive representation of its younger generation.

[22] http://gal-undesten.blogspot.ca/2012/06/blog-post_387.html
[23] http://www.news.mn/content/153784.shtml
[24] https://www.youtube.com/watch?v=8_ZhDLUVVEI

Acknowledgements

I would like to thank two anonymous reviewers and the English editor for their comments and suggestions on an earlier version of this paper.

Conflict of Interests

The author declares no conflict of interests.

References

Allman, D. (2013). The sociology of social inclusion. *Sage Open*, *3*(1), 1-16.

Appadurai, A. (1996). *Modernity at large. Cultural dimensions of globalization.* Minneapolis: University of Minnesota Press.

Avdai, C., Tömörjav, M., Songino, C., Dorj, B., Tsevegsüren, Z., & Natsagdorj, N. (2003). *Mongolyn nüüdelchdiin ündesnii ulamjlalt tekhnologi.* Ulaanbaatar, Mongolia: UNESCO, NSISOUCh [International Institute for the Study of Nomadic Civilization], Shinjlekh Ukhaany Akademi.

Asian Development Bank. (2013). *Education for the poor. Targeting strategies for the poor.* Ulaanbaatar, Mongolia: Asian Development Bank.

Baasanjav, Z. (1999). Surgan khümüüjüülekh setgelgee, surguul', bolovsrol. In *Mongol ulsyn tüükh (Tüükh onol-arga züin asuudluud)* (pp. 321-326). Ulaanbaatar, Mongolia: Ulsyn Ikh Surguul & Öchir Töv.

Batjargal, A. (1997). Bolovsrolyn salbart khiikh shinechleltiin yavtsad ankhaarakh zarim asuudluud. *Bolovsrolyn Medeelel*, *1*, 41-45.

Bira, S. (1998/1999). Mongolyn nüüdliin irgenshil ba ulamjlalt medleg ukhaan. *Bulletin. The IAMS News Information on Mongol Studies*, *22*(2)/*23*(1), 7-22.

[25] At present 45% of Mongolian households live in a *ger* ("Khün am", 2010).

Bloch, A. (2003). *Red ties and residential Schools: Indigenous Siberians in a Post-Soviet state*. Philadelphia: University of Pennsylvania Press.

Bruun, O. (1996). The herding household: Economy and organization. In O. Bruun & O. Odgaard (Eds.), *Mongolia in transition: Old patterns, new challenges*, (pp. 65-89), Richmond: Curzon.

Call for increased focus on education. (1997, August 20). *The Mongol Messenger*.

Chagdaa, C. S. (2002). *Mongol malchny am'drakhuin ukhaan*. Ulaanbaatar, Mongolia: "EV 2000" Khevleliin Gazar.

Chakrabarty, D. (2000). *Provincializing Europe. Postcolonial thought and historical difference*. Princeton, New Jersey: Princeton University Press.

Child, B. J. (1998). *Boarding school seasons. American Indian families 1900–1940*. Lincoln and London: University of Nebraska Press.

Chuluunbaatar, L. (2002). *Nüüdelchin mongolchuudyn bichig üsgiin soyol*. Ulaanbaatar, Mongolia: MUIS-iin Buddyn Soyol Sudalgaany Töv.

Clammer, J. (2003). Europe in Asia's imaginary. Disciplinary knowledges and the (mis)representation of cultures. In S. Lawson (Ed.), *Europe and the Asia-Pacific. Culture, identity and representations of region* (pp. 17-32). London and New York: RoutledgeCurzon.

Connell Szasz, M. (1999). *Education and the American Indian. The road to self-determination since 1928*. Albuquerque: University of New Mexico Press. (Original work published 1974).

Dash, M. (1966). *Mongol orny bilcheeriin mal mallagaany arga turshlaga*. Ulaanbaatar, Mongolia: Ulsyn Khevlelijn Khereg Erkhlekh Khoroo.

Dorjgotov, N. (2002). Zarim ügiin tukhai. In International Institute for the Study of Nomadic Civilization (Ed.), *Nüüdliin niigmiin olon ulsyn tüvshind sudlakh n'. Nomadism—International Study* (p. 109). Ulaanbaatar, Mongolia: Nüüdliin Soyol Irgenshliig Sudlakh Olon Ulsyn Khüreelen.

Dorzhsuren, Y. (1981). The flowering of art and culture. In *The 60th Anniversary of People's Mongolia* (pp. 108-122). Ulaanbaatar, Mongolia, and Moscow: Unen Editorial Board and Novosti Press Agency Publishing House.

Düger, K. (1999). Bichig üseg medekhgüi 200 myangan zaluus bidnii dund baina. *Zuuny Medee, 08.09*(174), 3.

Dyer, C. (2001). Nomads and education for all: Education for development or domestication? *Comparative Education, 37*(3), 315-327.

Dyer, C., & Choksi, A. (1998). Education is like wearing glasses: Nomad's views of literacy and empowerment. *International Journal for Educational Development, 18*(5), 405-413.

Enebish, J. (2002). Nüüdelchdiin baigal'-khögjim-khünii khariltsan shüteltsee. In International Institute for the Study of Nomadic Civilization (Ed.), *Nüüdliin niigmiin olon ulsyn tüvshind sudlakh n'. Nomadism—International Study* (pp. 130-134). Ulaanbaatar, Mongolia: Nüüdliin Soyol Irgenshliig Sudlakh Olon Ulsyn Khüreelen.

Enebish, J. (2004). The nomadic roots of Mongolian music & song. *Mongol Survey, 13*, 18-21.

Enkhtuvshin, B. (2002). Pressing problems of dialogue among civilizations and study of nomadic civilization in international and regional level. In International Institute for the Study of Nomadic Civilization (Ed.), *Nüüdliin niigmiin olon ulsyn tüvshind sudlakh n'. Nomadism—International Study* (pp. 8-26). Ulaanbaatar, Mongolia: Nüüdliin Soyol Irgenshliig Sudlakh Olon Ulsyn Khüreelen.

Enkhtuvshin, B. (2004). New challenges for nomadic civilization and pastoral nomadism in Mongolia. *Nomadic Studies, 9*, 69-81. Ulaanbaatar, Mongolia: International Institute for the Study of Nomadic Civilization.

Enkhtuvshin, B., & Tumurjav, M. (2001). Nomads and pasture use. In *Open Symposium on "Change and Sustainability of Pastoral Land Use Systems in Temperate and Central Asia"* (pp. 11-17). Ulaanbaatar, Mongolia: MAS/IISNC/LUTEA.

Escobar, A. (1997). The making and unmaking of the third world through development. In M. Rahnema & V. Bawtree (Eds.), *The post-development reader* (pp. 85-93). London and New Jersey, Dhaka, Halifax, and Cape Town: Zed Books, University Press LDT, Fernwood Publishing and David Philip.

Fernández-Giménez, M. E., & Huntsinger, L. (1999). Sustaining the steppes: A history of pastoral land use in Mongolia. *The Geographical Review, 89*(3), 315-342.

Finke, P. (2000). *Changing property rights systems in Western Mongolia* (Working Paper No. 3). Munich, Germany: Max Planck Institute.

Finke, P. (2004). Contemporary pastoralism in Central Asia. In G. Rasuly-Paleczek, & J. Katschnig (Eds.), *Central Asia on display. Proceedings of the VII. Conference of the European Society for Central Asian Studies* (pp. 397-410). Vienna, Austria: Lit-Verlag.

Fratkin, E. (1997). Pastoralism: Governance and development issues. *Annual Review of Anthropology, 26*, 235-261.

Galaty, J. G., & Johnson, D. L. (Eds.). (1990). *The world of pastoralism. Herding systems in comparative perspective*. New York: The Guilford Press.

Ganbaatar, J. (2001). *Ikh nüüdliin tüükh*. Ulaanbaatar, Mongolia: Mongol Ulsyn Ikh Surguul', Gadaad Khel, Soyolyn Surguul'.

Ginat, J., & Khazanov, A. M. (Eds.). (1998). *Changing Nomads in a changing world*. Sussex: Academic Press.

Ginsburg, T. (1997). Mongolia in 1996: Fighting fire and ice. *Asian Survey, 36*(1), 60-64.

Giordano, C., & Kostova, D. (2002). The social production of mistrust. In C. M. Hann (Ed.), *Postsocialism. ideals, ideologies and practices in Asia* (pp. 74-91). New York: Routledge.

Government of Mongolia. (2006). *Masterplan to develop*

education in Mongolia. Ulaanbaatar, Mongolia: Government of Mongolia.

Gundsambuu, K. (2002). *Social stratification in contemporary Mongolian society*. Ulaanbaatar, Mongolia: "Zotol" Club of Professional Sociologists.

Humphrey, C., & Sneath, D. (1999). *The end of nomadism? Society, state and the environment of Inner Asia*. Durham, UK: Duke University Press.

Innes-Brown, M. (2001). Democracy, education and reform in Mongolia: Transition to a new order. In M. Bray & W. O. Lee (Eds.), *Education and political transition: Themes and experiences in East Asia* (pp. 77-99). Hong Kong: Comparative Education Research Centre.

Kerven, C. (Ed.). (2003). *Prospects for pastoralism in Kazakstan and Turkmenistan. From state farms to private flocks*. New York: RoutledgeCurzon.

Khazanov, A. M. (1994). *Nomads and the outside world*. Madison: The University of Wisconsin Press. (Original work published 1984).

Khün am, *oron suutsny 2010 ony ulsyn toollogyn ür dün*. (2010). Retrieved from http://tuv.nso.mn/uploads/users/4/files/XAOCT%20uls.pdf

Krätli, S. (2000). *Education provision to nomadic pastoralists. A literature review*. Unpublished manuscript.

Lave, J., & Wenger, E. (1991). *Situated learning. Legitimate peripheral participation*. Cambridge: University of Cambridge Press.

Leibold, J., & Yangbin, C. (Eds.). (2014). *Minority education in China. Balancing unity and diversity in an era of critical pluralism*. Hong Kong: Hong Kong University Press.

Lkhagva, O. (2003). Ikh talyn nüüdelchdiin soyolyn undraga. *Mongolica. An International Annual of Mongol Studies, 13*(34), 92-103.

McGinn, N. F., & Borden, A. M. (1995). *Framing questions, constructing answers. Linking research with education policy for developing countries*. Harvard: Harvard Institute for International Development.

Mearns, R. (1993a). *Pastoral institutions, land tenure and land policy reform in post-socialist Mongolia* (PALD Research Report 3). Sussex, UK: Policy Alternatives for Livestock Development in Mongolia.

Mearns, R. (1993b). Territoriality and land tenure among Mongolian pastoralists: Variation, continuity and change. *Nomadic Peoples, 33*, 73-104.

Ministry of Education, Culture and Science. (2015). Baga, dund bolovsrolyn statistik, 2014–15. Retrieved from http://www.meds.gov.mn/data/1503/BDB14-15.pdf

Mongol Ulsyn Zasgyn Gazar & UNDP (1997). *Mongol Khünii Khögjliin iltgel*. Ulaanbaatar, Mongolia.

Munkhjargal, D. (1999). *Mongolian national report on Education for All assessment—2000*. Ulaanbaatar, Mongolia: Ministry of Science, Technology, Education and Culture, UNDP, UNESCO, UNICEF, UNFPA, World Bank.

Monkhor, D., & Damdinsüren, B. (1998). Bolovsrolyn khögjliin talaarkh sudalgaag chukhalchil'ya. *Bolovsrol Medeelel (Education & Information), 7*(11), 47-54.

Moock, P. R., & Namsraidorj, B. (2013). Suggestions for revisions of the per student funding formula for general secondary education in Mongolia. In *Education for the poor. Targeting strategies for the poor* (pp. 6-57). Ulaanbaatar, Mongolia: Asian Development Bank.

Myadar, O. (2011). Imaginary nomads: Deconstructing the representation of Mongolia as a land of nomads. *Inner Asia, 13*(2), 335-362.

Namkhainyambuu, T. (2000). *Bounty from the sheep. Autobiography of a herdsman*. Cambridge: The White Horse Press.

Natsagdorj, S. (1967). The economic basis of feudalism in Mongolia. *Modern Asian Studies, 1*(3), 265-281.

Ontsgoi tomilolt. (2011). Ulaanbaatar, Mongolia: Mongol Ulsyn Batlan Khamgaalakh Yaam.

Postiglione, G., Jiao, B., Xiaoliang, L., & Tsamla. (2014). Popularizing basic education in Tibet's nomadic regions. In J. Leibold & C. Yangbin (Eds.), *Minority education in China. Balancing unity and diversity in an era of critical pluralism* (pp. 107-129). Hong Kong: Hong Kong University Press.

Rinchen, B. (1964). *Mongol bichgiin khelnii züi. Tergüün devter*. Ulaanbaatar, Mongolia: Shinjlekh Ukhaany Akademiin khevlekh üildver.

Samoff, J. (1999). Education sector analysis in Africa: Limited national control and even less national ownership. *International Journal of Educational Development,19*(4/5), 249-272.

Sandshaasüren, R., & Shernossek, I. (1981). *Das Bildungswesen der Mongolischen Volksrepublik. Beiträge zur Pädagogik*. Berlin: Volk und Wissen.

Sanzhasuren, R. (1981). The torch of knowledge. In *The 60th Anniversary of People's Mongolia* (pp. 89-91). Ulaanbaatar, Mongolia, and Moscow: Unen Editorial Board and Novosti Press Agency Publishing House.

Schmidt, S. (1995). *Mongolia in transition. The impact of privatization on rural life* (Bielefelder Studien zur Entwicklungssoziologie Vol. 62). Saarbrücken: Verlag für Entwicklungspolitik.

Shagdar, S. (2000). *Mongol ulsyn bolovsrolyn tovchoon*. Ulaanbaatar, Mongolia.

Shagdarsüren, O. (1969). *Baigalyn shalgaral ba belcheeriin mal aj akhui*. Ulaanbaatar, Mongolia.

Shagdarsüren, L. (1976). *BNMAU-yn yerönkhii bolovsrolyn khödölmör politekhnik surguuliin üüsel, khögjilt*. Ulaanbaatar: Ardyn Bolovsrolyn Yaamny Khevlel.

Sneath, D. (1996). Combining ecological and social studies in the contemporary study of pastoralism in Inner Asia. In V. A. Koptyug & M. Uppenbrink (Eds.), *Sustainable development of the Lake Baikal region. A model territory for the world* (pp. 265-284). Berlin: Springer.

Sneath, D. (1999). Mobility, technology, and decollectivization of pastoralism in Mongolia. In S. Kotkin & B. A. Elleman (Eds.), *Mongolia in the twentieth century*.

Landlocked cosmopolitan (pp. 223-236). Armonk, USA: M.E. Sharpe.

Sneath, D. (2000). Producer groups and the decollectivisation of the Mongolian pastoral economy. In. J. Heyer, F. Stewart, & R. Thorp (Eds.), *Group behaviour and development.* Oxford: Oxford University Press.

Sneath, D. (2002). Mongolia in the 'age of the market': Pastoral land-use and the development discourse. In R. Mandel & C. Humphrey (Eds.), *Markets and moralities. Ethnographies of postsocialism* (pp. 191-210). Oxford: Berg.

Sneath, D. (2003). Lost in the post: Technologies of imagination, and the Soviet legacy in post-socialist Mongolia. *Inner Asia, 5*, 39-52.

Solga, H. (2014). Education, economic inequality and the promises of the social investment state. *Socio Economic Review, 12*, 18-25.

Steiner-Khamsi, G., Stolpe, I., & Tümendelger, S. (2003). Bolovsrolyn tölöökh nüüdel. *Shine Toli, 45*(4), 82-112.

Steiner-Khamsi, G., Stolpe, I. (2006): *Educational import: Local encounters with global forces in Mongolia*. New York: Palgrave Macmillan.

Stolpe, I. (2008). *Schule versus Nomadismus? Interdependenzen von Bildung und Migration in der modernen Mongolei*. Frankfurt, Germany: Peter Lang.

Stolpe, I. (2010). Earthing eternal heaven: Towards a mongolization of educational philosophies. *Mongolian Studies, XXXII*, 1-32.

Stolpe, I. (2011). Zud in der Mongolei: Perspektiven auf wiederkehrende endemische Katastrophen. *Mongolische Notizen, 19*, 44-60.

Stolpe, I. (2015). Truly nomadic? Die Mongolei im Wandel. *APuZ, 26/27*, 25-31.

Sükhee, S. (1988). *Mongol ardyn surgan khümüüjüülekh züin ulamjlal, devshliin zarim asuudal.* Ulaanbaatar, Mongolia: Ulsyn Khevleliin Gazar.

Sum'yaa, B. (2005). *Mongolyn nüüdelchdiin soyol.* Ulaanbaatar, Mongolia: International Institute for the Study of Nomadic Civilization.

Szynkiewicz, S. (1998). Contemporary concepts of being pastoralist: institutional continuity, change and substitutes. In J. Ginat & A. M. Khazanov (Eds.), *Changing nomads in a changing world* (pp. 202-222). Sussex: Academic Press.

Tatto, M. T. (1999). Education reform and state power in Mexico: The paradoxes of decentralisation. *Comparative Education Review, 43*(3), 253-278.

Taube, M. (2005). *Die Geheime Geschichte der Mongolen: Herkunft, Leben und Aufstieg Dschingis Khans.* Munich: Verlag C.H. Beck.

Tavakolian, B. (2003). Multiplicities of nomadism and varieties of anthropological theory. *Reviews in Anthropology, 32*, 297-314.

Tömörjav, M. (1989). *Belcheeriin Mongol Mal. (Ashig, shim, biologiin gol chanar).* Ulaanbaatar, Mongolia: Ulsyn Khevleliin Gazar.

Tömörjav, M. (2002). Töv Aziin nüüdellekhüi yoson, tüünd garch bui öörchlöölt: Surgamj, dügnelt. In International Institute for the Study of Nomadic Civilization (Ed.), *Nüüdliin niigmiin olon ulsyn tüvshind sudlakh n'. Nomadism—International Study* (pp. 38-44). Ulaanbaatar, Mongolia: Nüüdliin Soyol Irgenshliig Sudlakh Olon Ulsyn Khüreelen.

Tsanjid, A. (2005). *Mongol soyol irgenshil.* Ulaanbaatar, Mongolia: Mönkhiin Üseg.

UNESCO. (1993). *World education report.* Paris: UNESCO.

UNESCO. (2011). *World data on education. Mongolia* (7th ed.). Geneva: International Bureau of Education.

United Nations Development Programme, & Government of Mongolia. (2011). *Mongolia human development report*. Ulaanbaatar, Mongolia: Government of Mongolia, UNDP, SIDA.

United Nations Development Programme in Mongolia. (2014). Sustainable urban development in Mongolia. UNDP *in Mongolia.* Retrieved from http://www.mn.undp.org/content/mongolia/en/home/presscenter/development-dialogues-/DevelopmentDialogue8.html

Upton, C. (2012). Mining, resistance and pastoral livelihoods in contemporary Mongolia. In J. Dierkes (Ed.), *Change in democratic Mongolia: Social relations, health, mobile pastoralism, and mining* (pp. 224-248). Leiden: Brill Press.

World Bank. (2002). *Public expenditure and financial management review. Bridging the public expenditure management gap*. Washington: World Bank.

Yembuu, B. (2008). *National report on the situation of Adult Learning and Education (ALE) Mongolia*. Ulaanbaatar: National Centre for Non Formal and Distance Education, Ministry of Education, Culture and Science.

About the Author

Dr. Ines Stolpe

After graduating in Mongolian Studies and Education in Berlin and Ulaanbaatar, Ines Stolpe obtained her PhD in Central Asian Studies from Humboldt-University Berlin on the interdependencies of social and spatial mobility in contemporary Mongolia. Since 2013, she has been professor for Mongolian Studies at the Department of Tibetan and Mongolian Studies at the University of Bonn. Her research interests and areas of teaching include Mongolian language, cultural and political history and social change, educational philosophy, civil society, and Post-Socialist studies.

2

Who We Are Is What We Believe? Religion and Collective Identity in Austrian and German Immigrant Integration Policies

Astrid Mattes

Department of Political Science, University of Vienna, 1010 Vienna, Austria; E-Mail: astrid.mattes@univie.ac.at

Abstract

Immigrant integration is a contested policy field in which boundaries of membership are drawn and re-negotiated whereby groups of immigrants are partially included and excluded. Building on the concept of collective identity and theories of boundary making, this paper illustrates how religion functions as a category to mark and fill notions of self and otherness. As several studies have shown, immigrants in Europe are increasingly addressed as Muslims, a development that also serves the promotion of a Christian 'us'. Focusing on Austria and Germany, two countries where this is especially observable, the paper outlines the functioning of religion as symbolic boundary. The empirical study on national integration policies demonstrates how—within the relational process of boundary drawing against Muslims—a Christian identity narrative is established, how it functions as a marker of unity and how it relates to liberal and secular notions. Results from the qualitative content analysis of governmental policy programs from 2005 onwards show different patterns of boundary drawing on religion and the way they shape and limit the possibilities of inclusion. To understand this development, we have to look at Christian-democratic policy-makers, who currently dominate the political struggle for the power to define features of collective identity in immigrant integration policies.

Keywords

boundary making; collective identity; Christian-democrats; immigrant integration; Islam; religion

Issue

This article is part of the issue "International Migration and Ethnic Integration", edited by Yaojun Li (University of Manchester, UK) and Anthony Heath (University of Oxford, UK).

---

1. Introduction

As shown by various studies, Islam and Muslims have become 'the other' in European immigrant integration debates (Allievi, 2005; Grillo, 2010; Modood, 2009). The literature gives different explanations for the difficulty European societies experience with the integration of their Muslim populations. Within a broad spectrum of approaches, I identify four distinctive lines of argument. Some authors argue that Europe is essentially Christian, 'deeply rooted in a Christian tradition' and that Islam is therefore problematized in discourses on immigrant integration (Zolberg & Woon, 1999). In this view, the conflict comes down to the unwillingness to adapt predominantly Christian settings to religious pluralism and the refusal to include another religion into Christian self-perception. Conversely, other authors argue that Europe is essentially secular (Cesari, 2009; Foner & Alba, 2008), in fact the 'most deeply secularized of all corners of the globe' and the 'real issue in the Islam challenge is a vitally felt religion meeting a thoroughly non-religious (but not other-religious) environment' (Joppke, 2013, p. 611). This argument sees the Muslim presence (and the religious demands it might entail) as a challenge to the now essentially secular Europe. A third argument focuses on the essentially liberal identity of European states and the illiberal threat Islam might pose to it (Hansen, 2011). While similar to the idea of a secular Europe, this line of argument does not read the presence of a vibrant religion per se as a problem but the illiberal ideas it is argued to transmit. A fourth view on the problematization and the othering of Islam argues on a meta-level, seeing 'Muslim' as a racialized category to name a 'visible other' to white Europeans in a 'colour-blind' Europe (El-Tayeb, 2011, p. 16). This way of thinking would view the three other arguments as proof of the underlying—essentially racial—boundary at play. All these arguments have in common that they link the problematization of Islam to the constitution of the European self. This follows the logic of identity politics in which unity is produced by pointing out what is 'not us'. While the portrayal of Muslims and Islam as problematic is common to most European immigrant integration debates, there is less clarity about the unifying elements of the perceived 'us'. To put it bluntly: Are we all Christian, are we all secular, are we all liberal or are we just white?

Much scholarly attention has been paid to the application of 'Muslim' as a category of other-identification in immigrant integration debates and its exclusionary implications, but fewer studies analysed the resulting construction of the 'us' that is necessarily implied (valuable insights can be found in Brubaker, 2010; Eder, 2006; Korteweg & Yurdakul, 2014). Several authors have noted a new emphasis on Christianity as one particular aspect of this 'us' in European immigrant integration policies (Joppke, 2013; Modood, 2012). However, there is little understanding of this addressing of religion, how it functions as a marker of unity and how it relates to liberal and secular self-perceptions. The sole focus on the exclusion of an out-group obstructs any understanding of the underlying controversy over what makes up a collective identity. Not taking into account the political attempts to shape these perceptions, ignores ongoing power struggles over who 'we' are and what might or might not be in 'our' interest.

On that score, this paper focuses on the ways in which religion is involved in collective identities articulated in the context of immigrant integration. An empirical case study on governmental immigrant integration policies in Germany and Austria looks at the construction of symbolic boundaries that draw on religion as a marker for self and otherness. During the periods of observation (2005–2009 in Germany, 2008–2013 in Austria) both countries developed immigrant integration policy programs at national level, which were predominantly shaped by Christian-democratic policy makers (CDU/CSU in Germany, ÖVP in Austria). The analysis shows how Christianity is related to liberal and secular ideas almost to the same extent as Islam is assumed to oppose them. In the relational process of boundary drawing, Muslims (constructed as a homogenous group) are continuously portrayed as illiberal in their religious beliefs and practices while Christianity is constructed as an essential marker of unity in a variety of ways. Here, Christian-democratic parties might have found a way to overcome their struggle to successfully combine a Christian identity with a liberal democratic setting in increasingly secular societies. Rather than viewing this new emphasis on Christianity as a religious conflict, as a response to multiculturalism or as a sign of liberal disorientation, we can understand it as an expression of a political ideology Christian-democratic policy makers foster.

2. Collective Identity and Boundary Making in Immigrant Integration Policy

Immigrant integration policies produce membership boundaries through a notion of 'into what' immigrant populations are supposed to be integrated. As many authors have pointed out, it is the very idea of integration itself that provokes the issue of a common self-perception (Joppke, 2013; Korteweg & Yurdakul, 2014). This preoccupation with characteristics of a perceived unity allows policy makers to create and position narratives about 'us'. Consequently, we can understand immigrant integration policy debates as 'negotiations over how best to craft a shared national identity in a social context transformed by immigration' (Korteweg & Triadafilopoulos, 2013, p. 115). National identity mostly revolves around the idea of a common past, ancestry and culture of the people living in a certain territory (Guibernau, 2004, p. 126). Viewing nations as 'imagined political communities', national identity has to be seen as a permanent discursive process resulting in a kind of habitus which people 'internalize through socialization' (De Cillia, Reisigl, & Wodak, 1999, p. 153). It would be a foreshortened view to equate the aspects of identity promoted within immigrant integration policies with national identities. They are better understood as collective self-identifications, which is to 'identify oneself and others at the same time: to speak not just of but for others, to subsume others, along with oneself, into a collective "we"' (Brubaker, 2013, p. 2).

I use the term collective identity, as the construction of sameness does not necessarily rely on the notion of nation but mostly promotes a collective identity that is embedded in the European context as well as in particular national ones. Complementary to the 'Europeanization of exclusion', which subsumes the extensively researched othering of Islam across Europe (El-Tayeb, 2011, p. 23), there might be a Europeanization of inclusion, which cannot be observed if promoted identities are analysed as nationally bound.

The promotion of collective identity serves the creation of a majority, as well as the making of minorities (Wimmer, 2013), both shaped by the 'delineation of "us" and "not us"' (Zolberg & Woon, 1999, p. 8). Theories of boundary making view this as a relational process whereby in-groups and out-groups form around boundaries. Scholarship on boundaries covers a multitude of micro- and macro-social and socio-political categorization processes (see Pachucki, Lamont, & Pendergrass, 2007). Interested in how religion becomes a feature of collective identity, this paper's focus lies on categorization in governmental policy programs as a specific aspect of symbolic boundary formation.

Symbolic boundaries are 'conceptual distinctions' social actors make to 'separate people into groups and generate feelings of similarity and group membership' (Lamont & Molnár, 2002, p. 168). State institutions, such as governments, are in a dominant position to make their preferred distinctions 'politically relevant, publicly acknowledged and culturally legitimate' (Wimmer, 2013, p. 64). In the literature on boundary formation, symbolic boundaries are differentiated from social boundaries, which manifest in institutions and limit access to resources for certain groups (Bail, 2008). While social boundaries are reinforced and made salient using discrimination, collective organization and physical violence, means of symbolic boundary making include symbolic actions and discursive practices.

This paper analyses symbolic boundary formations, which function along distinct modes. Andreas Wimmer describes these modes as mostly building on existing group concepts that might change through processes of contraction or expansion, transvaluation, positional moves or boundary blurring (2013, p. 57). Boundaries shift (contract or expand) when terms for membership and non-membership are redefined, narrowing or widening the set of accepted attributes. Transvaluation occurs, when the normative order of a stratified system changes. Individual or collective positional moves might allow boundary crossings. However, bright boundaries can only be overcome by giving up distinctive elements of one's identity as they require assimilation in its strictest sense (Alba, 2005) and persist despite individual crossings (Barth, 1998). When boundaries get blurred by contrast, the in-group and its structures change. Former characteristics of the out-group become accepted within the in-group, the overlapping of previously mutually exclusive identity markers and multiple memberships are tolerated (Korteweg & Yurdakul, 2014). While especially Wimmer's modes of boundary making are more complex and comprehensive, the general applicability to categorization processes makes theories of boundary making a useful analytical tool to understand how institutions shape religion as a notion of difference.

3. Religion and Collective Identity

In terms of the composition of collective identities promoted in European immigrant integration policies, there is broad agreement on two aspects: First, Muslims have become 'the other' to European immigrant integration debates, which strongly relates to the securitization of this policy field and the simultaneous regulation of Islamic religion within it (Cesari, 2009). Second, there is a widespread acceptance that liberalism has become a cornerstone of the 'us' that collective identities refer to (Triadafilopoulos, 2011). The uniting element we can observe in most European integration policies of recent years is a postulated value consensus among the established population (Adamson, Triadafilopoulos, & Zolberg, 2011). This consensus is mostly presented as building on a set of liberal norms and the upholding of human rights. Conversely, the addressees of immigrant integration policies are characterized as not having internalized this set of norms (yet). This characterization of an out-group, marked by illiberal ideas (or the insufficient support of liberal ones) happens concurrently with conceiving immigrant populations as Muslims.

On the other hand, a renewed emphasis on Christianity has been observed by several authors but is rarely discussed more closely. Tariq Modood views this new emphasis as a 'response to the challenge of multiculturalism' in the light of 'the primacy given to religion as the basis of identity, organization, political representation, normative justification, etc.' (2012, pp. 139–140). The problematization of Muslims is—as demonstrated by Riem Spielhaus (2011)—not self-evident, nor is it simply related to the presence of believers. Equally, I suggest, the new emphasis on Christianity cannot be viewed as a self-evident reaction to the presence of Muslims in Europe and the primacy that is given to Islam. It is perfectly possible to encounter a religiously defined other with a non-religious line of argument.

Liberalism is however, insufficient to promote a specific national identity, as the universal character of liberal norms limits their scope to build a collective identity on particularistic elements (Joppke, 2008, p. 536). Christian Joppke therefore concludes that the new emphasis on Christianity is an attempt to capture a particularistic identity element (2008, p. 540). This is unconvincing: a Christian collective identity is neither particularistic—Christianity is not French, Austrian or German, it is just not Muslim—nor easily combined with liberal norms. Joppke addresses this issue in a later paper by calling Christianity and liberalism 'different words for the same thing observed over time' and attesting the term Christian to function as 'a code word for national particularism' (2013, p. 612). This ignores not only the vital theoretical debate about the relation of Christianity and Liberalism (Dombrowski, 2014; Gillespie, 2014; Laborde, 2013; Maffettone, 2014), but also the lively diversity of religious and secular political positions that exist within Europe and compete in many policy fields. In a way, this approach also contributes to the simplifying dichotomy of 'good religion/bad religion' many authors speak of, when religion is endorsed by state actors as long as it is useful to their own agenda (Wilson & Mavelli, 2014, p. 19).

Rather than viewing the new emphasis on Christianity just as a quasi-automatic response to the challenge of multiculturalism, as a search for particularistic identity elements of disoriented liberal states or even a religious conflict between Islam and Christianity, I suggest understanding it as the result of a contested process of competing sets of possible identity elements. The new emphasis on Christianity is primarily the expression of a political struggle for the power to define features of collective identity.

I will argue that Christian-democratic parties are pushing for this new emphasis on Christianity to solve their internal dilemma with proximity and distance to religion. Parties of the radical right use anti-Islamic ideas to promote a nationalist and exclusionary notion of 'us'. Social-democratic policy-makers have the tendency to disregard the role of religion (and culture) for immigrant integration (Laurence, 2013), instead focusing on socio-political aspects as markers for equality and difference (Scheffer, 2011). Christian-democratic parties, however, are seen as traditionally concerned with 'philosophical, ethical and, in a broader sense cultural issues' (Dierickx, 1994, p. 17).

4. Immigrant Integration, Religion and Christian-Democrats in Austria and Germany

Immigrant integration programs from Austria and Germany are the empirical basis for this case study on religion as a marker for self- and otherness. The two countries share similar migration histories and resemble each other in their approach towards integration (Koopmans, 2005). Up until the 1990s, despite significant histories of immigration, politicians in both Germany and Austria widely refused to identify their country as a country of immigration. Like other countries that installed guest worker regimes, Germany and Austria neglected badly needed integration policies for long-term residency. Rather, measures were limited to the labour market while return migration was equally fostered (Bommes & Kolb, 2012). Not until the turn of the millennium did integration issues finally climb up on the governmental political agenda. Comprehensive and systematic development of integration policy in Germany began after 2005 under a grand coalition government. Similar efforts at national level in Austria only started in 2008 (for a detailed overview of both countries immigrant integration policy development see Zincone, Penninx, & Borkert, 2011). The empirical analysis focuses on this period in which immigrant integration became a more closely defined and actively addressed policy field in both states.

Over the period of this project, Christian-democratic parties shaped both countries' immigrant integration policies. For Austria, it can be reasonably assumed that it was primarily the Austrian People's Party (ÖVP) that shaped outputs from 2000 onwards: Holding the relevant office (Ministry of Interior until 2011, State Secretariat for Integration from 2011 to 2013) can be seen as exceptionally influential in that particular policy field. In Germany during the empirical study period (2005–2009), Christian Democratic Union (CDU) held the governmental offices in charge of immigrant integration policy (Ministry of Interior, Federal Chancellery). Therefore this papers' findings are also limited to this party family.

Religion is a contested issue within those parties. In Germany, this became particularly evident during the 'Leitkultur' debate from 2000/01 onwards (Manz, 2004). This debate, in which CDU politicians picked up a term coined by the political scientist Bassam Tibi (1998), addressed the role of Christianity for collective identity. This was also contested within the party and it became one of many occasions when the meaning of the 'C' in the party's name was discussed controversially. German Chancellor Angela Merkel emphasized the importance of Christianity in various contexts, from demanding migrants to 'accept' Christian values (Der Spiegel, 2010) to the call on young party members to be more 'excited' about their Christian beliefs (Schwarze, 2010). The role of religion for and within the Austrian ÖVP is also ambivalent but less openly debated. When the party was re-established after World War II, they did not call themselves Christian to address a wider electorate and to demonstrate distance to the pre-war experience of Catholic authoritarianism (Binder, 2001). Throughout its post-war history, emphasizing conservative values and the role of Christianity was frequently used to counter criticism on neoliberal economic policies (Müller, 2014, p. 245).

Concerning state-religion relations, Austria and Germany are classified as 'systems of shared tasks' (Minkenberg, 2002), characterized by the exclusive collaboration of state institutions and religious communities acknowledged in law. These selected communities enjoy tax benefits, state-funded religious education in public schools, special legal protection and other privileges. In Austria, the Catholic Church is in a particularly dominant position. Over sixty per cent of the Austrian population are members of this church and Christianity is granted an outstanding role in the public sphere (e.g. crucifixes in classrooms). Because of its history as a multi-ethnic empire, Austria officially recognized Islam in 1912, following the annexation of Bosnia-Herzegovina. A state-recognized Islamic religious community was then established in 1979, long before Islam became a politicized issue. Many aspects of institutional embedding which are disputed in other European countries are regulated and not very contentious (Mattes & Rosenberger, 2015).

More than Austria, Germany is characterized by a distinct internalization of intra-Christian religious pluralism. Two Christian churches of almost equal size (Catholic and Protestant) dominate the religious landscape and, similar to Austria, enjoy the status of statutory bodies under public law. The state recognition of Islamic communities is a contentious issue that is not limited to religion politics but closely related to immigrant integration. The German Islam Conference (Deutsche Islamkonferenz, DIK) was established in 2006 to address both the institutional embedding of Islamic religious communities and the integration of Muslims in Germany (Rosenow-Williams, 2012). Participants included state authorities, Muslim representatives and individuals, as well as experts from academia and practice. In the course of the DIK it became clear that the initial hope for state recognition held by Islamic associations was only a distant prospect. While the DIK was at first scheduled as a three-year process, its mandate was renewed for the third time in 2014.

5. Methods and Material

Immigrant integration policies from Austria and Germany build a case in which processes of boundary drawing on religion can be identified. The empirical work builds on a qualitative content analysis of immigrant integration policy documents. Two central research questions where addressed: 1) How are different religions constructed in immigrant integration policies? and 2) What is the relationship between these constructions and the collective identity promoted in immigrant integration policies? As immigrant integration policies developed at different tempos, it is more accurate to investigate periods surrounding a key event than choosing a concrete time span. The period of analysis starts with the initial development of national policy strategies and is limited to one term in office of the respective government. This allows to investigate a timespan in which most influential factors stayed constant and varied party strength did not affect policy outputs. German integration policy programs analysed cover the period between November 2005 and October 2009, Austrian policies were analysed from December 2008 to November 2013. During these periods, each government issued eight major documents (see Table 1) covered in this analysis. The data material also includes selected information material, campaigns and press releases that explicitly address the issue of collective identity.

In the initial round of coding, text passages that draw on religion in the context of collective identity have been identified. A coding scheme, derived from relevant literature on symbolic boundary formation (Alba, 2005; Bail, 2008; Korteweg & Yurdakul, 2014; Lamont & Molnár, 2002; Wimmer, 2013) was used to perform a qualitative content analysis using semi-structured coding (Mayring, 2008). The coding of categorization practices ('defining relevant groups' and 'defining who belongs', Wimmer, 2013, p. 46) and types of boundaries (as discussed above) allowed for the identification of recurrent elements. After several rounds of coding, clusters of similarly structured elements were identified, out of which three patterns of relating religion to collective identity emerged.

6. Analysis and Discussion: Three Patterns of Religion as a Symbolic Boundary

Below I will present and discuss three patterns of religion as a symbolic boundary identified in the empirical case study. Direct quotes from the data material (translated by the author) are used to exemplify the results of the analysis. The subsequent discussion focusses on Christian-democratic parties as drivers of the observed emphasis on Christianity that mostly occurs in relation to Islam. Other minority religions by contrast, are hardly ever referred to in the policy documents analysed.

6.1. Muscular Liberalism

This first pattern is particularly relevant because it is not an alternative to the other patterns identified, but mostly works as an underlying structure. The categorization practice in this pattern defines the majority as unified by liberal values. Here, religion is not a feature of collective identity. The out-group by contrast is named as Muslims, marked by lacking willingness or ability to implement liberal norms.

> '[I]t is important to communicate Austrian fundamental values and rights and install a sense of belonging among Muslims.' (Bundesministerium für Inneres [BMI], 2012, p. 24)

Patterns like this have been discussed in the literature referring to 'muscular liberalism', which is based on the idea 'that it is the business of a liberal state to produce liberal individuals and promote a liberal way of life' (Modood, 2012, p. 143). Muscular Liberalism is not necessarily linked to religion and can be found in both Germany and Austria. In Germany, however, this pattern is most common in the context of the DIK. Muslim representatives had to profess their commitment to liberal norms throughout the process. The location of these claims of muscular liberalism in the context of the DIK links questions of shared values structurally to religion and to Islam in particular. Identity narratives are rarely found in general integration policy documents, while 'collective identity and shared values' is one of four core subjects of the DIK, almost like an outsourcing of value debates.

The boundary drawn here does not demarcate a clear in-group. Liberal is the only attribute the majority shares; no categories of difference are applied. The out-group however, is described as 'Muslims' and characterized as illiberal. This limits the possibilities of boundary crossing to individual positional moves. A formal 'commitment to the value system' by Muslim representatives is requested to allow for boundary blurring and the acceptance of the former mutually exclusive combination of 'liberal' and 'Muslim': Still, as the following statement from German National Integration Plan shows, boundaries might be uphold despite a given commitment:

> '[T]he committee pointed out that it is now crucial to connect the given commitment to the value system of the Basic Law to issues of everyday life, such as equality of men and women and unlimited school attendance of children from Muslim families.' (Deutsche Bundesregierung, 2007, p. 207)

6.2. Christian Ancestry

Within the 'Christian Ancestry' pattern, doubts about the extent to which Muslims are able or willing to accept liberal and secular structures are opposed with the construction of both secularism and liberalism as a historical product of Christianity and therefore insolubly linked. This takes two forms:

In the first argument, Christianity is given an active role in the promoted collective identity as secular structures are attributed to this religion.

Table 1. Overview data material.

	Austria		Germany	
2006			— 'Declaration of Intent', Federal Government — Opening Declaration of the German Islam Conference	Press releases and campaigns by Ministry of Interior, Federal Chancellery
2007			— National Integration Plan	
2008	— Expert Analysis on Integration 'Gemeinsam kommen wir zusammen'	Press releases and campaigns by Ministry of Interior	— National Integration Plan, 1st Progress Report — German Islam Conference, 3rd Plenum Report	
2009	— Survey 'Integration in Austria'		— 'Three years German Islam Conference' — German Islam Conference, 4th Plenum Report — Survey 'Muslim Life in Germany'	
2010	— National Action Plan for Integration			
2011	— Work Program Experts Council Integration — Annual Progress report on the National Action Plan for Integration	Press releases and campaigns by State Secretariat for Integration		
2012	— Annual Progress report on the National Action Plan for Integration — Report on the Dialogue Forum Islam			
2013	— Annual Progress Report on the National Action Plan for Integration			

> 'The German legal framework for the relation between the state and religious communities developed in the historical confrontation with Christian churches.' (DIK, 2009, p. 264)

The historical role of Christian churches is applied as a boundary against Islam in the context of the DIK. Continuous references to the historic role of Christian churches in the development of a secular state order portray Christianity as a religion that is already fulfilling such secular standards and has even co-founded them. Islam is viewed as opposed to these values. This relates to Talal Asad's view on secularism, as the effect of heterogeneous power relations, rather than as a substantial concept. As he argues, certain constructions of the secular are reproduced against Muslims, constructing them as 'external to the essence of Europe' (2003, p. 151).

In the second argument that works within this pattern, the description of Muslims as potential danger to liberal values is contrasted with the construction of these universal ideas as derived from Christianity and therefore essentially linked to it. Here universal values are portrayed as derived from Christian scriptures, Christian theology or Christian ethics, and the normative foundations of contemporary Europe are attributed to Christianity.

An example for such boundary construction can be found in the preamble of an early Austrian policy program:

> 'The following discussion will show that the problem of integrating foreigners predominantly concerns members of the Islamic culture, to a lesser extent also those of other (for example African or Asian) cultures.' (BMI, 2008, p. 18)

This statement is followed by a discussion of 'Austrian values', a listing of liberal norms. On the basic principle of equality the document states:

> 'The principle of equality derives from statements of the Old and especially the New Testament, that all men are equal before God.' (BMI, 2008, p. 20)

Despite a reference to the French Revolution as another source for the principle of equality that follows this statement, a binary opposition is constructed between liberal democracy, which is portrayed as a result of Christian belief, as part of 'us', and a certain idea of Islam, which is characterized by its non-compatibility with universal norms. Both membership and non-membership are defined on religious grounds. However, only few paragraphs in the analysed material are so illiberal in character. In general, references to Christianity are more carefully embedded in the discussion of collective values and identity. This quote from then Minister of the Interior in Germany, Wolfgang Schäuble, expresses this development:

> '[W]e have expectations of Muslims. Following the German legal and moral order, we understand the way towards a thriving coexistence as a process in which cultural and religious differences have to be acknowledged, but also in which the complete acceptance of liberal-democratic basic principles is required as a precondition....Within this order—which is shaped by Christian ethics, this has to be said—Islam has to find its place.' (DIK, 2009, p. 15)

In different forms, this pattern of boundary drawing subsumes the construction of a Christian ancestry to which Islam and Muslims, as the other, are opposed. Christianity, Christian norms or Christian ethics are portrayed as a cultural tradition or a heritage, rather than an actual religion. Joppke calls this a 'demotion of "religion" to the status of "culture"'. In Joppke's argument this promotion of religion through a demotion to culture makes it less of a violation of the neutrality mandate liberal democratic states ought to hold (2013, p. 606). While Christianity is treated as a cultural element, it is debateable to what extent this treatment is a demotion and not just a decoy or even an enhancement. It builds on the pattern of muscular liberalism that merges with a 'neutralized' Christianity. This only relates to a historic development but lacks any reference to believers, churches or religious practice. Tariq Modood speaks of a 'secular Christian', 'analogous to the term 'secular Jew' to describe someone of Jewish descent who has a sense of Jewish identity but is not religiously practicing and may even be an atheist' (2012, p. 142).

Yet this apparently secular Christianity functions to keep Islam outside of the bright boundary of collective identity. More than in the pattern of muscular liberalism, this boundary defines members of the in-group. Compared to the pattern of muscular liberalism, this is a contracting boundary shift as membership is now defined narrower as determined by Christian ancestry.

6.3. Universal Religion

In this pattern unwanted, illiberal and radical behaviour is attributed to 'wrongly understood' religion (then State Secretary for Integration in Austria Sebastian Kurz in Kathpress, 2011) as opposed to a universal religion that reinforces liberal values. No longer is Islam explicitly the marker for an out-group and Christianity the in-group characteristic but a religious community ('we') is opposed by illiberal people who misinterpret religious concepts.

This pattern of boundary drawing is particularly prominent in Austrian policy documents, e.g. in the statement below from the 2011 Integration Report:

> 'A major factor in the integration debate is the question of religious practice....For acknowledged religious communities, there is a need to examine how privileges granted by the state can be utilized to support integration and in turn to impede or avoid behaviour, which is not in accordance with the constitutional laws, under the "cloak" of religion.' (Staatssekretariat für Integration, 2011, p. 13)

Religion, portrayed as generally positive and compatible with universal norms, is differentiated from practices and beliefs described as happening 'under the cloak of religion'. Overall the positive evaluation of religion's ability to promote values comes to the fore, as in the following quote from Sebastian Kurz, on the topic of (Islamic) religious education in public schools:

> 'I believe that religion is very important to people in principle, that values are something important and religion is a good approach to examining personal fundamental values.' (Die Presse, 2011)

This involvement of universal religion in immigrant integration is even recommended to influence other policy fields:

> 'The Expert Council for Integration recommends a broad discussion among state actors, researchers and religious authorities about the role of religion in the public and private spheres. The findings of this process should not only influence religious education and ethics lessons in school, but should also be reflected in labour law, regional development and other legal issues.' (BMI, 2013, pp. 25–26)

This pattern of boundary drawing on religious grounds is an enhancement of religion. 'Universal religion' as part of the collective identity promotes a shared value basis in which the religious, not the secular, is seen as universal. My usage of this term draws on Lori Beaman's concept of the 'will to religion'. Here she discusses a more general trend towards increasing the relevance of religion in various aspects of public life and its consequences. Beaman describes universal religion as 'Christianity's transmutation as representing universal values', able to include a spectrum of religious traditions but remaining 'fundamentally Christian in its shape' (2013, pp. 149–151). While this opens up a possibility for the inclusion of Islam, at the same time it raises the questions of how to assess whether a religion is understood wrongly or rightly and who would be entitled to make this decision. Although integration policy documents do not name concrete examples, critical assessment of religion—as, for example, the Dialogue Forum Islam and its working group on 'gender relations', which aims to 'strengthen women's roles in community work' (BMI, 2013)—is limited to Islam and never involves illiberal aspects of Christianity. Islam and Christianity are not constructed in opposition but religion in general is understood as a positive, even necessary, part of Austrian society. A boundary is drawn between a collective identity of which religion is a central feature and some vague 'other' characterized as incompatible with liberal norms and 'under the cloak of religion'. We can understand universal religion as a boundary expansion: through an emphasis shift, it is no longer Islam in general that is associated with illiberal and therefore outgroup-characteristics but 'misconceived religion'. The boundary that is maintained—the demarcation of misconceived religion, characterized as illiberal and problematic—is clearly used to address (some) Muslims.

All three identified patterns of boundary drawing (see Table 2) can be observed in both Germany and Austria, yet they are unequally distributed between the cases. In Germany, many integration policy documents avoid addressing collective identity and common values beyond references to the Basic Law as a set of universal norms. This focus on the constitution as a point of reference for collective identity, which is much less common in Austrian documents, brings to mind the concept of 'constitutional patriotism' (Habermas, 1991; Sternberger, 1990). Unlike the Austrian constitution, the historic development of the German Basic Law holds a significant meaning for post-war German society (Kommers, 2012). Instead, the German debate on collective identity is mainly outsourced to the Islam Conference and therefore structurally connected to religion. The out-group here becomes defined a priori by the specific setting. The muscular liberalism pattern, whereby a boundary between liberal values and Muslims as an illiberal other is drawn, can be found within the DIK documents and beyond. The Christian ancestry pattern, which connects the liberal self to Christianity by 'secularizing' it, is also common in German policy documents and in particular in DIK documents or general documents that refer to the DIK. The opposite is true of Austrian policy documents. The muscular liberalism pattern is as common as in German documents, although it is not expressed through references to the constitution. While Christian ancestry is less present than in German documents, the pattern of universal religion characterizes Austrian immigrant integration policy documents of the study period. This might be related to the relatively active role of religion that can be found in Austria beyond the field of immigrant integration policies (Avramopoulou, Çorbacioğlu, & Sanna, 2012; Mattes & Rosenberger, 2015).

6.4. Two Christian-Democratic Parties Resolving a Common Dilemma?

While differences between Austria and Germany are small, the similarities are striking. A new emphasis on Christianity, in form of *Christian ancestry* and *universal religion* has been observed in both countries. As actors behave strategically to shape boundaries in their interest (Wimmer, 2013, p. 205) I want to discuss the particular strategies of Christian-democratic policy-makers, who shaped the immigrant integration programs analysed.

Historically, Christian-democratic parties emerged somewhat in conflict with the political system they operated in and often functioned 'as interest groups within a system whose legitimacy the church continued to reject' (Müller, 2014). Early Catholic parties were not in favour of the democratic development of European nation states. Obviously, this anti-democratic attitude has given way to a positive assessment of the modern liberal state and is no longer a characteristic of today's Christian-democratic parties. The shift to a democratic and more liberal political orientation happened at the expense of a narrow Christian (Catholic) agenda (Van Hecke & Gerard, 2004, p. 316). Early on in their history, Christian-democratic parties experienced close ties to the Catholic Church as restraining. Not only did the influence of church officials constrain political margins, but the parties' confessional character also narrowed their potential electorate. Christian-democratic parties found

Table 2. Patterns of religion as a symbolic boundary.

	In-group characteristics	Who belongs to in-group?	Out-group characteristics	Who belongs to out-group?	Type of boundary	Potential of boundary crossing
Muscular liberalism	liberal values	undefined majority	illiberal	Muslims	(potentially) blurred	collective: commitment? individual: assimilation
Christian ancestry	liberal values, determined by Christian history	secular and Christian majority	illiberal	Muslims	bright, contracted	collective and individual: assimilation
	liberal values, determined by Christian theology					
Universal religion	values determined by religions as moral authorities	religious majority	illiberal, 'under the cloak of religion'	(some) Muslims	bright, expanded	collective and individual: dissociation

themselves in what Stathis Kalyvas calls 'the confessional dilemma' and had to figure out 'how to escape from the constraints of their confessional origins while maintaining a distinctive identity' (1996, p. 223).

The role of Christianity for today's Christian-democratic parties is ambivalent and subject to intense internal and external debate. As Andreas Wagner demonstrates, traditional Christian positions on economic policies (aiming at a Christian understanding of a social market economy), welfare (oriented on the male-breadwinner model) or sexuality and gender (e.g. in opposition to gay rights) are controversial even within Christian democratic parties (2014, pp. 211–213). Nowadays, these parties mostly combine groups with different, more liberal, conservative or strictly Christian preferences. Calls for a stronger focus on Christianity—or even just for a reflection on religious foundations—are regularly heard. The central objection against this is the unpopularity of traditional religious arguments for an electorate increasingly unaffiliated to religion (Florin, 2014).

The historical internal dilemma of Christian-democratic parties—to successfully combine a Christian identity with a liberal democratic setting—is highly topical today. Within the field of immigrant integration, however, this dilemma seems to be dissolved by promoting a collective identity that interweaves Christianity with liberal norms against an equally religiously defined other. While religion was always an explicit part of Christian-democratic ideology, the extent to which it was highlighted and communicated varied. Unlike in other policy fields, the emphasis on Christianity is hardly contested here. Apparently, the outsourcing of a broader value debate to the field of immigrant integration allows Christian-democratic policymakers to both solve their internal dilemma and position a collective identity narrative clearly associated with their parties.

7. Conclusion

To conclude, I want to go back to the rhetorical question I raised at the beginning: Are we all Christian, are we all secular, are we all liberal or are we just white? Analysing the construction of religions as symbolic boundaries has allowed assessing the role of religion in the collective identities promoted in German and Austrian immigrant integration policies. To start with the obvious: This analysis supports the well-established claim that liberal norms are a strong, if not the central, element that European collective identities draw on in the context of immigrant integration. The investigated policies correspond to the notion of muscular liberalism as described in the literature. Promoted *collective identities are essentially liberal*.

Regarding the question whether this liberal collective identity is Christian or secular in character, the analysis found both. As references to religion were the central focus of this study, notions of identity that draw on secularism were not analysed systematically. Here lies great potential for further research that relates theoretical debates on conceptualizations of the secular (e.g. Warner, Van Antwerpen, & Calhoun, 2010) to an empirical analysis of collective identity constructions. The focus on religion in this empirical analysis, though, clearly showed that *Christian and secular values are not set in contradiction*, which results in the notion of a 'Christian secular'. If this, as Tariq Modood suggests, is an emerging identity that is Christian but not related to religious practice, the answer to the question if the observed collective identity is Christian or secular is: it is both. Taking into account the observed promotion of a universal religion somewhat changes the picture. Here a *vital religiousness, not exclusively limited to Christianity, is promoted* and results in a marginalization of the secular and the question becomes even less answerable within the limited scope of this study. These dynamics warrant further comparative research on a larger scale, in particular among countries with distinct experiences in terms of religion-state relations and party political settings.

Together the observed boundaries build a clear hierarchical order based on religion, establishing a superiority of Christianity as marker of Europeanness over Islam as the illiberal other. This analysis shows that religion—both Christianity and Islam—is used to uphold difference. Muslims are constructed as inferior to Christianity and the 'truly' European populations produced by it. This supports Fatima El-Tayeb's argument of *Muslim as a racialized category*.

The way Christianity gets linked to secular structures, liberal norms and their transmission merges Christianity and the structural and normative foundations of Austrian, German and European societies. Within immigrant integration policies, the contradictions between those ideologies are argumentatively eliminated, often even reversed. The Christian-democratic policymakers who shaped those policies did not aim to promote a Christian identity instead of a liberal one but seem to have succeeded in equating the primarily liberal collective identities promoted within immigrant integration policies with Christianity.

Acknowledgments

I want to thank Anna Korteweg and Sieglinde Rosenberger for their helpful commentary on previous versions of this paper. This article was supported by the Short-term grant abroad and the Open Access Publishing Fund of the University of Vienna.

Conflict of Interests

The author declares no conflict of interests.

References

Adamson, F., Triadafilopoulos, T., & Zolberg, A. (2011). The limits of the liberal state: Migration, identity and belonging in Europe. *Journal of Ethnic and Migration Studies*, *37*(6), 843–859. doi:10.1080/1369183X.2011.576188

Alba, R. (2005). Bright vs. blurred boundaries: Second-generation assimilation and exclusion in France, Germany, and the United States. *Ethnic and Racial Studies*, *28*(1), 20–49. doi:10.1080/0141987042000280003.

Allievi, S. (2005). How the immigrant has become Muslim. *Revue Européenne des Migrations Internationales*, *21*(2), 135–163. doi:10.4000/remi.2497

Asad, T. (2003). *Formations of the secular: Christianity, Islam, modernity*. Stanford: Stanford University Press.

Avramopoulou, E., Çorbacioğlu, G., & Sanna, M. (2012). Thinking through secularism: Debates on the Muslim veil in Europe. In S. Rosenberger & B. Sauer (Eds.), *Politics, religion and gender: Framing and regulating the veil* (pp. 37–55) New York: Routledge.

Bail, C. A. (2008). The configuration of symbolic boundaries against immigrants in Europe. *American Sociological Review*, *73*(1), 37–59. doi:10.2307/25472513

Barth, F. (1998). *Ethnic groups and boundaries: The social organization of culture difference*. Long Grove: Waveland Press.

Beaman, L. (2013). The will to religion: Obligatory religious citizenship. *Critical Research on Religion*, *1*(2), 141–157. doi:10.1177/2050303213490040

Binder, D. (2001). Die österreichische Volkspartei nach 1945. In M. Gehler, W. Kaiser, & H. Wohnout (Eds.), *Christdemokratie in Europa im 20. Jahrhundert* (pp. 399–424. Vienna: Böhlau Verlag.

Bommes, M., & Kolb, H. (2012). Germany. In C. Joppke L. F. & Seidle (Eds.), *Immigrant integration in federal Countries* (pp. 113–134). Quebec: MQUP.

Brubaker, R. (2010). Migration, membership, and the modern nation-state: Internal and external dimensions of the politics of belonging. *Journal of Interdisciplinary History*, *41*, 61–78.

Brubaker, R. (2013). Categories of analysis and categories of practice: A note on the study of Muslims in European countries of immigration. *Ethnic and Racial Studies*, *36*(1), 1–8. doi:10.1080/01419870.2012.729674

Bundesministerium für Inneres. (2008). *Gemeinsam kommen wir zusammen*. Retrieved from http://www.pakte.at/attach/1gemeinsam_kommen_wir_zusammen_gesamt.pdf

Bundesministerium für Inneres. (2012). Dialogforum Islam. *Öffentliche Sicherheit*, *3/4*, 24.

Bundesministerium für Inneres. (2013). Dialogforum Islam. *Öffentliche Sicherheit*, *1/2*, 36–37.

Cesari, J. (2009). The two pillars of state regulation of European Islam. In J. Heynes (Ed.), *Routledge handbook of religion and politics* (pp. 231–248). New York: Routledge.

De Cillia, R., Reisigl, M., & Wodak, R. (1999). The discursive construction of national identities. *Discourse & Society*, *10*(2), 149–173. doi:10.1177/0957926599010002002

Der Spiegel. (2010, October 15). Integration: Seehofer und Merkel befeuern Leitkultur-Debatte. *Spiegel Online*. Retrieved from http://www.spiegel.de/politik/deutschland/integration-seehofer-und-merkel-befeuern-leitkultur-debatte-a-723466.html

Deutsche Bundesregierung. (2007). Der Nationale Integrationsplan Neue Wege—Neue Chancen Deutschland. Retrieved from https://www.bundesregierung.de/Content/DE/Publikation/IB/nationaler-integrationsplan.html

Deutsche Islamkonferenz. (2009). *Drei Jahre Deutsche Islamkonferenz (2006–2009): Muslime in Deutschland—Deutsche Muslime*. Retrieved from http://gsb.download.bva.bund.de/BAMF/DIK/090616_DIK-Broschuere_gesamt_ONLINE.pdf

Die Presse. (2011, August 25). Kurz: 'Eingangsphasen für jedes Studium'. *DiePresse.com*. Retrieved from http://diepresse.com/home/politik/innenpolitik/688329/Kurz_Eingangsphasen-fur-jedes-Studium

Dierickx, G. (1994). Christian Democracy and its ideological rivals. In D. Hanley (Ed.), *Christian democracy in Europe: A comparative perspective* (pp. 15–30) London: A&C Black.

Dombrowski, D. (2014). *Rawls and religion: The case for political liberalism*. Albany: SUNY Press.

Eder, K. (2006). Europe's borders: The narrative construction of the boundaries of Europe. *European Journal of Social Theory*, *9*(2), 255–271. doi:10.1177/1368431006063345

El-Tayeb, F. (2011) *European others: Queering ethnicity in postnational Europe*. Minneapolis: University of Minnesota Press.

Florin, C. (2014). Christliche Leitkultur—Das ist vorbei. *Christ&Welt*, Nr. 22. Retrieved from http://www.christundwelt.de/detail/artikel/christliche-leitkultur-das-ist-vorbei

Foner, N., & Alba, R. (2008). Immigrant religion in the U.S. and Western Europe: Bridge or barrier to inclusion? *International Migration Review*, *42*(2), 360–392. doi:10.1111/j.1747-7379.2008.00128.x

Gillespie, R. (2014). Reason, religion, and postsecular: Liberal-democratic epistemology. *Philosophy & Rhetoric*, *47*(1), 1–24. doi:10.5325/philrhet.47.1.0001

Grillo, R. (2010). British and others: From 'race' to 'faith'. In S. Vertovec & S. Wessendorf (Eds.), *The multiculturalism backlash: European discourses, policies and practices* (pp. 50–71) London: Routledge.

Guibernau, M. (2004). Anthony D. Smith on nations and national identity: A critical assessment. *Nations and Nationalism*, *10*(1/2), 125–141. doi:10.1111/j.1354-5078.2004.00159.x

Habermas, J. (1991). *Staatsbürgerschaft und nationale Identität: Überlegungen zur europäischen Zukunft*. St. Gallen: Erker.

Hansen, R. (2011). The two faces of liberalism: Islam in contemporary Europe. *Journal of Ethnic and Migration Studies*, *37*(6), 881–897. doi:10.1080/1369183X.

2011.576192
Joppke, C. (2008). Immigration and the identity of citizenship: The paradox of universalism. *Citizenship Studies, 12*(6), 533–546. doi:10.1080/13621020802450445
Joppke, C. (2013). A Christian identity for the liberal state? *The British Journal of Sociology, 64*(4), 597–616. doi:10.1111/1468-4446.12041
Kalyvas, S. (1996). *The rise of Christian democracy in Europe*. Ithaca: Cornell University Press.
Kathpress. (2011, June 9). Kurz: Religionen sind Partner für gelungene Integration. *Kathpress.at*. Retrieved from https://www3.kathpress.at/goto/meldung/423247/kurz-religionen-sind-partner-fuer-gelungene-integration
Kommers, D. (2012). *The constitutional jurisprudence of the Federal Republic of Germany* (3rd ed.). Durham: Duke University Press.
Koopmans, R. (2005). *Contested citizenship: Immigration and cultural diversity in Europe*. Minneapolis: University of Minnesota Press.
Korteweg, A., & Triadafilopoulos, T. (2013). Gender, religion, and ethnicity: Intersections and boundaries in immigrant integration policy making. *Social Politics: International Studies in Gender, State & Society, 20*(1), 109–136. doi:10.1093/sp/jxs027
Korteweg, A., & Yurdakul, G. (2014). *The headscarf debates: Conflicts of national belonging*. Stanford: Stanford University Press.
Laborde, C. (2013). Political liberalism and religion: On separation and establishment. *The Journal of Political Philosophy, 21*(1), 67–86. doi:10.1111/j.1467-9760.2011.00404.x
Lamont, M., & Molnár, V. (2002). The study of boundaries in the social sciences. *Annual Review of Sociology, 28*(1), 167–195. doi:10.1146/annurev.soc.28.110601.141107
Laurence, J. (2013). Islam and Social Democrats: Integrating Europe's Muslim minorities. *Dissent Magazine*. Retrieved from https://www.dissentmagazine.org/article/islam-and-social-democrats
Maffettone, S. (2014). Why liberalism is more important than secularism. *Telos, 2014*(167), 88–106. doi:10.3817/0614167088
Manz, S. (2004). Constructing a normative national identity: The 'Leitkultur' debate in Germany, 2000/2001. *Journal of Multilingual and Multicultural Development, 25*(5/6), 481–496. doi:10.1080/01434630408668920
Mattes, A., & Rosenberger, S. (2015). Islam and Muslims in Austria. In I. Michalowski & M. Burchardt (Eds.), *After integration, Islam, conviviality and contentious politics in Europe* (pp. 129–152). Wiesbaden: Springer.
Mayring, P. (2008). *Qualitative Inhaltsanalyse: Grundlagen und Techniken*. Weinheim: Beltz.
Minkenberg, M. (2002). Religion and public policy institutional, cultural, and political Impact on the shaping of abortion policies in western democracies. *Comparative Political Studies, 35*(2), 221–247. doi:10.1177/0010414002035002004
Modood, T. (2009). Muslims and the politics of difference. In P. Hopkins & R. Gale (Eds.), *Muslims in Britain: Race, place and identities* (pp. 191–209). Edinburgh: Edinburgh University Press.
Modood, T. (2012). Is there a crisis of secularism in Western Europe? *Sociology of Religion, 73*(2), 130–149. doi:10.1093/socrel/srs028
Müller, J. (2014, June 15). The end of Christian democracy. *Foreign Affairs*. Retrieved from https://www.foreignaffairs.com/articles/western-europe/2014-07-15/end-christian-democracy
Pachucki, M. A., Lamont, M., & Pendergrass, S. (2007). Boundary processes: Recent theoretical developments and new contributions. *Poetics, 35*(6), 331–351. doi:10.1016/j.poetic.2007.10.001
Rosenow-Williams, K. (2012). *Organizing Muslims and integrating Islam in Germany: New developments in the 21st century*. Boston: Brill.
Scheffer, P. (2011). The open society and its believers. In M. McTernan (Ed.), *Exploring the cultural challenges to social democracy* (pp. 61–69) London: The Policy Network.
Schwarze, T. (2010, October 16). Merkel gegen Seehofer: 'Der Islam ist Teil Deutschlands'. *n-tv.de*. Retrieved from http://www.n-tv.de/politik/Der-Islam-ist-Teil-Deutschlands-article1729166.html
Spielhaus, R. (2011). *Wer ist hier Muslim? Die Entwicklung eines islamischen Bewusstseins in Deutschland zwischen Selbstidentifikation und Fremdzuschreibung*. Würzburg: Ergon Verlag.
Staatssekretariat für Integration. (2011). *Arbeitsprogramm des Expertenrats für Integration*. Retrieved from www.bmi.gv.at/cms/cs03documents bmi/957.pdf
Sternberger, D. (1990). *Verfassungspatriotismus*. Frankfurt am Main: Insel Verlag.
Tibi, B. (1998). *Europa ohne Identität? Die Krise der multikulturellen Gesellschaft*. Munich: Bertelsmann.
Triadafilopoulos, T. (2011). Illiberal means to liberal ends? Understanding recent immigrant integration policies in Europe. *Journal of Ethnic and Migration Studies, 37*(6), 861–880. doi:10.1080/1369183X.2011.576189
Van Hecke, S., & Gerard, E. (Eds.). (2004). *Christian democratic parties in Europe since the end of the cold war*. Leuven: Leuven University Press.
Wagner, A. (2014). *Wandel und Fortschritt in den Christdemokratien Europas*. Wiesbaden: Springer.
Warner M., Van Antwerpen, J., & Calhoun, C. (Eds.). (2010). *Varieties of secularism in a secular age*. Cambridge: Harvard University Press.
Wilson, E., & Mavelli, L. (2014). *Faith and the asylum crisis: The role of religion in responding to displacement*. Groningen: University of Groningen.
Wimmer, A. (2013). *Ethnic boundary making: Institutions, power, networks*. Oxford: Oxford University Press.

Zincone, G., Penninx, R., & Borkert, M. (Eds.). (2011). *Migration policymaking in Europe: The dynamics of actors and contexts in past and present*. Amsterdam: Amsterdam University Press.

Zolberg, A., & Woon, L. L. (1999). Why Islam is like Spanish: Cultural incorporation in Europe and the United States. *Politics & Society, 27*(1), 5–38. doi:10.1177/0032329299027001002

About the Author

Astrid Mattes is a University Assistant at the Department of Political Science at the University of Vienna. She studied Political Science and Comparative Religious Studies in Vienna and Limerick and spent research visits at the University of Lucerne and the University of Toronto. Her main research interests are European migration and integration politics, religious pluralism, diversity in liberal democracies, and Islam in Europe.

3

Secularities, Diversities and Pluralities: Understanding the Challenges of Religious Diversity in Latin America

Edgar Zavala-Pelayo * and Manuel Góngora-Mera

Lateinamerika-Institut, Freie Universität Berlin, 14197 Berlin, Germany; E-Mails: ezavalap@zedat.fu-berlin.de (E.Z.-P.), manuel.gongora@fu-berlin.de (M.G.-M.)

* Corresponding author

Abstract

Latin America is experiencing today the greatest religious diversity in its entire history. However, it must also be noted that a large number of the growing religious minorities may be classified into types of Christianity with conservative overtones. In this paper we will suggest that the literature streams on multiple secularities in contemporary (Western) societies and religious diversity in Latin America do offer insightful perspectives yet fail to adequately convey the challenges raised by the religious across contemporary Latin America. Addressing Latin America's historical background, we will distinguish conceptually and empirically among different degrees of secularities, diversities and pluralities and will construct with these distinctions a descriptive-normative model that can guide future analyses of secular and religious phenomena in Latin America. It is only through a comprehensive understanding of diversities, pluralities and secularities that the debates on those human rights crucial for social inclusion—from sexual and reproductive rights to gender and religious equality—can be fruitfully conducted in and beyond Latin America.

Keywords

Christian hegemony; multiple secularities; pluralism; religious diversity

Issue

This article is part of the issue "Religious Diversity and Social Inclusion", edited by Gary Bouma (Monash University, Australia).

---

1. Introduction

Different realities require different analytical approaches and policy responses. Latin America,[1] like any other macro-region, has a complex religious history, ranging from the colonial predominance of Catholicism between the 16th and 19th centuries to a manifest multiplicity of religions in the last decades. However, whereas other world regions might have similar histories of colonial evangelizing regimes and comparable landscapes of religious diversity, the complexity of the Latin American experiences cannot be equated with the complexity of those regions' religious histories and configurations. In this paper we argue that perspectival biases in the idea of multiple secularities and conceptual inaccuracies in the analysis of religious diversities in Latin America may be contributing to misunderstandings of the challenges associated with social inclusion that the region faces today.

Firstly, we will offer a legal historical overview of Latin America's colonial background. We will argue that such a background and its religious dogmatism cannot be neglected in comprehensive accounts of contemporary religious issues in Latin America. In our view, such

[1] In this paper the term "Latin America" encompasses only Spanish and Portuguese-speaking countries on the mainland. The Caribbean requires a separate analysis due to its diverse historical experiences (e.g. the Cuban path towards state atheism in the aftermath of the Revolution).

accounts must also include reflections about the fact that the growing religious minorities in Latin America are mostly *Christian* minorities. We will then address the literature that deals with "multiple secularities" across the globe and the literature that analyses religious diversity in Latin America. We will point out the former's underrating of post-colonial cases and the latter's conceptual imprecisions regarding Christian minorities, religious diversity and pluralism. Our analysis will suggest how these gaps are detrimental to the understanding of secular and religious phenomena in Latin America. After these preparatory discussions, we will present a descriptive-normative analytical model that can be used to provide a more comprehensive understanding of the complexity of the religious fields in Latin America and their multiple degrees of secularities, diversities and pluralities. We will conclude with the observation that, by identifying and reflecting upon those complexities and degrees, it is possible to discuss with more precision the impact of religious phenomena on human rights and, by extension, on social inclusion.

2. Religious Diversity in Latin America: A Legal Historical Overview

In 1493 (shortly after receiving news about the West Indies), the Pope granted to the Spanish kings the administrative control of the Catholic Church in the new territories, later confirming this decision with the Papal Bulls of 1501 and 1508; in 1514 he extended this privilege to the Portuguese kings. The system was called Royal Patronage (*Patronato Real* or *Padroado Real*). Iberian crowns enjoyed the prerogative of appointing bishops in their colonies; hence, the civil and ecclesiastical administrations often overlapped. The Iberian empires throughout the colony banned non-Catholic religions (particularly Judaism, Islam and Protestantism) in the Americas with relative success. The Spaniards adopted a cross-and-sword policy of expulsion and forced Christianization in both the Iberian Peninsula and the Americas (Prien, 2013, pp. 3-11). Small numbers of Jews and Muslims fled to America after being expelled from Spain (1492) and Portugal (1497), but many of them converted to Christianity to avoid persecution from the Inquisition. A few native peoples (e.g. Cunas, Mapuches, Amazonian Indians) managed to escape from Iberian rule and were able to maintain, to a great extent, their cultural identity; similarly, Africans who escaped slavery and formed autonomous settlements could partially preserve their religious traditions. But most African and indigenous peoples (were) converted to Christianity—though some of their beliefs and religious practices remained, hidden, through syncretism (Rauhut, 2012). The absence of competing religions resulted in an absolute religious intolerance. While in Europe the Augsburg principle *cuius regio, eius religio* could not be effectively enforced, leading to a proliferation of edicts of religious tolerance throughout the continent, the Iberian empires in America implemented the Inquisition's goal of the systematic control and extermination of sects, heretics and nonbelievers (Chuchiak, 2012). The region became the ultimate expression of the Iberian Counter-Reformation and was unable to develop any significant form of social conviviality with other religions for almost four centuries.

After the wars of independence (early 19th century), relations between church and state became a central dispute between the emergent political factions: liberals, who usually advocated for religious tolerance and encouraged secular authorities, and conservatives, who aligned themselves with the Catholic Church as a rule. Although liberals dominated the new governments, they were aware that religion was a powerful force for social cohesion in the effort to build a national identity in the political chaos of the post-independence era. Thus, they assured the clergy that the Catholic Church would preserve its privileges. As a matter of fact, all the new nations were confessional states, and the Roman curia was forced to allow the new countries patronage rights (Prien, 2013, pp. 277-278, 291-297). All Latin American Constitutions of the early nineteenth century declared their unrestricted, and in some cases perpetual, devotion to Catholicism as the state religion; in some cases, even private worship in other faiths was banned.[2] All Latin American Constitutions adopted shortly after the Spanish *Reconquista* and restoration (1814–1820) maintained confessional clauses, excluding any other religion.[3] Two centuries later, Costa Rica remains as the only confessional State in Latin America. Non-confessional constitutions in the mid-nineteenth introduced freedom of worship and religious tolerance, allowing missionary Protestantism and immigration by Protestants,[4] especially in Brazil and the Southern Cone. Nevertheless, Catholicism was preserved as the state religion.[5] In 1910, at

[2] Cf. e.g. Article 1 (Chapter I) of the 1811 Federal Constitution of Venezuela; Article 4 (Title I) of the 1812 Constitution of the Republic of Cundinamarca; Article 10 of the 1823 Constitution of Chile.

[3] Cf. e.g. Article 8 of the 1823 Constitution of Peru; Article 5 of the 1824 Constitution of the Empire of Brazil; Article 5 of the 1824 Constitution of El Salvador; Article 11 of the 1824 Constitution of the Federal Republic of Central America; Article 3 of the 1824 Constitution of Mexico; Article 45 of the 1825 Constitution of Guatemala; Article 5 of the 1825 Constitution of Honduras; Article 3 of the 1828 Constitution of Chile; Article 8 of the 1830 Constitution of Ecuador; Article 6 of the 1831 Constitution of Bolivia.

[4] Mostly from German-speaking countries, Denmark and the Netherlands.

[5] According to Prien (2013, p. 360), several constitutions granted religious tolerance, while preserving Catholicism as the state religion; for instance, in the *Provincias Unidas del Río de la Plata's* (1819), and later in those of Argentina (1853), Brazil (1825), Uruguay (1830), Paraguay (1870), Chile (1833) and its

least 94% of Latin Americans were Roman Catholics; this percentage remained practically unchanged until the 1980s (Pew Research Center, 2014a, p. 26).

Today, non-confessional constitutions represent the absolute majority in the region. Nevertheless, there are notable differences, resulting from dissimilar historical paths and domestic political dynamics. Nine constitutions make at least a passing reference to God in their preambles (Argentina, Colombia, Ecuador, El Salvador, Honduras, Nicaragua, Panama, Paraguay and Peru). The concept of morals, which is invoked as a restriction on some rights and freedoms connected with religion, explicitly derives from one single religious tradition (Catholicism) in Costa Rica, Panama, and Peru. In some countries (e.g. Nicaragua, Panama, and Peru) religious instruction in public schools is based on Christian values. The right to conscientious objection to military service for religious beliefs is not recognized in several countries. In sum, when comparing Latin America's contemporary challenges associated with religious diversity and social inclusion to those in other world regions, one should consider the crucial role of the colonial experience in understanding the absolute predominance of one religion to the exclusion of any other; this background yielded divergent secularization processes, with specific regional and national paths, dynamics and targets.

3. Religious Diversity in Contemporary Latin America

Latin American nominal Catholics amount to nearly 40% of the world Catholic population (Pew Research Center, 2014a, p. 4; Parker, 2005, p. 36). However, the percentage of people identifying as Catholic has fallen significantly. According to Latinobarómetro (2014, p. 4), the percentage of Roman Catholics fell from 80% in 1995 to 67% in 2013. A recent report by the Pew Research Center (2014a, p. 14) suggests that there are some countries in Latin America whose nominal Catholics may amount to half (El Salvador, Guatemala, Nicaragua) or less than half (Honduras and Uruguay) of the total population. Atheism, however, has not necessarily increased.[6] The emergence of non-Catholic religions and organizations in Latin America has been acknowledged and studied in a number of works by social scientists (e.g., Beltran, 2011; Bidegain & Demera, 2005; De la Torre & Gutiérrez, 2007, 2008; Fediakova, 2007; Ferre, Gerstenblüth, & Rossi, 2009; Forni, Mallimaci, & Cárdenas, 2003; Freston, 2011; Garma, 2007; Garvin, 2005; Parker, 2005, 2012). In these works the concept of religious diversity has been put forward as an unmistakable fact in contemporary Latin America. The religious predominance that Catholicism enjoyed until the second half of the twentieth century has indeed been challenged by expanding religious minorities.

However, there is a factual particularity that is worth pointing out. The growing non-Catholic minorities in Latin America are mostly *Christian*[7] minorities. Describing Latin America as "the world center of Christianity" (Freston, 2012, p. 80; our translation) might perhaps be an over-statement, but it is an unequivocal fact that the majority of the non-Catholic minorities spreading across Latin America are historical or emergent forms of Protestantism. In this sense, we observe two complimentary processes of religious migration: an inter-American flow of religious denominations and a conversion from Catholicism to Protestantism. The former is a process that spreads from the United States and Brazil towards the rest of the continent. Apart from the historical Protestants who arrived starting in the 19th century, the first agents of this migration wave were U.S. missionaries who were no longer allowed to travel to China after 1949 and were sent instead to Latin America (Prien, 2013, p. 553). With the exception of Uruguay, a wide spectrum of Anglo-American denominations has achieved a remarkable presence in all Latin American countries, in particular, in Brazil and Central America (Table 1); these include Baptists, Pentecostals, Presbyterians, Methodists, and Adventists. Additionally, several Brazilian Pentecostal and neo-Pentecostal churches have also penetrated the Andean region and other Latin American countries—e.g. the *Igreja Universal do Reino de Deus* and *Deus é Amor*.

It could be said that the migration process above is being consolidated or extended through a complimentary process of conversion. That is, current religious minorities are also the result of individuals who decide to convert (Freston, 2012) to another Christian religion. At least a third of current Protestants were raised as Catholic and half or more say they were baptized as Catholics. Interestingly, 60% of converts to Evangelicalism said that one reason they left the Catholic Church was their desire for a more assertive teaching on moral questions and greater commitment, reflected in conservative positions on typical hot-button issues (Pew Research Center, 2014a, pp. 5-6). The resulting religious landscape is a particular one.

If figures from the latest survey by the Pew Research Center (2014a) are considered, only 8% of the total population in Latin America would be religiously unaffiliated, and 88% would be Christian (19% Protestants and 69% Catholics). Results from the World

Ley Interpretativa (1865), Bolivia (1906), Peru (1915), Venezuela (1874), Honduras (1848, 1865, 1873) and Costa Rica (1860).

[6] In countries like Chile and Uruguay, however, the numbers of atheists, agnostics and religiously unaffiliated has remarkably increased (Pew Research Center, 2014a).

[7] By referring to this comprehensive category, we want to convey not an idea of hierarchical "varieties" of a single religion (Catholicism) but their theological, ritualistic and socio-political coincidences—regardless of whether these are seen as derivative or independent.

Table 1. Percentage of Catholics and Protestants.

	Country	Estimated Population 2013 (millions)	Catholics	Protestants/ Evangelicals	Total Christians
Countries with absolute Catholic dominance (>70%)	Paraguay	6.6	90%	6%	96%
	Mexico	116.2	83%	5%	88%
	Peru	29.8	81%	13%	94%
	Ecuador	15.4	80%	11%	91%
	Colombia	45.7	80%	14%	94%
	Bolivia	10.5	78%	16%	94%
	Argentina	42.6	76%	5%	81%
	Panama	3.6	75%	20%	95%
	Chile	17.2	70%	15%	85.%
Countries with significant Evangelical influence (>20%)	Brazil	201	64.6%	22%	86.6%
	Costa Rica	4.7	63%	23%	86%
	Guatemala	14.4	59%	36%	95%
	Nicaragua	5.8	53%	28%	81%
	El Salvador	6.1	51%	33%	84%
	Honduras	8.4	47%	36%	83%
Countries without religious dominance	Uruguay	3.3	45%	10%	55%

Source: Bureau of Democracy, Human Rights and Labor, U.S. International Religious Freedom Report for 2013.

Table 2. Percentage of Christians and non-Christians.

Affiliation/Country	Argentina	Brazil	Chile	Colombia	Ecuador	Peru	Uruguay
Total Christians*	71.2	78.9	75	77.1	76.1	86.8	31.2
Total non-Christians	10.9	5.6	0.2	1.1	0.3	1.7	7.5
Other; Not specific	9.7	1.2	0	0.9	0.3	1.4	7.3
Spiritist	0	3.5	0	0	0	0	0
Espirit, candomble, umbanda, esoterism, occultism	0	0.5	0	0	0	0	0
Buddhist	0.5	0.2	0	0.1	0	0	0
Hindu	0.2	0	0.1	0	0	0.2	0
Jew	0.3	0.1	0.1	0	0	0	0.2
Muslim	0.2	0.1	0	0.1	0	0.1	0
None	16.9	15	23.1	21.4	23.5	10.1	60.7
Don't know/No answer	0.9	0.6	1.7	0.3	0.1	1.5	0.6
N=	1,030	1,486	1,000	1,512	1,202	1,210	1,000

Source: Adapted from figures obtained through World Values Survey's online-analysis tool, wave 6, 2010–2014. * Roman Catholics, Protestants, Christians, Evangelicals, Pentecostals, Jehovah Witnesses, Mormons, 7th Day Adventists and Orthodox.

Values Survey are somewhat more conservative, but the pattern is also noticeable. Table 2 presents the most recent figures (waves 2011–2014) from the World Values Survey on religious denominations in some countries in Latin America. Although there are exceptional cases like Uruguay, this survey suggests that more than 70% of the population in Latin America is nominally Christian even in countries such as Argentina and Brazil, where non-Christian minorities are comparatively significant.

If the figures in Table 2 are compared, for example, to the more even distribution in the Asia-Pacific zone of Christians (7%), Muslims (24%), Unaffiliated (21%), Hindus (25%), Buddhists (12%), Folk religions (9%), Other religions (1%) and Jews (<1%) (Pew Research Center, 2014b), it is possible to state that the "religious diversity" label might have been used in Latin America too liberally and without the necessary nuances. Granted, the unique institutional/group identity, the doctrinal-theological specificities, and the particular socio-political histories of Christian minorities—as well as the diversity within Catholicism[8]—must be acknowl-

[8] Catholicism, as a global religion, is not only a mirror of the diverse societies where it can be found (Levine 2014), it also comprises a number of sub-institutions (e.g. religious orders, convents, schools, charities, etc.) and hierarchical structures (e.g. parishes, dioceses, bishoprics) whose direction by different individuals or groups across a multiplicity of historical peri-

edged and carefully reflected upon. However, it would be misleading to assume that there are no similarities between some of these minorities' theological principles and moral-political stances and those found in Latin America's Catholicisms. From a global perspective, Latin America still exhibits low levels of diversity, comprising, as it does, a majority of Christian, mostly conservative, confessions. Notwithstanding the theological antagonisms and mutual distrust among Protestants, Evangelicals and Catholics, it is not unusual to find coinciding conservative stances among them on social issues such as marriage, family, sexual orientation, reproductive choices, gender relations, education and personal autonomy. In these areas crucial for social inclusion one could speak of a Christian hegemony. This is characterized by the persistence of unequal rules of the game in the religious market; high control by churches over the educational system; promotion of traditional (Christian) values and views on personal autonomy (which leads to discrimination in workplaces and in schools, for instance); legitimation of sexism, homophobia, transphobia and other forms of discrimination; and/or the criminalization of abortion and stigmatization of women. From a legal point of view, such a framework creates inconsistencies with international human rights standards.

From this brief overview we can conclude that Latin America's religious fields diverge from those in the U.S. and Europe, where challenges arise instead from large waves of immigrants bringing with them their Christian *and non-Christian* religions. Similarly, Latin America's challenges are not those of African and Asian states, which have adopted Islam as an official religion and where minority faiths are discriminated against, conversion is punished, and several forms of religious-related violence are common. The challenges in Latin America are different. While all Latin American countries ban religious discrimination, recognize religious freedom, and protect indigenous religiosity, most of them remain countries where Christian denominations prevail and where religious equality is far from being achieved outside of constitutional texts.

4. Perspectival and Conceptual Shortcomings

In our view, there are two sets of literature on secular and religious diversities that are crucial to understanding Latin America's religious fields. The first offers a comparative framework of multiple secularities across the globe; and the second refers to the religious diversity/pluralism in Latin America. We will argue that there are critical shortcomings in both sets and also potential contributions between them if those very shortcomings are worked out. We will argue that multiple-secularities approaches do not necessarily overcome the west-and-rest discourse and can be further improved by considering the case of Latin America, yet without the conceptual overlapping between the ideas of religious diversity, plurality and pluralism that can be found in some scholarly works on this region.

Modernity in the west-and-rest discourse is conceived as a European innovation that has been globally transferred and whose European standards are the arrival point of every modern society (Hall, 1996). For decades, postcolonial authors have deconstructed this discourse (Boatcă, 2015, pp. 201-226; Costa, 2006, pp. 83-97; see also Bhambra, 2007; Chakrabarty, 2000). Recently, some debates on secularisms and religious diversity have considered the postcolonial critique of Occidentalism and have adopted a "multiple modernities" approach. A group of scholars, for instance, has proposed a model of "multiple secularities" which "acquire different shapes in different countries", for they operate "according to different cultural logics that document specific social histories of conflict"; these secularities, in a sense, "'respond' to specific...reference problems and offer 'solutions' to them" (Schuh, Burchardt, & Wohlrab-Sahr, 2012, p. 358; see also Wohlrab-Sahr & Burchardt, 2012). In a later publication, Burchardt, Wohlrab-Sahr and Middell (2015) accounted for these problems and distinguished four analytically ideal (not normative) types of secularities (see Table 3).

Table 3. Multiple secularities.

Reference Problems	Ideal types (Secularity for the sake of...)
Individual freedom vis-à-vis dominant social units	...individual rights and liberties
Religious heterogeneity and the resulting potential or actual conflictuality	...balancing/pacifying religious diversity
Social or national integration and development	...societal or national integration and development
Independent development of institutional domains	...the independent development of functional domains of society

Source: Own elaboration based on Burchardt et al. (2015).

To these four problem-secularity type combinations the authors add four accompanying groups of "guiding ideas": freedom and individuality, toleration and respect, progress and modernity, and rationality and autonomy, respectively. These guiding notions are normative "reference point[s]" that legitimize "religious-

ods and world regions yields greater diversity in performative and ideological terms.

secular distinctions" (Burchardt, Wohlrab-Sahr & Wegert, 2013, p. 615) and are held by individuals, groups, states or functional domains. We agree with the authors as to the convenience of separating the notion of the secular from linear narratives of modernity and underlining the historically contingent meanings of the secular and the different starting and arrival points of the societies studied. We also prefer the concept of "secularity" over "secularism" (which is usually restricted to the relationships between organized religions and the state) as a way to extend the analysis to the relations between the triad of state, organized religions, and society with its functional domains, e.g. education, science, media, business. In this sense, the concept serves to remedy what Frigerio and Wynarczyk call the "dominant model" (2008, p. 248) in analyses of religious fields—the exclusivist emphasis on the churches and the state alone that can be found in the specialized literature on Latin America (e.g. Amuchastegui, Cruz, Aldaz, & Mejia, 2010; Blancarte, 1994; Levine, 2009; Masferrer, 2013; Moran, 2013; Parker, 2012; Sawchuck, 2004) and beyond (e.g. Lavinia & Turcescu, 2011; Robbers, 2005). Nevertheless, this model may not overcome the west-rest bias. The groups of "guiding ideas" in each combination above are analytically useful but include complex concepts which, at least in some post-colonial societies, constitute implicit or explicit (quasi)epistemologies—e.g. progress, modernity and rationality—that have guided secular *and non-secular* individuals, states, groups and functional domains alike in a variety of projects, controversies and disputes. It is therefore not surprising that the authors find difficulties in inserting the case of South Africa into their model. They acknowledge that whereas modernity in the West meant a "struggle between Christianity and secularizing and secularist forces," Christianity in South Africa "became fundamentally intertwined with modernity" (Burchardt et al., 2013, p. 621). What would happen then to the model if it were constructed from the outset with this type of "exceptional" (postcolonial) cases? The case of Latin America is a useful one because it represents, first off, a region where "cultures of secularity" (Wohlrab-Sahr & Burchardt, 2012, p. 888) *as well as* religious cultures and phenomena—emerging religious minorities included—fill the social landscape and the discursive space.

However, in our view, some scholarly debates about Latin America's religious diversity do not necessarily offer a sound analytical platform upon which an alternative model—aimed at understanding not just multiple secularities but multiple *religious phenomena* beyond those of the West—could be constructed. In some scholarly works on Latin America's religious phenomena the concepts of diversity, plurality and pluralism are used interchangeably either as descriptors of the simultaneous presence of different religious denominations or as counterparts to concepts such as religious monopoly, hegemony, uniformity or majority. For instance, in a work on religious diversity in Latin America, an author asserts that "there is already a Latin American religious pluralism which is based in a growing diversity of heterogeneous cultural expressions." Later on, however, he explains this "religious pluralism" by referring circularly to the "diversity of beliefs" (Garma, 2007, p. 50). In a major work on religious diversity in Mexico, the introductory chapter points to the need to study the scope of "the diversification and the religious plurality" in Mexican indigenous localities (De la Torre & Gutiérrez, 2007, p. 14), thus implying the occurrence of two different realities, yet no conceptual distinction between these two concepts is provided in the text—instead the terms religious pluralism, plurality, diversity and diversification seem to be used interchangeably (2007, pp. 7, 9, 11, 14, 15). Similarly, in an introduction to a co-edited volume on religious diversity in Colombia, "religious plurality" is accounted for by the "religious diversity" (African religions, Sephardic Judaism, Islam) reportedly found in Latin America during colonial and postcolonial times (Bidegain, 2005, p. 15).

These conceptual-analytical imprecisions have been pointed out by other authors. Frigerio and Wynarczyk (2008) refer to the importance of Beckford's conceptual distinction between pluralism as i) "the magnitude" of religious diversity, ii) the extent to which religious minorities are "accepted" in a society and iii) the acknowledgement of the "moral and political value" of religious diversity (2008, pp. 233-234). In the view of these authors, the mere presence or growth of religious diversity does not necessarily equate to pluralism in sense ii) and, more importantly, in sense iii), that is, pluralism as the positive sanction of the moral and political relevance of new religious expressions and organizations. For pluralism to exist, the authors assert, there must be a fair "regulation" of the "religious market" (2008, p. 248), where the state as well as non-state institutions, such as NGOs and mass media, sanction the extra-religious importance of religious minorities. Frigerio and Wynarczyk's conceptual distinctions are similar in principle to Levine's. Levine (2009) distinguishes between religious plurality and religious pluralism. The former equates to the existence of religious diversity, that is, the quantitative presence of religious groups, denominations, and churches; religious pluralism goes beyond this presence and amounts to "the construction of rules of the game" (2009, p. 407; see also Freston, 2012, pp. 87-88) that give equal rights and legitimacy to the newcomers in the religious field. For Levine plurality serves as a necessary, though insufficient, condition of pluralism. From a stronger normative position, Eck (2001) had suggested earlier a similar clarification of religious pluralism. For this author, as well, religious pluralism does not amount to religious diversity. Firstly, whereas religious diversity is just "an observable fact," religious pluralism, in the author's view, must be "real engagement" with the religious other; secondly, whereas religious diversity entails only tolerance, religious pluralism also demands the understanding of the religious other and the overcoming of "stereotypes and prejudices"; thirdly pluralism must not become "valueless relativism" but must rather strengthen "the health of religious faith" (2001, pp. 69-71). Eck notes as well that pluralism does not refer to a given state of affairs but to "the ongoing work of each generation" (2001, p. 72).

With the above shortcomings and conceptual guidelines in mind, we now propose an analytical frame focused on the concrete hegemonic framework of Latin America and the conceptual distinctions between, and degrees of, secularities, diversities and pluralities.

5. A Three-Dimensional Model of Religious Pluralisms

In this section we describe both a series of key dimensions and a scale of degrees by which those dimensions can be analysed and referred to in debates on religious diversity, religious plurality and social inclusion, as depicted in Figure 1.

Firstly, we propose three key dimensions as axial categories that represent, in our view, the most important subfields in a given region's religious field/s: society, organized religions and the state. What we suggest is to regard them as institutions but also as interdependent sub-fields of forces; that is, partly autonomous and partly dependent axial spaces where symmetric and asymmetric relations of power between individuals, groups and institutions take place either in manifest or latent forms (Lukes, 2005). By referring to them as currently existing sub-fields we do not mean clear-cut spaces whose analysis concerns only present-time phenomena. These are dimensions whose constitution is to varying degrees related to their historicity. Thus we understand the *organized religions dimension* as one of the religious field's subfields, where historical churches and emergent organized religions and syncretic cults can be found either separate from each other or connected through symmetric or asymmetric links. In the same fashion, we suggest looking at the state not as a macro-institution but as a dimension where struggles for, and the granting of, religious rights take place. Similar to Frigerio and Wynarczyk's proposal (2008), our axial spaces include the *society dimension*. Yet we do not understand "society" as particular organizations and mass media that regulate the religious market (2008, pp. 228-229), but more generally as a subfield that is constituted by a wide range of individuals and groups that interact or not in a given context and can range from the atheist or the non-believer to the religiously-unaffiliated and the religiously-(multi)affiliated.

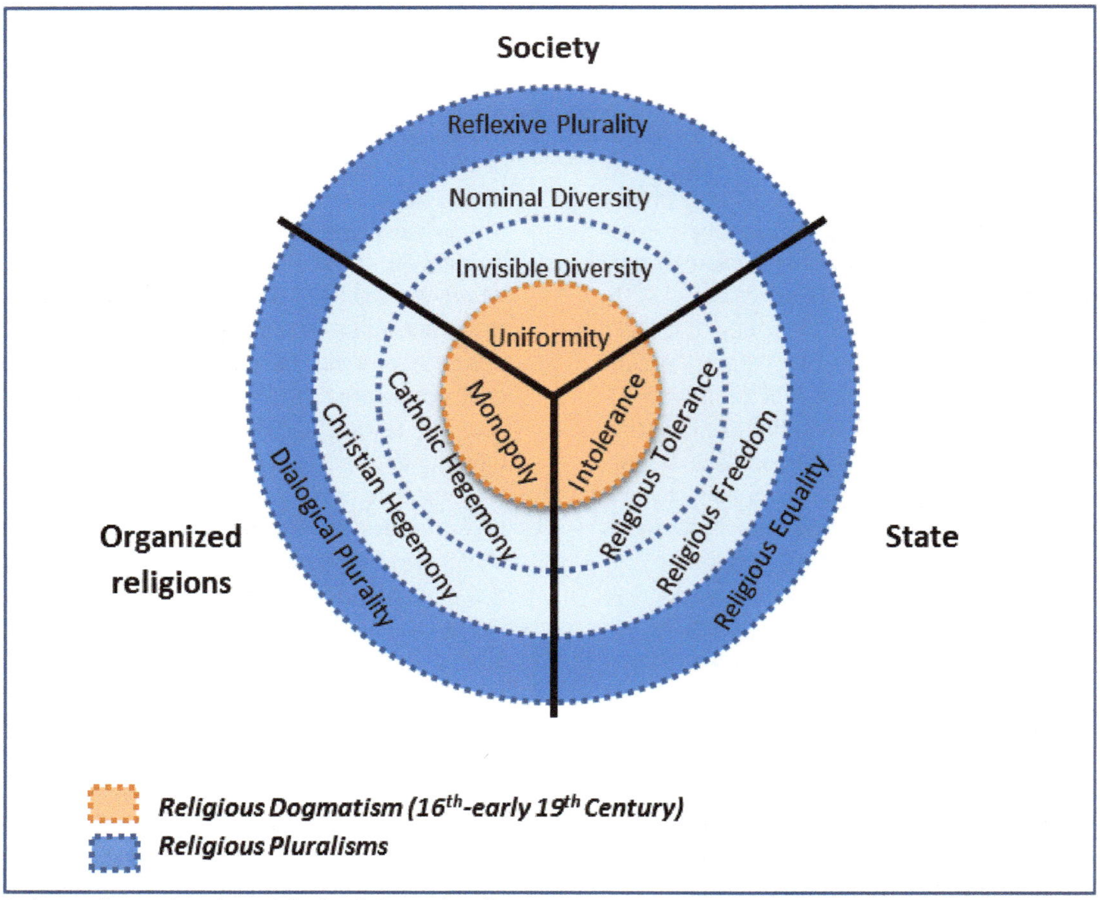

Figure 1. A three-dimensional model of religious pluralisms.

The second particularity of our model is aimed at overcoming the implicit and explicit binarisms in the literature on the emerging religious diversity in Latin America by adding degrees which can further qualify the three dimensions above. Like Eck (2001), Frigerio and Wynarczyk (2008) and Levine (2009), we sustain the analytical relevance of distinguishing between the quantitative emergence of religious diversity, the configuration of religious plurality, and religious pluralism as a combined and ceaseless process. Following this logic, instead of conveying in our model the idea of societies that are "uniform" or "diverse" in terms of religious (un)affiliation; "hegemonic" or "plural" in the subfield of organized religions, and "confessional" or "secular" with regard to the state, we want to convey multiple degrees of diversity, plurality and secularity that can be found in society, organized religions and state dimensions respectively. These degrees are not cumulative stages towards religious pluralisms; they are societal features that do not, and should not, necessarily unfold sequentially. Each degree is meant to be analysed qualitatively, quantitatively or both, to assess how much of, and which specific manifestations of, the degree in question can be empirically verifiable in a given case. We consider it important to point out as well that the degrees, which we will expand on below, are based mostly on descriptive analytics but also on a cautious normative standpoint, upon which a flexible concept of ideal religious pluralisms will be conveyed. These ideal religious pluralisms amount to the degrees illustrated in Figure 1's outer circular layer and are based on the idea that *complete* and *permanent* harmony, ecumenism and cooperation in societies (Mouffe, 2000) and religious fields might stand as desirable teleologies and even practical goals but should not be regarded as necessary requirements for a sound religious pluralism. We will expand on these realistic expectations in the sub-sections below.

5.1. The State Dimension

As observed, secularity in Latin America mainly relates to the state protection of the rights of religious minorities and the demise of the institutional privileges enjoyed by the Catholic Church, rather than to the decline of religiosity or the retreat of religion from public spaces. Due to the secular paths taken in Latin America (i.e. usually from Catholic confessionality to impartial but non-atheist states) we basically distinguish between: 1) *religious intolerance*: confessional states where non-adherents to the state religion are socially excluded and even private non-Catholic worship is expressly forbidden, creating favorable conditions for structural discrimination against persons who do not accept the official ideology or who oppose it; 2) *religious tolerance*: confessional states where religious minorities, although being socially excluded to different extents, are allowed (rather than entitled) to hold religious ceremonies in public, and the Catholic Church is supported by the government and enjoys other legal and political prerogatives; 3) *religious freedom*: confessional and non-confessional states that recognize the freedom to choose a religion or belief, consistently maintain a certain church-state separation and allow the legal recognition of non-Catholic religions (including their rights to possess properties, land and media; to form political parties; and to declare political positions), but where the Catholic Church might retain some privileges in consideration of its majoritarian status or cultural relevance for the nation; and 4) *religious equality*: non-confessional states that revoke the Catholic Church's privileges and establish principles of state evenhandedness vis-à-vis theistic, non-theistic and atheistic beliefs.

5.2. The Society Dimension

We suggest qualifying the degree of religious heterogeneity in society by contrasting the previous religious uniformity of Latin American colonial societies with their contemporary diversity and by breaking down the latter into a) *invisible diversity*, b) *nominal diversity* and c) *reflexive plurality*. Our starting point is the idea that a plural society should first and foremost know about the actual existence of the religious alternatives that can actually render that society plural. By proposing *invisible diversity* as an analytical distinction, we want to bring attention to the fact that there have been, and surely still are and will be, non-Catholic individuals and groups in Latin America whose religious or non-religious profile is unknown beyond limited circles of state and/or religious experts. When the religious others' local presence is ignored by the majority of individuals and major groups (e.g. media, educational institutions, business, political parties, civic organizations, etc.), we can speak about a situation of *invisible diversity*. Individuals and groups in one of Mexico's western-central states may be aware of the presence of publicly active Jehovah's Witnesses in the vicinity but individuals at large, and perhaps the local media or business sector, might not necessarily know about the presence of members of the "Marian Trinitarian Spiritualism" church (Sanchez, 2009). In such a case quantitative and qualitative assessments of what/how much religious diversity has been detected in a region can give a better sense of how much invisible diversity prevails there.

By *nominal diversity* we mean societies where there is both a factual presence of religious minorities as well as some major institutions, and/or individuals within those institutions, that do know about the presence and basic constitution of alternative religions and religious groups in that society. These are social institutions and individuals, beyond limited circles of religious or state experts, which are relatively knowledgeable about general facts of those religious alternatives—

their main doctrinal tenets or organizational characteristics, for instance. Within this category it is also possible to distinguish between a) actively hostile scenarios—where religious minorities are discriminated against or attacked (Dias, 2012; Vallverdu, 2005, p. 62); and b) passive scenarios—where individuals affiliated to the majority religion are aware of the presence and basics of the religious others but have little or no desire to understand them further—and vice versa (Mendoza, 2008, p. 202).

We suggest reserving the term *reflexive plurality* for societies where individuals from different religious groups—as well as atheists—know about the presence, the basics and at least some of the substantial views and background of their religious counterparts. These societies may or may not enter into cooperative relations based upon such knowledge. We do not see societies with reflexive plurality from a radical idealistic viewpoint, that is, as perfect societies where everybody knows with precision the history and doctrinal configuration of each religious alternative and where cooperation is therefore the norm (cf. Eck, 2001). For us, reflexive plurality does require openness and tolerance in order to be aware of prejudice (Eck, 2001), but such an openness can well remain as the base of a detached understanding.

5.3. The Organized-Religions Dimension

As to the plurality of churches and other organized religions, Latin America is characterized by the historical monopolistic position of the Catholic Church. In some cases, this monopoly remained uncontested even after the post-independence secular reforms that took place at different points in time across the region. What has followed, after the nominal challenge of this monopoly over the last two centuries, are different types of non-monopolistic dimensions of organized religion. From a descriptive position we distinguish two types: *Catholic hegemony* and *Christian hegemony*; from a normative position we distinguish one further type: *dialogical plurality*. Catholic hegemony describes dimensions where the Catholic Church, as an internally-diverse majority church in most countries, co-exists with Christian minority churches as well as other religious groups, associations or communities whose collective identity is not necessarily that of a church (as in the case of the Umbanda; Prandi, 2004, p. 229). Notwithstanding this co-existence, the Catholic Church and its ensemble of religious orders, Catholic groups and associations retain a clear religious and extra-religious (political, cultural, educational) pre-eminence (Levine, 2014; Levy, 1996). This Catholic hegemony is better apprehended if it is seen as the outcome of the historical religious and extra-religious activism of this church and its organizations. Regarding the case of Argentina, Carbonelli and Jones refer to such an outcome as a "cultural matrix" that has the capacity "to confer meaning on national identity and to shape state structures" (2015, p. 160; our translation).

Similar to a duopoly, a *Christian hegemony* could be described as a religious field where the Catholic Church and Christian denominations share a dominant position, which can result from various forms of cooperation or unintended alignment on moral and extra-religious issues (e.g. against reproductive rights, homosexuality, same-sex marriage, euthanasia, etc.). Through extra-religious activism, direct intervention in politics and the operation of media channels and radio stations, Christian morals, values and worldviews thus continue to shape social relations and define the rules of the game. Brazil illustrates this case. According to Freston (1998), Brazilian Pentecostal churches—which themselves seek a hegemony within the Brazilian Protestant milieu—tend to have no united political front but do have an active presence in the country's politics. Brazilian Pentecostal politicians have been elected as governors, federal deputies and city officials; in the most recent legislative period, they accounted for 12% of the seats in the Brazilian Congress (Machado & Burity, 2014, p. 601).

Dialogues are a main component of what we consider as an organized-religions dimension with *dialogical plurality*. This is a plurality that describes religious fields where majority and minority religions and religious groups not only value (Frigerio & Wynarczyk, 2008) their different or similar contributions to the religious and extra-religious dimensions but do so by openly communicating with each other (Vallverdu, 2005, p. 63). This particular type of religious plurality may include interfaith dialogues as well as other (socio-political) dialogues among the religious denominations' lay members or non-"authorized" voices (Levine, 2009, p. 406). Nevertheless, dialogical plurality, just as reflexive plurality in the society dimension, is not necessarily expected to produce cooperative engagement (cf. Eck, 2001) or a harmonious ecumenism (cf. Hagopian, 2009; Parker, 2005). Even less are such dialogues likely to be an effective means of overcoming asymmetries of power. Nonetheless, we consider dialogues as conducive to the creations of conditions of competence, dissent and negotiation that may well contribute significantly to progress towards more inclusive rules of the game. Here Frigerio and Wynarczyk's notes on the role of social institutions are relevant. A sound level of dialogical plurality is manifested when majority and minority religions/religious groups alike are able to dialogue, under equal conditions of openness, with state institutions as well as with society's civic groups, mass media, NGOs and other non-state organizations.

6. Conclusions

Drawing critically from the literature on religious diversity and the multiple-secularities approach, the analytical model we propose is aimed at overcoming Eurocentric categorizations and conceptual imprecisions. The model above contains both descriptive and normative analytical categories whose even and balanced distribution in Figure 1 is meant to represent neither symmetric dimensions in actual societies nor degrees of diversity, plurality and secularity that develop jointly in a linear fashion. Although the model does propose normative scenarios in the dimensions of state, religion and society, it is not meant to suggest a method which Latin American societies would have to undertake in order to develop and/or consolidate religious pluralism. The model above clarifies key concepts that can be used in specialized discussions and problematizes the interpretations of contemporary realities regarding the religious fields in Latin America. It is also a flexible analytical tool that can be adapted to local, national or transnational contexts and approaches. For instance, it can enable multi- or inter-disciplinary comparisons of degrees of secularities, diversities and pluralities that can be empirically observed across multiple local contexts—e.g. across Chiapas in Mexico, Chimborazo in Ecuador and Cauca in Colombia, where Protestant communities have apparently developed in comparable terms (Gros, 1999). Once operationalized, the model can also be used as a framework for comparative analyses of the degrees of religious pluralism across different Latin American countries or regions; these comparisons can be quantitative or qualitative and generate, for instance, *indexes* or *typologies* of religious pluralism. If the model is properly adapted—particularly the model's departure point, i.e. the region's historical background—it can also assist comparative analyses of the development of religious diversities/pluralisms, or other religious/secular dynamics, within and across postcolonial regions beyond Latin America. In any case, adaptations in our view would have to be cautious and preferably follow the non-Eurocentric, non-linear, complex (multiple dimensions and degrees) and realist rationale of the original model.

Above all, we consider both the discussion and the analytical proposal above to be key inputs for contemporary debates on social inclusion. As suggested in this paper, there are conceptual and empirical links between the consolidation of reflexive plurality in society at large, the development of dialogical plurality among organized religions and atheist organizations and the attainment of religious equality in terms of equal rights granted by the state to organized religions. More importantly, it can also be said that the development of reflexive and dialogical pluralities in the first two subfields may facilitate not only the consolidation of religious equality among organized religions but also the de-centering of Christian values in public education and the granting by the state of gender equality, as well as comprehensive sexual and reproductive rights for all individuals regardless of their sexual orientation—some of the crucial inclusive rights where there has been important progress on the legal and judicial fronts, but whose *de facto* fulfillment, and political debate at times, has been somewhat hindered by hegemonic churches and individuals' religious beliefs alike. The decrease of Catholic or Christian hegemony and the increase of dialogical plurality among organized religions, coupled with the presence of a reflexively plural society, may not be sufficient yet remains a necessary condition for the attainment of the aforementioned rights. A dialogical field of organized religions, together with societies whose reflexive plurality is high, may also facilitate the legal application and extra-legal consolidation of those inclusive rights. The resulting religious pluralisms—or the reflexive and dialogical cultures, and legal frames, of equality, understanding and dissent—provide, in principle, effective conditions for social inclusion.

Acknowledgements

We should like to thank the *Social Inclusion* journal's anonymous reviewers, the editor of this special issue as well as Paul Talcott and Carlos N. Mora, for their valuable comments on an earlier version of this paper.

Conflicts of Interest

The authors declare no conflicts of interest.

References

Amuchastegui, A., Cruz, G., Aldaz, E., & Mejia, M. (2010). Politics, religion and gender equality in contemporary Mexico: Women's sexuality and reproductive rights in a contested secular state. *Third World Quarterly, 31*(6), 989-1005.

Beltran, W. (2011). Descripción cuantitativa de la pluralización religiosa en Colombia. *Universitas Humanística, 73*, 201-237.

Bhambra, G. (2007). *Rethinking modernity postcolonialism and the sociological imagination*. Basingstoke and New York: Palgrave Macmillan.

Bidegain, A., & Demera, J. (2005). *Globalización y diversidad religiosa en Colombia*. Bogotá: Universidad Nacional de Colombia.

Blancarte, R. (1994). *Iglesia y Estado en México: Seis décadas de acomodo y de conciliación imposible*. México: IMDOSOC.

Boatcă, M. (2015). *Global inequalities beyond Occidentalism*. Farnham: Ashgate.

Burchardt, M., Wohlrab-Sahr, M., & Wegert, U. (2013). "Multiple secularities": Postcolonial variations and guiding ideas in India and South Africa. *International Sociology, 28*(6), 612-628.

Burchardt, M., Wohlrab-Sahr, M., & Middell, M. (Eds.)

(2015). *Multiple secularities beyond the West: Religion and modernity in the global age*. Boston, Berlin and Munich: De Gruyter.

Carbonelli, M., & Jones, D. (2015). Igualdad religiosa y reconocimiento estatal: Instituciones y líderes evangélicos en los debates sobre la regulación de las actividades religiosas en Argentina 2002–2010. *Revista Mexicana de Ciencias Políticas y Sociales, LX*(225), 139-168.

Chakrabarty, D. (2000). *Provincializing Europe. Postcolonial thought and historical difference*. Princeton: Princeton University Press.

Chuchiak, J. (2012). *The Inquisition in New Spain, 1536–1820: A documentary history*. Baltimore: John Hopkins University Press.

Costa, S. (2006). *Dois Atlânticos. Teoria social, anti-racismo, cosmopolitismo*. Belo Horizonte: UFMG.

De la Torre, R., & Gutiérrez, C. (Eds.) (2007). *Atlas de la diversidad religiosa en México*. México: CIESAS, COLJAL, COLEF, COLMICH, UQROO, SEGOB, CONACYT.

De la Torre, R., & Gutiérrez, C. (2008). Tendencias a la pluralidad y la diversificación del paisaje religioso en el México contemporáneo. *Sociedade e Estado, 23*(2), 381-424.

Dias de Oliveira, I. (2012). Religião e etnicidade: Novas sensibilidades num mundo multicultural. In C. Parker (Ed.), *Religión, política y cultura en América Latina. Nuevas miradas* (pp. 285-295). Santiago de Chile: Instituto de Estudios Avanzados, Universidad de Santiago de Chile.

Eck, D. (2001). *A new religious America. How a "Christian country" has become the world's most religiously diverse nation*. New York: Harper Collins.

Fediakova, E. (2007). Religión, política, ciudadanía: Cambio de paradigmas, iglesias evangélicas en Chile post-guerra fría. *Bicentenario. Revista de Historia de Chile y América, 6*(2), 71-98.

Ferre, Z., Gerstenblüth, M., & Rossi, M. (2009). Religión y religiosidad en Uruguay. *Cuadernos del CLAEH*, 32(99), 19-34.

Forni, F., Mallimaci, F., & Cárdenas, L. (Eds.) (2003). *Guía de la diversidad religiosa de Buenos Aires*. Buenos Aires: Biblos.

Freston, P. (1998). Pentecostalism in Latin America: Characteristics and controversies. *Social Compass, 42*(3), 335-358.

Freston, P. (2011). Religious pluralism, democracy, and human rights in Latin America. In T. Banchoff & R. Wuthnow (Eds.), *Religion and the global politics of human rights* (pp. 101-128). New York: Oxford University Press.

Freston, P. (2012). Las dos transiciones futuras: Católicos, Protestantes y sociedad en América Latina. In C. Parker (Ed.). *Religión, política y cultura en América Latina. Nuevas miradas* (pp. 77-97). Santiago de Chile: Instituto de Estudios Avanzados, Universidad de Santiago de Chile.

Frigerio, A., & Wynarczyk, H. (2008). Diversidad no es lo mismo que pluralismo: Cambios en el campo religioso argentino (1985–2000) y lucha de los evangélicos por sus derechos religiosos. *Sociedade e Estado, 23*(2), 227-260.

Garma, C. (2007). Diversidad religiosa y políticas públicas en América Latina. *Revista Cultura y religión, 1*(1), 48-60.

Garvin, N. (2005). Conversion & conflict Muslims in Mexico. *International Institute for the study of Islam in the Modern World, 15*, 18-19.

Gros, C. (1999). Evangelical Protestantism and indigenous populations. *Bulletin of Latin American Research, 18*(2), 175-197.

Hagopian, F. (2009). The Catholic Church in a plural Latin America. In F. Hagopian (Ed.), *Religious pluralism, democracy and the Catholic Church in Latin America* (pp. 429-466). Notre Dame: University of Notre Dame.

Hall, S. (1996). The West and the rest: Discourse and power. In S. Hall (Ed.), *Modernity: Introduction to the modern societies* (pp. 185-227). Oxford: Blackwell.

Latinobarómetro. (2014). Las religiones en tiempos del Papa Francisco. Retrieved from http://www.sciencespo.fr/opalc/sites/sciencespo.fr.opalc/files/LAS_RELIGIONES_EN_TIEMPOS_DEL_PAPA_FRANCISCO%20-%20copie.pdf

Lavinia, S., & Turcescu, L. (2011). *Church, State, and democracy in expanding Europe*. New York: Oxford University Press.

Levine, D. (2009). Pluralism as challenge and opportunity. In F. Hagopian (Ed.), *Religious pluralism, democracy and the Catholic Church in Latin America* (pp. 405-428). Notre Dame: University of Notre Dame.

Levine, D. (2014). *Popular voices in Latin American Catholicism*. Princeton: Princeton University Press.

Levy, D. (1996). *Building the third sector: Latin America's private research centers and nonprofit development*. Pittsburgh: University of Pittsburgh Press.

Lukes, S. (2005). *Power. A radical view* (2nd ed.). New York: Palgrave Macmillan.

Machado, M., & Burity, J. (2014). A ascensão política dos pentecostais no Brasil na avaliação de líderes religiosos. *DADOS: Revista de Ciências Sociais, 57*(3), 601-631.

Masferrer, E., (2013). *Religión, política y metodologías*. Buenos Aires: Libros de la Araucaria.

Mendoza, M. (2008). La Nueva Jerusalén y su relación con la población otomí de Querétaro. *Estudios de Cultura Otopame, 6*(1), 199-211.

Moran, J. (2013). Feminismo, Iglesia Católica y derechos sexuales y reproductivos en el Chile post-dictatorial. *Estudos Feministas, 21*(2), 485-508.

Mouffe, C. (2000). The democratic paradox. London and New York: Verso.

Parker, C. (2005). ¿América Latina ya no es católica? Pluralismo cultural y religioso creciente. *América Latina*

Hoy, 41, 35-56.

Parker, C. (Ed.) (2012). *Religión, política y cultura en América Latina. Nuevas miradas*. Santiago de Chile: Instituto de Estudios Avanzados, Universidad de Santiago de Chile.

Pew Research Center. (2014a). *Religion in Latin America: Widespread change in a historically Catholic region*. Retrieved from http://www.pewforum.org/files/2014/11/Religion-in-Latin-America-11-12-PM-full-PDF.pdf

Pew Research Center. (2014b). *Global religious diversity*. Retrieved from http://www.pewforum.org/2014/04/04/global-religious-diversity/#fn-20155-2

Prandi, R. (2004). O Brasil com axé: Candomblé e umbanda no mercado religioso. *Estudos Avançados, 18*(52), 223-238.

Prien, H. J. (2013). *Christianity in Latin America* (revised and expanded edition). Leiden and Boston: Brill.

Rauhut, C. (2012): *Santería und ihre Globalisierung in Kuba. Tradition und Innovation in einer afrokubanischen Religion*. Würzburg: Ergon.

Robbers, G. (2005). *State and Church in the European Union*. Baden-Baden: Nomos.

Sanchez, O. (2009). Vivir entre dos religiones. In S. Benard & O. Sanchez (Eds.), *Vivir juntos en una ciudad en transicion. Aguascalientes frente a la diversidad social* (pp. 189-212). Aguascalientes: Universidad Autónoma de Aguascalientes.

Sawchuk, D. (2004). *The Costa Rican Catholic Church, social justice and the right of workers 1979–1996*. Waterloo: Wilfrid Laurier University Press.

Schuh, C., Burchardt, M., & Wohlrab-Sahr, M. (2012). Contested secularities: Religious minorities and secular progressivism in the Netherlands. *Journal of Religion in Europe, 5*, 349-383.

Vallverdú, J. (2005). Violencia religiosa y conflicto político en Chiapas, México. *Nueva Antropología, 65*, 55-74.

Wohlrab-Sahr, M., & Burchardt, M. (2012). Multiple secularities: Towards a cultural sociology of secular modernities. *Comparative Sociology, 11*, 875-909.

About the Authors

Dr. Edgar Zavala-Pelayo

Edgar Zavala-Pelayo is a postdoctoral researcher based at the Institute for Latin American Studies and the Center for Area Studies of the Free University of Berlin. He holds a master's and doctoral degree in sociology from the University of Edinburgh. His theoretical and empirical research focuses on science-and-religions and politics-and-religions entanglements and their relations to the paradigms of modernity/ies, rationality/ies and secularisms/secularities.

Dr. Manuel Góngora-Mera

Manuel Eduardo Góngora-Mera is a postdoctoral researcher and lecturer at the Institute for Latin American Studies of the Free University of Berlin. He obtained his doctoral degree in Public Law from Humboldt University of Berlin. His publications deal mainly with constitutional and human rights issues, including international human rights law, inter-American constitutionalism, social rights, and categorical inequalities.

4

The Fog of Extremism: Governance, Identity, and Minstrels of Exclusion

Amyn B. Sajoo

Simon Fraser University, Faculty of Arts & Social Sciences, Vancouver, BC V6B 5K3, Canada; E-Mail: asajoo@sfu.ca

Abstract

An insistent focus on extremism and radicalization with regard to current Islamist trends masks the failures of pluralist citizenship, amid a larger crisis of identity. Whether in Muslim-majority societies or in the Euro-North American diaspora, "Islam" and "politics" are touted as explaining patterns of severe violence by state/non-state actors. Neither category accounts more than superficially for the complexities at hand, which revolve around exclusionary models of identity, faith and civil society. Successful narratives of inclusive citizenship depend on key markers outside of modernist secular orthodoxy. Theologies of inclusion are vital in fostering pluralist civic identities, mindful of the ascendance of puritanical-legalist theologies of exclusion as a salient facet of public cultures. Multiple surveys reveal the depth of exclusivist conservatism in diverse Muslim societies. These stances not only undermine civil society as a locus for engendering pluralist identities, but also undergird the militant trends that dominate the headlines. Targeting militants is often essential—yet is frequently accompanied by the willful alienation of Muslim citizens even within liberal democracies, and a growing "official" sectarianism among Muslim-majority polities. Convergent pluralisms of faith and civic identity are a vital antidote to the fog that obscures the roots as well as the implications of today's extremist trends.

Keywords

citizenship; civil society; exclusion; human rights; Islam; minorities; pluralism; radicalization; secularism; sectarianism; sharia; theology

Issue

This article is part of the issue "Religious Diversity and Social Inclusion", edited by Gary Bouma (Monash University, Australia).

The Balkan minstrels continued to tell their tales, now interrupting each other. In their desire to be accepted they had forgotten the insults, and humbly, almost awkwardly, begged: *We want to be like you. We think like you. Don't drive us away.* The old lady sensed that there was something missing from their tales.

'Could you sing the things you have been telling us?' she asked.

They were shaken as if they had been dealt a blow. Then, tearing themselves out of their stupor, one after the other, each in his own language, and finally in Latin, said 'No.' *Non.*

'Why not?' she asked kindly.

'*Non, domina magna*, we cannot under any circumstances. We are minstrels of war.'

They could not break out of the mold. Besides which, they would first have to consult their elders. Consult the dead...*Non*.

Ismail Kadare, *Elegy for Kosovo*, 1998

1. Introduction

For well over a decade—in the wake of the events of September 11, 2001, and most notably the US-led "war on terror"—responses to Islamist trends have been marked by an avowed focus on "extremism." A rising concomitant is the targeting of "radicalization" through legislation and social policy. Indeed, the latter is deemed a longer term and more subtle facet of the strategic response to Islamism, and to militant groups in particular. "We are engaged in a struggle that is fought on many fronts and in many forms," explains the United Kingdom home secretary, Theresa May, about a counter-terror law that includes banning "extremist" speakers from universities. "The threat we face right now is perhaps greater than it ever has been. We must have the powers we need to defend ourselves" (UK Government, 2014). This was echoed in France's response to the November 2015 terror attacks in Paris, where the language of "war" against a foreign "army" (Daesh/Islamic State) was coupled with an extended state of emergency allowing for special police powers, and constitutional changes relating to citizenship.[1] An embattled "we" is engaged in nothing more, or less, than self-defense against the depredations of radicals—the very sentiments that drove the expansive post-September 11 vision of mortal combat against global terror, and the war in Iraq.

What is new about this ominous threat that will engage us indefinitely? Terms such as "cosmic" and "irrational" are commonly associated with the professed religiosity of the extremists and radicals that threaten our wellbeing (Juergensmeyer, 2003; Neumayer & Plumper, 2009; Wilson, 2012). Whether in Muslim-majority societies or in the Euro-American diaspora, "Islam" or "politics" is touted as an explanatory category for patterns of severe violence by non-state actors. For some—scholars, politicians, journalists—it is not merely religion but Islam in particular that accounts for a *sui generis* propensity to violence. Orientalist tropes abound here, blithely oblivious or in spite of the trenchant critiques of that tradition offered up by Edward Said and others. For others, the explanations are about politics: in a secular age that demands sensitivity to scapegoating and persecution, Islam and Muslims are foils for struggles that are about perceptions of justice and the failure of democratic avenues of expression. To the extent that religion is a significant factor in radicalism and militancy, it is confined to extremist quarters that can be contained if not eradicated.

This article argues that neither category provides a tenable explanation, for all the historical and scientific rhetoric that is proffered in the guise of erudite critique. A binary view fails to account for a larger identity crisis that provides the setting for current Islamist trends, militant and otherwise. In a context where church and state find themselves in a complex relationship that does not fit the more familiar models—American, French, Saudi Arabian—religion no longer occupies the tidy institutional place that modernity assigned it in our individual and collective trajectories. Narratives of citizenship ignore this shift at their peril, if wedded to secularist claims about civic identities. Progressive theologies can play a vital role through inclusive discourse and action. As David Santillana observed nearly a century ago in this regard, "every question of law is also a matter of conscience, and jurisprudence is based on theology in the final analysis" (1926, p. 5). Today, puritanical-legalist stances on the shari'a are a prime basis for exclusive and repressive orthodoxies: multiple surveys reveal the depth of conservatism on matters of faith and civic culture among ordinary Muslims. These stances nurture the extremism that dominates the headlines, and undermine civil society as the locus of pluralist identities. Military and policy responses to actors such as al-Qaeda, Daesh ("Islamic State"), Boko Haram and al-Shabab are necessary. Yet strategic alliances are rife with and among governments that actively promote or shield anti-pluralist actors. And a deeper malaise of pluralist citizenship within the western diaspora is obscured in the war on extremism.

Without an ethos that takes seriously not only public religion but minority traditions in particular, secular frameworks of inclusion fall seriously short on effective citizenship. Our primary focus here is on the nexus of Islamist extremism and the larger malaise of identity in a globalized, secular modernity. Insecure identities seek shelter in a social and intellectual conservatism that may be religious and sectarian, but also secular, as in the case of nationalism. Examples of such trends in non-Muslim contexts are offered, though an elaborate survey is quite beyond the scope of this paper. I will first set forth the dichotomous claims about framing the militancy of actors that are deemed extremist in terms of "Islam" and "politics" as exclusive categories, before venturing into the underlying tensions of identity that find expression in religious conservatism and radicalization. Finally, I will address the ensuing challenges of pluralist citizenship that require an ethos of secular *and* religious inclusion—where material incentives are a necessary but insufficient condition.

An elucidation here on terminology. "Islamism" is an unsatisfactory descriptor of Muslim political action: it signals attachment to a faith tradition regardless of whether this actually has any merit. We do not standardly use such loose tags for political Judaism, Hinduism, Buddhism or Christianity. Nevertheless, "Islamism" has become a term of art in academic and media commentary (Martin & Barzegar, 2010). I use it in the sense of a drive to foster "an ideological community," one that strives for *state governance* through official "moral codes in Muslim societies and communities" (Bayat, 2013, p. 4). Such drives may be expressed in national and transnational movements—from al-Mourabitoun, Boko Haram, al-Shabab and the Taliban, to al-Qaeda and Daesh.[2] Islamists are distinguished

[1] Schofield (2015). The political and ethical perils of the "war metaphor" were promptly raised by *The Economist*—Prospero (2015).

[2] The term "Daesh" is used throughout this paper, as the appropriate acronym for al-Dawla al-Islamiya al-Iraq al-Sham (Islamic State of Iraq and the Levant) (Grayling, 2016). This is also

from non-political actors that advocate for spiritual or social welfare goals, and also "active pietist" groups that aspire to shape civil-political identities. The term *jihadi*, which tends to invoke a religiously-inspired struggle against "wordly" targets, including Muslim ones perceived as slack in their commitment to Islam, is highly diffuse; active pietists and civic movements may profess *jihad* as much as do militants (Abu-Rabi, 2010; Stephan, 2009). Many Islamists do not espouse militancy at all; some prefer the electoral route where available, as with prominent Egyptian and Tunisian and political actors in the "Arab Spring." Here, "militancy" and "extremism" refer to Islamist choices on this score, the acceptance of which is about "radicalization." The choices may be strategic or theological, informed or otherwise; it is our task to seek to understand why these choices are acted upon.

2. Framing Extremist Militancy

2.1. "Islam Is the Answer"

For an array of commentators, the self-proclaimed religiosity of actors who resort to violence suffices as the rationale for their choices. "Islam" accounts for a spectrum of motivations and realities that are summed up under the rubrics of extremism and radicalization, which characterize militancy ranging from that of major non-state groups to freelance terrorists. At its simplest, this equates the most aggressive forms of political Islam, or "Islamism," with Islam as a faith tradition. Typical are the post-September 11 writings of Bruce Bawer (2006, 2009), Gisele Littman (2005), Mark Steyn (2006), and Robert Spencer (2008, 2009). Populist in language, style and reach (many have been bestsellers), they perceive an "Islamified Europe" as the ultimate outcome of the mere existence of Muslim migrants—because "Islam itself is a political project," to quote Steyn. Muslim values, then, are not only incompatible with those of a Judeo-Christian West, but are ultimately ideological more than anything else. Indeed, the entirety of Muslim history and civilization are reduced—especially in the work of Spencer—to a linear narrative of animus against non-Muslims.

These populist writings, for all their tenuousness, have the benefit of an enabling analytical landscape. A key node is the "clash of civilizations" posited by Samuel Huntington (1996): an account of "Islamic culture" as a singular entity in perpetual conflict with western values, a teleology which Muslims fit into no matter where they are located. "The underlying problem for the West is not Islamic fundamentalism," according to Huntington, but rather "Islam, a different civilisation whose people are convinced of the superiority of their culture and are obsessed with the inferiority of their power" (1996, pp. 217-218). Although a plethora of critiques have undercut virtually all the serious claims in this account,[3] it remains influential after the events of September 11. Populist discourse draws on its sweeping assumptions and projections, stoking public fears about migration, Muslim minorities and national security (Abrahamian, 2003; M. Dunn, 2006; Wright, 2015). Then there is the work of scholars such as Daniel Pipes (2002a), Niall Ferguson (2004, 2006, 2011), and Bernard Lewis (1990, 2002, 2003), who have weighed in with insights on the histories of the Middle East/Islam, and the implications for western societies. Many of these insights are essentialist in casting Muslims and Islam as a unitary vector separate from and threatening to the stability and wellbeing of western societies.

Even for an eminent historian of the Middle East such as Lewis, "Islam" serves as a discrete category that ultimately trumps the diverse politics, economics and cultures of Muslim societies past and present. His tone is more temperate than Huntington's. Yet the same teleology is voiced, wherein western societies find themselves in the path of a "Muslim rage" that drives contemporary conflicts. Thus: "Islam, like other religions, has also known periods when it inspired in some of its followers a mood of hatred and violence. It is our misfortune that part, though by no means all or even most, of the Muslim world is now going through such a period, and that much, though again not all, of that hatred is directed against us" (Lewis, 1990). But he can be cavalier, as in his oft-cited 2004 proclamation to a German newspaper that "Europe will have a Muslim majority by the end of the twenty-first century at the very latest...Europe will be part of the Arab west—the Maghreb." (Schwanitz, 2004).[4] Demographics in this context is, of course, a charged subject with far-reaching implications for perceptions of identity as well as security. And this is reflected in western academic and populist commentary on extremist militancy and social radicalization.

At the most mundane level of linkage between religious identity and anti-western animus, Pipes pulls no punches: "A vast number of Muslims, those living in the Europe and the Americas no less than elsewhere, harbor an intense hostility to the West. For most Muslims, this mix of envy and resentment remains a latent sentiment, but for some it acquires operational significance" (2002b). Just as forthright is the Harvard scholar Niall Ferguson, no specialist on the Middle East or the Muslim world, but an authority on global history. "The greatest of all strengths of radical Islam...is that it has demography on its side. The western culture against

the term used by the UN with regard to Syria, as in Resolution 2254 (2015, December, 18), adopted by the UN Security Council.

[3] Edward Said (2001) labelled it as being about "a clash of ignorance" in which "the West" and "Islam" are analytically poor banners.

[4] A claim challenged by *The Economist* (2006).

which it has declared holy war cannot possibly match the capacity of traditional Muslim societies when it comes to reproduction" (2006). Apart from the intriguing claim that demography is a greater weapon than ideas or anything else in the extremist arsenal, it is worth noting the leap in reasoning from "radical Islam" to "traditional Muslim societies." Furthermore: "A youthful Muslim society to the south and east of the Mediterranean is poised to colonize—the term is not too strong—a senescent Europe...A creeping Islamicization of a decadent Christendom is one conceivable result: while the old Europeans get even older and their religious faith weaker, the Muslim colonies within their cities get larger and more overt in their religious observance" (Ferguson, 2004).

Bruce Bawer is almost regretful about the inexorable nature of this linkage, and the defensive impulse of its victims. "Many European Muslims," he asserts in his acclaimed *While Europe Slept: How Radical Islam is Destroying Europe From Within*, "may themselves be moderates, yet may have a concept of religious identity that makes it difficult for them to side with infidels against even the most violent of their fellow Muslims" (2006, p. 229). Evidence of this may heavily be to the contrary, judging by the volume of diasporic Muslim denunciation of acts of terrorism by fellow Muslims,[5] and the data on migrant integration and marginalization (Saunders, 2012). Yet if one accepts the premise that religious identity for Muslims is an undifferentiated whole—leaving scant room for distinction between a member of Daesh or al-Qaeda and a Muslim member of Amnesty International or Médecins Sans Frontières—then the apprehensions of Bawer, Lewis, Ferguson, and Pipes are warranted. Indeed, the premise was explicitly invoked by Anders Breivik, the Norwegian whose manifesto justifying his 2011 acts of mass terror repeatedly cited the writings of Bawer, among other influences (Breivik, 2011; see more generally Townsend & Traynor, 2011).

Those sentiments frequently lament the erosion of Europe's Christian identity, as a bastion against Islam and Muslims. How ironic, then, that the wider modernist discourse, even in much of the Muslim world, is about *secularism* as serving as a bastion against religion at large. At its most assertive, this latter view strips secularism down to the absence of public and private religion—a state of affairs which is deemed rational and friendlier to nonviolence. For the cluster of "new atheists," such as Richard Dawkins, Daniel Dennett, Sam Harris, Christopher Hitchens, and Ayaan Hirsi Ali, the trends in post-September 11 extremism have much to do with religious belief (Kettell, 2013; Jacoby & Yavuz, 2008). The intellectual integrity of this stance has been trenchantly challenged in assorted quarters, along with it ideological direction (Atran, 2010; Hedges, 2008; Ruse, 2010; Taylor, 2013). Suffice it to say that the new atheism plays into the politics of both the "clash of civilizations" *and* the demographic thesis, feeding public phobias about an invasive irrationality tied to Islam and Muslims. "We are at war with Islam," proclaims Sam Harris, "with precisely the vision of life that is prescribed to all Muslims in the Koran, and further elaborated in the literature of the hadith, which recounts the sayings and teachings of the Prophet" (2004, p. 110). A stronger reiteration of Huntington would be hard to find.

2.2. "Politics Is the Answer"

Secular globalization, argues the French sociologist Olivier Roy in *Holy Ignorance*, has snapped the premodern link between religion and culture. Religions today tend to regard culture as "profane, secular, or pagan" (2010, p. 28), which stakes a claim to authenticity by asserting a purity that renounces the political. But since politics, like culture, is everywhere, it is subsumed within faith traditions—thus sacralizing the world. For Roy, this is the ultimate counterpoint to modernity's secularization of the world, wherein everything that was once sacred is now subject to the appraisal of the economic, social and scientific. In the confrontation of faith and material culture, "holy ignorance" is rife: each side reimagines the other in its own image, a process that "is not contradicted by external social practice" (2010, p. 217). Roy's rich data is not merely about faith traditions resisting external social realities, but equally about the secular "formatting" of religious practices in public policy and corporate culture, with scant regard to the actual complexities of those practices.

The flipside of claiming that Islam explains extremist militancy and radicalism, then, is that hard political realities do so. A major strand of analysis aims to counter the secularist essentialism that frames religion, and Islam in particular. The cliché that "Islam is way of life" ends up signifying that everything is somehow about theology. Orientalism's long history of doing this is a matter of record, and the legacy remains with us (Said, 1997, 1994). Sami Zubaida's *Beyond Islam* offers a detailed account of Middle East modernity that strives to locate religion within economic and social contexts, pointedly rejecting the very idea of "Islamic society" so beloved of Orientalist narratives (2011). Instead, it is the "materiality of religion" in everyday life—expressed in "the shaping of political actors, alliances

---

[5] This extends to repeatedly petitioning mainstream newsmedia to cease using the term "Islamic State" in describing the group widely called "Daesh" in the Muslim world—and a graphic social media campaign launched in 2014 against the group under the banner #NotInMyName. See more generally Charles Kurzman's web-page, Islamic statements against terrorism. Retrieved from http://kurzman.unc.edu/islamic-statements-against-terrorism

and conflicts"—that Zubaida holds up for appraisal, notably in premodern Ottoman and present day Egyptian, Iranian and Turkish societies (p. 78). The tangibility of this approach to understanding religion, along with its humanizing quality, stand in stark contrast to the exoticization and othering of Orientalist accounts. Further, the ciphers of oppositional "western" and "Islamic" societal values are exposed, with substantial sociological data about their shared and overlapping realities, past and present.

At the same time, such approaches can secularize faith-centred impulses and actions. What Said called the "political actualities" entailed by the trends that proclaim a "return to Islam," tend here to overwhelm and obscure the theological drives that are real features of the landscape (1997). This is not necessarily the intent—which, typically, is to offer a sober counternarrative to essentialist accounts. Thus in Doug Saunders' *The Myth of the Muslim Tide: Do Immigrants Threaten the West*, the reader is offered an impressive corpus of statistical and historical data that map the social pathways of migrants in Europe and North America, including Catholics and Jews (2012). The debunking of anti-immigrant and anti-Muslim claims is cogent and, in the present climate, laudable. Still, Saunders echoes the view that secularizing trends among Muslim migrants should reassure us—along with the growing "privatization of religion" in Muslim societies such as Egypt, Iran and Turkey. Social inclusion and social peace rest on the conformity of Muslims to a version of modernity that is familiarly secular.

Again, in response to the puritanical tendency to separate religion from public culture noted by Roy, there are official attempts at doing the reverse. Cultural categories, after all, are more amenable to secular analysis and management in public policy/lawmaking—the "formatting" of religion (2010, pp. 187-191). This is accentuated in settings where official secularism is hard-wired into the constitution, as in France and Belgium; but Roy's evidence extends far beyond. In the US, where religion is well integrated into political culture, as well as Saudi Arabia and Iran, where official orthodoxies prevail, minority practices must fit into the approved administrative formats. The growing diversification among religions worldwide, institutional and otherwise, intensifies the challenge of "managing" them via existing formats (Bouma, 2008; Juergensmeyer, Griego & Soboslai, 2015). Moreover, new security regimes worldwide since the events of September 11, 2001, and the Edward Snowden revelations of 2013, have ushered in pervasive intrusions into group and individual domains (Lyon, 2015)—underscoring the need to format and control a range of "religious" behaviors, from piety and worship to socio-political activity. In a reminder of how surveillance schemes can violate the basic civil rights of religious groups, the US Court of Appeals rebuked New York City police for the arbitrary "classification" of Muslims along lines reminiscent of official abuses against African-Americans, Jews, and Japanese-Americans (Hassan vs. The City of New York, 2015).

For Will Kymlicka, a leading scholar of citizenship in diverse societies where Muslims live in diaspora communities, the emphasis has been on "cultural inclusion" as the gateway (2001; Kymlicka & Norman, 2000); this is rationalized in terms of democratic and social justice, and the imperatives of civic education. Minority rights are likewise framed in terms of the complexities of ethnic politics and effective legal-political accommodation (Pföstl & Kymlicka, 2015). Tariq Modood draws attention to the limits of such multicultural frameworks when it comes to religious minorities, calling for more effective forms of secularism to accommodate such citizens (2000). Being secular does not ipso facto mean being "value neutral;" secularism itself embodies a variety of value-postures on civic life (Berger, 1999; Bhargava, 1998; Martin, 2005). Recent literature has gradually taken this on board, as in Joshua Castellino and Kathleen Cavanaugh's seminal *Minority Rights in the Middle East* (2013), which is attentive to the dynamics of religious and socio-cultural identities in pursuit of equitable citizenship. It falls short, though, in engaging with the growing role of the shari'a with regard to the region's minorities, beyond normative statements (Sajoo, 2014). An incisive study of the Coptic minority in Egypt by Paola Pizzo explores the vital role of institutional faith actors on all sides in seeking both social and political inclusion—and importantly, links this to civil society (2015). There is a hint here of the evolving theologies of civic membership, though this remains unexplored.

The upshot is a thrust to frame the issues in political terms, at the expense of attention to theological components. Despite much criticism, the analytical vocabulary of human rights, minority claims, and social justice remains dominantly secular and secularizing. In significant part, this reflects frail public support even in liberal democratic societies for the accommodation of some religious expressions in the civic domain, especially when "multicultural tolerance" involves Muslims post-September 11 (Benton & Nielsen, 2013; Wright, Johnston, Citrin, & Soroka, 2016). Examples range from veiling to municipal zoning for mosques; a conspicuous display of civic resistance was the 2009 Swiss ban on minarets, after the results of a referendum that strongly overrode the official accommodationist stance (Cumming-Bruce, 2009). These public encounters with religion bring "sacred" laws and norms under the scrutiny of the political domain and can impart a strong sense of desacralization, if not secularization. Evidently, it is not only Islamists and their counterparts in other traditions who politicize their faith. Indeed, religious actors "struggle to come to terms with the very social landscape that the secular state was meant to address, namely the vast variation of identities housed within the borders of the nation" (Juergensmeyer et al., 2015, p. 32).

3. Extremism, Faith and Identity

3.1. Modernity's Orphans

Shortly after the arrest of Anders Breivik for the cold-blooded slaughter of civilians on the Norwegian island of Utøya on July 22, 2011, there was consternation among the police over his main preoccupation. Amid fresh corpses and pools of blood, Breivik demanded attention for a tiny cut on his finger, from a splintered piece of a victim's skull. "Look, I'm hurt. This will have to be bandaged up...I can't afford to lose too much blood," he complained. Later in prison, Breivik bitterly grieved the failure to upgrade his game console from Playstation2 to Playstation3, and also the grip on his institutional rubber pen. He strutted like a bodybuilder for a prison photo. On the basis of psychiatric reviews, the court ruled that Breivik was not psychotic. Recounting at length the narcissism, lack of empathy, isolated childhood, and the screed (noted above) that voiced a hate-filled politics, Karl Knausgaard argues that these cannot fully explain why Breivik committed what has been called "the worst attack on Norwegian soil since the Second World War":

> "Breivik's deed, single-handedly killing seventy-seven people, most of them one by one, many of them eye to eye, did not take place in a wartime society, where all norms and rules were lifted and all institutions dissolved; it occurred in a small, harmonious, well-functioning, and prosperous land during peacetime. All norms and rules were annulled in *him*, a war culture had arisen in *him*, and he was completely indifferent to human life, and absolutely ruthless. That is where we should direct our attention, to the collapse within the human being which these actions represent, and which makes them possible." (Knausgaard, 2015)[6]

For all the flaunting of anti-immigrant and anti-Muslim bigotry, Breivik's bizarre acts leading up to, during and after the massacre amount, for Knausgaard, to "role-playing, rather than political terrorism." One may quarrel with his conclusion, which seems to assume that such role-playing is necessarily distinct from terrorism; terrorists are often intent on posturing larger-than-life roles. Yet it is surely true that the erosion of basic human constraints against acts of mass murder in peacetime and prosperity is no ordinary thing, and suggests acute alienation. Knausgaard contrasts the internal collapse of constraints and instincts with their external/societal demise in situations like Iraq and Syria, and earlier in the Balkans and Rwanda. But the extraordinary brutality of Daesh, al-Qaeda, and the like is also perpetrated by recruits (and "supporters") from places of relative peace and prosperity across the world.[7] In other words, by individuals who have much in common with Breivik. Daesh's behavior, Knausgaard observes, "cannot be ascribed to people having suddenly become evil but, rather, to the disintegration of the mechanisms that in a civilized society typically prevent people from engaging in rape and murder." This social disintegration, then, runs with the internal collapse of individual constraints and instincts.

Modernity's alienating structural effects on individual identity—*anomie*—were evident over a century ago to Emile Durkheim, and are a core concern in the social sciences (Orru, 1987). The effects are heightened by secular globalization as a vital feature of the contemporary landscape. As noted, public culture is in tension with religion not only among communities of faith, but also in the policy frameworks of modern states that "format" religious practices and institutions. It is no surprise that the ensuing challenges to identity can provoke strong responses. The "politics of resentment" finds global expression along diverse avenues (Mazar, 2014), from fierce protests over dignity and national pride to violent insurgencies on behalf of imagined precolonial identities. Narratives of humiliation, grievance and fear are a staple not only of extremist groups, but also of nationalisms and "democratic" demagogues. Receptivity to them rests on political and social alienations. For the anthropologist Scott Atran, who has interviewed youths drawn to violence on six continents—including most recently in Iraq—the alienations feed a "dynamic countercultural movement":

> "Violent extremism represents not the resurgence of traditional cultures, but their collapse, as young people unmoored from millennial traditions flail about in search of a social identity that gives personal significance and glory. This is the dark side of globalization. They radicalize to find a firm identity in a flattened world where vertical lines of communication between the generations are replaced by horizontal peer-to-peer attachments that can span the globe." (Atran, 2015)

Social bonds and sacred values are key attractions in countering modernist alienations (Atran, 2010; Atran, Hammad, & Gomez, 2014). Groups like Daesh and al-Qaeda offer both: the intimacy of family-like group af-

---

[6] Knausgaard's account draws heavily on the comprehensive narrative in Sierstad (2013).

[7] The cumulative number of foreign recruits to Daesh is estimated to have doubled in the year since mid-2014, at 27,000–31,000 from 86 countries (*The Economist*, 2015).

filiation, and a view of the shari'a as sacred (2014). Beyond providing comfort and empowerment, sacred values confer legitimacy to narratives of grievance *and* of heroic response against long odds. Secular causes such as nationalism and ethno-cultural pride may similarly offer legitimating narratives, along with kinship-like support. But religious affiliations have the advantage of being inherently transnational, which allows for a greater repertoire of symbolic and social capital—with access to the digital tools of a globalized public sphere (Bunt, 2009; Eickelman & Anderson, 2003). Social media is not incidental to religious movements, but often a core aspect of their profiles and global reach; the gap between cyber and real communities offering social bonds and sacred values is rapidly shrinking (Bunt, 2009, pp. 291-292). Modernity's orphans are seldom averse to using its technological assets to the full.

Yet modernity's orphans are not confined to the margins of extremism or to "fundamentalist" religiosity. Anomie is a wider "malaise" (Taylor, 1991, 2007), and the responses to its secular forms are manifold. Multiple studies on both sides of the Atlantic over the past decade have found remarkably little to distinguish the demographic markers of "violent extremists" from the rest of the population (Atran, 2015; Patel, 2011; Travis, 2008). They are usually not well-schooled in religion; many are outright irreligious. Conventional family ties are common, and evidence of pathologies is no greater than for the mainstream. Although many come from lower economic strata—in western and Muslim-majority countries—there is also marked representation from the middle classes. In this vein, while most Muslims in the western diaspora feel that they belong to their countries of residence, local populations, notably in Germany and Spain, mostly believe the contrary (Benton & Nielsen, 2013; Saunders, 2012). Pew surveys of US Muslims over several years consistently find negligible levels of sympathy, much less support, for extremism, and far higher levels of satisfaction with American life than is found in the general public (Pew Research Centre, 2011). By contrast, only 33% of the US public believed that Muslim Americans wish to be an integral part of the nation. On the eve of Republican presidential candidate Donald Trump's call in December 2015 to exclude Muslims from entry into the US, 55% of Americans had an unfavorable view of Islam, and sentiments toward Muslims were the "coldest" of any religious community (Chalabi, 2015). Trump's proposal was supported by a majority of Republicans (43%) and 25% of all Americans, according to an NBC-Wall Street Journal poll (Bradner, 2015).

Isolating violent extremists from ordinary Muslims or mainstream society, it turns out, is harder for various publics, demagogues, and social scientists than identifying the sources and symptoms of modernist angst. It is harder still in the diverse societies of the "Muslim world"—from South-Central Asia and West Africa to the Middle East and North Africa—where fresh syntheses of Islam and modernity are in the making (Sajoo, 2008). Radicalization and violent extremism are real phenomena; yet they cast a fog over the complexity of modern social imaginaries, and hence to the nature of responses to those phenomena by states and civil societies.

3.2. Pluralism Revisited

In the aftermath of the 2010–11 uprisings in Tunisia, Egypt, Libya and Yemen that came to be described as "the Arab Spring," a study on youths aged 17 to 31 in 2013 yielded telling results (Al-Anani, 2015; Atassi, 2013). The new governing institutions were uniformly felt to be unrepresentative, and most had no party affiliation. Large majorities considered themselves as Muslims first, ahead of national citizenship; the exception was Egypt, where 35% did so. Majorities in all four countries—from 91% in Libya to 57% in Egypt—favored implementing the Shari'a as national law. In Tunisia, widely regarded as the success story of the Arab Spring, only 14% felt that the revolution which toppled the authoritarian government of Zine El Dine Ben Ali was a success. Constitutional reforms have since garnered much public support, and a civil society coalition won the 2015 Nobel Peace Prize (Chan, 2015). Yet Tunisia is among the highest sources of recruits per capita to Daesh and al-Qaeda, ahead of Saudi Arabia and exceeded only by Jordan (Sengupta, 2014).

The survey results are consistent with recent trends regarding citizenship, identity and religiosity across Muslim-majority societies. In tandem with fragile rule of law and democratic governance, citizenship tends to entwine with religious identity across the Middle East, South Asia, and Sub-Saharan Africa. Enacting the shari'a as the law of the land is favored by over 70% of the population in states ranging from Afghanistan, Iraq, Jordan, Nigeria and Pakistan to Indonesia, Morocco, Malaysia and the Palestinian Territories; the only regions where firm majorities oppose this are Central Asia and Southeastern Europe (Pew Research Centre, 2015). In sub-Saharan states where Muslims are a relatively small minority, the shari'a is still desired by more than half of Muslims (52%–74%) as national law. Religion is felt to be a precondition for individual moral standing by a majority of Muslims in all regions (Pew Research Centre, 2013). For large majorities the shari'a is the divine word, undistinguished from the corpus of legal rules or *fiqh* (An-Na'im, 2008; Moustafa, 2013; Pew Research Centre, 2013). It is also understood as subject to a single interpretation by the majority, especially in South Asia and the Middle East (Pew Research Centre, 2013); strong majorities in the Muslim world also hold to a singular understanding of Islam (Pew Research Centre, 2012).[8]

[8] Morocco and Tunisia stand out as exceptions to both claims:

Perhaps not surprisingly, the very acceptance of Muslim minorities is narrow. A majority of Egyptians, Indonesians and Jordanians, who are Sunni, do not recognize the Shi'a, whose origins are anchored in the earliest years of Islamic history, as fellow Muslims (Pew Research Centre, 2012). The Ahmadiyya minority, whose orientation is Sunni, enjoys even less acceptance. Sufi communities, most of which are also Sunni in orientation and whose esotericism has long been regarded as a core facet of Islam, are today recognized as Muslim by about half of Egyptians, Tunisians and Iraqis (Pew Research Centre, 2012). Post-September 11 initiatives to broaden the theological fold, such as the Amman Declaration by leading Sunni and Shi'a institutional figures who affirmed an inclusive and tolerant Islam (International Islamic Conference, 2005), have since run into hardline sectarian polemic at the highest levels (Fahim, 2015). Given the level of sectarianism not only in civil conflicts in Afghanistan, Bahrain, Iraq, Lebanon, Syria, and Yemen, but more broadly in tensions across the Muslim world, the theological backdrop—how the shari'a is perceived, and how individual/communal identities are tied to particularistic interpretations of Islam—can hardly be dismissed as merely captive to politics.

Theology stirred with politics has long been a staple of al-Qaeda, despite the hollow claims to juristic competence by Osama bin Laden (Lawrence, 2005). If the leaders of Boko Haram, Daesh, al-Shabab and the Taliban are even less versed on the finer points of theology, this has not stood in the way of their claims to authenticity and orthodoxy (Burke, 2015; McCants, 2015; Nordland, 2015). Even Arabic poetic traditions are marshalled in the service of these claims (Creswell & Haykel, 2015). And Daesh has invoked ritual, scripture and tradition, embodied in a manual, to rationalize the sexual enslavement of female children (Callimachi, 2015). This is endemic to the misogynistic attitudes that find their way into interpretations of gender in theology, far beyond the confines of "extremism" (Mir-Hosseini, Al-Sharmani, & Rumminger, 2015).

The conservative trends in the politics of identity that have provided such fertile ground for extremist theologies of exclusion are not confined to Muslim societies. Pew's "Social Hostilities Index," a complex measure of religiously-inspired acts of abuse/aggression by individuals and groups, has spiked—with intense majoritarian attacks against vulnerable minorities (often Muslims) in India, Myanmar, Sri Lanka, Vietnam, and China, as well as in the Middle East, Sub-Saharan Africa, and Indonesia (Pew Research Centre, 2014). For the celebrated Indian writer Arundhati Roy, "intolerance" is an utterly inadequate term to describe the "terror" that minorities such as Christians, Dalits, and Muslims now experience in her country (Roy, 2015). Much the same can be said of Rohingya Muslims in Myanmar, where Buddhist "extremism reflected in the laws suggests a future of even greater violence" (Mathieson, 2015; Physicians for Human Rights, 2013). Of late, researchers in the US describe thus the vulnerability of Muslims there:

> "It is not just that hatred against Muslims is extremely high today. It's that it's exceptional compared with prejudice against every other group in the United States. We examined prejudicial searches against black people, white people, gay people, Asians, Jews, Mexicans and Christians. We estimate that negative attitudes against Muslims today are higher than prejudice against any group in any month since 2004, when Google began preserving detailed data on search volumes." (Soltas & Stephens-Davidowitz, 2015)[9]

Hostility toward individuals and groups on the basis of their perceived faith affiliation inevitably privileges one kind of identity—religious—over others. Likewise, the stated theological agendas of extremist organizations, no matter how shallow or manipulative, make exclusive claims on the religious identities of their recruits and victims alike. Where does this leave the multiple identities that are central to pluralist civil society, and to countering violent extremism (Sen, 2006; Maalouf, 2001)? Modernist discourse has hitherto insisted on a "secularist" basis for the former. But secularist orthodoxy collides with hard realities about the place of religion in individual and group identities. Casting civic culture and citizenship as "bulwarks against religion" does not empower secular reason so much as narrow the reach of social inclusion in diverse public spaces (Taylor, 2011, p. 56; Stepan, 2011; Nandy, 1998). A nuanced appreciation of what is "secular," beyond the reflexive antagonism toward religion that is too often found in secular orthodoxy, brings us closer to the kind of pluralist citizenship that is professed in liberal ideology (Stepan, 2011).

A wariness of theologies of exclusion, religious or secular, is entirely proper in defending pluralist civic cultures. Far from being confined to the extremist/radicalized margins, exclusionary theologies are pervasive and fuel for recruitment to the former. A conspicuous example: "mainstream" Wahhabi interpretations of the shari'a as spearheaded by Saudi Arabia's clerical and political establishments are foundational for the theologies of groups such as Daesh and al-Qaeda (Armstrong, 2014; Daoud, 2015; Matthiessen, 2015; McCants, 2015).[10] That Saudi Arabia is a key

firm majorities subscribe to multiple interpretations, though in both countries majorities insist that the shari'a is divine.

[9] This is accompanied by a spike in actual hate crimes (Lichtblau, 2015). Similar trends prevail not only in Europe, but also in Australia (K. Dunn, 2015).

[10] Amid the competitive animosity between Riyadh and those

western economic and political ally has obvious implications: a mutual interest prevails in isolating extremism/radicalization as the "real" foe (Black, 2015). In neighboring Bahrain, the "extremist" tag serves not only to fuel sectarian repression of the Shi'a majority, but to undermine democratic accountability, with Saudi Arabia playing a leading role; as noted by Human Rights Watch (HRW), among others, this is abetted by Britain and the United States (Americans for Human Rights & Democracy in Bahrain, 2015; HRW, 2015; Ramesh, 2016). The extremist tag has also been exploited in Central Asia, where perceived Wahhabi tendencies have led to authoritarian crackdowns on *any* overt religiosity—as in Tajikistan, where even beards and dark clothing are suspect (Paraszczuk, 2015; Sarkorova, 2016). In an echo of the Soviet era, citizenship is construed strictly along lines of exclusive *secular* orthodoxy. Nor is there a dearth of such baggage today within western mainstreams, with the ascendance of the far-right and the banality of hate speech, in which religious identities are engaged willy-nilly.

Pluralisms that draw on theologies of inclusion, beyond mere accommodation or tolerance, offer the prospect of bridging modernist divides toward a richer civic identity. Scholars such as Diana Eck, Ashis Nandy and Charles Taylor have wrestled with Hindu and Judeo-Christian makings of fresh cosmopolitanisms—alongside Abdullahi An-Na'im, Tariq Ramadan and Omid Safi on the Muslim side—in fragmented public domains (Aga Khan, 2015a, 2015b; Karim, 2012; Marshall, 2013; Poor, 2015, pp. 152-158). To the questions "who is a Muslim" and "what is Islam," we have responses that engage fully with civic domains as well as with theology (Ahmed, 2015; An-Na'im, 2008). A fresh initiative in this regard is the Marrakesh Declaration (on Religious Minorities in Muslim-majority Countries), adopted in January 2016 by over 300 religious and political leaders from across the Muslim world (Marrakesh Conference on the Rights of Religious Minorities in Predominantly Muslim Majority Countries, 2016). In its focus on minority rights and citizenship, the Declaration calls for a vigorous Islamic jurisprudence, alongside a review of educational curricula—while invoking the inclusive spirit of the Charter of Medina drawn up by the Prophet Muhammad as a *civic* expression of religiosity.

Rather than transcend difference with universalist rhetoric and secular "reason," or merely enable differences to co-exist, the aspiration here is to mobilize religious affiliation as a contributor to civic ethics. The Rawlsian "overlapping consensus" is thickened, so that faith affinities cease being treated as outliers that must be privatized (Aga Khan, 2006; Taylor, 2011). Controversies over the wearing of Muslim head/face coverings in public spaces (courts, citizenship ceremonies, public schools, et al.) point to the dominance of a thin description of inclusion, despite its exclusionary impact. Likewise, sectarian trends are a reminder of the rigidities of identity among faith traditions: distinctiveness is equated with exclusivity, pluralism with dilution.[11] The queries "Who is Shi'a?" or "Who is Sunni?" or "Who is Protestant?" call for responses that are mindful of the slippage to chauvinism (Sajoo, 2015).

terror groups, a shared sectarian narrative directed at the Shi'a and Iran continues to serve overlapping interests (Mathieson, 2015).

4. Conclusion

Exclusionary theologies that are fed by, and in turn reinforce, the narrowing of religious identities flourish well beyond the periphery, in Muslim *and* non-Muslim domains today. It is not that exclusivism, much less conservatism, simply turns into violent extremism on a "conveyor belt" of displeasure. Rather, the former validates ideologies that enable and incite extremism, including its sectarian expression. Theologies of inclusion matter because they draw on diverse heritages that are a legitimate part of a global landscape where religious identities matter. Faith traditions have long embodied a "rooted worldliness," a transnational sensibility with local commitments, as integral to their ethics. This is inconsistently nourished: religions, like secular cultures, have historic ups and downs in the generosity accorded the Other. Both require cultivation on this score, and convergence.

Yes, deficits in the quality of life, employment, equality, and accountable governance fuel disaffection that extremist violence thrives on. The Arab Spring had much to do with such disaffection, and the appeals to empowerment offered by Islamist actors (Bishara, 2013; Hamid, 2014). But neither material incentives nor military responses can obliterate extremist violence, even if they were to succeed in disposing of Daesh, al-Qaeda, and their like. Still less can they answer the challenge of exclusive identities that undermine civil society, citizenship and gender equity.

"*Non, domina magna*, we cannot under any circumstances." This is the response in diverse tongues of the minstrels of war when asked to sing their shared narratives, in our epigraph from Ismail Kadare's *Elegy for Kosovo*. The mold that holds the minstrels captive is too embedded, and the compulsion for war too robust, to let them partake in the grander narrative which they find so attractive. Kadare's lyrical account of the con-

[11] In a graphic illustration, Wheaton College, a prestigious Christian evangelical institution located near Chicago, suspended a tenured professor who donned a *hijab* in solidarity with Muslims who "worship the same God." Her statement was deemed unacceptable on the basis that the Christian concept of God is uniquely Trinitarian and thence different from the unitarian Allah. After protests against her suspension among students and faculty, a settlement was reached for the professor to leave Wheaton (Hauser, 2016).

flicts in ex-Yugoslavia may be taken as symbolic of the ethno-religious inheritance that plagues the orphans of modernity. Yet this leaves out the role of modernity's own minstrels, notably those wedded to secular ideologies that impel wars on the Other. In Miroslav Volf's striking engagement with the stakes in the Balkan conflicts, the "character of social agents and their mutual engagement" is central to a *theological* exploration (Volf, 1996, 2016). Social inclusion, then, is as much a religious as a secular preoccupation—which calls for a more sophisticated appreciation of what these categories stand for. When the minstrels on each side have woken from what Kadare calls their "stupor," can they afford to say "*non*" to a fresher pluralism? Syria, Yemen, Iraq, Afghanistan and a host of other broken societies await the response.

Acknowledgements

I am grateful to the journal's editors as well as the anonymous reviewers of this article for their thoughtful remarks on the draft version.

Conflict of Interests

The author declares no conflict of interests.

References

Abrahamian, E. (2003). The US media, Huntington, and September 11. *Third World Quarterly*, *24*(3), 529-544.

Abu-Rabi, I. (Ed.). (2010). *The contemporary Arab reader on political Islam.* Edmonton, Canada: University of Alberta Press.

Aga Khan, K. (2006, February 12). Symposium on "Cosmopolitan Society, Human Safety and Rights in Plural and Peaceful Societies". Évora University, Portugal. Retrieved from http://www.akdn.org/Content/228/Evora-University-Symposium

Aga Khan, K. (2015a, November 12). The cosmopolitan ethic in a fragmented world. *Weatherhead Center for International Affairs.* Retrieved from http://wcfia.harvard.edu/jodidi/2015/transcript-aga-khan

Aga Khan, K. (2015b, November 12). A conversation between His Highness the Aga Khan and Professor Diana L. Eck. *Weatherhead Center for International Affairs.* Retrieved from http://wcfia.harvard.edu/lectureships/jodidi/2015/transcript_AgaKhan-DEck

Ahmed, S. (2015). *What is Islam? The importance of being Islamic.* Princeton, NJ: Princeton University Press.

Al-Anani, K. (2015). *Inside the Muslim brotherhood: Religion, identity and politics.* Oxford: Oxford University Press.

Americans for Human Rights & Democracy in Bahrain. (2015). *Shattering the facade: A report on Bahrain's implementation of the Bahrain Independent Commission of Inquiry (BICI) four years on.* Retrieved from http://ADHRB_BICI_Web-rev2-2

An-Na'im, A.A. (2008). *Islam and the Secular State: Negotiating the Future of Shari'a.* Oxford: Oxford University Press.

Armstrong, K. (2014, November 27). Wahhabism to ISIS. *The New Statesman.* Retrieved from http://www.newstatesman.com/world-affairs/2014/11/wahhabism-isis-how-saudi-arabia-exported-main-source-global-terrorism

Atassi, B. (2013, July 29). Poll: Arab youth feel alienated from politics. *Aljazeera.* Retrieved from http://www.aljazeera.com/news/middleeast/2013/07/2013729103126233170.html

Atran, S. (2010). *Talking to the enemy: Faith, brotherhood, and the (un)making of terrorists.* New York: HarperCollins.

Atran, S. (2015). Here's what the social science says about countering violent extremism. *Huffington Post.* Retrieved from http://www.huffingtonpost.com/scott-atran/violent-extremism-social-science_b_7142604.html?utm_hp_ref=Science

Atran, S., Hammad, S., & Gomez, A. (2014). Devoted actors sacrifice for close comrades and sacred cause. *Proceedings of the National Academy of Sciences*, *111*(50), 17702-17703. Retrieved from http://www.pnas.org/content/111/50/17702.full

Bawer, B. (2006). *While Europe slept: How radical Islam is destroying the West from within.* New York: Doubleday.

Bawer, B. (2009). *Surrender: Appeasing Islam, sacrificing freedom.* New York: Random House.

Bayat, A. (2013). *Post-Islamism: The changing faces of political Islam.* Oxford: Oxford University Press.

Benton, M., & Nielsen, A. (2013, May 10). Integrating Europe's Muslim minorities: Public Anxieties, policy responses. *Migration Information Source.* Retrieved from http://www.migrationpolicy.org/article/integrating-europes-muslim-minorities-public-anxieties-policy-responses

Berger, P. (Ed). (1999). *The desecularization of the world: Resurgent religion and world politics.* Grand Rapids, MI: Erdmans.

Bhargava, R. (Ed.). (1998). *Secularism and its critics.* Oxford: Oxford University Press.

Bishara, M. (2013). *The invisible Arab: The promise and perils of the Arab revolutions.* New York: Nation Books.

Black, I. (2015, December 15). "Saudi Arabia's anti-terrorism alliance: A political message sketchy on details. *The Guardian.* Retrieved from http://www.theguardian.com/world/2015/dec/15/saudi-arabia-anti-terrorism-alliance-political-message-sketchy-details?CMP=share_btn_fb

Bouma, G. (2008). The challenge of religious revitalization and religious diversity to social cohesion in secular societies. In B. Turner (Ed), *Religious diversity and civil society* (pp. 13-25). Oxford: The Bardwell Press.

Bradner, E. (2015, December 10). GOP primary voters split over Trump's Muslim ban, poll finds. *CNN Politics*. Retrieved from http://www.cnn.com/2015/12/10/politics/donald-trump-muslims-poll/index.html

Breivik, A. (2011, July, 22). 2083: A European declaration of independence. *Archives.org*. Retrieved from https://archive.org/details/2083_A_European_Declaration_of_Independence

Bunt, G. (2009). The digital umma. In A. B. Sajoo (Ed.), *A companion to the Muslim world (pp. 291-310)*. London: I.B. Tauris.

Burke, J. (2015, September). The truth about the caliphate. *Prospect*. Retrieved from http://www.prospectmagazine.co.uk/features/state-of-terror

Callimachi, R. (2015, August 14). Enslaving young girls, the Islamic state builds a vast system of rape. *New York Times*, p. A1.

Castellino, J., & Cavanaugh, K. (2013). *Minority rights in the Middle East*. Oxford: Oxford University Press.

Chalabi, M. (2015, December 8). How anti-Muslim are Americans? Data points to extent of Islamophobia. *The Guardian*. Retrieved from http://www.theguardian.com/us-news/2015/dec/08/muslims-us-islam-islamophobia-data-polls

Chan, S. (2015, October 10). Peace prize goes to Tunisian group for backing democracy after Arab Spring. *New York Times*, p. A6.

Creswell, R., & Haykel, B. (2015, June 8). Battle lines: Want to understand the jihadis? Read their poetry. *The New Yorker*. Retrieved from http://www.newyorker.com/magazine/2015/06/08/battle-lines-jihad-creswell-and-haykel

Cumming-Bruce, N., & Erlanger, S. (2009, November 30). Swiss ban building of minarets on mosques. *New York Times*, p. A6.

Daoud, K. (2015, November 20). Saudi Arabia, an ISIS that has made it. *New York Times*. Retrieved from http://www.nytimes.com/2015/11/21/opinion/saudi-arabia-an-isis-that-has-made-it.html?_r=0

Dunn, K. (2015). *The resilience and ordinariness of Australian Muslims: Attitudes and experiences of Muslims report*. Sydney: Western Sydney University-Islamic Sciences & Research Academy Australia. Retrieved from www.uws.edu.au/__data/.../12441_text_challenging_racism_WEB.pdf

Dunn, M. (2006). The 'Clash of Civilizations' and the 'War on Terror'. *49th Parallel*, *20*, 1-20.

Eickelman, D., & Anderson, J. (Eds.). (2003). *New media in the Muslim world: The emerging public sphere* (2nd ed.). Bloomington, IN: Indiana University Press.

Fahim, K. (2015, October 18). Sectarian leaders fan flames in Middle East. *New York Times*, p. A14.

Ferguson, N. (2004, April 4). "Eurabia?" *New York Times Magazine*. Retrieved from http://www.nytimes.com/2004/04/04/magazine/04WWLN.html

Ferguson, N. (2006, May 21). The march of Islam. *The Telegraph*. Retrieved from http://www.telegraph.co.uk/culture/3652572/The-march-of-Islam.html

Ferguson, N. (2011). *Civilization: The West and the rest*. London: Allen Lane.

Grayling, A. C. (2016, January). Daesh: It is not Islamic, or a state and this isn't a war. *Prospect*. Retrieved from http://www.prospectmagazine.co.uk/opinions/the-power-of-words-daesh-islamic-state-iraq-syria-terrorism

Hamid, S. (2014). *Temptations of power: Islamists and illiberal democracy in a new Middle East*. New York: Oxford University Press.

Harris, S. (2004). *The end of faith: Religion, terror, and the future of reason*. New York: W.W. Norton.

Hassan v. The City of New York. (2015, October 13). United States Court of Appeals, Third Circuit. Case No. 14-1688. Retrieved from http://www2.ca3.uscourts.gov/opinarch/141688p.pdf

Hauser, C. (2016, February 8). Wheaton College and Professor to 'part ways' after her remarks on Muslims. *New York Times*. Retrieved from http://www.nytimes.com/2016/02/09/us/larycia-hawkins-wheaton-college.html?_r=0

Hedges, C. (2008). *When Atheism becomes religion: America's new fundamentalists*. New York: Free Press.

Human Rights Watch. (2015). The blood of people who don't co-operate: Continuing torture and mistreatment of detainees in Bahrain. Retrieved from https://www.hrw.org/node/283352

Huntington, S. P. (1996). *The clash of civilizations and the remaking of world order*. New York: Simon & Schuster.

International Islamic Conference. (2015, July 4-5). *Amman Declaration: Statement issued by the Internation Islamic Conference*. Amman, Jordan. Retrieved from http://ammanmessage.com/index.php?option=com_content&task=view&id=20&Itemid=34

Jacoby, W., & Yavuz, H. (2008). Modernization, identity and integration: An introduction to the special issue on Islam in Europe. *Journal of Muslim Minority Affairs*, 28(1), 1-6.

Juergensmeyer, M. (2003). *Terror in the mind of God: The global rise of religious violence*. Berkeley, CA: University of California Press.

Juergensmeyer, M., Griego, D., & Soboslai, J. (2015). *God in the tumult of the global square: Religion in global civil society*. Oakland, CA: University of California Press.

Kadare, I. (1998). *Elegy for Kosovo*. New York: Arcade Publishing.

Karim, K. (2012). Cosmopolitanism: Ways of being Muslim. In A. Sajoo (Ed.), *A companion to Muslim cultures* (pp. 201-220). London: I.B. Tauris.

Kettell, S. (2013). Faithless: The politics of new atheism. *Secularism and Nonreligion*, *2*, 61-78. Retrieved from http://www.secularismandnonreligion.org/articles/1

0.5334/snr.al

Knausgaard, K. (2015, May 25). The inexplicable: Inside the mind of a mass killer. *The New Yorker*. Retrieved from http://www.newyorker.com/magazine/2015/05/25/the-inexplicable

Kymlicka, W. (2001). *Politics in the vernacular: Nationalism, multiculturalism, and citizenship*. Oxford: Oxford University Press.

Kymlicka, W., & Norman, W. (Eds.). (2000). *Citizenship in diverse societies.* Oxford: Oxford University Press.

Lawrence, B. (2005). Messages to the world: The statements of Osama Bin Laden. London & New York: Verso.

Lewis, B. (1990). "The Roots of Muslim Rage." *The Atlantic Monthly.* 266: 3, pp. 47 - 60.

Lewis, B. (2002). *What went wrong: The clash between Islam and modernity in the Middle East*. New York: Oxford University Press.

Lewis, B. (2003). *The crisis of Islam: Holy War and unholy terror*. New York: Random House.

Lichtblau, E. (2015, December 18). Crimes against Muslim Americans and mosques rise sharply. *New York Times*, p. A26.

Littman, G. (2005). *Eurabia: The Euro-Arab axis.* Madison, NJ: Fairleigh Dickinson University Press.

Lyon, D. (2015). *Surveillance after Snowden.* Cambridge, UK: Polity.

Maalouf, A. (2001). *In the name of identity: Violence and the need to belong*. New York: Arcade.

Marrakesh Conference on the Rights of Religious Minorities in Predominantly Muslim Majority Countries. (2016, January 25-27). Retrieved from http://www.marrakeshdeclaration.org/index.html

Marshall, K. (2013). *Global institutions of religion: Ancient movers, modern shakers.* London: Routledge.

Martin, D. (2005). *On secularization: A revised general theory*. Aldershot, UK: Ashgate.

Martin, R., & Barzegar, A. (Eds.). (2010). *Islamism: Contested perspectives on political Islam*. Redwood City, CA: Stanford University Press.

Mathieson, D. S. (2015, June 16). *Religious extremism looms over Myanmar*. New York: Human Rights Watch. Retrieved from https://www.hrw.org/news/2015/06/16/religious-extremism-looms-over-myanmar

Matthiesen, T. (2015, August). The domestic sources of Saudi foreign policy: Islamists and the state in the wake of the Arab Uprisings. In *rethinking political Islam series*. New York: Brookings. Retrieved from http://www.brookings.edu/research/reports2/2015/08/~/media/371341741F72445E8269110C5504E327.ashx

Mazar, M. J. (2014, July 3). The age of grievance. *Foreign Affairs*. Retrieved from https://www.foreignaffairs.com/articles/russian-federation/2014-07-03/age-grievance?cid=nlc-foreign_affairs_this_week-071014-the_age_of_grievance_5-071014&sp_mid=46430687&sp_rid=YW15bl9zYWpvb0Bob3RtYWlsLmNvbQS2

McCants, W. (2015). *The ISIS apocalypse: The history, strategy and doomsday vision of the Islamic State*. New York: St. Martin's Press.

Mir-Hosseini, Z., Al-Sharmani, M., & Rumminger, J. (Eds.). (2015). *Men in charge? Rethinking authority in Muslim legal tradition*. Oxford: Oneworld.

Modood, T. (2000). Anti-essentialism, multiculturalism, and the 'recognition' of religious groups. In W. Kymlicka & W. Norman (Eds.), *Citizenship in diverse societies* (pp. 175-195). Oxford: Oxford University Press.

Moustafa, T. (2013). Islamic law, women's rights, and popular legal consciousness in Malaysia. *Law & Social Inquiry*, *38*(1), 168-188.

Nandy. A. (1998). The politics of secularism and the recovery of religious tolerance. In R. Bhargava (Ed.), *Secularism and its critics* (pp. 321-379). New Delhi: Oxford University Press.

Neumayer, E., & Plumper, T. (2009). International terror and the clash of civilizations. *British Journal of Politics*, *39*, 711-734.

Nordland, R. (2015, December 17). Dealing a blow to extremists but not ideology. *New York Times*, p. A16.

Orru, M. (1987). *Anomie: History and meanings*. Boston: Allen & Unwin.

Paraszczuk, J. (2015, October 29). Tajikistan's crackdown on Islam 'helps IS recruiters'. *Radio Free Europe*. Retrieved from http://www.rferl.org/content/tajikistan-crackdown-helping-islamic-state-recruiting/27333859.html

Patel, F. (2011). *Rethinking radicalization*. New York: Brennan Centre for Justice, New York University School of Law. Retrieved from https://www.brennancenter.org/sites/default/files/legacy/RethinkingRadicalization.pdf

Pew Research Centre. (2011, August 30). *Muslim Americans: Mainstream and moderate attitudes*. Washington, DC: Pew Charitable Trusts. Retrieved from http://www.people-press.org/2011/08/30/muslim-americans-no-signs-of-growth-in-alienation-or-support-for-extremism

Pew Research Centre. (2012, August 9). *The world's Muslims: Unity and diversity*. Washington, DC: Pew Charitable Trusts. Retrieved from http://www.pewforum.org/files/2012/08/the-worlds-muslims-full-report.pdf

Pew Research Centre. (2013, April 30). *The World's Muslims: Religion, politics and society*. Washington, DC: Pew Charitable Trusts. Retrieved from http://www.pewforum.org/2013/04/30/the-worlds-muslims-religion-politics-society-overview

Pew Research Centre. (2014, January 14). *Religious hostilities reach six-year high*. Washington, DC: Pew Charitable Trusts. Retrieved from http://www.pewforum.org/2014/01/14/religious-hostilities-reach-six-

year-high
Pew Research Centre. (2015, December 7). *Muslims and Islam: Key findings in the U.S. and around the world*. Washington, DC: Pew Charitable Trusts. Retrieved from http://www.pewresearch.org/fact-tank/2015/12/07/muslims-and-islam-key-findings-in-the-u-s-and-around-the-world

Pföstl, E., & Kymlicka, W. (2015). Minority politics in the Middle East and North Africa: The prospects for transformative change. *Ethnic and Racial Studies, 38*(14), 2489-2498.

Physicians for Human Rights. (2013, May). *Massacre in Central Burma*. Cambridge, MA. Retrieved from https://s3.amazonaws.com/PHR_Reports/Burma-Meiktila-Massacre-Report-May-2013.pdf

Pipes, D. (2002a). *Militant Islam reaches America*. New York: W.W. Norton.

Pipes, D. (2002b). Faces of American Islam. *Daniel Pipes: Middle East Forum*. Retrieved from http://www.danielpipes.org/441/faces-of-american-islam-muslim-immigration

Pizzo, P. (2015). The 'coptic question' in post-revolutionary Egypt: Citizenship, democracy, religion. *Ethnic and Racial Studies*, *38*(14), 2598-2613.

Poor, D. M. (2015). *Authority without territory: The Aga Khan Development Network and the Ismaili imamate*. New York: Palgrave Macmillan.

Ramesh, R. (2016, February 9). Bahrain's UK-funded police watchdog fails to investigate torture claims. *The Guardian*. Retrieved at http://www.theguardian.com/world/2016/feb/09/bahrains-uk-funded-police-watchdog-fails-to-investigate-torture-claims-mohammed-ramadan?CMP=share_btn_fb

Roy, O. (2010). *Holy ignorance: When religion and culture part ways.* New York: Columbia University Press.

Roy, A. (2015, November 5). Why I am returning my award. *The Indian Express*. Retrieved from http://indianexpress.com/article/opinion/columns/why-i-am-returning-my-award

Ruse, M. (2010). *Science and spirituality: Making room for faith in the age of science*. New York: Cambridge University Press.

Said, E. (1994). *Orientalism* (25th anniversary edition). New York: Vintage Books.

Said, E. (1997). *Covering Islam: How the media and the experts determine how we see the rest of the world.* New York: Vintage Books.

Said, E. (2001, October, 4). The clash of ignorance. *The Nation*. Retrieved from http://www.thenation.com/article/clash-ignorance

Sajoo, A. B. (Ed.). (2008). *Muslim modernities: Expressions of the civil imagination*. London: I.B. Tauris.

Sajoo, A. B. (2014). Review: Minority rights in the Middle East. *Ethics and Global Politics*, *7*(1), 41-45.

Sajoo, A. B. (2015). Modernity: The ethics of identity. In F. Daftary, S. Jiwa, & A. Sajoo (Eds.), *The Shi'i World: Pathways in tradition and modernity* (pp. 349-370). London: I.B. Tauris.

Santillana, D. (1926). *Istituzioni di diritto musulmano Malichita con riguardo anche al sistema Scifiita* (Vol. 1, p. 5).

Sarkorova, A. (2016, January 21). Tajikistan's battle against beards to 'fight radicalisation'. *BBC News.* Retrieved from http://www.bbc.com/news/world-asia-35372754

Saunders, D. (2012). *The myth of the Muslim tide: Do immigrants threaten the west?* New York: Random House.

Schofield, H. (2015, November 16). Paris attacks: 'France will destroy IS'—Hollande. *BBC.* Retrieved from http://www.bbc.com/news/world-europe-34836439

Schwanitz, S. (2004, July 28). Europa wird am Ende des Jahrhunderts islamisch sein. *Die Welt.*

Sen, A. (2006). *Identity and violence: The illusion of destiny*. London: W.W. Norton.

Sengupta, S. (2014, September 13). Nations working to stop citizens from aiding ISIS. *New York Times*, p. A1.

Sierstad, Å. (2013). *One of us*. New York: Farrar, Strauss and Giroux.

Soltas, E., & Stephens-Davidowitz, S. (2015, December 13). The rise of hate search. *New York Times*, p. SR1.

Spencer, R. (2008). *Stealth Jihad: How radical Islam is subverting America without guns or bombs.* Washington, DC: Regnery.

Spencer, R. (2009). *The complete infidel's guide to the Koran*. Washington, DC: Regnery Publishing.

Stepan, A. (2011). The multiple secularisms of modern democratic and non-democratic regimes. In C. Calhoun, M. Juergensmeyer, & J. VanAntwerpen (Eds.), *Rethinking secularism* (pp. 114-144). New York: Oxford University Press.

Stephan, M. J. (Ed.). (2009). *Civilian Jihad: Nonviolent struggle, democratization, and governance in the Middle East*. New York: Palgrave Macmillan.

Steyn, M. (2006). *America alone: The end of the world as we know it*. Washington, DC: Regnery Publishing.

Taylor, C. (1991). *The malaise of modernity*. Toronto: House of Anansi Press.

Taylor, C. (2007). *A secular age.* Cambridge, MA: Harvard University Press.

Taylor, C. (2011). Why we need a radical redefinition of secularism. In J. Butler, J. Habermas, C. Taylor, & C. West (Eds.), *The power of religion in the public sphere* (pp. 34-59). New York: Columbia University Press.

Taylor, J. (2013, April 12). Atheists Richard Dawkins, Christopher Hitchens and Sam Harris face Islamophobia backlash. *The Independent.* Retrieved from http://www.independent.co.uk/news/uk/home-news/atheists-richard-dawkins-christopher-hitchens-and-sam-harris-face-islamophobia-backlash-8570580.html

The Economist. (2006, June 26). Tales from Eurabia. p. 11.

The Economist. (2015, December, 12). Islamic State: Unfriended. *The Economist*. Retrieved from http://www.economist.com/news/middle-east-and-africa/21679805-there-are-signs-islamic-states-propaganda-machine-losing-its?cid1=cust/ednew/n/bl/n/20151210n/owned/n/n/nwl/n/n/n/n

The Economist—Prospero. (2015, November, 19). The war metaphor. *The Economist*. Retrieved from http://www.economist.com/blogs/prospero/2015/11/johnson-fighting-words

Townsend, M., & Traynor, I. (2011, July 30). Norway attacks: How far right views created Anders Behring Breivik. *The Guardian*. Retrieved from http://www.theguardian.com/world/2011/jul/30/norway-attacks-anders-behring-breivik

Travis, A. (2008, August 21). MI5 report challenges views on terrorism in Britain. *The Guardian*. Retrieved from http://www.theguardian.com/uk/2008/aug/20/uksecurity.terrorism1

UK Government. (2014). Home Secretary Theresa May on Counter Terrorism. Retrieved from https://www.gov.uk/government/speeches/home-secretary-theresa-may-on-counter-terrorism

Volf, M. (1996). *Exclusion and embrace: A theological exploration of identity, otherness, and reconciliation.* Nashville, TN: Abingdon Press.

Volf, M. (2016). *Flourishing: Why we need religion in a globalized world*. New Haven, CN: Yale University Press.

Wilson, E. K. (2012). *After secularism: Rethinking religion in global affairs*. New York: Palgrave Macmillan.

Wright, R. (2015, February 25). The clash of civilizations that isn't. *The New Yorker*. Retrieved from http://www.newyorker.com/news/news-desk/clash-civilizations-isnt

Wright, M., Johnston, R., Citrin, J., & Soroka, S. (2016). Multiculturalism and Muslim accommodation: Policies and predisposition in three political contexts. *Comparative Political Studies*, forthcoming.

Zubaida, S. (2011). *Beyond Islam: A new understanding of the Middle East*. London: I.B. Tauris.

About the Author

Dr. Amyn B. Sajoo

Amyn B. Sajoo lectures in global politics and history at Simon Fraser University in Vancouver, where his research is at the interface of law, ethics, and religion. He was the 2010 Canada Department of Foreign Affairs Visiting Academic in the Middle East, and is the editor of the Muslim Heritage Series (I.B. Tauris, UK). Dr. Sajoo is the author/editor of numerous books, including most recently *The Shi'i World: Pathways in Tradition and Modernity* (co-edited with F. Daftary & S. Jiwa).

5

Contradictory and Intersecting Patterns of Inclusion and Exclusion of Street Youth in Salvador, Brazil

Marit Ursin

Norwegian Centre for Child Research, Norwegian University of Science and Technology, 7491 Trondheim, Norway;
E-Mail: marit.ursin@svt.ntnu.no

Abstract

Drawing on longitudinal qualitative research in Brazil involving participant observation and narrative interviews with young homeless persons, and semi-structured interviews with middle class residents, local businesses, and patrolling police officers, three overlapping yet contradictory dimensions of inclusion and exclusion are developed. First the hegemonic exclusionary discourse that tends to produce stigmatizing labels on poor people in general, and boys and young men on the street in particular, is mapped out. Second, socio-spatial exclusionary mechanisms involving architectural measures, surveillance cameras and violent policing, guarding the neighbourhood from stigmatised 'others' are examined. Third, the less recognised but equally important inclusionary mechanisms, facilitating street life and enabling a sense of belonging among young homeless people are explored. A simplistic and unidimensional conceptualisation of social exclusion is critiqued while demonstrating the multifaceted, intertwined, and contradictory character of homeless people's social relationships with middle class residents, businesses, and police. Furthermore, the exclusion/inclusion dualism that is vivid in the existing literature is questioned. It is suggested that a nuanced picture is vital to increasing our understanding of the everyday lives of homeless populations and that further investigation and theorization of their exclusion as well as inclusion is needed.

Keywords

Brazil; homelessness; social exclusion; social inclusion; street youth

Issue

This article is part of the issue "Homelessness and Social Inclusion", edited by Isobel Anderson (University of Stirling, UK), Maša Filipovič Hrast (University of Ljubljana, Slovenia) and Joe Finnerty (University College Cork, Ireland).

---

1. Introduction

Homeless populations, particularly in the global North, have increasingly been studied and theorised through the lens of social exclusion (e.g. Horsell, 2006; Pleace, 1998; Somerville, 1998), focusing on structural exclusionary mechanisms such as unequal material distribution and discriminatory job and housing markets. Within the burgeoning literature, street dwellers are also described in terms of socio-spatial exclusion, demonstrating how they are perceived as 'unwelcome elements' in metropolitan areas in all corners of the world (e.g. Beazley, 2003; Caldeira, 2000; Scheper-Hughes, 2005; Swanson, 2007; Young, 2003). The mapping of exclusionary processes is of vital importance to unravel the dynamic as well as relational character of social exclusion of vulnerable populations. However, the unilateral focus on exclusion has rendered us incapable of recognising parallel processes of social inclusion (Cameron, 2006). In order to grasp the complexity of social exclusion, it is important to look for experiences of social inclusion among people who appear to be marginalized (Fangen, 2010), bearing in mind that the distinction between inclusion and exclusion is not sharp-cut but ambiguous (Samers, 1998).

This article is inspired by Parr's (2000) claim that ethnographic research can disrupt understandings of 'others' as homogenous individuals who are straightforwardly excluded from 'the mainstream' and moved into marginal spaces. Furthermore, it supports Hall's (2005) conceptualisation of social inclusion and exclusion as not absolute positions, but rather as relational and entangled in particular ways and in particular contexts. I explore the social relations between young street dwellers and middle class residents, businesses, and police in one specific neighbourhood in urban Brazil with the aim to: (1) examine the hegemonic exclusionary discourses that 'other' poor people in general and boys and young men on the street in particular; (2) map out exclusionary mechanisms that guard the socio-spatial boundaries of an elite neighbourhood; and (3) explore less known but equally important inclusionary mechanisms, facilitating street life and enabling a sense of belonging among the young homeless. Drawing on longitudinal, ethnographic research among boys and young men on the street, I document patterns of prejudice across both inclusionary and exclusionary practices. Each of the above objectives is pursued consecutively following the sections on literature review on street youth and urban space, the socio-historical contextualisation of homelessness in Brazil, and the study's methodology, to which I now turn.

2. The Street as Site for Empowerment and Exclusion

The geographical order of urban space is imposed mainly from 'above' by the adult dominant class, police, politicians, and city planners. Yet, young people establish parallel modes of belonging to the streets (Holloway & Hubbard, 2001; Young, 2003). The street allows youth to contest social conventions and assert independence (Matthews, Limb, & Taylor, 2000), and for many poor boys and young men from the deprived *favelas* in Brazil, the street is a site of agency and empowerment (Gough & Franch, 2005). A growing body of research shows how young homeless populations often use 'tactics' of spatial resistance (De Certeau, 1984), encroaching upon the space of the dominating power in a language of protest, defiance, and refusal (Naterer & Godina, 2011; Ruddick, 1998; Scheper-Hughes & Hoffman, 1998; Young, 2003). Street youth appropriate public (as well as private) space opportunistically, using marginal spaces at marginal times (Ruddick, 1998), including spaces normally perceived as impossible, impractical, or impure by mainstream society (Young, 2003). However, studies also reveal their ambiguous position as socially marginalized yet partly accepted and incorporated in particular socio-spatial settings involving leisure or livelihood activities (Moyer, 2004; Naterer & Godina, 2011; Ursin, 2011, 2012; Ursin & Abebe, 2016; Young, 2003).

Young men on the street have been seen as disorderly and deviant by authorities throughout history (Pearson in Robinson, 2009), and are commonly met with 'moral panic' (Matthews et al., 2000). In the context of urban Brazil, poor young men are being scapegoated for criminal activity (Caldeira, 2000; Soares, Bill, & Athayde, 2005). The most controversial category of young people who occupy public space is the category of 'street youth', who are positioned as an abject and dangerous underclass that poses a serious threat to the social fabric. They are commonly ignored as rights-bearing citizens in terms of public policy (Scheper-Hughes, 2005) and instead referred to in terms of culpability: 'They' cause problems for ordinary citizens, scare away tourists, and make the streets unsafe (Gaetz, 2004). Moreover, they are often described in negative and stereotypical ways in the media, public opinion, and policymaking, labelled as threatening as opposed to threatened, offenders rather than victims, and fearless instead of fearful (Pain, 2003).

As Koskela (1997) argues, fear can reflect power relations in society as a product of systematic structural violence. This fear should not be primarily interpreted as a result of factual crime but as an indicator of the power relations in which young street dwellers are embedded. Discursive exclusion is intrinsically linked with spatial exclusion, justifying and reinforcing each other (Sibley, 1995). By being constructed as a threat, marginalised young men regularly experience exclusion from both social life and urban space (Pain, 2001). Social inclusion and exclusion can therefore be understood in terms of (im)mobility, as social inclusion is a matter of overcoming spatial constraints to gain access to desired places, related to work, leisure, and social life (Cass, Shove, & Urry, 2005). For homeless populations—who rely on public spaces to conduct essential aspects of their private lives—this access is even more crucial.

In response to the fear of crime and as a process of 'othering', society seeks to regulate public space (Koskela, 2009) through criminal justice and community safety policies, such as legal prohibitions of 'loitering', discriminatory policing, and the privatisation of public space with private security forces and close circuit television (Caldeira, 2000; Valentine, Skelton, & Chambers, 1998). Young people who domesticate public space are often met with extreme forms of sanctioning, ranging from arrests and deportation to torture and extermination (Pain & Francis, 2004; Ruddick, 1998; Ursin, 2012; van Blerk, 2013). Although such sanctions aim to improve the safety of some groups at the expense of others, they more often generate cumulative fear, distrust, isolation, social exclusion, and further marginalisation (Davis in Pain, 2001; Koskela, 2009; Ursin, 2012).

3. Longitudinal Research in a Street Ambience

Reviewing literature from the global North, Pain (2000) found that young homeless men are commonly defined as 'hard-to-reach' and regularly excluded from research on social relations in urban space, thus we know little about their experiences. To redress this, I draw on a longitudinal and ethnographic study, stretching over a decade, following the same group of boys originally inhabiting one specific neighbourhood in their transitions into adulthood. The study has a multi-method design, including participant observation, narrative interviews with young street dwellers, and semi-structured interviews with middle class residents, businesses, and police officers. Repetitive participant observation was employed, including participation in everyday life and in-depth informal social interaction with the young people on the street, pursuing "an intimate familiarity with the 'world of the other', through getting close to the dilemmas, frustrations, routines, relationships, and risks that are a part of everyday life" (Grills, 1998, p. 4). This meant earning the young men's trust and experiencing their everyday routines of eating, sleeping, 'chasing money' (correr atras), using drugs, and hanging out. In so doing, I also managed to map interactional patterns between the street population and other users of public space.

Jackson (2002) claims that the voices of marginal groups tend to be silenced—denied public recognition—despite their potential to enlighten new perspectives. In order to explore dimensions of social inclusion and exclusion from the 'bottom-up', I conducted narrative interviews with 14 key participants, whereof 10 engaged in two to three rounds of interviews, depending of their accessibility. The key participants were between 12 and 24 years old at the start of the study. All interviews were carried out in private at hours and in places the participants recommended, and they were given pseudonyms to protect their identities.

I also conducted interviews with middle class residents, businesses, and the police living and/or working in the chosen neighbourhood. This includes structured and open-ended interviews with 20 residents, both male and female, ranging from youth to elderly, including both users and non-users of public space; eight owners of shops, restaurants, and hotels in the neighbourhood; and the head of the neighbourhood association. In addition, I used the local newspaper as a source to increase my understanding of residents' and businesspersons' relation to public space, since letters to the editor frequently addressed neighbourhood concerns. I also carried out eight interviews with patrolling police officers (see Ursin, 2013, for a more detailed explanation on methodological and ethical issues related to the study).

4. Social Inequality and Street Populations in Brazil

In order to understand street populations in urban Brazil, it is necessary to trace the historical roots of contemporary social relations and the spatial segregation of Portuguese colonial rule and slavery in which the situation of homeless people is embedded. Slavery was abolished in 1888, but Brazil failed to integrate the freed into educational and labour institutions (Risério, 2004). This resulted in an escalation of young vagrants surviving on intermittent odd jobs in the growing urban centres in the late 19th century and onwards (Fraga Filho, 1994). Post-colonial and post-slavery politics preserved social inequalities, and Brazil continued to be highly divided into hierarchical groups, situating poor, dark-skinned manual labours at the bottom of the social strata (Borges, 1992).

The European-descendent elite perceived the social mixture in the growing metropolitan areas as threatening, bringing together "an unknown and frightening demographic mixture...Amid the ostentatious display of wealth could be found all manner of people loitering about: impoverished workers, vagabonds, beggars, ruffians, prostitutes, and street urchins" (Rizzini, 2002, p. 167). Worrying about decline of urban centres, poor people's access to city centres was increasingly restricted, including through arrest orders of vagrants (Caldeira, 2000; Sangodeyi-Dabrowski, 2003). This criminalisation of the poor has marked the state's response to social problems throughout history (Fernandes, 2013). Fuelled by gentrification processes (Vaz, 1994) but also post-industrialization, rural migration, and rapid urbanization (Kenny, 2007), deprived neighbourhoods expanded in urban peripheries throughout the last century.

These neighbourhoods—today renowned as favelas—continue to expand. Wooden shacks and muddy paths have been replaced by brick houses, asphalted streets, and cemented alleys, and water, sewage, electricity, and public transportation have become easier accessible. In addition to poverty, drug cartels have a strong foothold in many of these communities, which has resulted in an alarming rate of crime, drug trafficking, and violence (Lyra, 2013; Fernandes, 2013). The country experienced a decrease in the number of families living below the poverty line during the leftist government of President Lula da Silva (2003–2011), but is currently struggling with an economic crisis and corruption scandals. School enrolment among poor children and youth has drastically increased (Bush & Rizzini, 2011), but the public educational system is characterized by overcrowded classes, lack of resources, poorly remunerated teachers, and frequent strikes (Kenny, 2007).

The formal labour market has increased expectations in regards to educational qualifications, often demanding a minimum of completed high school (Menezes-Filho & Scorzafave, 2009). This has led to extreme competition for job positions that require low educational levels (Barker, 2005) and an increased unemployment rate among poor youth. A quantitative study in a favela in Northeast Brazil revealed that by the age of 18, nearly half of the residents were neither in school nor at work (Cardoso & Verner, 2006). Livelihood possibilities are not neutral, but engender processes of inclusion and exclusion, and bureaucracy, corruption, and nepotism are common obstacles for poor young Brazilians who seek formal employment (Hecht, 1998). Many *favelado* youth depend on self-employment and livelihood opportunities in the informal sector (Menezes-Filho & Scorzafave, 2009). As competition is high and purchasing power is low in their communities, many descend to wealthier areas in the city in search of income-generating opportunities (Kenny, 2007). One such area is the neighbourhood in which this study took place, where the material wealth of its middle class residents, businesses, and tourists generates legal as well as illegal livelihood opportunities for the homeless population (Ursin & Abebe, 2016). However, as Gough and Franch (2005) suggest, understanding the movements of young people is important to comprehend the meanings young people ascribe to urban space, the possibilities these spaces open up, and the multiple layers of social inclusion and exclusion, which will be further explored in the following sections.

5. Creating Social Boundaries Through Processes of 'Othering'

The site of this study—the neighbourhood of Barra—is a reference place (Jakle, Brunn, & Roseman, 1976, p. 51), with strong symbolic value for both its middle class residents and the tourism industry. It is presented as a homogenous, clean, safe, and modern space. As places are stereotyped not only by the characteristics ascribed to them but also by the kinds of people found in them (Jakle et al., 1976), the presence of poor boys and young men working and living on the streets threatens the social status of the residents and contributes to an impression of 'social decay' (Caldeira, 2000, p. 32). One male resident (31-year-old) argued that the street population causes discomfort as it makes "the social difference visible. When you go out with your car, you don't want to see horrible things". This reveals an 'out-of-sight, out-of-mind' mentality (see Swanson, 2007), emphasising the 'out-of-place-ness' as problematic instead of focusing on the root causes of homelessness—deep-seated poverty and socio-economic inequality. Entrepreneurs in tourism were often preoccupied with the foreigners' reactions, as one male hotel owner (33-year-old) explained:

> "I felt embarrassed the other day when a tourist left the hotel and saw all the kids sleeping [on the pavement outside]. I called and complained to Bahiatursa [tourist department]. How can they let this happen?"

The presence of street workers was perceived as destructive to tourism, as a letter to the editor of the local newspaper demonstrates:

> "It's incredible what the government allows to happen at one of the postcard images of Salvador: The lighthouse of Barra. We only see street vendors with their cool boxes...A great filth is spread throughout Barra, without anyone to inspect it or a minimum of civilization. It is impossible for Salvador to continue to be so messy, filthy, causing an awful impression on the tourists who fill the city" (*A Tarde*, 1 January 2009).

The letter reduces poor people's livelihoods into 'filth' and labels street vendors as dirty and uncivilised, and eliminates poor people from the status of the neighbourhood as a global tourist destination. It also shows an argumentation for state regulation and a displacement of the poor from their means of survival. This resembles the ways in which revanchist urban policies not only legitimised but also exacerbated existing socio-spatial divides in Ecuador, erasing spaces for the poor and working class while creating spaces for tourists (Swanson, 2007). As Swanson argues, while focusing on urban revitalisation to exhibit success as modern metropolises, these policies reframe persistent social problems as an issue of socio-spatial characteristics of a particular place. The street dwellers were aware of the desire to homogenise the neighbourhood, as a young man (20-year-old) said:

> "There are residents who want to preserve Porto da Barra. They think about removing the street youth, making it into a world for themselves and the tourists".

Residents' and businesses' perception of the young and poor as 'out of place' buttresses on processes of 'othering', defining who belongs and who doesn't. As exclusion is "not about gradations of inequality, but about mechanisms that act to detach groups of people from the social mainstream" (Giddens, 1998, p. 104), residents and business owners continuously define and re-define the street population. This process of discursive social exclusion involves a "projection of one's own values and expectations onto the environing world" (Rapport & Overing, 2000, p. 343). Rather than to describe and understand reality, they elaborate prejudices and eliminate ambiguities (Caldeira, 2000), attributing undesirable characteristics to the poor—boys and young men in particular—to emphasise distance and difference between 'us' and 'them'. This process of 'othering' is embedded in two not mutually exclusive discourses of *hygiene* and *urban danger* as captured in the words of the president of the Residents Association when defending actions to reduce the presence of street dwellers and vendors: "We have to defend our rights to the politicians, in terms of security and sanitation".

As seen above, hygienist semantics were used to argue for the purification and beautification of urban space for the sake of tourism, describing street vendors as 'filth'. This perception was not restricted to vendors but extended to poor people in general. Many people from surrounding favelas visit this neighbourhood during weekends, enjoying the beach, play areas, and increasingly also the shopping centres. The president of the Residents Association complained about this; "On Sundays at the lighthouse, when children are playing, even the poor ones come, all dirty", continuing; "They pollute the beach. They do the necessary in the water". Thus people from the lower social strata were perceived as a polluting presence in the cityscape. The homeless population was described in even more negative terms by a male resident (25-years-old): "They incommode the tourists. They are dirty, stinking, begging, robbing". A female resident (31-year-old) complained: "the aesthetics of the neighbourhood as well, it gets ugly. [The homeless] dirty the street, litter, faeces, urine". The problem is not defined as the lack of public facilities for street dwellers and other visitors but rather how the poor contaminate the neighbourhood. The majority of the young homeless men were highly aware of the hygienist discourse, disclosing that others perceived them as germs—invading, infectious, causing diseases. This resembles the hygienist discourse that had great symbolic and political significance during the gentrification process of urban space in the late 1800s and early 1900s (Fraga Filho, 1994; Rizzini, 2002; Vaz, 1994) where poor housing complexes in downtown areas in Rio de Janeiro and São Paulo were perceived as "cooking pots for the germs of yellow fever" (Chalhoub, 1993, p. 456). The rhetorics of modernisation and urban planning echoed quests of order, sanitation, and discipline, purifying urban space. As Sibley (1995) argues, disease metaphors are common to exclusionary mechanisms since the 'diseased other' defines normality and stability. The hygienist discourse reveals a preoccupation with aesthetics based on a narrow and elitist ideal of urban space. Moreover, it also appeals to and further incites sentiments of fear with references to bacteria, disease, and pollution.

Patrolling police in Barra also drew on hygienist semantics, referring to their occasional sweeping of homeless of the street (further explained below) as '*Barra limpa*', a clean Barra. By labelling someone as unclean, as imperfect members of a group, they are rendered discrepant and polluting (Douglas, 2002), not only in a literal sense but also in a symbolic sense, urging for social as well as spatial replacement. As Douglas asserts: "Dirt offends against order. Eliminating it is not a negative movement, but a positive effort to organize the environment" (p. 2). As one young street dweller (20-year-old) explained:

> "The residents want to chase us out of here because they've got education, right? Many have an education, it's easier to earn money, and they will have more if we aren't around. That's why they say they want a clean Barra with Pit Bull hearts".

The sanitation of space is thus perceived as encouraging spatial order—avoiding pollution and littering—as well as social order, preserving social homogeneity. Yet there is also a dimension of morality entwined in the hygienist discourse, where middle class residents and businesspeople often described the poor as lacking educação (education)—a male resident (65-year-old) explained; "On Saturdays and Sundays less educated people come here and litter". 'Educated' is used as synonymous with the middle and upper class who are morally superior as they do not litter but take care of the environment. The Brazilian term—educacão—is broader than the English understanding of the word education, meaning not only to be knowledgeable and have graduated but also to be well-mannered and civilized, which reveals colonial rhetorics of certain groups as ignorant and uncivilized (Sibley, 1995).

Fear and morality are also vital components in the urban danger discourse that 'other' the poor, especially adolescent boys and young men as non-conforming and malignant. A police officer described the vital differences between rich and poor boys as following:

> "A child on the street is completely different. He has a profile marked by evil, a bad person, do you understand? We know that at whatever moment he may have reactions, even of a crime of death. It's different with...the son of a rich person because we know he has education".

Likewise, a female resident (27-year-old) explained: "I would like to help them [street kids], let them live in my home, but I can't because they might kill you afterwards". This shows how young homeless men are seen as irrational, unpredictable, anti-social, and dangerous. Once again, the issue of education—or more precisely of being civilised—is accentuated. As Caldeira (2000) notes in her urban ethnography of São Paulo, poor 'others' are believed to be more vulnerable to crime and evil as they are closer to nature and irrationality. Hegemonic perceptions of poverty and crime amalgamate in Brazil as urban elites criminalize poverty by associating it with street crime and violence (Reis, 2005). Illustratively, the expression *marginal*—marginalized—signifies both being 'poorest of the poor' and an 'outlaw' (Perlman, 2009, p. 157). The criminalization of homelessness was reported by several young street dwellers, describing false accusations of theft and police punishment. The president of the Residents Association complained that the neighbourhood "has turned into hell. Even the car minders are thieves, they threaten to earn money, saying that they will slash your wheel". In criminalising the livelihoods of the poor, assimilating *marginais*, workers, and criminals, the enforcement of the class order and public order are merged (Da Matta, 1991).

Residents and business owners use their socio-political and economic superiority to establish young men as the society's 'other' and to ensure that stereotypes are generally accepted. In this way they legitimise the expulsion of the poor and the homeless and assert their 'rightful' belonging to the neighbourhood. Besides frequent meetings with local politicians, they talk to editors of local newspapers, expressing their concern of the presence of homeless. The president of the Residents Association was regularly in touch with the media, sometimes resulting in front-page stories such as 'The heavy Barra' (*Tribunal da Bahia*, 31 May 2005), accompanied by an illustration of two dark-skinned hands pointing guns towards the local light house, with the heading: "Prostitution, drugs and robberies are constant partners in a neighbourhood that used to belong to the bourgeoisie". On a discursive level, talks of urban danger and 'risk management' function as a primary mechanism of social control, excluding unwelcome people and behaviours (Fischer & Poland, 1998).

While discussing society's perception of young street dwellers, it became obvious that they are not only aware of their marginal status but also link it to distant social relations. One of the older men (27-year-old) living on the street reasoned: "The part of society which doesn't know me, perceive me as a marginal. I only stop being a marginal when they get to know me and see that I'm nothing like what they imagined". His street companion (27-year-old) expressed a similar view:

> "Because they [the residents] don't want to know how street youth feel; what the reason behind this is, being like this; why they are going through this; what kind of difficulties they encounter. No, they don't want to know, they only want to know what they see with their eyes...They only stay at home, that's why they get this 'trauma'".

By trauma, he is referring to the misconception of the street population as dangerous and the fear it causes. Another young man (20-year-old) described how the police sometimes would warn passers-by, saying that he was dangerous, lamenting: "The residents hear this from the police hence many draw their conclusions about me, totally different from who I am". When their life stories are reduced into 'a societal risk', exclusionary and discriminatory actions are stimulated and justified (Barker, 2005).

The social and spatial distance and distancing reduce possibilities of public encounters of heterogeneous groups, facilitating a lack of knowledge about 'the other'. Goldsmith's (2000) description of North American white middle class citizens is transferable to urban Brazil—they grow up in isolation, separated from others, and develop attitudes and behaviours towards African Americans that are based on simplified myths of difference, danger, and hostility rather than positive interaction. Todorov's (1992) description of the colonizer's relation to the 'other' along three axes—value judgement, rapprochement, and knowledge—helps understand middle class residents' and entrepreneurs' relation to the young street population. The moral condemnation (embedded in discourses of hygiene and danger) is allowed and sustained by distancing, which again creates and maintains ignorance, and which permits the continuance of the discourses of hygiene and urban danger. The three axes are interconnected, enabling and reinforcing each other, and maintaining a status quo of social relations in public space.

6. Creating, Maintaining, and Reinforcing Spatial Boundaries

Despite their superior position and their successful processes of 'othering', arguing for the expulsion of the poor and homeless in the neighbourhood, a strong sense of anxiety was observed among many residents and business owners. The president of the Residents Association was particularly explicit. She emphasized the preoccupation of vanishing boundaries between the worlds of the elite and the masses, stating that "Barra has turned into the periphery". When elaborating, she explained: "Today poor people buy clothes in cheap shops that sell clothes similar to ours. They enter [into shopping centres] with tennis shoes, caps, and everything, looking like a resident, and steal everything". This reveals the apprehension and insecurity generated by social encounters between diverse groups (Wilton, 1998). Residents and businesspeople feel a continuous need to create, maintain, and reinforce social as well as spatial boundaries between them and the 'others'. In excluding the poor and the homeless from the neighbourhood, they draw on their economic resources and socio-political influence. They were fighting a losing battle in restricting the access of the poor to the neighbourhood through trying to persuade politicians to stop direct bus routes from the suburban favelas, as the president of the Residents Association explained:

> "The city council said that they would only have buses from the suburbs to Lapa [the central bus station], not directly to Barra, but after the carnival he said that Lapa was nearly falling apart. They lied to gain votes. And then put up busses from far away to here".

If they had succeeded, *favelado* commuters would have had to pay two bus fares, which is a prohibitive cost for people with minimum wages.

A more successful approach is a costly investment in architectural measures to demarcate spatial boundaries, such as speared iron fences, broken glass cemented in the walls, electric gates and video cameras to create private and semi-private enclaves. As Caldeira (2000; see also Fischer & Poland, 1998) writes about insular upper class spaces in São Paulo:

> "These are privatized, enclosed, and monitored spaces of residence, consumption, leisure, and work. Their central justification is the fear of violent crime. They appeal to those who are abandoning the traditional public sphere of the streets to the poor, the marginalized, and the homeless" (p. 213).

Street dwellers often appropriate the interfaces between private and public spheres for sleeping, such as verandas, staircases, backyards, and garages, but such spaces are increasingly being fenced off. This not only reinforces boundaries but also makes urban space uninviting and less habitable for the homeless.

The city council also tried to make Barra less attractive for the street population. The decision to remove public benches some years ago was triggered by the presence of street youth. One street dweller (20-year-old) said:

> "They removed them because there were many homeless, many street dwellers there, sleeping...And that square had to be conserved to not disrespect the

> people who wanted to stroll there and couldn't because there were many homeless there, a lot of filth".

The municipality renovated great parts of the neighbourhood in recent years, including the main boulevard and many of the squares. When discussing these changes with one of the street dwellers (27-year-old) during the last fieldwork, some of the negative consequences became evident, including a reduced sense of belonging in the neighbourhood:

> "You know how we used to say that Barra was of the street people, do you remember? Today it isn't for the street people anymore. Today Barra is for the citizen, for those who have a business, a house, a home..."

He continued, elaborating on how they had lost public space to 'citizens', having fewer places to hang out due to restaurants' furnishing of the pavements, covering pavements with chairs, tables, and paying customers. As part of the revitalising of the neighbourhood, surveillance cameras were installed on street corners. This was particularly dreaded among the homeless population, as explained by a street dweller (27-year-old):

> "They took away the privacy of the homeless. There isn't any privacy anymore...because they put up more security for the population, it has become more transparent. It has become more difficult for the street kids".

The transparency and the feeling of being 'watched' invaded their 'private' sphere, as the homeless tend to privatise and domesticate public space by sleeping, eating, and bathing. Furthermore, he explained that it also impeded doing drugs, having sex, and committing petty theft. Another vital change was the privatization of car parking. To mind parked cars is one of the most lucrative legal livelihoods in the city centre for street dwellers, as it does not require any equipment and has a steady flux of clients. However, during the renovation some of the streets were turned into pedestrian precincts while parking was prohibited in others, encouraging drivers to park their cars in designated, private parking lots. As a result, several young men who had worked in Barra since childhood lost their main source of income.

Surveillance cameras are not the only security measure comforting the middle class residents and local business owners. They also invest large sums on private security forces to watch entrances and patrol streets. Rigid rules are instituted, for instance making the wearing of shoes obligatory and forbidding street vendors or street people from entering. One of the older street dwellers (35-year-old), interviewed in the last fieldwork, said that:

> "It has gone from bad to worse. Everyone discriminates those who live on the street, thinking that everyone who lives on the street is a thief. One cannot enter a super market because everyone is looking. The guards call the police to beat us. Often the guards, when we enter the super market to beg for something, like milk or something like that, the security guard hits us, pushes us, kicks us, pushing us out like we're dogs".

This reveals how transgressing visible and invisible boundaries is met with harsh sanctions. Many apartment buildings and business enterprises also pay the local police patrols regularly, establishing strong loyalty commitments. A male street dweller (27-year-old) reasoned:

> "If you own an apartment, an apartment building, you don't want anyone to bother your clients so they leave, right? If it's the homeless who are disturbing them, what you do is pay the police to remove them, right?"

Another street dweller (24-year-old) explained that the police leave them alone if the residents approve but shoo them away if there are complaints. This reveals that even though the harshest exclusionary mechanism is often executed by the police, it is incited by the attitudes of residents and business owners.

The police do not only defend the boundaries of semi-private and private space, but also seek to regulate and homogenize public space, pushing 'others' back to the geographical as well as social periphery. They decide who will have access to the neighbourhood through a "succession of little rituals of identification and humiliation" (Caldeira, 2000, p. 314). A police officer described how they decide who to approach; "Those who wear Mormaii, Cyclone, and Kenner [brands of clothes and sandals]. Bermuda shorts, big t-shirt, caps are characteristics of those who don't want to work, so we body search them". The style described, however, is one of the most common styles for poor youth in general, legitimizing everyday practices of discrimination and degradation of both street and *favelado* youth. The police draw on both the hygienist and urban danger discourse when explaining why certain groups need to be removed from the neighbourhood:

> "When we appear, the *neguinhos* [small negros] all tremble. This place is for the tourists, right? And for the residents as well, the majority middle class. We act to guarantee the security of these people. Street youth and prostitutes need to feel fear...Hence our work is to clean this area, removing these people".

The police frequently carried out operations to deport poor young people to the outskirts of the city (see also Ursin, 2012), as one of the more seasoned street dwellers (35-year-old) described:

> "You can't sleep on the street at night anymore because there are cars patrolling. If they catch you sleep-

ing...they put you in the trunk of the car, take you to a deserted place and beat you".

Violence is also employed as a preventive strategy, as a police officer related: "[W]e beat the children and the adolescents to see if they give up hanging around here and return to the periphery". According to Wacquant (2003), Brazilian police employ a 'zero tolerance' approach, which has proved beneficial in furthering politicians' and police forces' commitment to the elimination of street crime yet is inefficient in combating actual crime. Yet, brutal—and sometimes lethal—police violence targets poor, young men as they are perceived to be the main source of deviance and violence (Caldeira, 2000; Ursin, 2012). Given the hostility of the discursive as well as the spatial exclusionary mechanisms the young people on the street encounter, it may be difficult to understand why many of them chose to remain in the neighbourhood. In the last part of the article, the subtler acts of inclusion will be explored.

7. Subtle Acts of Social Inclusion in Everyday Encounters

Despite many exclusionary mechanisms, there are also parallel interactional patterns, which Young (2003) defined as socio-spatial acceptance of street youth, namely 'coexistence' and 'incorporation'. As Hall (2005, p. 18) suggests, "far from being absolute positions, social inclusion and exclusion are fragmentary and relational, 'entangled' within each other in particular ways and in particular contexts". Basically, these acts facilitate survival on the street, making it easier to stay. Most importantly, as mentioned above, city centres provide livelihood opportunities that are not available in the favelas. This is often enabled by supportive social networks of mainstream citizens, also called *fregueses*, as a young street dweller (24-year-old) stated; "I have a lot of friendships there [on the street], who always wanted my best, gave me an opportunity" (see also Conticini, 2005; Hecht, 1998). The majority of the homeless in this study engaged in intermittent informal jobs, such as minding cars and running errands, depending on trusting social bonds—although atypical—with residents and businesspeople (Ursin, 2012). Some were also offered more stable work at hotdog stands, beach barracks, and kiosks. Thus despite experiencing social exclusion, their jobs were often more profitable than those available in the *favelas*, emphasizing how spatiality shapes livelihood possibilities and homeless experiences of the young men (Ursin & Abebe, 2016).

As argued elsewhere, many of the street dwellers have lived in Barra since childhood and developed strong feelings of belonging, partly connected to their social relations with residents and business owners (Ursin, 2011). One young man described his relationship with residents as follows: "The majority is people who like me and don't speak badly about me, most of them. When I stay here [at my fixed spot] I feel at ease". A street dweller (27-year-old) who had injured his foot described how he survived on the street:

> "I get by due to my friendships....'I'm hungry, can you get some food for me?' Business owners, the local residents who know me since childhood. 'Damn, you know I don't like to bother people, but I need medicine'. One refuses, another gives. One refuses today but gives tomorrow".

Although there was never a guarantee of receiving help from anyone, having *fregueses* conquered through years of living on the street increases the chances of getting by. When poverty or indifference might encumber the help of family and friends, their extended socio-economic networks often work as much needed safety nets (Ursin & Abebe, 2016).

Some of the interviewed residents and business owners admitted to giving food to street dwellers, either regularly or occasionally. One of the restaurant owners (49-year-old) explained; "If they ask for food, I give. I do it out of pity, do you understand? Being hungry is awful". The discourse of pity is rooted in an idea of inferiority, rendering the young street dwellers as vulnerable and helpless. However, there were other reasons to donate food as well, as a female resident (38-year-old) illustrated; "When they approach me, I give [food]. But I give more out of fear than out of pity". This reveals the multifaceted and context-specific meaning of inclusionary and exclusionary processes, where even though the acts remain the same, the reasoning and rationale behind them differ. As Samers (1998) underscored, the distinction between social inclusion and exclusion is ambiguous. Although some acts increase opportunities of material inclusion (that is, access to food), they still buttress on imagined hierarchies of 'us' and 'them', regardless of whether the other is pitied or feared.

That said, inclusionary acts seem to extend beyond fear in many cases. Some residents and business owners develop individual and personal relationships with street dwellers based on mutually trust (see Ursin, 2012). These relationships facilitate the practicalities of street life in many ways besides food and money—for example, young men may use outdoor taps and store their clothes and valuables in their premises. A young man (22-year-old) who minded cars described how he used to wash the car of one of the residents and received a salary and other benefits:

> "I started to keep my belongings in the apartment building of this guy, in the garage. I even had his key, 'If you need, you enter, whatever occurs you just enter into the garage'. I took baths there, changed clothes".

The motivation behind letting him use the garage might be of both altruism and self-interest as the street dweller washed his car weekly, but either way it contains a dimension of social inclusion. A female resident (25-year-old) explained that she purposefully said 'good evening' to street youth hanging out in a small square close to her apartment building when she moved into the neighbourhood, hoping to ensure protection from street crime. Once again, inclusionary acts might be triggered by self-interest, such as cheap labour and safety, rather than based on ideas of equity, equality, and dignity.

From the point of view of the street dwellers, their social networks with members of the middle class signified more than a means of survival. Being amongst 'educated' people was appreciated, as a young man (27-year-old) explained: "Here I have my best family; residents, employees who work here in Barra, several workers such as port men, security guards, taxi drivers, hotel owners, beach workers". Many of the street dwellers expressed a sense of 'being seen' by mainstream society in ways that everyday life in the *favelas* did not allow. This suggests that the subtler forms of inclusion occurring on the street do not only have a material dimension but also a social one.

As argued elsewhere, this feeling of 'being seen' often enabled a strengthened notion of safety on the street (Ursin, 2011). In fact, safety was one of the main reasons stated for migrating to that particular neighbourhood—an escape from domestic as well as community violence. Several argued that because of the high density of security guards and police patrols, it was difficult to commit homicide in the neighbourhood (Ursin, 2012). Many street dwellers had become acquainted with security guards working in residential or business premises, and told stories of how they keep guard over them while they sleep (Ursin, 2016) or call for help when they are injured. Others explained that the presence of the police was comforting as this reduced the chances of being attacked (Ursin, 2011). This seems odd, considering the brutal police strategies to push them back to the periphery. However, the relationship between the homeless population and the police is riddled with ambiguity, switching between protection and danger. When street dwellers befriend security guards and sleep in vicinity of the police, they capitalize on security measures financed by the middle class. This is not an inclusionary act as exclusionary discourses cause these measures in the first place. However, it demonstrates the ambiguous and complex character of social relations in terms of inclusion and exclusion.

Last but not least, these subtle acts of inclusion do not necessarily embrace all street dwellers. Through honest work, relations of inclusion and trust with the surroundings emerge (Ursin, 2014). To maintain this trust and their networks, it is crucial to avoid (visible) illegal activities, especially violence and property crime (Ursin, 2012; Ursin & Abebe, 2016). However, as demonstrated elsewhere (Ursin, 2014), it is important to emphasize that there is no causal link between crime involvement and social exclusion. Rather, as explored in this article, social exclusion reinforces—and is reinforced by—derogatory images of public discourse, reduced legal livelihood possibilities, and aggressive policing, contributing to further marginalization of the homeless.

8. Conclusions: Is There Such Thing as Social Inclusion on the Street?

This study was based on a multi-method approach to explore the social relations between middle class residents, business owners and the police on the one hand, and poor, young men inhabiting the streets on the other. This exploration of the ways in which discursive and spatial boundaries are created and reinforced reveals a socio-cultural time-lag when it comes to the processes of 'othering' the urban poor in Brazil that is rooted in colonial and post-colonial mind-sets. This othering is embedded in an enduring desire to impose a social as well as a geographical distance for the elite to be able to remain in their insular worlds. The result (and perhaps a precondition) of these 'not-in-my-backyard' practices of exclusion is that underlying social, economic, and political conditions are ignored (Fischer & Poland, 1998) and that attempts are made to displace 'problematic' groups such as street vendors and homeless people.

The exclusionary discourses dominant among middle class residents, business owners, and police render the boys and young men on the street as dirty and dangerous. By drawing on hygienist and urban danger semantics they appeal to sentiments of fear of contamination and street crime, and ideas of superiority in terms of morality, rationality, and civility. Hegemonic discourse constructs different identities as either valued or devalued, yet it is naive to treat life as just a social construction. These discourses greatly influence the ways in which the homeless population is encountered, defined, and debated, and impacts their everyday lives and livelihoods. As Ward (2009, p. 239) reminds us; "lives are lived, experienced and enacted; people feel and respond to social constructions, whether negative or positive". The production and reproduction of difference occurs through the imposition of boundaries, which are not only social constructs of dichotomous and hierarchical relations ('us' and 'them') but also inherently spatial, directing issues of mobility, access, and expulsion. Spatial exclusion is thus both the outcome of, and integral to the production of, social difference (Wilton, 1998). Moreover, the prejudice in which exclusionary discourses is embedded is allowed and sustained by ignorance, which again is nurtured by the very same social and spatial distance and distancing it creates.

Patterns that encourage inclusion of street populations are often ignored in academic literature (Young, 2003) and the dimension of social inclusion is undertheorised in the literature on homelessness. The empirical material presented in this article reveals that despite harsh exclusionary mechanisms, such as stigmatization, hostility, and physical abuse, there are also subtle acts of acceptance and inclusion at the street level. This includes, amongst other things, greetings, food, livelihood possibilities, and protection. Although hostility towards homeless population deserves great attention, there are several implications of discounting more inclusionary dimensions of urban life. First, it reduces the so-called 'mainstream' society into homogenous populations. Second, it misrepresents social encounters across 'us' and 'them' as one-dimensional and static patterns of interaction. Third, it creates an understanding of the 'other' as homogenous social groupings who are straightforwardly excluded from 'the mainstream' to marginal spaces. Fourth, it increases incomprehension of street youth by masking reasons and rationales for remaining on the street.

An ethnographic approach is beneficial in the study of homeless people as it allows a more nuanced picture of exclusion and inclusion. The empirical material presented above reveals ambiguous patterns of social interaction and challenges the inclusion/exclusion dualism that is so present in the existing body of literature. To further unravel the complex character of these patterns, three points will be made. First, although the processes of 'othering' are fundamentally hierarchical, they may be rooted in opposing sentiments of pity and fear, which again are interlinked through the notion of inferiority. Second, both inclusionary acts—such as hand-outs and greetings—and exclusionary acts—such as beatings and physical removal—can be driven by exclusionary discourses based on the inferiority of the 'other'. This suggests that even though acts are inclusionary they are not necessarily based on ideas of equity, equality, and dignity but might be inherently instrumental. Many of these acts are vital in order to survive on the street thus highly valued by street youth. Yet, as they are embedded in diverging discourses of pity, fear, and pragmatism—not necessarily that different from the discourses that support their exclusion—it raises questions on whether all inclusion is positive, especially if the character of it and reason behind it might be exploitative and unequal. Third, inclusionary and exclusionary acts are not only imposed on street youth, but youth also actively enact and interpret them. For example, street youth capitalise on security measures financed by the middle class and businesses to exclude them to be able to feel safer and more 'at home' in the street (see also Ursin, 2011). This not only reveals the ambiguous and complex character of social relations in terms of inclusion and exclusion but also suggests limitations of the concepts of social inclusion and exclusion for being unidirectional and objectifying of the persons involved, reducing them into mere victims. In sum, this article demonstrates the multifaceted, intertwined, and contradictory character of social relations, encouraging further investigation and theorization of exclusionary as well as inclusionary mechanisms involving street dwellers.

Conflict of Interests

The author declares no conflict of interests.

References

A Tarde. (2009, January 1).

Barker, G. (2005). *Dying to be men*. London: Routledge.

Beazley, H. (2003) The construction and protection of individual and collective identities by street children and youth in Indonesia. *Children, Youth and Environments, 13*(1). Retrieved from http://colorado.edu/journals/cye

Borges, D. (1992). *The family in Bahia, Brazil, 1870–1945*. Stanford: Stanford University.

Bush, M., & Rizzini, I. (2011). *Closing the gap between rights and realities for children and youth in urban Brazil: Reflections on a Brazilian project to improve policies for street children*. Rio de Janeiro: CIESPI/PUC-Rio.

Cameron, A. (2006). Geographies of welfare and exclusion: Social inclusion and exception. *Progress in Human Geography, 30*(3), 396–404.

Caldeira, T. (2000). *City of walls: Crime, segregation and citizenship in São Paulo*. Berkeley: University of California.

Cardoso, A. R., & Verner, D. (2006). *School drop-out and push-out factors in Brazil: The role of early parenthood, child labor, and poverty*. Bonn: IZA.

Cass, N., Shove, E., & Urry, J. (2005). Social exclusion, mobility and access. *The Sociological Review, 53*(3), 539–555.

Chalhoub, S. (1993). The politics of disease control: Yellow fever and race in nineteenth century Rio de Janeiro. *Journal of Latin American Studies, 25*(3), 441–463.

Conticini, A. (2005). Urban livelihoods from the children's perspectives: Protecting and promoting assets on the streets of Dhaka. *Environment and Urbanization, 17*(2), 69–81.

Da Matta, R. (1991). *Carnivals, rogues, and heroes: An interpretation of the Brazilian dilemma*. Notre Dame, IN: University of Notre Dame.

De Certeau, M. (1984). *The practice of everyday life*. Berkeley: University of California.

Douglas, M. (2002). *Purity and danger* (6th ed.). London: Routledge.

Fangen, K. (2010). Social exclusion and inclusion of young immigrants: Presentation of an analytical framework. *Young, 18*(2), 133–156.

Fernandes, F. L. (2013). Youth gang members in Rio de Janeiro: The face of a 'lost generation' in an age of fear and mistrust. *Bulletin of Latin American Research, 32*(2), 210–223.

Fischer, B., & Poland, B. (1998). Exclusion, 'risk', and social control—Reflections on community policing and public health. *Geoforum, 29*(2), 187–197.

Fraga Filho, W. (1994). *Mendigos e vadios na Bahia do século XIX* (MA thesis in history). Salvador: Universidade Federal da Bahia.

Gaetz, S. (2004). Safe streets for whom? Homeless youth, social exclusion, and criminal victimisation. *Canadian*

Journal of Criminology and Criminal Justice, 46(4), 423–455.

Giddens, A. (1998). *The third way: The renewal of social democracy*. Cambridge: Polity Press.

Goldsmith, W. (2000). Still a global city: The racial and ethnic segmentation of New York. In P. Marcuse & R. van Kempen (Eds.), *Globalizing cities: A new spatial order?* (pp. 37–55). Oxford: Blackwell.

Gough, K. & Franch, M. (2005). Spaces of the street: Socio-spatial mobility and exclusion of youth in Recife. *Children's Geographies, 3*(2), 149–166.

Grills, S. (1998). *Doing ethnographic research—Fieldwork settings*. Thousand Oaks, CA: Sage Publications.

Hall, E. (2005). The entangled geographies of social exclusion/inclusion for people with learning disabilities. *Health & Place, 11*(2), 107–115.

Hecht, T. (1998). *At home in the street*. Cambridge: Cambridge University.

Holloway, L., & Hubbard, P. (2001). *People and place: The extraordinary geographies of everyday life*. London: Routledge.

Horsell, C. (2006). Homelessness and social exclusion: A Foucauldian perspective for social workers. *Australian Social Work, 59*(2), 213–225.

Jackson, M. (2002). *The politics of storytelling: Violence, transgression and intersubjectivity*. Copenhagen: Museum Tusculanum Press.

Jakle, J., Brunn, S., & Roseman, C. (1976). *Human spatial behaviour: A social geography*. California: Duxbury Press.

Kenny, L. M. (2007). *Hidden heads of households: Child labor in urban Northeast Brazil*. Toronto: Broadview Press.

Koskela, H. (1997). Bold walks and breakings: Women's spatial confidence versus fear of violence. *Gender, Place and Culture, 4*(3), 301–319.

Koskela, H. (2009). Crime/Fear of crime. In R. Kitchin & N. Thrift (Eds.), *International Encyclopedia of Human Geography*. London: Elsevier.

Lyra, D. (2013). *A república dos meninos: Juventude, tráfico e virtude*. Rio de Janeiro: Mauad.

Matthews, H., Limb, M., & Taylor, M. (2000). The street as "third space." In S. Holloway & G. Valentine (Eds.), *Children's geographies: Playing, living, learning* (pp. 63–79). London: Routledge.

Menezes-Filho, N., & Scorzafave, L. (2009). *Employment and inequality outcomes in Brazil*. São Paulo: Insper. Retrieved from http://www.oecd.org/dataoecd/54/53/42546065.pdf

Moyer, E. (2004). Popular cartographies: Youthful imaginings of the global in the streets of Dar es Salaam, Tanzania. *City & Society, 16*(2), 117–143.

Naterer, A., & Godina, V. (2011). Bomzhi and their subculture: An anthropological study of the street children subculture in Makeevka, eastern Ukraine. *Childhood, 18*(1), 20–38.

Pain, R. (2000). Place, social relations and the fear of crime: A review. *Progress in Human Geography, 24*(3), 365–387.

Pain, R. (2001). Gender, race, age and fear in the city. *Urban Studies, 38*(5-6), 899–913.

Pain, R. (2003). Youth, age and the representation of fear. *Capital & Class, 27*(2), 151–171.

Pain, R., & Francis, P. (2004). Living with crime: Spaces of risk for homeless young people. *Children's Geographies, 2*(1), 95–110.

Parr, H. (2000). Interpreting the 'hidden social geographies' of mental health: Ethnographies of inclusion and exclusion in semi-institutional places. *Health & Place, 6*(3), 225–237.

Perlman, J. (2009). *Favela—Four decades of living on the edge of Rio de Janeiro*. New York: Oxford University.

Pleace, N. (1998). Single homelessness as social exclusion: The unique and the extreme. *Social Policy & Administration, 32*(1), 46–59.

Rapport, N., & Overing, J. (2000). *Social and cultural anthropology*. London: Routledge.

Reis, E. (2005). Perceptions of poverty and inequality among Brazilian elites. In E. Reis & M. Moore (Eds.), *Elite perceptions of poverty and inequality* (pp. 26–56). London: Zed books.

Risério, A. (2004). *Uma história da Cidade da Bahia*. Rio de Janeiro: Versal Editores.

Rizzini, I. (2002). The child saving movement in Brazil. Ideology in the late nineteenth and early twentieth centuries. In T. Hecht (Ed.), *Minor omissions: Children in Latin American history and society* (pp. 165–180). Madison: University of Wisconsin.

Robinson, C. (2009). Nightscapes and leisure spaces: An ethnographic study of young people's use of free space. *Journal of Youth Studies, 12*(5), 501–514.

Ruddick, S. (1998). How homeless youth sub-cultures make a difference. In G. Valentine & T. Skelton (Eds.), *Cool places: Geographies of youth cultures* (pp. 344–362). London: Routledge.

Samers, M. (1998). Immigration, 'ethnic minorities', and 'social exclusion' in the European Union: A critical perspective. *Geoforum, 29*(2), 123–144.

Sangodeyi-Dabrowski, D. (2003). As raízes ideológicas da segregação no Brasil: O exemplo de Salvador. In M. Esteves Júnior & U. Montoya Uriarte (Eds.), *Panoramas urbanos: Reflexões sobre a cidade* (pp. 165–184). Salvador: Edufba.

Scheper-Hughes, N. (2005). Dangerous and endangered youth: Social structures and determinants of violence. *Annals of the New York Academy of Science, 1036*(1), 13–46.

Scheper-Hughes, N., & Hoffman, D. (1998). Brazilian apartheid: Street kids and the struggle for urban space. In N. Scheper-Hughes & C. Sargent (Eds.), *Small wars* (pp. 352–388). Berkeley: University of California.

Sibley, D. (1995). *Geographies of exclusion*. London: Routledge.

Soares, L., Bill, M. V., & Athayde, C. (2005). *Cabeça do porco*. Rio de Janeiro: Objetiva.

Somerville, P. (1998). Explanations of social exclusion:

Where does housing fit in? *Housing Studies*, *13*(6), 761–780.

Swanson, K. (2007). Revanchist urbanism heads south: The regulation of indigenous beggars and street vendors in Ecuador. *Antipode*, *39*(4), 708–728.

Todorov, T. (1992). *The conquest of America*. New York: Harper Perennial.

Tribunal da Bahia. (2005, May 31).

Ursin, M. (2011). 'Wherever I lay my head is home'—Young people's experience of home in the Brazilian street environment. *Children's Geographies*, *9*(2), 221–234.

Ursin, M. (2012). 'The city is ours': The temporal construction of dominance among poor young men on the street in a Brazilian elite neighbourhood. *Journal of Latin American Studies*, *44*(3), 467–493.

Ursin, M. (2013). *'The place where I buried my bellybutton'—A longitudinal study of transitions and belonging among young men on the street in Salvador, Brazil* (PhD thesis). Bodø: University of Nordland. Available at https://brage.bibsys.no/xmlui/bitstream/id/315237/Ursin.pdf

Ursin, M. (2014). "Crack ends it all?" A study of the interrelations between crack cocaine, social environments, social relations, crime, and homicide among poor, young men in urban Brazil. *Contemporary Drug Problems*, *41*(2).

Ursin, M. (2016). Geographies of sleep among Brazilian street youth. In K. Nairn, P. Kraftl, & T. Skelton (Eds.), *Geographies of children and young people. Space, landscape, and environment*. London: Springer. Retrieved from http://link.springer.com/referencework/10.1007%2F978-981-287-044-5

Ursin, M., & Abebe, T. (2016). Young people's marginal livelihoods and social transitions in urban Brazil: A tale of four lives. In T. Abebe, J. Waters, & T. Skelton (Eds.), *Geographies of children and young people. Labouring and learning*. London: Springer. Retrieved from http://link.springer.com/referenceworkentry/10.1007/978-981-4585-97-2_16-1

Valentine, G., Skelton, T., & Chambers, D. (1998). Cool places: An introduction to youth and youth cultures. In T. Skelton & G. Valentine (Eds.), *Cool places: Geographies of youth cultures* (pp. 1–32). London: Routledge.

van Blerk, L. (2013). New street geographies: The impact of urban governance on the mobilities of Cape Town's street youth. *Urban Studies*, *50*(3), 556–573.

Vaz, L. V. (1994). Dos cortiços às favelas e aos edifícios de apartamentos—A modernização da moradia no Rio de Janeiro. *Análise Social*, *xxix*(3), 581–597.

Wacquant, L. (2003). Toward a dictatorship over the poor? Notes on the penalization of poverty in Brazil. *Punishment & Society*, *5*, 197–205.

Ward, N. (2009). Social exclusion, social identity and social work: Analysing social exclusion from a material discursive perspective. *Social Work Education*, *28*(3), 237–252.

Wilton, R. D. (1998). The constitution of difference: Space and psyche in landscapes of exclusion. *Geoforum*, *29*(2), 173–185.

Young, L. (2003). The 'place' of street children in Kampala, Uganda: Marginalisation, resistance, and acceptance in the urban environment. *Environment and Planning D: Society and Space*, *21*, 607–627.

About the Author

Marit Ursin is Associate Professor at the Norwegian centre for Child Research at Norwegian University of Science and Technology. She has executed a longitudinal study with young people on the verge of adulthood on the street in urban Brazil as part of her MA in anthropology and PhD in sociology. She has also worked with children in institutional settings in Brazil and Mexico, as well as explored the impact of the drug trade in poor youth's everyday lives in Brazil.

6

Social Exclusion/Inclusion for Urban Aboriginal and Torres Strait Islander People

Maggie Walter

School of Social Sciences, University of Tasmania, Hobart, TAS 7001, Australia; E-Mail: maggie.walter@utas.edu.au

Abstract

Social exclusion social inclusion are useful concepts for making sense of the deeply embedded socio-economic disadvantaged position of Aboriginal and Torres Islander people in Australian. The concepts not only describe exclusion from social and economic participation; but seek to understand the dynamic processes behind their creation and reproduction. Yet few Australian studies go beyond describing Aboriginal over-representation on social exclusion indicators. Neither do they address the translatability of the concepts from non-Indigenous to Indigenous contexts despite mainstream studies finding the pattern of social exclusion (and therefore what social inclusion might look like) differs for Aboriginal and Torres Strait Islander people to that of other disadvantaged groups. This paper uses data from the Longitudinal Study of Indigenous children to explore patterns of social exclusion across social, economic, well-being and community dimensions for urban Aboriginal and Torres Strait families. The paper then develops a contextual understanding of the processes and patterns that create and sustain social exclusion and the opportunities and challenges of moving to greater social inclusion for urban Aboriginal and Torres Strait Islander people/s.

Keywords

aboriginal; social exclusion; social inclusion; Torres Strait Islander

Issue

This article is part of the issue "Social Inclusion and Indigenous Peoples", edited by Pat Dudgeon (University of Western Australia, Australia), Waikaremoana Waitoki (University of Waikato, New Zealand), Rose LeMay (Wharerātā Group, Canada) and Linda Waimarie Nikora (University of Waikato, New Zealand).

1. Introduction

The concepts of social exclusion and its policy ambition, social inclusion, are directly applicable to making sense of the longstanding marginalisation of Aboriginal and Torres Islander people within Australian society. These concepts extend our understanding of Aboriginal and Torres Strait Islander's people's position as being much more than economic disadvantage. Social exclusion not only describes exclusion from social and economic participation, but seeks to understand the dynamic processes behind their creation and reproduction. The complexity and multidimensional nature of social exclusion, therefore, is inclusive of negative social participatory aspects and the diminished citizenship that is inherent in, and compounded by, exclusion from social resources. Yet, gaining a greater understanding of Aboriginal and Torres Strait Islander positioning is more than translating the concepts from non-Indigenous to Indigenous contexts. What little work exists on the topic (see Hunter, 2009) suggests that the concepts of social inclusion and exclusion for Indigenous peoples have complexities not found in their application to dominant White settler populations. The dearth of theoretically informed literature also raises questions of the pattern of Indigenous social exclusion (and therefore what social inclusion) might look like.

This paper uses data from the Longitudinal Study of Indigenous children (LSIC) to explore patterns of social exclusion across social, economic, community and well-being dimensions for urban Aboriginal and Torres Strait families. This study, while using the study child as the unit of analysis, contains a wealth of data pertaining to family and parent circumstances and lived realities. The paper then uses these results to inform a contextual discussion of the processes and patterns that create and sustain social exclusion and the opportunities and challenges of moving to greater Indigenous social inclusion. The geographic terms used in this analysis are based on the index of Level of Relative Isolation which has five categories of isolation. Areas defined as having no level of isolations ('None') are metropolitan areas; those defined as having low levels of isolation are small cities or large towns. 'Moderate' refers to smaller towns located a significant distance from the nearest city and 'High' and 'Extreme' refers to small communities, often discrete Indigenous communities, situated in remote parts of Australia, a long distance from any urban areas (Department of Families, Housing, Community Services and Indigenous Affairs, 2011).

The study is confined to urban and regional families ('None' and 'Low' levels of relative isolation). The LSIC sample is divided because the contexts of social and community participation for Aboriginal and Torres Strait Islander people living in urban centres, and those living in remote areas of Australia are not directly comparable. Life circumstance similarities for respondents from 'None' and 'Low' level of relative isolation localities include that life is lived within a dominant non-Indigenous social and cultural setting. Levels of Relative Isolation are a proxy for the proportion of Indigenous and non-Indigenous population in a location. Indigenous people in areas defined as 'None' or 'Low' relative isolation are likely to make up just two to three percent of the total population of those areas. Conversely, those living in areas defined as 'High' and 'Extreme' are likely to be living in locations where the large majority of the population are Aboriginal or Torres Strait Islander people. The other reason for exploring urban and regional families separately is that most current statistics on Aboriginal and Torres Strait Islander people are presented at state or national aggregates, despite the very different life circumstances across geographic areas. As a result the actualities of social exclusion for urban/regional populations are rarely explored separately and social exclusion among Aboriginal and Torres Strait Islander families living in cities and regional towns is under-researched.

2. Social Exclusion and Aboriginal and Torres Strait Islander People

Social exclusion refers to the exclusion of people or groups from participation in mainstream social and economic life. In doing so the concept recognises the social aspects of poverty as well as the power relationship dimensions. As Burchardt, Le Grand and Piachaud (2002) argue, the exclusion of some groups from social resources support the privileged position of other groups. In turn, this distribution of social resources is reinforced by how those socially excluded interact with their wider society, and wider society with them. In this way social exclusion, includes the social processes involved in the underlying causes of poverty and inequality as well as outcomes (Fincher & Saunders, 2001, p. 9). As Sen (2000) argues, the helpfulness of the concept of social exclusion, is in its focussing attention on the role of the social and relational dimensions of deprivation.

One issue complicating the measuring of social exclusion is the complexity of the concepts. Many researchers, therefore, have argued it is more useful to develop a general conception of social exclusion rather than pursue a precise definition (Bradshaw, 2003; Burchardt et al., 2002; Saunders, 2003). Lister (2004), for example, states that social exclusion can be most usefully understood and used as a multifocal lens that illuminates aspects of poverty. The multidimensional nature of exclusion also translates to a wide array of potential elements to be included and this variety is reflected in the varying research constructions of the concept. Gordon et al. (2000), for example, identifies four dimension of social exclusion: income below poverty income threshold; labour market exclusion, service exclusion; and exclusion from social relations. Similarly, the Brotherhood of St Laurence, in collaboration with the Melbourne Institute of Applied Economic and Social Research, developed a social exclusion measure drawing on seven domains (BSL-MIAESR) (Azpitarte & Bowman, 2015). This multi-dimensional index includes measures of: material resources; employment; education and skills; health and disability; social connection; community and personal safety. Regardless of items included, however, such measures must always encompass the basic idea that social exclusion is both multi-dimensional concept *and* that it is clustered among vulnerable groups rather than evenly experienced across the broader population.

Social exclusion and social inclusion, by definition, are contextual, locational and situational. The form that social exclusion takes, the groups that are most vulnerable to that form of social exclusion, and the social inclusion measures needed to address the social exclusion, are particular to the society and the location and times in which they are found. These central aspects of social exclusion are particularly salient for Aboriginal and Torres Strait Islander people. Consistently identified in the literature as over-represented on measures social exclusion (see Brotherhood of St Laurence, 2015; Saunders, Naidoo, & Griffiths, 2007) there is, however, little literature that specifically addresses the Aboriginal dimensions of social exclusion or social inclusion. What literature does exist, such as the Overcoming Indigenous Disadvantage Key Indicators (Steering Committee for the Review of Government Service Provision, 2014) report from the Productivity Commission tend to explore social exclusion as a set of measures rather than as a concept that has structural foundations. Yet, social exclusion is a social, not individual, phenomenon, informed by patterns that emerge from examining linked social problems (Lister, 2004; Sen, 2000). As Saunders (2003, p. 5) argues, viewed as an individual attribute, social exclusion can become 'a vehicle for vilifying those who do not conform and an excuse for seeing their problems as caused by their own "aberrant behaviour'. Rather, as per Sen (2000), social exclusion might be better seen as capability deprivation with capability conceptualised as a reflection of the freedom to achieve core functionings such as being healthy, having a good job, safety and self respect. The restriction of capability limits or denies the ability of the individual, or groups of individuals to achieve outcomes that are valued and have reason to be valued; to achieve what Sen labels 'a decent life'.

The mainstream literature on social exclusion/inclusion is informative, but the validity of transposing of the understandings, strategies and policies from one place, or one population, to another is questionable. Hunter (2009) argues that the translatability of social exclusion and social inclusion from non-Indigenous to Indigenous contexts is problematic. Yet the conceptualisation of social exclusion implicit in the *Overcoming Indigenous Disadvantage* framework based on exclusion from the mainstream norm. There are no Indigenous specific indicators and the definition of social exclusion and the measurement of that exclusion is undertaken outside of Indigenous understandings. The validity of Hunter's (2009) arguments are borne out by research indicating that the pattern of social exclusion for Aboriginal and Torres Strait Islander people differs to that of other disadvantaged groups. For example, Saunders et al. (2007) in their examination of the extent of social exclusion find their Indigenous sample, drawn from the city of Sydney, less negatively affected by indicators of social disengagement relating to contact with others and participation in community activities. Indeed, on these indicators, the Indigenous outcomes were higher than the national figure. On indicators relating to service and economic exclusion, however, such as inability to pay utility bills, lack of emergency savings and inability to spend money on a special treat the Indigenous sample does worst.

Two conclusions can be drawn from these studies. First it is clear that social exclusion and inclusions are concepts that are resonant in the lives of urban Aboriginal people. It is also clear that the forms and shapes that social exclusion takes for Aboriginal people is not a duplicate of that other groups in Australian society traditionally associated with socio-economic disadvantage. The proportion of the Aboriginal and Torres Strait Islander population who can be regarded as socially excluded is also unclear, even from the literature that encompasses the topic. The BSL-MIAESR measure for example, estimates the prevalence of social exclusion among Indigenous Australians at more than 40 percent. However, the data for this estimate is the Household Income and Labour Dynamics Australia (HILDA) survey where the sample of Aboriginal and Torres Strait Islander people is small in size and groups all Aboriginal and Torres Strait Islander households into the one base 'Indigenous' category. Similarly the Social Policy Research Centre (Saunders et al., 2007) report notes that Indigenous people made up only 0.8 of their random Australian sample of 2704 community participants.

There is, therefore, despite assumptions of high levels of social exclusion among Aboriginal and Torres Strait Islander populations limited evidence to support those assumptions. The cumulative effect of limited literature, limited translatability of measures, limited evidence on the rates and types of social exclusion lead to a gap in understanding how social exclusion is maintained and sustained for Indigenous individuals, families and communities. This is especially so for the majority of Aboriginal and Torres Strait Islander people who live in urban and regional areas of Australia. As such strategies for social inclusion will also have to be tailored to meet Indigenous realities of social exclusion. To redress, at least partially, the gap in knowledge of Indigenous social exclusion, this paper uses data from the Longitudinal Study of Indigenous Children, Australia's only longitudinal Indigenous specific survey, to explore the patterns and nature of social exclusion of urban/regional Aboriginal and Torres Strait Islander families.

3. Method/Methodology

The Footprints in Time, Longitudinal Study of Indigenous Children (LSIC) is a national panel study that in Wave 1 (2008) surveyed the families of 1,670 Indigenous Children from 11 sites across Australia. These locations ranged from very remote communities to major capital cities (Department of Social Services, 2015). LSIC data are collected via face-to-face interviews between the Study Child's primary parent (named Parent 1) and locally employed Indigenous Research Administration Officers. Study children are divided into two cohorts; the B or baby cohort who were aged 6- 18 months at Wave 1 and the K or kid cohort, aged 3.5–5 years at Wave 1. The results presented in this chapter are, unless otherwise noted, drawn from Wave 6 conducted in 2013 (n=1239) when the younger cohort was aged 5.5–7 years of age and the older cohort 8.5–10 years of age.

While not a random sample, the spread of LSIC households are similar in geographic distribution to the total Indigenous population with three quarters located in areas classified as having 'None' or 'Low' levels of remoteness and a quarter in areas deemed remote and very remote (Australian Bureau of Statistics [ABS], 2011). In Wave 6, this distribution of Parent 1 households were 28 percent in areas classified as having a remoteness level of 'None', 51 percent in 'Low', 13 percent 'moderate' and nine percent as 'high/extreme' remoteness. The sample for this study are restricted to those households classified as 'None' and Low' level of remoteness. In Wave 6 this results a sub-sample of 973 households. The dimensions of social exclusion explored in this study are socio-economic; household and service; Community and Health and Socio-Emotional Well-Being.

Key socio-demographic details of these households are outlined in Table 1. As shown two thirds of the families are in areas of 'Low' remoteness, most Parent 1's are mothers and aged under forty years, although the primary carer for more than 10 percent of the children is a family member other than the child's mother.

Table 1. Study child and parent 1 demographic details: LSIC Wave 6 (n=973).

Variable	Category	Percent %
Level of Remoteness	None	35.4
	Low	64.6
Study Child Cohort	B Younger Cohort	58.9
	K Older Cohort	41.1
Gender of Parent 1	Male	3.3
	Female	96.7
Age of Parent 1	20-29	24.0
	30-39	47.5
	40-49	21.7
	50+	6.2
Indigenous Status of Parent 1	Aboriginal	70.7
	Torres Strait Islander	3.9
	Both	3.1
	Not Indigenous	22.3
Relationship of Parent 1 to Study Child	Mother	87.7
	Father	3.1
	Grandmother	5.9
	Other female relative	1.4
	Other	1.9

4. Socio-Economic Social Exclusion

This correlation between Indigeniety and poverty argued by Walter (2008) is evident in the LSIC data. As shown in Table 2, 40 percent of Parent 1s, the majority of whom are mothers, were in paid work at the time of data collection, with around half of that group working full-time. This rate is significantly lower than that of non-Indigenous mothers in Australia where over two thirds of mothers of children with children aged 6–9 years are in the paid workforce (Baxter, 2009). In the free text responses to why they were not in paid work the overwhelming majority (more than 400 of the 537 responses) gave reasons related to child rearing, predominantly stating that they wanted to look after their children themselves. Only 57 respondents gave lack of employment opportunity reasons. These responses indicate a clash between Aboriginal and Torres Strait Islander primary parents' values on appropriate child rearing and the policy push for mothers receiving welfare payments to return to the workforce when or before their youngest child turns six (Parenting Payment). The impact of this values differentiation is magnified given that nearly half of the Parent 1 group were unpartnered at the time of data collection.

Of those Parent 1s who were partnered, nearly 29 percent had partners not in the labour force. A small number of these were retired (n=10), permanently unable to work (n=9) or not well enough to work (n=23) but the majority of reasons given for not being in the paid workforce related to lack of employment opportunity. Just under half of the Parent 1s reported salary or wages as their main source of income and more than 80 percent reported that Government pensions, benefits or allowances as a main source of income. Nearly two thirds of Study Child households were reported as having weekly income from all sources, after deductions, under $1000. Unlike non-Indigenous parents therefore, who are evenly spread across the socio-economic spectrum, for a significant proportion of LSIC parents, social exclusion as defined by economic dimensions is the norm.

Socio-economic exclusion is also evident through more objective measurements included in LSIC Wave 6. On household deprivation measures (n=963) around one third (33%) reported that they could not pay their bills on time; nearly one in five (19%) reported receiving assistance from a welfare organisation; pay housing

Table 2. Parent 1 socio-economic status details: LSIC Wave 6 (n=973).

Variable	Category	Percent %
Parent 1 Employed	Yes	39.7
	No	60.2
Parent 1's Employment Type (n=380)	Full time	46.8
	Part time/Casual	49.5
	Other	3.7
Partnership Status of P1	Unpartnered	45.6
	Partnered	54.6
Parent 1's Partner Employed	Yes	71.3
	No	28.7
Parent 1's Partner Employment Type	Full-Time	76.7
	Part-time/Casual	15.0
	Self Employed	5.8
	Other	2.5
Main Source of Income*	Wages/Salary	45.7
	Govt Benefit/Pension/ Allowance	81.9
	Child Support/ Maintenance	10.6
Household Weekly Income After Deductions	$0-$499	21.2
	$500-$999	41.0
	$1000-$1499	21.2
	$1500-$1999	10.8
	$2000 plus	5.6

Note: * respondents could nominate more than one nine percent could not main source of income.

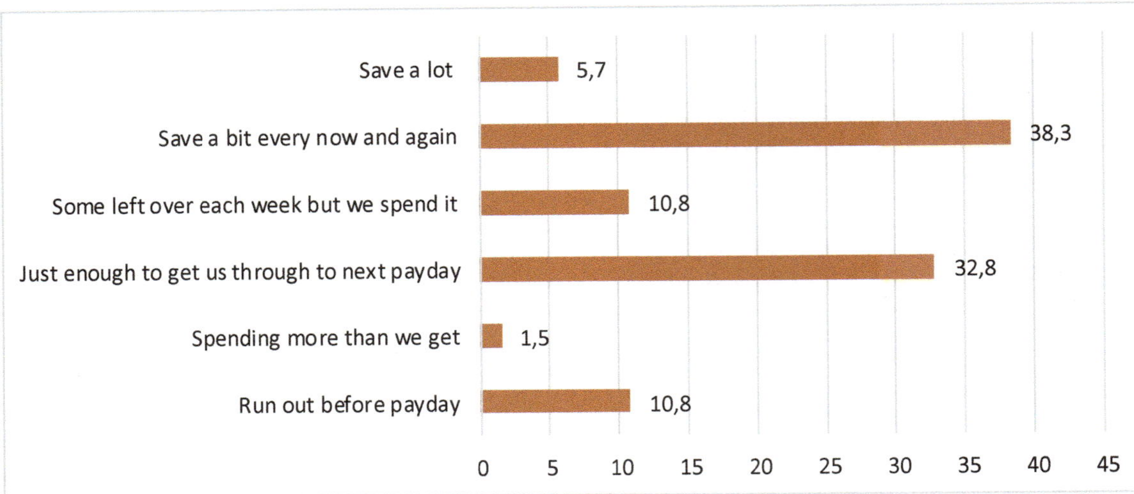

Figure 1. LSIC household self rating on financial stress (percentage).

payments in time; 12 percent had pawned or sold something to make ends meet; and around five percent respectively had been unable to heat their home, went without meals, or their child did not do school activities because of a shortage of money. On the financial hardship measures, as shown in Figure 1, despite evidence of relatively low household incomes, only 12 percent indicated they were not managing on current income and 44 percent indicated they save some money, at least some of the time. The norm of economic disadvantage within the community in which most LSIC parents live, perhaps, leads to coping money management systems that include aspects of social relationality. For example, analysis of Wave 6 data related to household meals (not shown here) finds that around 60 percent of Parent 1's report feeding people from outside of their household on a weekly or fortnightly basis.

5. Housing/Service Social Exclusion

The LSIC dataset capacity to measure levels of service exclusion for urban Aboriginal and Torres Strait Islander families is predominantly in the data related to housing. In line with census data (Walter, 2008) the majority of LSIC households occupy rental housing. In Wave 1 (2008) around 80 percent of households in rental accommodation with half of this group renting from public housing authorities. In consequent waves housing type was only asked of those who had moved since the previous wave. Analysis of these data (not shown here) indicate despite a small increase in the proportion paying off their home in each wave, the predominant pattern of renting remains.

The LSIC households also present a pattern of housing occupation. As shown in Table 3, around one quarter of households have more than two adults present and over 85 percent have two or more children present. In another deviation from non-Indigenous norms, 27 percent of households contain only one adult yet 46 percent of the Parent 1's report that they are unpartnered. A significant proportion of unpartnered Parent 1 households must therefore include adults who are not a partner. Walter and Hewitt (2012) confirm this likelihood, with grandmothers and sisters of the Parent 1 reported the most common adult type, other than partners, to reside in the LSIC household.

A substantial proportion (34%) of Parent 1 households also report their housing as in need of substantial repair as also shown in Table 3. Responses to 18 discrete categories show the most common major repairs needed are: plumbing in baths and showers (5.2%); structural problems (5.3%); major electrical problems (5.2%) or other major problem (6.2%). Further analysis of these data found housing repair inadequacy was clustered with the more than 15 percent of households reporting more than one major repair was needed.

Table 3. Study child's household (Wave 6 n=973).

Variable	Category	Percent %
Housing Type (n=240)*	Rental Public/Community	37.8
	Rental Private	47.2
	Owned (mortgage/outright)	10.5
	Other	4.5
Number of Adults in Household	One	27.5
	Two	47.5
	Three	15.3
	Four or more	9.6
Number of Children in Household	One	12.6
	Two	26.1
	Three	30.5
	Four or more	23.0
Household needs Major Repairs	No	66.4
	One major Repair	17.8
	Two major repairs	7.5
	Three or more major repairs	8.3

Note: * Only asked of those who moved house between Wave 5 and Wave 6.

6. Community Social Exclusion

Community social exclusion is assessed through analysis of Wave 6 neighbourhood and community data. As shown in Table 4, community safety was rated relatively highly by Parent 1 with 70 percent rating their community as good or very good for little kids and nearly two thirds rated overall safety of the community as very safe of quite safe. These findings, given the level of socio-economic deprivation and high level of rental accommodation among the LSIC families indicate that other factors are the main influence on respondents understanding of why a community is safe or good for little kids.

7. Well-Being Social Exclusion

As shown in Table 5, in Wave 6 (n=973) that more than 80 percent of Parent 1's rate their own health as excellent or very good. Close to three quarters of Parent 1s, however, report that they have at least some problems in their life. Regardless, more than 80 percent of respondents stated that they were coping fairly well, very well or extremely well, indicating a substantial level of resilience, despite the socio-economic adversity they face.

Racism is also an indicator social exclusion for urban Aboriginal and Torres Strait Islander families. The results from LSIC Wave 5 racism related question find over 60 percent of Parent 1s indicated that racism was never or hardly ever an experience for them. Nearly 40 percent, however, reported experiences of racism. Cultural experiences are also a common factor in the LSIC families. In Wave 1 the cultural activity questions were asked about the Study Child rather than Parent 1. Analysis of these data show that although few urban Study Children speak an Indigenous language (4%), two thirds were regularly taken to cultural events.

8. How Social Exclusion Dimensions are Spread between Households

The results in the previous sections show the incidence of different social exclusion measures in Parent 1 households. The next question is whether experience of different types of social exclusion are also clustered. Table 6 displays the results of inter-dimension correlations which show significant correlations. As can be seen, with the exception of 'P1 feels their life is difficult at present' and 'community safety' there is a statistically significant correlation of varying strengths between each dimension of social exclusion and all other dimensions. These results indicate that there is a relationship between the level of social exclusion on one measure and the level reported on others. Those with higher levels of exclusion on the individual measures are also more likely to have higher measures on other dimensions. Similarly, those with lower levels on exclusion on one measure are also more likely to record lower levels of exclusion on others.

Table 4. Parent 1 community safety ratings (wave 6, n= 973).

Variable	Parent 1 Rating %				
	Very good %	Good %	Okay %	Not so good %	Really bad %
Good community for little kids	38.5	31.7	19.8	7.6	2.4
	Very Safe %	Quite safe %	Okay %	Not very Safe %	Dangerous %
Overall Safety of Community	22.3	40.2	26.7	9.4	1.3

Table 5. Parent 1 social and emotional well-being measures.

Variable	Parent 1 Rating			
	Excellent %	Very Good %	Good %	Fair/Poor %
Parent 1 Global Health Measure (Wave 6: n= 973)	41.0	39.2	17.3	3.1
	No problems %	Few problems %	Some problems %	Many/Very many problems
Feels their life is difficult at present (Wave 6: n=970)	27.3	38.1	26.7	8.0
	Not at all %	A little %	Fairly Well %	Very/Extremely well %
Thinks they are coping (Wave 6: n=970)	0.9	6.8	42.4	40.8
	Every day %	Every week/ Sometimes %	Occasionally %	Never or hardly ever %
Family experiences racism, discrimination or prejudice (Wave 5: n=970)	3.1	19.3	15.4	61.3
	Very often %	Often %	Occasionally %	Never %
How often Study Child goes to Indigenous cultural event (Wave 1: n=1252)	7.6	14.8	41.8	36.2

Table 6. Correlations between social exclusion measures.

		P1 global health measure	Major repairs needed to house summary number	Safe community	Family money situation	P1 feels their life is difficult at present
P1 global health measure	Pearson Correlation	1	.107**	.069*	-.155**	.232**
	Sig. (2-tailed)		.001	.032	.000	.000
	N	973	972	963	969	969
Major repairs needed to house summary number	Pearson Correlation	.107**	1	.073*	-.127**	.118**
	Sig. (2-tailed)	.001		.023	.000	.000
	N	972	972	963	969	968
Safe community	Pearson Correlation	.069*	.073*	1	-.124**	.009
	Sig. (2-tailed)	.032	.023		.000	.781
	N	963	963	963	960	959
Family money situation	Pearson Correlation	-.155**	-.127**	-.124**	1	-.194**
	Sig. (2-tailed)	.000	.000	.000		.000
	N	969	969	960	969	965
P1 feels their life is difficult at present	Pearson Correlation	.232**	.118**	.009	-.194**	1
	Sig. (2-tailed)	.000	.000	.781	.000	
	N	969	968	959	965	969

Notes: ** Correlation is significant at the 0.01 level (2-tailed); * Correlation is significant at the 0.05 level (2-tailed).

9. Discussion and Conclusion

The first task of this paper was to explore patterns of social exclusion across social, economic, neighbourhood and well-being dimensions for urban and regional Aboriginal and Torres Strait families. The socio-economic data point to high rates of socio-economic exclusion. Low rates labour market activity, high rates of sole parenthood; high rates of rental housing and a substantial minority with inadequate housing due to disrepair. These measures all support the conclusion that LSIC households are likely to be among the poorest of households within their neighbourhoods. This finding aligns with Biddle's (2013) finding that, Australia wide, there was not a single Census area where the Indigenous populations has better or even relatively equal outcomes compared to the non-Indigenous population.

On the social participatory aspects the results are not as clear cut. The LSIC households are likely to be multiple person households with a majority rating their community as safe. A majority of Parent 1s are also physically and socio-emotionally able. Also, a substantial minority of Parent 1's report the experience of racism and two thirds of Study Children regularly attend Indigenous cultural events, signifying cultural and racial elements remain strongly evident in household's lived experience. The correlation results indicate there is a significant overlap in those experiencing poorer outcomes across measures social exclusions. The central finding of these results, therefore, is that, in line with Saunders et al. (2007) that evidence of 'deep' social exclusion across dimensions is present, but for an, albeit substantial, minority of LSIC households. What nearly all LSIC households share, however, is significant levels of socio-economic exclusion.

The next task of this paper is to explore the processes that create and sustain this social exclusion. That Aboriginal and Torres Strait families are socio-economically excluded is central to these processes, not because of its own inherent dimensions but as a stark reflector of social inequality. The first process, therefore, is the continued widespread exclusion of the LSIC families from mainstream economic, social, cultural and human capital resources of Australian society. This socio-economic exclusion is also socio-economic exclusion experienced within mainstream Australian urban and regional social settings. Identifying the economic correlates therefore does not do justice to the complexity this social exclusion. Social exclusion, as a concept, is culturally, socially and economically not the same for Aboriginal and Torres Strait Islander people as it is for non-Indigenous populations, in Australia or elsewhere.

The patterns shown in this research are, as argued by Lister (2004) and Sen (2000) are social structural; the results of social processes. Moreover, this inequality is racialised and directly related to the history and contemporary realities of black–white relations in Australia. The substantial proportion of urban/regional households who reported the experience of racial discrimination underscores the racialised nature of Indigenous inequality. Indigeneity is the central core, with other aspects intimately interwoven and interpreted through that Indigeneity (Walter, 2009). For example, as argued by Hunter (2000) and Walter (2015), the link between Indigenous unemployment and social exclusion is not clear in its causal direction. Are Indigenous people socio-economically excluded because they are unemployed or are Indigenous unemployment rates a consequence of broader social exclusion? The patterns of Indigenous/non-Indigenous unemployment from across Australia, where Indigenous rates are always multiples those of the non-Indigenous population suggest the second explanation (Walter, 2008). For example, 2011 Census data show Aboriginal unemployment rates as 18 per cent in the regional town of Dubbo and 17 per cent in the city of Perth compared to less than five percent for the non-Indigenous population both sites.

The second related process is that Indigenous socio-economic exclusion, as a lived reality, is also different. As Hunter (1999) established, material deprivation and living in overcrowded conditions are found even among relatively high income Indigenous households. Aboriginal material well-being is also different. Even for households with higher incomes these data are not necessarily an indicator of life-course advantage (Walter & Saggers, 2007). Such higher income is more likely to be a temporary phenomenon for Indigenous families. An analysis of the job descriptions of LSIC Parent 1s (Walter, 2015), finds at least one quarter are in Indigenous specific roles, such as community worker. Loss of that employment will likely lead directly back to low income, rather than another job at similar or higher wages. It is these two processes that determine the opportunities and the challenges of moving to greater social inclusion for urban/regional Aboriginal and Torres Strait Islander families. The deeply embedded, well-documented, long term nature of Indigenous socio-economic social exclusion suggest there is, first, no easy answer and second, that what policies have been implemented to date have been unsuccessful.

The work of Sen (2000) offers a way forward. Critical words in Sen's prescription for a minimally decent life are 'freedom to achieve' or opportunity freedom. These words denote both agency and the notion that freedom of choice is of, in itself a central aspect of capability and functioning. Without the ability to participate, in a way that is valued, in social, economic and political actions an individual or group does not have agency. Also critical is Sen's focus on the definition of a 'good life' not being determined by others but rather is about achieving the functionings to live a life that is valued by the person. As Hunter (2009) notes, social inclusion in whatever form it takes needs to include Indigenous perspectives in policies and programs as well as the promotion of full and effective participation in decisions that affect Indigenous people.

How then do current social inclusion aligned policies promote Indigenous agency to participate, in a way that is valued by Aboriginal and Torres Strait Islander people? The answer is, predominantly, that they do not. For example in the 2015 Closing the Gap Report Prime Minister Abbott, while expressing disappointment that in this 7th annual report, little progress had been achieved, began his message by stating ' it is hard to be numerate without attending school, it's hard to find work without basic education, and hard to live well without a job'. The failure of the Government to achieve progress, therefore, is framed immediately, on the opening page, through a discourse of individual Aboriginal failure. The long-standing, overwhelming social and societal pattern of Indigenous disadvantage and social exclusion is elided. Rather, failure of policy is linked tightly to discourses individual inadequacy and agency is implied as being negatively used by Aboriginal and Torres Strait Islander people to *not* make the choices they 'should'. The values here are not reflective of, or seemingly interested in, the values of the peoples to which the Closing the gap policy is being applied. They are also seemingly developed through a worldview of Indigenous people in Australia as incapable of living a decent life.

How might Indigenous policy look if a capability approach was applied? If social inclusion is interpreted as supporting the freedom to achieve the capability to live a decent life? Two criteria need to be in place. First, capability needs to be defined as socially relational, not instrumental. As argued earlier, the concept of social relationality recognises that urban Indigenous people are more than a group of disadvantaged individuals with a shared racial heritage. Aboriginal and/or Torres Strait Islander identity and culture shapes worldviews, understanding of social place and space and relationships with others. The correlation of Indigeneity and a reduced capacity to access social, economic, cultural and political resources (Walter, 2008) is intertwined within social relationality. Setting goals for individuals is unlikely to lead to increased social inclusion.

Second, strategies to increase social inclusion need to be based on Indigenous interpretations of a decent life. Sen's (2000) core functionings of being healthy, having a good job, safety and self-respect still apply, but within an Indigenous socially relational framework. The functionings of safety and self-respect, for example, exist within a social environment in which exposure to racism is a common experience. Being healthy is inclusive of social and emotional well-being which in turn is intimately related to connected to community, culture and country. Maintaining and sustaining cultural connections, as shown in these data, remains a core functioning for urban Indigenous people. Functionings around raising happy healthy children are, as shown by the data presented here, are shaped by values around mothering that differ from the dominant norms of an early maternal return to the labour market.

Would an Indigenous policy environment based on an Indigenous socially relational understanding of Sen's Capability Approach deliver better social inclusion outcomes for Aboriginal and Torres Strait Islander people? It has not been tried so no claims on its efficacy can be made. However, the current policy directions have been demonstrated, again and again, to be ineffective in social inclusion terms and probably doing more harm than good. Adopting an Indigenized Capability Approach requires a radical change of mindset from non-Indigenous politicians and policy makers.

Conflict of Interests

The author declares no conflict of interests.

References

Australian Bureau of Statistics. (2011). *Position paper: ABS review of counting the homeless methodology* (Aug 2011 Cat No. 2050.0.55.002). Canberra: Australian Bureau of Statistics.

Azpitarte, F., & Bowman, D. (2015). *Social exclusion monitor bulletin*. Melbourne: Brotherhood of St Laurence and Melbourne Institute of Applied Economic and Social Research, University of Melbourne.

Baxter, B. (2009). 'Mothers' timing of return to work by leave use and pre-birth job characteristics. *Journal of Family Studies, 15*(2), 153-166.

Biddle, N. (2013). *CAEPR indigenous population project: 2011 census papers, No 13/2013*. Canberra: Centre for Aboriginal Economic Policy Research, Australian National University.

Bradshaw, J. (2003). *How has the notion of social exclusion developed in the European discourse?* Plenary address to the 2003 Australian Social Policy conference, Social Policy Research Centre, University of New South Wales, Sydney.

Brotherhood of St Laurence. (2015). Social exclusion monitor. Retrieved from https://www.bsl.org.au/knowledge/social-exclusion-monitor

Burchardt, T., Le Grand, J., & Piachaud, D. (2002). Introduction. In T. Burchardt, J. Le Grand, & D. Piachaud (Eds.), *Social exclusion*. Oxford: Oxford University Press.

Department of Families, Housing, Community Services and Indigenous Affairs. (2011). *Footprints in time: The longitudinal study of indigenous children. Key summary report from wave 2*. Canberra: Department of Families, Housing, Community Services and Indigenous Affairs.

Department of Social Services. (2015). *Footprints in time: The longitudinal study of indigenous children wave 5*. Canberra: Department of Social Services.

Fincher, R., & Saunders, P. (2001). *Creating unequal futures? Rethinking inequality, poverty and disadvantage*. Sydney: Allen & Unwin.

Gordon, D., Adelman, L., Ashworth, K., Bradshaw, J., Levitas, R., Middleton, S., . . . Williams, J. (2000). *Poverty and social exclusion in Britain*. York: Joseph Rowntree Foundation.

Hunter, B. (1999). *Three nations not one: Indigenous and other Australian poverty* (CAEPR, working paper no. 1). Canberra: Australian National University.

Hunter, B. (2000). *Social exclusion, social capital and Indigenous Australians: Measuring the social costs of unemployment* (Discussion Paper No. 204). Canberra: Centre for Aboriginal Economic Policy Research, The Australian National University.

Hunter, B. (2009). Indigenous social exclusion: Insights and chgallenges for the concept of social inclusion. *Family Matters, 82*, 52-61.

Lister, R. (2004). *Poverty*. Cambridge: Polity Press.

Saunders, P. (2003). *Can social exclusion provide a new framework for measuring poverty?* (SPRC discussion paper no. 127). Sydney: Social Policy Research Centre, University of New South Wales.

Saunders, P., Naidoo, Y., & Griffiths, M. (2007). *Towards new indicators of disadvantage: Deprivation and social exclusion in Australia*. Sydney: Social Policy Research Centre, University of New South Wales.

Sen, A. (2000). *Social exclusion: Concept, application and scrutiny* (Social Development Papers No. 1). Manila: Asian Development Bank.

Steering Committee for the Review of Government Service Provision. (2014). *Overcoming Indigenous disadvantage: Key indicators*. Canberra: Steering Committee for the Review of Government Services Provision, Productivity Commission.

Walter, M. (2008). *Lives of diversity: Indigenous Australians* (Occasional paper 4/2008, Census Series#2). Canberra: Australian Academy of the Social Sciences.

Walter, M. (2009). An economy of poverty: Power and the domain of aboriginality. *International Journal of Critical Indigenous Studies, 2*(1), 2-14.

Walter, M. (2015). The vexed relationship between social mobility and social capital for aboriginal and Torres Strait Islander People. *Australian Journal of Social Issues, 50*, 69-88.

Walter, M., & Hewitt, B. (2012). Post separation parenting and indigenous families. *Family Matters, 91*, 83-91.

Walter, M., & Saggers, S. (2007). Poverty and social class. In B. Carson, T. Dunbar, R. Chenhall & R. Bailie (Eds.), *Social determinants of indigenous health* (pp. 87-104). Crows Nest: Allen and Unwin.

About the Author

Dr. Maggie Walter

Maggie Walter (PhD) descends from the parerebeenne people of tebrekunna country in North Eastern Tasmania. She is Professor of Sociology and the inaugural Pro Vice-Chancellor of Aboriginal Research and Leadership at the University of Tasmania. She is a long term member of the steering committee of the Longitudinal Study of Indigenous Children and has published extensively in the field of race relations, inequality and research methods and methodologies.

7

Social Stratification of Education by Ethnic Minority Groups over Generations in the UK

Laurence Lessard-Phillips [1,*] and Yaojun Li [2,3]

[1] Institute for Research into Superdiversity, School of Social Policy, University of Birmingham, Birmingham, B15 2TT, UK; E-Mail: l.lessard-phillips@bham.ac.uk
[2] Department of Sociology, University of Manchester, Manchester, M13 9PL, UK; E-Mail: yaojun.li@manchester.ac.uk
[3] Cathie Marsh Institute for Social Research, University of Manchester, Manchester, M13 9PL, UK

* Corresponding author

Abstract

A large body of research has been conducted both on the social stratification of education at the general level and on the educational attainments of ethnic minority groups in the UK. The former has established the increasing fluidity in the class–education association, without paying much attention to ethnicity, whilst the latter has shown reinvigorated aspirations by the second generation without fine-grained analyses. This paper adds to this literature by examining the relationship between family class, ethno-generational status and educational attainment for various 1st, 1.5, 2nd, 2.5, 3rd and 4th generations in contemporary UK society. Using data from Understanding Society, we study the educational attainment of different ethno-generational groups. Our analysis shows high educational selectivity among the earlier generations, a disruptive process for the 1.5 generation, high second-generation achievement, and a 'convergence toward the mean' for later generations. Parental class generally operates in a similar way for the ethno-generational groups and for the majority population, yet some minority ethnic groups of salariat origins do not benefit from parental advantages as easily. An 'elite, middle and lower' structure manifests itself in the intergenerational transmission of advantage in educational attainment. This paper thus reveals new features of class-ethno relations hitherto unavailable in UK research.

Keywords

class; educational attainment; ethnicity; minorities; multiple-generation groups; social stratification; UK

Issue

This article is part of the issue "International Migration and Ethnic Integration", edited by Yaojun Li (University of Manchester, UK) and Anthony Heath (University of Oxford, UK).

---

1. Introduction

The national origins of ethnic minority groups to Britain have changed in recent decades. While Britain has had a very long history of immigration, most of the main visible ethnic minority groups came after the end of the Second World War via post-colonial, economic, asylum, or family reunification routes. For instance, members of the black Caribbean group mostly came from Jamaican islands in the 1950s and 1960s, Indians from India and Africa in the 1960s and 1970s, Pakistanis and Bangladeshis in the 1970s and 1980s, and black Africans in the 1980s and 1990s. Of course, many members of visible and non-visible ethnic minority origins such as Chinese and Eastern and Western Europeans did not come in groups in the same manner as the (mostly) post-colonial groups above, but individually, later joined by families. Some of these groups have been in the country for a very long time (Castles & Miller, 2009; Cheng, 1994; Cheung & Heath, 2007; Lessard-Phillips, Fleischmann, & van Elsas, 2014; Li & Heath, 2016). A considerable proportion of the visible minorities came at a quite young age, and a significant and a growing portion were born in the country, being second or even third generation at the current time (see Lessard-Phillips, Galandini, de Valk, & Fibbi, 2015, for details on the terminology). The share of ethnic minority groups in Britain has thus increased from 2.9% in 1951 (Cheung & Heath, 2007, p. 512) to 14% in 2011 (Office for National Statistics, 2012) and has been predicted to grow to approximately 20–30% over the next few decades (Lievesley, 2010; Rees, Wohland, Norman, & Boden, 2012). Those born in Britain or those who arrived at a young age will have received their schooling in Britain and have entered the labour market with British qualifications. The extent to which they fare well in the educational and occupational structures, as an integral part of socio-economic integration, has been a major concern of academic and policy research.

The inclusion of ethnic minority groups in British society, including both the migrant generation and their descendants who grew up in the country is, as Li and Heath (2016) commented, at the forefront of current policy debates, despite the lack of clear policies attempting to tackle the issue. Recent British governments have placed an emphasis on integration as an important societal goal (e.g. Department for Communities and Local Government, 2012; Casey, 2016), and the current government has set up a 'Race Disparity Unit' under the Cabinet Office to try to gauge ethnic disadvantages in education and in the labour market. However, such programmes tend to focus on piece-meal responses to local issues rather than implementing relevant policies (Hepburn, 2015). For instance, the centralist New Labour government put much emphasis on 'Education, Education and Education' but failed to tackle the underlying class difference in educational stratification (Goldthorpe, 2010). It is also apt to point out that race and ethnic issues remained largely out of the 'Middle England' political orientation. The coalition and Conservative governments claimed to place their priorities on the promotion of social mobility (Cabinet Office, 2011; Civil Service, 2016) and social justice (Department for Work and Pensions, 2012), but the strategies largely failed to engage with the particular challenges faced by marginalised groups, especially those from ethnic minority backgrounds. Without effective evidence-based policy interventions, the potential for marginalised groups to improve their mobility and integration chances is likely to be limited.

In this paper, we aim to provide evidence on the educational attainment of ethno-generational groups in Britain. In order to do this, we followed and developed the novel approach by Li and Heath (2016) in combining the stratification and ethnic studies traditions and, furthermore, making a more refined differentiation of ethno-generation groupings than found in any existing studies in the UK. In so doing, we seek to determine the socio-ethno-generational factors underlying educational attainment. Our results suggest a complicated story of immigrant advantage and a 'regression to the mean' for later generations. Our approach brings greater complexity to analysis on education and highlights the need to consider the diversity of origin and the multiplicity of generation along with family class in investigating educational stratification as a means of promoting social inclusion.

2. Educational Attainment: Bridging Stratification and Assimilation

Education is one of the most important components of human and cultural capital (Becker, 1962; Bourdieu, 1986) and its importance for the labour market position just as for other domains of people's socio-economic life is undisputed. Social scientists, sociologists in particular, have long been concerned with the unequal opportunities in educational attainment. Yet, there has been a sort of 'division of labour' on educational analysis, with the mainstream sociologists focusing on family class differences and ethnic studies scholars on ethnic differences in educational attainment (Li & Heath, 2016). Part of this divide is due to disciplinary traditions and part due to data limitations. Prominent mobility scholars have conducted studies on the class-educational association (Bukodi, Erikson, & Goldthorpe, 2014; Devine & Li, 2013; Halsey, Heath, & Ridge, 1980; Paterson & Iannelli, 2007) but ethnicity rarely enters the picture. Attention is focused on class gradients or on the extent and direction of possible changes in social fluidity in education (Breen, Luijkx, Müller, & Pollak, 2009). Early students of migration and ethnicity, on the other hand, have been concerned with the ethnic disadvantages in education rather than with family class effects (Bhattacharyya, Ison, & Blair, 2003; Connor, Tyers, Modood, & Hillage, 2004; Dale, Shaheen, Kalra, & Fieldhouse, 2002; Drew, Gray, & Sporton, 1997; Heath & McMahon, 1997), but this is changing (Jackson, 2012; Lenkeit, Caro, & Strand, 2015; Rothon, 2007).

From the point of view of mainstream stratification research, the primary concern is how origin class uses its superior socio-economic-cultural resources to help the educational attainment of their children, how social inequality is maintained over time and across countries, and whether or to what extent this rigidity is being loosened (Breen & Jonsson, 2005; Breen et al., 2009). If we think about the Origin-Education-Destination (OED) model of status attainment (Blau & Duncan, 1967; Sewell, Haller, & Portes, 1969), the focus is on the relationship between parental social origins and education, and the ways in which class-origin advantages are transmitted in the educational realm. Among the ways in which these advantages are transmitted, the focus is on social capital (Coleman, 1988), cultural capital (DiMaggio, 1982) and economic capital (Breen & Goldthorpe, 1999). Within this stream of research, there is no reason why origin class would function in different ways for different ethno-generational groups, and ethnicity is thus rarely acknowledged within social stratification research on education even though class may work differently for different ethnic groups (Platt, 2016). There have also been recent attempts to add migrant/ethnic status to the OED model (see, e.g., Heath et al., 2008; Li & Heath, 2016; Zuccotti, 2015), but research is still in its infancy.

From the ethnic studies perspectives, a long-held view foresees a gradual process of ethnic convergence across generations. The revised straight-line assimilation theory, as espoused by Alba and his colleagues (Alba, Lutz, & Vesselinov, 2001; Alba & Nee, 2003; Waters, Tran, Kasinitz, & Mollenkopf, 2010) and reformulated from the classical assimilation theory developed by the founders of the Chicago School of Sociology, predicts a 'process of interpenetration and fusion' of early 20th-century migrants with the host society (Park & Burgess, 1921, p. 735). The defining features of the process include the successive generational upward mobility, greater integration into the mainstream, and reduced ethnic distinctiveness in terms of language use, residential concentration and marriage patterns for most minority ethnic groups (Gordon, 1964). The most important implication of this revised theory for our present purposes is that, overall, the second and higher generations can be expected to make educational progress which will facilitate increasing integration into the host society's socioeconomic life. But origin class effects are overlooked in this account. In this latter regard, we need to note that the 'segmented assimilation theory' proposed by Portes and colleagues (Portes, Fernández-Kelly, & Haller, 2009) does acknowledge the role of parent class but only suggests a binary structure.

The foregoing discussion has suggested that as the proportion of ethnic minority groups in the UK has increased with many being second and higher generations, the educational disparities with the mainstream population may have reduced. Recent research shows that ethnic minority members tend to do well and some groups even outperform the majority group in education (Demack, Drew, & Grimsley, 2000; Dustmann & Theodoropoulos, 2010; Heath, Rothon, & Kilpi, 2008; Jackson, 2012; Rothon, Heath, & Lessard-Phillips, 2009; Strand, 2014). Yet there are various unsolved issues in existing research. Firstly, the distinction between ethnicity and generation is not explicitly made and research on third generation education has not been possible due to data limitations. Secondly, we do not know whether the possible increasing fluidity in the class-education association in Britain is due to narrowing class inequality as suggested by Breen et al. (2009) or to increasing ethnic outperformance over whites in spite of their lower parental class positions. By combining the stratification and the ethnic studies traditions could thus not only shed light on the apparent mystery in Breen et al.'s findings but also help us gain a deeper understanding of the class-education associations over different generations of ethnic groups in Britain. It could help test whether the revised assimilation theory could find its support in the British context.

With these considerations in mind, we aim to address the following questions:

- Do the minority ethnic groups over different generations in the UK have the same level of educational attainment as their White British peers without an immigration background?
- Are patterns of ethnic overperformance found in the existing literature supported when a more granular measure of ethno-generational status is used?
- Is social advantage and disadvantage (SAD) transmitted in the same way for minority ethnic groups as for the majority group?

Answering those questions will help further our understanding of the education of ethno-generational groups in Britain and provide a strong evidence base for studying the educational mobility of ethnic groups across generations.

3. Data and Methods

We use the first three waves of the United Kingdom Household Longitudinal Survey, also called Understanding Society (USoc; University of Essex, Institute for Social and Economic Research, & National Centre for Social Research, 2013) for this study. We pooled them together to maximise sample size. Our analytical sample size (N=37,846) includes individuals with valid values on all variables used in the analysis. The USoc has ethnic boost samples and contains information about grandparental, parental, and respondent's place of birth which, given its large sample size, allowing us to differentiate 48 ethno-generational groupings with sufficient sample sizes for analysis (see note 2 of Table 1). This is more refined than any existing research in the UK has attempted. We were able to differentiate, whenever possible, between individuals from the first generation (individuals born outside of the UK and who arrived to the UK after age 16); the 1.5 generation (individuals arriving to the UK during compulsory schooling—ages 6 to 16); the second generation (individuals born in the UK of non-UK born parents or who migrated before age 6); the 2.5 generation (individuals with one immigrant and one UK-born parent); the third generation (individuals born in the UK with at least one non-UK-born grandparent); and the fourth generation (individuals born in the UK with UK-born parents and UK-born grandparents). We were also able to differentiate between many of the ethnic groups usually found in British survey data. This allowed us to have fine-grained ethno-generational categories that also take into account immigrant parentage for the white groups, something not often found in research but nonetheless important given historical migratory flows to the UK from neighbouring or Old Commonwealth countries. Ethnicity is based on ethnic self-classification, a measure that is subjective and a changeable over one's life course (Simpson, Warren, & Jivraj, 2015) and may imply a mismatch between reported and externally perceived ethnicity. We focussed our analyses

Table 1. Ethnicity by generational status in Britain, respondents aged 25–64 (2009–2012).

	Generation (% of group)						
	1st	1.5	2nd	2.5	3rd	4th	N
White British	0.6%	0.5%	2.7%	5.4%	7.3%	83.4%	29,072
White Irish	24.6%	6.0%	21.0%	8.9%	3.8%	35.7%	793
White Other	82.9%	2.8%	5.5%	3.8%	*	5.0%	1,338
Mixed	35.6%	*	17.4%	40.0%	7.0%	*	511
Black Caribbean	21.1%	18.0%	55.4%	5.5%	*	*	738
Black African	79.8%	7.5%	12.7%	*	*	*	1,036
Indian	55.9%	12.3%	31.7%	*	*	*	1,405
Pakistani	54.8%	11.0%	34.2%	*	*	*	964
Bangladeshi	60.3%	17.7%	22.1%	*	*	*	563
Chinese	82.3%	*	17.7%	*	*	*	203
Other Asian	84.1%	6.0%	9.9%	*	*	*	489
Other	49.2%	12.5%	9.5%	8.1%	9.4%	11.4%	734
Total	10.5%	1.5%	5.3%	5.3%	6.3%	71.1%	37,846

Notes: 1. Weighted analysis and unweighted Ns (authors' analysis). Row totals may not add to 100% due to rounding errors;
2. Cell counts under 30 are considered too small for analysis and merged with the 'Other group'. Source: Understanding Society.

on respondents aged 25–64. As we can see from Table 1, there is quite a variation in the generational status distribution among the various ethnic groups, which tend to follow the migratory patterns of the different groups (Lessard-Phillips et al., 2014).

We investigated the patterns and trends of educational attainment in the UK by different ethno-generational groups in the following way. We constructed a measure of parental class by deriving the 3-class version of the National Statistics Socio-Economic Classification (NS-SEC) from the 2010 Standard Occupational Classification (SOC2010) of parental occupation when respondents were 14 years of age. Using the dominance approach, which will often use the occupation of the non-immigrant parent in the 2.5 generation, the three-fold parental class schema covers (1) professional/managerial salariat (I-II), (2) intermediate class (III-IV), and (3) manual working class (semi-routine, routine, V-VII). With regard to education, and given the importance of university-level education for gaining high-level occupations and for fostering social mobility (Garratt & Li, 2005), we looked at the respondents' highest level of educational attainment and differentiate between those with degree-level or above qualifications and those without. We also used indicators of age and sex of the respondents (the descriptive statistics of age, sex and parental class are shown in Table 2). In the analyses, we first look at descriptive statistics to examine gross differentials. We then use a logit model of degree-level attainment for the full sample, comparing each of the ethno-generational status groups with the 4th generation white British (our reference category), to investigate ethnic differentials in educational attainment. Our models include parental class as the main explanatory variable and controls for age and sex. As the logits (log odds ratios) from the models are less intuitive to understand, we present average marginal effects (Mood, 2010).

Table 2. Main control variables and their distribution in the data.

Age	
Mean	44.4
SE	0.09
Range	25–64
Sex (%)	
Men	49.1
Women	50.1
Highest parental class (%)	
Professional/managerial: salariat	33.3
Intermediate class	27.7
Manual working class (semi-routine, routine)	39.0
N	37,846

Source: Understanding Society.

4. Results

Figure 1 portrays the percentage of university degree holders among the various ethnic groups by generational status.

Before we enter detailed discussion, we alert readers that unlike bar charts we usually see in academic papers, the bars in Figure 1 do not add to one hundred percent. Rather, for each of twelve ethnic minority groups, we have 'stacked' the percentages of respondents in each generational status who have degree-level education or above. For large ethnic groups such as white British, we could differentiate six generational statuses (1st, 1.5, 2nd, 2.5, 3rd and 4th generations) whereas for small ethnic groups such as Chinese, we could only differentiate two generational statuses (1st and 2nd). The 4th generation white British comprise the largest majority of all groups

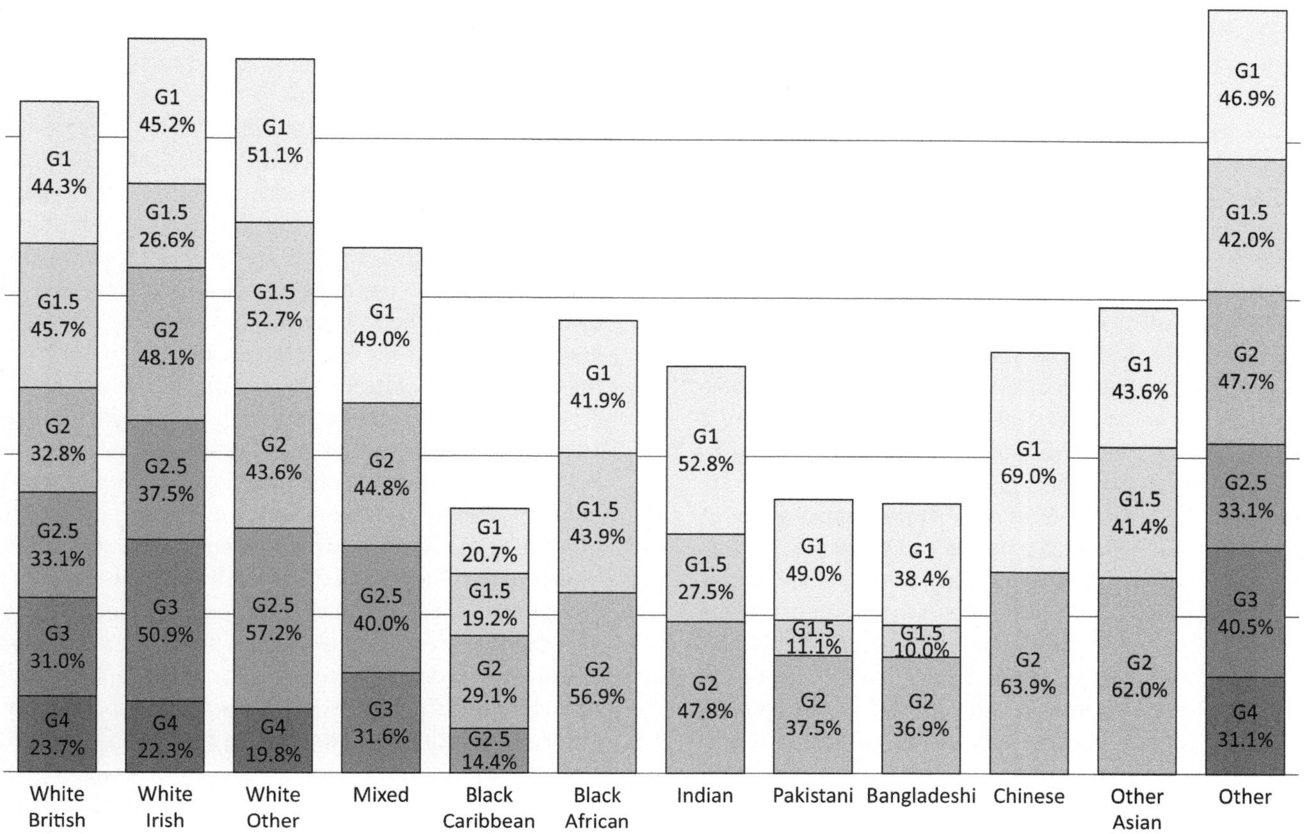

Figure 1. Degree-level attainment by ethno-generational status. Source: Understanding Society.

in our data. As such, they constitute the 'core' of the population and serve as the meaningful reference group for all other groupings.

Looking in closer detail at the patterns in Figure 1, we find features which tend to go unnoticeable in standard ethnic studies due to the crude measures of ethno-generational groups but which are brought into great relief thanks to our refined measurement. Firstly, we find clear evidence of first-generation positive selection for white groupings and for most of the visible ethnic minority groups alike, rendering support to claims by Borjas (1987) in the American context and to Li and Heath (2016) on the selection effects on ethnic social mobility. Thus, white British, white Irish (those from the Republic of Ireland), white Other (from North America, Western Europe, Australia and New Zealand, and Central and Eastern Europe), mixed (namely, white and black, white and Asian), Black African, Indian, Pakistani, Bangladeshi, Chinese, Other Asian, and 'Other' respondents of the migration generation are all highly educated, with two thirds of Chinese and over half of Indian first-generation respondents having degree level education or above. This forms a very sharp contrast to the 23.7% for the white British mainstream (fourth generation) with university education.

The first generation ethnic minority groups, in spite of their high level of education, tend to face great difficulties in the British labour market as their qualifications were obtained overseas and are not usually seen as having the same 'values' by employers. Thus, they tend to face higher levels of unemployment or find themselves in menial jobs (Heath & Li, 2008; Li, 2010). One of the possible implications is that those arriving in the young ages may, given the precarious employment position of their parents and financial difficulties in their families, opt for the labour market rather than continuing education at the end of compulsory schooling. Thus, we find that the 1.5 generation respondents of black Caribbean, Pakistani, and Bangladeshi heritages are all less likely to have degree level education than either their 1st or 2nd generation peers. This notwithstanding, it is also the case that other 1.5 generation respondents are not less likely to have degree levels than their 4th generation white British peers and this may indicate a pattern of additional investment to avoid hardship or discrimination on the labour market (Heath et al., 2008).

Thirdly, we find a quite consistent pattern of second-generation advantage among most groups (as compared to the 4th generation white British) that also applies to members of the 2.5 and 3rd generations, with very few exceptions. There also seems to be a clear case of 'regression to the mean' with regard to more established generations in the white groups. For these groups, the percentages with degree level qualifications decline over generations towards that of 4th generation white British, our core group (although some may be due to the younger age profile of some of these groups). This is a sign of 'integration' although it speaks of ethno-generational groups losing the competitive edge in education. We are unable to look into this issue further for ethnic minority groups because of sample size issues, but if their skin colour remains an inhibiting factor in employment and career advancement, this kind of integration could work to the disadvantage of visible ethnic minority groups.

The patterns highlighted above could be due to many factors, including selectivity and generational change in overall levels of education or different ages or historical times of arrival with different educational opportunities open to them, resulting in group-specific attainment profiles. But we also need to look at the profile from a class perspective. The data are shown in Figure 2, which depicts the distribution of degree qualifications by parental class and ethnic group. The patterns here are more in line with a narrative of higher educational attainment among higher parental social classes. This appears to hold for all ethnic groups, with the sole exception of black Caribbean respondents in the salariat. There are, however, some groups where the percentage of degree holders is much higher than for the White British across all socio-economic categories. This is especially the case for the Chinese and Indian groups. It is also worth noting that among those from working-class families, all other ethnic groups are more likely than the white British to have degrees, with the Chinese four times as likely (46.0% and 12.1% respectively). Thus, at least at prima facie level, class does not work in the same way for the majority as for the minority groups. The way in which class and ethno-generational status interact will be further investigated below.

To further explore the interrelations between class, ethnicity and generational status on educational attainment, we turn to the regression results. With regard to ethnic effects, as shown in Figure 3, the data points for most ethno-generational groups are clearly above the horizontal line denoting distance in degree-level attainment compared to the core white British, and there are no groups having lower levels of attainment than the mainstream white British. For most ethnic minority groups, we see a clear net effect of 'second generation advantage' that outweighs the 'first generation selectivity' once controls are added. Moreover, there is a trend of 'regression to the mean' among different generations of white British and mixed respondents, and a somewhat similar patterning among the white Irish and white Other groups. The black Caribbean respondents, for all their generational groupings, exhibit no signs of educational advantages as do most other groups who outperformed the white British. Class is, of course, very important for children's educational attainment, but to an expected and mostly similar extent across ethno-generational groups; there were very few significant interaction effects between ethnicity and class. An examination of the AMEs for ethnicity at each level of parental class show a

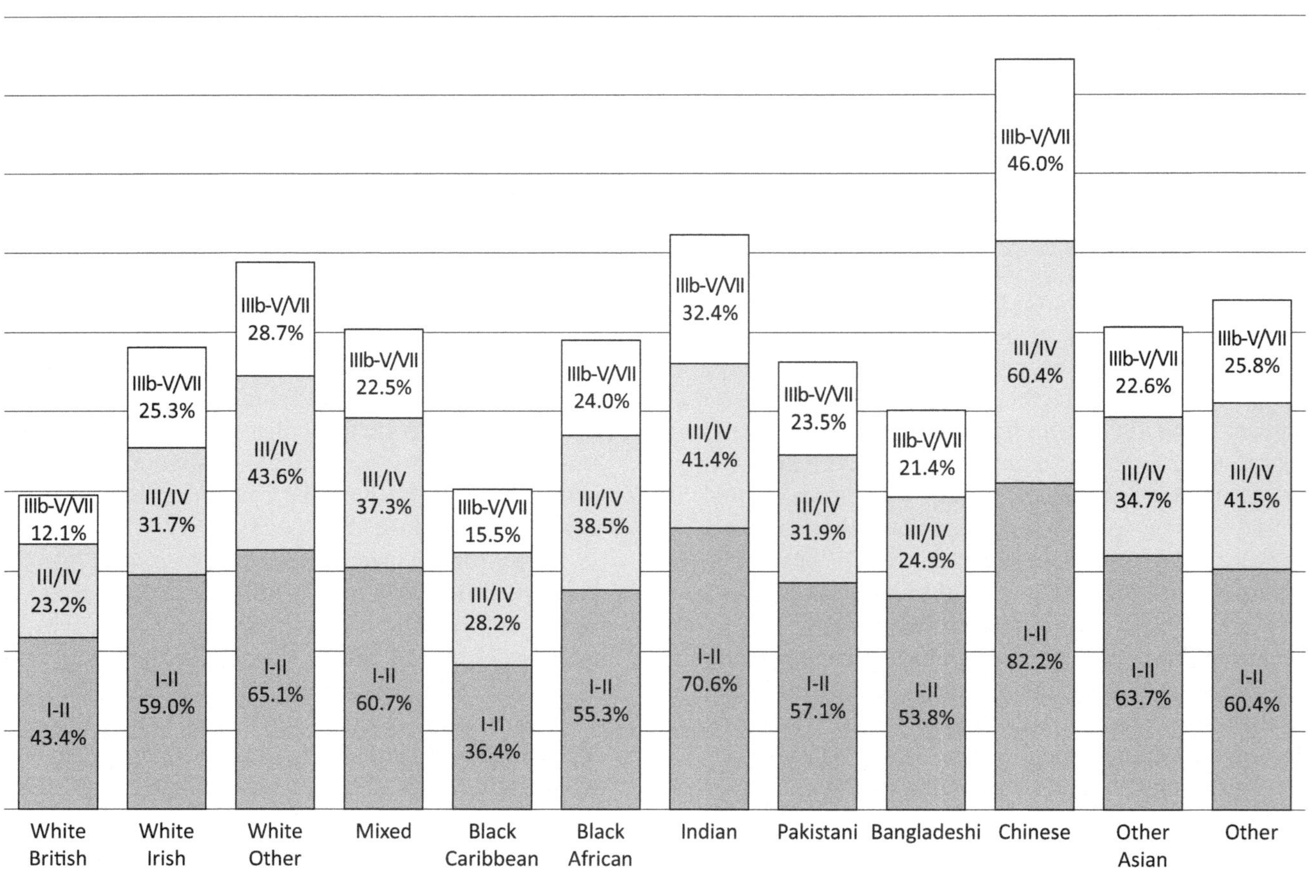

Figure 2. Degree-level attainment by ethnicity and parental social class. Source: Understanding Society.

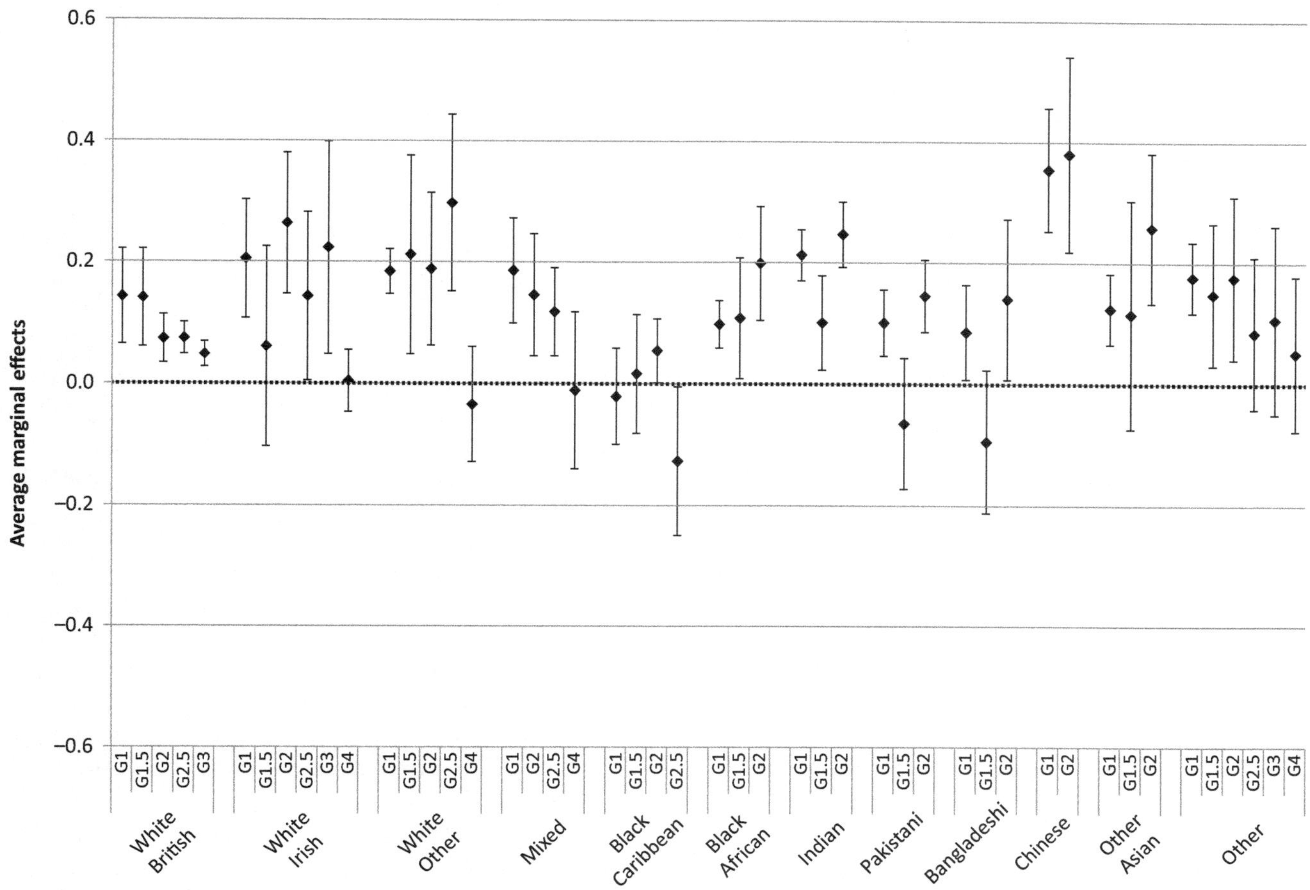

Figure 3. Average marginal effects of ethnicity on degree attainment, model controlling for class, age, and sex. Source: Understanding Society.

complex pattern of variation that generally reproduces the pattern shown above. Moreover, these results also show that the negative effects for the 2.5 generation black Caribbean respondents tend to be concentrated among the highest parental class and that 1.5 generation respondents of Pakistani (salariat) and Bangladeshi (intermediate) origins fail to achieve degree-level attainment. We have also conducted loglinear and unidiff analyses to look at the relationship between education and class for the different ethno-generational groups. The results (available on request) are largely in support of our discussion. For space reasons, we do not present the detailed modelling results here. Taken altogether, these results suggest that most ethno-generational groups seem to exhibit a greater defiance of origin effects, especially for more recent generations.

5. Discussion and Conclusions

With this paper, our aim was to further our understanding of the inclusion of ethno-generational groups within the UK educational structure by examining the educational attainment of ethnic groups across detailed immigrant generations. We did this by using insights from the social stratification literature and from scholarship on ethnic minorities. This was done to investigate whether the trends in the ethnic literature were supported by using more diverse measures of origin using the interaction of ethnicity and generation as a starting point for analyses. We also wanted to investigate whether the transmission of social advantage and disadvantage operates in a similar fashion for individuals with and without an immigration background. Using Understanding Society to investigate this, we were able to look at the educational attainments of 48 different ethno-generational groups.

Our results suggest four main features of interest regarding to the attainments of ethno-generational groups in the UK. In the first instance, we see a clear story of high educational selectivity among the first generation for most of the groups under study, which fits established literature about the positive selection of migrants. Even for the Black Caribbean group, which exhibits levels of attainment similar to that of the 4th generation white British, the story is still a positive one. In the second instance, and in line with established research, UK-born individuals with immigrant parentage fit overall narratives of 'immigrant advantage' present in the literature (Kao & Tienda, 1995).

Aside from these 'success' stories in securing a place at the top of the educational structure, we also found two other important features. Firstly, we see that the 1.5 generation does not seem to build on the skills selectivity advantage of the first generation or the 'immigrant advantage' of the second generation to the same extent. When it is possible to differentiate them from the 1st generation, we see that members of the 1.5 generation seem to experience some type of disruptive process of migration during the school-age years for their overall educational attainment. We suggested family financial disadvantage as a reason for their decision to enter the labour market rather than stay on in education, which is plausible but needs further corroboration. This is beyond the scope of this paper, requiring detailed data on both parents' and respondents' work-life histories and family financial conditions. Finally, for the more 'established' generations, we notice an overall convergence toward the level of attainment of the more established group, the 4th generation white British (or, in certain instances, lower levels of attainments relative to the comparison group). This also appears to be the case for individuals with some immigrant parentage, suggesting that having a non-immigrant parent may lead to convergence toward the mean rather than greater advantage. This supports the argument that, whenever possible, the 2.5 generation should be analysed separately, although for different reasons than those argued by Ramakrishnan (2004). Given that these groups tend to be relatively young, we will need to wait more time before we can say for certain whether this convergence is a trend or a demographic artefact. Moreover, more detailed analyses are needed to really disentangle the extent to which these ethno-generational effects add to the existing, separate, advantages and disadvantages of ethnicity and generation.

Overall, we see a complicated story of social advantage and disadvantage that highlights the need to take the diversity of ethnic, immigrant, and social background into account when looking into issues of educational attainments. This has mostly been ignored but tells interesting stories with regard to the inclusion of ethno-generational groups in the UK. This suggests that parental social background may work in varying ways within groups, as recently argued by Lenkeit and colleagues (2015) and that other influences may be at play. This approach may, we believe, be useful to study inclusion into other spheres, such as the labour market where we know important disadvantages exist.

Acknowledgments

We thank the ESRC (RES-163-25-0003; ES/I035168/1; ES/J020036/1; ES/K009206/1-2) for funding this research. We also thank attendants at the various conferences (ECSR/EQUALSOC, Stockholm, 2012; RC28, Trento, 2013; LIVEDIFFERENCE, Sheffield 2014) and the anonymous reviewers for very helpful comments and suggestions. Data visualization was aided by Daniel's XL Toolbox addin for Excel, version 7.1.4, by Daniel Kraus, Würzburg, Germany (www.xltoolbox.net). Both authors contributed equally to the paper. We are alone responsible for any errors in this paper.

Conflict of Interests

The authors declare no conflict of interests.

References

Alba, R., Lutz, A., & Vesselinov, E. (2001). How enduring were the inequalities among European immigrant groups in the United States? *Demography, 38*(3), 349–356.

Alba, R., & Nee, V. (2003). *Remaking the American mainstream: Assimilation and contemporary immigration*. Harvard University Press.

Becker, G. S. (1962). Investment in human capital: A theoretical analysis. *The Journal of Political Economy*, 9–49.

Bhattacharyya, G., Ison, L., & Blair, M. (2003). *Minority ethnic attainment and participation in education and training: The evidence*. Nottingham: DfES Publications.

Blau, P. M., & Duncan, O. D. (1967). *The American occupational structure*. New York: Wiley.

Borjas, G. J. (1987). Self-selection and the earnings of immigrants. *The American Economic Review, 77*(4), 531–553.

Bourdieu, P. (1986). The forms of capital. In J. G. Richardson (Ed.), *Handbook of theory and research for the sociology of education* (pp. 241–258). New York: Greenwood Publishing Group.

Breen, R., & Goldthorpe, J. H. (1999). Class inequality and meritocracy: A critique of Saunders and an alternative analysis. *The British Journal of Sociology, 50*(1), 1–27.

Breen, R., & Jonsson, J. O. (2005). Inequality of opportunity in comparative perspective: Recent research on educational attainment and social mobility. *Annual Review of Sociology, 31*, 223–243.

Breen, R., Luijkx, R., Müller, W., & Pollak, R. (2009). Nonpersistent inequality in educational attainment: Evidence from eight European countries. *American Journal of Sociology, 114*(5), 1475–1521.

Bukodi, E., Erikson, R., & Goldthorpe, J. H. (2014). The effects of social origins and cognitive ability on educational attainment Evidence from Britain and Sweden. *Acta Sociologica*. doi:10.1177/0001699314543803

Cabinet Office. (2011). *Opening doors, breaking barriers: A strategy for social mobility*. London: HMSO.

Casey, L. (2016). *The Casey Review: A review into opportunity and integration*. London: Department for Communities and Local Government.

Castles, S., & Miller, P. M. J. (2009). *The age of migration: International population movements in the modern world* (4th ed.). Cambridge: Palgrave Macmillan.

Cheng, Y. (1994). *Education and class: Chinese in Britain and the United States*. Aldershot: Avebury.

Cheung, S. Y., & Heath, A. F. (2007). Nice work if you can get it: Ethnic penalties in Great Britain. In A. F. Heath & S. Y. Cheung (Eds.), *Unequal chances: Ethnic minori-*

ties in Western labour markets (pp. 507–550). Oxford: Oxford University Press.

Civil Service. (2016). *Talent Action Plan 2016: Removing the barriers to success*. London: HMSO.

Coleman, J. S. (1988). Social capital in the creation of human capital. *American Journal of Sociology, 94*, S95–S120.

Connor, H., Tyers, C., Modood, T., & Hillage, J. (2004). *Why the difference? A closer look at higher education minority ethnic students and graduates*. Nottingham: DfES Publications. Retrieved from http://www.bristol.ac.uk/ethnicity/documents/educationreport.pdf

Dale, A., Shaheen, N., Kalra, V., & Fieldhouse, E. (2002). Routes into education and employment for young Pakistani and Bangladeshi women in the UK. *Ethnic and Racial Studies, 25*(6), 942–968.

Demack, S., Drew, D., & Grimsley, M. (2000). Minding the gap: Ethnic, gender and social class differences in attainment at 16, 1988–95. *Race Ethnicity and Education, 3*(2), 117–143.

Department for Communities and Local Government. (2012). *Creating the conditions for integration*. London: Department for Communities and Local Government.

Department for Work and Pensions. (2012). *Social justice: Transforming lives*. London: HMSO.

Devine, F., & Li, Y. (2013). The changing relationship between origins, education and destinations in the 1990s and 2000s. *British Journal of Sociology of Education, 34*(5–6), 766–791.

DiMaggio, P. (1982). Cultural capital and school success: The impact of status culture participation on the grades of US high school students. *American Sociological Review, 47*(2), 189–201.

Drew, D., Gray, J., & Sporton, D. (1997). Ethnic differences in the educational participation of 16–19 year-olds. In V. Kam (Ed.), *Ethnicity in the 1991 Census* (Vol. 4, pp. 17–28). London: The Stationary Office.

Dustmann, C., & Theodoropoulos, N. (2010). Ethnic minority immigrants and their children in Britain. *Oxford Economic Papers, 62*(2), 209–233.

Garratt, D., & Li, Y. (2005). The foundations of experimental/empirical research methods. In B. Somekh & C. Lewin (Eds), *Research methods in the social sciences* (pp. 198-206). London: Sage.

Goldthorpe, J. H. (2010). Analysing social inequality: A critique of two recent contributions from economics and epidemiology. *European Sociological Review, 26*(6), 731–744.

Gordon, M. M. (1964). *Assimilation in American life: The role of race, religion, and national origins*. New York: Oxford University Press.

Halsey, A. H., Heath, A. F., & Ridge, J. M. (1980). *Origins and destinations*. Oxford: Clarendon Press.

Heath, A. F., & Li, Y. (2008). Period, life-cycle and generational effects on ethnic minority success in the British labour market. *Kölner Zeitschrift fur Soziologie und Sozialpsychologie, 48*, 277–306.

Heath, A. F., & McMahon, D. (1997). Education and occupational attainments: The impact of ethnic origins. In V. Kam (Ed.), *Ethnicity in the 1991 Census* (Vol. 4, pp. 97–113). London: The Stationary Office.

Heath, A. F., Rothon, C., & Kilpi, E. (2008). The second generation in Western Europe: Education, unemployment, and occupational attainment. *Annual Review of Sociology, 34*(1), 211–235.

Hepburn, E. (2015). *Immigrant integration and policy divergence in Scotland since devolution*. Presented at the Political Studies Association, Sheffield.

Jackson, M. (2012). Bold choices: How ethnic inequalities in educational attainment are suppressed. *Oxford Review of Education, 38*(2), 189–208.

Kao, G., & Tienda, M. (1995). Optimism and achievement: The educational performance of immigrant youth. *Social Science Quarterly, 76*, 1–19.

Lenkeit, J., Caro, D. H., & Strand, S. (2015). Tackling the remaining attainment gap between students with and without immigrant background: An investigation into the equivalence of SES constructs. *Educational Research and Evaluation, 21*(1), 60–83.

Lessard-Phillips, L., Fleischmann, F., & van Elsas, E. (2014). Ethnic minorities in ten Western countries: Migration flows, policies and institutional differences. In *Unequal Attainments: Ethnic Educational Inequalities in Ten Western Countries* (pp. 25–61). Oxford: Oxford University Press.

Lessard-Phillips, L., Galandini, S., de Valk, H., & Fibbi, R. (2015). *Damned if you do, damned if you don't: The challenges of including and comparing the children of immigrants in European survey data* (NIDI Working Paper no.: 2015/01). The Hague: NIDI. Retrieved from http://www.nidi.nl/shared/content/output/papers/nidi-wp-2015-01.pdf

Li, Y. (2010). The labour market situation of minority ethnic groups in Britain and the US. *EurAmerica: A Journal of European and American Studies, 402*, 1–51.

Li, Y., & Heath, A. F. (2016). Class matters: A study of minority and majority social mobility in Britain, 1982–2011. *American Journal of Sociology, 122*(1), 162–200.

Lievesley, N. (2010). *The future ageing of the ethnic minority population of England and Wales* (Older BME People and Financial Inclusion Report). London: Runnymede Trust/Centre for Policy on Ageing.

Mood, C. (2010). Logistic regression: Why we cannot do what we think we can do, and what we can do about it. *European Sociological Review, 26*(1), 67–82.

Office for National Statistics. (2012). *2011 Census: Key statistics for England and Wales, March 2011*. London: ONS.

Park, R. E., & Burgess, E. W. (1921). *Introduction to the science of sociology*. Chicago: The University of Chicago Press.

Paterson, L., & Iannelli, C. (2007). Social class and educational attainment: A comparative study of England, Wales, and Scotland. *Sociology of Education, 80*(4), 330–358.

Platt, L. (2016). Class, capital, and social mobility. In H. Dean & L. Platt (Eds.), *Social advantage and disadvantage* (pp. 62–84). Oxford: Oxford University Press.

Portes, P. A., Fernández-Kelly, P. P., & Haller, D. W. (2009). The adaptation of the immigrant second generation in America: A theoretical overview and recent evidence. *Journal of Ethnic and Migration Studies, 35*(7), 1077–1104.

Ramakrishnan, S. K. (2004). Second-generation immigrants? The "2.5 Generation" in the United States. *Social Science Quarterly, 85*(2), 380–399.

Rees, P., Wohland, P., Norman, P., & Boden, P. (2012). Ethnic population projections for the UK, 2001–2051. *Journal of Population Research, 29*(1), 45–89.

Rothon, C. (2007). Can achievement differentials be explained by social class alone? An examination of minority ethnic educational performance in England and Wales at the end of compulsory schooling. *Ethnicities, 7*(3), 306–322.

Rothon, C., Heath, A., & Lessard-Phillips, L. (2009). The educational attainments of the "second generation": A comparative study of Britain, Canada, and the United States. *The Teachers College Record, 111*(6), 1404–1443.

Sewell, W. H., Haller, A. O., & Portes, A. (1969). The educational and early occupational attainment process. *American Sociological Review, 34*, 82–92.

Simpson, L., Warren, J., & Jivraj, S. (2015). Do people change their ethnicity over time? In *Ethnic identity and inequalities in Britain: The dynamics of diversity* (pp. 79-92). Bristol: Policy Press.

Strand, S. (2014). Ethnicity, gender, social class and achievement gaps at age 16: Intersectionality and "Getting it" for the white working class. *Research Papers in Education, 29*(2), 131–171.

University of Essex, Institute for Social and Economic Research, & National Centre for Social Research. (2013). Understanding Society: Waves 1-3, 2009-2012 [computer file]. 5th Edition. SN: 6614. UK Data Archive [distributor].

Waters, M. C., Tran, V. C., Kasinitz, P., & Mollenkopf, J. H. (2010). Segmented assimilation revisited: Types of acculturation and socioeconomic mobility in young adulthood. *Ethnic and Racial Studies, 33*(7), 1168–1193.

Zuccotti, C.V. (2015). Do parents matter? Revisiting ethnic penalties in occupation among second generation ethnic minorities in England and Wales. *Sociology, 49*, 229–251.

About the Authors

Laurence Lessard-Phillips is a Research Fellow at the Institute for Research into Superdiversity (IriS) at the University of Birmingham. Her main research interests lie in the perceptions, measurement, and dimensionality of immigrant adaptation; family influences on socio-economic and civic-political inclusion; ethnic inequalities in education and the labour market; the transnational behaviour across immigrant generations; and social inequalities and social mobility.

Yaojun Li is Professor of Sociology at the Department of Sociology and the Cathie Marsh Institute for Social Research, Manchester University, UK. His research interests are in social mobility and social stratification, social capital, and the socio-economic integration of ethnic minority groups. He has published widely in these areas, including papers in top sociology journals in Europe and the USA. He has also conducted numerous research projects funded by academic and government agencies in Britain, China, USA, Australia and Qatar.

8

The Prevalence of Rough Sleeping and Sofa Surfing Amongst Young People in the UK

Anna Clarke

Cambridge Centre for Housing & Planning Research, Department of Land Economy, University of Cambridge, Cambridge, CB3 9EP, UK; E-Mail: acc44@cam.ac.uk

Abstract

Whilst data on statutory homelessness is well recorded in the UK, there is a lack of data on informal homelessness (such as 'sofa surfing') and rough sleeping, other than that which relies on partial information and street counts. This paper presents findings from a recent online survey of young people and helps to fill this gap. It found that rates of sofa surfing and rough sleeping among young people were much higher than previously thought. Twenty-six percent of young people (aged 16–25) had slept rough at some point in their life and 35 percent had 'sofa surfed' (stayed with friends or family on their floor or sofa because they had nowhere else to go). The paper explores the implications of this for how we conceptualise homelessness. It suggests that homelessness may often be neither cause nor consequence of wider forms of exclusion, but that we may need to explore further the factors that enable some people to move swiftly out of homelessness more easily than others.

Keywords

boomerang generation; hidden homelessness; rough sleeping; sofa surfing; street homelessness; youth homelessness

Issue

This article is part of the issue "Homelessness and Social Inclusion", edited by Isobel Anderson (University of Stirling, UK), Maša Filipovič Hrast (University of Ljubljana, Slovenia) and Joe Finnerty (University College Cork, Ireland).

1. Introduction

In the UK, figures for the number of homeless people assisted by local authorities are collected, but other homeless people not in contact with homelessness services are particularly difficult to count. Those in contact with homelessness services, or who are sleeping on the street may be the 'tip of the iceberg' with many more experiencing homelessness but not using homelessness services, possibly because they rely on their own resources to solve their problems, or because they are unaware of the help available, or do not wish to use it.

This research, commissioned by youth homeless charity, Centrepoint, was part of a project estimating rates of youth homelessness throughout the UK (Clarke, Burgess, Morris, & Udagawa, 2015). This paper analyses the findings from the part of the research into 'hidden homelessness'—young people who experience homelessness but are not in contact with any agencies, including sofa surfers and rough sleepers. These groups are hard to find and therefore to count.

This paper aims to help fill that gap and to complement existing data from other sources. It draws on a 2014 survey conducted online of over 2000 young people (aged 16–25) in the UK to establish how many have experienced sofa surfing or rough sleeping. Sofa surfing was defined as "where individuals stay with friends or members of their extended family on their floor or sofa as they have nowhere else to go". Rough sleeping was defined as having slept in a list of non-housing locations including parks and cars because they felt they had nowhere else to stay.

The high numbers found by this research support the need for the growing body of work around pathways into homelessness, focussing not just on immediate triggers of homelessness, but also on the factors that differentiate the young people who move swiftly out of homelessness and those who do not. It also presents a challenge to notions that homelessness is necessarily extreme or something that effects only the most socially excluded.

2. Background

To quantify homelessness, it is first necessary to define what it is that is being counted. Whilst people sleeping on the streets are more visibly homeless, there are a variety of precarious, insecure or unsatisfactory living conditions often termed "hidden homelessness" (Reeve & Batty, 2011). The problem of definition has been a long running debate with little agreement or progress made on defining homelessness (Amore et al., 2011). The European Federation of National Organisations Working with the Homeless (FEANTSA) and the European Observatory on Homelessness have produced a classification system of different types of homelessness, termed ETHOS. However, this has been criticized for mixing up living situations, such as homeless shelters, with counts of people who are housed at present but at risk of future homelessness, such as people under threat of eviction or violence (Amore et al., 2011), reducing its utility as a definition that can be used to count homelessness at any one time. In practice, quantifying homelessness has tended to rely on data collected by governments—which is usually partial and relates mainly to specific categories of homeless people who are accessing services or have rights to be rehoused (Fitzpatrick, Pawson, Bramley, Wilcox, & Watts, 2015). In the UK, some efforts have been made to count rough sleepers, but they are known to present only a partial picture of rough sleeping, especially outside London.

There have been few studies which have tried to look at the rate of hidden homelessness—such as sofa surfing—among young people. A 2007 Danish study found a high prevalence of hidden homelessness in Denmark (Benjaminsen & Christensen, 2007). Sofa surfing has been mentioned in passing as an option used by women which may explain why there are fewer women found on the street (Reeve & Casey, 2006; Weber Sikich, 2008); as preferable to hostels for gay young people (Cull, Platzer, & Balloch, 2006) or as a precursor to more entrenched homelessness (Quilgars, Johnsen, & Pleace, 2008). Disability has received relatively little attention in relation to homelessness, though it is known that adults who had childhood learning difficulties are over-represented among the homeless population (Patterson, Moniruzzaman, Frankish, & Somers, 2012), with a recent UK study emphasising the need to understand disabled young people's role in shaping their own housing pathways (Mackie, 2012). Understanding the role of informal housing solutions such as sofa surfing could help develop this approach.

In the UK there are data collected from administrative sources on homeless people who are assisted by local authorities, but there appear to have been no real efforts made to systematically count people who are 'hidden homeless'—staying temporarily with friends or family members in what are very often quite precarious and insecure housing arrangements (Quilgars, Fitzpatrick, & Pleace, 2011). A study of single homeless people using homelessness services found that the majority of homeless service users had experience of hidden homelessness (Reeve & Batty, 2011) but we know very little about how many non-service users also have experience of hidden homelessness.

It is also as important to understand the duration and patterns of youth homelessness as it is to quantify it. This is particularly problematic with youth homelessness as is very often transient and connected to difficulties in making the transition from child to adult status (Chamberlain & Johnson, 2013; Hutson & Liddiard, 1994). A 2010 review of research (Quilgars, 2010) highlighted a 1998 research by the European Observatory on Homelessness which suggested that youth homelessness may be considered as a faltered or interrupted transition to adulthood which typically happens to vulnerable young people. It is well established that such transitions have become more protracted over the last two decades (Thomson, 2009) with the 'boomerang generation' gaining traction in the British press (Stone et al., 2014) and delayed independent household formation (Stone, Berrington, & Falkingham, 2014), home ownership, later marriage, cohabitation and increased insecurity in labour markets.

Studies on the needs of the homeless population have often focussed on the ones who use services or approach local authorities for assistance in the UK. These have found homeless young people to have very high rate of vulnerability—missing school, mental health problems or a history of having run away from home as a child (Hodgson, Shelton, & van den Bree, 2014; Quilgars et al., 2008). A high degree of overlap has been found between experience of homelessness and other domains of deep exclusion such as institutional care, childhood trauma, substance misuse, begging, street drinking, sex work, or 'survival' shoplifting (Fitzpatrick, Bramley, & Johnson, 2012; Fitzpatrick & Johnsen, 2011). A key aspect to debates around homelessness therefore concerns the nature and direction of causation. Do people become homeless as a result of other factor such as substance abuse or mental ill health? Or does homelessness contribute or directly cause these wider problems and difficulties for those who are living without a permanent home?

Whilst most studies suggest a degree of causation in both directions (Hodgson, Shelton, van den Bree, & Los, 2013), the focus in recent years has been on preventing the tendency of homelessness to cause or worsen other difficulties by focussing on a Housing First approach (Filipovič Hrast, 2014; Gaetz, 2014). This approach challenges the notion that it is necessary for homeless people to tackle any wider problems before they can sustain a tenancy and instead endeavours to house people into permanent homes first, and then to support them to tackle any other difficulties, such as mental health or substance abuse. The Housing First approach has shown good results throughout Europe (Busch-Geertsema, 2014), and presented a major challenge to the previous linear "treatment first" approach used in the United States (Johnsen & Teixeira, 2010). It is known that homeless people who suffer mental ill health or substance abuse tend to be homeless for longer than other homeless people, possibly because this leads them to become involved in a 'homeless sub-culture' associated with a street lifestyle to a greater extent than other homeless young people (Chamberlain & Johnson, 2013). The impact of street lifestyle on mental health and substance abuse has also been highlighted (Kidd, 2004; McCay & Aiello, 2013). The argument for a Housing First approach is, however, that wider difficulties do not in themselves prevent people from sustaining a tenancy, but rather that being homeless makes it harder to address other problems with proponents arguing that "becoming homeless may mean young people not only lose their families but other natural supports (friends, adults, extended family), and be forced to drop out of school" and can recover more quickly once housed (Gaetz, 2014). In other words, the underlying contention here is homelessness is more a cause than an automatic consequence of other difficulties.

The other major theme in policy around youth homelessness in the UK, as in much of Europe over the last ten years has been on homelessness prevention, rather than alleviation (Maher & Allen, 2014). In the UK this approach is tied in with the development of local authority led services to prevent young people losing their homes including mediation with parents and access to alternative housing before an existing tenancy is terminated (Pawson et al., 2007). The success of this approach is also enhanced if homelessness is understood as being a cause of wider difficulties, which will therefore be avoided if homelessness is prevented.

3. Data on Youth Homelessness in the UK

Availability of data in the UK varies greatly between types of homelessness, and few data sources offer the ability to distinguish homelessness in general from youth homelessness among those aged under 25 (Homeless Link, 2014a).

Rough sleepers are notoriously difficult to count. Nevertheless, rough sleeping is a form of homelessness that has attracted much attention, and therefore efforts have been made throughout the UK to count rough sleepers, track them through support systems, and measure progress in reducing rough sleeping. These date back to the 1990 Rough Sleepers' Initiative. A key focus more recently has been on the 'No Second Night Out' project, which aims to ensure that no rough sleeper has to sleep out for more than one night after having made contact with services (Department for Communities and Local Government, 2011).

Street counts do not give a measure of the total number of people experiencing homelessness over the course of a year, because the duration of each person's rough sleeping is not known. However, they are accepted by the UK government as the most accurate method of measuring trends in rough sleeping over time (National Audit Office, 2005). They can also give some indication of the scale of rough sleeping in different locations, though this is dependent on rough sleepers' counts having taken place in comparable fashions.

Rough sleeping in London continues to receive the most political prominence and funding, though is by no means the only place where people sleep rough in the UK. Services for rough sleepers are better developed in London than in most other areas, and the Combined Homeless and Information Network (CHAIN) database is a key source of data here. CHAIN is a database for people who work with rough sleepers and the street population in London, maintained by a charity, St. Mungo's Broadway, and tracks individual rough sleepers across their contact with different services[1]. The latest report (St Mungo's Broadway, 2014) found there to be 6,508 known rough sleepers recorded in London in the year 2012–2013, of whom 773 were aged 16–25.

Outside of London, the government also produce snapshot figures for rough sleeping based on information collected by local authorities (Department for Communities and Local Government, 2014) The figures are based on street counts and also on other sources of information such as information from voluntary sector agencies in contact with rough sleepers, such as day centres. The autumn of 2014, street counts estimated that there were 2,744 rough sleepers on one night in England, an increase of 18 percent from autumn 2013, and of these, 2,002 were outside London. Just over a fifth of the rough sleepers counted in England were in London (742). There is much variation between authorities with some authorities, such as Cornwall, having higher rates of rough sleeping than most London boroughs, whilst in contrast 50 local authorities estimated or counted no rough sleepers at all on the night when data was collected. The DCLG data does not provide a breakdown by age group. However, data compiled by Homeless Link (Homeless Link, 2014b) does provide a split by age group, and suggests that ten percent of rough sleepers in London are aged 16–24, as are 20 percent of those outside London.

In Wales, a rough sleepers survey was undertaken in November 2015, the first for some years, and local authorities reported a total of 82 rough sleepers during one night, based on street counts of areas where rough sleepers were known to bed down . The survey also asked how many people were known to have slept rough in Wales over a two-week period, and this exercise produced a figure of 240. No breakdown by age was given.

Rough sleepers' counts have not been consistently carried out in Scotland for over ten years. However, the previous housing circumstances of those assessed

[1] www.broadwaylondon.org/CHAIN.html

under the homeless persons' legislation when applying for housing are recorded (Scottish Government, 2013). These show that in 2013–2014 a total of 1,787 applicants had slept rough the night before they approached the council for housing assistance, 6.4 percent of all applicants. This figure is not broken down by age. The data also recorded 17 applicants who were classified as long term roofless (Scottish Government, 2014). These figures are not quite comparable to the CHAIN data on the numbers rough sleeping over a year, as they may include some double-counting (people who were assessed more than once in a year) and would also exclude any rough sleepers who did not approach a local authority, or who did so after having spent the previous night somewhere other than rough sleeping.

In Northern Ireland too, there is very little data on rough sleeping. The Northern Irish Housing Executive report that there are fewer than ten rough sleepers at any one time in Belfast and none elsewhere (Northern Irish Housing Executive, 2012); however, it is not stated when this count took place.

Previous research has tried to pull figures together for the UK as a whole and fill some of the gaps. A 2011 report estimated the number of young people experiencing homelessness in the UK during a year to be around 78,000–80,000 in 2008–2009, including 3,800 who slept rough at some point in a year (Quilgars et al., 2011), though acknowledges that this is likely to be a partial picture.

In short, all existing data on rough sleepers is dependent on the rough sleeper having been observed at some point by someone counting them either whilst rough sleeping, or shortly afterwards when they make contact with a support agency. No data exists on sofa surfing in the UK.

4. Research Methods

To help fill the gap in knowledge and find out more about young people's experiences of rough sleeping and sofa surfing, an online survey of 2,011 young people (aged 16-25) in the UK was drawn from a representative sample of UK adults. The survey was undertaken in September 2014 by ComRes, a leading polling company, with established panels known to be representative of the UK population, large enough to provide the required sample size of young people. The questions were designed by the academics leading the study, with input from Centrepoint, who founded the research, and also from ComRes who contributed technical expertise in questionnaire design. To avoid self-selection bias, the survey was advertised under the topic of "people" with the focus on homelessness only made apparent to young people once they responded to the survey. In total 17,605 invites were sent out, from which 5,537 respondents clicked through to the survey and of those there were 254 who were screened out (for instance on grounds of age), 349 who only completed part of the survey and 2011 who completed it. Online survey methods do exclude people without internet access, though data from the Office for National Statistics (ONS) shows that 99 percent of 16–24 year olds were recent internet users by 2014[2]. Young people who were homeless at the time of the survey may have been less likely to have had reliable internet access, so could be somewhat under-represented.

The survey aimed to establish how many had experienced sofa surfing. Respondents were asked whether they had ever slept in a list of places such as in a park or in a car because they had nowhere else to stay (see Table 1 for the full list). They were also asked whether they had ever sofa surfed, which was defined for them as 'where individuals stay with friends or members of their extended family on their floor or sofa as they have nowhere else to go'—and if they had, whether they had done so in the last year, and the length of time they had spent sofa surfing.

The survey data was weighted by ComRes for region, age and gender and the full dataset supplied to the research team for analysis. In order to be sure of including only those who were actually homeless, the detail provided by those who answered that they had slept rough only 'in another place' and also those whose reason for having nowhere else to stay was given as 'other' were checked. Despite the question having asked about rough sleeping *because you had nowhere else to stay* some respondents gave reasons suggesting that they did have accommodation but were temporarily unable to get to it, or had chosen not to, for instance because they had lost their keys or missed the last train home. Any respondents whose answers indicated that they had slept rough through *choice*, whilst *outside of the UK*, or because they did have accommodation but that they were *unable to access* it were excluded from the rough sleepers group for the purposes of analysis. They have therefore not been counted as rough sleepers in the subsequent analysis. In total this led to 88 responses being recoded as not being rough sleepers.

5. Findings

5.1. Rough Sleepers

The 2,011 young people aged 16-25 surveyed were asked whether they had had to stay in one of a list of places because they had nowhere else to stay. They were then asked whether their experience of rough sleeping was in the last year, or longer ago. Table 1, below, shows the answers to this question:

Overall, the analysis suggested that 26 percent of young people in this age group had experience of rough sleeping because they were homeless, and 17 percent had done so within the last year. These have been termed hereafter as 'rough sleepers', though it should be noted that the definition of rough sleeping is a broad one

[2] www.ons.gov.uk/ons/publications/re-reference-tables.html?edition=tcm%3A77-395602

that includes not just those sleeping on the streets and in parks, but also those who have slept in cars or tents because they had nowhere else to stay.

A narrower definition of rough sleeping as including only those who were outdoors and open to the elements would include only those who had slept on the streets, in a car park or in a park or other open space. This narrower group of 'outdoors rough sleeping' comprised a total of 188 young people, or nine percent of all young people.

Young people answering yes to the question, where asked why they had had nowhere else to stay (Table 2).

Rough sleepers who had rough slept within the last year were asked how long they had slept rough for (Table 3).

From this information, it is possible to make minimum estimates of young people sleeping rough on any one night. Table 4 shows how this has been calculated.

If the young people answering this survey are representative of UK, the 0.53 percent sleeping rough on any one night would equate to 39,557 people (of a population of 7.45 million). This seems a very high figure in comparison to other sources, which are predominately based on rough sleepers counts and rough sleepers in contact

Table 1. "Have you ever had to sleep in one of these places because you had nowhere else to stay?".

Response	Number	Proportion of all young people	Proportion of rough sleepers
In a car	292	15%	55%
In a car park*	83	4%	16%
In a park or other open space*	82	4%	15%
In a squat	50	2%	9%
In a tent	180	2%	34%
In an abandoned building	53	3%	10%
In another place (please specify)	10	1%	2%
On a night bus	74	4%	14%
On the streets*	95	5%	18%
Yes to any of the above	**533**	**26%**	**100%**
Of whom had done so within the last year	*346*	*17%*	
Yes to any of the outdoor places (marked with *)	**188**	**9%**	**35%**
I have never had to sleep in one of these places	1,478	73%	—
Total	**2,011**	**100%**	—

Source: Clarke et al. (2015). Respondents could give more than one answer.

Table 2. "Which, if any, of the following reasons explain why you had nowhere else to stay? (All those who have rough slept)".

Reason	Number	Proportion of those who slept rough
My parents were unable or unwilling to accommodate me	110	21%
I left home due to the negative environment there	88	17%
My friends or extended family were unable or unwilling to accommodate me	79	15%
I split up from my partner	58	11%
The place I was living was overcrowded	44	8%
My tenancy came to an end through no fault of my own and I could not find a new place to live	38	7%
I was suffering from substance abuse (e.g. drugs or alcohol)	23	4%
I was evicted from where I was living due to rent arrears (i.e. unable to pay the rent)	17	3%
I was suffering domestic violence at my family home	16	3%
I am not a British citizen, and didn't know anyone in the UK I could stay with	13	3%
I had to leave foster care / a children's home and had nowhere to go	9	2%
I was suffering domestic violence from my partner	9	2%
I had just left prison and had nowhere to go	8	2%
I was evicted from where I was living due to antisocial behaviour (including noise, or damage to property)	8	2%
Other (please specify)	13	3%
Total	**520**	**100%**

Source: Young people's survey, September 2014. Respondents could only give one answer.

Table 3. Estimates of the average time rough sleepers aged 16–24 in the UK spent sleeping rough in the year to September 2014.

		Total	Proportion of those who slept rough in last year
Number sleeping rough in last year		*346*	*100%*
Length of time slept rough	1 night	137	40%
	Between 1 night and a week	119	34%
	More than a week, but less than a month	51	15%
	More than one month, but less than three months	20	6%
	More than three months, but less than six months	11	3%
	More than six months, but less than a year	6	2%
	A year or longer	1	*
	Don't know	1	*

Source: Young people's survey, September 2014. Respondents could only give one answer.

Table 4. Estimated number of people aged 16–24 rough sleeping on any one night in the year to September 2014.

	UK
Number of young people answering survey	2,011
Number who have slept rough during the last year	345
Minimum number of nights spent sleeping rough in last year (by all rough sleepers)[3]	3,899
Estimated number of young people in survey sleeping rough on any one night[4]	11
Proportion of young people rough sleeping on any one night	0.53%

Sources: Young people's survey, September 2014 and DCLG Mid-year population estimate; own calculations.

with agencies. It is difficult to estimate the margin of error here in statistical terms as the number sleeping rough on any one night (11) is based on responses from 345 people, but they have contributed unequally to this figure (a relatively small number of long-term rough sleepers constitute a large proportion of all rough sleeping). Nevertheless, even if only 11 rough sleepers had been responsible for all the rough sleeping, this would still give lower and upper confidence limits of 20,357 and 72,726 (at 95 percent confidence). Whilst a substantial range, even the lower figure is still greatly in excess of official estimates for rough sleeping. The fact that 345 people (not eleven) actually contributed something to the figure increases the level of confidence that the population total is closer to 39,557. Whether these people can all be considered "homeless" is also worth considering, as for many the experience was very short lived reflecting one-off events.

It is unsurprising that this is higher than the published data; making contact with rough sleepers can be difficult for agencies, or people trying to count them especially if the rough sleeping is for a short duration or away from areas popular with rough sleepers. It is also important to note the variety of places that people reported they slept rough, as shown above in Table 2. Of those sleeping rough, 18 percent had slept on the streets, with a further 13 percent sleeping in a car park, park or other open space. Most of the rest had slept in a car, tent or night bus. This may mean that only around a third of the young people sleeping rough were in the more visible outdoor places where they might be more likely to be found by people doing street counts or working with rough sleepers. The extent of the rough sleeping of all sorts found in this survey is however very much higher than was expected.

Even if we focus only on narrow definition of rough sleeping, discussed above the survey still suggests that over 10,000 young people were sleeping rough *each night*—this still very high and suggests that further research would be helpful to see if these results can be replicated, possibly drawing on further surveys.

5.2. Sofa Surfing

The 2,011 young people aged 16–25 surveyed were asked:

> "Thinking about 'sofa surfing' (where individuals stay with friends or members of their extended family on their floor or sofa as they have nowhere else to go), do you have any experience of doing this?"

Those who said yes, were then asked whether this experience was in the last year, or longer ago.

[3] The length of time spent rough sleeping was asked in bands. A conservative estimate has been used here by assuming all spent the lowest time for each band (e.g. 'more than a week but less than a month' has been assumed to be just eight nights). This means that the estimates of the proportion of young people sleeping rough on any one night and the total numbers sleeping rough are lowest possible estimates from the answers given in the survey.

[4] This has been calculated by dividing the total number of nights spent by the number of days in a year (365).

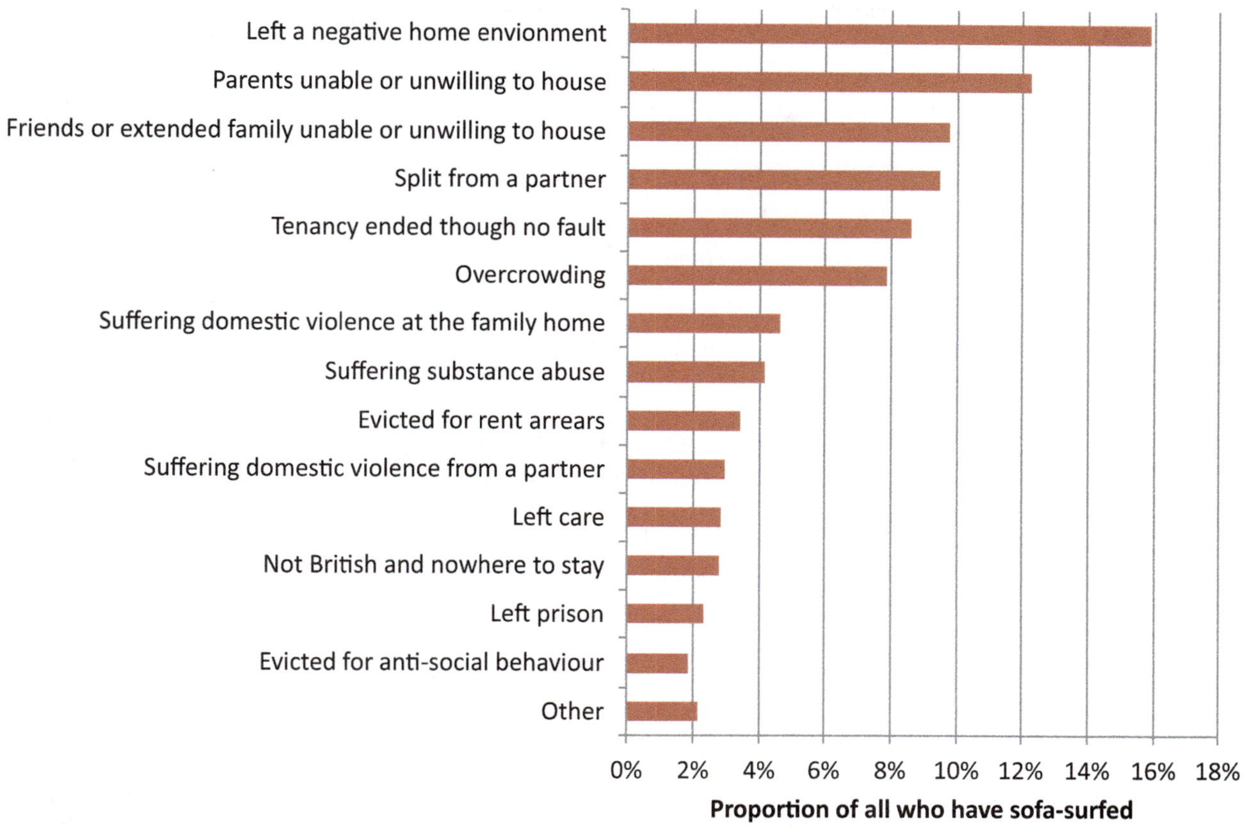

Figure 1. Reasons for sofa surfing among people aged 16–24 identified as sofa surfing in the year to September 2014. Source: Clarke et al. (2015). Respondents could only give one answer.

Overall, the survey suggested that 35 percent of young people in this age group (703 of the 2,011) had experience of sofa surfing, and 20 percent (409 people) had done so within the last year. In total 79 of the 409 people who had sofa surfed in the last year had also slept rough, meaning that a total of 675 out of the 2,011 (34 percent) had either sofa surfed or rough slept during the last twelve months. The survey explored the causes of sofa surfing (Figure 1).

As can be seen, the main reasons for young people sofa surfing relate to negative home environments or having been asked to leave by their parents. However there were substantial numbers also indicating that they had sofa surfed after a period of living independently, and were made homeless by a tenancy ending, splitting from a partner or no longer being able to stay with friends or extended family. Overcrowding was a reason in eight percent of cases.

The research found that some causes were associated with longer periods of sofa surfing. Overall, the median length of time that sofa surfers spent sofa surfing in the last 12 months was 25 days (3.5 weeks). Eighteen percent had sofa surfed for over three months, with four percent having done so for six or more out of the last twelve months. In contrast, 23 percent had sofa surveyed for a week or less. Figure 2 shows the relationship between the cause of sofa surfing reported the duration.

As can be seen, the reasons that are associated with having left home and then lost a home (evictions, leaving prison and domestic violence from a partner) are all associated with longer lengths of sofa surfing than are those associated with moving directly from the parental home to sofa surfing. This may suggest that for some young people a relatively short stay sofa surfing with a friend may be sufficient to enable them either to move back home or find a more permanent housing solution. In contrast, those who have lost a home of their own find it harder to move on from sofa surfing in a short timescale.

There were also significant differences between men and women, with men having sofa surfed for a median of five and a half weeks (38 days), as compared to two weeks (16 days) for women.

It is possible to make an estimate from the sofa surfing survey of the number of young people who are sofa surfing on any one night. Table 5 shows how this has been calculated.

The survey suggests that one in 35 young people of respondents were sofa surfing on any one night during the previous year. If the survey respondents are representative of the UK, this would equate to a total of 215,957 young people sofa surfing on any one night. As with the rough sleepers, it is hard to give a precise confidence interval to this estimate because some respondents contribute disproportionately to the total. If 57 people were responsible for all the sofa surfing this would give confidence limits of 160,379 to 272,319 young people sofa surfing on any one night. The fact that 409 people (not 57) actually contributed something to

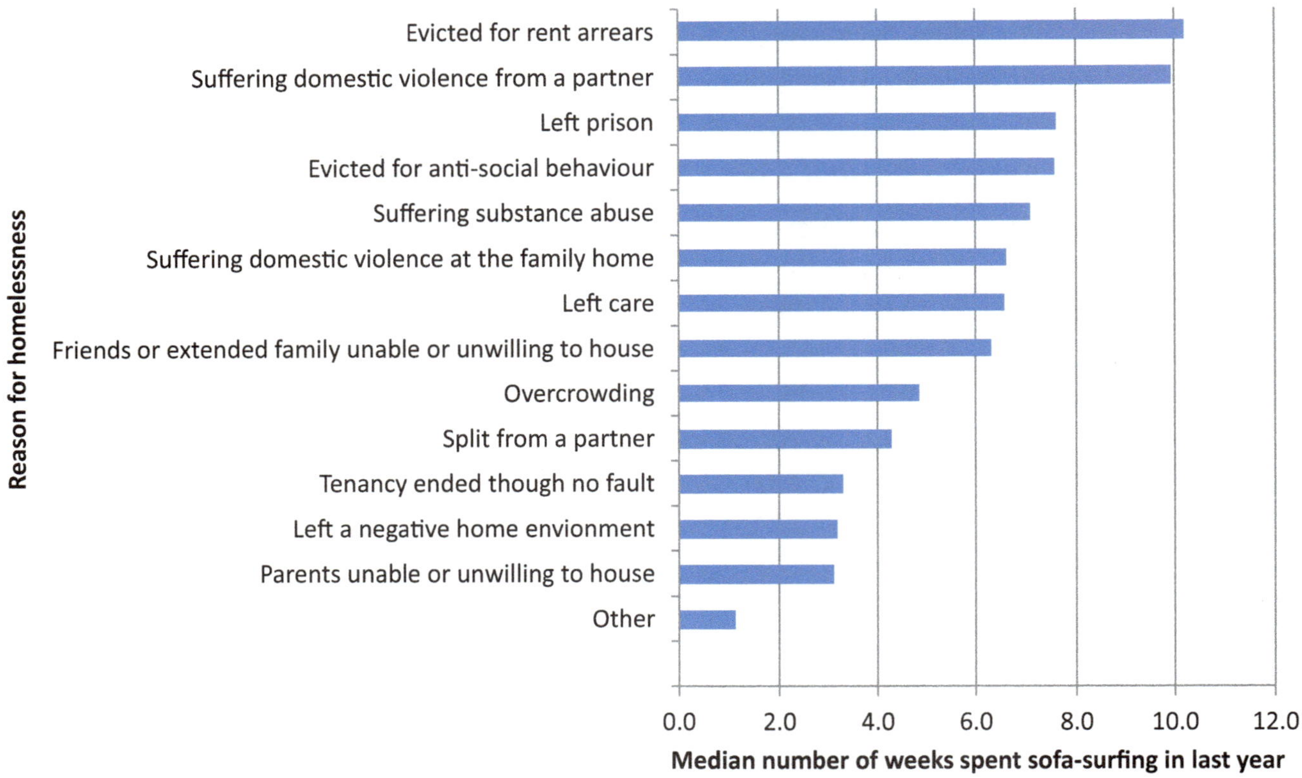

Figure 2. Median length of time spent sofa surfing by reason, among people aged 16–24 identified as sofa surfing in the year to September 2014. Source: Clarke et al. (2015).

Table 5. Estimated number of people aged 16–24 'sofa surfing' on any one night in the year to September 2014.

	UK
Number of young people answering survey	2,011
Number who have sofa surfed during the last year [From survey]	409
Total number of sofa surfing nights in last year [Sum of all lengths of time sofa surfing by all respondents]	20,977
Average number sofa surfing on any one night during last year [Total number of sofa surfing nights (20,977), divided by total number of nights in the year (365)]	57
Proportion of young people sofa surfing on any one night [Average number sofa surfing on any one night (57) divided by number of young people answering survey (2,011)]	2.9%

Sources: Young people's survey, September 2014, and DCLG Mid-year population estimate; own calculations.

the figure increases the level of confidence that the population total is closer to 215,957.

The research explored whether certain groups of young people were more likely to have sofa surfed than others. Four key factors could be identified which were related to the likelihood of having sofa surfed, as shown in Figure 3.

The correlation coefficients were: Gender (0.262); Disabled (0.079); Ever in care or had social worker (0.273); Citizenship (0.102). All were significant at the 0.01 confidence level.

As can be seen young men were substantially more likely than young women to have sofa surfed which is in contrast to the suggestions from previous research that women are more likely to sofa surf (Reeve & Casey, 2006; Weber Sikich, 2008). However the biggest risk factor appears to be having had contact with the social care system as a child; 90 percent of those who had ever been in the care of a local authority or had a social worker as a child said that they had sofa surfed. Those without British citizenship or who were disabled were also significantly more likely to report having sofa surfed (Table 6).

Of those who had sofa surfed, men, non-British citizens, disabled people and those who had been in care or had a social worker as a child were also more likely to report having done so for longer lengths of time.

There was no statistically significant difference between the qualification level and whether people had sofa surfed. However, this may be somewhat complicated by the fact that many in this age group are still in education and still living at home; the teenagers in the survey were less likely than the early 20s to have sofa surfed, and also more likely to lack qualifications. Comparing the qualification levels just of those in the older age groups (aged 22 or over) showed a clearer relationship between lacking qualifications and sofa surfing with

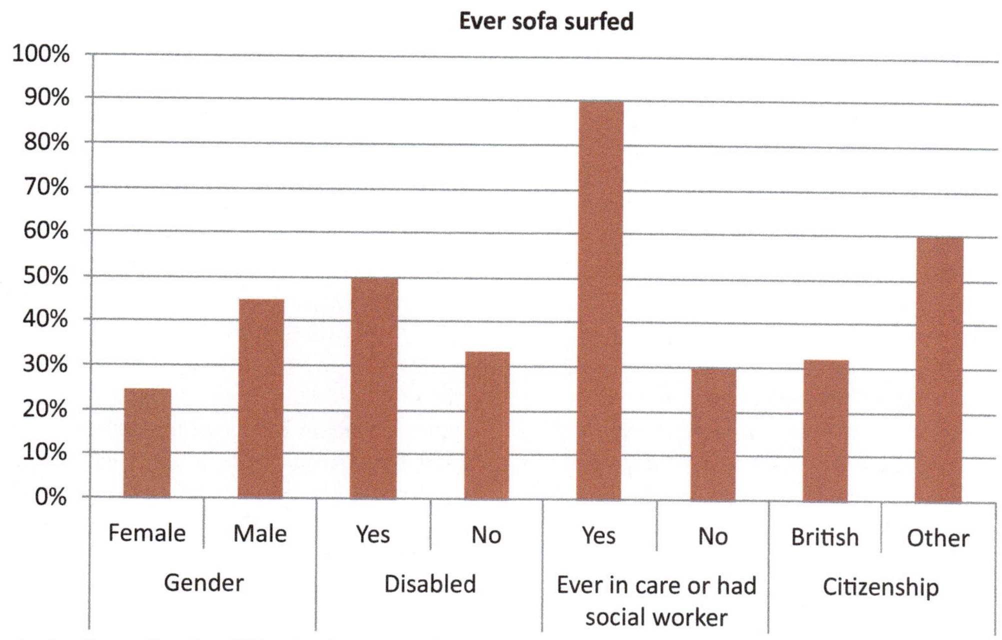

Figure 3. Extent of sofa surfing in different demographic groups, among people aged 16–24 identified as sofa surfing in the year to September 2014[5]. Source: Clarke et al. (2015).

Table 6. Vulnerability indicators of young people who had slept rough or sofa surfers.

		Ever rough slept	Ever sofa surfed	All young people	Proportion who have ever slept rough	Proportion who have ever sofa surfed	Proportion of rough sleepers	Proportion of sofa sufers
Ever in care or had social worker	Yes	134	142	**158**	85%	90%	25%	20%
	No	391	550	**1,833**	21%	30%	73%	78%
	Don't know	12	10	**20**	60%	50%	2%	1%
Citizenship	British citizen	426	579	**1,804**	24%	32%	79%	82%
	Non-British citizen	110	123	**206**	53%	60%	21%	17%
Employment status	Full-time employment	167	216	**471**	35%	46%	31%	31%
	Full-time student	175	242	**1,010**	17%	24%	33%	34%
	Part-time employment	73	98	**191**	38%	51%	14%	14%
	Part-time student	40	45	**88**	45%	51%	7%	6%
	Self-employed	17	22	**43**	40%	51%	3%	3%
	Unemployed	57	70	**187**	30%	37%	11%	10%
Disabled	Yes	68	78	**158**	43%	49%	13%	11%
	No	449	602	**1,800**	25%	33%	84%	86%
	Prefer not to say	20	22	**52**	38%	42%	4%	3%
Qualifications	None	13	13	**43**	30%	30%	2%	2%
	Level 1/GCSE grade D-G	44	62	**88**	50%	70%	8%	9%
	A*-C GCSE	111	135	**475**	23%	28%	21%	19%
	A level	157	217	**762**	21%	28%	29%	31%
	BTEC	44	58	**143**	31%	41%	8%	8%
	Degree/HND or above	168	216	**499**	34%	43%	31%	31%
Total		**536**	**703**	**2,011**	**27%**	**35%**	**100%**	**100%**

Source: Young people's survey, September 2014.

[5] 'Other' citizenship status includes: Asylum seeker; Indefinite leave to remain; Discretionary leave; Limited leave to remain with refugee status; Limited leave—other; Citizen of another EEA country; Humanitarian Protection. The numbers within each of these categories were too small to be statistically significant themselves.

57 percent of those lacking a degree having sofa surfed, compared with 40 percent of those with a degree (significant at the 0.01 confidence level).

Looking at the profile of rough sleepers and sofa surfers, however, it is clear that the large majority did not have any obvious vulnerabilities. Four out of five of sofa surfers had no prior involvement with the care system. And the large majority had British Citizenship, were not disabled and had left school with at least good General Certificate of Secondary Education (GCSE) grades (C and above). Nearly a third were graduates. This suggests that sofa surfing is not an uncommon experience for large numbers of young people from all backgrounds.

The research explored whether the young people felt that sofa surfing had had a negative or positive impact on various aspects of the respondent's life, as shown in Table 7.

As can be seen, there were very mixed views on this issue. Sofa surfing was often reported as a positive experience in most aspects of life, most likely because respondents were comparing to the situation they had left behind. Moving away from a home situation of conflict or severe overcrowding can help people to repair relationships with their families. Sofa surfing can also allow a young person to remain near a job or to move somewhere they hope to find work or housing.

Using the answers to the questions above, a 'positive rating' was created, using the sum of the scores given above (where 'very positive = 5; fairly positive = 4, etc.). The average score for all sofa surfers was 22.3 (Table 8).

Employment status was strongly correlated with positive views on sofa surfing, with an average rating of 19.3 for unemployed people, compared to 23.4 for full time students and 22.2 for employed people. This suggests that more vulnerable people with less secure employment or educational arrangements were more likely to find sofa surfing to be detrimental to their well-being.

Men were more positive than women, with average scores of 22.9 and 21.2 respectively. Young people who

Table 7. Impact of sofa surfing on the situation of people aged 16–24 identified as sofa surfing during the year to September 2014.

	Very negative	Fairly negative	Don't know	Fairly positive	Very positive	Total
Education	10%	27%	14%	32%	18%	100%
Work	13%	27%	11%	34%	16%	100%
Relationships	10%	26%	4%	37%	23%	100%
Well-being	15%	31%	6%	30%	19%	100%
Physical health	12%	33%	8%	29%	19%	100%
Finding housing	9%	28%	11%	33%	19%	100%
Finances	13%	25%	6%	38%	19%	100%

Source: Clarke et al. (2015).

Table 8. 'Positive rating' for sofa surfing by demographic group.

	Mean score	Std. Error	Significance	N
All sofa surfers	*22.3*			*703*
Female	**21.2**	**.448**	***	**244**
Male	**22.9**	**.313**	***	**459**
Aged under 22	22.7	.403		278
Aged 22 or over	22.1	.337		425
Working (FT, PT or self-employed)	22.2	.370		336
Unemployed	19.3	.827	***	80
Students	23.4	.386	***	287
Care leaver	25.4	1.277		34
Non-British citizen	23.9	.516		124
Living in England	**22.6**	**.284**	**	**568**
Living in Scotland	**20.6**	**.890**	**	**64**
Living in Northern Ireland	20.4	1.351		25
Living in Wales	22.4	1.071		45
Living in London	**24.8**	**0.684**	***	**106**
Rough slept in last 12 months	**23.8**	**.412**	***	**296**
Not rough slept in last 12 months	19.8	.516		138
Sofa surfed under 3 months	23.6	.359		335
Sofa surfed over 3 months	24.6	.970		74

Source: Young people's survey, September 2014. Notes: ** Significant at 90% confidence; ***Significant at 95% confidence.

had left care were more likely to report that sofa surfing had been a positive experience, with an average score of 25.4, though this was not statistically significant. Young people currently living in London were also more positive about sofa surfing with an average score of 24.8, possibly reflecting the more constrained housing options available in London and/or the value of being in London.

6. Conclusions

The findings from this research suggest that a third of young people have sofa surfed at some point, with a fifth having done so within the last year. If this survey is representative of the UK, it would suggest that around 1.5 million young people in the UK have sofa surfed within the last year. Estimates based on the survey would suggest that on any one night, a minimum of 216,000 young people are sofa surfing. Sofa surfing may, for some young people at least, not necessarily be a negative experience and can enable young people to move to a new area, or remain in their local area gaining or retaining access to education or employment. It may give young people a chance to repair relationships with their families and tends to be a short-term arrangement especially for young people who have had to leave the parental home. The emergence of websites such as couchsurfing.com, whilst targeted at travellers rather than people who are homeless, nevertheless highlights the positive way in which sharing living spaces can be seen. It may, as such, fulfil a necessary role in the transient and mobile nature of young people's lives. The extent to which sofa surfing was seen as a positive experience by young people responding to this survey presents a challenge to the way in which we conceptualise homelessness as necessarily negative and often damaging experience. The ways in which young people make choices over housing, maybe compromising housing security for other social goods (such as access to employment or breathing space to repair relationships) would benefit from further research.

It is harder to see rough sleeping in this same way—sleeping in parks, abandoned buildings, car parks or the street clearly places young people in a very unsafe situation and must be seen as a crisis situation, even if short-lived. Yet this survey suggests it is also not uncommon—experienced by a quarter of young people at some point in their lives, and by 17 percent of them within the last year. Even looking more narrowly just at the 'outdoor' places, nine percent of young people said that they had slept in one of these during the last year. Estimates based on the survey would suggest that on any one night, around 40,000 young people are sleeping rough in one of the places listed. At a time when access to mainstream housing is getting ever harder for young people and the welfare safety net further withdrawn, this is clearly a concern, suggesting the housing situations of many young people may already be precarious.

These figures for hidden homelessness are high, and significantly higher than has been found previously; analysis of official statistics for youth homelessness in the UK suggests a many-times lower figure of just 78,000–80,000 young people experiencing homelessness, with just tiny numbers known to be sleeping rough, and no data at all on sofa surfing. This clearly merits further research, and highlights the potential shortcomings of relying on administrative data and rough sleepers' counts for quantifying something that by its nature does not necessarily bring people into contact with those who collect the data.

These findings also support the argument that homelessness is not the primary cause of other problems, as most of the young people surveyed were—at the time of the survey—in adequate housing, and in work or studying. The widespread prevalence of hidden homelessness by young people and mixed views on the impacts of sofa surfing suggest that these kinds of homelessness do not for most young people lead on to wider forms of social exclusion.

However, the findings also suggest that nor is homelessness necessarily a consequence of wider vulnerabilities, as both sofa surfing and rough sleeping are undertaken by a large number of households most of whom are not entering a period of long term homelessness, or experiencing wider social exclusion, and are doing so without the involvement of external agencies or hostels. It is possible that by avoiding formal homeless provision young people also avoid becoming part of the 'culture of homelessness' (Chamberlain & Johnson, 2013; Ravenshill, 2008), and thereby avoid some of the other problems associated with homelessness and street lifestyles.

An important finding is also that the profile of young people surveyed here who had experienced homeless is significantly less vulnerable than found in other research (Quilgars et al., 2008) and quite different in profile to those suffering 'multiple exclusion homelessness (Fitzpatrick & Johnsen, 2011). This suggests that homeless people who turn to local authorities or other agencies for support are significantly more vulnerable than other young people experiencing a temporary situation of homelessness.

The findings also present a challenge for the focus on UK homelessness policies—which have very much been framed around the prevention agenda for the last ten years. Preventing something that occurs on such a wide scale is clearly challenging. The research suggests that a focus on causation alone may not be sufficient as the numbers who experience homelessness at some point are substantial. The findings instead suggest that there might be merit in improving further our understanding of why some young people move swiftly out of homelessness, whilst others fail to find a quick route out and suffer longer term effects.

Acknowledgments

This research was supported by Centrepoint, the Youth Homeless Charity. The polling was undertaken by Com-

Res. The author would like to thank Centrepoint and all the young people who took part in the survey.

Conflict of Interest

The author declares no conflict of interests.

References

Amore, K., Baker, M., & Howden-Chapman, P. (2011). The ETHOS definition and classification of homelessness: An analysis. *European Journal of Homelessness, 5*(2), 19–37.

Benjaminsen, L., & Christensen, I. (2007). *Homelessness in Denmark 2007: National survey*. Copenhagen: Det Nationale Forskningscenter for Velfard.

Busch-Geertsema, V. (2014). Housing First Europe: Results of a European social experimentation project. *European Journal of Homelessness, 8*(1), 13–28.

Chamberlain, C., & Johnson, G. (2013). Pathways into adult homelessness. *Journal of Sociology, 49*(1), 60–77.

Clarke, A., Burgess, G., Morris, S., & Udagawa, C. (2015) *Estimating the scale of youth homelessness in the UK*. London: Centrepoint. Retrieved from http://cdn.basw.co.uk/upload/basw_101305-9.pdf

Cull, M., Platzer, H., & Balloch, S. (2006). *Out on my own: Understanding the experiences and needs of homeless lesbian, gay, bisexual and transgender youth.* Brighton: Health and Social Policy Research Centre, University of Brighton.

Department for Communities and Local Government. (2011). *Vision to end rough sleeping: No second night out nationwide.* London: Department for Communities and Local Government.

Department for Communities and Local Government. (2014). *Rough sleeping statistics England—Autumn 2014 official statistics*. London: Department for Communities and Local Government.

Filipovič Hrast, M. (2014). Scaling up Housing First in Europe. *European Journal of Homelessness, 8*(2), 255–260.

Fitzpatrick, S., & Johnsen, S. (2011). Multiple exclusion homelessness in the UK: Key patterns and intersections. *Social Policy and Society, 10*(4), 501–512.

Fitzpatrick, S., Bramley, G., & Johnson, S. (2012). Pathways into multiple exclusion homelessness in seven UK cities. *Urban Studies, 50*(1), 148–168.

Fitzpatrick, S., Pawson, H., Bramley, G., Wilcox, S., & Watts, B. (2015). *The homelessness monitor: England 2015*. London: Crisis. Retrieved from http://www.crisis.org.uk/data/files/publications/Homelessness_Monitor_England_2015_final_web.pdf

Gaetz, S. (2014). Can Housing First work for youth? *European Journal of Homelessness, 8*(2), 159–176.

Hodgson, K. J., Shelton, K. H., & van den Bree, M. B. (2014). Mental health problems in young people with experiences of homelessness and the relationship with health service use: A follow up study. *Evidence Based Mental Health, 17*(3), 76–80.

Hodgson, K. J., Shelton, K. H., van den Bree, M. B., & Los, F. J. (2013). Psychopathology in young people experiencing homelessness: A systematic review. *American Journal of Public Health, 103*(6), 24–37.

Homeless Link. (2014a). *oung and homeless 2013*. London: Homeless Link.

Homeless Link. (2014b). *No second night out across England*. London: Homeless Link.

Hutson, S., & Liddiard, M. (1994). *Youth homelessness: The construction of a social issue*. Basingstoke: Palgrave Macmillan.

Johnsen, S., & Teixeira, L. (2010). *Staircases, elevators and cycles of change: 'Housing First' and other housing models for homeless people with complex support needs*. London: Crisis.

Kidd, S. A. (2004). "The walls were closing in and we were trapped": A qualitative analysis of street youth suicide. *Youth Society, 36*(1), 30–55.

Mackie, P. K. (2012) Housing pathways of disabled young people: Evidence for policy and practice. *Housing Studies, 27*(6), 805–821. doi:10.1080/02673037.2012.714464

Maher, C., & Allen, M. (2014). What is preventing us from preventing homelessness? A review of the Irish National Preventative Strategy. *European Journal of Homelessness, 8*(2), 119–136.

McCay, E., & Aiello, A. (2013). The need for early mental health intervention to strengthen resilience in street-involved youth. In S. Gaetz, B. O'Grady, K. Buccieri, J. Karabanow, & A. Marsolais (Eds.), *Youth homelessness in Canada: Implications for policy and practice* (pp. 229–242). Toronto: Canadian Homelessness Research Network Press.

National Audit Office. (2005). *More than a roof: Progress in tackling homelessness*. London: National Audit Office.

Northern Irish Housing Executive. (2012). *Homelessness strategy for Northern Ireland 2012–2017*. Belfast: Northern Irish Housing Executive.

Patterson, M., Moniruzzaman, A., Frankish, C. J., & Somers, J. (2012) Missed opportunities: Childhood learning disabilities as early indicators of risk among homeless adults with mental illness in Vancouver, British Columbia. *BMJ Open, 2*(6). doi:10.1136/bmjopen-2012-001586

Pawson, H., Netto, G., Jones, C., Wager, F., Fancy, C., & Lomax, D. (2007). *Evaluating homelessness prevention*. London: Communities and Local Government.

Quilgars, D. (2010). Youth homelessness. In E. O'Sullivan, V. Busch-Geertsema, D. Quilgars, & N. Pleace (Eds.), *Homeless research in Europe*. Brussels: FEANTSA.

Quilgars, D., Fitzpatrick, S., & Pleace, N. (2011). *Ending youth homelessness: Possibilities, challenges and pratical solutions*. London: Centrepoint.

Quilgars, D., Johnsen, S., & Pleace, N. (2008). *Youth homelessness in the UK: A decade of progress?* York: Joseph Rowntree Foundation.

Ravenshill, M. (2008). *The culture of homelessness*. Altershot: Ashgate.

Reeve, K., & Batty, E. (2011). *The hidden truth about homelessness: Experience of single homelessness in England*. London: Crisis.

Reeve, K., & Casey, R. (2006). *Homeless women: Still being failed yet striving to survive*. London: Crisis.

Scottish Government. (2013). *Operation of the homeless persons legislation in Scotland 2012–2013*. Edinburgh: Scottish Government.

Scottish Government. (2014). *Youth homelessness analysis 2013–2014*. Edinburgh: Scottish Government.

St Mungo's Broadway. (2014). *Street to home, CHAIN annual report, 1st April 2013–31st March 2014*. London: St Mungo's Broadway. Retrieved from www.mungos.org/documents/15617

Stone, J., Berrington, A., & Falkingham, J. (2014). Gender, turning points and boomerangs: Returning home in young adulthood in Great Britain. *Demography, 51*(1), 257–276.

Thomson, R. (2009). Transitions to adulthood. In W. Taylor, R. Earle, & R. Hester (Eds.), *Youth justice handbook: Theory, policy and practice* (pp. 23–33). Oxon: Routledge.

Weber Sikich, K. (2008). Global female homelessness: A multi-faceted problem. *Gender Issues, 25*(3), 147–156.

Welsh Government. (2016). *National rough sleeper count, November 2015—Experimental statistics—Revised* (SDR 13/2016). Cardiff: Welsh Government.

About the Author

Anna Clarke is a Senior Research Associate at the Cambridge Centre for Housing and Planning Research, within the University of Cambridge (www.cchpr.landecon.cam.ac.uk), where she has worked since 2004. Her research interests include housing need, homelessness, demand for social housing and low cost home ownership, worklessness and a growing area of work around welfare reform. She has published work for a wide variety of funders including the UK government, the National Housing Federation, Shelter, Centrepoint and the Joseph Rowntree Foundation.

Minority Embeddedness and Economic Integration: Is Diversity or Homogeneity Associated with Better Employment Outcomes?

Neli Demireva [1,*] and Anthony Heath [2]

[1] Department of Sociology, University of Essex, Colchester, CO4 3SQ, UK; E-Mail: nvdem@essex.ac.uk
[2] Nuffield College, University of Oxford, Oxford, OX1 3UQ, UK; E-Mail: anthony.heath@nuffield.ox.ac.uk

* Corresponding author

Abstract
Using data from the Managing Cultural Diversity Survey 2010 and the Ethnic Minority British Election Study 2010, we explore the activity and employment outcomes of majority and minority individuals in the UK, and examine their association with a variety of ethnic embeddedness measures. We do not find that white British respondents living in areas of high deprivation and diversity experience lower levels of economic activity or bad jobs. Deprivation rather than minority embeddedness stands out as the factor that serves to compound both majority and minority disadvantage. In the case of minorities, embeddedness does have some negative effects, although these are greatly attenuated once one takes into account the level of area deprivation.

Keywords
activity; employment; occupational attainment; migrants; minorities

Issue
This article is part of the issue "International Migration and Ethnic Integration", edited by Yaojun Li (University of Manchester, UK) and Anthony Heath (University of Oxford, UK).

1. Introduction

Recent attempts to quantify social inclusion in Europe have been focusing almost exclusively on the rates of activity and employment among migrants and their offspring (Kahanec, 2013). Policy makers have been widely supportive of this pragmatic approach. In a world facing a number of shortages, be it jobs or housing, continuing migrant dependency on the state rather than contribution has the potential to upset the social status quo, to unnerve a majority population concerned with falling standards of living and to undermine the social pact that provides support for welfare regimes in particular, and democracies in general. Furthermore, many politicians remain sceptical of selective acculturation, multiculturalism and a strong reliance upon the co-ethnic community (Cameron, 2013), and often question whether migrants and minorities can prosper under scenarios where minorities remain apart from the mainstream and live 'parallel lives'. In the context of the UK, the impact of migrants on employment prospects featured significantly in the debates surrounding Brexit and are an indispensable part of any immigration speech (Cameron, 2011; May, 2012). In contrast to this popular sentiment of escalating fears, the academic stance has been that migrants contribute to the system rather than undermine it—they usually have better health outcomes than the average Briton, pay more in taxes and do not really compete for jobs with the majority (Dustmann & Frattini, 2014).

Whereas this optimistic picture of migration can very well hold for the aggregate, different commentators have argued that it obscures the dire state of traditional working class white communities exposed to 'unbridled' diversity and the acute competition for resources in places which 'have been left behind'; that is to say, the ones that lack the structural means to weather profound changes (Casey, 2016; Goodhart, 2013).

Using data from the Managing Cultural Diversity Survey 2010 and the Ethnic Minority British Election Study 2010, we explore the activity and employment outcomes of majority and minority individuals in the UK, and examine their association with a variety of measures of community embeddedness. We do not find that white British respondents living in areas of high diversity experience lower levels of economic activity or bad jobs. Quite the contrary, they appear to benefit in such scenarios. Deprivation rather than percent migrant and minority in the local area stands out as the factor that serves to compound both majority and minority disadvantage.

2. The Impact of Minority Embeddedness and Deprivation

This paper focuses on the economic prospects of the white British, and migrants and minorities, accounting for their embeddedness in local communities. In order to do so, we take into consideration not only individual characteristics but characteristics of the local areas as well such as deprivation, degree of urbanization and level of minority embeddedness. We interpret minority embeddedness as the share of migrants and minorities present in the local area. The greater the share, the greater the minority embeddedness. Effectively, we consider the distinction between the white British on the one hand and on the other hand individuals who are 'outgroupers'; that is to say, the latter belong to an ethnic group other than white British. In this way, we argue that the paper is able to capture a fundamental distinction at the community level between the white British majority and a range of minority groups (comprising of migrants and the second generation); we can consequently comment on the overall implications of ethnic concentration and diversity both on minorities themselves and on their white British neighbours. However, we acknowledge that our sample sizes are not sufficiently large to permit a fine-grained analysis of specific local conflicts between particular ethnic groups and the white majority.

2.1. White British

Minority embeddedness for the majority group essentially entails more diversity (Abascal & Baldassarri, 2015). The literature on this association has focused on social trust rather than economic outcomes, but for a few exceptions. Dustmann, Frattini and Preston (2013), Dustmann, Frattini and Halls (2010) and Manacorda, Manning and Wadsworth (2012) show that regional migration flows hardly affect the mean wage; however, there are indications that majority members positioned at the lower end of the majority wage distribution are adversely impacted by incoming migrants who create a surplus in the economy by virtue of having greater human capital than the majority population while being ready to settle for unskilled jobs. In other words, low-skilled majority members are possibly worse off due to migration.

One thing to point out is that, unlike the research on social trust, these studies focus on the consequences of migration rather than on the consequences of diversity, and explore regional differences rather than local area variation. In this paper, we have chosen to align ourselves more closely with the postulates of conflict theory, which suggest that as societies diversify, there is growing competition for resources which brings about tensions between the majority groups, migrants and their descendants (Putnam, 2007). Our focus is on local communities. Conflict can be expected to be greater in deprived areas—the fewer the resources to be redistributed, the greater the competition. The literature from the US finds some support for these ideas (Alesina & La Ferrara, 2002; Putnam, 2007); however, the data from the UK suggests a much more moderate effect of diversity which usually disappears once controls for deprivation and economic competition are introduced at the community level (Demireva & Heath, 2014; Laurence, 2011; Laurence & Heath, 2008; Letki, 2008; Sturgis, Brunton-Smith, Read, & Allum, 2011). It appears that, at least in Britain, it is deprivation that undermines the social glue rather than diversity.

In this paper, we argue that similarly to social trust, the economic prospects of individuals merit greater attention. Some authors speculate that with growing diversity there might be greater competition for jobs (Reyneri & Fullin, 2011). Under such conditions, it is not only the wages of majority members that can be undercut. It is possible that their labour market activity as well as the opportunity to achieve a higher status job is threatened. Other scholars insist that migrants and the majority occupy different economic niches and that this occupational segregation can extend to the second generation as well (Dustmann & Frattini, 2014). If the latter is true the activity and employment status of the white British should be unaffected by diversity. This association can be of particular interest to policy makers who are concerned with the levels of unemployment both among majority and minority members, and the possible burden on the welfare system (Cameron, 2011).

If minority embeddedness induces greater competition for jobs, we would expect that:

> Hypothesis 1: As diversity increases, the employment probability of white British respondents will decrease. If migrants and minorities are rewarded proportionately to their human capital, there will be greater competition for high status jobs since migrants in general have higher levels of human capital than white British individuals (Dustmann et al., 2013); and the second generation has surpassed the majority in terms of educational attainment (Heath & Brinbaum, 2007).

Yet, it is possible that diversity just captures the selective sorting of individuals—white British individuals with poorer economic prospects concentrate into more deprived areas that happen to be also more diverse. Thus:

> Hypothesis 2: Deprivation rather than levels of diversity will account for the deterioration in the economic

prospects of the white British. It is also likely that diversity does not increase competition in all areas but only in the poorly resourced ones. That is to say, in areas experiencing economic strain, diversity will be associated with the exacerbation of conflict. In this case, we will observe a significant interaction effect between deprivation and diversity.

2.2. Migrants and Minorities

The question of whether it is possible for migrants and minorities to achieve upward social mobility while being embedded in communities of co-ethnics and pan-ethnics has been a long standing concern for migration scholars and policy makers. Notably, segmented assimilation theory postulates that some immigrants (Portes & Rumbaut, 2001; Portes & Zhou, 1993) may never catch up in terms of earnings with the white middle class, acculturating into the poor, underdeveloped segment of the receiving society (Zhou, 1994); while for others strong ethnic community may nevertheless lead to economic advancement.

Providing a consistent empirical test for segmented assimilation has proved difficult. Segmented assimilation places a focus on the second generation and their chances of occupational mobility (Zhou, 1994). Yet, it is in the first generation that the impact of ethnic embeddedness can be particularly strong: migrants who have little knowledge about institutions in the receiving society can be greatly helped by the existence of co-ethnic organizations that facilitate the first contact with majority employers (Waters, 1999). Important jobs can exist in ethnic economies that minimize unemployment spells (Alba & Nee, 1997). In contrast, other scholars argue that over time, for women, and in the second generation, this positive impact can attenuate and even disappear (Koopmans, 2015). Women with little access to the mainstream society can be encouraged to observe strict social norms and withdraw from the labour market; reservation wages for the second generation individuals with strong co-ethnic ties can be high, leading to higher levels of unemployment. Ultimately, the quality of jobs in the ethnic economy (similarly if these have been obtained through ethnic networks) can be poor; thus, creating the opportunity for stickiness of low status outcomes across generations. Policy makers are particularly suspicious of growing minority embeddedness, usually interpreting it as refusal to embrace integration (Cameron, 2011). Such segregation from the mainstream society is often brought up as a possible explanation for the poor employment prospects of South Asian Muslim communities in Britain (Phillips, 2005).

If these pessimistic predictions hold:

Hypothesis 3: We will observe a negative association between levels of minority embeddedness and the employment prospects of migrant and minority members.

Hypothesis 4: If however, occupying migrant/minority niches reflects on a number of selective processes and constraints (apart from preferred proximity to family and co-ethnic support networks) such as the availability of cheap housing at the point of migration, when we control for deprivation, this association will disappear.

Thus, we will argue that if migrant and minority individuals (Fryer, Pager, & Spenkuch, 2011) are concentrated in disadvantaged neighbourhoods and regions—the ones with greater economic volatility, unemployment, and bad jobs—leaving behind poor employment prospects can prove near impossible. Local area deprivation can impact both the pool of available jobs as well as the information transmitted about openings (Cutler, Glaeser, & Vigdor, 1997).

Several studies provide an examination of segmented economic assimilation with UK data. Using UKLFS 1992–2009, Patacchini and Zenou (2012) find some support for a positive association of local social interaction between people of the same ethnicity which is significant for Bangladeshi and Chinese workers, but not for Pakistanis or Indians. These associations are strongest for the most recent arrivals. Feng, Flowerdew and Feng (2015) establish that the ethnic penalty associated with the risk of becoming unemployed and the probability of finding employment is partly explained by geographical deprivation. Ethnic diversity helped women to retain employment but did not affect men. Deprivation partially explained the ethnic minority disadvantage in the English labour market. This research was based on the ONS Longitudinal Study (1991–2001). These studies demonstrate the need for a more comprehensive investigation of local area embeddedness and for a distinction between majority and minority populations; and the present paper aims to fill this important gap.

2.3. Data and Methods

In order to test our hypothesis, we need data for both majority and migrant and minority members. This study makes use of two major datasets with comparable questionnaire structures designed to measure a range of economic, social and political outcomes. Both were administered in 2010. The first is the Managing Cultural Diversity Survey (MCDS). This survey was a random location quota sample of 1650 individuals: 864 white British respondents; and through an ethnic minority booster sample, 786 minority individuals.[1] The second dataset is the 2010 Ethnic Minority British Election Study (EMBES) which focuses only on minority respondents. We would have liked to be able to use the British Election Study 2010 for our majority sample; however, this survey does not ask about the activity and occupational status of respondents. The EMBES was a random probability sample that covers the major ethnic minority groups in the UK with

[1] Of the 1666 respondents, there were 5 missing values for the variable age. All retired respondents and students have been excluded.

a sample of 2782 minority individuals. Thus, while the first dataset allows us to compare white British individuals with migrant and minority ones, the second brings us closer to understanding the differences between minority groups. The minority sample in MCDS is small and does not allow for a fine distinction between migrant and minority groups; yet, we achieve this with EMBES.

2.4. Geographical Units

A frequent criticism of diversity studies, such as that of Putnam (2007), is that they employ area units of analysis that vary greatly in size and, therefore, in their potential diversity mix, and are thus incomparable (Dawkins, 2008). The MCDS uses Middle Super Output Areas (MSOAs: minimum number of households 2000, maximum 6000) as the primary sampling unit while the EMBES sample uses Lower Super Output Areas (LSOAs: minimum number of households 400, maximum 1200). Compared to wards, MSOAs and LSOAs are felt to be more appropriate for this analysis due to the fact that wards differ greatly in size. We are also better placed to capture economic local area effects along the lines of ethnic niches through MSOAs and LSOAs rather than regions. We acknowledge however the difference in size between the two geographical units and the difficulties this may present for the analysis. However, the use of two datasets, bearing in mind their constraints, allows us to cross-check our results; and in this way yields the analysis to spatial sensitivity. The MCDS sampled 200 areas with the average of 7.95 respondents per unit. The EMBES sample consists of data points spread across 582 LSOAs with the average size of the cluster being 5.5 individuals.

2.5. Dependent Variables

We distinguish between several outcomes which reflect the economic prospects of individuals: the probability of being active (excluding retired respondents and students) and the probability of being employed, which are standard measures of labour market engagement (Van Tubergen, Maas, & Flap, 2004). To this, we add a measure of occupational status which reflects on the mobility prospects of individuals (Heath & Yu, 2005). Unfortunately, the measure of wage remuneration is imprecise, with lots of non-response, in both datasets. In addition, in MCDS, the occupational status variables captures occupational status of current or any job that the respondent has held, with those that have never held a job excluded; while in EMBES, the measure refers to the status of the current position of the respondent.

2.6. Independent Variables

2.6.1. Demographics

2.6.6.1. Ethnic Group

The UK studies on minority embeddedness highlight the necessity of distinguishing between the outcomes of different ethnic groups (Patacchini & Zenou, 2012). We distinguish between the outcomes of the majority and four minority groupings with MCDS data: Black Caribbeans and Black Africans, Indians, Pakistani and Bangladeshis and other respondents. With EMBES data, we can draw a more detailed distinction between minority groups. Unfortunately, however, EMBES has poor coverage of other white respondents, which we acknowledge as a limitation of the data.

We know from previous research that *age*, *gender* and *generational status* (Lessard-Phillips, 2015; Luthra, Platt, & Salamońska, 2014) have profound effects upon the opportunities and constraints faced by migrant and minority groups, with South Asian minority women experiencing lower levels of activity and second generation members usually hypothesized to have similar outcomes to the majority. Our EMBES data would allow us to closely examine generational patterns.

At the individual level we distinguish between *co-ethnic organizations* and *co-ethnic friends* which have been shown to be very important as they reflect on the bridging and bonding opportunities of individuals (Demireva & Heath, 2014; Heath & Demireva, 2014; Lancee, 2012).

2.6.2. Minority Embeddedness

We operationalize minority embeddedness at the local area level as the percentage of non-white British, thus drawing distinction to the exposure of minorities to the majority population and vice versa.[2]

2.6.3. Deprivation

The possible negative effect of socio-economic disadvantage will also be examined through looking at the Index of Multiple Deprivation (IMD)—economic cleavages are strong predictors of societal disintegration and may signal higher rates of competition (Laurence, 2011; Sturgis et al., 2011). We use IMD 2010 which is an official measure of small areas. It is based on seven domains: income, employment, education, skills and training, health, crime, barriers to housing and services, and living environment deprivation (for information on its range, see the Appendix).

[2] We have replicated the results with percentage of co-ethnics as well. Full tables are available upon request.

2.6.4. Other Individual Level Factors

Qualifications are at the heart of the human capital framework (Heath & Yu, 2005). We introduce them in our last model because we want to compare their explanatory power with that of community level predictors. Thus, community level measures can hold an important place in the aggregate but individual selection along the propositions of the human capital framework can be a much more powerful predictor of disadvantage. Social housing has been shown to significantly lower the odds of different ethnic groups in terms of trust and engagement (Demireva & Heath, 2014); and religiosity can potentially tap important cultural differences (Koopmans, 2015). With the MCDS data we can also control for factors such as residential stability and degree of urbanization.

2.6.5. Models

Our response variables are dichotomous; therefore we use the logit link:

Pr(economic integration outcome = 1) = β_0 + βage + βgender + βmarital status + βethnic group (in minority models) + βgeneration (in minority models) [Model 0] + βpercent non-white British [Model 1] + βco-ethnic bonding [Model 2] + βlnIMD [Model 3] + βreligiosity + βeducation + degree of residential stability [Model 4]

We also have models with degree of urbanization and tenure and those are available upon request.

2.6.6. Interpretation of Effects

We use average marginal effects, computed at different values of the X variables. This allows us to interpret the results intuitively as percentage point differences and provides a basis for comparison between different coefficients.

3. Descriptive Statistics

Several clear patterns emerge from the descriptive Tables 1 and 2. As is well-known, minorities are much more likely than the white British to live in diverse areas. Thus on average white British respondents in MCDS live in relatively homogeneous areas (containing on average 22 percent minorities) whereas minority respondents are much more likely to live in diverse areas: Pakistanis and Bangladeshis for example live in areas where roughly 50 percent of residents belong to a minority group. Pakistanis and Bangladeshis also live in areas with the highest scores on the index of multiple deprivation. However it is important to note that not all spatially concentrated minority groups reside in very deprived areas. Indians, who live in areas with a relatively high presence of minorities, nevertheless experience less local area deprivation than the black or other South Asian groups. However, if we zoom in on the most deprived areas (those above the 75th percentile of deprivation), we see that the levels of minority presence jump for all groups—for example, white British respondents who live in these most deprived areas are much more likely to have minority neighbours (the percentage of minorities in their area rising from 22 to 36 percent). These patterns highlight the importance of conditioning on deprivation when analysing the effect of minority embeddedness.

The ethnic groups differ not only in regards to the areas in which they live but also in terms of their individual characteristics as well. In general, minority respondents in our data are younger than their white British counterparts, especially the combined Pakistani/Bangladeshi group. Minorities on average appear better educated (higher percentages with degrees) than the white British.[3] In the EMBES data, Black Africans and Indians are among the most educated respondents; almost half of the respondents in these two groups have a de-

Table 1. Demographic, socio-economic, and community characteristics by ethnic group. Source: MCDS (2010); 298 retired and 113 in full time education respondents excluded from working age sample of 1666.

Ethnicity	Mean Prop Non-white Brit	Mean Prop non-white Brit at high deprivation	Mean IMD	Education Degree	Co-ethnic Organization	Co-ethnic Friends	Married	Mean Prop Co-ethnic	N
White British	0.22	0.36	2.85	35.65	42.71	5.32	57.41	0.78	625
Black Caribbean and African	0.47	0.49	3.29	42.66	10.49	24.48	37.06	0.07	127
Indian	0.54	0.49	2.99	60.12	12.27	20.25	63.8	0.18	155
Pakistani and Bangladeshi	0.54	0.61	3.43	44.06	10.49	16.08	66.43	0.17	139
Other	0.43	0.55	2.96	50.45	13.06	35.61	56.68	0.05	306
Total									1,255

[3] It is possible that having Pakistanis and Bangladeshis in a joint group in the MCDS masks the disadvantaged position of Bangladeshis in this respect. In comparison, the proportion of Bangladeshi with a degree in the EMBES sample is 0.22 well below the 0.29 for white British.

Table 2. Demographic, socio-economic, and community characteristics by ethnic group. Source: EMBES (2010); 238 retired and 277 in full time respondents were excluded from sample of working age population of 2753.

Ethnicity	Mean Prop Non-white Brit	Mean Prop non-white Brit at high deprivation	Mean IMD	Education Degree	Co-ethnic Organization	Co-ethnic Friends	Married	Social Housing	2nd Generation	Mean Prop co-ethnic	N
Black Caribbean	0.34	0.42	4.22	28.81	29.90	42.04	33.33	37.52	56.28	0.08	500
Black African	0.36	0.43	4.31	49.81	33.79	47.52	40.27	48.47	13.55	0.07	505
Indian	0.39	0.55	3.97	49.15	41.70	46.76	65.70	8.19	32.08	0.16	513
Pakistani	0.47	0.60	4.34	32.34	23.41	56.29	66.62	11.98	36.98	0.26	641
Bangladeshi	0.50	0.59	4.39	22.59	26.32	62.59	67.04	43.70	25.93	0.18	257
Other ethnicity	0.33	0.44	4.25	20.56	8.41	21.50	27.10	51.4	71.03	0.08	98
Total											2238

gree. Social housing, which is closely related to deprivation is high among Black Africans and Bangladeshis whereas the proportion of social renters among Indians is rather small.

4. Multivariate Analysis

Tables 3, 4 and 5 present logistic regression results on the likelihood of achieving economic integration. In each table we show the results for three sets of model, one set looking at rates of economic activity, the second set looking at the probability of employment (among those who are economically active), and the third set looking at the probability of achieving a professional or managerial position. We first introduce the potentially 'confounding' variables of age, gender and marital status (and the ethnic minority groups and generation in the models confined to minorities in Tables 4 and 5). We then introduce a measure of minority embeddedness (the percentage in the area who are not white British) in order to provide a first test of Hypotheses 1 and 3. To this we add two further measures of embeddedness—membership of a co-ethnic organization and of co-ethnic friends—in order to provide a more nuanced test: arguably minority embeddedness at the local area level, as measured by the percentage non-white British, represents just an opportunity for contact rather than established networks. These measures of co-ethnic friends and organizations provide a more direct test of theories of embeddedness.

The next stage is to introduce our measure of area deprivation in order to test hypotheses 2 and 4. Finally we include further predictors (educational level, and residential stability) which might be, to varying extents, endogenous to our key concepts of embeddedness and area deprivation. Thus growing up in a deprived area may limit one's educational opportunities. Tables 3 and 4 are based on the MCDS data, and enable us to compare patterns for ethnic minority and white British respondents. Table 5 is based on the EMBES data and is restricted to ethnic minority respondents only.

Table 3 uses the MCDS data to look at the patterns among white British respondents, thus enabling us to test Hypotheses 1 and 2.

Model 1 introduces the measure of the percentage non-white British in the area, which provides us with our first test of Hypothesis 1. This measure has no significant effect whatsoever on the economic activity or employment chances of the white British, and surprisingly has a significant positive effect on white British occupational chances. Furthermore, the more nuanced measures of co-ethnic organization and friends in model 2 also prove to be non-significant in the case of economic activity and employment chances, although they have contradictory effects (which will tend to cancel out) in the case of occupational attainment.

These results thus rather conclusively lead us to reject Hypothesis 1: the presence of minorities does not harm the employment patterns and prospects of the white British. If anything the reverse is the case especially in terms of occupational attainment with this positive association stronger controlling for deprivation.[4]

Moving on to our test of Hypothesis 2 with model 3, we find that area deprivation impacts negatively on the chances of the white British being economically active, gaining employment and securing higher-level jobs. Model 4 shows that educational level has the expected

[4] Full tables with interaction effects available upon request.

strong and positive effects on all three outcomes, and that it also partially explains the effects of area deprivation. (This could be due either to negative selection of less educated individuals into deprived areas, or it might be that living in a deprived area lowers educational attainment. Both processes may well occur but we cannot disentangle their importance from cross-sectional data such as we are using here). Nevertheless, the effect of area deprivation remains significant and negative for all three outcomes among white British respondents. This thus provides strong support for Hypothesis 2, namely that it is deprivation rather than diversity which accounts for any white British disadvantage, at least with respect to economic activity and employment chances.

In Table 4 we then use the MCDS dataset to explore the effects of embeddedness and area deprivation on the economic outcomes of ethnic minorities. First we find some significant differences between minorities, with the Black and combined Pakistani/Bangladeshi groups having lower rates of economic activity, employment and occupational attainment than the Indian group. This is consistent with previous research using other sources. We also find that age, gender and marital status work in the same was as they did for the white British in Table 3, although among minorities the effect of gender on economic activity is much stronger, while the age effects are relatively small. This raises some interesting questions for future research about minority career progression.

Moving on to the test of Hypothesis 3, we find that, unlike the situation among the white British, minority embeddedness does indeed have significant negative effects on economic activity, supporting Hypothesis 3, although not on the other two outcomes. Moreover, the more nuanced measures of embeddedness (at the individual level) in model 3 do not in general have the anticipated mediating role, except in the case of occupational attainment. The sign of the association differs in MCDS and EMBES but we are inclined to go with the much larger and richer sample of EMBES. The positive association with friends in MCDS could be due to the fact that the measure of occupational attainment captures the status of any job of the respondent and co-ethnic friends are perhaps important for holding a good job over the life time of the individual. Area deprivation does have the expected negative effect on economic activity and employment chances, supporting Hypothesis 4. In model 4 this effect turns out to be largely mediated by level of education, which, as in the case of the white British, is one of the most powerful predictors of occupational attainment.

In Table 5 we then check these results for ethnic minorities using the larger EMBES dataset, which also enables us to make finer differentiations between the minority groups. As with the MCDS data, models 2 supports the hypothesis that minority embeddedness has negative implications for economic activity; in the EMBES data embeddedness also has negative effects on employment and occupational chances, providing greater support for Hypothesis 3. However, area deprivation in model 4 proves to have large and significant negative effects, and substantially reduces the estimated effect of embeddedness for all three outcomes. Indeed embeddedness remains significant only for the chances of employment. The other interesting finding from EMBES is that co-ethnic friends tend to have a negative effect on economic outcomes whereas co-ethnic organizations tend to have either a positive or a non-significant effect.

The latter result is in line with the research of Lancee (2012). Thus, informal bonding with co-ethnics is associated with lower chance of getting the really good jobs, in contrast with bridging social capital which involves ties with members of the mainstream. Note that the survey was administered however at the end of the economic crisis in the UK when perhaps minority contacts were particularly weakened. In contrast, formal bonding with co-ethnics through organizational participation seems to have if anything a positive effect, perhaps reflecting the additional cognitive and practical skills which organizational membership is believed to foster.

Thus, on the whole, it is the deprivation of the area that appears to be associated with the undermining of the economic prospects of individuals rather than the mere presence of ethnic minorities, supporting Hypothesis 2 and Hypothesis 4. Only in the models restricted to minority members (Tables 4 and 5) do we find that economic outcomes are negatively associated with minority embeddedness. However, these negative effects are attenuated once we take account of area deprivation. Moreover, we do not find that white British respondents living in more deprived areas suffer disproportionately from greater diversity—on the contrary, in such scenarios their occupational attainment prospects improve.

5. Discussion

This paper examines the predictors of economic integration—economic activity, being in employment, and occupational status. Our central focus is a comparison of the effects of ethnic diversity and area deprivation. Do we find that diversity hinders the prospects for both majority and minority groups alike, or is area deprivation the main factor leading to poor economic outcomes? And do these processes operate in the same way for the white British majority group and for ethnic minorities, or do we find that there is an asymmetry in the patterns?

While the results from the different datasets differ in detail, we also have some rather clear-cut conclusions. First, area deprivation is a major source of poor economic outcomes both for the white British and for ethnic minorities. Secondly, the presence of minorities does not appear to have any harmful effects for the White British—in none of the models in Table 3 were the effects negative. Thirdly, in the case of minorities, embeddedness did prove to have some negative effects although these were attenuated by controls for area deprivation.

Table 3. Labour market outcomes of white British respondents. Source: MCDS (2010).

	Activity				Employment				Occupation			
	Model 1 Coef/se	Model 2 Coef/se	Model 3 Coef/se	Model 4 Coef/se	Model 1 Coef/se	Model 2 Coef/se	Model 3 Coef/se	Model 4 Coef/se	Model 1 Coef/se	Model 2 Coef/se	Model 3 Coef/se	Model 4 Coef/se
lnAge	0.343*** (0.056)	0.340*** (0.057)	0.320*** (0.058)	0.317*** (0.066)	0.113** (0.048)	0.100** (0.050)	0.085* (0.047)	0.086* (0.044)	0.203*** (0.041)	0.194*** (0.040)	0.171*** (0.042)	0.283*** (0.049)
Gender	−0.072* (0.039)	−0.077** (0.039)	−0.084** (0.039)	−0.083** (0.041)	0.078** (0.032)	0.074** (0.030)	0.068** (0.029)	0.068** (0.027)	−0.040 (0.033)	−0.055* (0.033)	−0.058* (0.033)	−0.033 (0.034)
Marital status	0.116** (0.040)	0.110** (0.039)	0.110** (0.039)	0.115** (0.039)	0.070** (0.032)	0.061** (0.031)	0.058* (0.030)	0.058** (0.029)	−0.042 (0.027)	−0.040 (0.026)	−0.034 (0.027)	−0.036 (0.029)
Minority Embeddedness												
Percentage non-white British	0.022 (0.104)	0.064 (0.108)	0.121 (0.106)	−0.047 (0.112)	0.048 (0.077)	0.079 (0.079)	0.104 (0.072)	0.031 (0.065)	0.245** (0.090)	0.383*** (0.092)	0.448*** (0.092)	0.153* (0.091)
Co-ethnic Organization		0.060 (0.046)	0.046 (0.047)	0.003 (0.045)		0.053 (0.036)	0.040 (0.035)	0.017 (0.033)		0.172*** (0.037)	0.160*** (0.036)	0.095** (0.036)
Co-ethnic Friends		−0.052 (0.097)	−0.066 (0.094)	−0.010 (0.087)		−0.055 (0.073)	−0.074 (0.077)	−0.045 (0.067)		−0.135** (0.051)	−0.129** (0.050)	−0.064 (0.067)
Deprivation												
lnimd			−0.103** (0.032)	−0.071** (0.032)			−0.052** (0.024)	−0.038* (0.021)			−0.105*** (0.024)	−0.042* (0.024)
Secondary (ref: Basic)				0.244*** (0.066)				0.132*** (0.036)				0.246*** (0.061)
Tertiary				0.362*** (0.058)				0.161*** (0.042)				0.611*** (0.054)
Residential Stability				−0.007 (0.025)				−0.009 (0.017)				−0.039** (0.017)
N	625	625	625	625	466	466	466	466	864	864	864	864

Notes: * $p < 0.10$; ** $p < 0.05$, *** $p < 0.01$; Results are explained as Marginal effects; The models of Active exclude retired respondents whose proportions is high among minority member; the employment and occupational models focus only on the Active population.

Table 4. Labour market outcomes of minority respondents. Source: MCDS (2010).

	Activity				Employment				Occupation			
	Model 1 Coef/se	Model 2 Coef/se	Model 3 Coef/se	Model 4 Coef/se	Model 1 Coef/se	Model 2 Coef/se	Model 3 Coef/se	Model 4 Coef/se	Model 1 Coef/se	Model 2 Coef/se	Model 3 Coef/se	Model 4 Coef/se
lnAge	0.361*** (0.068)	0.361*** (0.068)	0.367*** (0.068)	0.368*** (0.068)	0.045 (0.050)	0.048 (0.049)	0.057 (0.047)	0.074* (0.043)	0.163*** (0.049)	0.158** (0.048)	0.156** (0.049)	0.169** (0.052)
Gender	−0.281*** (0.036)	−0.280*** (0.036)	−0.281*** (0.037)	−0.277*** (0.038)	−0.056** (0.025)	−0.055** (0.025)	−0.051** (0.024)	−0.046** (0.023)	−0.044 (0.033)	−0.048 (0.033)	−0.048 (0.033)	−0.022 (0.030)
Marital status	0.077* (0.042)	0.075* (0.042)	0.074* (0.042)	0.074* (0.043)	0.051* (0.028)	0.049* (0.028)	0.044* (0.026)	0.036 (0.025)	0.012 (0.031)	0.014 (0.031)	0.016 (0.031)	0.023 (0.029)
Minority Embeddedness												
Percentage non-white British	−0.327*** (0.096)	−0.332*** (0.098)	−0.257** (0.099)	−0.243** (0.100)	−0.100 (0.062)	−0.107* (0.062)	−0.051 (0.059)	−0.053 (0.060)	−0.125 (0.080)	−0.111 (0.080)	−0.059 (0.092)	−0.019 (0.075)
Co-ethnic Organization		0.044 (0.060)	0.040 (0.061)	0.046 (0.059)		0.005 (0.041)	0.007 (0.040)	0.002 (0.040)		−0.045 (0.046)	−0.045 (0.047)	−0.048 (0.041)
Co-ethnic Friends		−0.012 (0.052)	−0.010 (0.051)	−0.019 (0.052)		−0.043 (0.037)	−0.046 (0.036)	−0.048 (0.035)		0.105** (0.040)	0.106** (0.040)	0.098** (0.038)
Deprivation												
lnimd			−0.062* (0.036)	−0.043 (0.037)			−0.051** (0.025)	−0.043* (0.026)			−0.041 (0.028)	−0.010 (0.023)
Secondary (ref: Basic)				0.159** (0.060)				0.046 (0.031)				0.114 (0.087)
Tertiary				0.286*** (0.061)				0.065* (0.036)				0.407*** (0.064)
Residential Stability				0.025 (0.022)				−0.011 (0.014)				−0.003 (0.018)
N	727	727	727	727	466	466	466	466	786	786	786	786

Notes: * $p < 0.10$; ** $p < 0.05$, *** $p < 0.01$; Results are explained as Marginal effects; The models of Active exclude retired respondents whose proportions is high among minority member; the employment and occupational models focus only on the Active population, controls also for ethnic group and generation.

Table 5. Labour market outcomes of minority respondents. Source: EMBES (2010).

	Activity				Employment				Occupation			
	Model 1	Model 2	Model 3	Model 4	Model 1	Model 2	Model 3	Model 4	Model 1	Model 2	Model 3	Model 4
LnAge	0.281*** (0.039)	0.285*** (0.040)	0.281*** (0.040)	0.289*** (0.040)	0.048 (0.042)	0.043 (0.042)	0.035 (0.041)	0.026 (0.040)	0.055 (0.058)	0.059 (0.058)	0.040 (0.059)	0.014 (0.063)
Gender	−0.243*** (0.020)	−0.241*** (0.020)	−0.240*** (0.020)	−0.231*** (0.020)	−0.049** (0.020)	−0.049** (0.020)	−0.048** (0.020)	−0.047** (0.019)	0.084** (0.027)	0.086** (0.028)	0.086** (0.028)	0.103*** (0.030)
Marital status	0.038* (0.020)	0.038* (0.020)	0.038* (0.020)	0.044** (0.020)	−0.008 (0.019)	−0.005 (0.019)	−0.007 (0.018)	0.001 (0.018)	0.026 (0.026)	0.025 (0.026)	0.024 (0.026)	0.044 (0.027)
Generation												
1st+ citizen (ref:1st)	−0.014 (0.030)	−0.021 (0.030)	−0.019 (0.030)	0.004 (0.030)	0.010 (0.031)	0.009 (0.031)	0.010 (0.030)	0.024 (0.029)	−0.156*** (0.037)	−0.154*** (0.037)	−0.151*** (0.038)	−0.108** (0.041)
1.5	−0.025 (0.035)	−0.033 (0.035)	−0.032 (0.035)	−0.019 (0.035)	0.032 (0.034)	0.030 (0.034)	0.027 (0.034)	0.040 (0.032)	−0.061 (0.047)	−0.061 (0.047)	−0.065 (0.047)	−0.001 (0.053)
2nd	0.094*** (0.027)	0.084** (0.027)	0.084** (0.027)	0.086** (0.028)	0.022 (0.031)	0.018 (0.031)	0.016 (0.031)	0.022 (0.030)	−0.006 (0.042)	−0.010 (0.043)	−0.014 (0.043)	0.020 (0.046)
Minority Embeddedness												
Proportion Non-white British	−0.082* (0.042)	−0.066 (0.042)	−0.024 (0.045)	−0.007 (0.046)	−0.161*** (0.043)	−0.153*** (0.042)	−0.098** (0.044)	−0.086** (0.043)	−0.128** (0.065)	−0.114* (0.066)	−0.034 (0.070)	0.029 (0.076)
Co-ethnic Organization		0.047** (0.020)	0.046** (0.020)	0.042** (0.021)		0.015 (0.022)	0.016 (0.022)	0.007 (0.022)		−0.030 (0.030)	−0.029 (0.031)	−0.033 (0.033)
Co-ethnic Friends		−0.035* (0.019)	−0.033* (0.019)	−0.025 (0.019)		−0.005 (0.018)	−0.004 (0.018)	−0.002 (0.018)		−0.075** (0.026)	−0.076** (0.026)	−0.070** (0.028)
Deprivation												
LnIMD			−0.058** (0.023)	−0.042* (0.023)			−0.078** (0.029)	−0.056** (0.028)			−0.081** (0.026)	−0.047* (0.026)
Secondary (ref: Basic)				0.158*** (0.036)				0.071** (0.036)				−0.171** (0.069)
Tertiary				0.249*** (0.032)				0.197*** (0.036)				0.284*** (0.067)
N	2485	2485	2485	2485	1707	1695	1695	1695	1344	1337	1337	1337

Notes: * $p < 0.10$; ** $p < 0.05$, *** $p < 0.01$; Results are explained as Marginal effects; The models of Active exclude retired respondents whose proportions is high among minority member; the employment and occupational models focus only on the Active population: controls also for ethnic group and generation.

Concerns about the effects of competition from minorities on the economic fortunes of the White British do not therefore receive any support from our data. In contrast concerns about ethnic embeddedness appear not to be wholly without foundation. This is in line with recent research by Zuccotti and Platt (2016) who, using linked census data, show that growing up in areas of high minority embeddedness leads to lower levels of economic activity subsequently. They interpret this as due to the preservation of traditional gender norms and roles in homogeneous minority communities. This argument has considerable plausibility, although we note that, in our data, area deprivation attenuates these negative effects of minority embeddedness. This suggests that it may be the lack of alternative opportunities that may provide the conditions for traditional norms to be perpetuated. We suggest that policy-makers should concentrate on providing greater opportunities for people, white British and minority alike, who live in deprived communities.

Acknowledgments

We want to thank the Leverhulme Trust for funding the ODP of which team the two authors are members, and the nationally representative survey, Managing Cultural Diversity Study, used in this article. The EMBES 2010 has been funded by the ESRC.This research was made possible thanks to funding from the European Commission: grant number H2020 649255.

Conflict of Interests

The authors declare no conflict of interests.

References

Abascal, M., & Baldassarri, D. (2015). Love thy neighbor? Ethnoracial diversity and trust reexamined. *American Journal of Sociology*, *121*(3), 722–782.

Alba, R., & Nee, V. (1997). Rethinking assimilation theory for a new era of immigration. *International Migration Review*, 826–874.

Alesina, A., & La Ferrara, E. (2002). Who trusts others? *Journal of Public Economics*, *85*(2), 207–234.

Cameron, D. (2011, February 5). Speech at the Munich Security conference. Retrieved from www.number10.gov.uk/news/pms-speech-at-munich-security-conference

Cameron, D. (2013). Speech on immigration and welfare reform. Retrieved from https://www.gov.uk/government/speeches/david-camerons-immigration-speech

Casey, L. (2016). *The Casey Review: A review into opportunity and integration*. London: Department for Communities and Local Government.

Cutler, D. M., Glaeser, E. L., & Vigdor, J. L. (1997). *The rise and decline of the American ghetto*. Retrieved from http://www.nber.org/papers/w5881.pdf

Dawkins, C. J. (2008). Reflections on diversity and social capital: A critique of Robert D. Putnam's "E Pluyibus Unum: Diversity and Community in the Twenty-First Century. The 2006 Johan Skytte Prize Lecture". *Housing Policy Debate*, *19*(1), 208–217.

Demireva, N., & Heath, A. (2014). Diversity and the civic spirit in British neighbourhoods: An investigation with MCDS and EMBES 2010 Data. *Sociology*, *48*(4), 643–663.

Dustmann, C., & Frattini, T. (2014). The fiscal effects of immigration to the UK. *The Economic Journal*, *124*(580), F593–F643. doi:10.1111/ecoj.12181

Dustmann, C., Frattini, T., & Halls, C. (2010). Assessing the fiscal costs and benefits of A8 migration to the UK. *Fiscal Studies*, *31*(1), 1–41.

Dustmann, C., Frattini, T., & Preston, I. P. (2013). The effect of immigration along the distribution of wages. *The Review of Economic Studies*, *80*(1), 145–173.

Feng, X., Flowerdew, R., & Feng, Z. (2015). Does neighbourhood influence ethnic inequalities in economic activity? Findings from the ONS Longitudinal Study. *Journal of Economic Geography*, *15*(1), 169–194.

Fryer Jr, R. G., Pager, D., & Spenkuch, J. L. (2011). *Racial disparities in job finding and offered wages*. Retrieved from http://www.nber.org/papers/w17462.pdf

Goodhart, D. (2013). *The British dream: Successes and failures of post-war immigration*. London: Atlantic.

Heath, A., & Brinbaum, Y. (2007). *Guest editorial: Explaining ethnic inequalities in educational attainment*. London: Sage Publications.

Heath, A., & Demireva, N. (2014). Has multiculturalism failed in Britain? *Ethnic and Racial Studies*, *37*(1), 161–180.

Heath, A., & Yu, S. (2005). Explaining ethnic minority disadvantage. In A. Heath, J. Ermisch, & D. Gallie (Eds.), *Understanding social change* (pp. 187–224). Oxford: Oxford University Press.

Kahanec, M. (2013). Labor mobility in an enlarged European Union. *International Handbook on the Economics of Migration*, 137–152.

Koopmans, R. (2015). Does assimilation work? Sociocultural determinants of labour market participation of European Muslims. *Journal of Ethnic and Migration Studies*, 1–20.

Lancee, B. (2012). The economic returns of bonding and bridging social capital for immigrant men in Germany. *Ethnic and Racial Studies*, *35*(4), 664–683.

Laurence, J. (2011). The effect of ethnic diversity and community disadvantage on social cohesion: A multilevel analysis of social capital and interethnic relations in UK communities. *European Sociological Review*, *27*(1), 70–89. doi:10.1093/Esr/Jcp057

Laurence, J., & Heath, A. (2008). *Predictors of community cohesion: Multi-level modelling of the 2005 Citizneship survey*. Retrieved from http://www.learningandwork.org.uk/lifelonglearninginquiry/docs/CIT0001.pdf?redirectedfrom=niace

Lessard-Phillips, L. (2015). Exploring the dimensionality of ethnic minority adaptation in Britain: An analysis across ethnic and generational lines. *Sociology*. doi:10.1177/0038038515609030

Letki, N. (2008). Does diversity erode social cohesion? Social capital and race in British neighbourhoods. *Political Studies, 56*(1), 99–126.

Luthra, R. R., Platt, L., & Salamońska, J. (2014). *Migrant diversity, migration motivations and early integration: The case of Poles in Germany, the Netherlands, London and Dublin* (LEQS Paper 74). London: London School of Economics and Political Science.

Manacorda, M., Manning, A., & Wadsworth, J. (2012). The impact of immigration on the structure of wages: Theory and evidence from Britain. *Journal of the European Economic Association, 10*(1), 120–151.

May, T. (2012). Home Secretary speech on 'An immigration system that works in the national interest'. Retrieved from https://www.gov.uk/government/speeches/home-secretary-speech-on-an-immigration-system-that-works-in-the-national-interest

Patacchini, E., & Zenou, Y. (2012). Ethnic networks and employment outcomes. *Regional Science and Urban Economics, 42*(6), 938–949.

Phillips, T. (2005). After 7/7: Sleepwalking to segregation. Speech given at the Manchester Council for Community Relations.

Portes, A., & Rumbaut, R. (2001). *Legacies*. Berkeley: University of California Press.

Portes, A., & Zhou, M. (1993). The new 2nd-generation: Segmented assimilation and its variants. *Annals of the American Academy of Political and Social Science, 530*, 74–96.

Putnam, R. D. (2007). E pluribus unum: Diversity and community in the twenty-first century. The 2006 Johan Skytte Prize Lecture. *Scandinavian Political Studies, 30*(2), 137–174.

Reyneri, E., & Fullin, G. (2011). Labour market penalties of new immigrants in new and old receiving West European countries. *International Migration, 49*(1), 31–57.

Sturgis, P., Brunton-Smith, I., Read, S., & Allum, N. (2011). Does ethnic diversity erode trust? Putnam's 'hunkering down' thesis reconsidered. *British Journal of Political Science, 41*, 57–82. doi:10.1017/S0007123410000281

Waters, M. C. (1999). *Black identities: West Indian immigrant dreams and American realities*. New York: Cambridge.

Van Tubergen, F., Maas, I., & Flap, H. D. (2004). The economic incorporation of immigrants in 18 western societies: Origin, destination and community effects. *American Sociological Review, 69*(5), 704–727.

Zhou, M. (1994). Segmented assimilation: Issues, controversies and recent research on the new second generation. In C. Hirschman, J. Dewind, & P. Kasinitz (Eds.), *The handbook of international migration: The American experience* (pp. 196–212). New York: Russell Sage Foundation.

Zuccotti, C. V., & Platt, L. (2016). Does neighbourhood ethnic concentration in early life affect subsequent labour market outcomes? A study across ethnic groups in England and Wales. *Population, Space and Place*. doi:10.1002/psp.2041

About the Authors

Neli Demireva (PhD) is a Senior Lecturer in Sociology at Essex University. Her research interests include migration, inter-ethnic ties, social cohesion, ethnic penalties and multiculturalism. She currently holds a BA grant on "Understanding the Ecology of Disadvantage: Betting Agents, Crime and the British Neighbourhood". From September 2015, she started working on the project: "GEMM: Growth, Equal Opportunities, Migration and Markets" (as part of the Horizon 2020 programme of the European Commission, "EURO-2-2014: The European growth agenda Research and Innovation action 4: Migration, prosperity and growth"). This project addresses the challenges and barriers that European countries face in managing the mobility of persons to realize competitiveness and growth.

Anthony Heath (CBE, FBA) is currently Director of the Centre for Social Investigation, Nuffield College, Oxford and Professor of Sociology at CMIST, University of Manchester. His research interests cover social stratification, ethnic inequalities, national identity and social integration. His recent books include *Unequal Attainments: Ethnic Educational Inequalities in Ten Western Countries* (Proceedings of the British Academy), *Migrants and Their Children: Generational Change in Patterns of Ethnic Minority Integration* (Routledge), *Hard Times: The Divisive Toll of the Economic Slump* (Yale) and *The Political Integration of Ethnic Minorities in Britain* (OUP). He has carried out work for a range of public bodies including OECD, UNDP and a range of government departments in Britain.

10

Participation and Sharing, or Peaceful Co-Existence? Visions of Integration among Muslims in Switzerland

Michael Nollert and Amir Sheikhzadegan *

Department of Social Sciences, University of Fribourg, 1700 Fribourg, Switzerland; E-Mails: michael.nollert@unifr.ch (M.N.), amir.sheikhzadegan@unifr.ch (A.S.)

* Corresponding author

Abstract
At least three traditions in sociological thought address the question of social inclusion. In the systems theory proposed by Luhmann, inclusion means that individuals are able to adapt and gain access to functional subsystems, such as the labor market or the welfare state. In the tradition of Simmel, social inclusion is seen as an outcome of "cross-cutting social circles". Both perspectives are addressed in Lockwood's distinction between social integration and system integration. Building on these theoretical traditions, the study proposes a typology of migrant integration in which inclusion requires a realization of both social and system integration. Against this theoretical background, the paper deals with the question of which kind of integration the Swiss Muslims strive for through civic engagement. Drawing on narrative autobiographical interviews, the study reveals two main tendencies among the studied Muslims. While some seek an opportunity to engage with people of other worldviews through civic engagement (social integration), others limit their civic engagement only to those religious communities that cultivate a strong collective Muslim identity, and reduce their contact with non-Muslims to a peaceful co-existence (system integration). The study also shows that these two attitudes are associated with two views on outgroup tolerance. While the advocates of social integration are for *liberal* tolerance, the supporters of system integration show tendency towards *multicultural* tolerance.

Keywords
coexistence; inclusion; Muslims; participation; segregation; social integration; Switzerland; systemic integration; voluntary associations

Issue
This article is part of the issue "Religious Diversity and Social Inclusion", edited by Gary Bouma (Monash University, Australia).

---

1. Introduction

Without a doubt, one of the most common markers of social inclusion and exclusion throughout the history of mankind has been religious affiliation. Numerous examples of religious repression can be seen throughout history (Schneider, 2002). The traumatizing experiences of the World Wars and the Civil and Human Rights Movements in the second half of the 20th century have given rise, in Western countries, to extensive measures to institutionalize a culture of tolerance. However, with the rise of Islamic consciousness in the Islamic world and its expansion into Western countries in the last two decades there have been increasing calls to underscore the limits of tolerance. Thus, the integration of Muslims has acquired an unprecedented political relevance.

In the presented study, we do not analyze the objective inclusion of Muslims. Instead, we focus on one of the subjective aspects of integration, namely Muslims' normative views on their inclusion. We begin the paper with a survey of sociological theories of integration/inclusion as well as a review of the state of research. We then draw on narrative autobiographical interviews to analyze Swiss Muslims' views of integration and their preferred type of inclusion in Swiss society. Finally, we address the question of outgroup tolerance among the interviewees.

2. Theoretical Framework and Research Questions

We begin this section by discussing two traditions of sociological thought that have addressed the question of social inclusion. We then develop a conceptual framework merging both traditions. Finally, we outline our research questions.

2.1. Inclusion through Access to Functional Subsystems

Inclusion is a new and extensively discussed concept in modern systems theories. Lockwood (1964) distinguishes between *social* integration, the interaction between individuals, and *system* integration, the interaction between institutions. Luhmann's systems theory (1997) differs from Lockwood's typology as it first replaces the concept of system integration with that of *integration*. In addition, he argues that social integration should no longer refer to the relationships between human individuals but to the communicative relationship between people and functional subsystems. As a result, Luhmann (1997) proposes a substitution of Lockwood's concept of social integration with the notion of *inclusion/exclusion*. Hence, people who lack of civil, political and social rights (Marshall, 1950), such as the residents of the Brazilian Favelas, are more or less excluded (see also Farzin, 2006; Stichweh, 2005). In summary: Luhmann's concept of social inclusion highlights individuals' ability to adapt to and access *functional subsystems*. Of particular relevance for Luhmann is the inclusive function of the welfare state in providing all individuals with similar life opportunities and social security. However, Kronauer (2010) has argued that inclusion goes beyond material subsistence and poverty containment to also include social interaction between individuals and groups. This position is advocated in the second tradition outlined in the following section.

2.2. Inclusion by Bridging Networking

Even though Simmel is rarely discussed as an integration theorist, his reflections on modernity can also be read as an implicit theory of integration. According to Simmel (1908a), modern societies are characterized by the "intersection of social circles", as individuals go beyond their original social circles to join new social networks. Although a modern person continues to be a member of his/her family, he/she also establishes contacts with other social circles, including voluntary associations. As he/she stands at the intersection of the social circles he/she is a member of, he/she develops an individual identity distinct from that of other individuals. Individualization is, therefore, the result of the accumulation of affiliations with different social circles (see also Nollert, 2010).

While the individualization process increases freedom of action, it also creates uncertainty. A modern person suffers from similar unease as Park's *Marginal Man* does: "One who is poised in psychological uncertainty between two (or more) social worlds, reflecting in his soul the discords and harmonies, repulsions and attractions of these worlds" (Stonequist, 1937/1961, p. 8). Therefore, it is unsurprising that people who engage in cross-cutting social circles sometimes lack a sense of community and suffer from a resulting attachment deficit (Nollert, 2014).

Instead of having a dominant or *solitary* identity (Sen, 2006), modern individuals develop *cross-cutting identities* (Bell, 1980, p. 243), with the consequence that they do not *a priori* know which part of their identity is salient. Modern individuals are often faced with loyalty conflicts. This is a result of being constantly confronted with divergent, if not contradicting, expectations from the circles they are affiliated with. In short, modern people are faced with a variety of intra-role and inter-role conflicts (Dahrendorf, 2006).

Although affiliation with cross-cutting social circles can cause much distress at the intrapersonal level, in the realm of social relations, it can also be a source of social integration. Thus, as an individual's attachment to his/her circle of origin is lessened and he/she is partially integrated into new social circles, he/she becomes more open-minded and his/her prejudice is reduced. Quoting from Simmel's (1908b) essay "The Stranger", Park describes the Marginal Man as follows: "He is the freer one, practically and theoretically. He views his relation to others with less prejudice. He submits them to more general, more objective standards, and he is not confined in his action by custom, piety, or precedents" (Park, 1928, p. 888).

Finally, one has to take into consideration that increasing and intensifying social contacts contribute to the erosion of homogeneous group identities. Welsch (2009), for instance, has argued that intercultural contacts ultimately result in a vanishing of cultural differences und the emergence of *transcultural* individuals with hybrid identities.

To sum up, social integration requires that individuals are not restricted in their social contacts by normatively homogeneous communities with rigorous boundaries. Thus, in line with Putnam's social capital theory (Narayan, 1999; Putnam, 2000), it can be argued that social integration requires social ties that would build *bridges* between social circles. This notion is also in line with Berry (1997)'s concept of integration in his typology of *acculturation strategies*, according to which integration goes beyond a mere side-by-side existence of separate, normatively homogeneous social circles to also include interactions between individuals and groups.

2.3. Inclusion as Realization of System and Social Integration

An encompassing definition of *social inclusion* can be derived from Lockwood's (1964) distinction between social and system integration. Lockwood defines social integration as orderly or conflictual relationships between actors, and system integration as orderly or conflictual relationships between the parts of a social system. One aspect, namely social relations, is the focus of network approaches. The other aspect, the relations between institutions, is the focal point of systems theories. Thus, on one hand, network approaches underscore the engagement of individuals in social groups alien to their ingroups. On the other hand, systems theories emphasize the congruency and coordination between markets, businesses, governmental institutions, and churches.

While systems theory is often criticized for neglecting social relations (Granovetter, 1985), the network perspective is reprehended for disregarding the impact of institutions (Brinton & Nee, 1998). In fact, social networks and associations are not sufficiently integrated unless they are embedded in a variety of political, economic and cultural institutions.

In our view, a thorough integration requires both system and social integration. Moreover, we regard system integration as something more than a mere coordination between institutions. In line with Luhmann's concept of inclusion, we argue that individuals also need access to these institutions in general, and to the labor market and welfare state in particular. In other words, individuals have to be "anonymously" integrated into the labor market and, if unemployed, sick, or old, into welfare institutions that guarantee their maintenance.

Our typology (see Figure 1) is based on two dimensions. From the network perspective, integration is realized when people maintain face-to-face contacts with a broad range of people (*social integration*). In contrast, systems theories regard integration as harmony between institutions as well as people's access to these institutions (*system integration*). From the intersection of these two dimensions, there emerge four types of integration: *inclusion, interaction, co-existence, and exclusion.*

Inclusion refers to a situation in which both system and social integration occur. Therefore, people can only be regarded as included if they are endowed civil, political, and social rights (Marshall, 1950), and if they can establish crosscutting social ties (Kronauer, 2010). This premise is compatible with Bourdieu's theory of capital (Bourdieu, 1983), according to which social inclusion can only be achieved if people have access to institutional resources, and that these resources are often made available through economic and cultural capital, or when social capital is generated through active participation in social networks. In the opposite case, *exclusion* happens when both social and system integration are absent. *Interaction* refers to a situation in which individuals (or groups) have social contacts to one another, but lack universal access to the core institutions of society. Extreme examples of this type of integration are slaves, child laborers, or illegal workers. *Co-existence* can be defined as system integration without bridging social ties. This type of integration can

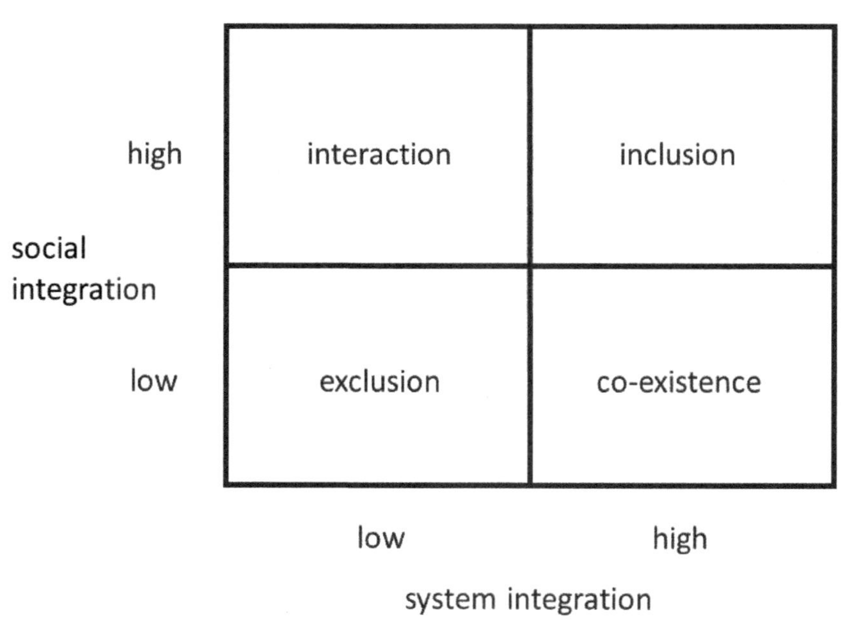

Figure 1. Social inclusion as realization of system and social integration.

even be, paradoxically enough, achieved in a highly segregated society, provided that the labor markets provide jobs and the state guarantees for welfare and equal rights. Hence, co-existence implies a segregationist multiculturalism, or, as Sen (2006) has put it, a *plural monoculturalism*. This is for instance the case when a minority prevents its members from contacting with the dominant population and strives instead for a segregated lifestyle, albeit in peaceful co-existence with other social groups. Co-existence is also compatible with a neo-liberal regime. In the United Kingdom, for instance, the co-existence model was supported for a long time by political neoliberalism. Thus, the cultural minorities were allowed to experience their own lifestyles, so long as they minimized their claims on social welfare. However, because this kind of co-existence can transform into spatial segregation, it has lost political support in the last few decades (Kivisto, 2013).

2.4. Research Questions

Our concept of social inclusion assumes, in line with Lockwood, a positive coordination of functional subsystems, and, in line with Luhmann, access to the core institutions of society. Moreover, drawing on Putnam's concept of bridging social ties, we assume that inclusion requires people to have cross-cutting group memberships.

In the public debate on integration of migrants, religious affiliation is of special interest. This is simply because orthodox religious leaders usually demand from their followers strict adherence to specific normative standards and restricted contact with "non-believers". In this sense, members of religious minorities are constantly exposed to psychic tensions, having to choose between retreating into the religious community and being socially open. Indeed, both alternatives pose their own risks. While retreat often leads to isolation, stigmatization, and orthodoxy, becoming open might lead to a loss of identity (see Coser, 1956).

Regarding the foregone reflections, the paper deals with following questions. First, it explores the question of which kind of integration the Swiss Muslims strive for through civic engagement, and which kind of normative positions they advocate when it comes to their integration into Swiss society. Second, we explore the question of the attitude of the interviewees towards outgroup tolerance.

3. State of Research

So far, sociological studies on the subjective dimension of migrants' integration have been mainly focused on the views and perceptions of the native population. In contrast, the views of Muslims on the topic of integration are widely under-researched. Studies based on World Values Surveys, as well as European Values Surveys, usually focus on the attitudes of natives towards Muslims, thus neglecting value orientations of Muslims (an exception is Davidov, Schmidt, & Schwartz, 2009), as well as their attitude towards integration. However, some studies address the extent of tolerance among different religious communities including Muslims. For instance, the studies by Inglehart and Norris (2012) and Tausch (2014b, 2015) based on PEW-data, indicate that the tolerance of Muslims varies widely between countries. Tausch and Karoui (2011) and Tausch (2014a) also show that the Salafist position is marginal in Europe. Miligan, Andersen and Brym (2014) have documented that tolerance within Europe varies not only between countries but also between Muslims and Christians and between practicing and non-practicing believers. Finally, drawing on a survey of Muslims of Turkish and Moroccan origin in six European countries, Koopmans (2015) has argued that religious fundamentalist attitudes among Muslims are more widespread than among native Christians.

However, the mentioned studies and data from the European and World Values Studies are of limited value for our research as they do not analyze behavior, and do not inform what integration means to Muslims and which type of integration the latter prefer. Furthermore, the studies also presuppose a stability of values over the course of life, while our qualitative research suggests, in line with Park (1928), that values might change as a result of migration and interaction with the native population (see also Rudnev, 2013).

Closer to our research question is the study carried out by Van Oudenhoven, Prins and Buunk (1998). The authors analyzed the adaption strategies of Moroccan and Turkish immigrants in the Netherlands, and compared them with members of the Dutch majority. They identified four adaption strategies: assimilation (original culture is considered unimportant, whereas contact with the majority is regarded as important), integration (both the original culture and contact with the majority are regarded as important), separation (original culture is considered important, whereas contact with the majority is not), and marginalization (both the original culture and contact with the majority are considered unimportant). Most Moroccans and Turks preferred integration, whereas the Dutch had positive attitudes toward both assimilation and integration. However, the Dutch believed that separation would be the strategy chosen most frequently by the immigrants.

According to Brettfeld and Wetzels (2007), who combined qualitative interviews and a survey of Muslims in Germany, most Muslims (more than 70%) argued against assimilation. However, more than 45% also thought that foreigners should adapt to the native culture, and only 9% favored separation. The survey also showed that segregation is mostly favored by fundamentalist and orthodox Muslims. A small minority of the fundamentalists also supported religiously motivated violence, disliked democracy, and indicated intolerance. Moreover, the authors emphasized that the combination of beliefs of segregation and radicalism among these Muslims closely resembles the position of the Neo-Nazis.

A telephone survey of 1350 young Muslims and non-Muslims in Germany (Frindte, Boehnke, Kreikenborn, & Wagner, 2012) indicated that the two studied groups have similar positions on integration. The findings suggest that the most radical views (anti-Semitism, authoritarianism, religious fundamentalism) are supported by a sub-group of non-German Muslims (i.e., Muslims without German citizenship), who also favor separation. The non-German Muslims who favored integration were those who had more social contacts with Germans. Neither German nor non-German Muslims favored assimilation.

In their interviews with 21 Muslim intellectuals or those active in public or community debates, Modood and Ahmad (2007) examined what these Muslims think about multiculturalism. The analysis shows that the respondents advocate multiculturalism, as long as it includes faith as a dimension of difference. In most of the other aspects of the multicultural ideal, the respondents seemed to share the views of non-Muslim British multiculturalists. Yet some of the interviewees believed that Islam's multicultural concepts are superior to the offers of any other faith or civilization. This view was advocated by those who are specialized in engaging with contemporary Western discourses rather than by religious authorities.

Finally, the qualitative studies of Yasmeen (2014) and Duderija (2014) both underline that certain Muslim minorities, in particular Salafists, cherish exclusionary practices. On one hand, they develop a sense of superiority towards the religiously other and therefore have little interest in social interaction with non-Muslims. On the other hand, they also take an exclusionary stance towards non-Salafi Muslims and Muslim women.

In summary, the research on integration views and preferences of Muslims in Europe suggests that a large majority of them favor a combination of conservation of their original culture and partial assimilation. This also includes making social contacts with the dominant population. Only a very small minority prefers separation while advocating radical worldviews and intolerance.

4. Methods and Data

4.1. Collecting Data

Regarding methodology, this study was based on a combination of document analysis, participatory observation, semi-structured interviews, and narrative autobiographical interviews. The *document analysis* was used to investigate the content of the websites, bylaws, communiqués, and other documents of the selected associations. Insight into the ways in which association members negotiate their collective identities was gained by *participatory observation*. *Semi-structured interviews* were conducted with association principals (President, Vice-President, or Imam), who acted as gatekeepers for us. The goal of these interviews was to collect information on the history, objectives, and internal relations of each association. The semi-structured interviews also helped to establish the trust of the gatekeepers.

Narrative autobiographical interviews, the main data-gathering method of the study, were conducted in order to gain insight into the narrative identities of the selected active members of the associations. In line with Lucius-Hoene (2000), narrative identity was understood as "a situated, pragmatic, autoepistemic and interactive activity drawing on culturally transmitted narrative conventions which is performed within the research context".

The transcribed interviews were analyzed according to the so-called "reconstruction of narrative identity" method developed by Lucius-Hoene and Deppermann (2004). Since this method is relatively new, its fundamentals are described below. Prior to this description, a brief explanation of the three dimensions of narrative identity (*temporal*, *social*, and *self-referential*) will be given, which the authors have accorded a prominent position in their evaluation.

The *temporal dimension* primarily relates to the question of how the story is structured in terms of time. Narrative autobiographical constructions include justifications and explanations for how the self became what it is. Thus, they also form the basis for orientation of actions and plans for the future (Lucius-Hoene & Deppermann, 2004, p. 57). Also important to the temporal dimension is the question of *agency*; one would like to establish if the narrator presents him/herself as an active and acting subject in his/her narration, or as the passive object of forces and powers that he/she cannot control.

The *social dimension* is concerned with the following questions:

- *Positioning:* What roles does he/she assign to him/herself and his/her interaction partners (both in the narrated episodes as well as in the interview situation)?
- *World construction* (*Weltkonstruktion*)*:* How does he/she describe the physical and social environment and the general conditions of his/her stories?
- *Narrative conventions*: To which culturally transmitted narrative conventions does he/she have recourse in his/her narration?

The *self-referential dimension* is about the self-reflections of the narrator. The following questions are of particular interest:

- What characteristics does the narrator ascribe to him/herself?
- Which attachments are thus expressed?
- How does his/her "theory of self" express itself? What assumptions about him/herself does he/she make as an "expert on his/her own ego"?
- What discoveries does the narrator make about him/herself during the narration (*autoepistemic processes*)?

4.2. The Analysis Procedure

Once the interviews are transcribed, one starts with the analysis of the collected texts. The reconstruction of narrative identity consists of three main steps: rough macroscopic analysis, detailed microscopic analysis, and reconstruction of the case structure.

- In the macroscopic structural analysis, one attempts to reconstruct how the narrator structured his/her story chronologically and thematically.
- A detailed microscopic analysis is a sequential analysis of a selection of interview passages that appear particularly relevant to the enquiry. Here, "general heuristics" are analyzed first ("Questions regarding the data": *What* is shown; *how*, *why*, and *why thus* and not otherwise?). Thereafter, one tries to find clues about the three dimensions of narrative identity in the respective passage. Due to the fact that narrative identity, by definition, represents a linguistic performance, one should also employ a series of linguistic and communicative methods in undertaking such analyses (see Lucius-Hoene & Deppermann, 2004, chapter 9).
- Once the analyses on the macro and micro levels are completed, one attempts to assemble the many fragments into a *case structure*.

For the sake of brevity, in this article we present only an abridged report of our analyses.

4.3. Sampling

Although our premises apply to all people, for the following reasons we focused our project on Muslims in Switzerland. The mass media in Switzerland and wider Europe often define Muslims as members of a minority that is difficult to integrate. They therefore face prejudice and discrimination (Cesari, 2004; Kivisto, 2013; Kühnel & Leibold, 2007; Sheridan, 2006; Stolz, 2005), which exacerbates their opportunities and willingness to establish and maintain contact with other communities. Moreover, many migrants are from countries with weak civil society structures (Gellner, 1994) and are therefore likely to have little experience with voluntary organizations (Amacker & Budowski, 2009). Finally, they are sometimes drawn into the maelstrom of religiously inspired anti-systemic movements in the Islamic world. This involvement may manifest itself as alienation from the local civil society. For these particular reasons, it seemed all the more interesting to examine whether Muslims' civic engagement has a significant impact on their attitude toward outgroups and toward the whole society.

The study was based on purposeful, two-step sampling. Firstly, eight Muslim voluntary organizations in Switzerland were selected, some with an outspoken bridging character, others with a pronounced bonding culture. Secondly, 26 members of the selected organizations (16 men and 10 women) were chosen for narrative autobiographical interviews.

5. Integration from the Point of View of Muslims: Two Prototypical Cases

As the narratives we analyzed in our research project corresponded to either the type *inclusion* or the type *co-existence*, with nobody matching any of the other two types, in this section we deliver two prototypes that almost perfectly represent the types *inclusion* and *co-existence*. In section six we refer to other autobiographical narratives of our project to underpin the findings presented in the two prototypes.

5.1. Case Study 1: Akbar

Along with his parents, Akbar (52) arrives in Switzerland from Pakistan at the age of two. His father, a lawyer and religious scholar, has the task of looking after the affairs of the Ahmadiyya community, which represents a minority within Sunni Islam, in the Diaspora. Akbar is sent to an international boarding school where he comes into contact with a variety of nationalities and religions. After graduation, he studies linguistics and graduates with a degree in German literature. He is self-employed, and through his office, he coordinates teaching assignments, translations, consultations, and volunteer activities. He works both as a high school teacher and as a lecturer in intercultural studies at a technical college. Although Akbar is very active professionally, volunteer activities take up much of his time. He maintains several charitable projects, holds a post of responsibility in a mosque organization, and is very active in the Swiss Green Party, a secular leftist party. He is also committed to development aid, plays an active role in local politics, and is active in associations for the integration of marginalized people, as well as intercultural dialogue. Akbar is married and has two children.

Akbar's worldview points to a carefree childhood in a social and missionary upper-middle class environment. When asked how he became the man he is today, Akbar replies:

"It was primarily my parents who pointed me in this direction. I did, as I said, grow up in the mosque. And that's a mosque to which African kings had come; Muhammad Ali had come, the boxer. Presidents of different countries had come, but also the tramp, the poor man from the street. Even a Swiss tramp. My parents took equal care of everybody. I cannot remember any man ever coming to my parents and saying that he was hungry, or needed somewhere to stay the night, or that he was cold, that they would not have taken care of. And that, of course, is something that has affected me very much, you know? And everything else is in consequence of the fact that my parents have influenced me thus, you know? I think that has been the key point. And then, of course, there was the international school. There [we talked about everything, for instance] the Israeli-Palestinian conflict. And there were Israelis at the school, and there were Arabs. And we discussed things all night long."

The experiences of his formative years affect him to the present day. As a humanistic understanding of Islam dominates his family's culture, being helpful and charitable is prominent in Akbar's sense of self.

"Education is my identity, women's rights are my identity, these I promote most of the time, you see? Or, to put it roughly, standing up for people who are in distress or who are underprivileged. It does not matter which country they are in. I campaign for such people in Pakistan, but I equally campaign for such people in Switzerland. This may be my identity or it is identity-forming."

Given this sense of self, Akbar's numerous civic activities are not surprising. In this respect, a high degree of continuity can be observed with respect to the temporal dimension of his narrative identity. This is particularly noticeable in his identification with his lifework—a school project for marginalized girls in Pakistan—because the project is a realization of his childhood dream:

"There [at school] when I was fourteen, I decided this, and I typed this on my first electric typewriter which I had bought or got as a present, that later, when I had grown up, I myself would build such a boarding school, though not for the richest people, but for the poorest, you know?....And I have now made this a reality."

As the first generation of female students approaches the end of high school, a college with a two-year degree course is being planned. It is with pride that Akbar points out that about half of the 200 girls enrolled come from Christian families, who often live a marginalized existence in Pakistan. Thus, he wants to counter the widespread notion that Muslims only support their co-religionists.

"The important point is that all of these girls attend our school without paying fees. They belong to the lower class. These are [also] people who are underprivileged because of their religious affiliation—they are Christians. We have a disproportionate number of Christians, considering that we have roughly fifty percent Muslim girls and fifty percent Christians, you know?"

Akbar's strong inclination toward charitable activities is in line with the humanitarian objective of his religious community. However, this does not mean that he identifies exclusively with his religion. Rather, he identifies with his many activities and memberships, which contribute to a complex and varied social identity.

5.2. Case Study 2: Urs

In his autobiographical narration, Urs (30) depicts a difficult adolescence. The reason seems to lie within his family. His mother divorces his father, who is struggling with addiction problems. She places Urs in the care of a foster family and emigrates. Urs finds support in the new family, whose members are deeply religious. His foster parents are puritanical Protestants and followers of a free church. He enjoys a warm family life and practices Christian rituals with the family. For a young man who was raised far from religion, his new life as a disciplined, practicing Christian is a fascinating experience. After a while, Urs leaves the family and moves abroad to be with his mother. The familial, religious life of the young teen now gives way to a much more permissive adolescent life.

Upon his return to Switzerland, Urs initially joins a strongly patriotic, conservative political movement. Later, he takes an interest in the Palestine question. In particular, the bombing of an airport in the occupied territories by the Israeli army seems to have had a drastic effect on him ("I lost it completely")—the more so, as the airport was built with the funds of SDC (The Swiss Agency for Development and Cooperation). He is now committed to the Palestinian cause. During a short stay in the Gaza Strip, he becomes fascinated by the hospitality of the Palestinians, their human warmth, and their supportive communal life.

He attributes the hospitality of the Palestinians to Islamic principles. It also excites him that Islam is a vibrant, community-based religion that permeates the everyday life of the faithful. His adoption of Islam is made easier by the fact that he did not give up his faith in God. At age 21, he converts to Islam.

In the foreground of Urs' conversion to Islam, we find first of all the *re-socialization* of a young person who longs for the *warmth of a community* (Bauman, 2000). This also explains his earlier involvement in a patriotically oriented political movement. In addition, his longing for a "normative edifice", which would give him guidance, testifies to Durkheim's understanding of an anomic state before conversion. In this respect, it is also possible here to speak of a *methodizing of life* (Weber, 1905/2002; Wohlrab-Sahr, 1999) as a result of conversion.

After conversion, Urs becomes a strictly practicing Muslim who places religious ritual at the center of his life. Henceforth, he dedicates himself to the cause of Muslims in Switzerland as well as abroad.

> "I really want to practice my faith consistently and don't want it pushed into a corner again and again through argument and discussion about the centrality of Western modernity. If something has to be at the center, then, conversely, I want religion, faith in God, and religious rituals to be at the center and the world to be organized around them. And this I thought I had found in Islam at the time, hadn't I? Yes, this is how I became the person I am today."

It is in this association that Urs finally finds the stability, nest warmth, and sense of family he has been missing for so many years.

> "The stability and constancy of an association, an organization, I only found here, in this association. At the same time, it has become a kind of center of life for us, has it not?"

When questioned if he had any sympathy with a particular political party or identified with a specific political orientation beyond his commitment to Islam, Urs gave this answer.

> "That's for me...how should I say? As already mentioned, my identity is Islam, and from this life-order perspective [Lebensordnungsperspektive] I am a little bit eclectic, when it comes to voting for a party.
> [...]
> [Moreover,] I simply couldn't be in a party at all. That's the reason. However, I think, nowadays many people believe that this political system is just too narrow."

What Urs strives for is the greatest possible autonomy of the Muslim community and its freedom to live up to its religious code. At the same time, he attaches great importance to the recognition of Islam and its acceptance as "normal" by the host society.

> "We see ourselves as a family with an idea. And the idea is that Islam gets naturalized in Switzerland. That one day the Muslims can say: We live here in Switzerland, not as guests, but as Muslims who are a recognized part of Switzerland.
> [...]
> Actually, we want to do away with the Muslim migrants' guest mentality that has prevailed up to now....We should not always ask for whatever we need. We should just take it. We should, for example, be able to build a mosque without having to beg society for a friendly gesture and without having to bow our heads. We should simply build it, as soon as we have the money for it and we have sought permission. This is more or less the idea, that we have a normalization discourse and try to normalize Islam in Switzerland, to normalize it according to the meaning of Jürgen Link's normalization theory."

By being a "normal" part of Swiss society, Urs means that practicing Muslims should be allowed to live up to their religious code of conduct in the public sphere without being stigmatized for it. In order to demonstrate this, he mentions the example of the normalization of homosexuality in Switzerland.

> "We remember, for instance, the homosexuals here in Switzerland. They too had...let's say in the 1950s, they could have been arrested if they outed themselves as homosexuals. Today, they are even allowed to marry, as homosexuals, aren't they? So we want to impose [on] society a similar normalization discourse, in the sense of 'We are normal. What we do here is normal. We belong to Switzerland', and that the tolerance imperative, the freedom rights, and the plural, democratic system of Switzerland oblige the society to accept this normality."

"Normal" does not primarily mean that Muslims have the same civic, political, and social rights. Rather, it implies a peaceful co-existence between Muslims and non-Muslims. Consequently, his association is not looking for interaction with the dominant population but separation from it. It attaches importance to possessing the right to an orthodox education of children, as well as segregated sports (both after gender and faith) and separated burial grounds. Finally, it denounces Muslims who campaign for the modernization of Islam.

6. Discussion

As typical cases of the two main groups of interviewees, Akbar and Urs have contrasting views on integration.

Akbar is engaged in numerous volunteer associations beyond the cultural/religious community he belongs to. Islam is only one part among others in his identity, and he shows strong identification with the many social projects he is engaged in. In Akbar's narration, neither excessive identification with an ingroup nor hateful demarcation against any outgroups can be noticed. It is only from the jihadists that Akbar distances himself. The active role he plays in the secular and left Green Party is also an indication of his deep concern for social welfare issues. Therefore, it can be said that he is in favor of *social integration*.

Urs, on the other hand, prefers *co-existence*. He is exclusively engaged in the Islamic organization which he co-founded. His most important cause is the equal treatment of Islam in Switzerland, achieving maximum autonomy for the community of practicing Muslims, and the separation of Muslims from non-Muslims. He relies on the democratic tradition and the liberal values of Swiss society to justify the demand of his organization for tolerance vis-à-vis practicing Muslims. His primary concern is the tolerance of his ingroup by outgroups and not vice versa. During the entirety of the interview he does not mention any other social groups that suffer from stigmatization. When he refers to the successful campaign of the Swiss homosexuals in "normalizing" their sexual orientation, he does so to demonstrate the strategy of his association. Any expression of sympathy that goes beyond this cognitive level is absent from his assertions.

His devotion to Islam and the Muslim community prevents him from engaging in secular organizations, such as trade unions, political parties, or neighborhood associations, in which religious affiliation is expected to be a personal, private issue. His position can therefore be interpreted as advocacy for high *systemic integration* but low overall *social integration*. According to our typology, he is primarily interested in a peaceful co-existence between the native population and Muslims. Thus, he demands the integration of *Islam,* while rejecting the requirement that Muslims should engage with the non-Muslim population of Switzerland.

As for the second focal point of the study, Akbar and Urs also represent two distinct types of outgroup tolerance. From a libertarian perspective, Urs demands that the Swiss native population should respect and even guarantee the autonomy of his ingroup and should not interfere in its internal affairs, thus allowing it to live up to its specific norms and rituals in its exclusive spaces. This attitude is based on putting collective rights of social groups over the rights of individuals. Hence, we suggest labeling this kind of attitude as *multicultural tolerance*.

In Akbar's narrative, there is no explicit reference to tolerance. However, his pride in being open to the views of different social groups (for instance the views of both Israeli and Arab students on the Palestinian conflict at the boarding school), his sensitivity towards human rights issues and his "standing up for people who are in distress or who are underprivileged" are all indicative of his openness, sympathy and care for marginalized people beyond their group attachments. Such an attitude is based on putting the rights of individuals over the collective rights of social groups. Hence, we suggest labeling such an attitude as *liberal tolerance*.

As already mentioned, Urs and Akbar represent two main groups among our interviewees. While the one group favors system integration as well as multicultural tolerance, the other group is supportive of both social integration and liberal tolerance (for a detailed description of this typology see Nollert & Sheikhzadegan, 2014, 2016). Furthermore, we could identify two subgroups among the latter. While one group showed clear shift towards liberal tolerance through civic engagement, the members of the other group were raised as tolerant individuals in the first place. Taking Akbar's childhood into consideration, it is fair to characterize him as a person whose tolerance was due primarily to his socialization in a tolerant environment.

The insight won by the above-discussed narratives can be well supported by other narratives. For the sake of brevity, we focus on the question of tolerance.

Respondents like Akbar have generally numerous civic engagements, a relatively complex social identity, and are supportive of liberal tolerance. For instance, Bekim, a 55-year old Kosovan migrant (who was also a trade-unionist) told us that in the course of his commitment to diverse volunteer associations, he has overcome both his distaste for religion and homosexuals. Similarly, Aras, a 58-year old Marxist-oriented trade-unionist of Turkish origin, developed a greater tolerance towards right-wing religious workers. A Syrian woman reported how civic engagement in her neighborhood helped her to overcome her social isolation as a housewife, to establish contact with people of different ethnic and social origins, and to restore her self-image as a socially active person. Regaining her self-consciousness, she co-founded an association of Arab women as well as a "roundtable of religious dialog".

Conversely, orthodox Muslims such as Urs, who are exclusively committed to a single association, tend to grow in distance from other social circles, including their original peer groups, and are generally supportive of multicultural tolerance. Mehmet (36), the son of a Turkish labor migrant family joined the organization of Urs after experiencing a spiritual transformation. Since then, he sees his religion with new eyes. He uses all his leisure time to empower practicing Muslims and to enhance their ability to live up to their faith. Sara (22), the daughter of a Kosovan labor migrant family, had to endure bitter experiences of discrimination because of her head scarf. She joined the same organization in order to participate in its collective action to protect the rights of practicing Muslims.

Indeed, the notion that membership in different social circles promotes tolerance is not new. For instance, de Tocqueville has underscored the role of voluntary associations in promoting mutual understanding and cooperation. Durkheim (1897/1951), has argued that in modern societies, neither the family, the religion, nor the state have an integrative function in society (see also Pescosolido & Georgianna, 1989). According to him, the only source of integration is voluntary association because social circles crosslink their members and curb any excessive emotions within in the group. Moreover, Allport (1954) has postulated the contact hypothesis, according to which, people who belong to a variety of social groups have more contacts and, therefore, tend not only to overcome their stereotypes and prejudices, but to also develop more generalized tolerance (see also Frölund Thomsen, 2012). Finally, Roccas and Brewer (2002) have argued that people with complex social identities are more open to change and more tolerant of otherness: "In sum, both cognitive and motivational factors lead us to predict that complex social identities will be associated with reduced ingroup favoritism and increased tolerance and positivity toward outgroups in general" (Roccas & Brewer, 2002, p. 102; see also Brewer & Pierce, 2005).

7. Conclusions

The research project outlined in this article focused on the subjective dimension of integration. It did this through investigating the views of Muslims in Switzerland on the optimal way of their integration into Swiss society. The autobiographical narratives we analyzed suggest that Muslims in Switzerland prefer one of two options. The preferences are either a combination of social and system integration (social inclusion) or a peaceful co-existence that would provide equal rights to Muslims, but also foster segregation of Muslims from non-Muslims. Accordingly, we found two distinct types of outgroup tolerance. The interviewees who supported social inclusion showed a *liberal* tolerance, based on the primacy of individual over collective rights. On the other hand, the interviewees who advocated peaceful co-existence between autonomous faith communities showed a *multiculturalist* tolerance, which means that they were more concerned about the collective rights of the communities than the rights of individual members of social groups.

Although only two prototypical cases are discussed here, our research has important implications for the future research. Firstly, it underlines the multi-dimensionality of the term integration. Secondly, it shows the linkages between the attitude towards integration and the outgroup tolerance. Thirdly and finally, it shows the importance of biography and habitus for the development of outgroup tolerance and of personal attitude towards integration.

Acknowledgements

This research with the German title "Freiwillige Assoziationen, multiple Identitäten und Toleranz. Eine Rekonstruktion narrativer Identitäten von Assoziationsmitgliedern mit besonderer Berücksichtigung von MuslimInnen in der Schweiz" was supported by the Swiss National Science Foundation (grant no. 100017_134841).

Conflict of Interests

The authors declare no conflict of interests.

References

Allport, G. W. (1954). *The nature of prejudice.* Reading, MA: Addison-Wesley.

Amacker, M., & Budowski, M. (2009). Exclusión social y sociedades paralelas: ¿Círculos sociales disyuntivos inclusivos y exclusivos? In J. F. Tezanos (Ed.), *Tendencias sociales. Juventud y exclusión social* (pp. 51-88). Madrid, Spain: Editorial Sistema.

Bauman, Z. (2000). *Community: Seeking safety in an insecure world.* Oxford, UK: Polity Press.

Bell, D. (1980). *The winding passage: Essays and sociological journeys 1960–1980.* Cambridge, MA: Abt Books.

Berry, J. (1997). Immigration, acculturation, and adaption. *Applied Psychology: An International Review, 46*(1), 5-68.

Bourdieu, P. (1983). Forms of capital. In J. C. Richards (Ed.), *Handbook of theory and research for the sociology of education* (pp. 241-285). New York: Greenwood Press.

Brettfeld, K., & Wetzels, P. (2007). Muslime in Deutschland: Integration, Integrationsbarrieren, Religion sowie Einstellungen zu Demokratie, Rechtsstaat und politisch-religiös motivierter Gewalt. Retrieved from http://www.islamdebatte.de/studien/2007-studien/brettfeld-katrin-wetzels-peter-2007-muslime-in-deutschland

Brewer, M. B., & Pierce, K. P. (2005). Social identity, complexity and out-group tolerance. *Personality and Social Psychology Bulletin, 31*(3), 428-437.

Brinton, M. C., & Nee, V. (1998). *The new institutionalism in sociology.* New York: Russell Sage Foundation.

Cesari, J. (2004). *When Islam and democracy meet.* New York: Palgrave.

Coser, L. A. (1956). *The functions of social conflict.* Glencoe, IL: Free Press.

Dahrendorf, R. (2006). *Homo sociologicus. Ein Versuch zur Geschichte, Bedeutung und Kritik der Kategorie der sozialen Rolle.* Wiesbaden, Germany: VS.

Davidov, E., Schmidt, P., & Schwartz, H. (2009). *Value orientations of Muslims in Europe*. Paper presented at the 3rd ESRA Conference, Warsaw, June/July 2009.

Duderija, A. (2014). Neo-traditional Salafis in the West: Agents of (self)-exclusion. In S. Yasmeen, & N. Markovic (Eds.), *Muslim citizens in the West: Spaces and agents of inclusion and exclusion* (pp. 125-142). Farnham, UK: Ashgate.

Durkheim, E. (1951). *Suicide: A study in sociology*. New York: The Free Press. (Original work published 1897)

Farzin, S. (2006). *Inklusion/Exklusion. Entwicklung und Probleme einer systemtheoretischen Unterscheidung.* Bielefeld, Germany: Transcript.

Frindte, W., Boehnke, K., Kreikenborn, H., & Wagner, W. (2012). *Lebenswelten junger Muslim in Deutschland.* Berlin, Germany: Bundesministerium des Innern.

Frölund Thomsen, J. P. (2012). How does intergroup contact generate ethnic tolerance? The contact hypothesis in a Scandinavian context. *Scandinavian Political Studies, 35*(2), 159-178.

Gellner, E. (1994). *Conditions of liberty: Civil society and its rivals*. London, UK: Hamish Hamilton.

Granovetter, M. (1985). Economic action and social structure: The problem of embeddedness. *American Journal of Sociology, 91*(3), 481-510.

Inglehart, R., & Norris, P. (2012). Muslim integration into western cultures: Between origins and destinations. *Political Studies, 60*(2), 228-251.

Kivisto, P. (2013). (Mis)Reading Muslims and multiculturalism. *Social Inclusion, 1*(2), 126-135.

Koopmans, R. (2015). Religious fundamentalism and hostility against out-groups: A comparison of Muslims and Christians in Western Europe. *Journal of Ethnic and Migration Studies, 4*(1), 33-57.

Kronauer, M. (2010). *Exklusion. Die Gefährdung des Sozialen im hoch entwickelten Kapitalismus.* Frankfurt am Main and New York: Campus.

Kühnel, S., & Leibold, J. (2007). Islamophobie in der deutschen Bevölkerung: Ein neues Phänomen oder nur ein neuer Name? Ergebnisse von Bevölkerungsumfragen zur gruppenbezogenen Menschenfeindlichkeit 2003 bis 2005. In M. Wohlrab-Sahr & L. Tezcan (Eds.), *Soziale Welt. Konfliktfeld Islam in Europa* (Sonderband 17, pp. 201-220). Baden-Baden: Nomos.

Lockwood, D. (1964). Social integration and system integration. In G. Zollschan & W. Hirsch (Eds.), *Explorations in social change* (pp. 244-257). Boston, MA: Houghton Mifflin.

Lucius-Hoene, G. (2000). Constructing and reconstructing narrative identity. *FQS Online.* Retrieved from http://www.qualitative-research.net/index.php/fqs/article/view/1087/2379

Lucius-Hoene, G., & Deppermann, A. (2004). *Rekonstruktion narrativer Identität. Ein Arbeitsbuch zur Analyse narrativer Interviews.* Opladen, Germany: VS.

Luhmann, N. (1997). *Die Gesellschaft der Gesellschaft.* Frankfurt am Main, Germany: Suhrkamp.

Marshall, T. H. (1950). *Citizenship and social class, and other essays.* Cambridge, UK: Cambridge University Press.

Miligan, S., Andersen, R., & Brym, R. (2014). Assessing variation in tolerance in 23 Muslim-majority and Western Countries. *Canadian Review of Sociology, 51*(3), 239-261.

Modood, T., & Ahmad, F. (2007). British Muslim perspectives on multiculturalism. *Theory, Culture & Society, 24*(2), 187-213.

Narayan, D. (1999). *Bonds and bridges. Social capital and poverty.* New York: World Bank.

Nollert, M. (2010). Kreuzung sozialer Kreise. Auswirkungen und Wirkungsgeschichte. In C. Stegbauer & R. Häußling (Eds.), *Handbuch Netzwerkforschung* (pp. 159-167). Wiesbaden, Germany: VS.

Nollert, M. (2014). Die integrative Kraft multipler Zugehörigkeiten und Identitäten. In M. Löw (Ed.), *Vielfalt und Zusammenhalt. Verhandlungen des 36. Kongress der Deutschen Gesellschaft für Soziologie in Bochum und Dortmund 2012* (pp. 957-969). Frankfurt am Main, Germany: Campus.

Nollert, M., & Sheikhzadegan, A. (2014). Vereine als Quelle von Identität und Toleranz. Narrativbiografische Interviews mit engagierten MuslimInnen in der Schweiz. In K. B. Schnebel (Ed.), *Europäische Minderheiten: Im Dilemma zwischen Selbstbestimmung und Integration* (pp. 297-336). Wiesbaden, Germany: Springer VS.

Nollert, M., & Sheikhzadegan, A. (2016). Kreuzung sozialer Kreise, multiple Identitäten und Toleranz: Eine Analyse zivilgesellschaftlich engagierter MuslimInnen in der Schweiz. In M. Nollert & A. Sheikhzadegan (Eds.), *Gesellschaften zwischen Multi- und Transkulturalität* (pp. 129-165). Zürich, Switzerland: Seismo Verlag.

Park, R. E. (1928). Human migration and the marginal man. *American Journal of Sociology, 33*(6), 881-893.

Pescosolido, B. A., & Georgianna, S. (1989). Durkheim, suicide, and religion: Towards a network theory of suicide. *American Sociological Review, 54*(1), 33-48.

Putnam, R. (2000). *Bowling alone: The collapse and revival of American community*. New York: Simon & Schuster.

Roccas, S., & Brewer, M. B. (2002). Social identity complexity. *Personality and Social Psychology Review, 6*(2), 88-106.

Rudnev, M. (2013). *Value adaption to a new social environment: Impacts from country of birth and country of residence on values of intra-European migrants* (Working Papers, 13/SOC/2013). Moscow, Russia: National Research University Higher School of Economics

Schneider, G. (2002). *Ungläubig sind immer die anderen. Weltreligionen zwischen Toleranz und Fanatismus.* Stuttgart, Germany: Klett-Cotta.

Sen, A. (2006). *Identity and violence: The illusion of destiny*. New York: W. W. Norton.

Sheridan, L. P. (2006). Islamophobia Pre- and Post-September 11th, 2001. *Journal of Interpersonal Violence, 21*(3), 317-336.

Simmel, G. (1908a). Die Kreuzung sozialer Kreise. In G. Simmel (Ed.), *Soziologie. Untersuchungen über die Formen der Vergesellschaftung* (pp. 305-344). Berlin, Germany: Duncker & Humblot.

Simmel, G. (1908b). Exkurs über den Fremden. In G. Simmel (Ed.), *Soziologie. Untersuchungen über die Formen der Vergesellschaftung* (pp. 509-512). Berlin, Germany: Duncker & Humblot.

Stichweh, R. (2005) *Inklusion und Exklusion. Studien zur Gesellschaftstheorie*. Bielefeld: Transcript.

Stolz, J. (2005). Explaining islamophobia: A test of four theories based on the case of a Swiss city. *Schweizerische Zeitschrift für Soziologie, 31*(3), 547-566.

Stonequist, E. V. (1961). *The marginal man: A study in personality and cultural conflict*. New York: Russell and Russell. (Original work published 1937)

Tausch, A. (2014a). *Armut und Radikalität. Soziologische Perspektiven zur Integration der Muslime in Europa*. Bremen, Germany: EHV AcademicPress.

Tausch, A. (2014b). Further insights into global and Arab Muslim opinion structures: Statistical reflections on the 2013 Pew report "The world's Muslims". *Middle East Review of International Affairs, 18*(1), 8-24.

Tausch, A. (2015). Hofstede, Inglehart and beyond. New directions in empirical global value research. *MPRA Paper No. 64282. Munich, Germany*

Tausch, A., & Karoui, H. (2011). *Les musulmans: Un cauchemar ou une force pour l'Europe?* Paris, France: L'Harmattan.

Van Oudenhoven, J. P., Prins, K. S., & Buunk, B. P. (1998). Attitudes of minority and majority members towards adaptation of immigrants. *European Journal of Social Psychology, 28*(6), 995-1013.

Weber, M. (2002). *The protestant ethic and the spirit of capitalism*. Los Angeles: Roxbury. (Original work published 1905)

Welsch, W. (2009). Was ist eigentlich Transkulturalität? In L. Darowska & C. Machold (Eds.), *Hochschule als transkultureller Raum? Beiträge zu Kultur, Bildung und Differenz* (pp. 39-66). Bielefeld, Germany: transcript.

Wohlrab-Sahr, M. (1999). *Konversion zum Islam in Deutschland und den USA*. Frankfurt am Main, Germany: Campus.

Yasmeen, S. (2014). The dynamics of exclusion/inclusion: Australia as a case study. In S. Yasmeen & N. Markovic (Eds.), *Muslim citizens in the West: Spaces and agents of inclusion and exclusion* (pp. 15–32). Farnham, UK: Ashgate.

About the Authors

Dr. Michael Nollert

Michael Nollert is professor at the Department of Social Sciences of the University of Fribourg, division of Sociology, Social Policy and Social Work. His research focuses on social inequalities and social exclusion and the impact of policies on social stratification. He has analyzed inequalities in the world system, in Latin America, in the intergenerational reproduction of social status (social mobility regimes), in the reproduction of economic elites and in the gendered division of unpaid work. Two of his current research projects deal with transnational networks of Bulgarian migrants in Switzerland and civic engagement of Muslims in Switzerland.

Dr. Amir Sheikhzadegan

Amir Sheikhzadegan, PhD in sociology from the University of Zurich, is a senior lecturer and researcher at the Department of Social Sciences of the University of Fribourg, division of Sociology, Social Policy and Social Work. He has been a visiting fellow at the "Zentrum Moderner Orient" (ZMO) in Berlin (DE) as well as at the "Religion and Society Research Cluster" of the Western Sydney University (AU). His fields of interest include Islam and modernity, Islam in Europe, minority-majority relations, multiculturalism, and civil society.

11

More Than a Checklist: Meaningful Indigenous Inclusion in Higher Education

Michelle Pidgeon

Faculty of Education, Simon Fraser University, Surrey, BC V3T 0A3, Canada; E-Mail: michelle_pidgeon@sfu.ca

Abstract

Since the 1970s there has been increased focus by institutions, government, and Indigenous nations on improving Aboriginal peoples participation and success in Canadian higher education; however disparity continues to be evident in national statistics of educational attainment, social determinants of health, and socio-economic status of Aboriginal compared to non-Aboriginal Canadians. For instance, post-secondary attainment for Aboriginal peoples is still only 8% compared to 20% of the rest of Canada (Statistics Canada, 2008, 2013). A challenge within higher education has been creating the space within predominately Euro-Western defined and ascribed structures, academic disciplines, policies, and practices to create meaningful spaces for Indigenous peoples. Indigenization is a movement centering Indigenous knowledges and ways of being within the academy, in essence transforming institutional initiatives, such as policy, curricular and co-curricular programs, and practices to support Indigenous success and empowerment. Drawing on research projects that span the last 10 years, this article celebrates the pockets of success within institutions and identifies areas of challenge to Indigenization that moves away from the tokenized checklist response, that merely tolerates Indigenous knowledge(s), to one where Indigenous knowledge(s) are embraced as part of the institutional fabric.

Keywords

Aboriginal peoples, Canada; indigenous higher education; indigenization; post-secondary education; recruitment; retention

Issue

This article is part of the issue "Social Inclusion and Indigenous Peoples", edited by Pat Dudgeon (University of Western Australia, Australia), Waikaremoana Waitoki (University of Waikato, New Zealand), Rose LeMay (Wharerātā Group, Canada) and Linda Waimarie Nikora (University of Waikato, New Zealand).

1. Introduction

Higher education has a responsibility to Indigenization, that is, to empower Indigenous self-determination, address decolonization, and reconcile systemic and societal inequalities between Indigenous and non-Indigenous Canadians. Since the 1970s there has been increased focus by institutions, government, and Indigenous nations on improving Aboriginal peoples participation and success in Canadian higher education. However, disparities of educational attainment continue (e.g., from the most recently available data, 8% of Aboriginal peoples have some form of a post-secondary credential compared to 20% of non-Aboriginal Canadians) (Statistics Canada, 2008, 2013). This educational disparity has repercussions to the individual, their families, and communities as lower educational attainment negatively impacts one's socio-economic status, health, and overall wellbeing. In thinking of what it means to have a truly socially inclusive society within the Canadian context, systemic barriers and inequities, along with other barriers to social inclusion (e.g., discrimination, racism, etc.) need to be addressed. In this work, Aboriginal refers to the first peoples of Canada, First Nations, Métis, and Inuit; in using the term Indigenous I am connecting myself and other Aboriginal peoples of Canada to an interconnected global community of Indigenous nations.

Indigenous higher education began in the 1960s with the establishment of Native Education and Native Studies programs in public universities (Battiste & Barman, 1995; Brant Castellano, Davis, & Lahache, 2000; Stonechild, 2006) and later the development of Aboriginal student support services (Pidgeon & Hardy Cox, 2005). While this article is focusing on public non-Indigenous institutions, it is important to acknowledge the early leaders in Indigenous post-secondary institutions who were the Gabrielle Dumont Institute (est. 1980) in Saskatchewan (Dorion & Yang, 2000) and the Nicola Valley Institute of Technology (est. 1982) in British Columbia (Billy Minnibarriet, 2012).

Indigenization as a discourse through academic writing and research emerged the early 2000s (Mihesuah & Wilson, 2004) and has increased in scope and depth to become a transformative movement globally. The long-term impact of this movement continues to take shape; it is hoped that future generations of Indigenous communities have different stories to tell—stories of equity, empowerment, and self-determination.

The purpose of this article explores what Indigenization means through institutional initiatives (e.g., policy, programs, and practices) that are aimed to support Indigenous success. To begin, the article provides a brief overview of the history of Aboriginal engagement with public post-secondary education and then transitions into exploring how the Indigenization movement has been articulated and critiqued from within and outside the academy. In understanding the landscape of Indigenization, I situate the work that I have witnessed over 10 years of research and practice in British Columbia, Canada through an Indigenous Wholistic Framework (Pidgeon, 2008a, 2014). It is used to understand how institutions have (or have not) been responding to Indigenization from Indigenous perspectives. The Framework includes the work of Kirkness and Barnhardt (1991) on the 4Rs of respect, relevance, reciprocal relationships, and responsibility; the 4Rs become the guiding structure for discussing the tensions within the Indigenization movement to move institutional approaches away from the tokenized checklist response that merely tolerates Indigenous knowledge(s) to one where Indigenous knowledge(s) are embraced as part of the institutional fabric. The article concludes with questioning and providing a response to: What does an Indigenized institution look like? The conclusions provide visioning of the next steps to collectively move towards becoming a socially inclusive society.

2. An Overview of the Relationship between First Nations, Métis, and Inuit and Post-Secondary Education

First Nations and Inuit kindergarten to grade 12 (or equivalent) is a federal responsibility as dictated through the Indian Act 1876 (and amendments) and while initially concerned with on-reserve schools now includes transfer payments to the provincial public system for Aboriginal students who attend off-reserve public schools. Métis peoples have a different historical relationship with the federal government in terms of education provision (Dorion & Yang, 2000). This relationship changed once legal changes to s.35 of the *Canadian Constitution 1982* recognized the unique culture and rights of Métis peoples. Gabriel Dumont Institute, established in 1980, was Canada's first Métis post-secondary institution that "focused on the education through cultural research as a way of renewing and strengthening the heritage and achievement of Métis and non-status Indian peoples in Saskatchewan" (Dorion & Yang, 2000, p. 180).

For the rest of Canada, kindergarten to post-secondary education is a provincial jurisdiction with financial transfer payments from the federal government. This unique relationship has created a dual system in that the federal government does not see itself legally responsible for the post-secondary education of Indigenous peoples (Battiste & Barman, 1995; Paquette & Fallon, 2014; Royal Commission on Aboriginal Peoples, 1996). Under the guise of social responsibility (rather than legal), the federal government began providing more support programs through federal funding for access programs, some academic initiatives, and financial support programs for First Nations learners, who were under the jurisdiction of the Indian Act, starting in 1970s to 1990s (Human Capital Strategies, 2005; Malatest & Associates Ltd., 2004; Stonechild, 2006; Usher, 2009; White, Maxim, & Spence, 2004).

Indian Control over Indian Education, a foundational Indigenous position paper written by the National Indian Brotherhood (now known as the Assembly of First Nations) in 1972, remains a corner stone in the articulation of First Nations visions for education. This document was an Indigenous response to the federal governments' White Paper, a proposed policy that aimed to change the nature of the relationship and responsibilities of the federal government to First Nations peoples. Indian Control over Indian Education clearly positioned the role of education across the lifespan (e.g., from early childhood to post-graduate education) for First Nations peoples in Canada (National Indian Brotherhood, 1972). Forty years later, the aims articulated in 1972 are even more relevant and pertinent to the conversation of what it means to meaningfully engage with Indigenization of higher education (Pidgeon, Muñoz, Kirkness, & Archibald, 2013). Building on this history, we have seen the emergence and recent resurgence in Indigenized-programs and services and Indigenous-specific post-secondary institutions across the country (Association of Universities and Colleges of

Canada (AUCC), 2010; Human Capital Strategies, 2005; Pidgeon, 2005, 2014; The Aboriginal Institutes' Consortium, 2005; Usher, 2009).

In many ways, Canada is in a unique moment in history as the national gaze has focused on the complexity of issues facing Indigenous communities. This national attention is influenced by the grassroots and community based advocacy such as the Idle No More Movement (e.g., http://www.idlenomore.ca) and the calls for a national inquiry for the missing and murdered Aboriginal women (e.g., http://canadians.org/sites/default/files/publications/missing-women-factsheet.pdf). Further to this, the Truth and Reconciliation Commission (TRC) of Canada bought the nation together to witness, reflect, and react to the cultural genocide experienced by Aboriginal peoples and the ongoing intergenerational legacy of the residential school era (1831–1996). In the TRC final report and *Calls to Action,* there was a call for the Canadian educational system to change "in order to redress the legacy of residential schools and advance the process of Canadian reconciliation" (Truth and Reconciliation Commission of Canada (TRC), 2015b, p. 1).

Indigenization of higher education is part of this reconciliation and to move forward, all involved- Aboriginal and non-Aboriginal need to consider what Indigenization means. For example, as Indigenous researchers, faculty members, students, Elders, and staff bringing our knowledges, practices, and ways of being into this colonial space must honors and respects who we are as Indigenous peoples. Non-Aboriginals seeking this "Indigenization" of their institutions must understand what Indigenization really means, and that Indigenization can not be defined or bounded by their expectations of what it should mean. Indigenization provides insight into Indigenous envisioning for the educational experiences for the next seven generations.

3. Indigenization: What Does It Really Mean?

From Indigenous perspectives, Indigenization of the academy refers to the meaningful inclusion of Indigenous knowledge(s), in the every day fabric of the institution from policies to practices across all levels, not just in curriculum. Marlene Brant Castellano (2014) envisions Indigenized education to mean "that every subject at every level is examined to consider how and to what extent current content and pedagogy reflect the presence of Indigenous/Aboriginal peoples and the valid contribution of Indigenous knowledge" (para. 1). Mihesuah and Wilson's (2004) *Indigenizing the Academy: Transforming scholarship and empowering communities* is one of the first texts put forward by Indigenous scholars who reflect on what it meant to Indigenize the academy. It clearly laid out the challenges of this process not only ideologically but also practically from a variety of Indigenous scholars from Canada and the United States. For example, in his chapter of the same text, Taiaiake Alfred (2004) reflects on Indigenizing the academy as a process where "we are working to change universities so that they become places where the values, principles, and modes of organization and behavior of our people are respected in, and hopefully even integrated into, the larger system of structures and processes that make up the university itself" (p. 88). Cupples and Glynn (2014) explored what it meant for a group within Nicaragua's coast to form their own decolonized and intercultural university with the "aim to support political and social struggles with culturally and epistemologically appropriate modes of teaching, learning, and research" (Mato, 2011 cited by Cupples & Glynn, 2014, pp. 56-57). Cupples and Glynn (2014) explained how the university provide access to individual students "but without losing sight of education as a collective good" (p. 57) based on principles of interculturality.

Daniel Heath Justice (2004) writing to the field of Indigenous literary studies shares lessons that are useful for other Indigenous academics, who are invested in the Indigenization of the academy. He reminds Indigenous peoples that the academy is just as much our inheritance as being part of the land and we have a right and entitlement to be part of the meaning making of this world and while we are in these spaces, "we must not forget to be both responsible and humble" (p. 101) and to "be generous of spirit, in war as well as in peace" (p. 103). These recommendations support the decolonizing work of Marie Battiste (Battiste, 1998; Battiste, Bell, & Findlay, 2002), who views education as a tool of decolonization where Indigenous people are empowered in who they are. Other Indigenous scholars (such as Kuokkanen, 2007; Smith, 2012) argue that higher education through Indigenization is becoming decolonized and perhaps more importantly, an active resistor to the ongoing colonization of Indigenous peoples. Kuokkanen's (2007) logic of the gift refers to meaningful inclusion of Indigenous knowledge(s) within the academy. Battiste (2013) in calling on educators to decolonize their pedagogy and practices, provides a way for us to address cultural misappropriation in our institutions. This call applies to all involved in higher education, whether a government bureaucrat, policy analyst, administrator, faculty, staff, or student, Aboriginal or non-Aboriginal. She states:

> "educators must reject colonial curricula that offer students a fragmented and distorted picture of Indigenous peoples, and offer students a critical perspective of the historical context that created that fragmentation. In order to effect change, educators must help students understand the Eurocentric assumptions of superiority within the context of history and to recognize the continued dominance of these assumptions in all forms of contemporary knowledge". (Battiste, 2013, p. 186)

There are criticisms of this movement from non-Indigenous and Indigenous communities, albeit their arguments come from difference places. The critiques who are non-indigenous peoples tend to position their arguments (or questions about or resistance too) Indigenization by stating that the academy already has a cannon of knowledge in which Aboriginal knowledges are part of- so why does the academy need to Indigenize? This resistance is particularly strong in academic disciplines with long colonial legacies and an unwillingness to alter their thinking. Another group adopts a multiculturalism stance, where they argue the inclusion of Indigenous knowledges and practices means that the academy will have to include all other groups in society (e.g., race, class, gender). They push back arguing the work of Indigenizing the academy is too difficult or complex. There are yet others who put forward a fiscal argument that given the current economic cutbacks and declining enrollment, providing such institutional commitment to a relatively small percentage of the university or college community is fiscally irresponsible. While many will state, of course if they could make their institutions better for Aboriginal students they would, but to undertake that task means that they will have to devolve their power, position, and prestige to create space for other ways of knowing and being (Pidgeon, 2008a, 2014).

While criticisms, or cautions, from Indigenous scholars regarding Indigenization are framed with an awareness that this movement is occurring within a deeply seated colonial structure with long histories in the colonization of Aboriginal peoples and still influencing the ongoing colonial project (e.g., Alfred, 2004; Mihesuah & Wilson, 2004; Paquette & Fallon, 2014). For Indigenization to occur, Indigenous scholars argue it must also be a decolonizing process; Indigenity has to go beyond what "others" are comfortable with, beyond the tokenistic representations of culture, or one-off events, programs, and services and misrepresentations of Indigenous peoples and their cultures (Arndt, 2013; Jacobs, 2014; King & Springwood, 2001; Lee & Castagno, 2007; Paquette & Fallon, 2014). These Indigenous scholars also inherently recognize these misrepresentations and forms of resistance perpetuate the colonial project of "othering" and sustain the inherent systemic racism, both overt and covert, that result in inappropriate uses of Indigenous culture and images within society.

Daniel Heath Justice (2004) aptly describes the tensions, in that if Indigenous scholars see the higher education institutions as:

> "enforce[ing] an understanding of 'knowledge' as that body of mores that have emerged more from a clash of ideas than a thoughtful consideration of them....Such a goal turns our attention away from lands and cultural traditions and into inequitable power dynamics of an increasingly corporatized academic world. Such an academy may well be beyond redemption." (p. 101)

However, if the view of the academy is one of "a place of intellectual engagement, where the world of ideas can meet action and become lived reality....[It] can also be a site of significant cultural recovery work, a place where all people who are disconnected from their histories can begin their journeys homeward" (p. 102). It is this later view, where Indigenization of the academy is embodied in the work of Indigenous peoples engaging as active participants in society and higher education to the broader goals of decolonization and empowerment. The questions that remain within this movement, is what is the process of indigenization and what does a successful Indigenized institution look like? To better understand this movement, and to provide a framing of the discussion through an Indigenous lens, the next section provides an overview of the Indigenous Wholistic Framework.

4. Indigenous Wholistic Framework: Theory and Process

An Indigenous Wholistic[1] Framework (see Figure 1) is just one way to represent Indigenous ways of knowing and being; it represents for me, as a person of Mi'kmaq ancestry a way of centering who I am as a scholar (Pidgeon, 2008a, 2014). This Framework connects not only the philosophical underpinnings of Indigenous knowledges but attempts pictorially to represent the complexity of wholistic interconnections that we have as individuals, to our communities, nations, and global communities. It recognizes that one's physical needs are linked to the spiritual, intellectual, and emotional and that living a balanced life is about meeting each of these needs sustained by one's inter-relationships. The Indigenous Wholistic Framework provides an anchor to move forward a discussion of Indigenizing the academy, in that we can locate it in place (geographically, institutionally, etc.) and see the interconnections of a broader educational system (e.g., country, province, territory) to the individual student, administrator, faculty, staff, Elder, and others in the institution and surrounding communities (Pidgeon, 2008a, 2014). This framework allows us to locate in place the Indigenous territories and lands, whether unceded or ceded through treaty, upon which post-secondary institutions were built. Acknowledging territory is increasing as an institutional practice in Canada; it acknowledges the Indigenous peoples of the area and, in a symbolic way, recognizes the colonial legacy of the institution in place and time.

As Figure 1 demonstrates the interconnections of indi-

[1] Wholistic is intentionally spelled with a W to be mindful of the whole being; it honors the practice begun by Archibald et al. (1995).

vidual to family to community (local, provincial/territorial, national, global) illustrates how an Indigenous student's educational journey or Aboriginal community engagement in research or academic programming is connected to a broader success and empowerment of Indigenous peoples. Within a post-secondary setting, for one to solely think of education as an intellectual exercise ignores keys components of the learning journey that fosters Indigenous understandings of success and well being (Pidgeon, 2008b). The 4Rs, first proposed by Kirkness and Barnhardt (1991), and later revisited by Marker (2004), are the cornerstone of my own work (e.g. Pidgeon, 2014). Other Native American scholars have also been taken up the 4Rs in their work in the US higher education system (e.g., Shotton, Lowe, & Waterman, 2013). The 4Rs represent Indigenous perspectives on how Respect for Indigenous knowledges, Responsible relationships, Reciprocity, and Relevant programs and services can transform institutional cultures and practices for Indigenous peoples. The 4Rs were offered by Kirkness and Barnhardt (1991) to help build understanding between Indigenous and non-Indigenous ways of thinking of supporting Aboriginal student success, in this article the 4Rs are extended to help bridge understanding of Indigenization where the Wholistic Framework centers the work from the Indigenous perspective.

Building on Figure 1, Figure 2 provides a visual representation of the interconnections in an institution between senior administration, faculty/departments, and faculty/staff/student with policies, programs, and practices. It shows the inter-relationships of the global-national-local to higher education, particularly evident in Canada's structure of provincial jurisdiction of education but federal responsibility of First Nations, Métis, and Inuit education. Indigenization as a form of social inclusion requires recognizing the work and dedication that has happened from the grass roots of an institution to the senior executive leadership to create systemic and broader societal change.

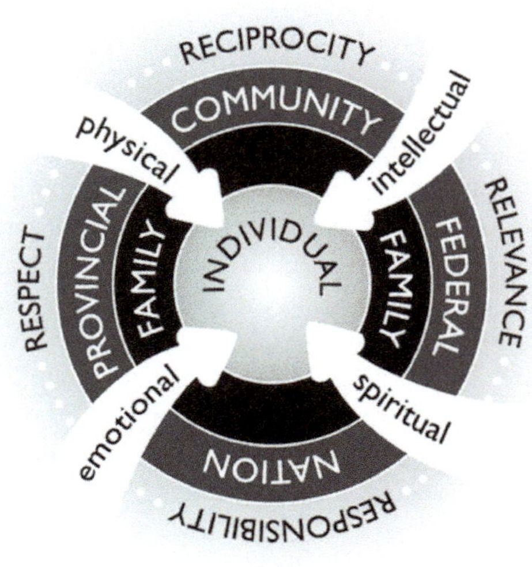

Figure 1. Indigenous Wholistic Framework.

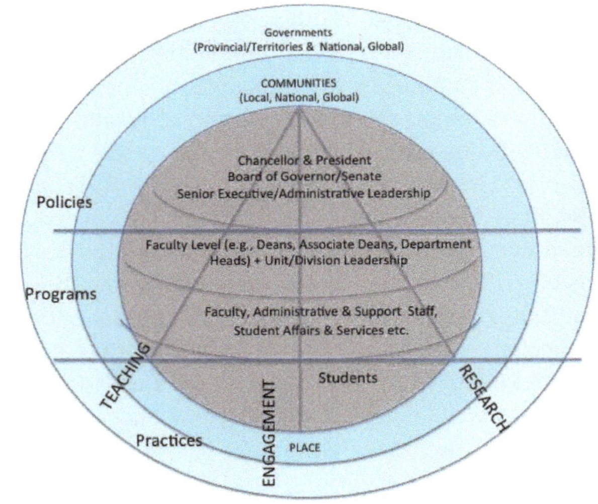

Figure 2. Visual representation of inter-connections of higher education.

5. Lessons Learned: Indigenizing the Academy through the 4Rs

Indigenizing the academy is not one strategy, or one policy change—it is a culminating and complex living movement that aims to see post-secondary institutions empowering Aboriginal peoples' cultural integrity through respectful relationships through relevant policies, programs, and services. This transformation will take time and it is time. It is important to remember that post-secondary institutions are not some abstract ideal or philosophy, nor are they unknown entities; institutional structures, values, and cultures are complex and the people who reside, engage, and interact (internally or externally) with these institutional communities all shape and influence the institution. Therefore, Indigenous and non-Indigenous peoples all have a responsibility to act to transform post-secondary education to benefit all, as illustrated within the Indigenous Wholistic Framework through Responsible Relationships & Governance; Relevance to Curriculum and Co-Curricular; and Respect in Practice.

5.1. Responsible Relationships & Governance

Canadian universities and colleges primarily operate on a bi-cameral governance model (e.g., senate and board of governors for universities or governance boards and education council for colleges) (Jones, 2014). The roles and responsibilities of these governing bodies are outlined in the College and Institutes Act or University Act (or comparable policy) in each province and territory. As Figure 2 illustrates, governance also encompasses the senior leadership of the President, Vice-Presidents, Deans, and Associate Deans, department heads and directors in addition to staff, faculty, and student unions and student leadership across the various areas of our campuses.

It is important to acknowledge the Indigenous institutes, such as Nicola Valley Institute of Technology (NVIT), the En'owkin Centre, Gabriel Dumont Institute, and other Indigenous institutions operate under an Indigenous governance framework, with Elders and Aboriginal senior leadership. Their entire institution from policy to program development and pedagogical practice imbeds and honours Indigenity. However, the focus of this article is on non-Indigenous public post-secondary institutions, for this is where the meaningful inclusion of Indigenity is a challenge.

Leadership in the Indigenization movement comes from a variety of individuals and groups within and outside the institution. It is the student affairs staff working to recruit and retain Indigenous students alongside Aboriginal student services, Aboriginal academic transition programs, and other culturally relevant supports. It occurs when faculty members begin to dialogue and enact changes in their programs, curriculum, and pedagogical practices that are more inclusive, respectful, and responsible of Indigenous knowledge(s) and of the Indigenous learners in the classroom. It also is exemplified at the most senior level- the president. For example, during the period of the TRC, the University of Manitoba publically apologized for its role in the training of teachers who worked in residential schools and its overall role in the colonial project against Indigenous peoples. In July 2015, the incoming president of the University of Saskatchewan, Peter Stoicheff, publically announced that he is making Indigenization his top priority. He explained that "the university must be a leader in closing the gaps between Aboriginal and non-Aboriginal people, he continued, calling this a 'moral imperative'"(Academia Group, 2015 para. 1).

Indigenization of the academy occurs when Indigenous community members, Elders, aunties, uncles, and other family members come to the institution to support their learners and/or become involved in the governance of the institution (e.g., members on Advisory council). Community involvement (or lack of it) also highlights a tension in Indigenizing the academy—Canadian higher education is primarily based on the bicameral system and in many ways operates with values and practices that are contrary to Indigenous governance models and cultural protocols. While more institutions are honouring of territory at formal and public institutional events, they can do more to ensure that the day-to-day operations of an institution, particularly related to Indigenous matters, honour and follow Indigenous models of governance (e.g., Aboriginal advisory committee; Indigenous leadership positions) and policies (e.g., Aboriginal strategic plans or specific policies).

5.1.1. Aboriginal Advisory Committee

Within British Columbia, there are 26 universities, colleges, and institutes, of whom 17 (65%) have institutional level Aboriginal strategic plans. However, only 8/17 have some form of an Aboriginal Advisory Committee, whose representatives include Elders, Aboriginal community leaders, and others who have an interest in Aboriginal higher education from within the institution. These positions are typically voluntary members from the community and staff from the institution. These advisory committees can be simply "window dressing," with limited power to make changes and simply provide the institution with a check mark of "have-it" but without influence or change on the institution itself. However, in most cases, these committees do bring together leaders from within and outside the institution and have terms of reference that forge powerful relationships and leadership within the university for Indigenous initiatives between the communities and the institution.

5.1.2. Indigenous Leadership Positions

Within BC's public post-secondary system, many institutions have created formal leadership positions such as Special Advisor to President (e.g., University of Victoria, Thompson Rivers University, University of British Columbia, Vancouver Community College) at the senior executive level. While some faculties have created leadership positions at the Associate Dean level for Indigenous initiatives (e.g., University of British Columbia). These positions are typically held by tenure-track professors, usually at the rank of associate or full, this academic credibility has been seen as an important "power" relationship in negotiating in the academy. At the senior administration level, these positions tend to have administrative staff of one to two people, have an operating budget for program planning and initiatives, and articulated terms of reference and goals. There are also leadership roles created under the responsibilities of a Vice President (e.g., VP Academic) or Associate Dean (e.g., Associate Dean, Academic) at the faculty level, such as a Director, who may or may not have an academic position within the institution, typically they are hired under an administrative position, and their mandate is related to implementing the institutions' Aboriginal strategic plan or implement a faculty-level plan (e.g., University of Victoria, Simon Fraser University).

The power of this senior leadership, whether from the senior executive to a faculty position, is largely dependent on how the position was negotiated within the institution, the reporting structure, budget attached to the position (e.g., financial and human resources), and most importantly, the mandate and goals of the position and the authority to enact change (e.g., scope, role, authority— symbolic or otherwise) (Pidgeon, 2014). Such positions create a unique opportunity to make systemic change through role-modeling and mentoring other in living Indigenous values and principles of governance in practice (Alfred, 2004;

Pewewardy, 2013). Such positions have also been created in the United States, as Francis-Begay (2013) described the establishment of special advisor to the president at the University of Arizona in 1999, and noted other institutions who have also created that liaison position between the institution and tribal nations (e.g., Montana State University, University of Idaho, University of New Mexico, Washington State University, University of Oregon, Northern Arizona University, and Arizona State University) (p. 82).

First Nations Student Associations (FNSA) are also a growing component of student leadership and governance on campus. As part of the undergraduate student union for the institutions, some FNSAs have negotiated funding allocation for Indigenous-student initiatives and programming on campus that benefits Indigenous and non-Indigenous students. FNSAs and student-representative positions within Senate, departments, and faculties are other opportunities for Indigenous students to have an active voice within their institutions (Pidgeon, 2008a; Pidgeon, 2014).

5.2. Institutional Policy

5.2.1. Aboriginal Strategic Plans

Institutional level policy relates to the work of the governance bodies (e.g., Senate) and the day-to-day operations of an institution and institutional-wide strategic initiatives. The majority of the 124 public universities, colleges, or institutes across Canada had some form of institutional plan which outlines the institutional mission and purpose within a three to five year cycle; these strategic reports are also accountability frameworks and reporting mechanism to the provincial ministry. For the purposes of this paper, I conducted an environmental scan of publically available strategic plans at 124 public colleges and universities in Canada, only 35% of these institutions had a specific institution-wide Aboriginal strategic plan, which was also referred to as Aboriginal Student Success Strategy or Indigenous Initiatives. Indigenous strategic plans tend to cover policy, programs, and broader institutional goals around Aboriginal student success rates.

Other policies that are important to note, are those that intentionally focus on Indigenous education, normally focusing on support Aboriginal student success. For example, the Indigenous Education Accord (Association of Canadian Deans of Education (ACDE), 2009) and the Indigenous Education Protocol for Colleges and Institutes (College and Institutes Canada, 2014b).

The ACDE (2009), with the leadership Jo-ann Archibald, John Lundy, Cecilia Reynolds, and Lorna Williams, developed the accord to enhance teacher education preparation for working with Indigenous learners and their communities. It states "recognizing the need for transformative educational change and acknowledging the unique leadership responsibilities of deans, directors, and chairs of education within Canadian university context, the ACDE supports and encourages the following goals" (p. 5): respectful and welcoming learning environments; respectful and inclusive curricula; culturally responsive pedagogies; mechanisms for valuing and promoting Indigenity in education; culturally responsive assessment; affirming and revitalizing Aboriginal languages; Indigenous education leadership; non-Indigenous learners and Indigenity; and culturally-respectful Indigenous research (pp. 5-8).

Colleges and institutes are key providers to post-secondary education to Indigenous peoples, who represent diverse cultures, languages, histories, and contemporary perspectives (College and Institutes Canada, 2014b). The College and Institutes Canada, representing 135 public and private colleges and institutes, developed an Indigenous Education Protocol for Colleges and Institutes. This document was launched on December 31, 2014 and "underscores the importance of structures and approaches required to address Indigenous peoples' learning needs and support self-determination and socio-economic development of Indigenous communities" (para. 4). As of June 8, 2015, 34 colleges and institutes from Alberta, British Columbia, Manitoba, Saskatchewan, Quebec, Ontario, New Brunswick, North West Territories, and Yukon (College and Institutes Canada, 2014a) had signed this document with the commitment to the following seven principles: 1) Commitment to make Indigenous education a priority; 2) Ensure governance structures recognize and respect Indigenous peoples; 3) Implement intellectual and cultural traditions of Indigenous peoples through curriculum and learning approaches relevant to learners and communities; 4) Support students and employees to increase understanding and reciprocity among Indigenous and non-Indigenous peoples; 5) Commit to increasing the number of Indigenous employees with ongoing appointments throughout the institution, including Indigenous senior administrators; 6) Establish Indigenous-centred holistic services and learning environments for learner success; and 7) Build relationships and be accountable to Indigenous communities in support of self-determination through education, training, and applied research (College and Institutes Canada, 2014a).

The principles that are common to these two policies are also evident in university Aboriginal strategic plans, with the addition of the area of research (e.g., Indigenous research strategies, methodologies, and relevant research to Indigenous communities). These strategic plans often influence specific policies to be implemented regarding Indigenous students as the next section outlines.

5.2.2. Aboriginal Specific Policies.

In researching student experiences of university and

college, there were notable places in institutional policy that were pertinent to the Indigenous student experience and Indigenization. The first would be around admissions, considering prior-knowledge and ensuring culturally relevant admissions processes for students. Two areas of tension around admissions are: 1) self-identification of whether or not they are Aboriginal and 2) financial barriers. To support Aboriginal access, some institutions have developed third-party billing policy. Third party billing allows for the institution and provider of funding to directly work together and allows an Aboriginal student (or any student who is receiving funding from an outside source (e.g., not student loans, personal bank loans, or scholarships/grants)) to not have to negotiate receipt of funding. Examples of this funding policy are on the websites of Dalhousie University, University of Victoria, and University of Manitoba. This policy creates a direct relationship between the institution and the funder and in this agreement, some institutions will "cover" fees for the student (from application, tuition, and books) and work with the Band (or other funding organization) to receive the funds.

In terms of self-identification, in an educational system where being "labelled" Aboriginal has had negative consequences for many (e.g., special education or non-academic streaming), Aboriginal students are leery of institutional requests for self-identification (Hare & Pidgeon, 2011; Royal Commission on Aboriginal Peoples, 1996; Wotherspoon & Schissel, 1998). While institutions may be simply asking for this information for 1) enrolment numbers and/or 2) referrals to Aboriginal student services; many students are sceptical on how that information is actually used and do not want to be labelled in any way (Pidgeon, 2008a, 2008b). As a researcher and teacher, I have observed many Aboriginal students choose not self-identify at admissions but will later in their educational journey whether it was during a visit to the Aboriginal student services centre, in a class where they had an Indigenous faculty member or instructor, or in later applications for Indigenous-specific scholarships or at the time of graduation. Many of these students will never formally notify the institution of their Indigenous identity hence, there are discrepancies in reporting institutional statistics on how many Indigenous students may be enrolled and graduation rates.

Admissions policies also occur at the program level, where some academic areas intentionally designate "seats" or proportional representation policies for Aboriginal students. The goal is to increase Aboriginal representation in particular fields of study, notably medicine, nursing, law, dentistry, and other professional programs such as engineering or business. There are also similar policies related to on-campus accommodations and financial supports (e.g., scholarships, grants).

Within Aboriginal admissions or other policies in some institutions, a tension does exist with self-identification and institutional processes that require "proof" of Aboriginal ancestry. For students who are registered Band members and/or have status through the Indian Act, this documentation is relatively easy to provide. However, for other Indigenous students, getting this required documentation is more problematic due to the political tensions within their Band or community, separation from their community (e.g., Sixty scoop, foster care, adoption, etc.), or relocation (e.g., growing up in urban settings or communities outside of their ancestral connections or being Indigenous from other countries) (Pidgeon, 2008a, 2008b; Pidgeon, Archibald, & Hawkey, 2014). University and college then becomes a time for these Aboriginal students to explore, understand, and empower themselves with a better sense of what it means to be Aboriginal. This journey is not an easy one; it is one that must be supported within the Indigenization of the institution and is part of the broader decolonizing project of Canada's education system.

5.3. Relevance to Curricular & Co-Curricular

5.3.1. Teaching & Learning

The academic programs of Native Teacher Education Programs and Native Studies were the first academic points of entry for many Aboriginal students in the late 1960s and to the 1970s (Battiste & Barman, 1995; Stonechild, 2006). Since the 1990s there has been a diversification of academic majors, minors, and program focuses specifically related to Indigenous perspectives. There have also been targeted recruitment initiatives within the Science, Technology, Engineering, and Mathematics (STEM) fields and medicine to recruit and retain Indigenous engineers, scientists, medical doctors, and nurses (Human Capital Strategies, 2005). Within Teaching and Learning Centers there have been efforts to hire Indigenous curriculum experts to help support faculty to support Indigenous learners in their classrooms through culturally relevant curriculum and pedagogical practices. Libraries are also beginning to embrace Indigenous knowledge system(s) within the library sciences and consequently, hire Indigenous librarians to work specifically with Indigenous content. Within the reconciliation section, the Truth and Reconciliation Commission of Canada (TRC) (2015a) call to action for education for reconciliation calls for curriculum, intercultural competencies, and teacher training—all of these recommendations apply to teaching and learning at university and colleges and certainly align with the Indigenization movement.

Such policy and practices do influence the classroom experiences of students. For example, the Association of Canadian Deans of Education (2011) follow up report demonstrated how the 19 Faculties of Education implemented the Accord on Indigenous Education from a one-time course to an integrated approach throughout the curriculum. Some institutions have not only created a required course but also have furthered their support in the work of Aboriginal language revitalization and extended (or renewed) their relationships with local First Nations (e.g., St. Francis Xavier University).

In addition to a required course, the Faculty of Education at York University have also moved towards an Infusion model were "it is centered on developing respectful relationship with First Nations, Métis, and Inuit partners and creating space in the program for thoughtful construction of new pedagogy and understandings" (Vetter & Blimkie, 2011 cited in ACDE, 2011, p. 7) that respect Indigenous ways of knowing and being. Some examples of the work being done across the country include the University of British Columbia where in 2013 the Dean of Education and Associate Dean of Indigenous Education supported the establishment of a professorship in Indigenous Education in Teacher Education, which was directly related to implementation of the Accord. At Simon Fraser University, this mandate has taken a more integrated approach through the Professional Development Program supported through new tenure track hire in Indigenous education and the creation of the Office of Indigenous Education, with an advisory committee to implement the Accord across the Faculty. In 2014, the University of Toronto's Ontario Institute for Studies in Education (OISE) received a gift of five million dollars to strengthen Indigenous education research in Canada. OISE created the endowed chair of William A. Macdonald, Q.C Distinguished Fellow in Indigenous Education ("Indigenous education initative at OISE: Advancing leadership in Indigenous knowledge and education," 2015) and Chief Shawn A-in-chut Atleo was the first appointed to this distinguished chair.

While the Accord was developed for Faculties of Education it does provide a replicable process and relevant programmatic changes for other academic disciplines to follow. The first would be to have Indigenous faculty within the discipline take a leadership role in developing the accord with the support of the Deans of the faculties across the country. This work would center Indigenous knowledge, pedagogies, and practices within the discipline and provide models of how the discipline could take up the work (e.g., required courses to infused across the curriculum). The Deans would be responsible for supporting the implementation of the accord within their respective faculties, as the Deans of Education have done so with the Accord they unanimously signed.

Given the 2015 TRC *Calls to Action* and recommendations, the Accord leads to the broader question: What about a required course for all undergraduate students? This is the exact call made by the Aboriginal Student Council and the University of Winnipeg Student Union in February 2015, which would require all undergraduates complete an Indigenous studies course as part of their degree program as a graduation requirement (CBC News, 2015). The Senate of the University of Winnipeg approved in principle the Indigenous course requirement on March 26, 2015 and it will be implemented for Fall 2016 (Communications, 2015). The University of Lakehead is also working towards requiring all incoming undergraduate students to take an Indigenous content course as part of their degree requirements for graduation. The motivation for both institutions is based on social justice, acknowledging the systemic and societal racism and the general lack of awareness and understanding non-Aboriginal Canadians have about Aboriginal peoples history and contemporary issues across the country (Halsall, 2015).

5.3.2. Student Services

Student services is considered to oversee the co-curricular aspects of the student experience which include, but are not limited to, housing, counseling, wellness, student leadership, student engagement, financial services, learning commons, and other such support services. Aboriginal student services in Canada were first established in the 1970s in response to a recognized need for culturally relevant support services for Indigenous learners (Pidgeon, 2005; Pidgeon & Hardy Cox, 2005). The 1990s saw a period of growth due to provincial target funds to further support Aboriginal students in their transition to university with culturally-relevant support services; in 2001 approximately 45% of public universities had some form of Aboriginal student support (Pidgeon & Hardy Cox, 2005), and in 2014–2015 my recent review of this original research found more than 90% of Canadian colleges and universities now have some form of Aboriginal student services.

Across the research projects I have been engaged in, administrators, student service providers, and Aboriginal students expressed some tensions about providing culturally-relevant services to a small percentage of the student population, despite recognizing the inherent value of such services (Pidgeon, 2008a, 2014). Institutionally, this tension arises from government cutbacks to funding post-secondary education generally and establishing Aboriginal-initiatives based on short-term, often external funding. For student service providers, not only were fiscal limitations expressed, but the acknowledgement that providing Aboriginal student services without institutional commitment to human resources and campus space continues to be difficult. Aboriginal student services provide a home-away-from-home for students and both practitioners and Aboriginal students shared experiences of how limited operating budgets impacted services (e.g., limited access to tutoring, computer resources, etc.). Some students shared their observation that while there was a lot of institutional promotion of support of Indigenization, such programs, policies, and services become irrelevant if Aboriginal students themselves were not seeing institutional changes that directly impacted their curricular and co-curricular experiences (Pidgeon, 2008a, 2014).

5.3.3. Research

Academic research within Canada is funded primarily through the Tri-Council, which is comprised of three national research councils: Canadian Institute of Health Research (CIHR), Social Sciences and Humanities Research Council (SSHRC), and National Science and Engineering Research Council. Pertinent to this discussion is the Tri-Council's collaborative work with Aboriginal scholars on developing a specific chapter within the Tri-Council Ethical Guidelines that address ethical issues when working with Aboriginal communities. Even in following Chapter 9 of the Tri-Council, researchers must also be aware they need to consult with relevant organizational bodies (e.g., Health or Educational authorities) and of course, Aboriginal communities ethical protocols (Mi'kmaq Ethics Committee and College Institute, 1997; Piquemal, 2001).

Indigenous research methodologies and processes cannot be excluded from this discussion for several reasons. Indigenous scholars are incorporating culturally relevant and responsible research practices in their scholarship. As a result they are bridging relationships with Aboriginal communities that are bound by cultural expectations of ethics as well as academic ethical standards. In the inclusion of Indigenous research methods in the academy, there is a need to change tenure and promotion policies and procedures to not only understand the work of Indigenous researchers. There has to be institutional recognition through policies, like those of tenure and promotion, that acknowledge Indigenous scholars using Indigenous research methodologies will have different research trajectories and dissemination processes within this body of work will look different from traditional research profiles of non-Indigenous scholars (Kovach, 2009; Smith, 2012).

The Canadian Association of University Teachers (CAUT) has been holding bi-annual forums for Aboriginal academic staff to better understand their unique issues of being within the academy and to better support their work. These forums are:

> "organized with the guidance of CAUT's Working Group on Aboriginal Post-Secondary Education, this the Forum will be an important opportunity for Aboriginal academic staff from across Canada to get together to share information, discuss issues of common interest, and provide advice to CAUT and our member associations." (Canadian Association of University Teachers (CAUT), 2015, para. 5)

Specific workshops are held regarding tenure and promotion with the aim to change the system structures to be more inclusive for Indigenous academics and those working with Aboriginal communities.

5.4. Respect in Practice

Through my research (Pidgeon, 2011, 2014; Pidgeon et al., 2014), I have learned of pockets of presence in our institutions where Indigenization thrives and this work also highlights some ongoing tensions with Indigenization of the academy: How does Indigenization live in practice? How are Indigenous knowledge(s) being respected in our institutions? In thinking about meaningful social inclusion and Indigenization, I have chosen to focus on three tensions that are currently hindering advancing Indigenization in the academy: token checklists vs. meaningful practice, Indigenization vs. Internationalization, and identity contestations.

5.4.1. Checklist vs. Meaningful Practices

The institutional checklist approach to Indigenization can be an easy one to write and to say, "Done, done, and done". However, in using the Indigenous Wholistic Framework to create this list, there are deeper questions to ask for. For example, does the institutions Indigenization strategy positively change the lived experiences of Indigenous students, staff, and faculty? Are Aboriginal peoples seeing themselves reflected in the curriculum, the classroom, the hallways, in their academic programs of choice, in the staff room, or at Senate?

In a period of austerity measures for post-secondary education, one avenue for financial support still available is through targeted funding programs (e.g., government, endowments etc.) for Indigenous programs and services (albeit short term and often externally sourced). However, such special initiative funding becomes pointless if the institutions do not commit institutional resources (both human and financial) to the long term sustainability of such initiatives (Pidgeon, 2014). This is not an argument against special initiative funding as such funding can be key catalysts to support institutional change however Indigenization cannot stop here nor be dependent solely on such short-term funding.

In the review of the development of Aboriginal specific student affairs and services, early establishment of such services was a direct result of specific provincial funding programs aimed at increasing support for Aboriginal students (Pidgeon, 2005; Pidgeon & Hardy Cox, 2005). During the early development of these centres they were often located on the outskirts of campus or located in buildings that required major repair. For other institutions they created Aboriginal-specific buildings or gathering spaces in existing buildings were externally funded through endowments and fund raising (Pidgeon, 2014). These buildings, such as the Longhouse at UBC or the Aboriginal Student Centre at the University of Winnipeg represent culturally appropriate Indigenous architecture. Other models, such as the services provided at Western University through Indigenous Services, the First Nations House at University of Toronto, or the Indigenous student centre and Aboriginal gathering spaces at Simon Fraser University all of which reclaimed institutional space and included culturally-appropriate artwork, physical spaces (e.g., circle lounges), and other modifications that represented Indigenity.

Indigenous initiatives for systemic change and sustainability require clear funding commitments that are not dependent on the securing of the next grant. Governments change as do political will—so for Indigenization of the academy to have a lasting legacy for the next seven generations it must be sustainable and integrated, not an add on approach that is limited by funding. This funding flux is also related to another tension evident in higher education between Indigenization and internationalization.

5.4.2. Indigenization & Internationalization

The increasing influence of globalization and neoliberalism on the discourses of access to higher education requires institutions to be mindful of the tensions in the internationalization movements and the Indigenization movements (Garson & Dumouchel, 2013). In today's reality there is a competition of resources that challenges how institutional resources (both human and financial) are directed to each initiative. In some instances, these two movements are seen as opposing and competing for institutional resources. However, assumptions can not be made that creates a binary of Indigenous or International. When in fact, Aboriginal peoples can also be from international context and attend Canadian post-secondary institutions. What is needed are equitable approaches to decolonization and intercultural development, as part of Indigenization, to not only meet Indigenous peoples were they are (e.g., physically increasing access to digital and face-to-face learning environments) but also ensuring high quality programs and services. Indigenization, as the Truth and Reconciliation Report calls for, is about increasing understanding of non-Aboriginal peoples to become decolonized in order to truly value the contributions of the past, present, and future of Indigenous peoples.

5.4.3. Identity Contestations

The politicization of Indigenous identity plays out in the academy, from those claiming identity that is not theirs to claim for personal financial or professional gain (Pewewardy, 2004), to those students and scholars reclaiming their Aboriginal identity as a decolonization process (Huffman, 2001; Pidgeon, 2014). As Daniel Justice Heath reminds us:

> "If nationhood and liberation are our goals, we must truly acknowledge the diversity of Native experiences by avoiding both the traps of 'mixed-blood angst' and of 'full-blood purity'—if we focus on blood quantum as an indicator of Indian 'authenticity,' we emphasize a colonist paradigm that was imposed on Native peoples for the sole purpose of destroying our Nations, traditions, and landbases. Such a focus ignores the wide variety of response to different communities to colonialism and it sets up arbitrary idea of what makes a 'real' Indian....Similarly these trips ignore the fact that we aren't just another immigrant ethnics group—we're independent tribal Nations, with governments and distinctive identities of our own that emerge from our spiritual and cultural relationships to this land." (p. 104)

Building on the earlier discussion of whether students choose to self-identify as Aboriginal, Indigenous students who enter university and/or college with their own aspirations of success. Indigenous student success is not only about graduation but is also about being empowered as Indigenous peoples with their cultural integrity intact (Pidgeon, 2008b). It is critical Indigenous and non-Indigenous peoples remain cognizant of the colonial project of "divide and conquer", where by what counts as "Indigenous" becomes another colonial tool to further distract Indigenous peoples from their own rights of self-determination and defining nationhood for themselves. For this to occur, for Indigenization to thrive within the academy—the next section explores the question "What do Indigenized public colleges and universities look like?"

6. What Does a "Successfully" Indigenized Public College or University Look Like?

System transformations require not only recognition of institutional responsibility to Indigenous peoples, but also articulated accountability to these responsibilities (Pidgeon, 2014). Indigenization of the academy has truly transformed higher education when Indigenous students leave the institution more empowered in who they are as Indigenous peoples and when non-Indigenous peoples have a better understanding of the complexities, richness, and diversity of Indigenous peoples, histories, cultures, and lived experiences. Indigenizing the academy can be enacted Indigenous representation from the Board of Governors, Senate, and senior administration to the faculty, staff, and students. It is about having relevant curricular and co-curricular program, policies, and services in place that truly honor who Indigenous students are in their journey (Pidgeon, 2008b).

There is still the question of when will we know that an institution has successfully Indigenized (from Indigenous understandings of what that means). For example, an Indigenized public post-secondary institution may have institution-wide policies, such as Aboriginal strategic plans; proportional representation of administrators, faculty, and staff who are Indigenous; culturally relevant programs, policies, services, and practices across each faculty and department, and an ongoing commitment to Indigenization. Several questions might be posed to institutions undertaking Indigenization: what changes can we see in the lived experiences of Indigenous student? Are there changes in recruitment and retention of Indigenous students, faculty, and staff? How do Aboriginal communities experience these institutions and the students who return home from these places? Even more broadly, to ask Indigenous peoples what their expectations are of such institutions and what societal and systemic changes will need to be witnessed and more importantly experienced by Indigenous peoples. These questions will be answered in the near future as we will be able to examine institutional practices and outcomes related to their Indigenization efforts.

7. Conclusions

The overall theme of this journal relates to social inclusion of Indigenous peoples and this article positions Indigenization in higher education as one movement that can reconcile disparities that currently exist in our educational systems and societies for Indigenous peoples. System wide and institutional transformation will take time and while Indigenous peoples have been experiencing colonization for over 500 years, we do not have another 500 years to wait for change. The change is happening as Indigenous peoples live in these academic spaces and Indigenization must continue to regenerate and live for generations to come. The true Indigenization of higher education and for meaningful social inclusion of Indigenous peoples, Indigenity must remain at the core of the transformation, centred and grounded in the local territories and nations upon which colleges and universities reside. Non-Aboriginal peoples must take responsibility and be part of their own decolonizing process and move towards reconciliation. In a Indigenized institution, Indigenous peoples remain empowered in their self-determination and cultural integrity. Ultimately, higher education through Indigenization becomes a place for Aboriginal peoples to journey to attain their envisioned futures.

Acknowledgments

I raise my hands in thanks to those who have participated and partnered in research with me over years. It is the voices of Aboriginal students, Elders, administrators, faculty, and staff that are central to this work and the continued efforts each of them make in moving forward Indigenization in the academy. I would also like to acknowledge and pay respect to the non-Indigenous administrators, faculty, and staff who have worked alongside with Indigenous peoples to make transformational change within the institution for Indigenous peoples and their communities.

Conflict of Interests

The author declares no conflict of interests.

References

Academia Group. (2015, July 13). *New uSask President committes to indigenization*. Retrieved from http://academica.ca/top-ten/new-usask-president-commits-indigenization

Alfred, T. (2004). Warrior scholarship. In D. A. Mihesuah & A. C. Wilson (Eds.), *Indigenizing the academy: Transforming scholarship and empowering communities* (pp. 88-99). Lincoln, Nebraska: University of Nebraska Press.

Arndt, G. (2013). Indigenous dance and dancing indian: Contested representation in the global era by Matthew Krystal (review). *The Americas*, *70*(1), 109-111. doi:10.1353/tam.2013.0082

Association of Canadian Deans of Education (ACDE). (2009). *Accord for Indigenous Education*. Retrieved from http://www.csse-scee.ca/docs/acde/acde_accord_indigenousresearch_en.pdf

Association of Canadian Deans of Education (ACDE). (2011). *Accord for indigenous education: Progress report 2011*. Retrieved from http://www.csse-scee.ca/docs/acde/acde_indigenousaccord_progressreport.pdf

Association of Universities and Colleges of Canada (AUCC). (2010). *Answering the call: The 2010 inventory of Canadian university programs and services for Aboriginal students*. Retrieved from Ottawa: http://www.univcan.ca/wp-content/uploads/2012/01/aboriginal-directory-repertoire-autochtone-2010.pdf

Battiste, M. (1998). Enabling the autumn seed: Toward a decolonized approach to Aboriginal knowledge, language, and education. *Canadian Journal of Native Education*, *22*(1), 16-27.

Battiste, M. (2013). *Decolonizing education: Nourishing the learning spirit.* Saskatoon, SK: Purich.

Battiste, M., & Barman, J. (Eds.). (1995). *First Nations education in Canada: Circle unfolds.* British Columbia: University of British Columbia.

Battiste, M., Bell, L., & Findlay, L. M. (2002). Decolonizing education in Canadian universities: An interdisciplinary, international, Indigenous research project. *Canadian Journal of Native Education*, *26*(2), 82-95.

Billy Minnibarriet, V. (Ed.). (2012). *Aboriginal post-secondary education in British Columbia: Nicola valley institute of technology—"An eagle's gathering place"*. University of British Columbia, Vancouver. Retrieved from http://www.collectionscanada.gc.ca/obj/thesescanada/vol2/BVAU/TC-BVAU-42089.pdf

Brant Castellano, M. (2014). *Indigenizing education*. Retrieved from http://www.cea-ace.ca/blog/marlene-brant-castellano/2014/06/2/indigenizing-education

Brant Castellano, M., Davis, L., & Lahache, L. (Eds.). (2000). *Aboriginal education: Fulfilling the promise*. Vancouver: UBC Press.

Canadian Association of University Teachers (CAUT). (2015). *Forum for Aboriginal academic staff*. Retrieved from http://events.caut.ca/aboriginal-2015/

CBC News. (2015). *UWinnipeg students' union calls for mandatory indigenous course*. Retrieved from http://www.cbc.ca/news/canada/manitoba/uwinnipeg-students-union-calls-for-mandatory-indigenous-course-1.2958811

College and Institutes Canada. (2014a). *Indigenous education protocol*. Retrieved from http://www.collegesinstitutes.ca/policyfocus/indigenous-learners/approaches-and-exemplary-practices-to-guide-implementation

College and Institutes Canada. (2014b). *Indigenous learners*. Retrieved from http://www.collegesinstitutes.ca/policyfocus/indigenous-learners

Communications. (2015, March 26). *Senate approves principle of Indigenous course requirement*. Retrieved from http://news-centre.uwinnipeg.ca/all-posts/senate-approves-principle-of-indigenous-course-requirement

Cupples, J., & Glynn, K. (2014). Indigenizing and decolonizing higher education on Nicaragua's Atlantic Coast. *Singapore Journal of Tropical Geography, 35*(1), 56-71. doi:10.1111/sjtg.12051

Dorion, J., & Yang, K. R. (2000). Métis post-secondary education: a case study of the Gabriel Dumont Institute. In M. Brant Castellano, L. Davis, & L. Lahache (Eds.), *Aboriginal education: Fulfilling the promise* (pp. 176-189). Vancouver: UBC Press.

Francis-Begay, K. (2013). The role of special advisor to the president on Native American Affairs. In H. Shotton, S. C. Lowe, & S. J. Waterman (Eds.), *Beyond the asterisk: Understanding native students in higher education* (pp. 81-94). Sterling, VA: Stylus.

Garson, K., & Dumouchel, L. (2013). *G2: Internationalization and Indigenization: Finding the synergies*. Paper presented at the CBIE, Vancouver, BC. Retrieved from http://www.cbie-bcei.ca/wp-content/uploads/2013/08/G2-Internationalization-and-Indigenization.pdf

Halsall, J. (2015, June 23). Some univerisities look to adopt indigenous course requirements. *University Affairs/Affaires universitaires*. Retrieved from http://www.universityaffairs.ca/news/news-article/some-universities-look-to-adopt-indigenous-course-requirements

Hare, J., & Pidgeon, M. (2011). The way of the warrior: Indigenous youth navigating the challenges of schooling. *Canadian Journal of Education, 34*(2), 93-111. Retrieved from http://search.proquest.com.proxy.lib.sfu.ca/docview/881643999?accountid=13800

Huffman, T. (2001). Resistance theory and the transculturation hypothesis as explanations of college attrition and persistence among culturally traditional American Indian students. *Journal of American Indian Education, 40*(3), 1-23.

Human Capital Strategies. (2005). *Review of Aboriginal post-secondary education programs, services, and strategies/best practices and Aboriginal special projects funding (ASPF) program*. Retrieved from http://www.humancapitalstrategies.ca/download/final_report_june_30-05.pdf

Indigenous education initative at OISE: Advancing leadership in Indigenous knowledge and education. (2015). Retrieved from https://www.oise.utoronto.ca/oise/UserFiles/File/IndigenousInitiaties2015.pdf

Jacobs, M. R. (2014). Race, place, and biography at play: Contextualizing American Indian viewpoints on Indian mascots. *Journal of Sport & Social Issues, 38*(4), 322-345. doi:10.1177/0193723514530568

Jones, G. A. (2014). An introduction to higher education in Canada. In K. M. Joshi & S. Paivandi (Eds.), *Higher education across nations* (Vol. 1, pp. 1-38). Delhi: B. R. Publishing.

Justice, D. H. (2004). Seeing (and reading) red. In D. A. Mihesuah & A. C. Wilson (Eds.), *Indigenizing the academy: Transforming scholarship and empowering communities* (pp. 100-123). Lincolin: University of Nebraska Press.

King, C. R., & Springwood, C. F. (Eds.). (2001). *Team Spirits: The Native American mascots controversy*. Retrieved from http://www.ebrary.com

Kirkness, V. J., & Barnhardt, R. (1991). First Nations and higher education: The four R's—Respect, relevance, reciprocity, responsibility. *Journal of American Indian Education, 30*(3), 1-15. Retrieved from http://jaie.asu.edu/v30/V30S3fir.htm

Kovach, M. (2009). *Indigenous methodologies: Characteristics, conversations, and contexts*. Buffalo: University of Toronto Press.

Kuokkanen, R. (2007). *Reshaping the university: Responsibility, Indigenous epistemes and the logic of the gift*. Vancouver: UBC Press.

Lee, S., & Castagno, A. (2007). Native mascots and ethnic fraud in higher education: Using tribal critical race theory and the interest convergence principle as an analytic tool. *Equity & Excellence in Education, 40*(1), 3-13. doi:10.1080/10665680601057288

Malatest, R. A., & Associates Ltd. (2004). Aboriginal peoples and post-secondary education: What educators have learned. Retrieved from http://www.millenniumscholarships.ca

Marker, M. (2004). The Four Rs revisited: Some reflections on First Nations and higher education. In L. Andres & F. Finlay (Eds.), *Student affairs: Experiences in and through Canadian post-secondary education* (pp. 171-188). Vancouver, BC: UBC Press.

Mi'kmaq Ethics Committee and College Institute. (1997). Mi'kmaq research ethics and protocols. Retrieved from http://mrc.uccb.ns.ca/prinpro.html

Mihesuah, D. A., & Wilson, A. C. (Eds.). (2004). *Indigenizing the academy: Transforming scholarship and empowering communities*. Lincoln, NE: University of Nebraska Press.

National Indian Brotherhood. (1972). *Indian control of Indian education*. Ottawa: National Indian Brotherhood.

Paquette, J., & Fallon, G. (2014). In quest of Inidgenity, quality, and credibility in Aboriginal post-secondary education in Canada: Problematic, contexts, and potential ways forward. *Canadian Journal of Educational Administration and Policy, 165*, 1. Retrieved from http://www.umanitoba.ca/publications/cjeap/pdf_files/paquette_fallon.pdf

Pewewardy, C. D. (2004). So you think you hired an "Indian" faculty member? In D. A. Mihesuah & A. C. Wilson (Eds.), *Indigenizing the academy: Transforming scholarship and empowering communities* (pp. 200-217). Lincoln, NE: University of Nebraska Press.

Pewewardy, C. D. (2013). Fancy war dancin on academe's glass ceiling: Supporting and increasing Indigenous faculty role models in higher education In H. Shotton, S. C. Lowe, & S. J. Waterman (Eds.), *Beyond the asterisk: Understanding native students in higher education* (pp. 139-150). Sterling, VA: Stylus.

Pidgeon, M. (2005). Weaving the story of Aboriginal student services in Canadian unviersities. *Communique, 5*(3), 27-29.

Pidgeon, M. (2008a). *It takes more than good intentions: Institutional accountability and responsiblity to Indigenous higher education* (Doctoral Thesis). University of British Columbia, Vancouver, Canada.

Pidgeon, M. (2008b). Pushing against the margins: Indigenous theorizing of "success" and retention in higher education. *Journal of College Student Retention: Research, Theory & Practice, 10*(3), 339-360. doi:10.2190/CS.10.3.e

Pidgeon, M. (2011). *Imagining Douglas College as a successful place for Aboriginal students*. Unpublished Research Report, Vancouver, BC.

Pidgeon, M. (2014). Moving beyond good intentions: Indigenizing higher education in British Columbia universities through Institutional responsiblity and accountability. *Journal of American Indian Education, 53*(2), 7-28.

Pidgeon, M., Archibald, J.-a., & Hawkey, C. (2014). Relationships Matter: Supporting Aboriginal graduate students in British Columbia, Canada. *Canadian Journal of Higher Education, 44*(1), 1-21. Retrieved from http://proxy.lib.sfu.ca/login?url=http://search.ebscohost.com/login.aspx?direct=true&db=eric&AN=EJ1028743&site=ehost-live

Pidgeon, M., & Hardy Cox, D. (2005). Perspectives of Aboriginal student services professionals: Aboriginal student services in Canadian universities. *Journal of Australian & New Zealand Student Services, 25*, 3-30.

Pidgeon, M., Muñoz, M., Kirkness, V. J., & Archibald, J.-a. (2013). Indigenous control of Indian education: Reflections and envisioning the next 40 years. *Canadian Journal of Native Education, 36*(1), 5-35.

Piquemal, N. (2001). Free and informed consent in research involving Native American communities. *American Indian Culture and Research Journal, 25*(1), 65-79.

Royal Commission on Aboriginal Peoples. (1996). *Gathering of strength, Volume 3. Report of the Royal Commission on Aboriginal Peoples (RCAP)*. Ottawa: Minister of Supply and Services.

Shotton, H., Lowe, S. C., & Waterman, S. J. (Eds.). (2013). *Beyond the asterisk: Understanding Native students in higher education*. Sterling, VA: Stylus.

Smith, L. T. (2012). *Decolonizing methodologies: Research and indigenous peoples*. New York: Zed Books.

Statistics Canada. (2008). Aboriginal statistics at a glance. Retrieved from http://www.statcan.gc.ca/pub/89-645-x/89-645-x2010001-eng.htm

Statistics Canada. (2013). 2011 National Household Survey. Retrieved from http://www12.statcan/gc/ca/nhs-enm/2011/as-sa/99-011-x/2011001/tbl/tbl02-eng.cfm

Stonechild, B. (2006). *The new buffalo: The struggle for Aboriginal post-secondary education in Canada*. Winnipeg, MB: University of Manitoba Press.

The Aboriginal Institutes' Consortium. (2005). *Aboriginal institutions of higher education: A struggle for the education of Aboriginal students, control of Indigenous knowledge, and recognition of Aboriginal institutions.* Retrieved from http://caid.ca/AboHigEdu2005.pdf

Truth and Reconciliation Commission of Canada (TRC). (2015a). *Honoring the truth, reconciling for the future: Summary of the final report of the Truth and Reconciliation Commission of Canada.* Retrieved from http://www.trc.ca/websites/trcinstitution/File/2015/Honouring_the_Truth_Reconciling_for_the_Future_July_23_2015.pdf

Truth and Reconciliation Commission of Canada (TRC). (2015b). *The Truth and Reconciliation Commission of Canada: Calls to action*. Retrieved from http://www.trc.ca/websites/trcinstitution/File/2015/Findings/Calls_to_Action_English2.pdf

Usher, A. (2009). *The Post-Secondary Student Support Program: An examination of alternative delivery mechanisms.* Retrieved from http://www.educationalpolicy.org/publications/pubpdf/INAC.pdf

White, J. P., Maxim, P. S., & Spence, N. D. (2004). An examination of educational success. In J. P. White, P. S. Maxim, & D. Beavon (Eds.), *Aboriginal policy research: setting the agenda for change* (Vol. 1, pp. 129-148). Toronto: Thompson.

Wotherspoon, T., & Schissel, B. (1998). Marginalization, decolonization and voice: Prospects for Aboriginal education in Canada. Retrieved from http://proxy.lib.sfu.ca/login?url=http://search.ebscohost.com/login.aspx?direct=true&db=eric&AN=ED467991&site=ehost-live

About the Author

Dr. Michelle Pidgeon

Dr. Michelle Pidgeon's ancestry and family are from Newfoundland and Labrador and she is currently living and working in the traditional and unceded territories of the Coast Salish peoples. She is an Associate professor in the Faculty of Education at Simon Fraser University, British Columbia. She is also the Editor of the *Canadian Journal of Higher Education*. Dr. Pidgeon is passionate about higher education, student services, and Indigenity. A central tenant of her work is that success is defined and articulated through an Indigenous wholistic framework and research process.

12

Double Disadvantages: A Study of Ethnic and *Hukou* Effects on Class Mobility in China (1996–2014)

Yaojun Li [1,2,*] and Yizhang Zhao [3]

[1] Department of Sociology, University of Manchester, Manchester, M13 9PL, UK; E-Mail: yaojun.li@manchester.ac.uk
[2] Cathie Marsh Institute for Social Research, University of Manchester, Manchester, M13 9PL, UK
[3] Department of Social Statistics, University of Manchester, Manchester, M13 9PL, UK;
E-Mail: Yizhang.Zhao@manchester.ac.uk

* Corresponding author

Abstract
This paper examines the ethnic and household registration system (*hukou*) effects on intergenerational social mobility for men in China. Using national representative surveys covering almost two decades (1996–2014), we assess both absolute and relative rates of mobility by ethnicity and *hukou* origin. With regard to absolute mobility, we find that minority men had significantly lower rates of total and upward mobility than Han men, and those from rural *hukou* origins faced more unfavourable chances. With regard to relative mobility, we find men of rural ethnic origins significantly less likely to inherit their parental positions. Even with parental and own educational qualifications and party memberships controlled for, we still find ethnic minority men of rural *hukou* origins behind others in access to professional-managerial positions. Overall, our findings suggest that the preferential policies have largely removed the ethnic differences in the urban sector but ethnic minority men from rural *hukou* origins are faced with double disadvantages: in addition to the inequality of opportunity rooted in the institutional divide which they share with the majority group from similar backgrounds, they face much greater inequalities in conditions, namely, in having poorer socio-economic and cultural resources.

Keywords
China; ethnicity; household registration system (*hukou*); social mobility

Issue
This article is part of the issue "International Migration and Ethnic Integration", edited by Yaojun Li (University of Manchester, UK) and Anthony Heath (University of Oxford, UK).

---

1. Introduction

The aim of this paper, drawing on national representative sample surveys in China, is to examine the social inequality in intergenerational class mobility in terms of ethnic and structural relations. We address ethnic and structural inequalities simultaneously by exploring the mobility differences between the ethnic minority and the majority (Han), and for people from urban and rural origins. The ethnic dimension is easy to understand but unlike the situation in western countries, ethnicity has added complexity in China due to the scale, diversity, geography and political importance of the ethnic minority groups. The structural differences refer to the inequalities embedded in the household registration (*hukou*) system which was implemented in the 1950s and which has limited the upward mobility chances of people from rural origins for over half a century. Any mobility research on China would be incomplete without taking into account the *hukou* effects. Quite a few studies have been conducted examining the *hukou* effects on mobility but to the best of our knowledge, no research has been conducted on intergenerational social mobility by ethnicity in China. To this end, this paper seeks to understand the ethno-*hukou* intersection in contemporary China by providing evidence on both the absolute and the relative rates of social class mobility.

Social mobility research and ethnic studies are, as Li and Heath (2016) note, both concerned with the same underlying issue, that of social equality and social justice. Social inequality, be it manifested in terms of family background, ethnicity/race, gender, age, disability, sexuality or other ascribed characteristics, is economically inefficient, morally indefensible and politically illegitimate. In the western capitalist countries, ethnic issues are mainly concerned with the difficulties faced by immigrants and their descendants in education, employment and career advancement, and are thus a matter of inter-ethnic relations and of socio-economic integration. In China, ethnicity has, in addition to socio-economic equality, extra considerations such as political stability, national unity and border safety as most of the ethnic minorities live in the western part of the country which tends to be mountainous, under-developed and bordering other countries. The Chinese government attaches great importance to ethnic unity and equality and has, especially in the last few decades, instigated numerous preferential policies to try to help the minorities in their socio-economic development. Quite a few studies have been made to evaluate the effects of such policies but owing to the lack of appropriate data on parental class position, researchers have thus far been unable to assess whether ethnic minorities have similar mobility chances to those by the majority, the extent of difference, and the possible reasons that may underlie such differences. The present analysis wishes to provide evidence to these questions for the first time.

This paper is structured as follows. In the next section, we give a brief review of the socio-economic-demographic profile of China's ethnic minorities, the preferential policies adopted by the Chinese Government towards the minorities to improve their life chances, and the research findings about the education, employment and income situations of the ethnic groups. A brief discussion will also be made of the main findings from the social mobility research perspective for the urban and the rural populations in China. After that, we explain the data and methods to be used in the paper, followed by presentation of our findings on both the absolute and the relative mobility rates along ethnic and *hukou* dimensions. In the final section, we summarize our findings with some discussion.

2. Ethnic Minorities in China

China is a vast country with a very large population. It is also a multi-ethnic and multicultural country. There are currently 55 officially-designated ethnic minority groups in addition to the Han majority. According to the 2010 Census of the Population of the People's Republic of China (PRC), 114 million people were of ethnic minority heritages, accounting for 8.49% of the overall population (National Bureau of Statistics of the People's Republic of China, 2011).

Whilst ethnic minorities take up a relatively small proportion in the overall population in China, they occupy a strategically important position as they live in areas comprising around two thirds of the nation's territory. The Chinese Communist Party (CCP) enacted pro-ethnic policies in its controlled areas even during the war years, promising equal rights for all ethnic minorities (Sautman, 1999). After the PRC was founded in 1949, the central government made numerous efforts to protect minority interests and promote their socio-economic development such as by giving them official legal status, creating written language for some of the groups, guaranteeing equal rights in the 1982 Constitution, promoting equal opportunities in the 1984 Law of Regional Autonomy and many subsequent laws and regulations at the central and provincial levels (Gladney, 1996; Lin, 1997).

Owing to the low population density and the vast areas of territory the ethnic minorities populate, the central government gave areas with relatively high ethnic concentrations a special political and administrative status called 'ethnic autonomous regions'. Five such autonomous regions were created at the provincial level (Inner Mongolia, Guangxi, Tibet, Ningxia, and Xinjiang), 30 autonomous areas at the prefectural level and 120 autonomous administrative units at the county level (National Bureau of Statistics of the People's Republic of China, 2015). Being an autonomous region does not necessarily mean that ethnic minorities comprise the overwhelming majority of the residents in the area. As a matter of fact, they only consist of 45% of the population in the five regions. But the overall socio-economic levels in the areas are below those in the rest of the country, especially the big cities and the coastal areas which have witnessed rapid development since the reform programme was launched in 1978.

China has a tradition of treating all ethnic groups as members of a big family in the nationhood building. In fact, in the Chinese language, the word 'country' (*guo jia*) literally means 'nation family'. To ensure equal rights amongst the family members (the different ethnic groups in this case), the central government and the CCP have adopted many measures to enhance the political, social and economic wellbeing of the ethnic minority groups. Several social movements were launched in the 1950s and 1960s to combat Han chauvinism in minority areas, to show full respect to the cultural traditions of the ethnic minority groups, to avoid condescendence in attitudes, behaviours and practices when working with people of ethnic minority heritages, and to fight against discrimination of one kind or another, especially in recruitment and promotion (Chao, 1994; McMillen, 1979, p. 114). At the same time, tens of thousands of educated youths and technical personnel were sent from the majority population to the autonomous areas to help with the socio-economic development, and to strengthen the national security of the border areas (Attané & Courbage, 2000).

The ethnic minorities, like people in the rest of the country, suffered during the chaotic period of the Cultural Revolution (1966–1976), with minority cultural customs labelled as primitive, minority cadres exposed to ridicule, and pro-ethnic policies regarded as unnecessary (Dreyer, 1968; He, 2005, p. 69; Lin, 1997). Since the early 1980s, a wide range of policy measures have been adopted to mitigate the adverse influence of the Cultural Revolution and to support the socio-economic development of minorities including, most importantly, the 1982 State Constitution of China in which equal rights were enshrined in law for all ethnicities in the country. The previous autonomous administration system was reinstated at the provincial and lower levels, and numerous preferential policies were enacted and implemented from the central to the local governments to help the minorities, including exemptions from the one-child family-planning policy, lower marks for university admissions, economic assistance and tax reduction, and more favourable opportunities for recruitment and promotion. The overall aim of the policies was not only for the minorities to have better opportunities, but also to achieve the ultimate aim of equal outcomes among all ethnic groups (Chen, 1991).

As compared with 'affirmative action' or 'positive discrimination' programmes in some other countries, China's preferential policies are, as Sautman notes, 'broader (encompassing a wider array), deeper (affecting almost all minority people) and more variegated (due to decentralization)' (1998, p. 86). Perhaps the most notable example of such policies pertains to the minorities' exemption from the strict regulations on family planning. The one-child policy was implemented nationwide in the 1980s, but most of the minority groups were allowed to have two children in the urban areas and three or four in the rural areas (Attané & Courbage, 2000; Bulte, Heerink, & Zhang, 2011; Sautman, 1999). Although the policy varied to some extent over time and across regions, the principle of showing respect to minority cultures by allowing them to have more children remained unchanged. Yet, as we are going to see, this preferential treatment in the form of 'greater opportunities' may have yielded an unintended consequence, in the sense of aggravating the already existing inequality of condition and creating additional barriers for mobility. We shall come to this later when we discuss the findings. Here we focus on policies that might have had direct and positive impacts on the minorities' life chances, including those on education, employment, and economic support.

With regard to education, China's Compulsory Education Law (1992) covers all children for nine years, from primary to lower secondary schools. Yet full coverage was not achieved in the remote areas, most of which were in minority autonomous regions. Many people in these areas were in dire poverty and could not even afford the basic teaching materials. In order to improve the coverage and ensure the basic standard of education in the minority areas, the central government allocated special resources called the Ethnic Minorities Education Aid Special Fund. In 1994, the state raised the funding to one billion Chinese Yuan per year, a fivefold increase as compared with the previous years. With the assistance of the fund, hundreds of boarding schools were built in the remote areas. Students were exempted from fees for tuition and books and, in many cases, were guaranteed free food, clothing, lodging, and supplementary study materials (Sautman, 1998, p. 91). Ethnic autonomous regions were also encouraged to develop their own curriculum and use their own language in the local schools. These programmes catered for the special needs on language, culture and historical traditions of the local ethnic communities, and the expenses in teacher training, curriculum designing and extra printing were partly funded by the government budget (Postiglione, 2009, p. 504). Yet the special treatment for teaching ethnic languages and cultures also added to the students' difficulty in learning, making them proficient in neither the local nor the national language and lowering their prospects for advancing into higher levels of education.

As for higher education, ethnic minority students enjoy a range of preferential policies. For university admission, ethnic students were given extra points on the basis of their original marks in the national entrance examination or were offered a lower threshold for admission. For example, Sautman (1998) reported that in Xinjiang in 1987, the Han (majority) students needed an average score of 470 points in science and 445 points in liberal arts for access to key universities, while the minorities only needed an average score of 313 and 269 points respectively. In addition, the government has established more than 20 universities for ethnic minorities, mostly located within the minority areas, so that the minority students could have access to higher education near their hometown (Huang, 2000). These universities mainly enrol students from minority backgrounds and offer special subjects based on the needs of different ethnic regions. In order to enhance the education quality of minority students, the state has initiated a programme for top national universities to form partnerships with those in minority autonomous regions for cooperation and assistance, such as teacher training, facility donation, library resource sharing, and various other forms of exchange (Yang & Wu, 2009).

The preferential treatment does not stop at education. Ethnic minorities in China also enjoy favourable treatment in recruitment and promotion, especially in the autonomous regions. The 1993 Regulations on Work with the Urban National Minorities called on enterprises to recruit more minority workers in return for lower taxes or tax breaks. As in the case of university admission, when examinations were required for job seekers, minority applicants would have bonus points. For instance, in the employment examination for an oil and chemical factory in Urumqi, the capital city of Xinjiang autonomous region, applicants from the Han majority needed 250 points whereas the minimum for minorities was 120. In some cases, the minority status is necessary as employers need to meet the job quotas to reflect the ethnic composition of the population in the local area (Sautman, 1998).

The preferential policies give even greater advantages to ethnic minorities for access to cadre positions or promotions within government agencies. According to the 1982 State Constitution of China, the head of ethnic autonomous regions must be a member of the ethnic group that comprises the majority of the population in that particular location, and the preference was then extended to such an extent as to prioritise minority candidates in the recruitment of lower-level government personnel as well (Gustafsson & Li, 2003). As a result, many places have seen an upsurge of hiring and promoting minority cadres since the 1980s. Of particular note in this context is the fact that China has a dual leadership system, consisting of CCP leaders and administrative officials at all levels of government agencies and state-run enterprises. The party leaders in the minority areas do not have to be members from the ethnic minorities and thus the minorities are more represented in the administrative than in the party organisations.

The Chinese government has not only provided financial and other kinds of help to individuals of ethnic minority heritages in education and employment but also enacted favourable economic policies for the autonomous regions where minority ethnics tend to reside. In the more recent times, the government has initiated two grand projects, The Development of the Western Region (2000) and The Silk Road Economic Belt (2013), in which all the five autonomous regions were included as key areas for national and international investment. In addition, various preferential policies were introduced to support economic growth in minority autonomous areas. As instigated in the 1982 Constitution, the minority autonomous areas are allowed lower tax rates and greater fiscal controls over their local revenues (Zang & Li, 2001). At the meso level, programmes such as government-subsidized microcredit have also been set in motion prioritising poor households in minority areas, and direct subsidies and tax breaks have been granted to these areas and to businesses run by minorities. Given the vast array of economic and other favours enjoyed by ethnic minorities, having an ethnic minority status is, or is perceived as being, advantageous, which can be seen from the fact that millions of people changed their ethnic identity from Han to minority status in the 1980s and the 1990s to benefit from the preferential policies conferred upon the minorities (Sautman, 1999, p. 286), and those of mixed ethnic backgrounds have also been found to prefer a minority identity, which have contributed to the increase in the proportion of the minorities in the overall population (Hoddie, 1998). A study using a more recent census data arrived at a similar conclusion, namely, that children from inter-ethnic families are more inclined to be registered as minority ethnic rather than as majority Han (Guo & Li, 2008).

Given the breadth and depth of preferential policies implemented in China in the last few decades, one might ask whether ethnic minorities are still disadvantaged or whether they have caught up with or even surpassed the majority group in socio-economic life. Existing studies have explored this question from different perspectives and we here give a brief summary of the effects in education, income, and occupational attainment.

With regard to educational attainment, studies have shown that, after decades of government assistance, ethnic differences in primary schooling have been largely removed, but disparities remain at the transition to lower and higher secondary schools (Hannum, 2002; Hong, 2010). As for college education, although the number of minority students has been increasing rapidly, the percentage is still lower than expected. The ethnic minorities accounted for 8.41% and 9.44% of the national populations in 2000 and 2005 respectively,[1] but only 5.71% and 6.10% of the university students came from minority backgrounds in the two years (Zhu, 2010). Moreover, one-fourth of these students were enrolled in ethnic minority colleges, which means the percentages of students studying at universities outside the autonomous regions were even lower (Qin, 2004).

Why are ethnic minorities underrepresented in higher levels of education? Scholars believe that regional economic differentiations and household socioeconomic disparities were the most important factors. The ethnic disadvantages tended to increase after the market transition as the local economic conditions have been playing an increasingly important role in local school resources and educational quality (Hannum, 2002). A lower level of proficiency in Mandarin has also been reported as a crucial contributing factor to the ethnic minority children's poorer school performance. Minority students with a family background using Mandarin were around twice as likely to be enrolled in high school as those who used minority languages at home (Hong, 2010). Bilingual education using Mandarin plus a minority language was an attempt to preserve minority cultures, but it added burdens to minority students from poor homes who were already struggling with their studies (Lin, 1997), incurring dissatisfaction among ethnic parents (Ma, 2007). On the other hand, the preferential policies enjoyed by the minority students also caused dissatisfaction from among the majority students and their parents who lived alongside the minorities in the minority regions (Ma, 2008).

Turning to income, findings are mixed. Some studies have shown that minorities are economically worse off than are the Han majority. For example, Gao and Teng (2006) showed that the ethnic regions in northwest China had an underdeveloped industrial economy

[1] The data on the proportions of ethnic minorities in China for 2000 and 2010 are from the Censuses of the Population in the two years, but those for 2005 are from the 1% population sampling survey. See http://www.stats.gov.cn/tjsj/tjgb/rkpcgb/qgrkpcgb/200603/t20060316_30326.html. Thus while all three proportions (8.41%, 9.44%, and 8.49% for 2000, 2005 and 2010) are official figures on ethnic compositions, that for 2005 may not be as accurate as the other two.

which accounted for the ethnic poverty in those regions. Gustafsson and Sai (2009) found that the minorities had a poverty risk almost twice as high as that for the majority in rural China, but they attributed the difference to location. When location and household characteristics are both taken into account, they conclude, ethnicity does not 'have much of an independent effect on poverty status' and the most promising policies for narrowing the inter-ethnic poverty gaps should, according to the authors, be those 'promoting growth in low-income villages (that are concentrated to western China) irrespective of the ethnicity of the inhabitant' (Gustafsson & Sai, 2009, p. 604; see also Gustafsson & Li, 2003). In other words, the authors believe that, in fighting against poverty-related inequality, it is location, rather than ethnicity, that matters.

Yet ethnicity is found to matter in terms of occupational attainment. Hannum and Xie (1998) examined occupational differences between the Han majority and the ethnic minorities in Xinjiang. Using census data from 1982 and 1990, they found a rising occupational dissimilarity between Han and the minorities. For example, the overall percentage of the labour force in agricultural occupations declined from 58.9% to 49.6% between the two-time points, but the percentage for the minorities increased from 69.4% to 76.7%. The rising concentration of the minorities in agricultural work was accompanied by a falling representation in almost all other occupational categories, and educational inequality was held as a key factor for the increasing dissimilarity, especially in the attainment of high-status occupations. In a similar vein, Sautman (1999) found that whilst ethnic minorities had an overrepresentation of cadres as benefiting from the preferential policies in cadre appointment, they were underrepresented among technical and professional occupations. As both studies were based on Xinjiang, it is not possible to know whether the findings would be generalizable to the ethnic occupational difference in the overall population.

These and other studies which we have not been able to include here due to space limit of the paper have much enhanced our understanding of the ethnic minority disadvantages in the different domains of socio-economic life in China. Yet, there is one common feature, or rather a common limitation, in all such analyses, namely, the lack of information on parental social position which has prevented researchers from exploring the family origin effects on the ethnic minorities' mobility chances. In other words, much work has been conducted comparing the inequalities of opportunity but little work has been carried out that examines the inequalities of condition and the consequences of such inequalities on life chances between the minority and the majority groups.

With regard to studies that do explore the effects of family class, another deficiency is shown. Parallel to what Li and Heath (2016) observed for Britain, ethnic and mobility research scholars in China have also been travelling on separate tracks with the former ignoring family class and the latter ignoring ethnic effects. China's situation is more complicated than that in Britain though, due to additional layers of stratification. The most significant of such layers is that of the household registration (*hukou*) system. As earlier noted, this system was implemented in 1955 requiring all new-born babies to be registered following mother's status, forcing the great majority of the Chinese people at that time and in most of the subsequent periods to have rural *hukou*, unable to enjoy the benefits provided by the government to urbanites in education, employment, housing, medical insurance and a host of other areas. For decades, the *hukou* system has served as the most important institutional divide preventing rural citizens from upward mobility. Given this, almost all important mobility analyses in China have taken *hukou* into consideration.

Within the mobility domain, one of the most important studies is that by Wu and Treiman (2007). Using a national representative sample called Life History and Social Change (conducted in 1996), the authors conducted a thorough analysis of intergenerational social mobility for men in China and found a large-scale downward mobility into agriculture, a feature not elsewhere found in international mobility research. Yet this apparently surprising finding is exactly what would be expected from the *hukou* system: rural sons cannot follow in their fathers' footsteps if the fathers were professionals or managers working in the countryside such as teachers, doctors or cadres but their mothers were agricultural workers (peasants). Only a small proportion, 'the best and the brightest', of those from rural origins could gain entry tickets to urban life, mainly by gaining admission to university. On the other hand, given the huge size of China's countryside, even a small proportion from the rural backgrounds who managed to achieve *hukou* transition could make a big presence in the cities and, what is more, the exceptionally gifted, highly educated, new urbanites tend to take up elite positions. The *hukou* system had a hugely negative effect on rural people's mobility chances, which is also reported by Chen (2013) using the 2005 and 2006 China General Social Survey (CGSS). More recently, Li, Zhang and Kong (2015) used more data from the CGSS (2005, 2006, 2008, 2010) for China, and the General Household Survey (2005), the British Household Panel Survey (2006) and the UK Household Longitudinal Survey (2010) for Britain to compare the mobility profiles in the two countries. They found that social inequality in China was much greater than that in Britain, especially for Chinese women. This, the authors showed, was chiefly due to the *hukou* system. Within each *hukou* sector, social inequality in China was little different from that in Britain.

Yet, in spite of the advances in mobility research in China, none of the available studies have looked at the ethnic differences in mobility chances. Thus, sadly, ethnic research has failed to look at the family origin effects just as mobility research has neglected the ethnic dimension in social stratification. Given this, it is imperative to know whether social reproduction mechanisms operate in a similar way among the ethnic minorities to that among the majority in China, or whether the ethnic minorities face additional barriers over and above those caused by class origin and *hukou* status.

3. Data and Variables

In the present study, we use the Life History and Social Change (LHSC, 1996), China General Social Survey (CGSS, 2005, 2006, 2008, 2010, 2011, 2012, 2013) and China Labour-force Dynamics Survey (CLDS, 2014). Although conducted by different institutions, all three survey series employed multistage probability sampling methods to draw national representative samples for mainland China. While there are some differences in geographical coverage between individual surveys, overall, all 31 provinces, autonomous regions and municipalities in mainland China are covered in the surveys.[2] The CGSS series also includes data for 2003 but that survey covers urban residents only and is therefore not used in the present analysis.

In this study, we use 'ethnic minority' as an overall category without further differentiating between the 55 minority groups. This by no means implies that they are homogenous. The Korean minority, for instance, have been found to have the best educational attainment in China (Lee, 1986). Thus, different ethnic groups do have considerable demographic, socioeconomic, and cultural differences including fertility, mortality, education, occupation, and use of Mandarin (Ma, 2008, 2010; Poston & Shu, 1987; Yusuf & Byrnes, 1994). We group them together based on two considerations: first, all ethnic minorities enjoy similar preferential policies despite their specific historical and cultural characteristics, which sets them apart from the Han majority. Secondly, as the minorities account for less than 10% in the population, further differentiations would lead to very small sample sizes for the groupings, making it untenable in statistical analysis.

With regard to father's and respondent's class, we use the EGP class schema (Erikson, Goldthorpe, & Portocarero, 1979), which is the most widely used class schema for intergenerational social mobility research adopted by practitioners in many countries including China (Chen, 2013; Li et al., 2015; Hannum & Xie, 1998; Wu & Treiman, 2007). We acknowledge that other markers of institutional division such as workplace unit (*danwei*), *hukou* status or political power might add complexity to the social stratification of the Chinese society, and mobility students on China may apply class-, status- or power- based schemas. In order to take account of the unique characteristics of the Chinese society and to make the results comparable to mobility findings from other countries, we adopt the EGP schema. In our further analysis, we also, where appropriate, control for other attributes relevant to mobility such as age, education and CCP membership. We take the *hukou*-ethnicity combination in much of our analysis as a key explanatory variable on people's mobility trajectory alongside father's class. The EGP class schema is based on employment status and occupational position (current or last main job). All information with regard to respondent's and father's employment status and occupational position was collected in the surveys and was coded in a consistent way into own and parental class variables. In the present study, we differentiate, for fathers and respondents alike, five classes: (1) professional and managerial salariat, (2) routine non-manual (clerical), (3) self-employed (own-account), (4) routine manual, and (5) agricultural workers (also called 'peasant' in China). For *hukou* status, we use the respondent's origin *hukou*, namely, the status in the adolescent years (around age 14–18). We confine our analysis to men aged 16 to 65 in this analysis, and exclude those who have never worked such as students, which gives us a sample size of 35,147 for analysis. Gender and workplace affiliation (danwei) are also very important dimensions of social stratification in China (Li et al., 2015; Lin & Bian, 1991) but space limitations do not allow us to explore these in this paper.

4. Analysis

Following standard approaches in the literature we address both absolute and relative rates of mobility by ethnicity and *hukou* status. To assess absolute mobility rates, we start with the class distributions by the various ethno-*hukou* groups, supplemented by an analysis of gross and net amounts of mobility. The former is measured by using the dissimilarity index (DI) and the latter by using Lieberson's (1975) net difference index (NDI). The DI indicates the percentages of cases that would have to be reallocated to make the two distributions identical and thus measures the overall difference between any two distributions. As the DI is insensitive to the local concentrations in or the direction of differences between, father's and son's classes, we use the NDI to show the net class decline or advancement of the son's relative to the father's class.[3] Proceeding from this, we analyse the total,

---

[2] The data files, including technical reports, for LHSC, CGSS and CLDS are available at https://dataverse.harvard.edu/dataset.xhtml?persistentId=hdl:1902.1/M889V1, http://www.cnsda.org/, and http://css.sysu.edu.cn/Data respectively. Qinghai and Ningxia were not covered prior to 2010 and Xizang (Tibet) was only covered in 2010. Nevertheless, this is the best social survey series available covering mainland China. The response rates in the CGSS are 62.1%, 60.4%, 59.7%, 74.3%, 72.6%, 71.5% and 72.2% for 2005, 2006, 2008, 2010, 2011, 2012 and 2013 respectively. The CLDS is a panel study, with the wave 2 (2014) response rate being 75.7% of the wave 1 (2012). See http://css.sysu.edu.cn/Data/List?type=%e4%b8%ad%e5%9b%bd%e5%8a%b3%e5%8a%a8%e5%8a%9b%e5%8a%a8%e6%80%81%e8%b0%83%e6%9f%a5

[3] The NDI is defined as NDxy = pr(X > Y) – pr(Y > X) and further defined as $\sum_{i=2}^{n} x_i \left(\sum_{j=1}^{n=i-1} y_j \right) - \sum_{i=2}^{n} y_i \left(\sum_{j=1}^{n=i-1} x_j \right)$ where, in our case, X indicates father's class and Y that of the respondent. It is noted here that we reversed the class order in calculating the NDI with 1 referring to agricultural workers and 5 to the salariat.

upward and downward mobility rates and examine each by ethno-*hukou* differentiations. To address relative mobility, we use loglinear and log-multiplicative layer effect (also called uniform difference, UNIDIFF) models. These are then supplemented with logit models on son's access to the professional-managerial salariat controlling for ethno-*hukou* status, father's class, and a range of socio-demographic attributes.

4.1. Overall Distributions and Absolute Mobility

We begin with the overall class distributions of fathers and sons, distinguishing the Han majority and the ethnic minorities and, for each, within the urban and the rural sectors. The data are shown in Table 1 where we also show the DI and the NDI. Looking first at the urban sector, we can see that there is not much difference between the Han majority and the ethnic minorities in terms of father's or son's class distributions. Minority fathers have, if anything, a somewhat higher percentage in salariat positions (27.3%) than Han fathers (25.2%). Minority sons are less likely to find themselves in salariat or clerical, and more likely to find themselves in own-account, positions relative to their majority peers. When we look at the rural sector, we see a clear manifestation of ethnic divide. As expected, the overwhelming majority of fathers from both groups were agricultural workers, 80% for Han and 84% for minority fathers, and there is little difference in the distributions to the other class categories. Yet, this overall similarity in fathers' distributions is not shown for sons. Sons from the Han majority group were clearly more likely to occupy higher social positions, from the salariat to the manual working class and are therefore much less likely to find themselves in agricultural positions (44.6%) as compared with minority men (64.8%). The DI and the NDI also show greater gross mobility and net class advancement by Han than by minority men, and that in both urban and rural sectors.

The data in Table 1 thus show that men from ethnic minority backgrounds were disadvantaged. This, of course, is an overall profile, without taking into account the effects of father's class on son's class. In Table 2, we show the class distribution of sons by father's class. For simplicity, we do it by ethnicity but in the 'summary statistics', we also report findings from further analyses by *hukou* status and by the ethno-*hukou* combination.

The ethnic differences are clearly shown in the two panels. For those from salariat families, we see that 38.2% of Han but only 28.7% of minority sons were able to get salariat positions and the risks in downward mobility into agriculture was three times as high: 34.5% versus 10.5%, or a difference of 24 percentage points. The difference in intergenerational stability in agricultural jobs is at a similar level: 68.5% for minority sons and 49.3% for Han sons. And comparing the figures under columns 1 and 5, we can see that the majority (Han) sons from each class backgrounds were more likely to find themselves in salariat, and less likely to find themselves in agricultural, jobs.

The data in the two panels of Table 2 are colour-coded and presented in row percentages. Had we conducted the analysis in cell percentages, we could have easily obtained the total immobility and mobility rates, with the latter further differentiated into upward and downward mobility. The details are shown in the lower part of the table called 'summary statistics' where, in addition to ethnic rates, we also present the rates by *hukou* and, furthermore, by ethno-*hukou* combinations. Also shown are results of statistical tests with Han, Urban, and Han urban as reference groups in the three domain respectively.

At the overall level, over half (53.5%) of the Chinese men were in different class positions to their fathers, with 41.8% having better jobs than their fathers and only 11.7% faring worse. Yet the ethnic differences were self-evident, with the minority men having significantly lower rates in both total and upward mobility rates than their majority peers. The *hukou* differences were less clear-cut, though. Men of rural origins had lower total mobility rates than their urban peers but their upward mobility rates were actually significantly higher, and downward mobility rates significantly lower, than those of their ur-

Table 1. Fathers' (F) and Respondents' (R) class distribution by ethnicity and *hukou* status.

	Urban				Rural			
	Han		Minority		Han		Minority	
	F	R	F	R	F	R	F	R
1 Salariat	25.2	31.2	27.3	26.8	6.3	12.5	6.5	8.2
2 Clerical	14.2	17.3	15.1	11.4	3.1	5.9	2.2	3.4
3 Own account	4.8	9.9	8.3	17.8	1.9	12.2	1.5	8.1
4 Routine manual	44.0	39.7	36.6	39.7	8.7	24.8	5.6	15.5
5 Agricultural	11.9	1.8	12.6	4.2	80.0	44.6	84.1	64.8
Dissimilarity index		14.1		12.1		37.8		22.7
Net difference index		15.7		4.6		36.8		21.6
N		7,995		463		23,225		2,375

Source: The Life History and Social Change survey (LHSC, 1996), China General Social Survey (CGSS, 2005, 2006, 2008, 2010, 2011, 2012, 2013) and China Labour-force Dynamics Survey (CLDS, 2014).

ban peers. This is most likely due to the occupational upgrading witnessed in the last thirty years, with 260 million migrant workers moving to cities to find jobs not all of which were routine manual in nature. Further analysis shows that of those from rural origins and currently still holding rural *hukou* status but not engaged in agricultural work, 13% were doing professional or managerial work, and 9% were doing clerical work. The rural sector has been held at a much lower place since the 1950s and it is thus easier for rural residents to move up and more difficult for them to move further down relative to the urbanites. And looking at the data on the ethno-*hukou* combination, we find what we have suspected: minority men of rural origins have benefited least from the socio-economic development of the country—they have significantly lower rates in both total and upward mobility than do the urban majority peers.[4]

4.2. Relative Social Mobility

We now turn to a different way of looking at class reproduction, namely, relative mobility. Our research questions can be expressed as follows: do we find a weaker association between class origins and destinations among the minority than among the majority group? Do we find a 'perverse openness' where minority status tends to 'trump' class so that minority men are held back irrespective of their fathers' class situation?

Relative mobility (often termed 'fluidity' or 'openness') refers to the competition between people from different origins in obtaining advantaged and avoiding disadvantaged destinations, and is expressed in odds ratios. The closer the odds ratio is to 1, the weaker the class reproduction (and the greater the level of social fluidity or openness). Our interest, then, is whether the odds ratios for the minority group are closer to unity than they are for the majority group. Standard techniques for testing the relationships are to fit three models: the conditional independence model which serves as the baseline; the common social fluidity model (CmSF), which allows for an association between origin and destination but not the three-way interactions; and the log-multiplicative layer effect (also called uniform difference, or UNIDIFF) model which provides an assessment of the extent to which the minority group differs from the majority in the magnitude of the origin/destination odds ratios. This third model provides us with a general test of differences in fluidity, testing whether there is a uniform pattern for the odds ratios to be closer to (or further away from) 1 in a particular layer of the table. To save space, we do not provide the statistical formulae of the three models (interested readers could see Li & Heath, 2016). For the same reason and as the model fit statistics are quite abstract, we are not going to show the statistic details here (results available on request). Basically, none of the three models fit the data by ethnicity, *hukou*, and ethno-*hukou* combination to an acceptable degree but the UNIDIFF models do provide a significant improvement in fit over the CmSF models. Yet, it is of interest to present the UNIDIFF parameters for the ethno-*hukou* combination (Figure 1), which shows that the association between father's and son's class positions is significantly weaker for the minority men of rural origins than for the majority of urban origins.

The UNIDIFF model is good at capturing the magnitude of difference in the origins-destinations association between one layer and another, but it is not good at pinpointing the aspect in which the odds ratios defining the origins-destinations association is particularly strong or weak. As Li and Devine (2011) and Li and Heath (2016) show in the British context, the relative mobility can be much more salient in some aspects of the class competition than in others. To see this more clearly in the Chinese context, we show the symmetrical odds ratios.

[4] As we pooled the data from 1996 to 2014, the question arises as to whether there are significant changes in the net association between father's and son's classes over the years covered. Our analysis shows, quite reassuringly (see Footnote Figure 1 below), that whilst some fluctuations manifest themselves in the year-by-year pattern, the changes are not of a clearly directional order or to a significant extent. It is also noted here that as the LHSC and the CGSS are individual-level samples and the CLDS is a household-level survey, we randomly selected one adult respondent from each household in the CLDS.

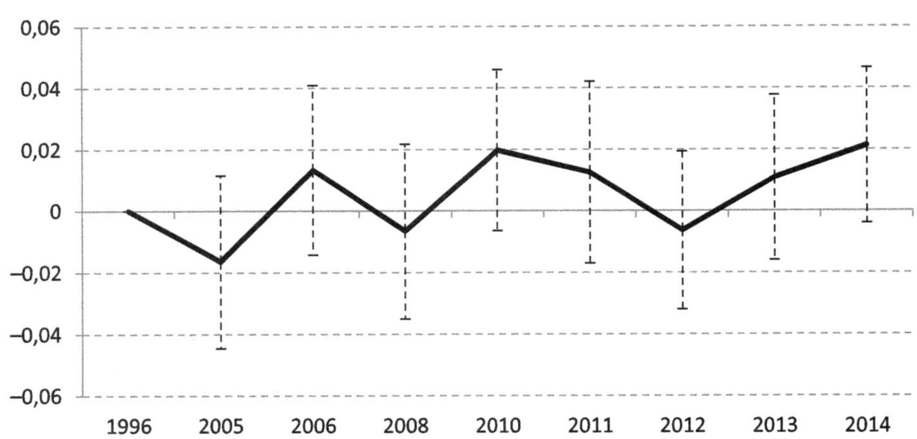

Footnote Figure 1. UNIDIFF parameter estimates and confidence intervals for survey years.

Table 2. Class distribution by class of origin (percentage by row).

	Class of destination				
Class of origin	1	2	3	4	5
Panel 1: Han					
1 Salariat	38.2	13.4	11.1	26.7	10.5
2 Clerical	29.0	19.7	12.1	30.6	08.6
3 Own account	26.7	12.1	25.5	28.6	07.1
4 Routine manual	21.4	14.2	11.2	46.2	06.9
5 Agricultural	10.5	05.1	11.1	23.8	49.3
Panel 2: Minority					
1 Salariat	28.7	5.5	14.2	17.0	34.5
2 Clerical	23.1	10.8	12.8	33.5	19.7
3 Own account	13.8	11.4	39.9	27.7	7.3
4 Routine manual	15.9	12.3	11.8	47.2	12.7
5 Agricultural	06.9	02.8	07.4	14.5	68.5

■ Immobility ■ Downward mobility ■ Upward mobility

Summary statistics

	Total	Upward	Downward
All	53.5	41.8	11.7
By ethnicity			
Han (ref)	54.7	43.0	11.7
Minority	40.4***	28.9***	11.5
By *hukou*			
Urban (ref)	61.9	39.8	22.1
Rural	55.1***	42.6***	8.5***
By ethno-*hukou*			
Han urban (ref)	62.0	40.2	21.9
Han rural	52.6***	44.2***	8.4***
Minority urban	59.2	33.1*	26.0
Minority rural	37.4***	28.4***	9.1***

Note: Significance tests are conducted on the summary statistics. * $p < 0.05$; ** $p < 0.01$; *** $p < 0.001$. Minority rural men have significantly lower levels of total and upward mobility than Han rural men at the 0.001 level in both respects.

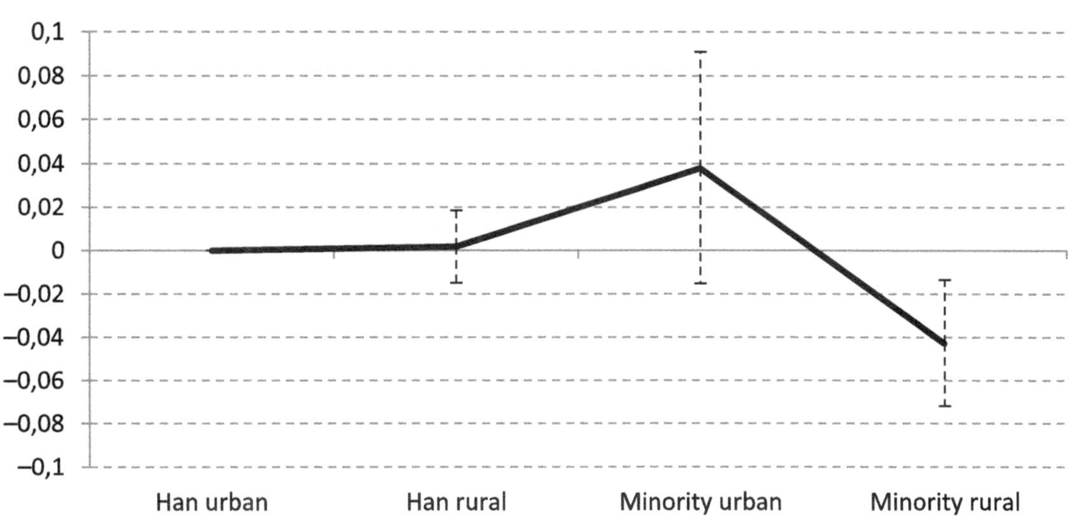

Figure 1. UNIDIFF parameter estimates and confidence intervals.

The data in Table 3 show the relative social advantages and disadvantages associated with different classes and along the ethnicity, *hukou* and ethno-*hukou* dimensions. Take the top left-hand cell of the table for example. The figure (1.93) means that for men from the majority group (Han), they are nearly twice as likely to find themselves in salariat rather than clerical positions if they are from salariat families as compared with men from clerical families in the same kind of competition (for salariat rather than clerical jobs). The figure below it (2.45) refers to the odds ratio for the ethnic minority men. The minority figure is slightly higher than that for the majority but the difference is not significant.

Now if we turn our gaze to the top-right cell, we see 16.99 and 8.26 as odds ratios for the competitions between Classes 1 and 5 for the majority and the minority men respectively. Thus, among the Han, as compared with a peasant's son, a salariat's son is 17 times as likely to find himself in a professional or a managerial position rather than as an agricultural worker. Compared with the majority, the minority is less unequal, with the odds ratio being half the magnitude, and the differences between the two sets of odds ratios are significant at the 0.001 level. The lesser inequality as shown here implies a much greater disadvantage faced by the ethnic minorities in being less able to inherit their father's superior class positions.

Table 3. Symmetrical odds ratios for mobility tables by ethnicity, *hukou* and ethno-*hukou* combination.

	Class			
Class	2	3	4	5
Panel 1: by ethnicity				
1 Salariat	1.93	3.28	3.09	16.99
	2.45	5.77	4.99	8.26***
2 Clerical		3.43	2.08	21.87
		2.95	1.24	13.55
3 Own account			3.68	15.87
			5.73	–a
4 Routine manual				13.95
				17.60
Panel 2: by *hukou*				
1 Salariat	1.79	5.15	2.97	18.33
	2.11	2.22**	3.41	6.40***
2 Clerical		3.81	1.83	42.80
		2.28	2.36	7.56**
3 Own account			4.57	17.18
			2.92	12.21
4 Routine manual				16.29
				5.75***
Panel 3: by ethno-*hukou*				
1 Salariat	1.74	4.92	2.91	16.51
	3.86	7.04	4.60	26.25
	2.19	2.09**	3.33	7.20**
	0.84	4.73	5.27	3.28***
2 Clerical		3.47	1.88	45.14
		7.38	1.30	36.28
		2.38	2.48	7.84**
		0.77	0.70	2.75**
3 Own account			4.26	14.22
			6.43	—
			2.79	5.55
			5.63	7.47
4 Routine manual				14.22
				—
				5.55***
				7.47

Notes: The odds ratios in each cell are for Han and minority in Panel 1; for urban and rural *hukou* origins in Panel 2, and for Han urban, minority urban, Han rural, and minority rural in Panel 3, respectively; For cell counts below 5, the odds ratios are not shown (as indicated by -); Significance tests are conducted with Han in Panel 1, urban in Panel 2 and Han urban in Panel 3 as reference groups. * $p < 0.05$; ** $p < 0.01$; *** $p < 0.001$.

There are, as expected, pronounced *hukou* effects on mobility chances, particularly surrounding Class 5 (agricultural workers). Thus, as we see in Panel 2, men of urban *hukou* origins tend to have more favourable chances, at three times or higher, than do men of rural origins in the class competitions, namely, in competing to avoid agricultural positions. For instance, in the Classes 1 versus 5 competitions, the odds ratios are 18.3 and 6.4 for urban and rural sectors respectively, and 16.3 and 5.8 for the routine manual versus peasant sons, both pairs being significantly different at the 0.001 levels.

There are thus both ethnic and *hukou* differences which are most concentrated in the class competition in trying to arrive at higher, and to avoid agricultural, jobs. The combined effects, as shown in Panel 3, bring the disadvantages of minority rural men to the sharpest relief. It is true that among these men, coming from salariat families still have an advantage of around 3.3 times being themselves found in salariat rather than peasant jobs as compared with their peasant peers in the same kind of competition, but this is less than half than for their Han peers (7.2), and well below that for the urban co-ethnics (26.3) or for the urban Han (16.5). Further analysis, using minority rural men as the reference group, shows that all three groups are significantly more advantaged (p. 0.001, 0.016 and 0.009 respectively).

We have, in the preceding analysis, looked at the absolute and the relative mobility rates associated with ethnicity and *hukou* origins. Family class, ethnicity and *hukou* statuses are shown as being very important markers of social inequality in China. There are, however, other factors which we could not consider due to constraints in descriptive and loglinear modelling. For instance, minorities tend to reside in underdeveloped areas and face more structural barriers. In our data, only 22% of minority men as against 35% of the Han have high-school education or above. The former are also less likely than the latter to be CCP members (12% and 15% respectively). In the remaining part of this section, we turn to logit analysis on access to professional-managerial salariat to try to control for these and other factors. We construct five models. Model 1 includes father's class and respondent's own age; model 2 adds father's education and CCP membership as well as respondent's ethno-*hukou* status (we use rural Han as the reference group for modelling stability as this is the largest group in our data); models 3 and 4 add respondent's education and CCP membership respectively (as indicators of cultural and political capital); and model 5 further adds an interaction term for ethno-*hukou* and education (level of education is used as a continuous variable here following Li & O'Leary, 2007).

With regard to data in Table 4, we find, in model 1, strong effects of father's class, and with clear gradients. Even with age differences taken into account, coming from salariat families is highly conducive to one's career life, increasing the odds of salariat access by around five-fold ($e^{1.604} = 4.97$). When father's education, CCP membership and respondent's ethno-*hukou* status are entered in Model 2, we find that these have highly significant effects and that the effect of father's class, albeit reduced, is still highly significant. In Model 3, respondent's own education is taken into consideration which is shown as being of chief importance in explaining salariat access while the effects of father's education and CCP membership as well as respondent's own ethno-*hukou* status are reduced to a general insignificance, suggesting that these effects are mediated via respondents' education. Surprisingly, we see that father's class is still highly significant. In Model 4, we further control for respondent's own CCP membership which is found to be highly conducive to salariat access (in our data, 37% of the salariat, 23% of the clerical workers but only 8% of the agricultural workers are CCP members: joining the CCP is usually a first step in one's career advancement in China). Finally, in Model 5, we control for the interaction effects of ethno-*hukou* status and education. The pattern of the coefficients for the other variables in the model are little changed as compared with those in Model 4 but we do find that the returns to the majority men of urban *hukou* status are negative, echoing Wu and Treiman's (2007) finding that given the institutional divide, only the 'best and brightest' from rural origins could gain their passport to urban life via higher education and those who do manage to do so tend to occupy the elite positions. Also noticeable is the fact that the coefficients for the minority rural men remain strongly negative and persistently significant from Models 2 to 5.

Finally, we present a bird's eye view of mobility chances conditional on father's class and ethno-*hukou* status (Figure 2). The data are obtained from the predicted probabilities based on Model 5 of Table 4, with the effects of the covariates taken at their mean values. Hence the data pertain to the net effects of father's class and ethno-*hukou* statuses. The stratification order is clearly shown. Other things being equal, a minority man of rural *hukou* origin would still have a smaller chance of becoming a professional or manager than his Han compatriot with urban *hukou* even if the former comes from a salariat family and the latter from agricultural origin (typically working on state farms): 21.5% versus 22.6%. And the disparity runs seven times as high between urban Han men from salariat families and rural minority men from peasant families in the competition for salariat destinations (44.9% and 6.6%).

5. Discussion and Conclusion

We have, in this paper, made what we believe as the first attempt to study intergenerational social mobility by ethnicity in contemporary China. Drawing on the best available data containing the key variables for the analysis (father's and own class, ethno-*hukou* statuses and a range of other factors), we conducted the analysis of both absolute and relative rates of mobility for men from minority and majority ethnic groups and of rural and urban

Table 4. Logit regression results on access to the professional-managerial salariat.

	Model 1	Model 2	Model 3	Model 4	Model 5
Father's class (peasant = ref)					
Salariat	1.604***	0.889***	0.793***	0.790***	0.728***
Clerical	1.247***	0.666***	0.458***	0.469***	0.431***
Own account	1.032***	0.666***	0.457***	0.474***	0.384**
Routine manual	0.823***	0.376***	0.256***	0.268***	0.213**
Age	−0.007	−0.011	0.046***	0.041***	0.042***
Log age	0.020	0.391	−0.624	−0.787	−0.812
Father's education (primary = ref)					
Higher professional+		0.931***	−0.178	−0.130	0.011
Lower professional		0.807***	−0.107	−0.067	0.007
Higher secondary		0.594***	−0.038	−0.021	0.015
Lower secondary		0.498***	0.174**	0.183**	0.191**
Father's CCP membership		0.192***	−0.026	−0.121	−0.107
Ethno-*hukou* (Han rural = ref)					
Han urban		0.507***	−0.026	0.034	0.957***
Minority urban		0.193	0.026	0.079	0.108
Minority rural		−0.473***	−0.234*	−0.234*	−0.478*
R's education (lower sec = ref)					
Degree+			4.130***	3.759***	4.205***
Higher professional			3.341***	3.043***	3.326***
Lower professional			2.326***	2.152***	2.282***
Higher secondary			1.439***	1.314***	1.320***
R's CCP membership				0.900***	0.887***
Ethno-*hukou**education (Han rural = ref)					
Han urban					−0.329***
Minority urban					−0.030
Minority rural					0.116
Constant	−2.007*	−3.297**	−2.281	−1.600	−1.611
Pseudo R^2	0.073	0.094	0.296	0.309	0.314
N	34712	33014	32990	32753	32753

Note: The coefficients for years (1996 = ref) are not shown. We also checked using the list-wise approach (using the same data as available in all models) and found the same patterns (data from the list-wise approach and those on years are available on request). * p < 0.05; ** p < 0.01; *** p < 0.001.

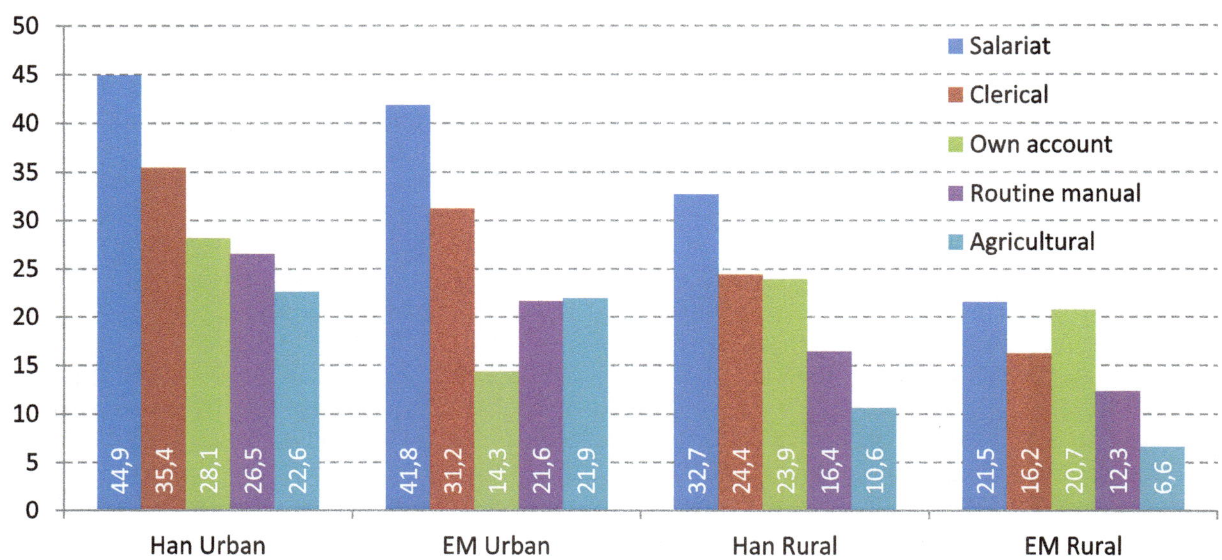

Figure 2. Predicted probability of access to the salariat.

hukou statuses. Our main findings can be summarised as follows.

In terms of gross mobility, we found that minority and majority men from the urban sector were not much different from each other but those from rural origins had greater mobility, especially those from the majority group who had the greatest net class advancement. This is most likely due to the massive internal migration in the reform period where an estimated 260 million people of rural status went to cities to find jobs in the burgeoning and rapidly developing industries and commercial enterprises. Rural men of minority backgrounds also made use of the opportunities but to a lesser extent. Coming from a much lower starting point, ethnic minority men from rural origins not only had lower total mobility, but their upward mobility rates were also the lowest as compared with the other groups. They had fewer family resources to start with and even those from similar backgrounds were less able to inherit their family resources, as shown in the 'symmetrical odds ratios', resulting in the significantly weaker association between origins and destinations. Even with parental and own cultural and political capital taken into account, we still found that ethnic minority men from rural origins were significantly behind other groups in access to the salariat. The net mobility profiles, as we saw in Figure 2 on predicted probabilities, show a clear stratification order in China with three main features. Firstly, family class has a very important influence for all ethno-*hukou* groups but more so for the majority men from urban origins than for others. Secondly, those of minority rural statuses faced the gravest disadvantages, much more so than their majority peers from similar (rural) origins. Thirdly, ethnicity is also shown to have some influence for the urban sector but the effects are generally weaker than for the rural sector.

How do we explain the findings? A great deal has been written about the household registration (*hukou*) system in creating the barriers against the rural citizens in upward social mobility (Bian, 2008; Chen, 2013; Li et al., 2015; Lin & Bian, 1991; Wu & Treiman, 2007) and the disadvantages faced by rural citizens are expected. We have also seen above that a whole range of preferential policies, especially in the last thirty years or so, have been adopted by governments at all levels to create more favourable opportunities for the ethnic minorities, and such policies cover a host of areas from education, employment to economic development. Given such favourable opportunities, why do ethnic minority men from rural origins still lag behind?

There are of course many reasons accounting for our findings the most important of which would be the long-standing poverty due to the relative underdevelopment of the local economy in the minority regions, especially in rural areas. The government assistance, in the forms of preferential policies, direct funding and investment, has no doubt helped the minority populations to ameliorate the situation. Without such generous support, the ethnic gaps in mobility would have been much larger. Yet some of the policies, well-intended as they were in respecting and preserving minority cultures such as the exemption from the family-planning policies, might have had the unintended consequences of perpetuating their poverty. For rural ethnic families already struggling in poverty and with rather limited upward mobility chances available in the local economy, having three, four or more children would only reduce their chances for improvement as compared with urban families with smaller family sizes or even with the majority peers in the rural, more developed, area where the family-planning policies were generally reinforced.

The bilingual education adopted for some ethnic schools may also have had the unintended consequences of adding to the learning difficulties of ethnic children, making it harder for them to compete with Mandarin speakers (Lin, 1997; Ma, 2007). This might not be a serious problem in the developed areas with high quality of education, such as areas where ethnic Koreans are located, but it may have aggravated the educational disadvantage for most of the other ethnic minority groups. Furthermore, the lower marks required of ethnic students for college admissions, whilst a clear boost to ethnic equality, may also have lowered their competitive edge as compared with that of the majority students studying in national universities. In an increasingly market-oriented economy, demonstrated competence, rather than a formal diploma or certificate, is becoming the order of the day in China.

There are many other reasons which we cannot cover here. Overall, we would say that ethnic minorities may have enjoyed equal or better opportunities (as entailed in the preferential policies) relative to the majority group but it is the inequality of condition that sets the two groups apart. Thus, the government should do more, rather than less, to help the minorities, especially those in the rural, poverty-stricken, regions.

Finally, we need to draw the readers' caution that, even though we have used what are the best data sources currently available for ethnic mobility analysis, there are limitations in our study. Firstly, due to the lack of data between 1996 and 2005, we could not explore mobility trajectories in the intervening years. On the other hand, given the pattern as shown in Footnote Figure 1, there is little reason to believe that the mobility trajectories in those years would have diverged greatly from what is revealed in the analysis had data for the years been available. Changes in the mechanisms of social reproduction usually take place at a rather slow pace, as the voluminous mobility research in the world over half a century has shown. Secondly, although our pooled data cover all 31 provinces, autonomous regions and municipalities, Tibet, Qinghai and Ningxia were underrepresented as they were not covered in the earlier years. Thus, the minority groups in those areas were less represented than in other areas. While this is less than desirable, we need to bear in mind that the minority groups in these provinces are mainly Zang and Hui ethnic minorities who are also found in large numbers in other provinces and cities such as

Sichuan, Chongqing, Shaanxi, Gansu, Henan and Shanxi which were well represented in the data used in the analysis, and this would give us fairly good reasons to believe that the mobility chances of their co-ethnics who were surveyed in the other provinces will have been generally representative of their own trajectories. This having been said, the lower growth rates of the local economies in the three provinces in the last few decades might have had negative effects on the upward mobility chances of the ethnic minorities, resulting in an underestimation of the ethnic gaps in the provinces concerned. This needs to be further examined in future studies if and when appropriate data become available. Thirdly, as the minority groups constitute only a very small proportion in the overall population, we have not been able to make further differentiations amongst the ethnic groups in the present study. Fourthly and for similar reasons, we have not been able to examine the spatial effects on ethnic stratification. Our findings of overall similarity between the minority and the majority groups among the urban sector suggest, as Gustafsson and Li (2003) and Gustafsson and Sai (2009) showed in their poverty studies, that there might be strong spatial effects. Maybe ethnic mobility chances are similar in the more developed, coastal, provinces. Overall, while this is the first systematic study of social mobility by ethnic groups in contemporary China based on the best data currently available, there are many other domains of social mobility that we have not been able to explore. Our analysis has also opened up some new channels of exploration which future analyses could undertake, with more and better-quality sample surveys that are being collected in China.

Acknowledgments

We wish to thank the UK's *Economic and Social Research Council* (ESRC) for funding the projects for this research: *Social mobility and social capital in China and Britain* (ES/I035168/1, Li as PI), *Socio-economic position of the minority ethnic groups in Britain* (RES-163-25-0003, Li as PI) and *Understanding the dynamics of ethnic identity and inequality in the UK* (ES/J020036/1, Li as Co-PI). We are also grateful to the Sam Chan Alumni Studentship and the University of Manchester's top-up funding for the *Happiness in China* project (Li as PI and Zhao as research student). We alone are responsible for any errors in the paper.

Conflict of Interests

The authors declare no conflict of interests.

References

Attané, I., & Courbage, Y. (2000). Transitional stages and identity boundaries: The case of ethnic minorities in China. *Population and Environment*, *21*(3), 257–280.

Bian, Y. (2008). Urban occupational mobility and employment institutions: Hierarchy, market, and networks in a mixed system. In D. Davis & F. Wang (Eds.), *Creating wealth and poverty in China* (pp. 165–183). Palo Alto: Stanford University Press.

Bulte, E., Heerink, N., & Zhang, X. (2011). China's one-child policy and 'the mystery of missing women': Ethnic minorities and male-biased sex ratios. *Oxford Bulletin of Economics and Statistics*, *73*(1), 21–39.

Chao, C. (1994). The procedure for local legislation in mainland China and legislation in national autonomous areas. *Issues & Studies*, *30*(9), 95–116.

Chen, K. (1991). Study the Marxist nationality theory and correctly understand the nationality issues of the new period [in Chinese]. *Time*, *10*, 4–17.

Chen, M. (2013). Intergenerational mobility in contemporary China. *Chinese Sociological Review*, *45*(4), 29–53.

Dreyer, J. (1968). China's minority nationalities in the Cultural Revolution. *The China Quarterly*, *35*, 96–109.

Erikson, R., Goldthorpe, J. H., & Portocarero, L. (1979). Intergenerational class mobility in three Western European societies. *British Journal of Sociology*, *30*(4), 415–441.

Gao, X., & Teng, T. (2006). An analysis of the economic underdevelopment and industry economy of the ethnic region of the Northwest of China [in Chinese]. *Ethno-National Studies*, *1*, 21–30.

Gladney, D. C. (1996). *Muslim Chinese: Ethnic nationalism in the People's Republic* (No. 149, Chapter 2). Cambridge: Harvard University Asia Center.

Guo, Z., & Li, R. (2008). Marriage age, number of children ever born, and the ethnic identification of children of inter-ethnic marriage: Evidence from China population census in 2000 [in Chinese]. *Sociological Studies*, *5*, 98–116.

Gustafsson, B., & Li, S. (2003). The ethnic minority–majority income gap in rural China during transition. *Economic Development and Cultural Change*, *51*(4), 805–822.

Gustafsson, B., & Sai, D. (2009). Temporary and persistent poverty among ethnic minorities and the majority in rural China. *Review of Income and Wealth*, *55*(S1), 588–606.

Hannum, E. (2002). Educational stratification by ethnicity in China: Enrollment and attainment in the early reform years. *Demography*, *39*(1), 95–117.

Hannum, E., & Xie, Y. (1998). Ethnic stratification in Northwest China: Occupational differences between Han Chinese and national minorities in Xinjiang, 1982–1990. *Demography*, *35*(3), 323–333.

He, B. (2005). Minority rights with Chinese characteristics. In B. He & W. Kymlicka (Eds.), *Multiculturalism in Asia* (pp. 56-79). Oxford: Oxford University Press.

Hoddie, M. (1998). Ethnic identity change in the People's Republic of China: An explanation using data from the 1982 and 1990 census enumerations. *Nationalism and Ethnic Politics*, *4*(1–2), 119–141.

Hong, Y. (2010). Ethnic groups and educational inequalities: An empirical study of the educational attainment of the ethnic minorities in Western China [in Chinese]. *Society*, *30*(2), 45–73

Huang, J. (2000). Issues in the development of Chinese higher education for minorities. *Higher Education Policy*, *13*(2), 203–214.

Lee, C. J. (1986). China's Korean minority. In *The Politics of Ethnic Education*. Boulder: Westview Press.

Li, Y., & Devine, F. (2011). Is social mobility really declining? Intergenerational class mobility in Britain in the 1990s and the 2000s. *Sociological Research Online*. Retrieved from http://www.socresonline.org.uk/16/3/4.html

Li, Y., & Heath, A. (2016). Class matters: A study of minority and majority social mobility in Britain, 1982–2011. *American Journal of Sociology*, *122*(1), 162–200.

Li, Y., & O'Leary, R. (2007). Progress in reducing Catholic disadvantages in Northern Ireland. In A. Heath & S. Y. Cheung (Eds.), *Unequal chances: Ethnic minorities in Western labour markets* (pp. 549–587). Oxford: Oxford University Press for the British Academy.

Li, Y., Zhang, S., & Kong, J. (2015). Social mobility in China and Britain: A comparative study. *International Review of Social Research*, *5*(1), 20–34.

Lieberson, S. (1975). Rank-sum comparisons between groups. In D. Heise (Ed.), *Sociological methodology* (pp. 276–91). San Francisco: Jossey-Bass.

Lin, J. (1997). Policies and practices of bilingual education for the minorities in China. *Journal of Multilingual and Multicultural Development*, *18*(3), 193–205.

Lin, N., & Bian. Y. (1991). Getting ahead in urban China. *American Journal of Sociology*, *97*, 657–688.

Ma, R. (2007). Bilingual education for China's ethnic minorities. *Chinese Education & Society*, *40*(2), 9–25.

Ma, R. (2008). Types of the ethnic relationships in modern China [in Chinese]. *Social Chinese Journal of Sociology*, *28*(1), 1–23.

Ma, R. (2010). The impact of leaving home for external employment on the ethnically mixed rural communities: A field survey of the villages in Wengniute Banner, Inner Mongolia, China [in Chinese]. *Chinese Journal of Sociology*, *30*(3), 107–129.

McMillen, D. H. (1979). *Chinese communist power and policy in Xinjiang, 1949–1977*. Boulder: Westview Press.

National Bureau of Statistics of the People's Republic of China. (2011). The main data bulletin of the sixth census, No. 1. Retrieved from http://www.stats.gov.cn/tjsj/tjgb/rkpcgb/qgrkpcgb/201104/t20110428_30327.html

National Bureau of Statistics of the People's Republic of China. (2015). Annual statistics. Retrieved from http://data.stats.gov.cn/easyquery.htm?cn=C01

Postiglione, G. A. (2009). The education of ethnic minority groups in China. In J. Banks (Ed.), *The Routledge international companion to multicultural education* (pp. 501–511). New York and London: Routledge.

Poston Jr., D. L., & Shu, J. (1987). The demographic and socioeconomic composition of China's ethnic minorities. *Population and Development Review*, *13*(4), 703–722.

Qin, H. (2004). Conflicts and amalgamation: Consideration on development of higher education of minority in China [in Chinese]. *Guizhou Ethnic Studies*, *24*(3), 130–136.

Sautman, B. (1998). Preferential policies for ethnic minorities in China: The case of Xinjiang. *Nationalism and Ethnic Politics*, *4*(1–2), 86–118.

Sautman, B. (1999). Ethnic law and minority rights in China: Progress and constraints. *Law & Policy*, *21*(3), 283–314.

Wu, X., & Treiman, D. J. (2007). Inequality and equality under Chinese socialism: The Hukou system and intergenerational occupational mobility. *American Journal of Sociology*, *113*(2), 415–445.

Yang, R., & Wu, M. (2009). Education for ethnic minorities in China: A policy critique. *SA-e DUC Journal*, *6*(2), 117–131.

Yusuf, F., & Byrnes, M. (1994). Ethnic mosaic of modern China: An analysis of fertility and mortality data for the twelve largest ethnic minorities. *Asia-Pacific Population Journal*, *9*(2), 25–46.

Zang, X., & Li, L. (2001). Ethnicity and earnings determination in urban China. *New Zealand Journal of Asian Studies*, *3*(1), 34–48.

Zhu, Z. (2010). Higher education access and equality among ethnic minorities in China. *Chinese Education & Society*, *43*(1), 12–23.

About the Authors

Yaojun Li is Professor of Sociology at Department of Sociology and Cathie Marsh Institute for Social Research, Manchester University, UK. His research interests are in social mobility and social stratification, social capital, socio-economic integration of ethnic minority groups and comparative analysis. He has published widely in these areas, including papers in top sociology journals in Europe and the USA, and research reports for government departments and think-tanks. He has also conducted many research projects funded by academic and government agencies in Britain, China, USA, Australia and Qatar.

Yizhang Zhao is a PhD student at the Department of Social Statistics, University of Manchester. Her research covers statistical methods, social stratification in health and wellbeing, internal migration, and social change in Chinese society. Her particular interest is on how different dimensions of social inequality affect people's health and subjective wellbeing, and how the influence changes over time and across space.

13

Bicycle and Car Share Schemes as Inclusive Modes of Travel? A Socio-Spatial Analysis in Glasgow, UK

Julie Clark and Angela Curl *

Urban Studies, University of Glasgow, Glasgow, G12 8RS, UK; E-Mails: julie.clark@glasgow.ac.uk (J.C.), angela.curl@canterbury.ac.nz (A.C.)

* Corresponding author

Abstract

Public bicycle and car sharing schemes have proliferated in recent years and are increasingly part of the urban transport landscape. Shared transport options have the potential to support social inclusion by improving accessibility: these initiatives could remove some of the barriers to car ownership or bicycle usage such as upfront costs, maintenance and storage. However, the existing evidence base indicates that, in reality, users are most likely to be white, male and middle class. This paper argues that there is a need to consider the social inclusivity of sharing schemes and to develop appropriate evaluation frameworks accordingly. We therefore open by considering ways in which shared transport schemes might be inclusive or not, using a framework developed from accessibility planning. In the second part of the paper, we use the case study of Glasgow in Scotland to undertake a spatial equity analysis of such schemes. We examine how well they serve different population groups across the city, using the locations of bicycle stations and car club parking spaces in Glasgow, comparing and contrasting bike and car. An apparent failure to deliver benefits across the demographic spectrum raises important questions about the socially inclusive nature of public investment in similar schemes.

Keywords

bicycle-sharing system; car-share; Glasgow; inclusive; modes of travel; shared transport; social inclusion; spatial analysis

Issue

This article is part of the issue "Transport Policy and Social Inclusion", edited by Miriam Ricci, Graham Parkhurst and Juliet Jain (University of the West of England, UK).

1. Introduction

Public bicycle sharing schemes and car clubs have proliferated in recent years and are increasingly part of the urban transport landscape (Enoch & Taylor, 2006; Fishman, Washington, & Haworth, 2013). There are car clubs in over 1,100 cities worldwide (Shaheen, Martin, Cohen, & Finson, 2012). Similarly, bicycle share schemes have grown both globally and in the UK: there are now nearly 900 bicycle share schemes worldwide (DeMaio & Meddin, 2015), including 3,000 vehicles in locations across the UK (CarPlus, 2015a). This growth in shared transport schemes is underpinned by considerable policy interest. From an urban transport management perspective, shared transport has the potential to reduce congestion and alleviate pressure on parking (Shaheen, Cohen, & Martin, 2010). Considered at a strategic level, these schemes can be seen as a means of encouraging modal shift towards more sustainable—and healthier—modes of transport (Dowling & Kent, 2015; Marsden, Mullen, Bache, Bartle, & Flinders, 2014; Ogilvie & Goodman, 2012; Parkes, Marsden, Shaheen, & Cohen, 2013). Within this context, car and bicycle sharing could offer a pathway towards lower levels of car ownership (Kent & Dowling, 2013). This, in turn, should achieve reduced fuel consumption and lower emissions of greenhouse gases and damaging particulates within the urban environment, simultaneously supporting environmental and health policy agendas.

As well as providing potential health benefits by increasing access to active travel and decreasing levels of pollution, it can be theorised that shared transport options have the scope for supporting social inclusion. In parallel with the growth of the compact city agenda towards the turn of the 21st Century, there was an upsurge of interest in transport disadvantage (DETR, 2000; Sinclair & Sinclair, 2001; Social Exclusion Unit, 2003). A growing understanding of the recursive relationship between urban form and modal choice shed light on the economic, educational and social disadvantages suffered by those unable to fulfill their mobility needs (Hine & Mitchell, 2003; Lee & Murie, 1999; Lucas, 2004; Turner & Grieco, 2000). Part of the promise of shared transport modes is that they offer a level of mobility which might otherwise be unaffordable, and in doing so, can mitigate financial disadvantage for less affluent members of society (O'Brien, Cheshire, & Batty, 2014; Shaheen et al., 2012).

Together, policy interest, the growth of shared modes, and the scope for enhancing levels of social inclusion seem a promising combination. The objectives of such schemes can be unclear; furthermore, there is little precedent for the evaluation of schemes against any objectives which might have been set (Ricci, 2015). This paper argues that there is a need to evaluate how socially inclusive transport sharing schemes are and, further, to develop appropriate evaluation frameworks. We open by considering car and bicycle schemes, outlining inherent tensions within transport and social inclusion. Thereafter, we propose a framework of what might constitute inclusivity in shared transport modes. In the next part of the paper, we undertake a spatial equity analysis of the schemes in terms of how well they serve different population groups across the city, using the locations of bicycle stations and car club parking spaces in Glasgow, comparing and contrasting bicycle and car.

2. Shared Transport and Social Inclusion

2.1. Shared Transport: Car and Bicycle Schemes

Car share schemes, often called car clubs, offer access to a fleet of vehicles without the need to own a car. The defining characteristics of both for- and not-for-profit schemes are that they involve short-term rental, with a range of charging structures adopted by different organisations at different times. Participation in a car club generally requires some form of registration and membership. Participants are then charged on duration of hire, distance travelled or some combination of these (Dowling & Kent, 2015). Users collect a vehicle from dedicated parking bays. Parking stations tend to be located in either city or neighbourhood centres or beside major employment areas (Dowling & Kent, 2015). More sophisticated, 'free-floating' schemes can accommodate a one-way trip, with the vehicle returned to another approved parking spot rather than the original parking bay (Firnkorn & Müller, 2011). Despite struggling in the UK, schemes where people share private vehicles have been particularly successful in the US; nevertheless, these peer-to-peer schemes require both an adequate proportion of car owners who are willing to share and setting agreements that allow a baseline of revenue to be generated (Stephany, 2015).

Evidence suggests that car schemes are predominantly used by employed men, aged 26–49 (Loose, 2010), who are also more likely to be well-educated, business users, and from the higher end of the income spectrum (Rabbitt & Ghosh, 2013). Compared with other drivers, those using car share schemes are likely to have lower levels of car ownership, take fewer private car trips, drive shorter distances, and exhibit more multi-modal and intermodal behaviours, in particular, holding public transport season tickets and having greater bicycle use (Kent & Dowling, 2013; Kopp, Gerike, & Axhausen, 2015; Loose, 2010). Evidence indicates that people who participate in a car share reduce the distance they travel by car by up to 45%, and, furthermore, that up to 55% will give up their private vehicle, while others abandon plans to purchase a new vehicle (Loose, 2010). As well as having lower levels of car dependency, car sharers generate significantly lower annual CO2 emissions (Rabbitt & Ghosh, 2013). Although there has been recent growth in the availability and popularity of car clubs, adoption of car sharing is still at relatively low levels (Loose, 2010).

Bicycle sharing involves access to bicycles docked at relatively 'desirable' points. Central locations and ease of access also make this a mode which is particularly appealing for visitors to the city. As with car share, no ownership is required and the schemes cover the cost of storage, maintenance and parking (Shaheen et al., 2012). Bicycle share has evolved from early honour or coin operated systems to more sophisticated electronic docking stations, utilising smart cards and requiring either short-term or annual memberships (Buck et al., 2013). Most recently, some schemes have made a further shift, from registration and membership business models to more casual usage, facilitated by the spread of smart, mobile technology, where anyone with access to a debit card can access a hire bicycle (Lathia, Ahmed, & Capra, 2012). Although bicycle share has been around for longer than car clubs, cycling remains a minority mode in many urban environments and some commentators consider that Europe is still amidst the adoption process of bike-share systems, with the US lagging behind by a further 5–7 years (Parkes et al., 2013).

While the economic barriers to participation in bicycle share are lower than with car share, there are still significant socio-economic and spatial variations in uptake (Pucher, Buehler, & Seinen, 2011). Bicycle scheme users are predominantly male, of relatively high income and, as with car club members, aged around 25–44 (Buck et al., 2013). Women and people from deprived areas are likely to be under-represented (Ogilvie & Goodman, 2012). Additional to gender, age and income, cultural factors may also be an issue; a Dutch study of urban policy and cycle use has found that immigrants with a different cultural background were less likely to cycle, while US research has also found that bicycle sharers were predominantly white (Buck et al., 2013; Rietveld & Daniel, 2004). Furthermore, although the proportion of white residents in a neighbourhood was found to be insignificant during research into car share usage in New York, the author theorised that the 'real' car share members were recently arrived young, white residents in gentrifying low-income areas (Kim, 2015).

Bicycle share participants in a major North American study of over 10,000 riders 'overwhelmingly' reported less driving, with concomitant reductions in vehicle kilometers and emissions (Shaheen et al., 2012). Additionally, cycling can be used as a secondary mode, travelling to train stations (Heinen, van Wee, & Maat, 2010), indicating that schemes can also support the use of public transport.

2.2. Transport and Social Inclusion

Recent decades have seen an increase in awareness of the social dimensions of mobility and accessibility (Lucas, van Wee, & Maat, 2015). However, while the growing field of environmental justice deals with the spatial patterning of amenities, transport exclusion constitutes both a literal and metaphorical disconnect which renders people unable to participate in society (Church, Frost, & Sullivan, 2000). Welch (2013) contends that the equity impacts of mismatched service needs and distribution are still under-researched. The rise of digital connectivity notwithstanding, physical copresence remains a necessity for multiple aspects of social inclusion. While virtual contact can replace physical mobility, particularly for more affluent members of society, many require to 'go' to work, visit medical services or attend places of education. Likewise, virtual contact might be best considered an enhancement of actually meeting with friends and family, rather than a substitute. For all the heralded 'death of distance', the digital age has, thus far, most favoured those who already have the greatest level of resource (Cairncross, 1997; Kenyon, Rafferty, & Lyons, 2003).

Many studies of accessibility-related exclusion focus on those without a car, which can, to some extent, be considered an implicit endorsement of the car as a solution to transport-related social exclusion. Access to private transport unquestionably provides benefits; however, the dominance of the car and the wider impacts of car ownership give rise to a number of environmental, economic and social concerns (Black, 2003; Goodwin, 1999; Hine & Mitchell, 2001). Fuel, maintenance, and running a car all generate externalities in terms of emissions covering air, water, noise, and ground pollution (Reid, 1995). Congestion is a stress on infrastructure, drivers, other road users including pedestrians, and business (Grant-Muller & Laird, 2006). Beyond environmental impacts, injuries and fatalities entail economic and human costs, and traffic creates an uncongenial environment, inimical to everyday exercise and social interaction (Appleyard, 1981). Furthermore, demand for private transport diverts resources from other modes (Pucher & LeFevre, 1996).

The role of place in disadvantage is a well-established feature of social inclusion/ exclusion discourse (Kristensen, 1995). Perhaps the most far-reaching impact of the dominance of the car lies in its effect on land use patterns. Freed from the constraint of following established public transport routes, urban activities become dispersed (Muller, 2004). Additionally, the increasing separation of work and home from social and leisure activities fosters isolation and a polarisation between those possessing and those lacking access to private transport, problematising the status of the private car within the modal mix of transport options.

It has been argued that urban compaction can have positive equity effects, in that dense, mixed use development can increase accessibility and reduce car dependence (Burton, 2001). Preston & Rajé (2007) identify three criteria as important in identifying the degree of transport-related social exclusion: area mobility (the level of travel in an area as a whole); individual mobility (the level of travel made by particular individuals or groups); and the overall accessibility of the area. Within a relatively dense urban environment, it might be hoped that car and bicycle schemes would mitigate exclusion along all of these dimensions. However, the growth of shared transport schemes has also been associated with the hollowing out of the state, as public provision has been withdrawn in favour of expectations the private sector should have primary responsibility for managing transport (Aldred, 2012). This perspective serves to undermine any easy assumption that shared transport will necessarily support greater social inclusion, in that less affluent members of society will be less able to participate in market-based activities.

Policy levers are crucial in supporting modal shift. Considering car club schemes, there are a number of business models: they might be for-profit, co-operatives or non-profit; they are also sometimes associated with a particular public transport network (Hampshire & Gaites, 2011). Like car clubs, bicycle share schemes have garnered significant policy support and are generally regarded as an uncontentious intervention because of their perceived social and environmental advantages (Parkes et al., 2013). In some cases, when parking spaces are converted from general use to 'car share only', public bodies have levied a charge on car share operators to compensate for lost revenue (Shaheen et al., 2010). However, it has been argued that many schemes can only be economically viable given a particular blend of cultural, economic, political and transport contexts and that policy collaboration and support are necessary for shared transport to flourish (Enoch & Taylor, 2006; Parkes et al., 2013; Ricci, 2015). Promotion, marketing and provision of parking bays, signage and cycling infrastructure are all means through which policy support for shared transport schemes can be demonstrated (Moore, Rodriguez, Tokuhiro, & Wang, 2012; Pucher, Dill, & Handy, 2010). In some schemes, this amounts to a de facto state subsidy of private enterprise for the public good. This can be considered questionable, in that the existing evidence base indicates an apparent failure to deliver benefits across the demographic spectrum, raising important questions about the equity of public investment in similar schemes. We therefore develop a framework of what might constitute inclusivity in shared transport modes. In the second part of the paper, we undertake a spatial equity analysis of the schemes in terms of how well they serve different population groups across the city, using the locations of bicycle stations and car club parking spaces in Glasgow, comparing and contrasting bike and car.

3. Evaluation Framework for Equity Analysis of Shared Transport Schemes

This section offers a preliminary evaluation framework for examining shared transport schemes in terms of inclusivity. While each scheme operates under different model of delivery and access, here we conceptualise how such schemes *might* be inclusive and what factors should be considered in an assessment of inclusivity, before focusing more specifically on the case of Glasgow in later sections. We draw on concepts from accessibility planning and equality impact assessments, discussing these with reference to shared bicycle and car schemes. Accessibility Planning is an approach to inclusive transport, designed to reduce barriers to access and address issues of social exclusion. The Social Exclusion Unit (2003) specifies barriers to accessibility, which we consider in analysing shared transport schemes as potentially inclusive modes of travel. Focusing on bicycle and car club parking stations as destinations in their own right, we evaluate their accessibility in relation to other modes, predominantly walking. Additionally, we consider how shared modes might improve accessibility to other destinations in the city, such as providers of employment, education or healthcare. Equality impact assessments evaluate how the positive and negative impacts of proposed transport schemes are distributed across population sub-groups. We therefore complement the accessibility planning approach by considering the distribution of shared transport facilities across the population.

3.1. Cost

The cost of transport is a potential barrier to movement which, on the basis of the relative cost of transport as a proportion of income, impacts unevenly upon lower income households (Hine & Mitchell, 2001). Car ownership is often used as a proxy for income and lack of car ownership is generally associated with lower income and risk of social exclusion (Goodwin, Hallet, Kenny, & Stokes, 2012; Hine & Mitchell, 2001).

High 'entry' costs present one of the key problems associated with private car ownership. This also means that once a vehicle has been purchased, it is usually more economical to use it as the main source of transport, rather than to engage with multiple modes. Within this framework, car ownership can be considered as a threat to sustainability and multi-modality agendas that seek to promote alternative modes of transport. In contrast, car clubs are marketed towards those whose transport needs might be partially or incompletely met by car ownership. These might be people who use cars infrequently, who might give up a car, or decide not to purchase a second car (e.g., City Car Club, 2015a). We posit that they also provide the potential to meet the transport needs of those who cannot afford a private vehicle and associated costs but who may require a car for some journeys, thus also having a role to play in transport justice by improving car-based accessibility. However, even though car clubs might offer a more financially viable means of accessing a car, a driving licence is a prerequisite in taking advantage of the opportunity and it should be remembered that the distribution of licences, as well as car ownership, is patterned by socio-economic status.

Similarly, bicycle schemes may provide a lower cost means of entry for those wishing to cycle, and hence can widen available transport options. Nevertheless, particularly in the UK, cycling is now commonly associated with middle class men in lycra (Daley & Rissel, in press; Goodman, Green, & Woodcock, 2014) and is likely to be seen as a mode of choice, rather than the 'necessity' which the car is considered by many (Sloman, 2006). However, although lack of car access due to affordability problems might be widely accepted as a problem of transport equity/justice, it can be forgotten that in deprived communities, a bicycle can also be an appreciable expense, especially for multi-member households (Clark & Kearns, 2014). Therefore, as noted by Goodman, Green, & Woodcock (2014), there is some evidence to suggest that bicycle sharing schemes can promote inclusivity by ameliorating the issue of entry cost and normalising cycling. However, as with car schemes, shared bicycle schemes usually entail user registration, and can require the use of a credit or debit card for access, as insurance or as a deposit. Similarly, internet access, a smart phone or a bank account can be necessary. While it is possible to find schemes that do not have these requirements, given that geography is a pertinent issue, many people may find access either more difficult or impossible, for practical purposes.

The cost of using shared transport, relative to other alternatives, is therefore a crucial consideration when addressing whether shared transport schemes can be seen as an inclusive mode of transport.

3.2. Physical Access

When considering physical access to public transport in the UK, the Disability Discrimination Act imposes duties on transport providers to support transport users who have a disability. These include: wheelchair space; step free access; priority seats; size and height of steps; handrails; colour contrast; and information displays (Metz, 2003). Concerns with regard to disability access and shared transport schemes might range from a complete lack of accessibility in relation to some car or bike sharing schemes because the vehicles themselves are unsuitable, to barriers imposed by the way in which schemes are operated.

Physical disabilities can restrict the ability of some individuals to drive or cycle and, although adaptable vehicles may mitigate this, it is perhaps unrealistic to assume that vehicle design will be versatile enough for all potential user needs. However, vehicle design can be inclusive as possible. For example, shared bicycles can be sturdy, have adjustable-height seats and typically have three gears, making them easy to use (Midgley, 2011) . There are increasing numbers of e-bike sharing schemes, removing some individual and built environment physical barriers to access. However, there needs to be wider debate about the extent to which such schemes should or can be designed to cater for all, for example, widening provision by offering a range of bicycles such as tricycles, e-bikes and children's bicycles or children's seats.

The discussion above relates mainly to medically diagnosed physical disability, which may lead to specific mobility requirements. Access to car and bike share schemes can also be restricted by other requirements: there are often age restrictions, excluding those below or above certain ages relating to car clubs. However, with regard to bicycle sharing in particular, physical *ability* is also a consideration. Concerns with physical health and fitness, both actual and perceived, may be a barrier to some people using these schemes. It might be possible to address this through marketing, to normalise the image of cycling (Goodman et al., 2014) or through training schemes such as 'bikeability' (Johnson & Margolis, 2013). However, to be truly inclusive, marketing and training must go alongside re-design of the built environment, including appropriate and well-maintained cycle infrastructure.

3.3. Safety & Security

Safety and security can be barriers to the use of certain modes of transport. For shared bicycle and car schemes there are issues of both actual and perceived safety, relating to the location of the stations, which may determine whether they are deemed safe to use. Furthermore, there are temporal considerations, which may make a location, for practical purposes, inaccessible at different times throughout the day. It is recommended that stations are both well lit and under surveillance (Midgley, 2011) .

In addition to the static location of facilities, safety concerns related to infrastructure and the wider built environment can act as a barrier to participation in cycling (Saelens, Sallis, & Frank, 2003) as well as having a role to play in driver safety (Ewing & Dumbaugh, 2009; Ewing, Hamidi, & Grace, 2014) , although we are not aware of any evidence as to whether road design acts as a deterrent to driving. Furthermore, infrastructure may have differential benefits or adverse impacts on different groups, leading to inequality in access and highlighting a need for inclusive design of the built environment. Finally, helmets are often perceived necessary for safety. These can be provided under some bicycle sharing schemes, usually in countries with compulsory helmet laws. In other instances the lack of a helmet may be a perceived barrier to using bicycle hire schemes.

3.4. Information

Awareness of shared transport schemes and understanding of how they operate may limit participation for individuals. There is evidence that private car owners have difficulty grasping the total cost of car ownership (Turrentine & Kurani, 2007) and so may not appreciated the cost-saving potential of car share. As noted previously, information about share schemes is usually provided online, which can be an exclusionary medium for those without internet skills or access. Furthermore, consideration should be given to who is the target audience of information campaigns. Given public investment, there should be consideration and targeting of groups to ensure inclusivity; however, this many not be a high priority from a commercial perspective.

3.5. Provision of Services

Bicycle share stations and car club parking spaces are unlikely to be evenly spread across the city they serve and will thus necessarily favour some population groups more than others. It is therefore important to consider whether the spatial patterning of provision excludes some groups from accessing these modes, as a factor which may explain the inequalities in usage patterns identified by others (Ogilvie & Goodman, 2012).

The location of destinations or geographical provision of services is an important component of accessibility to destinations and, as such, the component most usually measured by accessibility metrics. In the case study following, we use 400m as a walk distance to a bicycle or car. Of necessity, we consider the bicycle stations and car club parking spaces as destinations relative to the characteristics of the residential population; in reality these modes may form part of multi-modal journeys. Home, therefore, may not necessarily be the location from which we should be considering accessibility. However, in the absence of more detailed journey information we use this as a starting point.

3.6. Journey Time

Journey time is one of the most studied aspects of accessibility (Curl, Nelson, & Anable, 2013). It might also be important to consider how provision of shared transport modes contributes more widely to city level accessibility to destinations by making some destinations more accessible in terms of journey time to those without a private vehicle.

3.7. Travel Horizons

Travel horizons constitute another important aspect of accessibility, especially in relation to inclusion. Perceived accessibility may differ to that measured by any metric because individuals do not know or do not feel comfortable travelling to certain areas. Lack of awareness of transport options might be related to information or feeling uncomfortable related to safety, as previously discussed. Although shared transport modes have the potential to expand travel horizons, they may also exclude some by being located in destinations outwith their travel horizons.

3.8. Summary

Although each scheme will be different, we have outlined ways in which shared transport schemes in general might be considered inclusive or exclusive. In some respects, share schemes can be seen to be inclusive, through promoting cycling, normalising cycling (Goodman et al., 2014), widening travel horizons or adding to transport mode choices for those without access to their own car or bicycle. However, in many respects they can also be considered exclusive, benefitting some more than others. We have outlined the main aspects of inclusivity that we consider to be important for shared transport modes. In the following section we take two aspects, provision of services and cost, and examine these in relation to a case study.

4. Case Study: A Socio-Spatial Equity Analysis of Shared Transport Schemes in Glasgow

4.1. Introduction

This section presents a case study of socio-spatial analysis of car club and shared bicycle locations in Glasgow, Scotland. Glasgow is a post-industrial West European city, with a population in the metropolitan area of just over 1.1 million and approaching 600,000 in Glasgow City (National Records of Scotland, 2015). Over four in ten Glaswegians (41%) commute to work as a car driver or passenger, while smaller proportions use public transport (30%) or walk (26%), and only 1.6% cycle (Understanding Glasgow, 2015a). There are marked economic and health inequalities in Glasgow, with almost half of those within the city boundary living in the 20% of most deprived areas in the country (Understanding Glasgow, 2015b). Glasgow provides an interesting case study in that it was host to the 2014 Commonwealth Games, one of the world's most well-established multi-sport events. In support of a promised Games physical activity 'legacy', the city introduced a mass automated bicycle hire scheme, run by 'nextbike' in 2014. The city also has a car club franchise, which has recently changed from 'City Car Club' to 'Co-wheels' (Carplus, 2015b). However, 'City Car Club' has retained some operations in the city meaning there are now two schemes, 'Co-wheels' run under the City Council franchise and 'City Car Club'[1] operating privately. At this stage, the authors have been unable to obtain information relating to the way in which locations of car spaces or bicycle share stations are determined or to the usage of the schemes. However, we hope to pursue this in the future.

In this case study, we assess how the locations of these cars and bicycles are distributed relative to the resident population. Existing evidence suggests inequalities in who uses bicycle sharing (Buck et al., 2013; Ogilvie & Goodman, 2012; Pucher et al., 2011) and car sharing (Loose, 2010; Rabbitt & Ghosh, 2013) schemes. We seek to address whether the physical location favours such demographic groups and therefore whether the schemes can be considered inclusive on the basis of their distribution across the city. Then we consider the pricing structure and whether this promotes inclusivity.

4.2. Methods

Distance to stations has been reported as a significant predictor of usage of car and bicycle share schemes (Daddio, 2012; Katzev, 2003). In a study by Daddio

[1] Since the research was undertaken City Car Club has changed to Enterprise Car Club. We refer to City Car Club as this was the name, and therefore locations and costs, which were applicable at the time of research.

(2012), respondents took an average of 10.75 minutes to access a car sharing bay, 76% of users walked to the car station and 15% cycled. However, in other research, 400m has been used as a threshold for walking to car share stations (Abraham, 1999; Celsor & Millard-Bell, 2007). Loose suggests that a distance of 500m is optimal, with usage of car share schemes falling appreciably at higher distances (Loose, 2010). While recognising that there is a need for more research into acceptable walk distances to bicycle stations, we elected to adopt the lower 400m threshold for both analyses, given that a relatively dense urban environment means that there are likely to be alternative public transport options within the same distance.

The locations of the bicycle stations and car club car park spaces were manually geocoded in QGIS using the location information from the company websites (Nextbike, 2015a; Co-wheels, 2015a; City Car Club, 2015a). We then used the Network Analyst extension in ArcGIS to create 400m service areas, using the ITN road and path network, around each station as an approximation of the distance people are willing to walk to connect to another mode of transport. The service area polygons were imported back into QGIS and overlaid with datazones, which are a small-area geography used for census data in Scotland. The proportion overlaps between our service areas and datazones were calculated using polygon to polygon matching. We calculated both the proportion of each datazone which fell into service areas, and the proportion of the total service areas covered by each datazone so that we could apportion population data to the buffer zones around stations. This overlap was then exported to Excel and population calculations using census data were undertaken in Microsoft Excel.

For the majority of census groups, we report the proportion in each demographic category which can access a bicycle or car station within a 400m walk, relative to the total citywide population of each group. We calculated the number of each group living within the overall area covered by the service areas and then divided this by the total population of that demographic group in the city. The example below illustrates this calculation process (Figure 1).

As with any geographic analysis, there are issues related to the modifiable area unit problem. We are restricted by datazone geography for census data and our approach in matching this to service areas assumes that populations are spread evenly across each datazone, when in reality the population as a whole or certain sub-groups may be clustered within datazones. Secondly, by comparing to the population of Glasgow we face the issue that comparing with other geographical areas, such as the city centre only, or the greater Glasgow travel to work area, would yield different results. However, we chose this comparison given the allocation of public money to such schemes across the City Council area, so wish to understand whether the benefits are evenly spread across the population.

In the following sections, we use census data to compare the demographic composition of people living within 400m of car, bike or car and bike stations in Glasgow with the population of Glasgow City Council area as a whole. A schematic representation of the location of car club parking spaces and bicycles is given in Figure 2.

If a datazone contains 600 females, and 5% of the surface area of the datazone overlaps with the service area then 30 females are assumed to live within the area accessible to a station. This is repeated for all datazones which overlap the surface area to calculate the total of each demographic group living within the 400m buffer.

For continuous data, cars per household, cars per person and mean age we instead used the proportion of the service area covered by each datazone to weight the mean for each overlapping datazone according to the amount it 'contributes' to the total service area, based on surface area.

For example: *If datazone 1 (mean age 57) accounts for 45% of the total service area and datazone 2 (mean age 65) accounts for 55% overall mean age for the service area is (57×0.45)+(65×0.55)=61.4.*

Figure 1. Calculation Process for matching of census data to service areas.

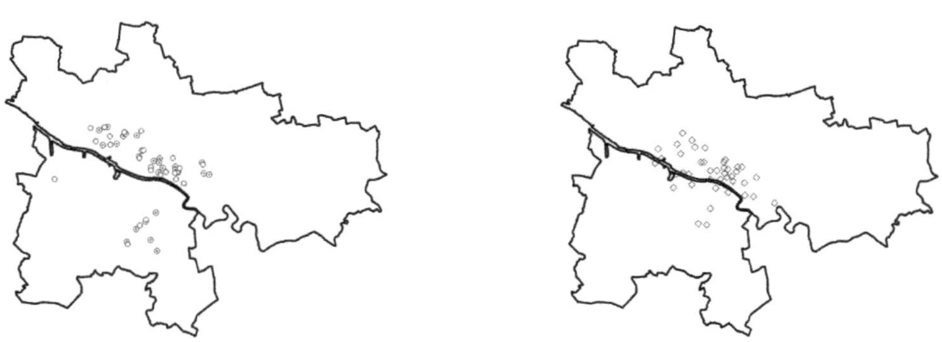

Figure 2. Location of car share (left) and bicycle share (right) schemes in Glasgow.

As might be anticipated, there is a clustering around the city centre. This is more pronounced in the case of bicycle stations, while there is a greater spread of car clubs, particularly towards the heavily residential south side of the city.

4.3. Glasgow City Population

We open by presenting Glasgow City population characteristics believed to be relevant to transport inclusion and associated with cycling. These include gender, age, ethnicity, and socio-economic indicators such as housing tenure, car ownership, qualifications, employment status, as well as main mode of travel to work (Ricci, 2015, Table 1).

Table 1. Population characteristics of Glasgow. Source: Census 2011.

	Glasgow City Council Area
Population	593,862
Households	285,899
Female	52%
Male	48%
Mean age	38
Age 0–15	4%
Age 16–29	24%
Age 30–45	22%
Age 45–65	24%
Age 65+	19%
white British	83%
non white British	17%
Owned	46%
social rented	37%
private rent	15%
no car	51%
at least one car	49%
cars per person	0.31
car per hh	0.64
No Qualifications	32%
Qualifications	68%
Employed	36%
Unemployed	6%
PT	28%
Car	42%
Other	20%

Table 2. Mean age and cars per person and household for those living within 400m of shared car and bicycle schemes.

	Bike share	Car club	Car club & bike share
Mean age	34	35	25
Mean cars per person	0.25	0.31	0.25
Mean cars per household	0.49	0.60	0.49

The reporting of this data is by necessity simplistic: we recognise the limitations, for example, of using binary variables for ethnicity, employment and education level in that such an approach does not offer depth of understanding; nevertheless, it has the merit of clarity and ease of comparison. Furthermore, our methodology assumes that the population within each datazone is homogenous: this is not the case, biasing the results to some extent. However, datazone geographies are decided on the basis of areas which are relatively homogenous in terms of socio-demographic characteristics. That some characteristics are reported at the household level and some at the individual level also introduces difficulties in terms of interpretation. Additionally, while household car ownership may benefit all household members, it is not necessarily the case that all individuals within a household will have access to a car. We do not have scope to examine these intra-household dynamics here. However, we can nevertheless offer important insights into which groups of people may have lower access to car and bike sharing stations.

Across Glasgow City, 9% of the population (10% of households) live within 400m of a bike share station. 14% of the population (14% of households) live within 400m of a car club space and 5% of the population (5% of households) are within 400m of both. The following sections show how access to car and bicycle sharing schemes varies by socio-demographic group. If all population groups had an equal level of access to car and bike stations, we would expect the proportion of the group which can access a station or parking bay to equal that of the population as a whole. Where there are differences, this can be considered an indication of socio-spatial inequality of access and an indication of potential exclusion of some groups with respect to accessing shared transport modes. Additionally, Table 2 shows the mean age, cars per person and cars per household of those who can access shared car and bicycle schemes within the specified walk radius.

4.4. Access to Bicycle Sharing Stations

There is some variation in access to bicycle station by gender, although the difference is slight (see Figure 3): 8% of females are within 400m of a bike station compared with 10% of males. The 16–29 year old population has greater access to bikes than other age groups. Perhaps surprisingly, higher percentages of the non-white British population fall within the specified walk radius. Furthermore, private renters have greater access than those who either own or are social renters. This can be considered a reflection of tenure patterns around the city centre and before suburban areas are reached.

Those households without car access have greater access to bicycle share stations (11%), in comparison with a figure of 10% for households across the city.

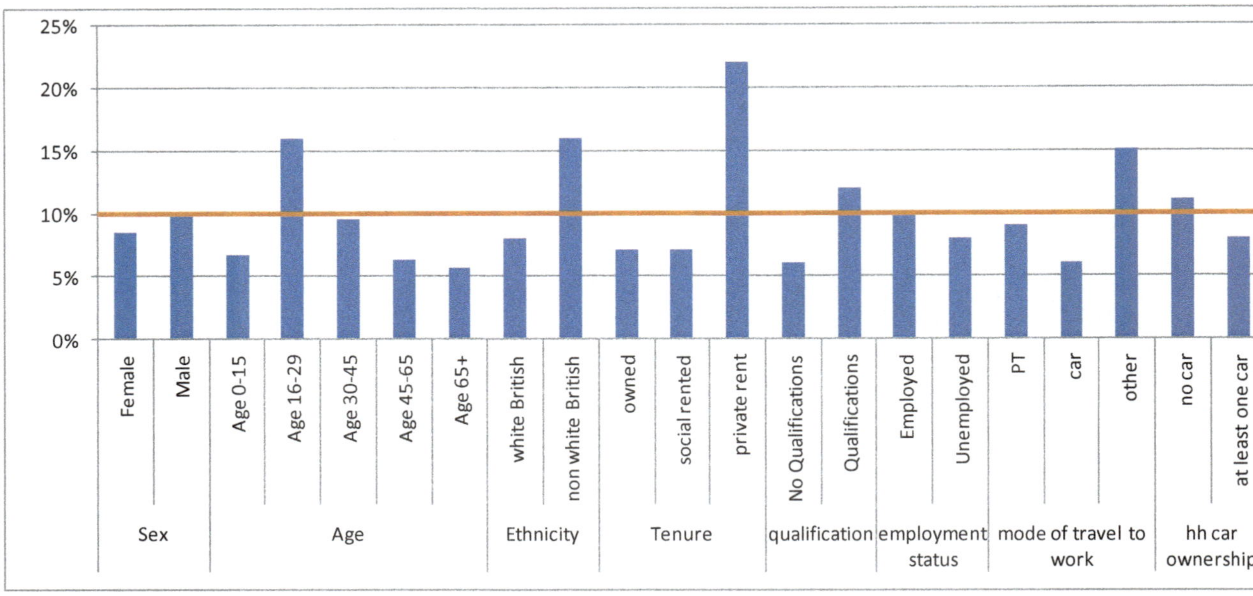

Figure 3. Proportion of the population who can access a bicycle sharing station within a 400m walk.

That the number of cars per household is lower than the Glasgow average for households within 400m of a bicycle station suggests bicycle share can be seen as inclusive, offering the option of another mode of transport for those without access to a car. However, given the clustering of stations in the city centre, it may also be that low levels of car ownership in the area reflect a lifestyle choice, rather than an issue with affordability. The latter possibility is strengthened when the demographic profile of those nearer stations is considered: people with qualifications and in employment also have higher rates of access to bicycle share, but in general are substantially more likely to be car owners than those without work or qualifications. This favours the possibility that, for at least some of this group, their education and employment might make car ownership an option which they have chosen not to exercise.

We analyse travel to work mode under three categories: public transport; car; and 'other', which would include walking or cycling. These data are from the 2011 Census, which was taken prior to the inception of bicycle share schemes in the city. Across Glasgow as a whole, an average of 9% of the population has access to a bicycle station within 400m. Of people who fall into the category of being relatively close to a bicycle share station, the proportion of public transport users is the same as the population average but considerably lower with respect to car users. For people who fell into the 'other' category at the 2011 Census, which would include those who walk or cycle to work, the proportion of people with ready access to bicycle rental is considerably higher. This indicates that the scheme appears to favour those who already live in areas where a high proportion of people cycle to work—a potentially fertile target market in terms of encouraging new users through social norms. Nevertheless, it also raises questions as to the ability of the schemes to achieve modal shift from car use.

4.5. Access to Car Club Parking Bays

Given the similarities in distribution of car and bicycle share stations, many of the patterns identified for bicycle sharing stations are similar for car club parking bays (see Figure 4). As might be anticipated, men have slightly better access than women. Similarly, when looking at age, people in the 16–29-year-old category have greater access than other age groups, although this is more evenly spread than for bicycle stations and, notably, a greater proportion of 30–45 year olds have access to cars than to bicycles.

As with the bicycle stations, the non-white British population have greater access, as well as there being considerably higher access among private renters than those who are either homeowners or social renters.

Access to car club cars is equivalent between car and non-car owning households. If car clubs were to be viewed as inclusive we might assume that access should be greater for non-car owning households, so that people without a private vehicle could benefit. However, household car ownership does not mean that all individuals have access to that vehicle and, for those within 400m of car club bay, the mean figure for cars per household is lower than the Glasgow average, 0.60 compared to 0.64 (Table 1 and Table 2).

Similar to bicycle stations, those with at least a school level qualification and who are in employment have greater access to car club bays.

Of those who travel to work by a mode other than car or public transport, 20% can access a car club bay within 400m. Again, this raises the issue of environmental sustainability as, on this basis, car clubs may actually lead to higher car use by attracting people who do not currently drive. On the other hand, in contrast to bicycle sharing schemes, there is no difference in access

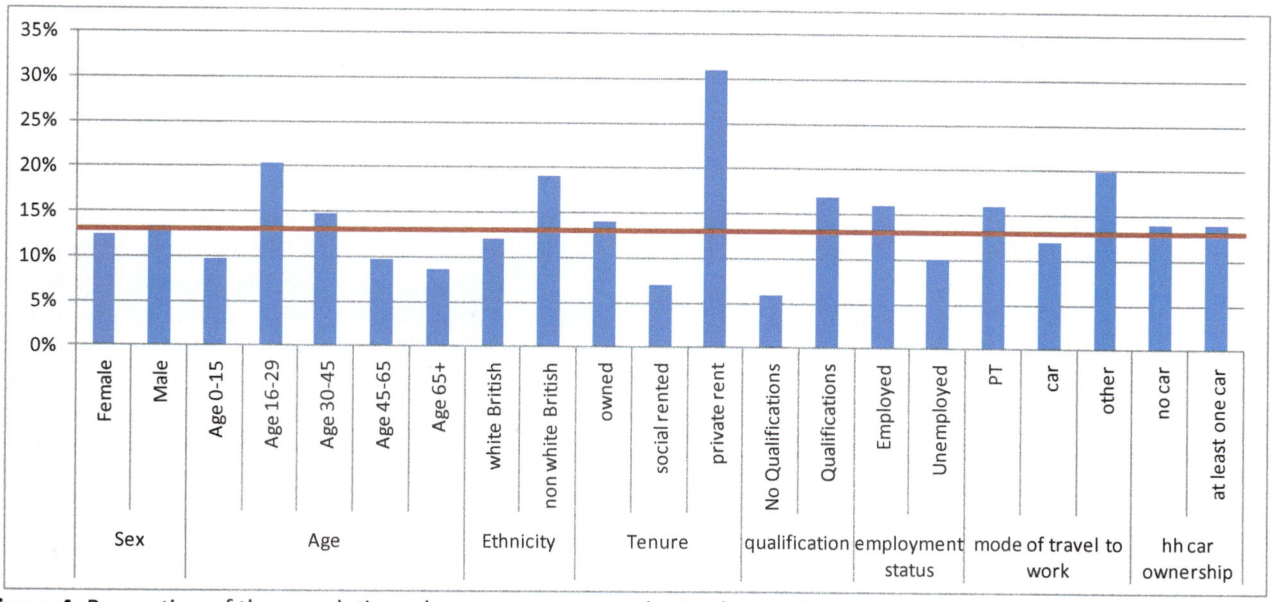

Figure 4. Proportion of the population who can access a car sharing bay within a 400m walk.

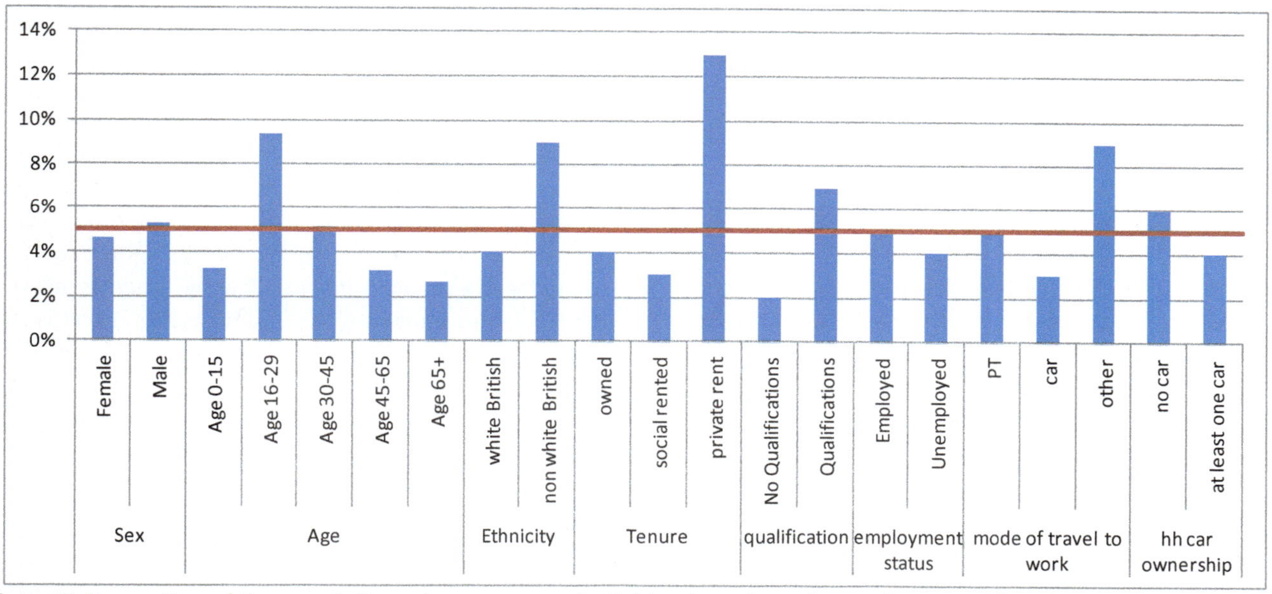

Figure 5. Proportion of the population who can access both bicycle and car share schemes within a 400m walk.

to car sharing bays between groups who do or do not have a car. The mean figure for cars per household and per person are both greater for people in areas where there are car parking bays than areas where bicycle share is available.

4.6. Access to Both Bicycle and Car Club Stations

Although fewer people (5%) can access both car bays *and* bicycle stations than either car or bicycle stations individually, the socio-spatial patterning remains similar: people who are aged 16–29, non white British, private renting, with educational qualifications, in employment and not travelling to work by car or public transport or owning a car have greatest access (see Figure 5).

We suggest that these results are a reflection of the clustered nature of the bicycle and car stations in central locations, which by default means that some population groups will have better access. At this point it is important to remember that proximity to stations does not equate to usage, although it is an important explanatory factor (Katzev, 2003). Groups show to have greater access in this analysis can be considered comparable to those who we identified as users of such schemes in the literature review, insofar as there is a slight predominance of men and those in younger age groups, and in some form of employment, with qualifications. Although these are not necessarily particularly affluent areas, they are also not areas of high deprivation, in that people within the walk radius tend to rent privately or own their homes, rather than live in social housing. This would suggest that targeting stations and parking bays in certain areas may lead to usage, and therefore act as a policy mechanism for furthering transport inclusion. Furthermore, targeting at areas with existing poor accessibility and higher unemployment *could* be one means of promoting these schemes as inclusive modes of transport, especially given that access is poorer for the unemployed and those without qualifications.

From a commercial perspective therefore, the spatial location of both car and bicycle schemes might make sense: they are in locations likely to lead to higher usage of the schemes, highlighting the role of market forces. However, given the public investment we need to consider whether they can be considered socially inclusive. Additional to considering the economic dimensions of social inclusion, our research shows relatively large proportions of non-white British residents living close to share stations, and factors affecting usage for these populations are unknown.

We have assessed the spatial accessibility by demographic group to the fixed locations where car and bicycle sharing can be accessed. However, we have not considered the fact that vehicles may not always be available at these locations and whether a lack of alternative transport modes may be a hindrance to using or relying on such modes.

4.7. Cost-Structure

As discussed in Section 3, cost is also a key consideration when evaluating the inclusivity of shared transport schemes. In theory, such schemes have lower entry costs than upfront car or bicycle ownership and therefore potentially present a low-cost means of using either a car or bicycle. The pricing structures for bicycle sharing and car clubs in Glasgow are shown in Figures 6–8.

Bicycle sharing offers a membership or non-membership option with slightly different usage rates. One of the car clubs charges an hourly or daily rate plus a mileage rate alongside a membership fee, whereas the other has a minimum monthly spend of £5, and hourly or daily rate plus a mileage rate. The daily and hourly rates depend on the type and size of vehicle.

A single bus fare within the city costs £2 (approximately €2.55/ $US2.90). This is likely to be more expensive than a bicycle hire for equivalent distance, but is substantially cheaper than a car club journey, although this is a broad comparison and will vary by journey and by time of day. Annual public transport tickets would provide savings, though we do not feel this is an appropriate comparison: if an individual were to purchase an annual public transport ticket, the assumption would be they would use it every day; using the shared car scheme every day would likely involve an unattractive (if not prohibitive) cost in comparison with actually buying a car. Comparing the daily fare provides a better reflection of the on-the-spot costs for casual users. Furthermore, paying annual or similar long-term advance charges for public transport travel tickets is also likely to be a problematic issue for those on lower incomes, even although daily fares may be more expensive on a per trip basis. The cost of an annual public transport 'zonecard', covering the city centre zones including the bicycle and car sharing schemes areas is £721 (approximately €910/ $US1045). We therefore feel that this is a more realistic comparison. On this basis, the bus is more inclusive than car sharing in terms of walk-on fares and no upfront membership fees. However, bicycle sharing offers both options.

FARES

	regular fare (£ 0 annually)	annual subscription (£ 60 annually)
first 30 min per ride	£ 1	free of charge
every additional 30 min	£ 1	£ 0.50
5–24 h	£ 10	£ 5

Registration is free of charge. You will be required to deposit credit of £ 10. This amount can be used in both fare types.

Figure 6. Nextbike cost structure. Source: Nextbike (2015b).

Vehicle type	New hourly rate	New daily rate
Small	£3.95	£25
EV	£3.20	£20
Medium	£4.45	£30
Large	£5.45	£35
7 Seat	£6.95	£40
Vans	£6.95	£40

Mileage rates:
No mileage fee for electric and Prius Plug-in! | 13p/mile for small, medium, large & 7 seat cars | 13p/mile for vans The daily rate is the maximum you pay in any 24 hour period, plus the mileage charge when applicable. Please refer to our FAQ's for more information

Sign up

Select your rate plan

Personal			Business	
Standard	Under 22	Van only	Standard	Van only
Select	Select	Select	Select	Select

Payment plan

This rate plan offers an annual or monthly membership fee.

Please select your preferred option: £60 annually £7 monthly†

† 30 day minimum term applies

Figure 7. Cost structure for City Car Club. Source: City Car Club (2015b).

	Individual	Organisation
Joining fee	£25	£25

This one-off fee covers the cost of your application, smart card and welcome pack.

	Individual	Organisation
Additional driver	£15	£12

You can add as many drivers to your account as you wish.

	Individual	Organisation
Monthly minimum spend	£5	-

This is like a membership fee, except if you make a booking that costs at least £5, you effectively don't pay it!

Size	Small	Medium	Large	7 seater	Electric
Car type	Aygo	Yaris Hybrid	Auris Hybrid	Prius+	Nissan Leaf
Per Hour	£4.50	£5.25	£6.00	£7.25	£3.75
Overnight	£9.00	£10.50	£12.00	£14.50	£7.50
Per Day	£27.00	£31.50	£36.00	£43.50	£22.50
Per Mile			£0.13		Free

Figure 8. Cost structure for Co-wheels. Source: Co-wheels (2015b).

The high entry costs, and relatively high usage costs for some of the car schemes may be a barrier to usage among those who do not have access to a vehicle. Furthermore the costs associated with driving lessons and a driving licence mean that this may not feasibly be seen as an inclusive mode of travel in terms of cost.

The costs associated with the bicycle scheme, on the other hand, are relatively low and, although the membership fee may be a deterrent to some, there is an option to avoid this. Anecdotally, we know that the bicycle share company is offering concessionary memberships through some employers (including some universities). This might limit its status as equitable in that all customers are not treated equally and those who may least need subsidised membership are being offered it, perhaps at a cost to other users, although we do not know this.

Both the car and bicycle schemes require individuals to be registered with the company and have a bank account. This excludes those without bank accounts, which is 12% of the population of Glasgow and 14% of those in the most deprived parts of Glasgow, compared with 7% in Scotland as a whole (Scottish Household Survey, 2015) therefore limiting the inclusivity of such schemes. In reality internet access may also be required.

4.8. Summary

On the basis of residential location, relatively low percentages of the population (10–15%) have the potential to benefit from bicycle and car sharing stations across the city as a whole, raising questions as to the inclusivity of the schemes. However, it is important to note that, while proximity is important in predicting use, access does not equal usage. Not all those who can access a bicycle or car will use them, and others may use share vehicles to travel further or use employment-location stations as hubs. It is therefore important to study usage alongside the provision, comparing the demographics of users to the demographic of the areas where stations and parking bays are located. Although we believe this data to be available for our case study area, we have as yet been unable to access it.

We have presented an aggregate level socio-spatial analysis of car and bicycle sharing schemes in terms of proximity to access points in Glasgow. This gives a broad overview of how the spatial locations of these schemes are distributed across the population. More detailed, mixed methods analysis, including speaking with users of each mode, would allow firmer conclusions to be drawn.

5. Conclusions

There has been a recent surge of academic interest in shared transport modes. However, limited attention has been paid to how inclusive car and bicycle sharing schemes are, and to whether they might contribute to or address problems of transport-related social exclusion. In this preliminary work, we have applied learning from the fields of accessibility and equalities impact analysis to consider shared transport schemes. In doing so, we aim to problematise the easy assumption that shared transport will necessarily support social inclusion and mitigate transport disadvantage.

Although there is evidence to suggest that the benefits from bicycle sharing schemes are unevenly distributed across socio-demographic groups (Ricci, 2015), it is not clear whether this is because the schemes themselves are unevenly distributed, spatially and socially, thereby influencing who can access shared modes of transport and perpetuating inequality of access. In our case study, the demographic characteristics of those with access to both car and bicycle schemes are broadly similar, reflecting the central location of the stations. Car sharing schemes may be able to contribute to transport justice by improving car-based accessibility for those without access to a private vehicle. However, we found no evidence of differences in household car ownership for those with ready geographic access to the car sharing schemes. Furthermore, given the cost structure, it seems unlikely that car share will fulfil this role in the city. Overall, the location of the stations for both car and bicycle schemes makes sense from both commercial and mode-shift perspectives, appearing to favour those most likely to participate. Nevertheless, in this case, the market imperative means that share schemes are less likely to extend to those most at risk of transport-related social exclusion. This raises questions as to whether there are ongoing tensions between sustainability and social justice agendas. Achieving modal shift targets related to sustainability requires limiting travel, whereas social justice possibly requires increased travel among some socio-demographic groups. Overall, we would assess bicycle sharing schemes as being more inclusive, in that they involve fewer barriers to participation, particularly in relation to cost. However, there are serious limitations to inclusivity in relation to both actual and perceived safety concerns, which may be a major factor; for those less physically able, or parents struggling with shopping and children, bicycles may be less practical.

We intend that this paper will act as a catalyst setting a research agenda for more critical consideration of social inclusion, equity and justice related to emerging forms of transport. Given that some level of public investment is required to support shared transport schemes, issues of equality and inclusivity should not be ignored. Related to this, more consideration needs to be given to policy structure, governance and regulation and whether such schemes should be considered as quasi-public transport, which will increasingly become part of the urban transport system and can be used to meet transport policy goals related to sustainability and inclusion. We have discussed the inclusive nature of shared transport schemes in relation to a number of dimensions of what might constitute inclusive transport and then empirically examined spatial access and cost, but there is a need for more empirical work examining the other aspects such as physical access, information and safety and security. There is a need for more research to understand who and more importantly *why* people are (or are not) using shared transport schemes. In particular, this study highlights a need for mixed methods research, investigating the extent of share scheme usage by non-white British residents and exploring any barriers to use. While many studies have looked at the demographic of users, further comparison of this data with the demographic of the areas in which schemes are provided would reveal who is *not* using them and so make known more regarding the inclusive and equitable nature of delivery. Qualitative engagement with individuals across the socio-demographic spectrum would help illuminate the points we have raised here regarding how the schemes may or may not be considered inclusive modes of transport. Further work might be approached from two angles: firstly, whether the schemes are delivered in an inclusive manner; and secondly, whether shared modes might contribute more broadly to an inclusive transport system.

Acknowledgments

The authors gratefully recognize support from Dr Sharon Wright and the University of Glasgow Urban Studies Research Incentivisation Fund. We would also like to thank Professor Rowena Murray, whose encouragement and enthusiasm were an inspiration throughout this project.

Conflict of Interests

The authors declare no conflict of interests.

References

Abraham, J. (1999). Carsharing: A survey of preferences. *World Transport Policy and Practice*, *5*(3), 189-200. Retrieved from http://trid.trb.org/view.aspx?id=747392

Aldred, R. (2012). Governing transport from welfare state to hollow state: The case of cycling in the UK. *Transport Policy*, *23*, 95-102. doi:http://doi.org/10.1016/j.tranpol.2012.05.012

Appleyard, D. (1981). *Liveable streets*. Berkeley, CA: University of California Press.

Black, W. (2003). *Transportation: A geographical analysis*. London: The Guildford Press.

Buck, D., Buehler, R., Happ, P., Rawls, B., Chung, P., & Borecki, N. (2013). Are bikeshare users different from regular cyclists? A first look at short-term users, annual members, and area cyclists in the Washington D.C. region. *Transportation Research Record: Journal of the Transportation Research Board*, *2387*, 112-119. Retrieved from https://www.academia.edu/6076965/Are_Bikeshare_Users_Different_from_Regular_Cyclists_A_First_Look_at_Short-Term_Users_Annual_Members_and_Area_Cyclists_in_the_Washington_D.C._Region

Burton, E. (2001). The compact city and social justice. Paper presented at *The Housing Studies Association Spring Conference University of York*, UK.

Cairncross, F. (1997). *The death of distance*. London: Orion.

CarPlus. (2015a). Key achievements. *CarPlus*. Retrieved from http://www.carplus.org.uk/about/background-2

CarPlus (2015b) Glasgow: All change as Co-wheels launches 32 car fleet. *Co-wheels Shared Mobility News*. Retrieved from http://www.carplus.org.uk/archived_newsletter/shared-mobility-news-september-2015

Celsor, C., & Millard-Bell, A. (2007). Where does carsharing work?: Using geographic information systems to assess market potential. *Transportation Research Record: Journal of the Transportation Research Board, 1992*. Retrieved from http://trrjournalonline.trb.org/doi/abs/10.3141/1992-08

Church, A., Frost, M., & Sullivan, K. (2000). Transport and social exclusion in London. *Transport Policy*, *7*(3), 195-205. Retrieved from http://www.sciencedirect.com/science/article/B6VGG-41WSBDT-4/2/5362c772da815916234fff5f7b8c63f9

Clark, J., & Kearns, A. (2014). *The Glasgow 2014 games: Regeneration and physical activity legacy*. Glasgow, UK: GoWell/ Glasgow Centre for Population Health. Retrieved from http://www.gowellonline.com/assets/0000/3691/Prospective_Assessment_of_Active_Legacy.pdf

City Car Club (2015a). Locations. *City Car Club*. Retrieved from https://www.citycarclub.co.uk/locations/glasgow-car-hire

City Car Club (2015b). Car hire. *City Car Club*. Retrieved from https://www.citycarclub.co.uk/locations/glasgow-car-hire

Co-wheels. (2015a) Locations. *Co-wheelers*. Retrieved from http://www.co-wheels.org.uk/locations

Co-wheels. (2015b). Pricing. *Co-wheelers*. Retrieved from http://www.co-wheels.org.uk/pricing

Curl, A., Nelson, J. D., & Anable, J. (2013). Same question, different answer: A comparison of GIS-based journey time accessibility with self-reported measures from the national travel survey in England. *Computers, Environment and Urban Systems*, 49, 86-97oi:http://doi.org/10.1016/j.compenvurbsys.2013.10.006

Daddio, D. (2012). *Maximizing bicycle sharing: An empirical analysis of capital bikeshare usage* (Masters Dissertation). University of North Carolina at Chapel Hill, Norh Carolina, NC.

Daley, M., & Rissel, C. 2011). Perspectives and images of cycling as a barrier or facilitator of cycling. *Transport Policy*. 18(1), 211-216

DeMaio, P., & Meddin, R. (2015). The bike-sharing blog: International bike-share database. *The bike-sharing blog* Retrieved from http://bike-sharing.blogspot.co.uk/2015/07/international-bike-share-database.html

DETR. (2000). *Social Exclusion and the Provision and Availability of Public Transport*. London: DETR

Dowling, R., & Kent, J. (2015). Practice and public-private partnerships in sustainable transport governance: The case of car sharing in Sydney, Australia. *Transport Policy*, *40*, 58-64. doi:http://doi.org/10.1016/j.tranpol.2015.02.007

Enoch, M. P., & Taylor, J. (2006). A worldwide review of support mechanisms for car clubs. *Transport Policy*, *13*(5), 434–443. doi:http://doi.org/10.1016/j.tranpol.2006.04.001

Ewing, R., & Dumbaugh, E. (2009). The built environment and traffic safety: A review of empirical evidence. *Journal of Planning Literature*, *23*(4), 347-367. doi:http://doi.org/10.1177/0885412209335553

Ewing, R., Hamidi, S., & Grace, J. B. (2014). Urban sprawl as a risk factor in motor vehicle crashes. *Urban Studies*, *53*(2), 247-266. doi:http://doi.org/10.1177/0042098014562331

Firnkorn, J., & Müller, M. (2011). What will be the environmental effects of new free-floating car-sharing systems? The case of car2go in Ulm. *Ecological Economics*, *70*(8), 1519–1528. doi:http://doi.org/10.1016/j.ecolecon.2011.03.014

Fishman, E., Washington, S., & Haworth, N. (2013). Bike share: A synthesis of the literature. *Transport Reviews*, 33(2), 148-165. Retrieved from http://www.tandfonline.com/doi/abs/10.1080/01441647.2013.775612

Goodman, A., Green, J., & Woodcock, J. (2014). The role of bicycle sharing systems in normalising the image of cycling: An observational study of London cyclists. *Journal of Transport & Health*, *1*(1), 5-8. doi:http://doi.org/10.1016/j.jth.2013.07.001

Goodwin, P. (1999). Transformation of transport policy in Great Britain. *Transportation Research Part A: Policy and Practice*, *33*(7-8), 655-669. doi:http://doi.org/10.1016/S0965-8564(99)00011-7

Goodwin, P., Hallet, S., Kenny, F., & Stokes, G. (2012). *Transport: The new realism*. Oxford, UK: Transport studies Unit, Working Paper number 1062, prepared for Rees Jeffreys Road Fund. Retrieved from http://www.tsu.ox.ac.uk/pubs/1062-goodwin-hallett-kenny-stokes.pdf

Grant-Muller, S., & Laird, J. (2006). *Costs of congestion: A literature-based review of methodologies and analytical approaches*. Edinburgh, Scotland: Scottish Executive Social Research. Available from: http://www.gov.scot/resource/doc/153566/0041321.pdf

Hampshire, R., & Gaites, C. (2011). Peer-to-peer carsharing. *Transportation Research Record: Journal of the Transportation Research Board*, *2217*, 119-126. doi:http://doi.org/10.3141/2217-15

Heinen, E., van Wee, B., & Maat, K. (2010). Commuting by bicycle: An overview of the literature. *Transport Reviews*, *30*(1), 59-96. doi:http://doi.org/10.1080/01441640903187001

Hine, J., & Mitchell, F. (2001). *The role of transport on social exclusion in urban Scotland: Literature review*. Edinburgh, Scotland: Scottish Executive Central Research Unit. Retrieved from http://www.gov.scot/Resource/Doc/156591/0042062.pdf

Hine, J., & Mitchell, F. (2003). *Transport disadvantage and social exclusion: Exclusionary mechanisms in transport in urban Scotland*. Aldershot, UK: Ashgate.

Johnson, R., & Margolis, S. (2013). A review of the effectiveness of adult cycle training in Tower Hamlets, London. *Transport Policy*, *30*, 254-261.doi:http://doi.org/10.1016/j.tranpol.2013.09.005

Katzev, R. (2003). Car sharing: A new approach to urban transportation problems. *Analyses of Social Issues and Public Policy*, *3*(1), 65-86. doi:http://doi.org/10.1111/j.1530-2415.2003.00015.x

Kent, J. L., & Dowling, R. (2013). Puncturing automobility? Carsharing practices. *Journal of Transport Geography*, *32*, 86-92. doi:http://doi.org/10.1016/j.jtrangeo.2013.08.014

Kenyon, S., Rafferty, J., & Lyons, G. (2003). Social exclusion and transport in the UK: A role for virtual accessibility in the alleviation of mobility-related social exclusion? *Journal of Social Policy*, *32*(3), 317-338.

Kim, K. (2015). Can carsharing meet the mobility needs for the low-income neighbourhoods? Lessons from carsharing usage patterns in New York City. *Transportation Research Part A*, 77, 249-260.

Kopp, J., Gerike, R., & Axhausen, K. W. (2015). Do sharing people behave differently? An empirical evaluation of the distinctive mobility patterns of free-floating car-sharing members. *Transportation*, *42*(3), 449-469. doi:http://doi.org/10.1007/s11116-015-9606-1

Kristensen, H. (1995). Social exclusion and spatial stress: The connections. In *Beyond the Threshold: The Measurement and Analysis of Social Exclusion*. Bristol: The Policy Press.

Lathia, N., Ahmed, S., & Capra, L. (2012). Measuring the impact of opening the London shared bicycle scheme to casual users. *Transportation Research Part C: Emerging Technologies*, *22*, 88-102. doi:http://doi.org/10.1016/j.trc.2011.12.004

Lee, P., & Murie, A. (1999). *Literature review of social exclusion*. Cambridge, Massachusetts, USA: Polity Press

Loose, W. (2010). *The state of European car-sharing* (Final Report D 2.4 Work Package 2).Intelligent Energy

Europe and Bundesverband CarSharing e. V. Retrieved from http://www.eltis.org/sites/eltis/files/tool/the_state_of_carsharing_europe.pdf

Lucas, K. (2004). Locating transport as a social policy problem. In K. Lucas (Ed.), *Running on empty: Transport, social exclusion and environmental justice* (pp. 7-13). Bristol, UK: Policy Press.

Lucas, K., van Wee, B., & Maat, K. (2015). A method to evaluate equitable accessibility: Combining ethical theories and accessibility-based approaches. *Transportation*, onlinefirst 3/3/2015 doi:http://doi.org/10.1007/s11116-015-9585-2

Marsden, G., Mullen, C., Bache, I., Bartle, I., & Flinders, M. (2014). Carbon reduction and travel behaviour: discourses, disputes and contradictions in governance. *Transport Policy, 35,* 71-78e.

Metz, D. (2003). Transport policy for an ageing population. *Transport Reviews, 23*(4), 375-386. Retrieved from http://www.scopus.com/scopus/inward/record.url?eid=2-s2.0-0242369155&partnerID=40

Midgley, P. (2011). Bicycle-sharing schemes: Enhancing sustainable mobility in urban areas. United Nations Department of Economic and Social Affairs: Commission on Sustainable Development Background Paper No. 8 CSD19/2011/BP8. New York: United Nations Retrieved from http://www.un.org/esa/dsd/resources/res_pdfs/csd-19/Background-Paper8-P.Midgley-Bicycle.pdf

Moore, J., Rodriguez, J., Tokuhiro, M., & Wang, C. (2012). Where should the public sector invest in alternative modes of transport? *A comparative study of car clubs and electric vehicles in London*. London: The London School of Economic and Political Science in conjunction with Arup. Retrieved from http://carsharing.org/wp-content/uploads/2012/03/Final_Capstone_Report_Arup.pdf

Muller, P. O. (2004). Transportation and urban form: Stages in the spatial evolution of the American metropolis. In S. Hanson & G. Giuliano (Eds.), *The geography of urban transportation* (3rd ed.). London: The Guildford Press.

National Records of Scotland. (2015). Settlements and localities. Mid-year population estimates: age distribution errors. *National Records of Scotland*. Retrieved from http://www.nrscotland.gov.uk/statistics-and-data/statistics/statistics-by-theme/population/population-estimates/special-area-population-estimates/settlements-and-localities

Nextbike. (2015a). Locations. *Nextbike*. Retrieved from http://www.nextbike.co.uk/en/locations

Nextbike. (2015b). Prices. *Nextbike*. Retrieved from http://www.nextbike.co.uk/en/prices

O'Brien, O., Cheshire, J., & Batty, M. (2014). Mining bicycle sharing data for generating insights into sustainable transport systems. *Journal of Transport Geography, 34,*262-273.

Ogilvie, F., & Goodman, A. (2012). Inequalities in usage of a public bicycle sharing scheme: Socio-demographic predictors of uptake and usage of the London (UK) cycle hire scheme. *Preventive Medicine, 55*(1), 40-45. doi:http://doi.org/10.1016/j.ypmed.2012.05.002

Parkes, S. D., Marsden, G., Shaheen, S. A., & Cohen, A. P. (2013). Understanding the diffusion of public bikesharing systems: Evidence from Europe and North America. *Journal of Transport Geography, 31,* 94-103. doi:http://doi.org/10.1016/j.jtrangeo.2013.06.003

Preston, J., & Rajé, F. (2007). Accessibility, mobility and transport-related social exclusion. *Journal of Transport Geography, 15*(3), 151-160.

Pucher, J., Buehler, R., & Seinen, M. (2011). Bicycling renaissance in North America? An update and reappraisal of cycling trends and policies. *Transportation Research Part A: Policy and Practice, 45*(6), 451-475. doi:http://doi.org/10.1016/j.tra.2011.03.001

Pucher, J., Dill, J., & Handy, S. (2010). Infrastructure, programs, and policies to increase bicycling: An international review. *Preventive Medicine, 50 Suppl 1,* S106-25. doi:http://doi.org/10.1016/j.ypmed.2009.07.028

Pucher, J., & LeFevre, C. (1996). *The urban transport crisis in Europe and North America*. Houndmills, UK: Macmillan.

Rabbitt, N., & Ghosh, B. (2013). A study of feasibility and potential benefits of organised car sharing in Ireland. *Transportation Research Part D: Transport and Environment, 25,* 49-58. doi:http://doi.org/10.1016/j.trd.2013.07.004

Reid, D. (1995). *Sustainable development: An introductory guide*. London: Earthscan.

Ricci, M. (2015). Bike sharing: A review of evidence on impacts and processes of implementation and operation. *Research in Transportation and Business Management*, 15, 28-38.

Rietveld, P., & Daniel, V. (2004). Determinants of bicycle use: Do municipal policies matter? *Transportation Research Part A: Policy and Practice, 38*(7), 531-550. doi:http://doi.org/10.1016/j.tra.2004.05.003

Saelens, B. E., Sallis, J. F., & Frank, L. D. (2003). Environmental correlates of walking and cycling: Findings from the transportation, urban design, and planning literatures. *Annals of Behavioral Medicine: A Publication of the Society of Behavioral Medicine, 25*(2), 80-91. Retrieved from http://www.ncbi.nlm.nih.gov/pubmed/12704009

Shaheen, S. A., Cohen, A. P., & Martin, E. W. (2010). Carsharing parking policy: Review of North American practices and San Francisco, California, Bay Area case study. *Transportation Research Record: Journal of the Transportation Research Board, 2187,* 146-156. doi:10.3141/2187-19 Retrieved from http://tsrc.berkeley.edu/carsharingparking

Shaheen, S. A., Martin, E. W., Cohen, A. P., & Finson, R.

S. (2012). *Public bike sharing in North America: Early operator and user understanding|research report.* San José, California, USA: Mineta Transportation Institute. Retrieved from http://transweb.sjsu.edu/project/1029.html

Sinclair, F., & Sinclair, S. (2001). *Access all areas: An assessment of social inclusion measures in Scottish local transport strategies.* Edinburgh, Scotland: Centre for Research into Socially Inclusive Services. Retrieved from http://www.amazon.co.uk/Access-All-Areas-Assessment-Strategies-ebook/dp/B00AVNUE70

Sloman, L. (2006) Car Sick: Solutions for our car addicted culture. Totnes, UK: Green Books.

Social Exclusion Unit. (2003). *Making the connections: Final report on transport and social exclusion.* London, UK: Social Exclusion Unit.

Stephany, A. (2015). *The business of sharing: Making it in the new sharing economy.* London: Palgrave Macmillan. Retrieved from http://www.palgrave.com/page/detail/the-business-of-sharing-alex-stephany/?sf1=barcode&st1=9781137376176

Turner, J., & Grieco, M. (2000). The impact of transport investment projects upon the inner city: A literature review. *Time and Society*, *9*(1), 129-136.

Understanding Glasgow. (2015a). Transport overview. *Understanding Glasgow.* Retrieved from http://www.understandingglasgow.com/indicators/transport/overview

Understanding Glasgow. (2015b). Poverty overview. *Understanding Glasgow.* Retrieved from http://www.understandingglasgow.com/indicators/poverty/overview

Turrentine, T. S., & Kurani, K. S. (2007). Car buyers and fuel economy? *Energy Policy*, *35*(2), 1213-1223. doi:http://doi.org/10.1016/j.enpol.2006.03.005

Welch, T. F. (2013). Equity in transport: The distribution of transit access and connectivity among affordable housing units. *Transport Policy*, *30*, 283-293. doi:http://doi.org/10.1016/j.tranpol.2013.09.020

About the Authors

Julie Clark is an interdisciplinary, mixed methods researcher, who is primarily motivated by the potential of academic research to inform policy and alleviate critical social issues. She gained a doctorate in Urban Studies at the University of Glasgow for her mixed methods investigation of the relationships between social inclusion and car ownership, and has project managed the award winning, multi-strand, research project *GoWell: Studying Change In Glasgow's East End,* since it began in 2012.

Angela Curl is a lecturer in health geography at the University of Canterbury, having previously worked in Urban Studies at the University of Glasgow and the OPENspace Research Centre at the University of Edinburgh. She completed her PhD (Geography) in 2013 at the University of Aberdeen, focussing on how perceptions of accessibility compare to objective measures. Angela's research interests are broadly in the area of transport and health with a particular focus on how the built environment contributes to travel behaviour, physical activity and health and wellbeing.

14

Mobility, Transport and Social Inclusion: Lessons from History

Colin Pooley

Lancaster Environment Centre, Lancaster University, Lancaster, LA1 4YQ, UK; E-Mail: c.pooley@lancaster.ac.uk

Abstract

This paper argues that although it is now possible to travel more quickly and easily than ever before, transport-related social exclusion is more likely than it was in the past. Using evidence drawn from life writing and oral testimonies I examine the ways in which people accessed everyday transport over the past two centuries. In the early nineteenth century mobility options were limited and most people travelled in similar ways, though the rich always had access to the fastest and most comfortable transportation. From the mid-nineteenth century the railways provided fast travel for most people. Progressively, in the twentieth century British society became car dependent so that those without access to a car were disadvantaged. Such transport-related social exclusion was exacerbated by the denuding of public transport, and by heightened expectations for mobility which often could not be achieved. It is argued that a return to a less differentiated mobility system could increase transport-related social inclusion.

Keywords

Britain; historical perspective; mobility; social inclusion; transport policies; travel diaries

Issue

This article is part of the issue "Transport Policy and Social Inclusion", edited by Miriam Ricci, Graham Parkhurst and Juliet Jain (University of the West of England, UK).

---

1. Introduction and Context

Social inclusion and exclusion have figured prominently on both political and social agendas in twenty-first century Britain, with numerous reports highlighting the continuing nature and implications of social exclusion. Although not always explicitly highlighted, exclusion from travel and transport lies at the heart of most of the issues that are discussed. For instance, the Joseph Rowntree Foundation (2000) identified four dimensions of exclusion: 'impoverishment, or exclusion from adequate income or resources; labour market exclusion; service exclusion; and exclusion from social relations'. Lack of access to transport contributes significantly to all these issues. Several studies have focused specifically on transport and social exclusion, with the Social Exclusion Unit report (2003) highlighting the issues and proposing an agenda for planning authorities to tackle the problem. However, a decade later there was little sign of significant change as demonstrated by a Sustrans report (2012) which showed that some 1.5 million people in Britain were experiencing serious transport poverty which cut them off from employment and services. This was defined as experiencing a combination of low household income which made running a car difficult, living more than a mile from the nearest bus or railway station, and living in areas where it takes more than an hour to access essential services by public transport, cycling or on foot. The persistent nature of transport-based social exclusion has also been highlighted in recent academic studies (Hine, 2012; Lucas, 2012; Mattioli, 2014). However, one dimension that has been lacking from most recent research and policy papers is an historical perspective. This paper seeks to redress the balance by demonstrating that an understanding of the ways in which transport-related social inclusion and exclusion have changed over time can inform twenty-first century transport policies.

An historical dimension is rarely considered in any arena of contemporary policy, although some historians have begun to highlight the relevance of an historical perspective (Guldi & Armitage, 2014; History and Policy, n.d.). With respect to transport, Colin Divall and colleagues have recently focused on the ways in which an understanding of transport history can inform current policy (Divall, 2011, 2015; Divall, Hine, & Pooley, 2016), but for the most part present-day policies seem to be formulated in an historical vacuum. It is not always easy to identify relevant data and demonstrate past trends and interventions that could be relevant today. In the context of social inclusion and exclusion this is further complicated by the complexity of the issues involved. Social exclusion is a multi-dimensional process (Popay et al, 2008): gaining good data on a complex range of issues, and untangling their interrelations in an historical context, can be daunting. Nonetheless, I suggest that it is possible to construct an argument about social inclusion in Britain that does have a strong historical dimension. All the complexities and contradictions that beset the analysis of transport-related social exclusion in a contemporary context also apply to the past. For instance, principles of social justice and environmental justice do not sit comfortably together, as social justice demands enabling maximum access to the fastest and most convenient forms of transport (for most people today motor vehicles) whereas environmental justice would require strict controls on such vehicles. As personal transport has become faster and more convenient it has also produced more pollutants, causing harm to both global and local environments and to individual health and quality of life for those most affected, usually those with least access to fast and convenient transport (Lucas, 2004, 2006; Pooley, 2016). Transport-related social exclusion has never been solely about transport itself, and often is more properly explained by associated non-transport factors and, particularly, by issues of power, accessibility and choice. Thus in rural areas, lacking most services, transport deprivation and 'forced' car ownership are well documented (Ahern & Hine, 2012; Currie et al., 2009; Johnson, Currie, & Stanley, 2010; Shergold & Parkhurst, 2012), but those with the money, time and good health to be able to drive have the luxury of choosing to live in an attractive rural environment while also accessing all the services they need. Only those whose mobility is constrained by poverty, ill health or other factors experience transport-related social exclusion. Even living close to services and facilities does not guarantee access. For instance, while distance and travel costs may be a disincentive for using health services for some, for others inconvenient opening hours, feelings of alienation or perceived social and cultural differences may be more important (Goddard & Smith, 2001; Gulliford et al., 2002; Gulliford & Morgan, 2013; Pooley et al., 2003). Thus social or cultural factors that discourage travelling even short distances to access services may be more important than the cost or convenience of the transport itself. However, separating the effects of such factors is difficult and there is an extensive transport literature discussing mobility and accessibility issues (e.g. Moseley, 1979; Preston & Rajé, 2007). Additionally, prejudices against, or preferences for, particular forms of transport may cause reluctance to travel if a more acceptable alternative is not available (Beirão & Cabral, 2007; Pooley & Turnbull, 2000a). For instance, public transport (especially the bus) is often perceived (particularly by men) as less attractive than driving or even cycling. In situations where the preferred form of transport is not available accessing services may be deferred. Notwithstanding the complexities outlined above, this paper argues that historical evidence suggests that, as transport options have increased, so too has transport-related social exclusion become more common. Although the very rich have always had access to the fastest and most comfortable forms of transport, in the past when modal choices were limited it can be assumed that most people travelled in much the same way. As transport choices increased, and some faster and more convenient modes became more widely available, differences in travel opportunities between different sectors of the population, and different parts of the country, became more obvious. It is argued that in twenty-first century Britain a more socially inclusive transport system, at least in terms of personal mobility, would be one that was more uniform and which therefore offered easy accessibility but less modal choice. Although no doubt perceived as less convenient and congenial for some, differences in travel opportunities and experiences could be minimised. Such a system, if based mainly on low-carbon public transport, walking and cycling, would also more closely meet the requirements of a more environmentally just transport system.

2. Sources of Evidence

Evidence about the patterns and experiences of past mobility is not readily available. Basic information on inter-area journey-to-work flows was first collected in the 1921 census and again in various forms from 1951 (Office for National Statistics: census 1911–2001). More details of everyday movements (including mode, purpose, distance etc.) have been collected in the National Travel Survey, first conducted in1965–66 and repeated at increasing frequency up to the present (Department for Transport [DfT], 2016a). Additionally, one-off surveys and planning reports from the first half of the twentieth century can provide some information on everyday travel (especially travel to work including the development of workmen's trains in London), but by their nature these are sporadic and do not provide readily comparable data (for instance Abercrombie, 1945; Abernethy, 2015; Barlow, 1940; Jones, 1934; Liepmann, 1944). Prior to the 1920s little readily-available data exists apart from data on passenger loads by mode for municipal providers of trams and motor buses (Barker & Robbins, 1963; Pooley & Turnbull, 2000b). However, most of these sources provide only aggregate level data and few give any evidence on the social composition of travellers or the purpose of the journey. In this paper the principal sources consulted are personal diaries, letters, autobiographies, life histories and evidence from oral history. Only by using life writing and, for the more recent past, oral evidence, do we have any chance of reconstructing the range of mundane and everyday journeys that most people regularly undertook.

There are, of course, many problems inherent in using such sources. Their survival is sporadic and random, and it is impossible to assess the representativeness of any set of sources used. All life writing is likely to be biased towards those who had both the literacy and leisure time to write a diary or life history, and some such writing comes from elites who were in the public eye and whose life writing was designed both for public consumption and as a justification of actions taken. Such sources are avoided in this research. There is no way of judging what was included and what was excluded from any form of life writing, and it is likely that unusual events were recorded more assiduously than mundane and repetitive occurrences. Thus a daily journey to work may be rarely commented on but exciting holiday travel recorded in full. In general, diaries which were written up daily, or at least frequently, were more likely to record immediate reactions to everyday occurrences than more considered and retrospective life histories and autobiographies. There is also some evidence of gender differences in life writing, with women more likely to write diaries and men autobiographies (Humphries, 2010, pp. 12-48; Lejeune, 2009; Smith & Watson, 2010; Vickery, 1998). Similarly, evidence from oral history depends on the skill of the interviewer, the relevance of the questions asked and the memory of the respondent. Recollections may be coloured by information gained later in life and, as with life writing, it is impossible to assess the representativeness of those interviewed (see for instance Fields, 1989; Perks, 1992; Ritchie, 2014; Thompson, 2000; Thomson, Frisch, & Hamilton, 1994).

Research reported in this paper draws mainly on evidence collected from three separate research projects concerned with different aspects of everyday mobility in the past and the present. Each has been reported elsewhere and only the briefest of details are presented here. First, on-going research is using a range of life writing (diaries, letters, life histories) to examine aspects of everyday life, including mobility, in Britain from circa 1800 to 1950 (Pooley & Pooley, 2015). Analysis of these diaries provides the basis for most of the discussion of social inclusion and transport prior to the availability of oral evidence and more widely-available twentieth-century sources. Second, research carried out in the 1990s on the journey to work in Britain in the twentieth century collected oral and survey evidence from three large cities (Glasgow, Manchester and London) on the ways in which travel to work has evolved over a century (Pooley, Turnbull, & Adams, 2005). This source is used for much twentieth-century evidence. Finally, more recent research on sustainable urban travel, especially walking and cycling, provides data on contemporary mobility patterns and their implications. A large database of oral evidence was collected from four English urban areas (Lancaster, Leeds, Leicester, Worcester) during 2008–11, and is fully reported in Pooley et al. (2013). Although none of these projects originally had social inclusion/exclusion as a main focus, and care must be exercised when making generalisations from a small body of data, all provide data that can be used productively to demonstrate the ways in which changing travel opportunities and experiences have affected access to everyday travel and transport over the past two centuries. Due to constraints of space only a small sample of the evidence available can be quoted here.

3. Before the Railway

In nineteenth-century Britain the railways provided a transport revolution at least as significant as the motor car in the first half of the twentieth century and low-cost air travel in the late-twentieth century (Kellett, 1969; Perkin, 1971; Simmons, 1968, 1986). By the 1850s most major cities, and many smaller settlements, were connected into the rail network, but prior to this the options for travel within Britain were limited. Movement was either by road (on foot, on horseback, in a farmer's or carter's waggon, by mail coach or in a private carriage), or on water (by canal barge or on a coastal vessel) (Albert, Aldcroft, & Freeman, 1983; Dyos & Aldcroft, 1969). All were relatively slow, and most meant that the traveller experienced some discomfort from the weather, and occasionally on poorly regulated and minimally-maintained roads, some danger from highwaymen or accidents. There were improvements in both the speed and safety of vehicles before the mid-nineteenth century as major roads came under the control of Turnpike Trusts, with improved surfaces but a toll to pay, and with improvements to the design of carriages. However, the fastest, most comfortable and most convenient means of transport could for the most part be accessed only by an affluent minority, with the bulk of the population travelling on foot, cart or, occasionally for longer journeys, by mail coach, though access to a horse would have been more widespread in rural than in urban areas (Albert, 1972; Bogart, 2005; Chartres & Turnbull, 1983; Freeman, 1980; Pawson, 1977). Thus, although there were certainly both social and spatial inequalities in access to travel and transport, for the vast majority of the population mobility experiences were quite similar. In this sense it can be argued that levels of transport-related social exclusion were relatively low or, to put it a different way, most people were equally excluded from the fastest and most comfortable forms of transport.

Scarce evidence from life writing in the eighteenth and early-nineteenth centuries confirms the extent to which travel was usually slow and potentially uncomfortable but was also taken for granted as the normal way of moving from one place to another. For instance, when Ellen (Nelly) Weeton, mistress in a small village school in South Lancashire, decided to move to Liverpool in 1808, she travelled with minimal belongings first on foot (walking some 18km on the first day) and then another 5.5km to catch the Wigan Packet boat to Liverpool along a portion of the Leeds-Liverpool canal. Her journey was recorded in a series of letters she sent to friends and relatives. Relevant extracts include: 'On 22nd inst. I left Leigh, walked to Holland, staid all night at my Aunt Barton's, and on the following morning set sail for Liverpool from Apply Bridge;'[1] and 'I left there [Up Holland] the next morning all in the rain, and how it begun to be fair soon after I got into the boat, and what an agreeable sail I had.'[2] After spending some 15 months in Liverpool Nelly Weeton took a position as a governess to the daughter and companion to the new (young) wife in a wealthy family who lived on the shores of Windermere in Cumbria. On this occasion she travelled by coach, possibly paid for by her new employer (though this is not stated), and she described her journey from Liverpool to Windermere in a series of letters: 'I left Liverpool on Tuesday the 12th and staid all night at Mr Barton's at Walton; the next morning he and I left Preston in the mail and arrived at Kendal soon after two that afternoon. We dined there and then took a post chaise to Mr Peddar's of Dove's Nest twelve miles from Kendal.'[3]

More celebrated diarists such as Dorothy Wordsworth have also described both their regular lengthy walks and more occasional longer journeys by coach (Owen, 2003; Wordsworth & Woof, 2002), and even for the affluent elite journeys by carriage could be uncomfortable and potentially hazardous. Raleigh Trevelyan, the son of Sir John Trevelyan whose London home was adjacent to New Bond Street, briefly kept a diary as a 13/14 year old schoolboy, and vividly described a winter journey by chaise (part of his trip back to boarding school after the Christmas holidays): 'Got up at 5 was in the chaise at 7 & at St Lawrence in 20 minutes. The snow there is 4 feet deep the road cut through it. Past the turnpike the snow is very deep in a road not used in winter & a deep chalk pit is full of water on account of the snow having melted into it. In another place the snow is 2 feet deep & the road cut through it. By 2 mills we went a little out of the road into a field for some way on account of the snow. In another place the snow is 5 feet & the river has overflowed several fields. The snow by Faversham is 3,4,5,6 feet & about the same depth all the way to Gravesend particularly on Chatham hill w[h]ere it is almost 7 feet & the road cut through almost all the way. Arrived at Charlton at 6 PM (when we dined) having had the same chaise all the way from Canterbury with a crack at the bottom you could put your fingers through.'[4] For these diarists at least almost all journeys were undertaken either on foot, by horse-drawn vehicle or on water and, although the rich had more choice and a little more comfort, differences in everyday experiences of travel were relatively small.

4. Expanded Travel Options in the 19th Century

From approximately the 1840s to the early twentieth century travel choices in Britain expanded significantly but, arguably, access to the different forms of transport remained relatively undifferentiated. The growing rail network allowed people to travel long distances more quickly and in greater comfort than before, and although the rich could separate themselves from less wealthy travellers in first-class carriages, railway travel became more affordable than mail coaches had been in the early-nineteenth century. The poorest in society could rarely afford rail travel, and not all locations in Britain were connected into the rail network, but by the 1870s at least travel by train was a real possibility for a large proportion of the population (Divall & Shin, 2012; Leunig, 2006). Within urban areas walking continued to be important for many, but horse-drawn omnibuses and trams (first steam and then electric) rapidly provided increased travel options for most people. In London in particular, the expanding suburban rail network, both over ground and underground, provided further travel options. Although both the bicycle and the motor car appeared on British roads from the late-nineteenth century, their major impact came later (Armstrong, 2000; Cannadine & Reeder, 1982; Dyos & Aldcroft, 1969; Simmons, 1986). Clearly travel experiences for the very rich and the very poor were different, but the increased range of rela-

[1] Letter 80, Ellen Weeton to Miss Bolton, August 27, 1808. Ellen Weeton: Letters to correspondents (Vol 2) October 25, 1807–January 3, 1809. Edward Hall Diary Collection, Wigan Archive Service (Leigh). EHC 165a.

[2] Letter 81, Ellen Weeton to Mr Weeton, August 31, 1808. Ellen Weeton: Letters to correspondents (Vol 2) October 25, 1807–January 3, 1809. Edward Hall Diary Collection, Wigan Archive Service (Leigh). EHC 165a.

[3] Letter 131, from Ellen Weeton to Mr Weeton, December 25, 1809. Ellen Weeton: Letters to correspondents (Vol 3) January 14, 1809–February 4, 1811. Edward Hall Diary Collection, Wigan Archive Service (Leigh). EHC 165b.

[4] Diary of Raleigh Trevelyan, February 1814, Edward Hall Diary Collection, Wigan Archive Service (Leigh). EHC 191.

tively affordable means of travel over both long and short distances meant that few were excluded from mobility, most locations offered a number of different transport options, and many forms of transport were shared by travellers drawn from a range of social groups. Life writing from the period can again be used to support this argument.

At the time of writing his diary in the mid-nineteenth century John Leeson was in his 40s, and a relatively affluent manager of property living in central London. With family and friends John Leeson travelled widely through the city and further afield using a variety of forms of transport. Short local journeys (particularly for pleasure) were often undertaken on foot; for longer trips he would often hire a Hansom cab (he did not keep a carriage) but also used the omnibus and local trains. Longer trips out of the capital were mostly by train, though when convenient he also used coastal vessels from the Thames. For much of his everyday travel his experiences would have been little different from those of many other Londoners, including those of much lesser means. For instance, in August 1847 Leeson recorded: 'Mother came home by Railway from Norwich—I met her at the station at 2 of clock. Fred came with her. She looks well pleased with her excursion there and likes Railway travelling;'[5] and a couple of years later he wrote: 'Left London and I went by Railway from Euston Square to Derby and Ambergate, Matlock, to Buxton, got there at 5.'[6] Many everyday journeys were only recorded on the occasions when something went wrong, but it is clear from John Leeson's diary that bus use was routine. For instance: 'Charlotte lost £3 in an omnibus, going to her sister's at Walworth;'[7] and 'I slipped down in London—Euston Road—on leaving an Omnibus and sprained my left arm, was confined to the house a few days with the arm in a sling.'[8] Collecting rent from the properties he managed was often combined with social calls, and for such trips he often hired a cab: 'I went to the tenants for the rents—took Mrs L, baby and Kate in the cab with me;'[9] but holidays on the south coast were usually undertaken by coastal steamer: ' I left London with Mrs Leeson, Lotty and nurse and went from London Bridge by steamer to Margate, took lodgings on the front—stayed there six weeks...a pleasant rural country town with nice walks out of it.'[10]

John Lee, born in 1842, was a young apprentice draper living in north Lancashire when he wrote his surviving diary in the mid-nineteenth century. Although of much lesser means than John Leeson, he travelled in much the same way as his London-based contemporary. Short trips made by Lee were usually on foot, longer journeys by train, with some use of bus or tram when available. He travelled frequently and apparently without significant constraints. There is certainly no indication that he experienced any transport-related social exclusion despite his young age and relatively limited finances. For instance, in 1862 he made the short trip from south Lancashire to his home town of Burnley in north Lancashire by rail: 'Went by the first train to Burnley to get some of my school books &c out of my large box and a few other things for the Bazaar which we are preparing for in Heywood.'[11] However he usually chose the cheapest means of travel as indicated by an entry for later the same year: 'Stayed with aunt till noon, then I took the half past 12 train to Heywood. I was disappointed in finding that it was a second class train instead of a third as the Time Table stated.'[12] On occasion, old and new forms of transport could interact as when he missed the train and had to resort to horse-drawn transport: 'Got up to go by the six o'clock train to Ripon, but I was about five minutes too late. I fortunately got to ride in a dray;'[13] but when the opportunity arose he also sampled the newest transport available as on a visit to Birkenhead on Merseyside: 'Train to Liverpool, dinner with Aunt and Uncle Walter. Over to Tranmere, walked from there to Birkenhead and got into one of the Americain [sic] Railway carraiges [sic], that have just been made here to run through the streets on rails.'[14]

In small towns and rural areas old and new forms of transport continued to interact much longer than in larger urban settlements. Although by the 1880s the railway had reached many rural locations, travel to and from a railhead was usually on foot or by cart. Mary Ann Prout (born 1861) lived with her parents in Cornwall when she wrote a diary in 1882. Her father was a coal merchant with part ownership of a coal vessel that traded out of Perranporth, and Mary, her family and visitors, travelled by a mixture of rail, cart and on foot. The nearest station was about eight kilometres away (a distance that was comfortably walked when necessary) and the nearest town (Truro) some 14 km. Necessity meant that most people travelled in similar ways and, although transport was probably a little slower and less convenient than in large urban areas, the diarists studied were not prevented from undertaking everyday tasks or longer journeys by a lack of transport. Rural

[5] Diary of John Leeson, August 21, 1847, Bishopsgate Institute Archives, London. GDP/ 8.

[6] Diary of John Leeson, August 2, 1849, Bishopsgate Institute Archives, London. GDP/ 8.

[7] Diary of John Leeson, February 8, 1851, Bishopsgate Institute Archives, London. GDP/ 8.

[8] Diary of John Leeson, March 3, 1860, Bishopsgate Institute Archives, London. GDP/ 8.

[9] Diary of John Leeson, April 17, 1852, Bishopsgate Institute Archives, London. GDP/ 8.

[10] Diary of John Leeson, August 5, 1852, Bishopsgate Institute Archives, London. GDP/ 8.

[11] Diary of John Lee, April 1, 1860, Private collection.

[12] Diary of John Lee, October 15, 1860, Private collection.

[13] Diary of John Lee, August 25, 1859, Private collection.

[14] Diary of John Lee, October 14, 1860, Private collection.

travel in the 1880s is illustrated by the following diary extracts: 'Mother sent Telegram to Truro for Father to meet Mr Brunt at Scorrier and sent Roberts's trap to station for them. They went from Scorrier to Perran to see the Willie [a boat] and then came back here...Mr Brunt walked to Chacewater station;'[15] 'Mr Henwood left about dinner time. Mrs Mitchel from Hayle came in just before he left she walked from Scorrier station this afternoon...Father has left this evening in the Willie for Padstow;'[16] 'Father and me went to Truro today the Buss [sic] was very full. I bought a hat, window curtains and several other things.'[17] Despite relative rural isolation there is little sense that Mary Ann Prout and others mentioned in her diary experienced significant transport-related social exclusion.

5. The rise of the Motor Vehicle in the 20th Century

Twentieth-century travel in Britain was dominated by the rise of the motorised vehicle, though with a significant subsidiary role for the bicycle in mid-century. In 1920 there were 591,000 registered motor vehicles in Britain, rising to 3,970,000 in 1950 and 28,897,600 by the year 2000. Most significantly, in 1920 private cars accounted for only 31.6 per cent of registered vehicles (38.6 per cent were motor cycles and scooters), but by 1950 cars formed almost half of all registered vehicles and in 2000 80.3 per cent (DfT, 2016c). The story of the twentieth century is not just that of the rise of the motor vehicle but, especially, that of the private motor car. By 2000 there was almost one registered private car for every household in Britain. However, cars were not distributed evenly across the population with 26.8 per cent of households in England having no car while 29.5 per cent had access to two cars or more in 2001 (Office for National Statistics [ONS], n.d.-a). In addition to the private car twentieth-century travellers did have a wide range of other options if they chose to use them. The Victorian railway network remained at approximately the same extent until the reductions of the 1960s, long-distance motor coach services provided an alternative to rail travel from the 1920s, trams and motor buses could provide a dense network of services in urban areas, and for many men in particular the bicycle provided a high degree of personal mobility over short to medium distances, especially in the mid-twentieth century (Dyos & Aldcroft, 1969; Hibbs, 1989; Pooley et al., 2005). What impact did such changes have on transport-related social exclusion and inclusion in Britain? Selected life writing and oral histories can again be used to explore the everyday experiences of travel in the twentieth century.

For at least the first 50 years of the twentieth century car ownership remained restricted to the more affluent, and even those who did own a car rarely used it for mundane everyday trips (O'Connell, 1998). Private motor vehicles were primarily reserved for leisure activities and special occasions. Ida Berry (born 1884) lived with her widowed mother in south Manchester and kept a (surviving) diary from 1902–07. Though living comfortably (she did not work), she recorded no occasions when she rode in a car, and only rarely mentioned male acquaintances that did have access to a car in the first decade of the twentieth century. When recorded, car rides were always for leisure activities, as on this occasion when she and her sister met a male friend in a car as they returned from a cycle ride: 'As we came home we met Harry, motoring, so he turned back and rode between us down Northen Grove, and we had a little chat at the gate.'[18] Similarly, in the 1920s in London the much more affluent junior lawyer Gerald Gray Fitzmaurice (born 1901) also did not have access to a car and only rode with friends for leisure and pleasure, as on this occasion in 1926: 'Staying weekend with the Van Lessens to celebrate Gladys's and my joint birthdays. Yesterday we went for such a lovely drive in Prue's new car, a 5 seater Fiat Saloon, a sweet little thing...Prue drove so well.'[19] Oral evidence from the mid-twentieth century tells a similar story as stated by respondents in Manchester and London: 'If you had access to a car at that stage...you would have used that for leisure only. It would not have occurred to you to use it for work' (Interview RJ04, Manchester, male, 1950s); 'Now taking the car involved driving to the Blackwall tunnel and going round that way, so I would never take the car just to go to work. I would only take it if I was doing something else in the evening' (Interview RJ43, London, male, 1950s).[20]

The ability to make such choices about car use, or to live car-free, was made possible in the first half of the twentieth century by continued provision of good public transport in both rural and urban areas, together with a willingness to walk or cycle for many shorter journeys. Catherine Gayler (born 1919) was a schoolgirl living with her parents in rural Lincolnshire when she kept a diary in the 1930s. Her father did not have a car and all travel was by bike, bus or on foot. Her most frequent trips were the approximately ten kilometre journey from home to Grantham (where she went to school), and the 21 km to her grandmother's house. On

[15] Diary of Mary Ann Prout, April 22, 1882, Bishopsgate Institute Archives, London. GDP/58.

[16] Diary of Mary Ann Prout, May 8, 1882, Bishopsgate Institute Archives, London. GDP/58.

[17] Diary of Mary Ann Prout, May 17, 1882, Bishopsgate Institute Archives, London. GDP/58.

[18] Diary of Ida Berry, March 27, 1905, Bishopsgate Institute Archives, London. GDP/28.

[19] Diary of Gerald Gray Fitzmaurice, October 24, 1926, Bishopsgate Institute Archives, London. GDP/52.

[20] Oral history data in this section was collected as part of a project on the journey to work in twentieth-century Britain, funded by The Leverhulme Trust (1996–99).

school days she mostly used the bus, but both journeys were also regularly undertaken by bike: 'Didn't get up very early in morning and biked over to grannies with Mum in afternoon. It rained quite hard coming back. Got home just after six.'[21]; 'Went to Grantham on 1 bus back on the 4 to do Xmas shopping.'[22] Even in the much more remote Eskdale valley in Cumbria, Jill Caldwell (born 1937) had numerous travel options as a teenage girl in the 1950s. Her father and some other male acquaintances had cars in which she sometimes cadged a lift, but she mostly travelled by bus, train or (less frequently) by taxi, bike or on foot. She often juggled different forms of transport but always seemed to complete a journey without undue difficulty, as in this instance when returning from a shopping trip to Carlisle: 'I'd no sooner got to June's than we were off shopping and we were in plenty of time for the train at Carlisle....We managed to catch a bus to Gosforth and I also managed to persuade June that a taxi was a NECESSITY if I was to keep alive.'[23] Urban dwellers had even more transport choices, and oral history respondents regularly travelled by tram, bus, bike, train or on foot in mid-century. Although not all travel was trouble free, three brief examples show the degree to which easy urban travel was taken for granted by most people: 'Well tram cars was...the mode of transport....That was the normal mode of transport and it was very cheap in these days' (Interview RJ49, Glasgow, male, 1930s); 'Well I had ridden a bicycle to school and it was just slightly easier. I didn't have the long walk to the bus stop...I didn't have to change buses, it was just easier to go on the bike' (Interview RJ03, London, female, 1950s); 'Yes [there was public transport], but I could walk as quickly then. Those were the days!' (Interview RJ15, Manchester, female, 1930s).

However, by mid-century changes were occurring that by the 1960s led to a large increase in everyday car use as well as car ownership. Many factors drove increased car dependence, including greater affluence, but for routine travel to and from work the dispersion of employment to the periphery of cities was significant. As work places became less easily accessed by public transport the car rapidly became the preferred means of commuting. This was stated by oral history respondents in Manchester and Glasgow: 'Yes, I got a car at that point because to travel to x was quite awkward. To do it by public transport would mean...a bus journey, an underground journey, and another bus journey...so it really wasn't terribly convenient, so I'd managed to accrue a little capital and I bought a car' (Interview RJ39, male, Glasgow, 1950s); 'Yes I got my first car in 1954....I didn't want a car to travel through Manchester to get to Blackley, but I knew when I was offered this job at Alderley Edge that I would have to do it because there was no cross-country transport at all. It was just hopeless, so I decided to have a car' (Interview RJ15, Manchester, female, 1950s). The continued dominance of car-use for most everyday travel, first predominantly by men but by the later twentieth century also by many women, together with the erosion (and in some rural areas often complete removal) of public transport in the later twentieth century is well documented (Docherty & Shaw, 2008; Sheller & Urry, 2000; Urry, 2004). As one London respondent stated: 'The trouble is my little eight-minute journey, to do it by public transport would be two buses...there's no direct route for me from work....It's door to door, it's just convenience' (Interview RJ92, London, male, 1990s). Gradually, travelling by any means other than a private car became more difficult and less attractive, and those without access to a car (especially in areas with the most denuded public transport) increasingly found their lives restricted by lack of everyday transport.

6. Conclusions: Into the 21st Century

In theory the twenty-first century traveller in Britain has more transport options than ever before, leading to enhanced expectations that movement both within Britain and internationally should be quick, easy and relatively cheap. Certainly the advent of low-cost airlines has enabled unprecedented levels of international travel for many (Lyth, 2016), and new mobile communication systems have further widened horizons and increased connectivity (Büscher, Urry, & Witchger, 2011). We live in an increasingly mobile world in which there is an assumption that travel and communication over both long and short distances should be unrestricted (Larsen, Urry, & Axhausen, 2007; Urry, 2007). However, one consequence of such high expectations is that disappointment and frustration is that much greater if expectations are not fulfilled. Those unable to participate fully in a highly mobile twenty-first century society are likely to experience both absolute and relative transport-related social exclusion, leading to reduced employment and social opportunities and, potentially, to ill-health due to feelings of frustration and isolation. While health effects of isolation have been most extensively studied among older people (Luo, Hawkley, Waite, & Cacioppo, 2012; Victor & Bowling, 2012), transport-related social exclusion can cause problems for any age group. Such sentiments were expressed by a number of interview respondents in a recent study of everyday travel in four English towns.[24]

[21] Diary of Catherine Gayler, September 29, 1934, Bishopsgate Institute Archives, London. GDP/16.

[22] Diary of Catherine Gayler, December 21, 1934, Bishopsgate Institute Archives, London. GDP/16.

[23] Diary of Anne (Jill) Caldwell, April 28, 1952, Bishopsgate Institute Archives, London. GDP/1.

[24] Interviews cited in this section were carried out as part of an EPSRC-funded research project on walking and cycling, 2008–11.

For instance: 'People still assume that there's something wrong with you if you don't drive' (Interview P121, Leeds, married couple interview); 'Personal safety is an issue and the car, people feel safe in their own car' (Interview P139, Leicester, male); 'Living without a car would be a high maintenance lifestyle' (Interview P80, Worcester, family interview). Although many respondents did seek to minimise car use (and some lived car-free), others clearly articulated their perceived need to have access to a car when needed.

Seen through an historical lens travel in the twenty-first century is something of a paradox. Travel and communication is easier than it has ever been and most people in Britain have access to transport that would have been beyond the imagination of most two centuries ago. However, at the same time a combination of heightened expectations and car dominance has meant that those who cannot access fast and convenient travel may experience some effects from transport-related social exclusion. In the past, when travel options were fewer, expectations were lower and travel experiences more uniform across much of the population. In 2011 approximately one quarter of English households did not have access to a car or van, but access to appropriate transport depends on more than just household car ownership. In large urban areas which have retained good public transport networks (especially London) a car is not needed for most everyday journeys. In contrast in many small towns and rural areas a car is essential. Age restrictions on car driving were enforced in Britain from 1930 and a driving test introduced in 1935 (Driver and Vehicle Standards Agency, 2016); thus in contrast to almost all other forms of transport certain groups are by definition excluded from driving. In all locations the young and the old (often excluded from driving by ill-health) will be most dependent on forms of transport other than the car, or on lifts from those who can drive. Although the gap is narrowing, women are also less likely to have a driving licence than men. In 1975–76 only 29 per cent of females aged 17 or over had a driving licence compared to 69 per cent of men. By 2014 the figures were 67 per cent and 80 per cent respectively (DfT, 2016c). To some extent variations in access to transport and mobility by location, age, gender and income have always been present but, as demonstrated by the evidence presented from life writing and oral testimonies, for the most part transport choices and opportunities in the past appear to have been more inclusive than is the case today. It can be argued that a society which is less car-dependent, and in which there are either fewer choices (for instance through greater restrictions on car use) or more evenly distributed choices, can produce greater transport-related social inclusion.

Acknowledgements

Thanks to Jean Turnbull for assistance with collecting oral life history data, to Dave Horton, Griet Scheldeman, Caroline Mullen and Tim Jones for the collection of interview data, and Marilyn Pooley for assistance with transcribing diaries.

Conflict of Interests

The author declares no conflict of interests.

References

Abercrombie, P. (1945). *Greater London plan 1944*. London: HMSO.

Abernethy, S. T. (2015). Opening up the suburbs: Workmen's trains in London 1860–1914. *Urban History, 42*(1), 70-88.

Ahern, A., & Hine, J. (2012). Rural transport—Valuing the mobility of older people. *Research in Transportation Economics, 34*(1), 27-34.

Albert, W. (1972). *The Turnpike road system in England: 1663–1840*. Cambridge: Cambridge University Press.

Albert, W., Aldcroft, D., & Freeman, M. (1983). *Transport in the industrial revolution*. Manchester: Manchester University Press.

Armstrong, J. (2000). From Shillibeer to Buchanan: Transport and the urban environment. In M. Daunton (Ed.), *The Cambridge urban history of Britain 1840–1950* (pp. 229-260). Cambridge: Cambridge University Press.

Barker, T. C., & Robbins, M. (1963). *A history of London transport: The nineteenth century*. London: Allen & Unwin.

Barlow, S. (1940). *Report of the Royal Commission on the distribution of the industrial population*. London: HMSO.

Beirão, G., & Cabral, J. (2007). Understanding attitudes towards public transport and private car: A qualitative study. *Transport Policy, 14*(6), 478-489.

Bogart, D. (2005). Turnpike trusts and the transportation revolution in 18th century England. *Explorations in Economic History, 42*(4), 479-508.

Büscher, M., Urry, J., & Witchger, K. (Eds.) (2011). *Mobile methods*. London: Routledge.

Cannadine, D., & Reeder, D. (Eds.). (1982). *Exploring the urban past: Essays in urban history by H.J. Dyos*. Cambridge: Cambridge University Press.

Chartres, J., & Turnbull, G. (1983). Road transport. In W. Albert, D. Aldcroft, & M. Freeman (Eds.), *Transport in the industrial revolution* (pp. 64-99). Manchester: Manchester University Press.

Currie, G., Richardson, T., Smyth, P., Vella-Brodrick, D., Hine, J., Lucas, K., . . . Stanley, J. (2009). Investigating links between transport disadvantage, social exclusion and well-being in Melbourne—Preliminary results. *Transport Policy,* 16(3), 97-105.

Department for Transport. (2016a). National Travel Survey. Retrieved from https://www.gov.uk/government

/collections/national-travel-survey-statistics

Department for Transport. (2016b). National Travel Survey 2014. Retrieved from https://www.gov.uk/government/statistics/national-travel-survey-2014

Department for Transport. (2016c). Vehicle Statistics, Table VEH0103. Retrieved from https://www.gov.uk/government/statistical-data-sets/veh01-vehicles-registered-for-the-first-time

Divall, C. (2011). Transport history, the usable past and the future of mobility. In M. Grieco & J. Urry (Eds.), *Mobilities: New perspectives on transport and society* (pp. 305-319). Farnham: Ashgate.

Divall, C. (2015). Introduction. In C. Divall (Ed.), *Cultural histories of sociabilities, spaces and mobilities* (pp. 3-16). London: Pickering and Chatto.

Divall, C., Hine, J., & Pooley, C. (Eds.). (2016). *Transport policy: Learning lessons from history*. Farnham: Ashgate.

Divall, C., & Shin, H. (2012). Cultures of speed and conservative modernity: Representations of speed in Britain's railway marketing. In B. Fraser & S. Spalding (Eds.), *Trains, culture, and mobility: Riding the rails* (pp. 3-26). Plymouth: Lexington.

Docherty, I., & Shaw, J. (Eds.) (2008). *Traffic jam: Ten years of 'sustainable' transport in the UK*. Bristol: Policy Press.

Driver and Vehicle Standards Agency. (2016). History of road safety, the highway code and the driving test. *GOV.UK*. Retrieved from https://www.gov.uk/government/publications/history-of-road-safety-and-the-driving-test/history-of-road-safety-the-highway-code-and-the-driving-test

Dyos, H. J., & Aldcroft, D. (1969). *British transport: An economic survey from the seventeenth century to the twentieth*. Leicester: Leicester University Press.

Fields, K. (1989). What one cannot remember mistakenly. *Oral History*, 17(1), 44-53.

Freeman, M. (1980). Road transport in the English Industrial Revolution: An interim reassessment. *Journal of Historical Geography*, *6*(1), 17-28.

Goddard, M., & Smith, P. (2001). Equity of access to health care services: Theory and evidence from the UK. *Social Science & Medicine*, *53*(9), 1149-1162.

Guldi, J., & Armitage, D. (2014). *The history manifesto.* Cambridge: Cambridge University Press.

Gulliford, M., Figueroa-Munoz, J., Morgan, M., Hughes, D., Gibson, B., Beech, R., & Hudson, M. (2002). What does 'access to health care' mean? *Journal of health services research & policy*, *7*(3), 186-188.

Gulliford, M., & Morgan, M. (Eds.). (2013). *Access to health care*. London: Routledge.

Hibbs, J. (1989). *The history of British bus services*. Newton Abbot: David & Charles.

Hine, J. (2012). Mobility and transport disadvantage. In M. Grieco & J. Urry (Eds.), *Mobilities: New perspectives on transport and society* (pp. 21-40). Farnham: Ashgate.

History and Policy. (n.d.). Retrieved from http://www.historyandpolicy.org

Humphries, J. (2010). *Childhood and child labour in the British industrial revolution.* Cambridge: Cambridge University Press.

Johnson, V., Currie, G., & Stanley, J. (2010). Measures of disadvantage: Is car ownership a good indicator? *Social Indicators of Research,* 97(3), 439-50.

Jones, D. C. (1934). *The social survey of Merseyside* (3 volumes). Liverpool: Liverpool University Press.

Joseph Rowntree Foundation. (2000). Poverty and social exclusion in Britain. Retrieved from http://www.jrf.org.uk/publications/poverty-and-social-exclusion-britain

Kellett, J. (1969). *The impact of railways on Victorian cities*. London: Routledge and Kegan Paul.

Larsen, J., Urry, J., & Axhausen, K. (2007). *Mobilities, networks, geographies*. Aldershot: Ashgate.

Lejeune, P. (2009). *On diary.* Honolulu: University of Hawaii Press.

Leunig, T. (2006). Time is money: A re-assessment of the passenger social savings from Victorian British railways. *The Journal of Economic History, 66*(3), 635-673.

Liepmann, K. (1944). *The journey to work: Its significance for industrial and community life.* London: K. Paul, Trench, Trubner.

Lucas, K. (2004). *Running on empty: Transport, social exclusion and environmental justice*. Bristol: Policy Press.

Lucas, K. (2006). Providing transport for social inclusion within a framework of environmental justice in the UK. *Transportation Research A*, 40(10), 801-809.

Lucas, K. (2012). Transport and social exclusion: Where are we now? *Transport policy*, *20*, 105-113.

Luo, Y., Hawkley, L., Waite, L., & Cacioppo, J. (2012). Loneliness, health, and mortality in old age: A national longitudinal study. *Social Science & Medicine*, *74*(6), 907-914.

Lyth, P. (2016). Plane crazy Brits: Aeromobility, climate change and the British traveller. In C. Divall, J. Hine, & C. Pooley (Eds.), *Transport policy: Learning lessons from history* (pp. 171-184). Farnham: Ashgate.

Mattioli, G. (2014). Where sustainable transport and social exclusion meet: Households without cars and car dependence in Great Britain. *Journal of Environmental Policy & Planning*, *16*(3), 379-400.

Moseley, M. (1979). *Accessibility: The rural challenge*. London: Methuen.

O'Connell, S. (1998). *The car and British society: Class, gender and motoring, 1896–1939*. Manchester: Manchester University Press.

Office for National Statistics. (n.d.-a). Census 1911–2001. Retrieved from http://www.ons.gov.uk/ons/guide-method/census/2011/how-our-census-works/about-censuses/census-history/200-years-of-the-census/census-1911-2001/index.html

Office for National Statistics. (n.d.-b). Census of England

and Wales 2001. Retrieved from http://www.neighbourhood.statistics.gov.uk/dissemination

Owen, S. (2003). *Nineteenth-century Lake District diaries: Personal experiences of landscape and sense of place*. Unpublished PhD thesis, Lancaster University.

Pawson, E. (1977). *Transport and economy: The turnpike roads of eighteenth century Britain*. New York: Academic Press.

Perkin, H. (1971). *The age of the railway*. Newton Abbot: David and Charles.

Perks, R. (1992). *Oral history: Talking about the past*. London: Historical Association.

Pooley, C. (2016). Balancing social justice and environmental justice: Mobility inequalities in Britain since circa 1900. In C. Divall, J. Hine, & C. Pooley, C. (Eds.), *Transport Policy: Learning lessons from history* (pp. 47-64). Farnham: Ashgate.

Pooley, C., Briggs, J., Gatrell, T., Mansfield, T., Cummings, D., & Deft, J. (2003). Contacting your GP when the surgery is closed: Issues of location and access. *Health & Place*, *9*(1), 23-32.

Pooley, C., Jones, T., Tight, M., Horton, D., Scheldeman, G., Mullen, C., . . . Strano, E. (2013). *Promoting walking and cycling: New perspectives on sustainable travel*. Bristol: Policy Press.

Pooley, C., & Pooley, M. (2015). 'Mrs Harvey came home from Norwich...her pocket picked at the station and all her money stolen': Using life writing to recover the experience of travel in the past. *Journal of Migration History, 1*(1), 54-74.

Pooley, C., & Turnbull, J. (2000a). Modal choice and modal change: The journey to work in Britain since 1890. *Journal of Transport Geography*, *8*(1), 11-24.

Pooley, C., & Turnbull, J. (2000b). Commuting, transport and urban form: Manchester and Glasgow in the mid-twentieth century. *Urban History*, *27*(3), 360-383.

Pooley, C., Turnbull, J., & Adams, M. (2005). *A mobile century? Changes in everyday mobility in Britain in the twentieth century*. Aldershot: Ashgate.

Popay, J., Escoral, S., Hernández, M., Johnston, H., Mathieson, J., & Rispel, L. (2008). Understanding and tackling social exclusion: Final report of the World Health Organization. *Social Exclusion Knowledge Network*. Retrieved from http://www.who.int/social_determinants/knowledge_networks/final_reports/sekn_final%20report_042008.pdf?ua=1

Preston, J., & Rajé, F. (2007). Accessibility, mobility and transport-related social exclusion. *Journal of Transport Geography*, *15*(3), 151-160.

Ritchie, D. (2014). *Doing oral history*. Oxford: Oxford University Press.

Sheller, M., & Urry, J. (2000). The city and the car. *International Journal of Urban and Regional Research*, *24*(4), 737-757.

Shergold, I., & Parkhurst, G. (2012). Transport-related social exclusion amongst older people in rural Southwest England and Wales. *Journal of Rural Studies,* 28(4), 412-421.

Simmons, J. (1968). *The railways of Britain: An historical introduction*. London: Macmillan.

Simmons, J. (1986). *The railway in town and country, 1830–1914*. Newton Abbot: David and Charles.

Smith, S., & Watson, J. (2010). *Reading autobiography. A guide for interpreting life narratives*. Minneapolis: University of Minnesota Press.

Social Exclusion Unit. (2003). *Making the connections: Final report on transport and social exclusion*. London: Office of the Deputy Prime Minister.

Sustrans. (2012). Locked out: Transport poverty in England. *Sustrans*. Retrieved from http://www.sustrans.org.uk/lockedout

Thompson, P. (2000). The *voice of the past: Oral history*. Oxford: Oxford University Press.

Thomson, A., Frisch, M., & Hamilton, P. (1994). The memory and history debates: Some international perspectives. *Oral History*, *22*(2), 33-43.

Urry, J. (2004). The 'system'of automobility. *Theory, Culture & Society*, *21*(4/5), 25-39.

Urry, J. (2007). *Mobilities*. Cambridge: Polity.

Vickery, A. (1998). *The gentleman's daughter: Women's lives in Georgian England*. New Haven, CT: Yale University Press.

Victor, C., & Bowling, A. (2012). A longitudinal analysis of loneliness among older people in Great Britain. *The Journal of psychology*, *146*(3), 313-331.

Wordsworth, D., & Woof, P. (2002). The Grasmere and Alfoxden journals. Oxford: Oxford University Press.

About the Author

Colin Pooley is Emeritus Professor of Social and Historical Geography at the Lancaster Environment Centre, Lancaster University, UK. His research focuses on the social geography of Britain and continental Europe since circa 1800, with recent projects focused on migration, mobility and sustainable travel. He has published over 100 journal articles and book chapters and 13 books including *Promoting Walking and Cycling: New Perspectives on Sustainable Travel* (Policy Press, 2013).

15

The 'Arc of Prosperity' Revisited: Homelessness Policy Change in North Western Europe

Isobel Anderson [1], Evelyn Dyb [2,*] and Joe Finnerty [3]

[1] Faculty of Social Sciences, University of Stirling, Stirling, FK9 4LA, UK; E-Mail: isobel.anderson@stir.ac.uk
[2] Urban and Regional Research Institute, Oslo and Akershus University College, 0130 Oslo, Norway;
E-Mail: evelyn.dyb@nibr.hioa.no
[3] School of Applied Social Studies, University College Cork, Cork, Ireland; E-Mail: j.finnerty@ucc.ie

* Corresponding author

Abstract

This paper compares continuity and change in homelessness policy in Ireland, Scotland and Norway with a particular focus on the period of post-crisis austerity measures (2008–2016). The analytical approach draws on institutional theory and the notion of path dependency, which has rarely been applied to comparative homelessness research. The paper compares welfare and housing systems in the three countries prior to presenting a detailed analysis of the conceptualisation and measurement of homelessness; the institutions which address homelessness; and the evidence of change in the post-2008 period. The analysis demonstrates that challenges remain in comparing the nature of homelessness and policy responses across nation states, even where they have a number of similar characteristics, and despite some EU influence towards homelessness policy convergence. Similarly, national-level homelessness policy change could not be interpreted as entirely a result of the external shock of the 2008 general financial crisis, as existing national policy goals and programmes were also influential. Overall, embedded national frameworks and institutions were resilient, but sufficiently flexible to deliver longer term policy shifts in response to the changing nature of the homelessness problem and national policy goals. Institutionalism and path dependency were found to be useful in developing the comparative analysis of homelessness policy change and could be fruitfully applied in future longitudinal, empirical research across a wider range of countries.

Keywords

homelessness; institutionalism; path dependency; policy change

Issue

This article is part of the issue "Homelessness and Social Inclusion", edited by Isobel Anderson (University of Stirling, UK), Maša Filipovič Hrast (University of Ljubljana, Slovenia) and Joe Finnerty (University College Cork, Ireland).

---

1. Introduction

> "We believe that Scotland can match the success of similar countries—Ireland to our west, Iceland to our North and Norway to our east, nations that sit at the top of world wealth league tables and form an arc of prosperity around our shores." (Scottish Government, 2007, p. 9)

This ambitious vision on the part of the Scottish Government pre-dated the global financial crisis (GFC) which commenced with the 2008 credit crunch and continued to affect all four countries mentioned to varying degrees. The quotation was also a point of departure for an earlier comparative analysis of homelessness policy in Ireland, Scotland and Norway (Anderson, Dyb, & Finnerty, 2008). Subsequently, the financial crisis hit large parts of Europe, with the implementation of austerity policies as national governments sought to address the impact of the crisis via contractionary fiscal policies.

Building on our earlier comparative analysis, this article explores whether and how homelessness policy changed in this economically challenging period, framed within theories of path dependency regarding welfare and housing systems, as well as homeless-specific policies. Prior to the GFC, the three countries exhibited some similarity in homelessness problems and policies (e.g. convergence on housing-led approaches to homelessness), despite being dissimilar in other aspects of homelessness governance, housing systems and welfare regimes. Given the differing nature and severity of how the GFC manifested and was responded to in the three countries, the paper explores whether this resulted in increasing divergence in homelessness policies and in the nature and scale of homelessness since 2008.

The three countries considered here were differently affected by the crisis: Ireland as one of the hardest hit countries in Europe, Scotland less so, and Norway with hardly any noticeable changes to the economy during the period in question. Though hardest hit by the crisis, Ireland responded as the 'model pupil' in relation to complying with the demands of the EU Troika programme (which provided aid through the European Commission, the European Central Bank and the IMF to Ireland and four other countries, Pisany-Ferry, Sapir, & Wolff, 2013) and implemented policies which prioritised cutbacks in capital expenditure programmes such as social housing construction (Dukelow, 2016). While the devolved nature of Scottish government makes it appropriate to consider Scotland as a distinct nation in relation to housing policy and responses to homelessness (McKee, Muir, & Moore, 2016), Scotland experienced severe cuts to public expenditure and welfare services as part of the UK response to the GFC, particularly in the post-2010 period (Lupton, Burchardt, Hills, Stewart, & Vizard, 2016), even though the UK avoided any troika 'bail out'. Due to a solid oil-based economy, Norway was largely shielded from the effects of the crisis until as recently as late 2015, although a sharp drop in oil prices at an early stage of the crisis created uncertainty in the oil dependent part of the economy. By 2016, investments in oil production and oil related activities were in a phase of rapid downsizing, with widespread consequences, in particular for the Western coastline of Norway with a rather dramatic increase in unemployment.

The connections between homelessness, wider societal structures and events such as the global financial crisis are complex. Although a detailed critique of the impact of the GFC on Ireland, Scotland and Norway is beyond the scope of this paper, it is possible to examine whether and how homelessness policies developed and changed during the subsequent period of profound economic and social change in Europe. In contrast, the immediate prior period (2000 to 2007), had been largely characterised by prosperity and a degree of convergence in progressive, inclusive homelessness policies, particularly embracing housing-led approaches, in and beyond our three countries (Anderson et al., 2008; Benjaminsen, Dyb, & O'Sullivan, 2009).

Our key research question then is whether and how homelessness policy changed across the three countries in the more economically challenging period after the GFC. Section 2 sets out our analytical approach to the question and our research method. Our comparison of welfare regimes and social housing systems is further developed in section 3. In section 4 we revisit the conceptualisation and measurement of homelessness in the three countries and the nature of the institutions which deliver homelessness policies and responses, before examining change in the post-2008 period. Taking account of differences in conceptualisation and measurement in the three countries, we examine whether there were changes in the nature of homelessness in the post-2008 period and what were the resultant policy challenges in sustaining a housing-led focus on resolving homelessness. Our analysis of homelessness in relation to notions of path dependency and institutional embeddedness enables development of our final comparative analysis and conclusions on homelessness policy continuity and change across the three countries (Sections 5 and 6).

2. Analytical Model and Research Method

Our analytical approach draws on institutional theory and the notion of path dependency. This approach is well suited to compare cases that share some overall features, however divergent in specific areas. Although the 'arc of prosperity' phrase seemed of limited validity in retrospect, the three countries continued to share some key characteristics which suggested they remained reasonably comparable with each other as case study examples (Yin, 1994). They are sited within the Northern arc of Europe and geographically at the fringe of the European Union. Ireland and Scotland/the UK are EU members (the research was completed prior to the 2016 UK referendum on EU membership) and although Norway is not a member of the EU, its economy is deeply woven into EU legislation and the wider economy of the European Economic Area (EEA). The countries have similar populations, ranging from just above 4.8 million inhabitants in Ireland, to 5.2 million in Scotland, with Norway in a middle position with just above 5 million inhabitants. They are all 'mature' welfare states with well-established welfare institutions, and included both as 'Northern European' countries and as 'high-income' countries in the United Nations (2015) classification of countries by major areas/region of the world. Comparing the three economies is complicated by the inclusion of Scotland within the larger UK economy with a population of 60 million (Figure 1). Scotland (UK)'s GDP has been consistently lower than that of Ireland, with Norway significantly more prosperous than the other two countries, though all three remained above the EU average GDP before and after the GFC.

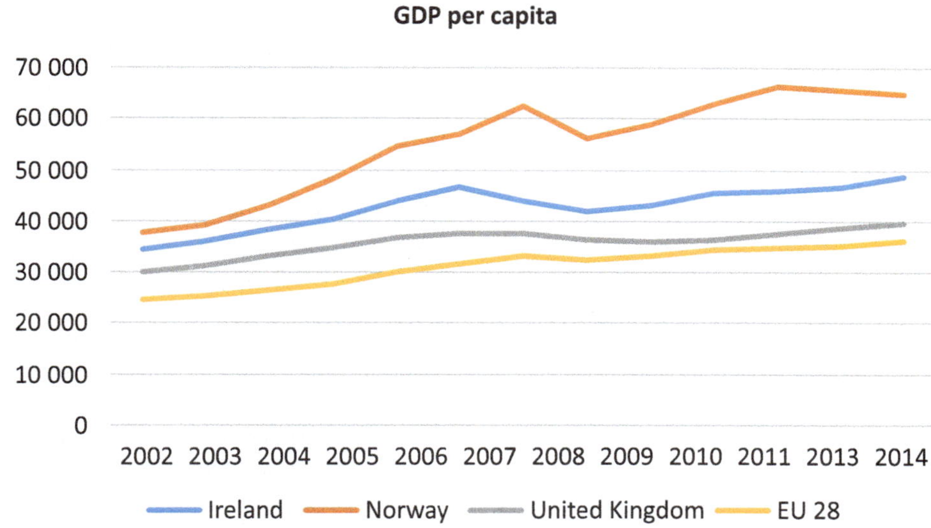

Figure 1. GDP per capita for the three countries and EU average. Source: OECD http://ec.europa.eu/eurostat/web/national-accounts/data/database (Scotland represented by UK figures).

Our comparison of the three countries is derived from desk-based research by the three authors drawing on the international research literature and publicly available official statistics and policy documentation for the three countries. The research method incorporated application of our theoretical approach to the comparative review of the evidence of continuity or change in homelessness and policy responses in our three case study countries. While other studies (e.g. Fitzpatrick & Stephens, 2014) have benefited from cross-national empirical data collection, this article focuses on change over time, utilising the existing data sets for the three countries.

Our theoretical approach draws on the notion of path dependence and institutional theory (Mahoney, 2000; North, 1990). That is to say, what are the conditions for emergence of institutions, for sustaining institutions and for institutional changes? The notion of path dependency does not predict a deterministic process, 'it is not a story of inevitability in which the past neatly predicts the future' (North, 1990). There might be, and usually are, several events influencing any one event, decision, policy programme etc., some of which perhaps lead to unintended results or to the final result (intended or unintended). The decisions made at one point in the historical pathway are likely to narrow the choices at a later point. However, while the main institutions in society may be solid and only change slowly, at a particular moment striking turns may occur or be activated, for example involving sudden economic shocks such as the GFC. These possible turns or developments are, however, dependent on and limited by former developments and structures.

The development of the divergent housing systems in the Nordic countries was rigorously investigated by Bengtsson, Annaniassen, Jensen, Ruonavaara and Sveinsson (2006) and Bengtsson and Rounavaara (2010) who argued that path dependency allowed for the possibility that single events might influence societal outcomes, but also that previous events might be distant in time from the outcomes explained by them. Importantly, explanation required a process or 'temporal' approach, analysing change over time: 'progress in the analysis of social, institutional and discursive change in housing...lies in combining historical and contextual sensitivity with a thinking in terms of social mechanisms' (p. 200). Discussing homelessness in relation to institutionalism and path dependency is rare in the European research literature on homelessness, though Irving-Clarke (2016) applied this framework to his analysis of policy development for supported housing in the UK. This paper seeks to contribute to the literature on homelessness and social inclusion by taking forward the longitudinal analysis of institutionalism, path dependency and homelessness. Figure 2 shows a simplified diagram of our analytical model relating institutional structures and path dependence to an analysis of homelessness policy.

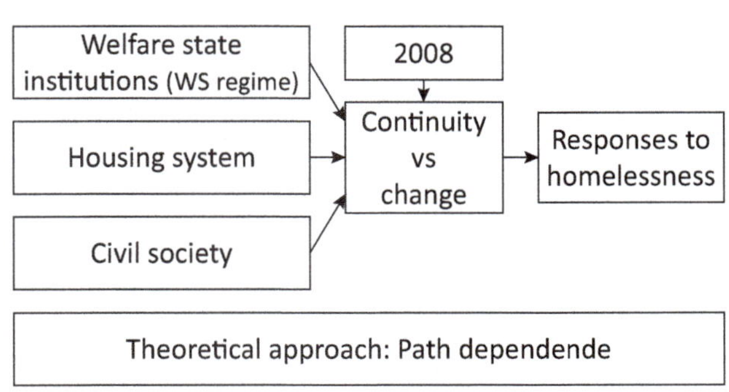

Figure 2. Institutional structures influencing homelessness policy change (source: authors).

Path dependency is the analytical concept of the model. From left to right, Figure 2 shows three sets of variables (welfare state institutions, the housing system and civil society) which to a larger or smaller degree in different national settings influence policy responses to homelessness. The welfare state institutions comprise the most comprehensive set of variables and cover all types of institutions involved in homeless policy in a broad sense. Esping-Andersen's (1990) typology of welfare regimes serves as a concept to narrow and handle the welfare state institutions. The relationship between the welfare system and the housing system is complicated (section 3 below). Stephens, Fitzpatrick, Elsinga, van Steen and Chzhen (2010) found welfare systems to be a vital factor in explaining levels of homelessness and interventions within nation states, but they also emphasised that the housing system and housing policies are important influences. Within civil society, voluntary organisations are particularly important players in the homelessness field, although their role varies across the three countries in this article. Private providers of homelessness services might also be included within the civil society set of variables, depending on the nature of their involvement in welfare arrangements to tackle homelessness. The 2008 point marks the onset of the GFC which was followed by a period of austerity politics, which may or may not trigger changes in responses to homelessness. The institutional arrangements covered by the independent or explanatory variables will also have developed along certain paths, with vital decisions taken at certain points in time. While it is important to acknowledge that 'politics matters' in the analytical frame of path dependency, selected policy alternatives are likely to depend on prior events and choices.

Delving into each of the three sets of variables in detail is beyond the scope of this article. Rather, our ambition is to shed light on how homelessness and policy responses were shaped by the footprints of the welfare and housing institutions in the three countries and to examine the responsiveness of institutions to austerity policy after 2008. For example, path dependence would suggest a preliminary hypothesis that policy reactions to increased risks of structural homelessness and associated changes in the profile of the homeless population would reflect both prior policy arrangements and some degree of institutional inertia, particularly in relation to social housing supports. Regarding the comparative aspect, DiMaggio and Powell (1991) argues that modern institutions tend to develop towards isomorphism and convergence. Processes and initiatives at EU level, such as the Open Method of Coordination, peer reviews of homelessness strategies across the EU members, and work by FEANTSA [European Federation of National Organisations Working with the Homeless] (the umbrella organisation for European organisations working with homelessness) to coordinate policy and research across the EU may also have driven convergence rather than differentiation (Gosme, 2014; Gosme & Anderson, 2015).

3. The Welfare State and Social Housing

Approaches to the comparative analysis of social policy, including housing and homelessness, have developed substantially since the ground breaking work of Gøsta Esping-Andersen (1990) which set out the thesis of three distinct, path dependent models of welfare capitalism (universalistic, corporatist and liberal). Criticisms have included neglecting the position of women (Sainsbury, 1999) as well as the role of housing systems. Esping-Andersen's analysis did not incorporate the Southern European nations and was completed before the post-communist Eastern European nations became integrated into European social policy, but scholars have subsequently sought to address these issues (e.g. Deacon, 2000; Ferrera, 1996; Gal, 2010). Our three countries diverge in their welfare state regime categorisation. Ireland and Scotland belong to the liberal welfare state model while Norway is an archetype of the social democratic (universal) welfare state. However, while accurately placed in the liberal model over many policy areas, Ireland had, up until the early 1990s, conformed to a more social democratic approach in some areas of housing, involving a lead role by local authorities in social housing provision (Finnerty, 2002; Finnerty & O'Connell, 2014a; Kenna, 2011). Similarly, Anderson (2004) argued that Scotland had more social-democratic roots forged in the 1945-1979 period of welfare and state housing expansion. What is less often noted in discussions of Esping-Andersen's welfare state typology is his emphasis on the similarities of modern (20th century) welfare state formation. Notably the three countries considered here are all mature welfare states with highly developed welfare arrangements.

While housing has typically been provided through both market and welfare mechanisms, services for homeless people in all three case study countries (shelters, temporary accommodation, day care, soup kitchens/food distribution, etc.) have been the responsibility of welfare services (particularly local authorities, social services, and to a varying degree, the voluntary organisations operating in the field). Housing provision plays a vital role in preventing and counteracting homelessness. The relationship of the housing sector to the welfare state has long been recognised as challenging and complex (Hoekstra, 2010; Kemeny, 1995; Malpass, 2005; Torgersen, 1987) with the housing sector mainly market-driven, even at the height of post-war welfare state provision. However, in parallel with the evolution of welfare states, Governments across Europe have supported the housing sector at certain points in time, in some countries quite heavily (e.g. all the Nordic countries, the UK, the Netherlands and Ireland) even though distinct housing systems developed in different countries. Social housing has been a key element in resolving homelessness and while generally a responsibility of local authorities (social service and/or housing authorities) or voluntary agencies, the development of social/affordable housing is connected to and interwoven with the general housing system.

In Ireland, post-2008 austerity policies initially accelerated the existing policy shift (since 2003) away from traditional local authority housing towards provision by housing associations and private landlords renting to tenants in receipt of some form of rental subsidy (eligibility for this means-tested subsidy is determined by the local housing authority.) Central to this policy shift was a deepening reliance on the private market for both the financing and supply of social housing, under the banner of creating the 'flexible and responsive social housing supports' envisaged in the *Social Housing Strategy 2020* (DECLG [Department of Housing, Planning, Community and Local Government], 2014, p. 51; Finnerty & O'Connell, 2014a, 2014b).

However, since 2014, an increasing shortage of affordable accommodation in the private rented sector has cast doubt on the wisdom of reliance on private landlordism in meeting social housing need, especially where policy had embraced housing-led solutions to homelessness. Policy responses to this shortage have included: landlord-tenant mediation services (including case-by-case discretionary increase in housing subsidy), more recently followed by an increase in the amount of housing subsidy paid to eligible renters; a two-year rent freeze, and the introduction of a new rental housing subsidy (the Housing Assistance Payment) whose novel feature is a tapered withdrawal of subsidy as household income increases.

Within the UK, Scotland was influential in the 20th century expansion of council housing (and later the housing association sector) both of which provided secure, affordable housing for the working classes. UK-wide policy influenced the subsequent residualisation of council housing through sales to sitting tenants, a policy emphasis on home ownership, and reduced investment in social housing from the 1980s onwards. Like Ireland, Scotland experienced a gradual process of tenure transformation over the long term, where the 21st century saw continuing pressures on social housing, stagnation of home ownership and a resultant resurgence in private sector renting. Scotland's social democratic welfare roots appeared to wither somewhat as income inequality increased in the devolved period (Morelli & Seaman, 2012). By 2015, while house prices and market rents showed an upward trend, overall housebuilding levels were well below their 2007 peak and social housing completions fell by 44% from 2010–2014, to just 3,217 in 2014 (Powell, Dunning, Ferrari, & McKee, 2015). These trends caused significant housing pressures including increased difficulty in entering home ownership. The estimated affordable housing requirement for Scotland was 12,014 dwellings per annum over five years, where the Scottish Government was committed to 6,000 per year in 2011–2016 (Powell et al., 2015).

In contrast to Ireland and Scotland, Norway was known as the social democratic homeowner nation (Annaniassen, 2006), with successive governments since the 1950s supporting homeownership. The main policy tool was the provision of low interest loans by the State Housing Bank combined with favorable taxation schemes which supported homeownership. According to Annaniassen, the decision to support homeownership was a moment creating a path dependency delimiting the choices of the next generation of politicians and entrepreneurs. In the mid-1980s a conservative government took the decisive step to liberate the housing and financial markets, followed by downscaling of state subsidies to the housing sector. The large sector of cooperative housing had been characterised as a type of solidarity homeownership and, to a certain extent, as social housing. Deregulation led to house price rises in the pure private owner market, and the cooperative sector (still with price regulation) had a strong case when arguing for repealing the regulations. The two sectors became more equal with respect to price and second hand sale (remaining restrictions in the cooperative sector have no impact on price setting). These crucial changes in housing policy affected homelessness policy, or rather, the future basis for homelessness policy. Firstly, the cooperative sector became too expensive for the poorer and more vulnerable households. Secondly, because the cooperative sector was built as a substitute for, and came to a certain extent to replace publicly owned dwellings, these were and remained relatively few in number. Council housing was an important tool in homelessness policy; however due to the shortage of dwellings (just 1.5% of the total housing stock), it had largely become transitional housing. The policy shift reducing the traditional responsibilities of the Housing Bank might have resulted in a dramatic downsizing of the institution, but, from the end of the 1990s, the Housing Bank became a major national player in social housing policy targeting vulnerable groups. As a vital welfare institution in implementing homelessness policy, the strong position of the Housing Bank also enhanced a housing led homelessness policy at an early stage (around 2000).

Housing systems in Ireland and Scotland historically had some characteristics of a social democratic (rather than a liberal welfare) system, resulting in 'social renting' in these two countries, while the Norwegian housing system developed 'social homeownership'. While momentum for far reaching changes in the structure of the housing systems may be identifiable in all three countries, the specific outcomes were not detached from the pre-existing structures in any of them. In all three countries a marked shift towards economic liberalism occurred during the 1980s, continuing through the 1990s and into the 21st century. In the Irish case, the large local authority housing sector was supplemented by housing association provision and from 2003, displacement of this public and housing association provision by private landlords. In Scotland, the late 1980s also marked a long-term shift to privatisation and residualisation of the council housing sector, while in Norway, 'social homeownership' evolved into a 'liberal' system (Stamsø, 2009, 2014) with limited public intervention to alleviate the negative effects of the market. Although Ireland saw further reliance on private provision of finance and accommodation supply in the social housing sector in parallel with austerity policy, there was no significant institutional turn in structures for social housing provision directly linked to the GFC in any of the three cases.

4. Homelessness, Institutional Embeddedness and Policy Change

4.1. Conceptualising Homelessness and Trends in the Homeless Population

How homelessness is defined in any country directly influences the measurement of homelessness, and the influential ETHOS (European Typology of Homelessness and Housing Exclusion) conceptualisation of homelessness (Edgar, 2009; FEANTSA, 2016) has aided international comparisons. The ETHOS typology identifies four broad conceptual categories (rooflessness, houselessness, insecure housing and inadequate housing) which can be utilised in comparing the definition and measurement of homelessness in Ireland, Scotland and Norway.

In Ireland, homelessness policy continues to understand homelessness as encompassing rooflessness and houselessness only. The official definition remains that of Section 2 of the Housing Act 1988, where a person is regarded as homeless if the housing department of their local authority judges that they have no accommodation that they can 'reasonably occupy', or they are living in some form of emergency accommodation, and are judged to have insufficient resources to secure reasonable accommodation. While this could encompass a wide range of housing need, in practice the definition is interpreted narrowly to focus on those sleeping rough and those living in emergency and transitional accommodation. In the 2008 revised national homelessness strategy, other groups at acute risk of homelessness such as soon-to-be released prisoners without an address were included in the definition DEHLG [Department of the Environment Heritage and Local Government] (2008a). Ireland also conducts national counts of homeless persons. Every three years, Irish local authorities conduct a point in time assessment of homelessness as provided for in section 9 of the Housing Act 1988. The 2008 count enumerated 1394 homeless persons (DEHLG, 2008b, p. 103), although homelessness NGOs disputed these official figures. The local authority three-yearly count has been superseded by a count of rooflessness and houselessness in the five-yearly Census of Population, and more significantly, by a new software system to provide monthly statistics on numbers using emergency shelters only. The most valid and reliable count of rough sleeping has been conducted twice yearly in Dublin since 2007 by the Dublin Regional Homeless Executive. The extent of rough sleeping was relatively low at around 70 persons in Dublin in 2010, predominantly (around 80%) male and single, with high levels of addiction and mental health issues (O'Reilly et al., 2015). A separate count of those in social housing need, including categories such as living in unaffordable accommodation and involuntarily sharing showed a much larger and growing population, reaching almost 90,000 persons by 2012.

Homelessness in Ireland is highly concentrated in the main cities, with the Dublin region accounting for 70% of the recorded houseless population. A significant factor impacting on demand for Irish homeless services prior to the global financial crisis was the growth in homeless persons of Eastern European origin (Bergin, Lawless, Lalor, & Pym, 2005), resulting from rising unemployment, enlargement of the EU, and the application of a Habitual Residency Condition (which barred anyone not resident in Ireland for the previous two years from claiming social welfare assistance and from eligibility for social housing assistance). From early 2014, houselessness (excluding rough sleepers) increased rapidly, to 6,611 persons nationally (4,248 adults and 2,263 dependent children) in August 2016 (DECLG, 2016). This increase is noteworthy for the number of families accommodated in emergency accommodation, involving a 215% increase in the number of families, and a 215% increase in the number of children, since July 2014 (DECLG, 2016). In Dublin, the numbers recorded as sleeping rough have fluctuated between 90 and 105 persons in the counts from Spring 2015 to Spring 2016 (DRHE, 2016). Increases in rough sleeping since late 2014 have been recorded by homelessness services in Cork City, with an average of 17 people sleeping rough in August 2016, and a total of 345 people sleeping rough and 124 people in squats throughout 2015 (Cork Simon Community, 2016). Although lagging behind the immediate impact of the 2008 GFC, rising homelessness has been clearly linked to structural/economic (rather than individual level) mechanisms, such as the shortage of available and affordable accommodation in the private rented sector (behind which lies a resumption of rental inflation in the private rental sector for which housing subsidies have failed to compensate; lack of private social housing new build; and policy reliance on private landlords to assume a social housing role) (Finnerty, O'Connell, & O'Sullivan, 2016; Walsh & Harvey, 2015). A statutory measure of the 'waiting list' for social housing is an unreliable indicator, as those in certain kinds of rent supplemented accommodation have been removed from the list as being 'adequately housed' in their current private rental accommodation.

For Scotland, the definition of homelessness was consolidated in Section 24 of the Housing (Scotland) Act 1987, and summarised for Government reporting purposes as: 'A person is homeless if he/she has no accommodation in the UK or elsewhere. A person is also homeless if he/she has accommodation but cannot reasonably occupy it, for example because of a threat of violence. A person is potentially homeless (threatened with homelessness) if it is likely that he/she will become homeless within two months.' (Scottish Government, 2008, p. 18). Although superficially similar to the Irish legal definition, Scottish practice embraces elements of all four ETHOS categories (rooflessness, houselessness, insecure housing and inadequate housing) through a wider interpretation of tests of 'reasonableness' of existing or previous accommodation. The legal definition underpins local authority statutory homelessness duties, and official homelessness statistics for Scotland have counted applicants who apply to local authorities for assistance under the legislative framework since 1977, resulting in a comprehensive annual data set spanning nearly 30 years. Some 34,662 applications were recorded in the year 2015–16, of which 16,395 were assisted into settled housing, following assessment (Scottish Government, 2016a). For international comparison however, the point in time data on the number of homeless households in temporary accommodation at the end of the annual statistical period is more useful. At 10,555 households on 31 March 2016, this was still significantly higher (pro-rata total population) than the level of homelessness in Ireland. The number of households in temporary accommodation had steadily increased from 3,995 in 2000, to 11,254 in 2011 but this reflected a pre-GFC policy change in the Homelessness etc. (Scotland) Act 2003 which widened the statutory homelessness safety net over the period up to 2012 (Anderson & Serpa, 2013; Scottish Government, 2015a) rather than the direct or exclusive impact of the GFC. Homeless people who apply for assistance are asked if they have previously slept rough but the Scottish Government has not maintained distinct rough sleeping counts, representing a weakness in the Scottish data on homelessness. However, the Scottish Household Survey indicated rough sleeping was experienced by as many as 5,000 persons a year with around 660 people (mostly men) sleeping rough on a typical night (Fitzpatrick, Pawson, Bramley, Wilcox, & Watts, 2015). National survey data also confirmed the key role of household-level poverty in the generation of homelessness in Scotland (Fitzpatrick et al., 2015). Over the long term, reasons for homelessness in Scotland have remained closely linked to the breakdown of a relationship or the breakdown of living arrangements in shared accommodation, reflecting a lack of alternative housing availability (Scottish Government, 2015a). The characteristics of homeless applicants were also reported as fairly consistent before and after the GFC: the majority of applicants tend to be single, younger males of White Scottish ethnicity (Scottish Government, 2016a) although the proportion of all applicants reporting needs for support beyond housing increased from 34% in 2012/13 to 42% in 2015/16.

Unlike Ireland and Scotland, Norway has no statutory definition of homelessness. Rather, the definition was adopted for research purposes. Inspired by a Swedish national homeless survey in the early 1990s, and informed by the similarities of the two countries' welfare arrangements, Norway adopted the Swedish definition and methods for the first Norwegian homelessness survey. The definition is, as in the Irish case, primarily convergent with the 'roofless' and 'houseless' ETHOS categories. Those counted as homeless in this and future surveys are those without an owned or rented dwelling and staying in one of the following situations: in casual or temporary accommodation, without an organised place of residence for the coming night; and living temporarily with family, friends or acquaintances. Also included are people who are in prison or in an institution, and who are to be released or discharged within two months without an address. Those in precarious housing situations (e.g. moving between short-term tenancies) are not defined as homeless. The Norwegian definition of homelessness may be characterised as rather narrow compared to the legislative driven definition in Scotland, but wider than in countries defining homelessness mainly or exclusively as sleeping rough and staying in homeless shelters. Norway's homelessness census is cross-sectional and measures homelessness during one specific week (usually week 48 or 49). Registration is carried out by service providers (social services, housing authorities, child welfare, correctional services, local and national health services and civil parties). Five homelessness surveys have been conducted since 1996 with the sixth due in late autumn 2016, creating time series data on homelessness in Norway over a period of 20 years (including the 2016 survey), with very little amendment to the definition and operationalisation since 1996. However, the number of variables in the survey was increased successively. The surveys represent a comprehensive picture of homelessness in the country in addition to enumeration of the population. Apart from a drop in the number of homeless people from the first to the second survey, homelessness in Norway has increased slightly with each survey. However, relative to the population growth the increase in homelessness figures were minimal from 2008 to 2012. In 2012 the number enumerated was 6,257, corresponding to 1.27 per 1,000 population (Dyb & Johannessen, 2013). As also noted by Benjaminsen and Lauritzen (2015) the homeless populations in the Nordic countries are dominated by people with multiple problems. The largest group is single males of national ethnic origin, with an addiction, and with social security benefit as main income. Despite an overall moderate growth in the number of homeless persons, the number of children homeless with their parent(s) increased by 70% (from 400 in 2008 to 679 in 2012) (Dyb & Johannessen, 2013), which may reflect a noticeable increase in the number of children living below the EU poverty limit of 26% from 2008 to 2015 (mainly a structural poverty problem). The 2012 census made an effort to include migrants living on the streets and in night shelters. The objective was only partly successful, not because of the rigid definition of homelessness, but because these groups have very limited rights to welfare services in Norway, and thus are exceptionally hard to reach.

Comparing our three cases, there is no simple correlation between conceptualisation and measurement of homelessness, and either housing system or wider welfare regime, with Ireland and Norway more similar in focusing on rooflessness and houselessness, compared to Scotland's more generous interpretation (including elements of insecure and inadequate housing) which resulted in a higher level of enumerated homelessness. All three countries have collected data on homelessness over the long term and have some post-2008 data, but differences in definition and frequency of enumeration still preclude straightforward numerical comparisons, though similarities in the profile of homeless households can be identified.

4.2. Institutions and Homelessness

Fitting a policy analysis approach, institutions sit below the level of welfare regime types, and include national and local government and other stakeholders governing homelessness (Beer, 2012). Bengtsson and Ruonavaara (2010) highlighted social exclusion and norms of eligibility for access to housing as factors which could contribute to the long term continuity of residential structures. While housing may be largely distributed through the market, homelessness interventions are rarely, if ever, delivered by market mechanisms (though they may reflect market failure). Comparative homelessness research has often used welfare state regimes as a background typology (Anderson & Ytrehus, 2012; Baptista & O'Sullivan, 2008; Benjaminsen et al., 2009) and there is some consensus that homelessness to some extent reflects welfare state regimes, the degree of decommodification of welfare and the generosity of welfare spending. Nordic welfare states would be characterised as least commodified/most generous, with the Southern European countries at the opposite end of the spectrum. Stephens et al.'s (2010) comparative study concluded that welfare regimes were of decisive importance for homelessness, although housing systems impacted the risk of becoming homeless. As well as defining homelessness in relation to position in the housing market, homelessness policy often also embraces individual vulnerability. The proportion of people with complex needs in the homeless population is at least partly explained by a low level of poverty and a higher threshold for becoming homeless in the Nordic welfare states compared to countries in the other regime clusters (Stephens et al., 2010). Broadly, the study found that structural homelessness (arising from prevailing social and economic conditions) was lowest where welfare safety nets were strong. The housing market was a major driver of structural homelessness, and access to affordable housing for vulnerable groups was a major concern even in countries with the strongest welfare protection. Targeted interventions could deliver reasonably good outcomes for homeless people, while homeless migrants were often the least well protected group. Drawing on data from the same six-nation study, Fitzpatrick and Stephens (2014) further identified social cohesion and egalitarianism (along with familialism and individualism) as factors influencing interventions and outcomes for vulnerable groups of homeless people. In this section, we examine continuities and changes in the key institutions which provide accommodation and services for homeless people in our case study countries.

In Ireland, the Housing Act 1988 remains the key piece of homelessness legislation, giving power to local authorities to intervene directly via cash payments to homeless persons (e.g. for emergency Bed and Breakfast (B&Bs)) or by direct provision of social housing (local authority and voluntary providers); or indirectly via cash assistance to voluntary bodies for providing emergency shelters, to assist homeless persons find accommodation. Another housing option is some form of rental housing subsidy, eligibility for which is determined by the housing authority (section 3 above). However, the 1988 Act left unclarified the relations between local authorities and the other statutory provider, the Health Boards (subsequently the Health Services Executive), and indeed with voluntary providers. The Housing Act gave considerable discretion to local authorities in terms of who was to be counted as homeless and what services were to be provided to them, while the Health Service Executive continues to have a broadly defined remit to meet the needs of homeless persons. The strong position of the church in Ireland has also been emphasised with respect to homeless policies (Baptista & O'Sullivan, 2008). This position has played out at a number of levels: in terms of the mixed economy of welfare, a strong reliance on charities (albeit now with quite high levels of state funding) to provide emergency responses; in attitudinal terms, a relatively high level of public support for tackling homelessness (in the abstract); and—in the face of loss of trust in a variety of institutions (including charities)—a continuing high level of public goodwill towards organisations providing services for, and advocating policy change in relation to, homelessness (Finnerty, 2014a, 2014b).

In Scotland, local authorities also emerged as state providers of housing and also became the institutional solution to homelessness from the introduction of the legal framework in for England and Scotland in 1977. An important difference from the Irish case is that Scottish legislation conveys statutory *duties* to assist certain households facing homelessness, rather than merely discretionary powers to intervene. By and large, up to the end of the 20th century, Scottish households who applied and were eligible for assistance were rehoused in secure council or housing association tenancies. However, the legislation worked least well for single people and couples without children, who were largely excluded from the benefits of the legislation as 'not in priority need'. The institutional role for local authorities was expanded in Scottish legislative change in the 21st century, with the abolition of the 'priority need test' by the end of 2012 effectively enhancing the strong legal framework, so that all applicants assessed as unintentionally homeless were entitled to settled accommodation (Anderson & Serpa, 2013). Institutionally, local authorities are assisted in their homelessness duties by third sector housing associations, advocacy agencies and support service providers, as well as by welfare policy (through UK and Scottish government health and social security services and local social care authorities), reflecting the dual requirement for both a housing policy and welfare policy solution to homelessness.

Although Norway has no homelessness legislation, the right to a roof over your head and to receive assistance with acquiring a permanent dwelling is legislated for in the Social Services Act, and institutionally embedded in welfare provision nationally in the Ministry of Social Affairs and locally by the municipal social services authorities. Homelessness policy is shaped and implemented by and between the institutional spheres of the national housing authority, which has no real counterpart at the municipal level, and the social welfare authorities both nationally and locally. Embeddedness of homeless policy within the national housing authority (the Housing Bank) has secured a steady focus on access to housing as an objective to counteract and alleviate homelessness. However, policy tools are limited, comprising targeted economic support and soft measures like programmes accompanied by support for developing competence and guidance. Local authorities exercise extensive autonomy in welfare service delivery, whereas social housing, with a weak legal status, varies widely between municipalities. The voluntary sector is an important stakeholder, however its role as advocate for homeless people is of greater importance than its share of total homeless service provision.

Looking at homelessness institutions in our three case study countries, we can see that core housing and welfare institutions have displayed considerable embeddedness since the post-world war II growth of the welfare state. Ireland and Scotland are most similar due to the institutional role of local authorities and housing associations in providing affordable rented housing, with Norway displaying a degree of institutional change in the role of the State Housing Bank in developing and implementing homelessness policy. The increasing role for voluntary sector institutions in homelessness advocacy and service provision has been identified in all three countries, albeit often in partnership with the state sector.

4.3. Homelessness After the 2008 Financial Crisis—Policy Change in Three Case Study Countries

In this section of the paper, we examine whether key policy shifts in homelessness occurred in the post-2008 austerity period, despite institutional embeddedness of housing systems and institutionalised homelessness structures. Given that the GFC was more directly associated with austerity policy in the two liberal welfare states, compared to the more economically resilient social democratic welfare state, we consider whether there has been associated divergence in homelessness and policy responses.

In relation to housing and housing policy in Ireland, a very sharp decrease in funding available for social housing construction occurred after 2008. However, the GFC merely intensified an existing trend, visible since 2003, toward increased reliance on the private rented sector to meet social housing need, via both leasing and housing subsidy arrangements (Finnerty et al., 2016). While this planned private provision of the social housing 'offer' was clearly inferior to the housing offer from local authorities and housing associations in relation to security of tenure, the principal problem continued to be the lack of participation by private landlords in these leasing and subsidy arrangements. Nonetheless, the three governments in power over this period remained committed to tackling homelessness and increasing social housing output in response to the wider context of growing housing insecurity amongst low-income households in the private rented and in owner-occupied tenures (including those in long-term mortgage arrears). The 'partnership government' of May 2016 created a new Department of Housing, and the new Minister of Housing rapidly produced an *Action Plan for Housing and Homelessness* which, inter alia, provides incentives to private landlords to participate in social housing delivery and accelerates the resumption of social housing construction by local authorities and housing associations (with a target of 47,000 new units by 2021 (Government of Ireland, 2016). In relation to homelessness, the national homelessness policy, published in 2008 just as the housing bubble was bursting, had as its key target the elimination of long term homelessness by end 2010 (DEHLG, 2008a). When this target was not met, and despite the backdrop of economic crisis, the target was restated briefly in the context of a 2011 housing policy statement by the incoming coalition government, and elaborated on in a 2013 homelessness policy statement (with 2016 as the revised target year for ending homelessness) (DECLG, 2013). A further significant intervention was the requirement placed on the main urban local authorities to prioritise homeless households in their allocations policies. While the Action Plan omits mention of the elimination of homelessness, it nonetheless lists a series of measures to prevent and address homelessness (such as 1,500 rapid-build units, higher rates of rental subsidy for those exiting homelessness, and an expanded tenancy protection service in urban areas) and to address aspects of housing precarity in the private rented and owner occupied tenures. The explanation for this high political salience of homelessness lies, as noted above, in the spread of housing precarity amongst low-income households who are private renters or are in mortgage arrears, and the increase in family homelessness, particularly in the Dublin region.

Scotland (as part of the United Kingdom) was subject to sweeping austerity measures in the post 2008 period, with an emphasis on the reduction of the public sector deficit through cuts in public expenditure which fell disproportionately on the poor and the young (Institute for Policy Research, 2015). The Scottish homelessness policy response was to promote homelessness prevention (known as Housing Options) alongside the existing legal safety net, acknowledging that it would not be feasible to 'build a way out of homelessness'. Homelessness prevention guidance was launched in 2009 with Scottish Government funding from 2010 to promote joint working and sharing of practice across local authorities. Policy change was governed through a joint stakeholder group with representation from central and local government (housing, health and social care services), third sector service providers and homelessness charities. From 2013 this Homelessness Prevention and Strategy Group had an explicit brief to further embed homelessness prevention activity in Scotland (Scottish Government, 2015b). The Housing (Scotland) Act 2014 gave greater discretion to social landlords in terms of who should be prioritised for housing, but also announced the abolition of the 'Right to Buy' in order to preserve the remaining social housing stock. The Private Housing (Tenancies) (Scotland) Act 2016 provided for modernisation of the terms of private rented tenancies in parallel with policy goals to better support access to private renting for lower income households. Further Housing Options guidance was issued in 2016 (Scottish Government, 2016b). Scottish Government (2016a) homelessness statistics reported a continuing fall in homelessness applications in the post-2008 period. However, this was acknowledged as reflecting the impact of housing options/homelessness prevention strategies rather than changes in the structural drivers of homelessness. It was further acknowledged that the reduction in homelessness had already slowed to a point where the impact of prevention was unlikely to lead to further large reductions in homelessness applications, with two thirds of homeless applicants having first been through the housing options service (Scottish Government, 2015a, 2015b).

Longitudinal, independent analysis of the impact on homelessness of economic and policy developments (from a baseline in 2012) concluded that Scotland faced a slow pace of economic recovery combined with the impact of welfare and housing reform (Fitzpatrick et al., 2015), but Scotland retained the most ambitious homelessness legislation in the UK. Enumerated homelessness actually peaked in 2005/6 ahead of the GFC, as Scotland expanded its homelessness safety net up to 2012. This was followed by a marked downward trend in the 5 years up to 2015, acknowledged to be a result of homelessness prevention and despite wider austerity measures (Fitzpatrick et al., 2015; Scottish Government, 2015a, 2015b). Anderson and Serpa (2013) interpreted these trends as a 'blurring' of homelessness policy in the austerity period, and the Housing Options approach was also reviewed critically by the Scottish Housing Regulator (2014) for lack of clarity in relation to the statutory homelessness system. Research by Mackie and Thomas (2015) revealed that 80% of approaches to homelessness prevention services were from single people, who remained more likely than families to become homeless, to experience drug/alcohol dependency or mental health issues, to be temporarily accommodated in hostels or B&Bs, and to wait longer for settled accommodation.

While homelessness has been an important policy issue in Norway for more than a decade, the number of homeless people saw a slight but steady increase in the post-2008 period. The Norwegian government had previously implemented two national schemes to prevent and combat homelessness. Project Homeless (2001–2004), included only the largest cities while Pathway to a Permanent Home (2005–2007) was implemented nationwide, and the subsequent national homeless census for 2008 coincided with the onset of the GFC. Although Norway was largely shielded from the effects of the crisis, some financial uncertainty was experienced in the housing market. People became more hesitant to buy housing, and so some of those in cohorts expected to move into homeownership lingered in the rental sector, thus 'occupying' dwellings that under other conditions would have been available for vulnerable households (Dyb, Helgesen, & Johannessen, 2008). This interpretation would explain why homelessness increased despite a nationwide program to combat homelessness, although pressures in the sparse municipal rental sector and similarly limited private rental sector also contributed. The national strategy had set some quite ambitious targets for combating homelessness, and evaluation found that the single most important explanation for not reaching those targets was shortage of available housing in the municipalities (Dyb et al., 2008). Since 2008, Norway has not had a homeless strategy or scheme. From around 2010 the Housing Bank coordinated the 'Social housing development program' in which selected municipalities facing considerable social housing challenges (including homelessness) were invited to cooperate with the Housing Bank. Contractually, the Housing Bank provided funding and assistance, while municipalities committed to working towards specific objectives (defined by the municipalities or with assistance from researchers/consultants). Evaluation (utilising 'soft' measurements) demonstrated that the participating municipalities implemented the programme in accordance with the contracts (Grønningsæter, Becken, Bakkeli, Klingenberg, & Strand, 2015), and the homeless census due in November 2016 was anticipated to provide a further measure of the effects of the programme. The 'Social housing development programme' was winding up during this research with the 'Housing for welfare' strategy being rolled out (2015–2020). Homelessness and housing exclusion were increasingly recognised as "wicked problems" in Norway, requiring involvement of all national welfare institutions and other stakeholders. 'Housing for welfare' was supported by five Ministries and was more far-reaching than the former scheme (Housing for Welfare, 2014). Among priority groups were families with children experiencing homelessness or at risk of homelessness, and refugees with a residence permit waiting in a refugee centre for settlement. The most visible change in homelessness and social housing policy since 2008 was to a broader approach, additionally including households in precarious housing situations and linking homelessness policy to anti-poverty and labour market policies. However, the Ministry responsible for housing and the Housing Bank were still the main stakeholders for the homelessness policies.

The evidence in this section has raised some further challenges in interpreting post-2008 homelessness policy change in terms of direct responses to the GFC and to austerity politics. The comparative analysis is further developed below (section 5).

5. Comparative Analysis

In this section, we refine our comparative analysis of homelessness policy change in the 'former arc of prosperity' drawing on our analytical model (Table 1) and the empirical evidence presented from the three case study countries. We consider in what ways politics and institutional settings may have mediated the homelessness policy responses, and whether conceptualisation of homelessness and policies have exhibited greater divergence or not in the period since 2008.

In Ireland, the national homelessness strategy published on the eve of the GFC embraced a housing-led approach to tackling homelessness, albeit that a heavy reliance was now placed on the private rented sector as a housing exit. Moreover, a preventative dimension also featured strongly in the strategy. The impact of the GFC (and the bursting of the property price bubble) led to a lagged impact on the scale and nature of homelessness, manifesting as a steady increase in the numbers of fam-

Table 1. Continuities and Changes in aspects of homelessness in post-2008 Ireland, Scotland and Norway. Source: authors.

Aspects of Homelessness	Ireland	Scotland	Norway
Nature and scale of homelessness	Increase in family homelessness due to structural (housing and economic) factors.	Decrease in homelessness explained by prevention strategy despite austerity; continuity in profile of homeless population.	Minimal increase in the relative number of homeless persons. Considerable increase in family homelessness.
New/updated strategy	Yes: a number of policy and legislative changes: Housing Act 2009, Homeless Policy Statement 2013, Implementation Plan 2014, Rebuilding Ireland 2016.	Continuation of strengthening of legislative frame work through GFC (2003–2012), combined with parallel strategy to enhance homelessness prevention though Housing Options services from 2009.	Continuous programmes since 2000. Post 2008: Homelessness is part of a wider programme addressing social housing and services.
Objectives	The target of eliminating homelessness remained, but the end-date was pushed back from 2010 to 2016.	From 2009, aim to prevent homelessness where possible (e.g. earlier intervention through Housing Options), while sustaining existing legal safety net.	Preventing and curbing homelessness. Soft measures: financial project support, development of qualifications. No changes post 2008.
Institutions	Establishment of Regional Homeless Fora.	National: multi-stakeholder Homeless Prevention and Strategy Group. Local: local authorities lead partnerships with other statutory and voluntary agencies.	National: Multi-stakeholder programmes, the Housing Bank is the coordinating agency. Local: Social services are the main stakeholder.
Basic idea/philosophy	Deepening of housing-led approach to what was conceived as a small number of 'chronic' homeless persons with individual-level deficits.	Housing-led since 1977, legal framework strengthened in 2001 and 2003 Acts. Increased recognition of need for improved joint working with health, care and support services in 21st century, continued post-2008.	Housing led from the first programme in 2000. No changes post 2008.

ilies in emergency accommodation, with the issue gaining high political salience from 2014. A new social housing strategy continued to emphasise the role of the private rented sector as an accommodation solution, despite rising rents and lack of participation of private landlords. A series of rather ad hoc policy responses to what is now widely deemed to be a homelessness crisis has been outlined by the new 'partnership government'. In retrospect, the ambition of the 2008 target of eliminating homelessness was based on the assumption of rooflessness and houselessness as (a) caused by individual level deficits and (b) as generating a small and stable number of 'chronic' homeless persons.

Scotland demonstrated 'positive path dependency' in the period immediately following the introduction of devolved government in 1999 when its 'rational' review of homelessness policy (Simon, 1959) through a Homelessness Task Force resulted in a strengthening of the longstanding legal framework at a time of economic prosperity and political confidence (Anderson, 2009). Post 2008, neither political change nor economic crisis produced sufficient pressure to undo the strongly inclusive policy and legislation in place since 2003. Rather, these embedded structures were more subtly affected by welfare reform, constraints on social housebuilding and a switch of emphasis to the 'soft policy' options of homelessness prevention and housing advice. Perhaps unusually, trends in homelessness reflected policy change more than economics. Homelessness applications increased during the period of prosperity (2000–2006) as the legislative framework was expanded and showed a modest decline during 2006–2012 as the expanded framework bedded down and the housing options/homelessness prevention services were introduced. Homelessness reduced significantly during 2011–2015 with the increased push to housing options services, but this may already have reached its full potential by 2016. While homelessness policy and practice may have mitigated some of the potentially worst effects of the financial crisis, avoiding a surge in homelessness post 2008, homelessness remained at a high level compared to Ireland and Norway, and other dimensions of hardship increased, such as time in temporary accommodation and use of new services such as food banks in the austerity period.

For Norway, the notion of path dependency demonstrates points of change and continuity in homelessness policy with the continuing presence of the Housing Bank as the main player. The transformation from a bank, although state owned with a social profile (it was first and formerly a finance institution), into a state welfare agency was not an obvious outcome of earlier rapid changes in housing policy. On the other hand, downsizing of the Housing Bank's traditional responsibilities coincided with an increased and renewed interest in homelessness research and policy. Unlike Ireland and Scotland, the definition of homelessness is not institutionally embedded in the housing legislation in Norway. The right to housing holds a weak position in the social welfare legislation phrased as the social services' duty to assist with acquiring a permanent dwelling, whereas the responsibility for homeless policy and intervention programmes is assigned to the housing sector at the national level. Responsibility of homelessness policy placed on the housing authorities represents a strong incentive for maintaining housing as part of the homelessness solution and from the very first national programme launched in 2001, a housing led homelessness policy became a principal objective. Distinct from the financial crisis, it is hard to detect any austerity policy in the homelessness sector from 2008 to 2016.

Overall, our comparative analysis suggests few distinctive characteristics of homelessness policy according to Esping-Andersen's welfare regimes. This conclusion differs somewhat from that of a comparative analysis of homeless strategies in five liberal welfare states (Ireland, England, Northern Ireland, Scotland and Wales) and four social democratic welfare states (Denmark, Finland, Norway and Sweden), in the period 2005 to 2011 (Benjaminsen et al., 2009). The 2009 analysis was based on a review of homeless strategy documents and not on the implementation of the strategies. All the strategies shared some common objectives, like ending street homelessness, reducing stays in shelters, providing long-term or permanent accommodation and providing individualised services and support. In the five liberal welfare states, a statutory definition of homelessness embedded in the housing legislation was evident in the strategy documents. Generally, the link to housing policy was less evident in the homelessness strategies of the social democratic welfare states. As demonstrated here, Norwegian homelessness policy shares a strong linkage to housing policy with its two liberal counterparts, although the ties to the housing system have different institutional sources; the Housing Bank in Norway and the legal framework in Ireland and Scotland.

Thus, while in Ireland and Scotland the concept of homelessness is shaped by the legal framework, in Norway the definition derives from research and policy purposes. The definition of homelessness in Ireland appears more elastic than that of Norway, with Scotland embracing the broadest interpretation of homelessness. In both Ireland and Scotland municipalities have some discretionary authority in their interpretation of the respective legal frameworks and national policies. This allows for a certain flexibility in assessing homelessness, but overall interpretation is driven at national level, albeit in partnership with municipalities. The Norwegian definition has been developed from homelessness censuses over a period of 20 years, and conformity to the definition throughout the censuses is an important part of maintaining the time series of homelessness data. Looking past the formal definitions, all three countries apply concepts of homelessness with extensive room for political priorities and shift of focus between different homeless subgroups.

In their analysis Benjaminsen, Dyb, & O'Sullivan (2009) observed that the strategy documents in the liberal cluster of welfare states were extremely detailed. The authors noted that this is was likely to reflect the relationship between central and local authorities, which left limited room for the local authorities to make their own plans. In contrast, the relatively greater autonomy of the municipalities in the social democratic welfare states afforded them far-reaching scope for local adaptation of the national strategy. The analysis in the present article nuances this conclusion from the homelessness strategy analysis. In Ireland and Norway, municipalities have a rather wider autonomy to prioritise between groups and shape a local service provision, compared to Scotland, where local autonomy in homelessness policy is more limited, although evidence does indicate some local discretion in practice. In Ireland, however, the centre has asserted greater control since 2008, with more stringent reporting requirements re process and outcome imposed on local authorities. Moreover, in all three countries, it is acknowledged that the high proportion of persons with multiple needs in the homeless population requires cooperation and coordination between housing, health, social services, child welfare and criminal justice services. The increasing effectiveness of their incorporation into national homelessness strategies and implementation demonstrates a gradual shifting of institutional embeddedness linked to the long term trend to better joined-up governance across public services.

The voluntary sector has traditionally played an important part in service provision to the poorest and most in need, including homeless households. Its size and the role differs considerably between Ireland, Norway and Scotland. Among the three case study countries, Ireland stands out as having a particularly influential voluntary sector in the homelessness field, with Norway and Scotland more equal regarding the role of homelessness voluntary organisations as partners of local authorities. A common characteristic of the present position of the voluntary sector in the North European countries is increased reliance on public funding, implying a degree of regulation of standards of service provision. However, the voluntary sector can still maintain some distance from statutory authorities, and define themselves as advocates for specific groups. Increasing dependence on public funding will require voluntary organisations to follow national and municipal priorities regarding homelessness groups and the orientation of public programmes, as public budgets reflect policy priorities.

Defining and redefining the concept of homelessness, and making decisions about who is entitled to support and who is not, is a way of governing homelessness policy. This observation was made by Sahlin (2004) analysing Swedish homeless policy more than ten years ago. One of the conclusions from the comparative analyses in this article is that, beyond diverging legal and/or research driven definitions of homelessness, governments in all three countries exercise power to define and redefine who and which groups are a focus of homelessness policy in any given period. The voluntary sector often represents one or several voices in the homelessness discourse, which may produce some challenge to government programmes and policy along with service user organisations. These voluntary and service user organisations are present in all three countries, but appear to have a particularly strong voice in the Irish case.

Although there are differences across the three countries in the conceptualisation and measurement of homelessness, it is evident that homelessness remains a persistent problem across Ireland, Scotland and Norway. Our analysis supports the path dependency approach that 'history matters' in housing policy analysis (also Malpass, 2000, 2005). Despite institutional inertia and converging processes at European level, the analysis here also suggests that national 'politics' matters—as policies can defend inclusive, housing led approaches to homelessness, even in an era of neoliberal political convergence, economic crisis and austerity politics.

6. Conclusion

Despite progress made by FEANTSA and the introduction of ETHOS (European Typology of Homelessness and Housing Exclusion), comparing the exact number of homeless persons between different countries is still a considerable challenge. However, a growing body of comparative policy reviews, analysis and, to some extent, research in the field of homelessness has contributed to increased mutual understanding of concepts and a mutual language for comparison across countries and welfare state regimes. Due to unsystematic differences in the housing systems without any obvious pattern, comparative research and analysis has been hugely challenging in the field of housing (e.g. Crook & Kemp, 2014; Oxley, 2001; Stephens, 2016). To some extent, these challenges of conducting comparative research in housing also affect the homelessness field. At the end of the day, regardless of the definition of homelessness and whether policy is primarily embedded in housing or welfare policies, housing is essential in order to end or alleviate homelessness. Definitions, discretions and prioritising thus still govern who should have access to social or subsidised affordable housing and who has less priority or is excluded from the 'deserving' groups.

Our analysis of Ireland, Scotland and Norway indicated that Esping-Andersen's notion of welfare state regimes is not the most fruitful approach to comparing homeless policy among a small group of countries that share some common features regardless of their welfare regimes. Nonetheless, welfare state regimes continue to offer researchers an attractive departure point for comparative analysis, despite longstanding acknowledgement that housing does not fit the typology at all well. Kemeny (2001) emphasised the difference between the welfare regimes and the welfare systems produced within the regimes. National welfare systems are not a static reflection of a specific welfare regime. The related approach of institutionalism led us to consider the significance of path dependency in relation to the institutions which underpin homelessness policy and practice in our three countries, the opportunities for change and the constraints which determine continuity in approaches to homelessness. This approach was fruitful in confirming strong formal linkages to housing policy in the homelessness strategies of all the three countries, and a considerable degree of resilience in relation to housing-led solutions to homelessness through varying political and economic pressures in the three countries since the GFC. Our analysis here points in the direction of curbing the use of the welfare state regimes as a comparative parameter and reconsidering the potential of institutional analysis as an alternative. Further empirical research across a larger number of countries and welfare regimes would enable more rigorous testing of this conclusion, and such research would require to be longitudinal in order to test for continuity or change in path dependency of housing and homelessness policies in relation to wider welfare structures.

Acknowledgements

The authors are grateful to colleagues who have commented on earlier versions of this paper presented at international conferences, and to the two anonymous referees who provided valuable comments on the earlier version submitted for publication.

Conflict of Interests

The authors declare no conflict of interests.

References

Anderson, I. (2004). Housing, homelessness and the welfare state in the UK. *European Journal of Housing Policy*, *4*(3), 369–389.

Anderson, I. (2009). Homelessness policy in Scotland: A complete safety net by 2012? In S. Fitzpatrick, D. Quilgars, & N. Pleace (Eds.), *Homelessness in the UK: Problems and solutions* (pp. 107–124). Coventry: Chartered Institute of Housing.

Anderson, I., Dyb, E., & Finnerty, J. (2008). Homelessness policy and housing options in three European countries: Ireland, Scotland and Norway. In D. Downey (Ed.), *Perspectives on Irish Homelessness: Past, present and future* (pp. 44–55). Dublin: Homeless Agency.

Anderson, I., & Serpa, S. (2013) The right to settled accommodation for homeless people in Scotland: A triumph of rational policy making? *European Journal of Homelessness*, *7*(1), 13–39. Retrieved from http://www.feantsaresearch.org/spip.php?article234&lang=en

Anderson, I., & Ytrehus, S. (2012). Reconceptualising approaches to meeting the health needs of homeless people. *Journal of Social Policy*, *41*(3), 551–568.

Annaniassen, E. (2006). Norge—det socialdemokratiska ägarlandet (Norway—the social democratic home-ownership country). In B. Bengtsson, E. Annaniassen, L. Jensen, H. Ruonavaara, & R. J. Sveinsson (Eds.), *Varför så olika? Nordisk bostadspolitik i jämförande historisk ljus* [Why so divergent? Nordic housing policy in a historical comparative light] (pp. 159–218). Malmö: Égalité.

Baptista, I., & O'Sullivan, E. (2008). The role of the state in developing homeless strategies: Portugal and Ireland in comparative perspective. *European Journal of Homelessness*, *2*, 23–41.

Beer, A. (2012). Housing governance. *International Encyclopedia of Housing and Home*, *3*, 497–501.

Bengtsson, B., Annaniassen, E., Jensen, L., Ruonavaara, H., & Sveinsson, J. R. (2006). *Varför så olika? Nordisk bostadspolitik i jämförande historisk ljus* [Why so divergent? Nordic housing policy in a historical comparative light]. Malmö: Égalité.

Bengtsson, B., & Ruonavaara, H. (2010). Introduction to a special issue on path dependence in housing. *Housing, Theory and Society*, *27*(3), 193–203.

Benjaminsen, L., Dyb, E., & O'Sullivan, E. (2009). The governance of homelessness in liberal and social democratic welfare regimes. *European Journal of Homelessness*, *3*, 23–51.

Benjaminsen, L., & Lauritzen, H. (2015). *Hjemløshed i Danmark 2015. National kortlægning* [Homelessness in Denmark 2015. National survey] (Report 15:35). Copenhagen: SFI.

Bergin, E., Lawless, K., Lalor, T., & Pym, M. (2005). *Settlement first.* Dublin: Simon Communities of Ireland.

Cork Simon Community. (2016). *Rough sleeping in Cork August 2016.* Retrieved from https://www.corksimon.ie/about-homelessness/homeless-watch

Crook, T., & Kemp, P. A. (2014). Introduction. In T. Crook & P. A. Kemp (Eds.), *Private rental housing. Comparative Perspectives* (pp. 1–26). Cheltenham: Edward Elgar Publishing Limited.

Deacon, B. (2000). Eastern European welfare states: The impact of the politics of globalization. *Journal of European Social Policy*, *10*(2), 146–161.

DECLG. (2013). *Homelessness policy statement.* Dublin: DoECLG.

DECLG. (2014). *Social Housing Strategy 2020.* Dublin: Stationery Office.

DECLG. (2016). *Homelessness report August 2016.* Dublin: DoECLG. Retrieved from http://www.housing.gov.ie/sites/default/files/publications/files/homeless_report_-_august_2016.pdf

DEHLG. (2008a). *The way home—A strategy to address adult homelessness in Ireland 2008–2013.* Dublin: Stationery Office.

DEHLG. (2008b). *Annual housing statistics bulletin 2008.* Retrieved from www.environ.ie/en/Publications/StatisticsandRegularPublications/HousingStatistics/

FileDownLoad,20957,en.pdf
DiMaggio, P. J., & Powell, W. W. (1991). The iron cage revisited. Institutional isomorphism and collective rationality in organization fields. In W. W. Powell & P. J. DiMaggio (Eds.), *The new institutionalism in organizational analysis* (pp. 63–82). Chicago: The University of Chicago Press.
DRHE. (2016). *Access to homeless services and move on to tenancies Q1 2016*. Dublin: DRHE.
Dukelow, F. (2016). The Irish welfare state in the twenty-first century: Challenges and change. In M. P. Murphy & F. Dukelow (Eds.), *The Irish welfare state in the twenty-first century: Challenges and change* (Ch. 14). Basingstoke: Palgrave Macmillan.
Dyb, E., & Johannessen, K. (2013). *Bostedsløse i Norge 2012—En kartlegging* [Homelessness in Norway 2012—A survey]. NIBR-report 2013:5. Oslo: The Urban and Regional Research Institute. Retrieved from http://biblioteket.husbanken.no/arkiv/dok/Sum/BostedsloseNorge2012_eng.pdf
Dyb, E., Helgesen, M. K., & Johannessen, K. (2008). *På vei til egen bolig. Evaluering av nasjonal strategi for å forebygge og bekjempe bostedsløshet* [The pathway to a permanent home. Evaluation of the national strategy to prevent and counteract homelessness 2005–2007] (NIBR-report 2008:15). Oslo: The Urban and Regional Research Institute. Retrieved from http://www.hioa.no/extension/hioa/design/hioa/images/nibr/files/filer/2008-15.pdf
Edgar, B. (2009). *European review of statistics on homelessness*. Brussels: FEANTSA.
Esping-Andersen, G. (1990). *The three worlds of welfare capitalism*. Cambridge: Polity Press.
FEANTSA (2016). Ethos typology on homelessness and housing exclusion. Brussels: FEANTSA. Retrieved from http://www.feantsa.org/spip.php?article120
Ferrera, M. (1996). The 'southern model' of welfare in social Europe. Journal of European *Social Policy*, *6*(1), 17–37. doi:10.1177/095892879600600102
Finnerty, J. (2002). Homes for the working classes? Irish public house-building cycles, 1947–2002. *Saothar: Journal of the Irish Labour History Society*, *27*, 65–71.
Finnerty, J. (2014a). *Ending adult homelessness in an age of austerity—Neither low-hanging fruit nor systemic change*. Paper presented at WELPHASE workshop, European Network of Housing Research 2014 conference, Edinburgh, July.
Finnerty, J. (2014b). Preventing and ending homelessness for adults with mental health disabilities in Ireland: Realities and aspirations. In C. Clarke (Ed.), *Homelessness. Prevalence, impact of social factors and mental health challenges* (pp. 1–16). New York: NOVA.
Finnerty, J., & O'Connell, C. (2014a). 50 years of the social housing 'offer' in Ireland: The casualisation thesis examined. In L. Sirr (Ed.), *Public and private renting in Ireland* (pp. 170–181). Dublin: IPA.
Finnerty, J., & O'Connell, C. (2014b). Housing ladders and snakes: An examination of changing residential tenure trajectories in the Republic of Ireland. In P. Kenna (Ed.), *Contemporary housing issues in a globalized world* (pp. 251–266). Farnham: Ashgate.
Finnerty, J., O'Connell, C., & O'Sullivan, S. (2016). The changing regime of social housing policy and provision. In M. P. Murphy & F. Dukelow (Eds.), *The Irish welfare state in the twenty-first century: Challenges and change* (Ch. 11). Basingstoke: Palgrave Macmillan.
Fitzpatrick, S., & Stephens, M. (2014). Welfare regimes, social values and homelessness: Comparing responses to marginalised groups in six European countries. *Housing Studies*, *29*(2), 215–234.
Fitzpatrick, S., Pawson, H., Bramley, G., Wilcox, S., & Watts, B. (2015). *The homelessness monitor: Scotland*. London: Crisis.
Gal, J. (2010). Is there an extended family of Mediterranean welfare states? *Journal of European Social Policy*, *20*(4), 283–300.
Gosme, L. (2014). Key steps towards a European Union homelessness policy. *Journal of European Social Policy*, *24*(3), 289–299.
Gosme, L., & Anderson, I. (2015). International learning as a driver of innovation in local-level policy making: Achievements and challenges from peer review of homelessness policies. *European Journal of Homelessness*, *9*(1), 37–59. Retrieved from http://www.feantsaresearch.org/spip.php?article377
Government of Ireland. (2016). *Rebuilding Ireland: Action plan on housing and homelessness*. Retrieved from http://rebuildingireland.ie
Grønningsæter, A. B., Becken, L-E., Bakkeli, V., Klingenberg, S., & Strand, A. H. (2014). *Evaluering av Husbankens kommunesatsing* [Evaluation of The Housing Bank's municipal program]. Oslo: Fafo. Retrieved from http://fafo.no/images/pub/2014/20398.pdf
Hoekstra, J. (2010). *Divergence in European welfare and housing systems* (Doctoral dissertation). Delft University of Technology. Amsterdam: IOS Press BV.
Housing for Welfare (2014). *National strategy for housing and support services (2014–2020)*. Oslo: The Norwegian Government. Retrieved from https://www.regjeringen.no/globalassets/upload/kmd/boby/housing_for_welfare_national_strategy_for_housing_and_support_services_2014_2020.pdf
Institute for Policy Research. (2015). *Alternatives to austerity*. Bath: University of Bath.
Irving-Clarke, Y. (2016). *Supporting people—How did we get here and what does it mean for the future?* (Doctoral dissertation). De Montfort University.
Kemeny, J. (1995). *From public housing to the social market: Rental policy strategies in comparative perspective*. London: Routledge.
Kemeny, J. (2001). Comparative housing and welfare: Theorising the relationship. *Journal of Housing and the Built Environment*, *16*, 53–70.
Kenna, P. (2011). *Housing law, policy and practice in Ire-*

land. Dublin: Clarus Press.

Lupton, R., Burchardt, T., Hills, J., Stewart, K., & Vizard, P. (2016). *Social policy in a cold climate: Policies and their consequences since the crisis*. Bristol: Policy Press.

Mackie, P., & Thomas. I. (2015). *Single homelessness in Scotland*. London: Crisis.

Mahoney, J. (2000). Path dependence in historical sociology. *Theory and Society*, *29*(4), 507–548.

Malpass, P. (2000). *Housing associations and housing policy*. Basingstoke: Palgrave Macmillan.

Malpass, P. (2005). *Housing and the welfare state. The development of housing policy in Britain*. Basingstoke: Palgrave Macmillan.

McKee, K., Muir, J., & Moore, T. (2016). Housing policy in the UK: The importance of spatial nuance. *Housing Studies*. doi:10.1080/02673037.2016.1181722

Morelli, C., & Seaman, P. (2012). Income and wealth inequalities in Scotland since 1997. In G. Mooney & G. Scott (Eds.), *Social justice and public policy in Scotland* (pp. 43–60). Bristol: Policy Press.

North, D. C. (1990). *Institutions, institutional change and economic performance. Political economy of institutions and decisions*. New York: Cambridge University Press

O'Reilly, F., Barror, S., Hannigan, A., Scriver, S., Ruane, L., MacFarlane, A., & O'Carroll, A. (2015). *Homelessness: An unhealthy state. Health status, risk behaviours and service utilisation among homeless people in two Irish cities*. Dublin: The Partnership for Health Equity.

Oxley, M. (2001). Meaning, science, context and confusion in comparative housing research. *Journal of Housing and the Built Environment*, *16*, 89–106.

Pisani-Ferry, J., Sapir, A., & Wolff, G. (2013). *EU-IMF assistance to euro-area countries: An early assessment*. Brussels: Breugel.

Powell, R., Dunning, R., Ferrari, E., & McKee, K. (2015). *Affordable housing need in Scotland* (Summary Report). Edinburgh: Shelter Scotland.

Sahlin, I. (2004). Central state and homelessness policies in Sweden: New ways of governing. *European Journal of Housing Policy*, *4*(3), 345–367.

Sainsbury, D. (1999). Gender, policy regimes, and politics. In D. Sainsbury (Ed.), *Gender and welfare states regimes* (pp. 248–260). Oxford: University Press.

Scottish Government. (2007). *Principles and priorities: The Government's programme for Scotland*. Edinburgh: Scottish Government. Retrieved from http://www.gov.scot/Resource/Doc/197113/0052743.pdf

Scottish Government (2008). *Operation of the homeless persons legislation in Scotland 2007–8*. Edinburgh: Scottish Government.

Scottish Government (2015a). *Operation of the homeless persons legislation in Scotland 2014–15*. Edinburgh: Scottish Government.

Scottish Government (2015b). *Housing options (PREVENT 1) statistics in Scotland 2014–15*. Edinburgh: Scottish Government. Retrieved from http://www.gov.scot/Topics/Statistics/Browse/Housing-Regeneration/RefTables/PREVENT1to31Mar15

Scottish Government (2016a). *Operation of the homeless persons legislation in Scotland 2015–16*. Edinburgh: Scottish Government.

Scottish Government (2016b). *Housing options guidance*. Edinburgh: Scottish Government.

Scottish Housing Regulator (2014). *Housing options in Scotland: A thematic enquiry*. Glasgow: Scottish Housing Regulator.

Simon, H. (1959). Theories of decision-making in economics and behavioural science. *American Economic Review*, *49*(3), 253–283.

Stamsø, M. A. (2009). Housing and the welfare state in Norway. *Scandinavian Political Studies*, *32*(2), 195–220. doi:10.1111/j.1467-9477.2008.00223.x

Stamsø, M. A. (2014). Norway. In T. Crook & P. A. Kemp (Eds.), *Private rental housing. Comparative perspectives* (pp. 125–147). Cheltenham: Edward Elgar Publishing Limited.

Stephens, M. (2016). Using Esping-Andersen and Kemeny's welfare and housing regimes in comparative housing research. *Critical Housing Analysis*, *3*(1), 19–29.

Stephens, M., Fitzpatrick, S., Elsinga, M., van Steen, G., & Chzhen, Y. (2010). *Study on housing exclusion: Welfare policies, housing provision and labour markets*. Brussels: European Commission. Retrieved from https://pureapps2.hw.ac.uk/portal/files/4727289/housing_exclusion_1_.pdf

Torgersen, U. (1987). Housing: The wobbly pillar of the welfare state. In B. Turner, J. Kemeny, & L. J. Lundqvist (Eds.), *Between state and market: Housing in the post-industrial era* (pp. 116–126). Stockholm: Almqvist & Wiksell International.

United Nations (2015). *Classification of countries by major area and region of the world* (World population prospects: The 2015 Revision). New York: United Nations Department of Economic and Social Affairs/Population Division.

Walsh, K., & Harvey, B. (2015). *Family experiences of pathways into homelessness*. Dublin: Housing Agency.

Yin, R. K. (1994). *Case study research. Design and methods*. Thousand Oaks: Sage Publications.

About the Authors

Isobel Anderson is Chair in Housing Studies and Associate Dean (Research) in the Faculty of Social Sciences at the University of Stirling, Scotland. She was founder/co-ordinator of the working group on Welfare Policy, Homelessness and Social Exclusion within the European Network for Housing Research (2003–2013) and is currently a Member of the International Advisory Committee of the *European Journal of Homelessness* and a board member of Homeless Action Scotland.

Evelyn Dyb is Research Professor at the Urban and Regional Research Institute, Oslo and Akershus University College, Norway. Her prime research interest is in housing and welfare. She is a member of the International Advisory Committee of the European Journal of Homelessness, one of the coordinators of the Welfare Policy, Homelessness and Social Exclusion within the European Network for Housing Research and national coordinator of the Nordic Network of Homelessness Research.

Joe Finnerty is Course Director of the Higher Diploma in Social Policy in the School of Applied Social Studies, University College Cork. His research interests are principally in the areas of housing and homelessness, poverty and social exclusion, and quantitative research methods. He is a coordinator of the Welfare Policy, Homelessness and Social Exclusion working group of the European Network of Housing Research, is Ireland correspondent for the *European Observatory on Homelessness*, and sits on the Cork Kerry Youth Out of Home Forum.

Secular New Zealand and Religious Diversity: From Cultural Evolution to Societal Affirmation

Douglas Pratt [1,2]

[1] School of Social Sciences, Faculty of Arts and Social Sciences, University of Waikato, Hamilton 3240, New Zealand; E-Mail: dpratt@waikato.ac.nz
[2] Faculty of Theology, University of Bern, 3012 Bern, Switzerland

Abstract
About a century ago New Zealand was a predominantly white Anglo-Saxon Christian nation, flavoured only by diversities of Christianity. A declining indigenous population (Maori) for the most part had been successfully converted as a result of 19th century missionary endeavour. In 2007, in response to increased presence of diverse religions, a national Statement on Religious Diversity was launched. During the last quarter of the 20th century the rise of immigrant communities, with their various cultures and religions, had contributed significantly to the changing demographic profile of religious affiliation. By early in the 21st century this diversity, together with issues of inter-communal and interreligious relations, all in the context of New Zealand being a secular society, needed to be addressed in some authoritative way. Being a secular country, the government keeps well clear of religion and expects religions to keep well clear of politics. This paper will outline relevant historical and demographic factors that set the scene for the Statement, which represents a key attempt at enhancing social inclusion with respect to contemporary religious diversity. The statement will be outlined and discussed, and other indicators of the way in which religious diversity is being received and attended to will be noted.

Keywords
Christian denominations; Christian missions; demographics; ethnic diversity; New Zealand; reception; religious diversity

Issue
This article is part of the issue "Religious Diversity and Social Inclusion", edited by Gary Bouma (Monash University, Australia).

---

1. Introduction

Although prior to the late 18th century there was some sporadic encounter of European explorers with this distant land deep within the South Pacific, it was, to use King's phrase, "as the eighteenth century merged into the nineteenth" (King, 2003, p. 116) that saw the beginnings of European colonial settlement. In this context two religious cultures collided. On the one hand there was the religion of the indigenous inhabitants, the Maori, who "had always been a highly spiritual people" (King, 2003, p. 139) even though, at first, the culturally embedded nature of this spirituality meant some Europeans did not think, initially, that Maori had any religion as such (Irwin, 1984). On the other hand, the religion of the Europeans, Christianity, arrived on these shores initially in the form of two Protestant missionary movements (Anglican and Methodist), followed soon by a Catholic one (Marist). Only in later decades of the 19th century did settler Christianity arrive in earnest to re-shape the religious landscape. Throughout, as sociologist Hans Mol (1982) has noted, profound change occurred to Maori religious life and sensibility in the wake of European colonization and evangelization (see also Pratt, 2015). And whilst the incoming European religious culture has been referred to as a 'transplanted Christianity' (Davidson & Lineham, 1989), Mol rightly observes that the incoming Europeans brought with them their own dissensions and disruptions: "migration to the other side of the world meant vast discontinuities with the past" (Mol, 1982, p. 1). If there was an expectation that colonisation and concomitant evangelisation would result in a homogenous society, the sociological and cultural reality was quite otherwise. In reality, even then, diversity ruled (Colless & Donovan, 1985).

Whilst, superficially, it could be said that there were two cultures—Maori and European (known colloquially as 'Pakeha')—and two religions, Maori and Christianity, in reality there was, and is, a diversity within and of Maori culture (Best, 1974) and a manifest variety of Christianities (Davidson, 1997). The arrival of European settlement brought with it the beginnings of the modern era of religious diversity. And although popular historical perception tends to elide this diversity—presuming but one homogenous form of Maori religiosity and one dominant (Western) form of Christianity (with at least a nod to the divide between Protestant and Catholic and perhaps an acknowledgement of Protestant denominationalism)—the fact of the matter is that diversity, at least within the dominant religion, was from the outset a major feature contributing to the cultural evolution of New Zealand as a modern secular state and society. As the nineteenth century progressed, and especially following the signing of a treaty between the British Crown and the Maori Chiefs (Orange, 1987), that diversity was extended with the arrival of other religions, further expanding and consolidating during the 20th century. This development has been largely within a context of liberal tolerance and acceptance of, albeit limited or constrained (cf. the history of immigration policies, for example), diversity—arguably a hallmark of what it is to be a secular society (Griffiths, 2011). At the same time, from the late 20th century on, changes in religious identity, demographics, and allegiances have seen a rise in non-religious identities and a concomitant contentious identification of 'being secular' with being 'non-religious' if not, in fact, signifying being 'anti-religion' as such.

Other than when caught up with the educational question as to whether and in what mode religion should be taught in schools (McGeorge & Snook, 1981; Turley & Martin, 1981), religion has not been a matter of deep interest or controversy in New Zealand in recent decades. Religious spats have certainly flared from time-to-time ever since free-thinkers, emerging new Church denominations, and other relatively fringe elements of Christianity accompanied the main Christian Church bodies to this far-flung British colony in the 19th century. But such dissensions, even when gaining publicity, were always matters internal to Christianity. Today New Zealand, as we shall see below, is one of the least overtly religious societies within the orbit of Western secular influence. It can be very hard for religion to get any kind of exposure in the media, unless it is for all the wrong reasons, such as paedophile priests or other forms of sexual misconduct and abuse. New Zealanders, I suggest, are arguably among the most studiously ignorant of religion; religion is a subject of discussion that is actively avoided and deemed better to ignore. As a result, misunderstanding and prejudice appears rampant.

In this paper I shall sketch the historical development of religious plurality since the 19th century—when Europeans, and so Christianity, arrived, settled and interacted with the indigenous Maori. I shall then outline the key demographic changes, with reference to census data, that demonstrate the nature and extent of a blossoming religious diversity, including the relationship between ethnic and religious diversities, together with a rising abjuring of religion that has become more prevalent in the last few decades and, with that, a challenge to what it means to be secular. I shall outline and discuss the National Statement on Religious Diversity and the reception it has received. Where has this statement come from, and what does it seek to assert and achieve? Finally, I shall review of a variety of other forms and avenues for engagement with religious diversity and offer some concluding remarks. Arguably, so far as social inclusion is concerned, it would appear that when it comes to religion New Zealand is happiest if religion is mute. But for some in this country, there are certain religions which they would rather not see included at all; and for others, religion as such should be a private matter only and not even on the agenda of social inclusion *per se*. How might this sit with the history and reality of religious diversity in New Zealand?

2. A History of Religious Diversity (I): Colonial Christianity

Prior to the arrival of Europeans in the late 18th and early 19th centuries, and with them missionary Christianity, the indigenous Maori followed their own primal religious traditions (Irwin, 1984). During the 19th century, missionary evangelical outreach and conversion among Maori, despite a relatively slow beginning, was on the whole quite successful. Christian missions began with the arrival of the Anglican Church Missionary Society (CMS) and its first missionary, Rev. Samuel Marsden (Davidson, 1997, pp. 8-10). Marsden came from Australia where his hospitality to Maori who visited him there garnered Maori protection and support to establish the first New Zealand mission. He conducted the first known formal service of worship, on a beach in the Bay of Islands (upper north of the North Island of the country), on Christmas Day 1814 and soon thereafter returned to his home in Sydney. By the time he came back to New Zealand in 1819 the CMS mission, which was premised on the principle of introducing 'civilisation' as the precursor to promoting Christianity, was in serious trouble. It almost collapsed, but in 1823 relocated to a new location where it fared better. An important contribution to the study of Maori language was made, including work on a translation of the Bible. The first baptism of a Maori occurred in 1825. Anglican missionary outreach to Maori was well underway, and its legacy persists to this day.

The Rev Samuel Leigh, the first Wesleyan (Methodist) minister to Australia, began the New Zealand work of the Wesleyan Missionary Society (WMS), also in the north of the country, in 1822 (Davidson, 1997, p. 13). However this, too, proved a difficult beginning, with considerable tension between the local Maori community and the Mission station emerging. Interpersonal difficulties among the missionaries were also factors involved. The station was sacked by Maori in 1827 and the Wesleyans withdrew for a short while. Rather like the Anglicans, in 1828 they relocated and regrouped at a new site—on the Hokianga harbour on the western side of the upper North Island—and soon expanded from there. By 1830 scant missionary success could be recorded as it would appear there was little or no understanding of the real task. Physical, spiritual and psychological isolation took their toll and there was considerable difficulty in language acquisition. Methodist missionaries seemingly had little to offer the Maori. But the venture was not a total failure. Maori language (*Te Reo Maori*) was learned eventually by some; significant points of contact were gradually made between missionaries and Maori and, as with the Anglican missionary endeavour, such contacts and attendant relationships played a significant role in the emergence and signing of the *Treaty of Waitangi* (see New Zealand History, n.d.), the 1840 document that marked the commencement of New Zealand as a modern nation State governed by England—so making it part of the English colonial empire.

In January 1838 a French Catholic bishop, Jean Baptiste Pompallier (1807–1871), arrived in New Zealand together with two members of the Society of Mary (Marists), a newly formed French missionary order (Davidson, 1997, p. 16). The first Mass was celebrated on January 13 in a private home—just across the harbour from the Wesleyan Mission Station. Pompallier himself was able to preach in Maori only three months after his arrival. He also had to learn English. He urged his missionary priests to be sensitive to Maori customs, on the one hand, but also to attack 'Protestant errors' on the other. On the whole the approach of the Catholics was much more accommodating towards Maori life and customs than that of the other two Christian missions. But the Catholics had less to offer the Maori, by way of material benefits, than the Anglicans and Methodists with their emphasis on education, health, and agricultural technology. "Catholic missionaries opted for a life of poverty which had difficulty competing with the attractions of the Protestant missions"; however "without the demands of families and mission stations, [they] were often able to get closer to Maori than their Protestant counterparts" (Davidson, 1997, p. 16). More French Marists joined Pompallier who established his headquarters at the township of Russell in the Bay of Islands which, for a while, was the capital of the colony. There he set up a printing press to rival the Protestants.

As a result of these developments a twofold suspicion and animosity attached itself to the Catholic missionary endeavour, namely Protestant vs. Catholic rivalry (religious); and French vs. British rivalry (political). This played a part in the urgency with which the British concluded the 1840 Treaty with the Maori chiefs. New Zealand was henceforth ruled by Britain, but without an established Church. Although New Zealand was a predominantly Protestant society, Catholics nevertheless had a free hand to be about their own religious business, as did the many varieties of Protestant denomination and sects that attended the burgeoning arrival of settlers seeking a brave—and religiously free (i.e. allowing of diversity)—new world. Thus a distinctive development foreshadowing the emergence of a broader religious diversity emerged around the middle of the nineteenth century, namely a secular polity that gave freedom to, as well as from, religion under the law.

At this stage religious diversity was really a matter of Christian denominational variety. "The pluralistic nature of New Zealand settler society, with denominations having to exist alongside one another in a religious mix very different from England, was already beginning to determine the reaction of the people to religious issues" (Davidson, 1997, p. 30). No one Church had pride of place, constitutionally, over any other; although, by dint of being a British colony the Church of England, transplanted into the colony as a missionary endeavour, then servicing a settler community and undergirding a new society, emerged as the *de facto* national Church. The matter of establishing the Church in a colonial context involved transplanting not just religion as a set of beliefs and values, but also its institution(s), with accompanying customs, polity, and agendas.

By 1874 the Anglicans were institutionally organised as 'The Church of the Province of New Zealand'. For many years generations of New Zealanders would not know what 'religion' (Church) they belonged to, as they seldom darkened the door of any. But when pressed, as for example to record a religious identity at census time, even with an opt-out option many simply said 'C of E' (Church of England). They might not be active believers, but they knew whence they would be buried, and in the meantime where they were most likely to marry and have any children christened. One did not have to commit to being Anglican; it was part of the British culture which had stamped its imprint upon New Zealand. By contrast, one committed to virtually every other Church.

Whereas the CMS was an exclusively missionary organisation, and the colonial (settler) Anglican Church came later, the Methodist WMS saw itself as having a responsibility to minister to both Maori and Pakeha (European) from the outset. This, together with its strong emphasis on lay participation and local initiative, meant the transition to, even co-development of, a settler Church alongside Maori mission work was perhaps more easily achieved. However, other varieties of Methodism (for instance: Primitive Methodists, Bible Christians) which came out with the settler ships were concerned exclusively with ministry to the settler communities, and they remained legally tied to their English Churches of origin for a long time.

As for the Catholics, who initially made no formal distinction between missionary and settler work, incoming settler communities soon predominated in terms of demand. In particular the needs of the Irish Catholic settlers—including educational as well as spiritual and pastoral needs—came to the fore and required much energy and effort (King, 1997). Indeed, as Davidson (1997, p. 38) notes: "The distinctive French Marist influence on early New Zealand Catholicism was overtaken by the impact of the Irish settlers and the Irish priests and nuns who gave their own special character to Catholic identity in New Zealand".

Coming out of Scotland, Presbyterians began in New Zealand as a settler colonial Church. Presbyterian worship began formally in 1840 and the first Presbyterian Church was opened in 1844 in Wellington. A mission to Maori, despite an early failed attempt, was a secondary concern that was pursued nevertheless, but the primary focus was the Scottish settlers. And just as Methodism out of England was itself a diverse affair, so too was Scottish Presbyterianism—the 'Kirk' (Church of Scotland) was the established Church in Scotland, but in the 1840s ministers also came to New Zealand from the dissenting Reformed Presbyterian Church of Scotland, and both the clergy and a Lay Association of the Free Church of Scotland set their sights on Otago, in the lower South Island, establishing a settlement as a Free Church colony there in the 1840s. But the dream of an Antipodean Free Church theocracy was doomed from the outset: most of the settlers to the South were, in the end, English rather than Scots, with a good measure of Irish as well. The tide of secularism was also high in the new settler communities: they hadn't come half-way round the world to be dominated by pontificating parsons yet again. In the event, the discovery of gold in Otago-Southland in the 1860s put paid to the remnants of a dream for a religious utopia of the south. But an imprint and a heritage had been created: Otago-Southland for a long time had greater than 50% of the population identified as Presbyterian, and the Scots' emphasis on education bore fruit with the establishment of the first New Zealand University (now the University of Otago) in Dunedin in 1869.

Along with the arrival of members of the Church communities noted above, the 1840s and 1850s saw members of other smaller Christian Churches begin to arrive. Communities of Brethren, Baptists, Congregationalists, Quakers (Society of Friends), and the Salvation Army, together with their institutions, were late 19th century transplants. A distinctive New Zealand colonial religious (Christian) identity began to emerge. The idea that there should be an 'established Church' was widely resisted by virtually all. No one denomination was to be predominant. However, together with the reality of sectarian tension and religious bigotry, this resulted in a strong secular flavour in the political development of the country from colonial outpost to self-governed dominion.

3. A History of Religious Diversity (II): The World Comes to New Zealand

If Christianity was by far the predominant religion, it was not to remain in a wholly singular position for long (Donovan, 1996). By the late 19th century the Church of Jesus Christ of Latter-day Saints—which is another world religion, in reality an alternate Christianity, not another denomination as such—had been established and pursued a vigorous outreach into the Maori community as well as into the settler European communities. Census and other records also show a varying and relatively early presence of Hindu, Buddhist, Muslim, Jewish and Sikh adherents. For the most part, numbers were so low as to vitiate the prospect of establishing their own religious communities, except for Jews who were able to have synagogues in the late 19th century in the capital city, Wellington, and also Auckland (Beaglehole & Levine, 1995; Gluckman, 1990).

By the late 19th century the religious landscape of New Zealand was one of Christian denominational diversity coupled with a smattering of other religions, and the decided flavour of Secularists and Freethinkers with, for the most part, an imported religious leadership (Stenhouse & Thomson, 2004). The quest to recruit and train colonial clergy was only in its infancy even quite late in the 19th century. However colonial Church architecture, as well as the distinctive use of timber, of which there was an abundance, made its mark quite early on. The legacy of this remains, even despite the combination of more modern approaches to Church buildings that emerged during the 20th century and, in the last couple of decades, the emergence of Middle Eastern and Asian architectural tropes with the erection of mosques, gurdwaras, and temples of various sorts.

4. New Zealand, Religion, and Secular Society

A very significant and far-reaching 19th century development was the Education Act of 1877. This declared

New Zealand to be a secular society in that the state would provide primary education that was "free and secular and compulsory" (King, 2003, p. 233). In response, the Churches for the most part initially backed a 'Bible in Schools' movement which, from 1879, agitated for the reading and teaching of the Bible in schools as an inherent element of culture and heritage. Sectarian division was, however, the Achilles' heel to any uniformity although, from 1895, the pattern of a negotiated half-an-hour per week teaching period during which, technically, a school would be 'closed'—that is, it would not during that period be operating as a state school—thus allowing volunteers from local Churches, very often clergy in the early days, to provide some form of Bible instruction. A point of contention then, and ever since, is that, for the most part, rather than meeting a cultural educational lacuna, the 'Bible in Schools' educational programme is often an agent for evangelical outreach. Much depends, especially today where it may be allowed—individual Boards of Trustees now determine whether or not to have the programme—, on the nature of the individual volunteer conducting the class and the choice of curriculum followed. Some are better than others; some more educationally appropriate, others clearly not.

The long-lasting legacy of this late 19th century development has been to obviate religion as a bona fide subject of educational study within the secular state system. The Catholic, Anglican, and Presbyterian Churches all developed their own private school systems to a greater (Catholic) or lesser degree. Smaller Churches, such as the Methodists, might have had one or two. Nowadays Jews and Muslims also have their own, as do some sectarian Christian Churches such as the Exclusive Brethren. Some religious education has ever been available for those who wish it, but its exclusion today from State primary and secondary education, together with its very late and limited appearance in the tertiary sector—now under significant threat—has had significant consequences for the prospect and quality of public debate about religious matters. The predominant cultural view has ever been that there are two subjects one never discusses in public—religion and politics. The latter may be allowable on some occasions; the former never—except when secular media and its supporting pundits go on the warpath against some aspect or other of religion or religious people.

During the 20th century the denominational diversity of Christianity consolidated and became institutionally established. Where initially there had been dependency on 'sending' authority, mostly out of England, in some cases Australia, independence of governance and identity was gradually gained. In 1907 New Zealand emerged from 19th century colonial status to being an independent Dominion of the British Empire. And where England went, as it did in 1914 (WWI) and again in 1939 (WWII), New Zealand would follow. But in the aftermath of the Second World War three factors emerged as highly significant for the religious landscape of New Zealand. First, the country itself moved from the status of a Dominion to being an autonomous member of the British Commonwealth. The ties to mother England loosened somewhat. And, in consequence, Christian denominational identity, whilst heading toward a post-War peak in terms of numerical strength and cultural influence, began also to self-question as a combination of war experience and the impact of Christian ecumenism was felt. The ecumenical movement flourished in New Zealand during the third quarter of the twentieth century to the extent that five Churches—Anglican, Presbyterian, Methodist, Congregationalist and Churches of Christ—entered formal negotiations to unite. However, despite a substantial expression of support from all sides, the failure of the Anglicans to carry a decisive vote saw their withdrawal in 1976. An attempt to proceed in the early 80s without the Anglicans also foundered; the ecumenical tide was on the turn.

Indeed, ecumenical energies were soon eclipsed by other cultural and demographic changes that had begun to impact New Zealand society, including a renaissance of Maori culture and language, and growing immigration with its attendant cultural and religious pluralities. These factors threw into sharp relief questions of national and Church identity. By the 1990s the country was officially bi-cultural (Maori and 'Pakeha'—meaning primarily European, but inclusive of all who are not Maori). The *Treaty of Waitangi* had been restored to its pivotal place of influence, and the major Churches which not so long ago had sought to 'become one' embarked, each in their own way, upon distinctively different bi-cultural journeys. But if diversity was somewhat dominated in the public and religious sphere by cultural duality, in reality this was already eclipsed by the upsurge in diverse races, cultures and religions that were arriving daily—whether as immigrants, or as refugees. Indeed, the 1987 Immigration Act ushered in a significant broadening of immigrant and refugee populations.

5. Demographic Developments: From Christian Predominance to Religious Diversity

By the late 20th century evidence from census data (Statistics New Zealand, various reports) suggest a close link between ethnic diversity and religious diversity. And, in more recent years, while the number of Christians has decreased, the numbers of believers of other faiths have increased. Although still a small percentage of the total population, they nevertheless are part of the changing religious landscape where diversity and not a relative homogeneity is the watchword. The recent (2013) census of the New Zealand population certainly produced some surprises, including that, as compared to the 1906 census when 92.9% of the then population of slightly less than one million recorded as Christian, now only 45.1% of the population (4.2 million) so identified themselves.[1] Whilst in one hundred years the raw number of Christians has more than doubled, from c. 881,000 to c. 1,913,000; as a proportion of the total populace the Christian bloc has halved. But perhaps what is more significant in terms of comparison is that in 1956, out of a population of 2,174,062 there were about 1,906,650 Christians (87.7%). Thus over the whole of the past half century or so total numbers have barely increased (not by virtue of remaining static, rather by a process of increase then steady erosion) but the demographic proportion has declined dramatically. What changed? Basically, two things—and these are found elsewhere in many secular western societies—namely an increase in religiously diverse populations, and an increase in the numbers who eschew any particular religious identity. In New Zealand's case, 1906 saw some 4,768 persons (c. 0.5%) in total recorded as belonging to a religion other than Christianity, in 1956 it was 6,612 (c. 0.3%—a proportionate decline) but in 2013 this had become 245,223 (5.98%).

Clearly, at almost 6% other religions are not a major component of the population as such. Diversity is present but not obvious. Yet significant demographic shift and development has taken place over recent decades, and is set to continue. A process of demographic change is underway. And this has consequences for religious diversity. For example, whereas Zoroastrians went from only 4 persons in 1956 to 972 in 2013, Buddhists leapt from 111 to over 58,000 in the same period, and Sikhs likewise from 133 to 19,191. But the largest growth has been that of Hindu adherents who went from about 1600 in 1956, to around 17,500 in 1990 and just on 90,000 at the 2013 census. Muslim increase was from 200 (1956), to some 6000 (1990) and around 46,000 in 2013. Jews were around 3800 in 1956 and in 2013 are at 6867. But in 2013 two new categories were included: Spiritualism/New Age (18,285) and Maori religion (2,595). The category 'Maori religion' reflects developments within contemporary Maori culture either toward a secular position, especially in the case of many urbanised Maori (and most Maori today are of mixed race and culture), or toward an intentional attempt to recover elements of 'lost' Maori religion and so religious identity.

Overall, it is evident that religion in New Zealand is diversifying, but arguably such diversity was not the main factor contributing to the decline of the proportional share of Christianity. That is more directly attributed to the dramatic rise in the population of persons recorded as having no religion (1906 = 1,709; 1956 = 12,651; 2013 = 1,635,345). In half a century this category has moved from less than 1% of the population to over 38%. Add to that the two long-standing census categories concerning religion: 'Object to answering' and 'Not stated' (combined figures: 1906 = 2.8%; 1956 = 8.8%; 2013 = 12.3%) and the proportion of the population abjuring any religious identity is now sitting on 50%, and climbing. So, in broad terms, we might say roughly half the population is religious, and half not. But if the half that are religious in terms of the census were fully active and engaged in the life of faith, religious leaders would be rejoicing.

In point of fact census religious identity is not, and never has been, reflected in life-of-faith behaviours, and that has been a sociological reality for a long time. Nevertheless, the chief conclusion drawn from this cursory examination of demographic changes vis-à-vis religion is that New Zealand can be said to lead the world in terms of secularism—provided this term is understood in its popular usage as denoting non- or irreligion, and not in what I would regard as the more usual sociological sense of denoting social acceptance of religious diversity *per se* and a social policy of equal allowance and treatment of diverse religious identities (Dobbelcare, 2002). New Zealand is officially secular in this latter sense, but popular discourse often belies a tendency to equate 'secular society' as one where religion is absent from the public domain, if not from society absolutely. Although there is evidence to suggest census disavowal of religious identity cannot rule out a propensity to hold various supernatural beliefs, advocates of ideological secularism trumpet the decline of Christianity as a triumph for rational humanism, and sometimes not even that. However, it seems often they are puzzled, or blind to—or in some cases even fearful of—the rise of other religions. But that is another matter.

A useful comparison of religiosity, as measured by census returns that aggregate religious categories, alongside categories indicative on no religion, yields the following in respect of recent data (see Table 1).

Table 1. Census returns.

Country/Year	% religious	% no-religion
New Zealand 2013	51.1%	38.6%
Australia 2011	68.3%	22.3%
USA 2008	83.1%	16.1%
Canada 2011	76.5%	23.5%
UK 2011	67.7%	25.1%

Sources: Statistics New Zealand 2013 Census; Australia 2011 Census; US 2008 Pew Center Report; Pew Report of Canada's Religious Landscape, 2013; UK Office for National Statistics 2011 Census.

[1] The census data has been comparatively analysed by Dr. Todd Nachowitz (2007), whilst a PhD candidate in the Political Science and Public Policy programme of the School of Social Sciences at the University of Waikato. I am grateful to Dr. Nachowitz for allowing me free access and use of his material.

Along with a rise in those declaring no-religion, New Zealand has seen a steady numerical decline of those identifying as Christian since the post-WWII peak in the late 50s and early 60s.

6. Ethnic Diversity and Religious Affiliation

As indicated by an analysis of census data, a distinct correlation exists between ethnic diversity and religious affiliation. Europeans constituted 93.7% of the population in 1906. Half a century later the change was miniscule—Europeans were still 92.7%. But in 2013 a considerable change is registered with Europeans now at 74.2%. Still a majority, but a significant decline nonetheless. Maori figures at the same points are 5%, 6.3% and 14.9%, respectively.[2] All others combined hovered around 1% until well into the 20th century when changes due to immigration took hold. In 2013, peoples of Pacific Island origins made up 7.4% of the population, the category of 'Asian' came in at just under 12% and all others combined at just on 3%. Of the nearly half million Asians recorded, Chinese comprise approx. 35% and Indians approx. 33%. The 2013 Census shows a correlation between ethnicity and religious affiliation as follows:

- European—Christian: 47.4%; no religion 45.7%; other religions less than 0.50% ea
- Maori—Christian: 46.1%; no religion 44%; other religions less than 0.40% ea
- Pacific—Christian: 73.8%; no religion 16.6%; other religions less than 0.70% ea
- Asian—Buddhist 9.4%; Christian 28.6%; Hindu 18%; Muslim 6%; no religion 29.4%

This is but a snap-shot, not a full picture. But it is sufficient to indicate the nature of the changes to religious diversity that are currently taking place, and will continue to do so as the demographic profile modifies further due to immigration, which is a function not only of policy but also of specific links the country has to the Pacific Islands, and also to Asian countries, especially China—with whom New Zealand was the first Western nation to sign a free trade agreement. In consequence, it is clear there will be significant implications for religious diversity as a direct result of on-going changes to the ethnic composition of the society.

7. The National Religious Diversity Statement

A project of the New Zealand Diversity Action Programme of the New Zealand Human Rights' Commission (HRC), supported by Victoria University of Wellington and the Ministry of Social Development, the 'Religious Diversity in New Zealand' document which was launched in 2007 seeks to provide a basis for raising awareness and promoting ongoing discussion of contemporary religious plurality in the country. It also aims to articulate aspirational ideals for the guidance of the wider community in matters of religion. It sets out a number of principles which are grounded in international human rights treaties and the New Zealand Bill of Rights Act. These include freedom of religion, conscience, and belief; freedom of expression; the right to safety and security; the right to reasonable accommodation of diverse religious practices in various settings.

The Statement has been endorsed by a wide range of faith communities and leaders as well as many citizens, of various religious persuasions, who wish to see a better public climate for the acceptance and discussion of religion within society. Many individuals endorsed, supported, and even contributed to the development of the Statement. It is largely regarded as representing a positive step in promoting better awareness and acceptance of religious diversity beyond the simple ethic of tolerance that has long been characteristic of New Zealand's social mores. And today this ethic, in the glare of hostile light trained upon the global hotspots of religious extremism, is under threat. From a post-WWII period when there was a climate of tolerance and liberal acceptance that often undergirded interest in the 'other', whether cultural, religious, or both, there is now an increasing xenophobia and reaction to the suspicion of a hostile other—as seen, for instance, in the current global phenomenon of Islamophobia. These are major factors which the Statement seeks to address, among others.

Early in the 21st century many western secular governments, previously none too concerned with their religious constituency so long as the peace was not disturbed, began, in the aftermath of 9/11, to address both counter-terrorism and the promotion of religious harmony as a matter of new social policy. Although being intensely secular in the sense that, apart from the daily prayer which opens the proceedings of parliament when in session, government in New Zealand has nothing to do with religion. It is a private matter for citizens to pursue as they see fit. Nevertheless the New Zealand government in 2004 joined with a number of other governments in the Southeast Asia and South Pacific region to meet more or less annually

[2] There are few, if any, full-blood Maori. Racial intermingling has been very widespread. However, by law, a person who can claim even one Maori in their ancestral lineage may register as Maori. Further, Maori culture has a strong communal dimension: being Maori means having a place of belonging not only within an immediate family (*whanau*) but also a wider familial group (*hapu*), and through that, affiliation to a sub-tribe and/or major tribe (*iwi*). It is tribes who have settled disputes and grievances with the Crown, arising from 19th century land confiscations and other abuses, upon which compensation has been settled in the order of millions of dollars in land and cash. Being identified as Maori no longer attracts the opprobrium it once did.

for a formal regional interfaith dialogue (Bouma, Ling, & Pratt, 2010). The emerging globalised expressions of a religiously motivated terrorism were brought closer to home by the Bali bombing in 2005, and perhaps even more so by the London bombings that same year—many more New Zealanders are familiar with the London Underground than they are with Balinese beaches. Thus wider political initiative and interaction sparked the awareness that something was needed at a local (national) level.

Indeed, the idea for a national statement concerning religious diversity grew directly from the New Zealand delegation that attended the first regional interfaith dialogue in Yogyakarta, Indonesia (the Asia-Pacific Dialogue on Interfaith Cooperation) in 2004. In effect, the proposal to create such a statement constituted part of the New Zealand response to concerns that interfaith harmony, as a tool of counter-radicalization, ought to be something of a political priority within the countries of the region.

As it happened, with the facilitative support of the Human Rights Commission and led by Professor Paul Morris of the Religious Studies Department at Victoria University, Wellington, the Statement was developed between 2004 and 2007. Morris had attended the first regional interfaith forum as a member of the New Zealand delegation. A public consultative process was pursued, together with the involvement of an ad hoc multi-faith reference group convened in Wellington, to draw up an initial draft.[3] As a product of that process, the statement was first published in 2007 with a print-run of 10,000 funded by New Zealand National Commission for UNESCO. It was soon endorsed by a wide range of faith communities and leaders and a second, revised, edition was published in 2009 in English and nine other languages.[4]

Four chief reasons (*Statement on Religious Diversity in Aotearoa New Zealand*, 2009, p. 5) underlying the Statement are given, namely the perceived need for a wide-ranging public discussion about religious diversity as such; the reality of instances of religious discrimination drawing attention to the need for awareness of religious rights, especially regarding minority groups; a recognition that increased religious diversity was impacting on many aspects of social and cultural life and in some cases resulting in discord, even violence—most typically the occasional assault on an individual; most dramatically the firebombing of a mosque in 1998, although for most the reference to religious violence is elsewhere, overseas; and the need for a succinct resource to which people may turn for some initial information and guidance.

In a society such as New Zealand, where the very consciousness of the presence of religion can disrupt and disturb the secular presumption of the absence of religion from public life, the Statement provides a basis for discussion of and about religious diversity. It affirms that the State seeks to treat all faith communities and those who profess no religion equally before the law. Following a Foreword from the Prime Minister, the booklet carrying the Statement comprises an Introduction followed by the eight clauses of the Statement. A note on the origins of the Statement, a succinct yet detailed commentary on the each of the clauses, acknowledgements and endorsements recorded at the time of printing, are also included.

The Introduction (*Statement on Religious Diversity in Aotearoa New Zealand*, 2009, p. 2) states quite straightforwardly that "New Zealand is a country of many faiths, with a significant minority who profess no religion. Increasing religious diversity is a significant feature of public life". The foundation for affirming this diversity is implied in an assurance, given by Governor Hobson, at the time of the signing of the 1840 *Treaty of Waitangi* between the Crown and the Maori Chiefs: "the several faiths (beliefs) of England, of the Wesleyans, of Rome, and also Māori custom shall alike be protected". The role the Christian religion has played, and continues to do so, with respect to the development of the overarching national "identity, culture, beliefs, institutions and values," is acknowledged (*Statement on Religious Diversity in Aotearoa New Zealand*, 2009, p. 2). Nevertheless, demographic change as a result of recent immigration is recognised to now be a driver of religious diversity: "It is in this context that we recognise the right to religion and the responsibilities of religious communities."

Furthermore, the Introduction situates the affirmation of diversity within the context of Human Rights and the fact New Zealand is a signatory to a number of international treaties, including the *Universal Declaration of Human Rights* and the *International Covenant on Civil and Political Rights*, which uphold the right to freedom of religion and belief. This includes the right to *hold* a belief; the right to *change* one's religion or belief; the right to *express* one's religion or belief and the right *not to hold* a belief. These are reflected in the New Zealand Bill of Rights Act and Human Rights Act, enacted in 1990 and 1993 respectively. The point is made that the right to religion entails affording this right to others and not infringing their human rights in respect to religious identity.

The eight clauses of the statement on religious diversity are as follows:

1. The State and Religion: *The State seeks to treat all faith communities and those who profess no religion equally before the law. New Zealand has no official or established religion.*

[3] The Statement is obtainable as a downloadable pdf from the Commission website: www.hrc.co.nz

[4] These languages are: Arabic, Chinese, Gujarat, Hindi, Korean, Maori, Punjabi, Tongan and Samoan.

2. The Right to Religion: *New Zealand upholds the right to freedom of religion and belief and the right to freedom from discrimination on the grounds of religious or other belief.*
3. The Right to Safety: *Faith communities and their members have a right to safety and security.*
4. The Right of Freedom of Expression: *The right to freedom of expression and freedom of the media are vital for democracy but should be exercised with responsibility.*
5. Recognition and Accommodation: *Reasonable steps should be taken in educational and work environments and in the delivery of public services to recognise and accommodate diverse religious beliefs and practices.*
6. Education: *Schools should teach an understanding of different religious and spiritual traditions in a manner that reflects the diversity of their national and local community.*
7. Religious Differences: *Debate and disagreement about religious beliefs will occur but must be exercised within the rule of law and without resort to violence.*
8. Cooperation and Understanding: *Government and faith communities have a responsibility to build and maintain positive relationships with each other, and to promote mutual respect and understanding.*

The Statement includes a commentary expanding on each clause. Some of the key points are as follows:

1. The State and Religion. The history of religion and religious diversity in New Zealand, beginning with the variety of Christian denominations and the accommodation of non-religious perspectives in "perfect political equality" is noted (*Statement on Religious Diversity in Aotearoa New Zealand*, 2009, p. 7) and attention drawn to the context of there being neither a strict constitutional demarcation nor the presence of a state religion; the country is, in effect, religiously neutral *qua* State, though historically—and until recently—dominantly Christian so far as the population is concerned.
2. The Right to Religion. Human rights legislation and norms are alluded to with specific mention of "the right not to be discriminated against on the basis of religion of other non-religious ethical beliefs" (*Statement on Religious Diversity in Aotearoa New Zealand*, 2009, p. 7).
3. The Right to Safety. In a context where there are occasional outbursts of vandalism of religious property and abuse directed to persons of faith, the right to be safe, in terms of both persons and property, is upheld. And this includes "the broader sense of being secure in being different" (*Statement on Religious Diversity in Aotearoa New Zealand*, 2009, p. 7).
4. The Right to Freedom of Expression. The importance to a democratic state of freedom of expression and of the media is acknowledged along with the need for these to be exercised in a responsible manner, both with "the right to religious expression and the right to express views about religion" (*Statement on Religious Diversity in Aotearoa New Zealand*, 2009, p. 8).
5. Recognition and Accommodation. The motif of "reasonableness" applied here is directly referenced to existing legislation. It goes to the heart of a positive apprehension of religious diversity within wider society: customs and practices that express the identity and life of those who are ethnically and religiously different need to be allowed for, and this includes "different dress codes and schedules and calendars for prayer and holy days" (*Statement on Religious Diversity in Aotearoa New Zealand*, 2009, p. 8).
6. Education. The nature of the history of secular education in New Zealand is noted, and a strong emphasis is placed on the need for genuine education about religion and religions, especially in a context of increased diversity and tensions arising from that diversity largely based on ignorance and suspicion. It is also noted that some of the best such educational programmes are found in Roman Catholic and Anglican integrated schools. Ironically, it is the education of some religiously confessional schools that serves the interests of the study of religion in a way completely lacking within the State school system.
7. Religious Differences. The potential for difference to lead to dissension is recognised, with the caveat that tensions arising from a clash of deeply held different, especially conflicting, beliefs and perspectives need to be managed within the law.
8. Cooperation and Understanding. Responsibilities accompany rights: the desire to live in peaceful mutuality of respect requires to be worked at. This is a duty resting on social, cultural and political institutions and individuals alike.

There is, of course, little in the statement that is new *per se*, or otherwise not to be found in existing legislation. However, as the Statement itself notes, its intention is to be aspirational; to focus attention upon religious diversity as such and so provide a platform for addressing issues that may from time to time arise from the fact of this diversity. It is a bold attempt at a public statement about religion in a society whose dominant and unexamined public understanding of 'being secular' would seem to amount to 'ignoring religion'. Certainly this is the case with the secular press: it is not that it is 'secular' in the sense it is not owned by a religious body; its very secularity is a stance taken that is a priori dismissive of matters religious—unless, being contentious, they either bring religion into disrepute, or else confirm religion as belonging to the realm of the ridiculous. Thus attempts to gain media interest in and exposure of such a positive development as suggested by even the fact of the statement—let alone some good developments since, as noted below—have been singularly unsuccessful.

8. Reception of the Statement

The Statement was first presented at the National Interfaith Forum held in Hamilton, New Zealand, in February 2007. This gathering, comprising interested individuals—it is not in any sense formally representative of religious communities as such—endorsed the Statement and urged communities to engage with it as a means of promoting dialogue and understanding. Subsequent to that event, the formal launch by the Prime Minister, Helen Clark, occurred at the *Asia Pacific Regional Dialogue on Interfaith Cooperation*. This May 2007 event was a meeting of the Southeast Asia and Pacific annual Regional Interfaith Dialogue Forum that had begun in 2004 (Pratt, 2010b).

Although widely received and attracting formal endorsement from Church and other faith community leaders, there was early strident opposition from some Christian quarters—broadly speaking, those who might be identified as 'evangelical-conservative' or simply 'right-wing' Christians. In other words, the very inception of the Statement attracted resistance from some Christians, among them the ultra-conservative Destiny Church, which did not wish to admit the acceptance of religious diversity. It wanted instead to promote the notion that New Zealand is exclusively a Christian country. Brian Tamaki, the self-appointed 'Bishop' leading this Church, proclaimed opposition to any promotion of religious diversity in New Zealand. Although resiling from advocating the outright expulsion of other religions, he nonetheless asserted that "alternative or foreign religions" should "not be afforded equal status" with Christianity. Tamaki represented an extreme conservative view that identifies "opening the door to a diversity of religions" with "dismantling our own Christian heritage" (New Zealand Herald, 2007).

This was not unlike similar exclusivist resistance to religious diversity as experienced in Australia (Bouma, 2012, 2013). Closer Economic Relations (CER) protocols between Australia and New Zealand, and other bilateral arrangements, are not the only forms of cultural connections that link these two countries—otherwise separated by over 1200 miles of ocean, as well as very different colonial histories and governmental arrangements. In the case of religion, many contemporary conservative evangelical Christian Churches and organisations enjoy trans-Tasman links and exchanges of personnel with the result of that there can be found similarities of religious outlook and theology. But resistance to a statement affirming of religious diversity was not just found in certain right-wing Christian quarters. It was also objected to by secular humanists, mostly by way of letters to the editor in local newspapers, who did not wish to see any apparent privileging of religion as such. Clearly, in differing ways, such a statement hit a raw nerve.

With a measure of support from some other conservative Christians for whom also the notion that New Zealand is not, officially, a Christian country was both novel and objectionable, Destiny Church New Zealand staged a demonstration outside the May 2007 Waitangi meeting and launch to express opposition to the Statement's reference to the separation of Church and state, arguing that New Zealand should, in fact, be a Christian state. Some representatives of Destiny Church and the Exclusive Brethren had also appeared at the February Interfaith Forum to voice their opposition. They were given a polite hearing and, ironically for them, experienced a measure of that tolerance and acceptance which inheres to the secular context of religious diversity to which they were objecting.

In existence now for a few years, the Statement may not be as well or as widely known as it should be, but it is readily available via internet sources and well referenced in respect to ongoing interfaith activities and resources (see Human Rights Commission, 2012). There is arguably a work of promotion and education that is yet to take place, although an interesting recent development is the inception of a new organisation, The Religious Diversity Centre in Aotearoa New Zealand, to be officially launched in early 2016. The Trust backing this new development has as its first aim that of providing "high quality research and educational resources on religious diversity" and references in its Trust Deed the Statement on Religious Diversity.

9. Engaging Religious Diversity

Along with the Statement, its reception, on-going influence, and use as a document of reference, there have been a number of other relevant initiatives and activities worth noting as they exemplify the affirmation of religious diversity within a context of social inclusion.

The Human Rights Commission (HRC) carries out many statutory functions as well as exercising initiative in promoting the greater good. Among the latter is its work in facilitating a national interfaith network, producing a monthly electronic interfaith newsletter, and its facilitating of the development of the Statement on Religious Diversity in the first place. In 2007, the Commissioner, Joris de Bres, observed that although an arm of secular government,

> "The primary functions of the Commission under the Human Rights Act are to promote respect for human rights, and to encourage the maintenance and development of harmonious relationships between the diverse groups that make up New Zealand society. No other public agency has such a clear statutory mandate to promote the right to religion (including the right not to hold a religious belief), and to promote understanding between faith communities....This does not in any way compromise the secular nature of the Commission or the separation of church and state: the state has as much of a responsibility to engage with citizens who share a community of belief as they do with those who share a community of culture, ethnicity or geography." (de Bres, 2007, p. 9)

Together with promoting the Statement, the HRC publishes a monthly e-newsletter (*Te Korowai Whakapono*) which has to do with all sorts of religious diversity matters. The HRC is behind the New Zealand Diversity Action Programme of which an Interfaith Network is one of a number facilitated by the Commission. Each August the HRC organises a religious diversity forum within its larger annual New Zealand Diversity Forum. It also publishes, within the annual Race Relations Report, a review of religious diversity developments. The HRC has produced a range of relevant sundry publications and is active in dealing with discrimination complaints involving religion and belief. In general terms, the Commission promotes freedom of religion and belief and the harmonious relations between people of different beliefs in a context of growing religious diversity of New Zealanders, in large measure as a result of increased immigration from Asia and elsewhere. Furthermore, global tensions and the rise of Islamophobia since the terror attacks of 9/11, as well as subsequent terrorist events, have made of religion and religious diversity an important human rights issue in New Zealand. Significant attention has been paid to the Muslim community (Pratt, 2010a, 2011).

The Office of Ethnic Affairs of the New Zealand government is also active in the field of religious diversity and the promotion of interreligious and intercultural relations. It provides a focal point for the United Nations' *Alliance of Civilizations* programme. Given the close linking of ethnic and religious diversity that tends to take place, the Office works across a wide range of ethnic communities and religious organisations that overlap including, in particular, the Muslim community and *inter alia* the Federation of Islamic Associations of New Zealand. It has pursued with this community a 'Building Bridges' project and hosted events such as in 2013 'The Muslim World Forum'.

Other positive responses to the fact of religious diversity include, since 2003, the holding of a regular, almost annual, National Interfaith Forum. As noted above, it was at one of these (2007) that the Statement was endorsed prior to being officially launched. In the foreseeable future, a likely pattern will be a bi-annual national gathering with, in the alternate years, one or more regional interfaith events. Since the 1990s there has been a gradual development of Regional Interfaith Councils or Forums. Although there is no overarching national Interfaith Council as such, the loose networking between the regional groups seems to be proving effective and workable. Indeed, there is resistance to having energies channelled into the establishment and maintenance of any interfaith bureaucracy. In this context, the ongoing facilitative support of the HRC, and to a lesser extent the Office of Ethnic Affairs, is important. However, it does tend to reinforce a public perception that religious diversity is more a sub-set of ethnic diversity and Human Rights concerns as opposed being but one societal response as a direct affirmation of religious diversity as such.

There are also a number of active bilateral councils, some of which have been quite long-standing. These include, for the most part, Councils for Christians and Jews (CCJ) and Councils for Christians and Muslims (CCM). At times, such as in the major city of Auckland, these councils organise joint events and consultations. And various faith communities, including many of the Churches—notably Anglican, Roman Catholic, Presbyterian, and Methodist—also have their own interfaith committees and/or allied structures with an interfaith component. The ebb and flow of organisational energy and priority notwithstanding, interfaith engagement seems to becoming a more integrated aspect of many religious communities, as opposed to being a comparative fringe activity for enthusiasts. But even this assessment may be somewhat optimistic.

A number of legal measures have been put in place that recognize and support religious diversity. These include an amendment to the Holidays Act in 2010 to allow the transfer of public holidays, such as Christmas and Easter, to days of other personal religious or cultural significance and, in 2011, a review of immigration policy to better provide for the immigration of religious workers. A number of significant resources have also been forthcoming in recent times, including the New Zealand Police manual, *A Practical Reference to Religious Diversity* (2005/2009), among others, for example Pio (2014).

10. Conclusion

New Zealand is an ethnically, culturally and religiously diverse nation, and the depth and nature of that diversity is set to increase. Overall, the European population is declining as a relative proportion compared to the increasing populations of Maori, Pacific Islanders, Asian and just about all other minor categories as well. The number and proportion of people at census time being recorded as having no religion looks set to increase. Significantly, since 2001 the total increase of those registering no religious affiliation has risen by almost 60%. It now comprises the largest single category after Christianity. And, as at 2013, the sum of all non-Christian religions combined is only about one third more than those who mark 'Object to answering' the question. It is clear the decline in the total Christian population is more a result of rising non-religious identity than it is a reflection of demographic changes wrought by immigration, although it is nevertheless true that among recent immigrants, especially from China, it is likely a good proportion profess no religious identity. In this context of changing demographics and increased religious diversification, the New Zealand Statement on Religious Diversity is both a beacon and a challenge. Only time will tell if the sentiments and hopes expressed therein result in lasting positive outcomes. But unless there is renewed effort to make good on the aspirational hopes and actions embedded in the Statement, such as in respect to Schools teaching "an understanding of different religious and spiritual traditions" for example—an aspiration that remains as red rag to a bull for many who confuse being secular with being non-religious—what time is likely to tell is the fading of a dream of true social inclusion in the face of religious apathy and rejection. Certainly it would seem since the demise of the Clark (Labour) government, the recent years of the Key (National) government displays much less interest in, let alone support of, interfaith matters and engagements within wider society, reflecting the default position of treating religion as an entirely private affair, not something that should concern the organs of state.

Acknowledgments

I am grateful for the helpful comments of the reviewers of early drafts of this article, and to Jocelyn Armstrong, Chairperson of the Religious Diversity Centre of Aotearoa New Zealand Trust, for her helpful final review.

Conflict of Interests

The author declares no conflict of interests.

References

Beaglehole, A., & Levine, H. (1995). *Far from the Promised Land: Being Jewish in New Zealand.* Wellington, New Zealand: Pacific Press/GP Publications.

Best, E. (1974). *The Maori as he was.* Wellington, New Zealand: A.R. Shearer, Government Printer.

Bouma, G. D. (2012). Religious diversity and social policy: An Australian dilemma. *Australian Journal of Social Issues, 48,* 281-295.

Bouma, G. D. (2013). Diversity of religions and freedom of religion and belief. In J. Arthur & T. Lovat (Eds.), *The Routledge international handbook of education, religions and values* (pp. 55-61). Abingdon and New York: Routledge.

Bouma, G. D., Ling, R., & Pratt, D. (2010). *Religious diversity in Southeast Asia and the Pacific: National case studies.* Dordrecht: Springer.

Colless, B., & Donovan, P. (Eds.). (1985). *Religion in New Zealand society* (2nd ed.). Palmerston North, New Zealand: Dunmore Press.

Davidson, A. K. (1997). *Christianity in Aotearoa: A history of church and society in New Zealand.* Wellington: New Zealand Education for Ministry Board.

Davidson, A. K., & Lineham, P. (1989). *Transplanted Christianity: Documents illustrating aspects of New Zealand Church history.* Palmerston North, New Zealand: Dunmore Press.

de Bres, J. (2007). Human rights and religious diversity. *Aotearoa Ethnic Network Journal, 2*(2), 9-11.

Dobbelacre, K. (2002). *Secularization: An analysis at three levels.* Brussels: Peter Lang.

Donovan, P. (Ed.). (1996). *Religions of New Zealanders.* Palmerston North, New Zealand: Dunmore Press.

Gluckman, A. (Ed.). (1990). *Identity and involvement: Auckland Jewry, past and present.* Palmerston North, New Zealand: Dunmore Press.

Griffiths, D. H. (2011). Defining the secular in the New Zealand Bill of Rights era: Some cases and controversies. *Otago Law Review, 12*(3), 497-524.

Human Rights Commission. (2012). *Te Korowai Whakapono: Religious diversity in Aotearoa 2004–2011.* Wellington, New Zaland: Human Rights Commission Religious Diversity Network

Irwin, J. (1984). *An Introduction to Maori religion.* Adelaide, Australia: Australian Association for the Study of Religions.

King, M. (2003). *The Penguin history of New Zealand.* Auckland, New Zealand: Penguin.

King, M. (1997). *God's farthest outpost: A history of Catholics in New Zealand.* Auckland, New Zealand: Penguin Books.

McGeorge, C., & Snook, I. (1981). *Church, State and New Zealand education.* Wellington, New Zealand: Price Milburn

Mol, H. (1982). *The fixed and the fickle: Religion and identity in New Zealand.* Ontario, Canada: Wilfrid Laurier University Press.

Nachowitz, T. (2007). New Zealand as a multireligious society: Recent census figures and some relevant implications. *Aotearoa Ethnic Network Journal, 2*(2), 17-25.

New Zealand Herald. (2007, May 29). Lookout sparks unholy row, p. A3.

New Zealand History. (n.d.). Treaty of Waitangi. Read the treaty. Retrieved from http://www.nzhistory.net.nz/politics/treaty/read-the-treaty/english-text

Orange, C. (1987). *The Treaty of Waitangi.* Wellington, New Zealand: Allen & Unwin/Port Nicholson Press.

Pio, E. (2014). *Work and worship: Religious diversity at workplaces in New Zealand.* Auckland, New Zealand: AUT Faculty of Business and Law.

Pratt, D. (2010a). Antipodean angst: Encountering Islam in New Zealand. *Islam and Christian-Muslim Relations, 21*(4), 397-407.

Pratt, D. (2010b). Secular government and interfaith dialogue: A regional Asia-Pacific initiative. *Studies in Interreligious Dialogue, 20*(1), 42-57.

Pratt, D. (2011). Antipodean Ummah: Islam and Muslims in Australia and New Zealand. *Religion Compass, 5*(12), 743-752.

Pratt, D. (2015). Religion fixed and fickle: The contemporary challenge of religious diversity. In D. J. Davies & A. J. Powell (Eds.), *Sacred selves, sacred settings: Reflecting Hans Mol.* Aldershot, UK: Ashgate.

Statement on Religious Diversity in Aotearoa New Zealand. (2009). Wellington: Human Rights Commission.

Stenhouse J., & Thomson, J. (Eds.). (2004). *Building God's own country: Historical essays on religions in New Zealand.* Dunedin, New Zealand: University of Otago Press.

Turley, B., & Martin, M. R. (1981). *Religion in education.* Wellington, New Zealand: Churches Education Commission.

About the Author

Dr. Douglas Pratt

Douglas Pratt is Professor of Religious Studies at the University of Waikato, New Zealand, Adjunct Professor of Theology and Interreligious Studies at the University of Bern, Switzerland, and the New Zealand Associate of the UNESCO Chair in Intercultural and Interreligious Relations—Asia Pacific. His research interests include interreligious dialogue, Christian-Muslim relations, religious diversity and extremism. Recent publications include *The Character of Christian-Muslim Encounter* (2015) and *Religious Citizenships and Islamophobia* (2016).

Academic Integration of Mainland Chinese Students in Germany

Hanwei Li [1,2]

[1] Faculty of Education, University of Tampere, 33100 Tampere, Finland; E-Mail: hanwei.li@staff.uta.fi
[2] Bielefeld Graduate School in History and Sociology, University of Bielefeld, 33615 Bielefeld, Germany

Abstract

This article presents an analysis of the academic integration experiences of mainland Chinese tertiary-level students in Germany. Using Tinto's model, the article explores the challenges that Chinese students face during their academic integration, the strategies they employ, and the relationship between academic and social integration. The data were collected in spring 2016 by interviewing 26 mainland Chinese students studying either in German universities or universities of applied sciences. Four major challenges were identified and analyzed: language barrier, knowledge gap, pedagogical differences, and cultural differences. An important outcome of the study presented is that social integration serves as a facilitator for enhancing academic integration, but is not a prerequisite for academic success. Group learning with peers was found to enhance learning outcomes. Overall, Chinese students have exploited their own advantages in academic integration by exploring feasible strategies and benefiting from their past learning experiences. It is suggested that academic integration as a long and challenging process for international students should be acknowledged by the German HEIs, and that more institutional support and guidance are needed.

Keywords

academic integration; Chinese student; Germany; higher education; social integration

Issue

This article is part of the issue "International Migration and Ethnic Integration", edited by Yaojun Li (University of Manchester, UK) and Anthony Heath (University of Oxford, UK).

---

1. Introduction

While the migration studies literature generally focuses on the integration of labor migrants, family migrants, and asylum seekers, there is less research focusing on the integration of international students. This is partly because international student mobility is often seen as 'temporary', and international students constitute a 'less problematic' group of foreign arrivals. However, the number of students pursuing studies abroad continues to surge as higher education institutions around the world compete for the most talented students, and university enrolment continues to increase worldwide. International students have become the key target of many countries' battlefields of global competition for brightest and best. Canada, for example, has recently changed its electronic immigration selection system to make it easier for international students to become citizens. It counts half of students' time spent studying in Canada toward the period of residence required for citizenship (Smith, 2017). Meanwhile, many European countries, such as Germany, France, the Netherlands, and Finland, have also pursued a policy of allowing international university graduates an extension to their residence permits for job seeking after graduation. International students are no longer classed as 'temporary migrants', rather it is hoped that their stay in the host country will increase motivation for long-term settlement, and that their temporary movement could be part of a deliberate strategy for permanent migration (Tremblay, 2005). Thus, integration of international students has become topical and deserves more scholarly attention.

Nevertheless, international students still only constitute a minority of the total tertiary student population. Chinese students are the most numerous of the international tertiary-level students (UNESCO Institute for Statistics, 2016). In 2013, over 4.1 million Chinese were studying abroad, representing 1.8 percent of all tertiary enrolments globally (UNESCO Institute for Statistics, 2016). Between the introduction of Deng Xiaoping's opening policy in the 1970s and 2015, around four million Chinese students went abroad to study, and this figure increases by approximately 19 percent annually. In 2016, about 520,000 Chinese students moved to study abroad (Ministry of Education of P. R. of China, 2016).

Chinese student migration mostly aims at the English-speaking countries (Chen & Ross, 2015; Gu & Schweisfurth, 2006; Kajanus, 2016), while Germany is the most popular destination among the non-English-speaking countries. According to the Institute of International Education, about 30,511 Chinese students were studying in Germany in 2015, making them the second largest group of international students in Germany (after Turkish students). The share of Chinese students of the international student population in Germany is around ten percent (Wissenschaft Weltoffen, 2016). Although most degree programs are still offered in German language (Bessey, 2012), Germany has become an increasingly popular choice for higher education among Chinese students.

Germany is a popular destination among Chinese students for several reasons. First, it is one of the few countries to offer all nationalities high quality higher education free of charge or for modest tuition fees, which is a major attractive factor for international students. Both English- and German-taught programs are provided for international students. Unlike many non-English-speaking countries that are recruiting international students for English-taught programs, most international students study on German-taught programs alongside native German students. German language is taught in universities across the globe and language institutes such as the Goethe Institut. Germany also arranges established standardized German language tests (DSH and TestDaF) in many countries in the world, where students can obtain a language certificate in support of their applications for studies in Germany. For those students who cannot reach the requirement to begin their academic studies in Germany, it is possible to start the studies in the *Studienkollegs* (*Studienkolleg für ausländische Studierende*) at German colleges and universities. These studies function as a 'bridge' to help international students enhance their German language skills, and become acquainted with German academic culture. Further, Germany has an organization specialized in promoting academic mobility between Germany and other countries. The German Academic Exchange Service DAAD (*Deutscher Akademischer Austauschdienst*) offers information on studying in Germany, on selecting a university, on admission criteria, and on preparing to embark on studies in Germany. It also offers various types of scholarships to students across the globe for exchange, studying German language, or studying on degree programs. The DAAD has offices in many countries of the world, including China, that actively offer information on how to apply to study in Germany, and on academic collaboration and mobility. For example, in China the DAAD has its own social network accounts on WeChat and Weibo that routinely distribute information on the application process for studying in Germany, presents introductions to specific German universities and cities, and reproduces testimonials from current students.

In addition, Germany is one of the first countries in the EU to actively seek to improve international students' access to the labor market. In the context of the recent political debate, international students were identified as future skilled workers. The aim was to make access to the labor market easier for them, especially in the information technology sector. International graduates holding a degree from a German university are in a favorable position for getting job offers. Moreover, due to their linguistic skills and intercultural communication skills, international students can serve as 'connectors' between their countries of origin and destination. The latter factor is particularly relevant for the export-oriented German economy (Aksakal & Schmidt-Verkerk, 2014).

Given this policy context, there has been growing concern over the extent to which German higher education institutions (HEIs) manage to provide appropriate and responsive academic and personal support for the integration of international students. While numerous surveys have examined the macro-level trends in student mobility and the quality of German HEIs, less attention has been paid to the experiences of individual international students.

The purpose of this paper is to investigate how Chinese students integrate into German academic environments, what challenges they encounter while studying in Germany, and what coping strategies they adopt for such challenges. The following research questions guided the study presented here: (1) what challenges do mainland Chinese students encounter while studying and living in Germany? (2) What strategies do Chinese students use to overcome challenges in their academic integration? and (3) Is there a connection between academic and social integration among Chinese students studying in Germany?

2. Integration of International Students: The Research Context

In earlier research on the academic and social integration and study progress of international students in a foreign academic setting, the terms 'integration', 'adaptation', and 'acculturation' have been used interchangeably in different settings, carrying largely similar connotations. This article chooses to use the term 'integration' because integration can be seen both as a goal and a process. When it comes to social relations, the goal of the German integration policy is that foreign newcomers will establish a relatively robust relationship with the host community, while not abandoning their home ethnic community and ethnic identity (Süssmuth, 2009). As a goal integration refers a situation in which newcomers have attained at least a moderate level of language and cultural competence within the country of settlement that ensures their ability to thrive. It also implies that migrants actively try to become a part of the surrounding society (Budyta-Budzyńska, 2011). It can be said that a successful adaptation presupposes that newcomers integrate into their new living environments, which in turn is usually a result of a successful acculturation process.

2.1. Academic and Social Integration

Tinto (1975, 1997) developed a model of student attrition that laid a theoretical foundation for studying tertiary student retention. In his model, Tinto established the approximate parity between social and academic integration in their effects on dropout. The central concept proposed in Tinto's model is that a student's integration into the social and academic systems of the higher education institution is what ultimately results in perseverance or dropout. The higher the degree of integration of the students into the college system, the less likely they are to fail to fulfill a commitment and achieve goals leading to the completion of their degree programs. A person's academic integration can be measured in terms of the grade performance and intellectual development achieved during studies. While international students enter university with various backgrounds and motivations, their integration into the higher education system will ultimately determine their perseverance or dropout. Tinto describes two imperative conditions for successful retention: (1) institutional experiences (involving the education system); and (2) academic and social integration. Those who feel at home, participate actively in extra-curricular activities, and feel connected with fellow students and teachers are more likely to persevere in their studies.

The predictive validity of Tinto's model was tested in various settings. One study suggested that students' academic integration, together with educational objectives, predicts their persistence in the HEIs (Bers & Smith, 1991). In addition to formal studies, informal interaction with faculty members plays a vital role in the students' academic integration (Terenzini & Pascarella, 1977). However, Tinto's model does not specify the process by which institutional experiences affect student learning. While student characteristics prior to entry may affect their academic integration, the institutional experience results in a certain study effort and ultimately in student persistence. A study by Severiens and Schmidt (2009) examining institutional experiences of student learning, found a direct positive effect of the learning environment on international students' progress in their studies. A problem-based learning environment, more than conventional programs, helped students to develop their cognitive skills and stimulated them to acquire new knowledge. Problem-based learning also appeared to be successful in stimulating students to obtain credits, and achieve a higher level of social and academic integration.

One of the key themes among the studies using Tinto's model is the relationship between academic and social integration. The findings of Mannan (2007) show that academic and social integration complement each other among undergraduates. However, Rienties, Beausaert, Grohnert, Niemantsverdriet and Kommers (2012), who examined the validity of educators' impressions, found that international students are insufficiently adjusted to higher education in their host countries, both academically and socially, and that the extent of their academic success is multifaceted. International students with a (mixed) western background were better academically and socially integrated, and achieved a higher study performance than did domestic students. By contrast, international students with a non-western background were less socially integrated, but still achieved a similar study performance. The social adjustment of students was negatively related to their study performance. These findings suggest that the relationship between academic and social integration processes is complex in nature and merits further investigation.

Research on the social integration of international students has particularly emphasized the positive effect of establishing social networks with host nationals (Bochner, McLeod, & Lin, 1977a; Coles & Swami, 2012). Research has also shown that international students report less homesickness, less loneliness, and greater satisfaction if they have more host-national friends (Church, 1982; Hendrickson, Rosen, & Aune, 2011). Contacts with host nationals have also been shown to enable international students to develop local networks, attain a better understanding of local cultures, and acquire the necessary social skills (Li & Gasser, 2005). Yet in practice it may be difficult to make contacts with host-nationals. It is relatively easy for international students to form friendship networks with co-national students (Bochner, McLeod, & Lin, 1977b; Furnham & Alibhai, 1985; Hendrickson et al., 2011). While contact with co-nationals can play a vital role in the international students' social networks, engagement with co-nationals may inhibit them from forming friendship networks with representatives of the host society (Church, 1982), and from acquiring or improving skills in the host language (Maundeni, 2001), which impedes intercultural learning processes (Kim, 2000). Accordingly, Kim (2000) argues that co-national contacts only offer short-term support, while contacts and friendships with host-nationals are more important for social integration.

2.2. Chinese Learners in Western Higher Education

Studies focusing on the academic integration of Chinese students in western HEIs have produced mixed and sometimes contradictory results. Kennedy (2002) found that Chinese culture has an influence on Chinese students' learning styles: Chinese students are low in individualism and high in collectivism, and exhibit a strong sense of belonging to a social group and a preference to work together to solve problems (Kennedy, 2002; Nield, 2009;

Sayers & Franklin, 2008) Some studies have found that students from a Confucian cultural background have more difficulties in adjusting to the western teaching style than do their western peers. They may adopt a less active learning strategy, and be hesitant about voicing their own opinions in the classroom, while western students are more used to participating actively in class (Auyeung & Sands, 1996; Duanmu, Li, & Chen, 2009; Strohschneider & Guss, 1999; Vita, 2001; Yuen & Lee, 1994). In addition, Cortazzi and Jin (1997) have shown that Chinese and British students are likely to have different expectations regarding students' and teachers' roles. The Chinese students expect a teacher to be a 'knowledge model' who gives students clear guidance for them to follow, while British teachers act more as facilitators of students' learning by encouraging the learners' own creativity and independence.

However, there are other studies which contradict these findings, suggesting that, contrary to the Chinese student stereotype, Chinese learners have a stronger preference for high-level, meaning–based learning strategies and prefer to avoid rote learning. Kennedy (2002) found that Chinese students can adopt new learning styles when the learning context changes and new learning approaches are needed. Thus, more active and communicative modes of learning may be preferred to a traditional teacher-centered style. According to Durkin (2008), Chinese students approach their learning tasks by adopting a strategic attitude to learning. She found that most East Asian master's students opted for a middle way which synergizes their own cultural approach to critical thinking with western-style critical thinking and debate that are culturally acceptable to them. In this way international students, without being fully acculturated, become 'empathetic insiders', who understand and value the new practices, perceiving them as opportunities for growth and development. Zhang (2013) also found that some Chinese students would choose a middle way to improve their linguistic competence for better academic integration. Instead of approaching native speakers, some Chinese students tried to make friends with other non-Chinese students to practice their English and thus gain more confidence in intercultural communication.

2.3. Chinese Students in Germany

Given the relatively large number of Chinese students in German HEIs, little research has so far been conducted on this group. The existing literature suggests that Chinese students studying in Germany share some problems with those in other countries, such as language issues, financial stress, loneliness, and difficulties in academic integration. Zhu (2012, 2016) explored Chinese students' academic adjustment in four phases: pre-departure, initial, developing, and final phase. She found that Chinese students' insufficient preparation (language proficiency and knowledge about German universities) in the pre-departure phase led to difficulties in the initial phase. The students often described their initial experiences as a 'catastrophe', as they were not at all familiar with the academic system in Germany. In the developing phase, Chinese students reported progress in German language and knowledge about German universities, which facilitated their further development. One major challenge in the developing phase was to negotiate the difference in academic expectations between home and host universities. In the final phase, Chinese students showed understanding and appreciation of the expectations at German universities. German language proficiency, academic support, and personal effort together influenced the Chinese students' academic adjustment at German universities.

Moreover, Chinese students studying in Germany with German as the language of instruction reported greater challenges in their academic and social integration (Zhou, 2009). The study by Mao (2011) showed that only half of the international students had studied German before arriving in Germany, while the rest began learning German only on arriving in the country. Consequently, less than one third of Chinese students taking part in the study could report that their proficiency in German was 'good' or 'very good', even though their studies in a German university had already begun (Mao, 2011).

By examining a group of German and a group of Chinese students, Luo and Kück (2011) examined the similarities and differences between these students' learning behaviors and styles. They found that the learning styles of the two groups were amazingly close, as both groups were oriented towards improving their competence and being creative through self-motivation. In addition, they used similar learning methods, such as self-learning and asking questions, and viewed the lecturers as professional and moral examples in academic settings. This demonstrates that cultural differences do not necessarily affect the learning approaches of German and Chinese students.

Guan (2007) compared Chinese and German students' adjustment at the University of Bremen and the University of Göttingen. His research at the University of Bremen the former research suggested that the concept of self played an important role in the adjustment of Chinese students; while at the University of Göttingen he found that when facing difficulties Chinese students used different resources from their German counterparts to deal with the problem. Most Chinese students preferred to turn to books and media instead of talking with native Germans.

In sum, much of the literature on the academic and social integration of international students adopts a cultural perspective focusing on the tensions caused by attempts to cope with cultural differences in a new environment. The research presented in this article was contextualized in different literatures concerning the nature of international students' intercultural communication and intercultural experience. Yet the emphasis was not placed on cultural difference as such, but encompassed various challenges facing the students arising from cultural, pedagogical, linguistic, and institutional perspectives that are also due to the stress of integrating into the larger societal context in addition to the academic context.

Meanwhile, while much attention has been paid to 'cultural difference', less has been paid to the processes of learning, which may be identical across different cultural and academic settings. As the foregoing literature review shows, learning styles may be similar among students from different cultural backgrounds. Strategies for the academic integration of international students may prove to be just as useful when implemented in a brand new academic setting.

For the purposes of the research presented here, the list of relevant questions concerned how students cope with pedagogical and cultural differences, participate in classroom and group learning, interact with teachers and classmates inside and outside class, and how they succeed in their assessments. Social integration refers to a process or state where students establish relatively robust relationships with host-national individuals or communities and take part in diverse social activities. Since the focus of this article is on the academic integration of Chinese students, the examination of their social integration is limited to whether their social integration facilitates their academic integration.

3. Data and Methods

Data collected through semi-structured interviews were used to explore the challenges and coping strategies of academic integration among Chinese students in Germany. The author interviewed 26 mainland Chinese tertiary-level degree students in two German universities during spring and summer 2016. Most of the interview questions (except those eliciting demographic information) were open-ended questions enabling students to talk freely and in depth within the range of the research questions, while also allowing flexibility to delve into topics which were not expected at the beginning of the study. All interviews were conducted by the author in Mandarin Chinese to lower the potential barrier of cultural and linguistic difference, while allowing the students to delve deeper into the subject of interest. Most of the interviews were conducted at two German universities. Both universities are large research and teaching HEIs offering instruction in the main academic disciplines.

Multiple methods were used to recruit interviewees. First, the author asked the international offices of the two participating universities to send invitations to all mainland Chinese students registered in these universities to participate in the research. The students who volunteered to participate in the research were contacted by email, instant message, or telephone. Second, snowball sampling was used. The research participants were encouraged to invite their friends and other mainland Chinese students who might be interested in joining the research. Third, a research assistant helped to distribute the invitation to interviews through the local Chinese students' association network. Among the interviewees, 16 were female and 12 male students. All participants were in their twenties with an average age of 24 years for female and 26 for male students. The interviewees came from various academic backgrounds: five were studying natural sciences, four social sciences, three mechanical engineering, three medicine, three computer science, three sports management, two arts and humanities, two German linguistics, one English literature.

Most of the interviewees came from urban middle and upper middle class family backgrounds in China. The group of interviewees included students who had just come to study in Germany for one semester, and those who had come to Germany for more than five years. As the time interval and integration phases of the interviewees were diverse, the author was able to explore which features of academic integration manifest in different phases. Students who had moved to Germany recently had fresh experience of 'culture shock', while the senior students gave lively accounts of how they had managed to overcome academic integration problems in different stages and on their development trajectories. The interviews lasted from one to three hours. The shared language and cultural background facilitated communication between the interviewer and the interviewees. All interviews were recorded and transcribed. The interview data were analyzed using interpretative content analysis; particularly interesting insights were written down during the interview, but most of the analyses were carried out on the basis of the interview transcripts.

In the following section, the challenges and coping strategies of Chinese students' academic integration into Germany will be discussed in detail. In presenting the findings, no such personal data is revealed that would make the interviewees recognizable. The anonymity of respondents is protected, and no real name is disclosed in the article. In the quotations, gender and major subject will serve to characterize the respondents. Citations from the interviews conducted in mandarin Chinese were translated into English by the author.

4. Findings

4.1. Challenges in Academic Integration

Most of the Chinese students in Germany were studying abroad for the first time in their lives. The challenges they encountered during their academic integration can be categorized into the following themes: language barrier, knowledge gap, cultural difference, and pedagogical difference.

4.1.1. Language Barrier

All Chinese students interviewed stressed the importance of German linguistic proficiency in their studies. Indeed, many interviewees had come to study in Germany specifically because they wanted to be fluent in German.

Some mentioned that they wanted to be fluent in German because they were influenced by German culture and its specifics, such as football or automobiles. Some interviewees estimated that, in addition to achieving academic success in their major subjects, fluency in German was a great added value for their future careers, as the quotation below shows:

> It is very common for my generation to go to study in the UK, the cost is higher but you can graduate with your M.A. in one year (after completing the bachelor's degree). However, I chose to study in Germany because there are relatively fewer people speaking German compared to English. When I graduate, I would not only have a diploma from a country with a good reputation for higher education, but also speak two foreign languages. (Female, Medicine)

The language barrier has been mentioned repeatedly in many earlier studies as a major challenge to the integration of international students. However, the extent and severity of the language problems among Chinese students are greater in Germany than in English-speaking countries for three reasons as follows: First, German is the second or third foreign language for most of the Chinese students. While there are international high schools that teach German as a foreign language in China, most of the students study German for one to two years in China or in Germany, and then take the German language test DSH or TestDaf in order to be enrolled in a German HEI. However, even if they succeed in obtaining the language certificate, their linguistic capacity is often far from sufficient to accomplish their academic tasks. The following quotations show that studying in German is not easy for Chinese students:

> I think the most difficult challenge in studying here is the language. You don't know what the teacher is talking about, don't know what your classmates are talking about, and when you read the book you want to tear the book apart....You know that when we were in China, we studied English for many years from primary school to university and when we go abroad it is still difficult to use English. Not to even mention mastering German in the short term. Even if we had passed the language test, and had studied the language for two years, when we entered the classroom, we still found ourselves far behind. I think it is necessary for the German universities to reform the DSH test because most foreign students who passed the test are still not fluent enough in German. (Male, Media Studies)

> Although I had passed the DSH exam, I still had difficulty adapting to using German language in daily life as well as in academic settings. I found that the German language that people used in daily life was totally different from what we studied in class back in China. The use of vocabulary is different, and people from different regions have different accents. They also tend to speak faster than the listening material we learned from in our classes. It took me about one to two semesters to get used to using German in my daily life. (Male, Sports Management)

Second, the German language taught in China was not the same as the German that the students used in their academic and daily lives. Even for the students of German linguistics it took some time to get used to this:

> After coming here (Germany), I found that the things we learned in China were just on paper. I only realized after living in Germany that the (German) language is not spoken in that way (that we learned in China). The cassettes that we listened to in class were very slow, while in reality they speak much faster. When I listened to the German teacher explaining in German, it still took some time before I could truly adapt....I think it took around two months. (Female, German Linguistics)

For some other students not involved in studying German linguistics, it might take up to two years to get used to studying in Germany.

Third, the students who passed the German language tests were adequate in communicating in daily life in German, but their academic vocabulary for their major subjects was still limited. However, in the German-taught classes, German and international students studied together as the teachers did not take them and their special demands into account. This caused problems for some interviewees:

> The teachers will teach according to the tempo of German students, without taking into consideration the difficulty of foreigners to follow the class in their second or third foreign language. The pace of the class is often really fast, and there is some vocabulary or even teachers' writing on the blackboard that are incomprehensible for us. (Male, Electrical Engineering)

However, those students who had participated in the *Studienkollege* before they began their bachelor's studies in Germany, generally had better linguistic proficiency than those who had only taken language classes before entering German universities.

By contrast, Chinese students on English-taught international master's programs seemed to encounter fewer problems. Although they still needed to expand their vocabulary and improve their proficiency in spoken English, the language alone was less of an issue for them compared to those who studied in German.

4.1.2. Knowledge Gap

Notably, Chinese students studying their major subjects in either German or in English reported difficulties in understanding the contents of teaching:

> At the beginning of my studies I could understand at most 30 to 40 percent of the teaching. For some classes that were difficult, my understanding was even less than 30 to 40 percent, because even if I had taken the class in Chinese I wouldn't have been able to understand everything. I feel I was not as good as my fellow classmates. (Male, Electrical Engineering)

The difficulty of understanding the content of teaching was often due to gaps in the Chinese students' knowledge background due to differences in curriculum content and structure between German and Chinese universities. Even for the students coming to study in Germany under bilateral agreements the courses they had taken in China were not entirely compatible with the German courses:

> What we learn here is very difficult, combined with the abstruse language, it is really torture to understand what the book is trying to say. The classes in which we have background knowledge from classes we took in China were a bit better. But if we hadn't learned something before, we needed to start from the beginning, and this the most difficult part....Once we were required to understand the mechanism of a machine. In China, we had never studied the mechanism behind this machine before. There were at least two to three classes of knowledge gap between our current knowledge reserve and the knowledge required to accomplish this task. We had to work for ten days from 9 a.m. to 11 p.m. in the library with help from others to solve that. It almost drove us crazy. (Male, Machine Mechanics)

The curricula and the focus of studies in China may be so completely different from those in Germany that some students had to study those courses over again. Failing a course was a frustrating experience for many:

> Media studies in China generally focuses on practical issues, like how to do an interview and how to produce TV programs. But the courses we took here were more focused on the theoretical side. We have courses in sociology, history, philosophy, literature, etc. It makes me frustrated....It was often that after one semester, I still had no clue what some courses were about. I have never failed classes before, but failing classes here became so common that I became numb...many things I know in Chinese. But I don't know how to express myself in German. Thus, although I have abundant knowledge in my head, I couldn't tell it to others. (Male, Media Studies)

> In the first semester, I could understand most of the basic courses. But for some classes that required content-specific background knowledge, such as one class that called *Althochdeutsch* (Old High German OHG), I basically could not understand everything. (Female, German Linguistics)

Surprisingly, failing a lot of classes was a common theme mentioned by several interviewees. Many of them mentioned that they had never failed a class in China, but after they came to Germany, the combined challenge of studying a rigorous module in a foreign language caused them to fail classes more often than before. According to the rules in Germany, if a student fails class three times, he or she will no longer be allowed to study that major in any German university. This increased the stress the Chinese students were enduring.

4.1.3. Cultural Difference

Some of the interviewees mentioned that their difficulties in academic integration were caused by differences in cultural practices. This was especially evident among students of humanities and social sciences. In most cases, the students were not able to specify what they meant by 'culture'. This is understandable as cultural phenomena are often immanent, and hidden culture featuring tacit cultural knowledge (such as values and norm systems) is difficult to recognize. The situation was different with visible cultural characteristics. Cultural differences were obvious in cultural studies, for instance in learning experiences which required the students to read literature or review films. One of the interviewees said:

> Sometimes in the class, the teacher mentioned a certain author, film director or element of a genre of film and my classmates immediately responded. However, I might not have any clue of what they were referring to, or at least I would not know how to express it in German. Also, the same element, such as a portrait of a dragon in a film, is also quite different in a German film and in a Chinese film. Such cultural differences often cause difficulty for me to follow in class. I found the same difficulty understanding a Chinese film when it was shown in my class. (Female, Film Studies)

In some cases cultural differences were reflected in different ways of thinking and approaching knowledge. One of the senior students compared the German tradition of analytical thinking and debate culture with Chinese traditions as follows:

> I think integration is a very bloody word, that after you become integrated, the uncomfortable feeling will always accompany you that on the surface you look like a German, but in fact it is a burden you have to carry with you. Take the critical thinking and debate culture in Germany for example, they like to think this is a constructive way of solving problems.....Germans like to tear the whole thing apart, and analyze where a problem is, then they will find the solution, and tell you point by point they are right. This kind of analytical thinking and debate culture is totally different from the humane way of dealing with conflict as low key as possible in China. It conflicts with the humane

> touch of Chinese society where unnecessary conflicts are usually avoided. (Male, Higher Education)

4.1.4. Pedagogical Differences

While the classes in China often took the form of teacher-centered lecturing, the learning methods used in German classrooms may be more diverse, including group assignments, classroom discussion, and so on.

Having been provided with answers for many years and having being taught to respect the views of authority, some Chinese students found questioning and challenging peers and lecturers engendered acute discomfort (Wu, 2015). Most of the Chinese students interviewed reported that they would not join in the classroom discussion. The language barrier was the main issue preventing them from active engagement in class. The following students, who had already studied in German HEIs for four years, reported still having problems in taking part in classroom discussions:

> Until now I can basically know what the teacher was talking about in class, because the teacher must be talking around the main topic. But I have no way to predict what the classmates were about to say. My response reflex is still much slower than the native speakers, and it is not possible for the other students to repeat the content again. That is why I couldn't join in the classroom discussion so well, because I could understand what the teachers were talking about because their expressions are predictable, but following what the classmates were saying is still difficult. (Male, Sociology)

Many other reasons also contributed to a perceived lack of participation of Chinese students in class: First, accustomed to the Chinese teaching and learning environment, some Chinese students felt they were expected to give the 'right answer' to the teachers' questions. They would be reluctant to articulate what came into their minds in class. Second, their silence in class might also be linked to individual personality traits, such as shyness and modesty. They were not accustomed to the western debate culture in class, and would prefer to say nothing. Lastly, a number of students felt a need to know more about the teaching content to provide their own feedback in class, as seen in the following remark:

> In the beginning, I would not participate in the classroom discussion because I was really afraid that I would make a mistake if I spoke up in class, and that would make me feel ashamed. So I was basically answering the teacher's questions by heart by myself. Even if sometimes I found the answers from my classmates were wrong, I would still not correct them. (Female, Computer Engineering)

Moreover, examinations in German HEIs take different forms from those in China. While in China most exams are written exams, the German exams may also be oral. This form of examination could be quite intimidating for Chinese students, since they had never encountered an oral exam before.

Besides different forms of exams, the final mark usually entails several pieces of essay writing. The students interviewed were still struggling to use German language or, lacking experience in essay writing, might fail to deliver what their teachers were looking for in their work. In addition, the students studying humanities and social sciences were often required to write several essays throughout the whole semester, which could be a daunting and demanding task for the Chinese students. As one of the students said:

> There were four modules in our major for each semester. For each of the modules one essay of around 30 pages was required. Together we needed to write about 120 pages for one semester. It took me about one semester to adapt to such intensity of reading and writing. (Female, English Linguistics)

Some of the exams might also be group projects in which the students needed to collaborate to develop a business project or industrial model by themselves. Some of the students interviewed stated that this was the most difficult form of assessment since their knowledge deficit was still too big to fulfill the demand of completing the project by themselves. Coupled with the pressure from working with classmates from other cultural backgrounds this created acute stress for them to cope with. However, it was also a perfect opportunity for them to learn from their peers while doing a group project on their own.

5. Chinese Students' Academic Integration Strategies

5.1. Social Integration and Academic Integration

The research findings imply that social integration could facilitate Chinese students' academic integration, but those students who were not socially integrated still managed to achieve their academic goals. This result is similar to the findings of the study by Rienties et al. (2012), but additional explanations and nuances can be presented in light of the present study.

Based on the interview data, it can be said that social integration facilitates academic integration mainly through enhancing the students' proficiency in German language and their understanding of German culture. The interviewees explained their experiences as follows:

> I intentionally chose to live in a WG (shared dormitory) with five German flat mates. They are very patient in helping me improve my German, and always speak more slowly when talking to me. One of my flat mates said to me, "Why you still say it the wrong way? You have to listen carefully how we say it." I followed

> her advice and now my German is much better than before. (Female, English Linguistics)

> Spoken German cannot be learned only through taking classes. You have to get into contact with people. Because different people have different habits of speaking, and use different expressions. Some speak fast, slow, clear, or unclear. You have to get used to different speaking habits of different people. (Female, Computer Science)

While some students were frustrated by their initial failure and communication problems, and would prefer to socialize with only Chinese students, those who managed to step out from the co-national network had benefited from their efforts, which had facilitated their academic integration and enriched their personal lives:

> I think one of the major losses of many Chinese after coming here is that they seemed to have lost the capacity to communicate with other people like they did in China. That they were all hiding at home, do not get in touch with the society or the people. I think a social network is not something that you only establish when you need it. Like some of the assignments I need to do for my class, I got help from a friend of a friend. An established network will also help you gain more trust when you are looking for a job. (Female, Mass Media Studies)

However, the students studying very demanding subjects expressed their frustration with the heavy burden of study assignments so that they could not afford to spend as much time on social activities as local or exchange students. For them, social integration might impede academic integration since their study tasks were so burdensome that the students needed to concentrate and devote all their time to their studies. To facilitate better academic integration, the students managed to achieve their study goals by utilizing their social networks with other Chinese students, especially senior ones, and relying on the professionals that they could find in the internet:

> We often have group tutor sessions with senior Chinese students. They do not necessarily understand everything, but it is nevertheless helpful for us. (Female, Chemistry)

The findings show that, no matter whether with host-national, international or co-national students, teaching and learning from others greatly facilitates learning. As one of the Chinese students described his experience:

> I often discuss with my classmates. Some knowledge I can read for a day without understanding anything. But discussing with others for one hour can be more efficient than studying by myself for many days. Some knowledge you don't understand but others might have comprehended very well. Just a few examples and you will get the clue....Most of us are helping each other. Nobody can say that I understand everything in this class that I don't need to discuss with others. (Male, Electronics)

Further, the Chinese students rely on online networks with other Chinese to facilitate their better academic integration in Germany. There are various online discussion forums, social media, or websites such as Zhihu[1] (similar to Quora) that are dedicated to helping netizens solve difficult issues. As in the example mentioned above, one of the students had a pressing task so that it was only with the help of professionals that the students found online through a Chinese website that they managed to complete the assignment.

It can therefore be stated in summary that social integration is helpful for Chinese students' better academic integration, since it enhances their linguistic proficiency in German and enlightens them about German culture, enriches their personal lives, and helps them open doors to new opportunities. However, even without a host-national network, most Chinese students still managed to achieve their academic goals since they relied on their Chinese peers and senior students, as well as on professionals that they found online. Teaching and learning from others or in a team have proven to be an effective means to achieve better academic integration, no matter if the others are co-national, host-national, or international students.

5.2. Critical Thinking and Debate Culture

The Chinese students generally had to go through a phase of gaining a clearer understanding of the learning content, and then to the next stage of critical thinking. The most academically successful students generally developed their capability for critical thinking through their studies. Their better understanding of learning content generally built upon their improved German/English language skills. To compensate for the difficulties in following teaching in class, they would generally invest extra hours at home to digest the material before and after class. After their understanding of the learning material improved through intensive reading, the students would gradually develop critical thinking skills so that they began to form their own judgments about the learning material and express these in their academic work and in class:

> Most of the education in China stopped at the phase of understanding. However, they didn't teach the students to ask 'so what?' after they have acquired the knowledge. I think the main difference in German higher education is that they will give a broad perspective of the field by asking you to read different articles

[1] Zhihu is an online platform to ask questions and connect with people who contribute unique insights and quality answers.

and book chapters in one semester. After you have established a systematic knowledge of the field, you will need to critically form your own opinion. This is what is lacking in Chinese higher education. And the process of critical and innovative thinking is also the beginning of academic research. I think it will take a long process to adjust to acquire the critical thinking capability. It is an enlightening process, and this process is lacking in Chinese higher education system. (Female, German Linguistics)

However, there were also students who took a negative view of the critical thinking strategy as a learning approach in German universities. One of the interviewees said:

I think the critical thinking I witness in the classes here is quite superficial. Sometimes the students give their opinions and judgments on a certain topic based on their own experience or sometimes based on partial examples from reality. In the classes in China, the teacher told us in the first class: 'I don't expect you to give any opinion on the text for now. You need to fully understand the content first. So I will guide you to read the original text word by word so that you can have a better understanding of the author.' (Female, Sociology)

5.3. Benefit from Past Learning Experience

While the challenges posed by studying in a German HEI were great, some Chinese students could benefit from their previous study experiences in China that smoothed the transition. Their previous education in China had trained them to be resilient and tenacious, so that the challenges they faced in Germany were overcome by a 'can-do spirit'. One interviewee thought that Chinese students have been well trained to cope with learning tasks abroad after years and years of training in a highly competitive education system:

I think my western peers can be easily frustrated since they are more self-centered and used to getting what they want. And when they cannot get what they want, they feel pain. They are the best and brightest students so that they always feel they can control their lives. But for us, we are used to not being able to have full control over our lives. No matter where you are born, after being through a college entrance exam, we have all experienced an abundant amount of failure training. Most of the Chinese students I know, as long as they have the perseverance to proceed, can finish their studies. I have never seen anyone develop psychological issues because of study pressure. (Female, Law)

Unlike many studies that assume rote learning is only a surface learning method adopted strategically by students to pass exams, one of the interviewees said that through memorizing, he managed to achieve a better understanding than before:

There is an old Chinese saying that, read for a thousand times, the meaning will reveal itself. For some of the formulas I don't understand I will try to memorize them. After reciting, reiterating, and comparing with other examples, slowly you will know what it is about. (Male, physics)

Those students with adequate language skills felt that completing the study tasks was no longer a cause of concern. Adopting a strategic approach towards learning, one female student described her experience:

I think an exam is something that the Chinese worry about the least, because we grew up with exams. Although you don't understand one hundred percent of what the teachers were saying in class, there is still hope. They will give us all the PowerPoints to study by ourselves. Even if you still don't understand, you can ask the teacher. (Female, Medicine)

6. Conclusion

In conclusion, the difficulty of using a foreign language in academic contexts combined with knowledge gap, pedagogical differences, and cultural differences posed challenges for the Chinese students to achieve academic success. Many students expressed frustration at their lack of linguistic proficiency and adequate general knowledge causing them to fail many classes like never before. However, these challenges also served as a stimulus to come up with new strategies that were more appropriate for their own learning habits and personal dispositions.

Social integration has been proven to facilitate Chinese students' better academic integration by enhancing their linguistic proficiency and improving their cultural awareness. Nevertheless, this is not an absolute prerequisite for better academic integration since the Chinese students without strong social ties with German students also managed to achieve their academic goals by turning to other Chinese for help. The key strategy for studying difficult subjects appeared to be learning in a team with others, regardless of nationality, so that through mutual teaching and learning, the students' study efficiency was greatly enhanced.

The western way of critical thinking and debate was another key barrier that also revealed the underlying cultural difference between east and west. Some interviewees thought that criticism is a missing phenomenon in Chinese education, and that Chinese students only begin to achieve critical awareness after coming to study abroad. However, others doubt the efficiency of putting it into practice prematurely in class when the students have not yet reached advanced comprehension of the learning material. Meanwhile, analytical and critical thinking are claimed to be incompatible with Chinese culture, which emphasizes being humane and avoiding unnecessary conflict.

Contrary to the conventional stereotype of Chinese students who only rely on 'learning by rote' and passively listening to teachers in class, this research shows that the students were actually resourceful and innovative in pursing their academic goals through active participation and learning through various sources and platforms. Rote learning was utilized as a pathway to better deep learning. Some interviewees argued that the Chinese students are well-equipped to meet academic challenges in a foreign context since they are used to high pressure exams, and have acquired resilience and tenacity to meet the challenges of academic integration since they have lived through one of the most competitive education systems in the world.

Recognizing the challenges of Chinese students' academic integration and the strategies used to cope with these challenges helps the HEIs to adapt to the demands of foreign students. Most German HEIs provide orientation lectures and activities to facilitate the integration of international students. However, according to the findings of this study, such orientation activities did not sufficiently address the challenges international students face in adapting to German academic environments. It is recommended that the German HEIs organize specific initiatives to address the academic integration of international students, such as mentoring projects that help the students to adapt to their new learning environments more easily. Offering extensive language courses would also be helpful for students using a foreign language in an academic setting. Lastly, academic institutions could organize more social activities with faculty members and students to promote social networking between international students, faculty members, and other fellow students, thereby enhancing international students' class communication, and facilitating their integration into the academic and social environments of the host country.

Acknowledgments

The study was conducted at Bielefeld University, Germany. It was a part of the Marie Curie project TRANSMIC, funded by the European Union's 7th Framework Programs, coordinated by Maastricht University, which the author gratefully acknowledges. The author would like to thank Pirkko Pitkänen, Virve Kallioniemi-Chambers, and Luuk van der Baaren for providing constructive and useful comments on an earlier version this paper.

Conflict of Interests

The author declares no conflict of interests.

References

Aksakal, M., & Schmidt-Verkerk, K. (2014). Characteristics of temporary transnational migration: The German case. In *Characteristics of temporary transnational migration, collected working papers from the EURA-NET project*.

Auyeung, P., & Sands, J. (1996). A cross cultural study of the learning style of accounting students. *Accounting & Finance*, *36*(2), 261–274.

Bers, T. H., & Smith, K. E. (1991). Persistence of community college students: The influence of student intent and academic and social integration. *Research in Higher Education*, *32*(5), 539–556.

Bessey, D. (2012). International student migration to Germany. *Empirical Economics*, *42*(1), 345–361.

Bochner, S., McLeod, B. M., & Lin, A. (1977a). Friendship patterns of overseas students: A functional model. *International Journal of Psychology*, *12*(4), 277–294.

Bochner, S., McLeod, B. M., & Lin, A. (1977b). Friendship patterns of overseas students: A functional model. *International Journal of Psychology*, *12*(4), 277–294.

Budyta-Budzyńska, M. (2011). *Adaptation, integration, assimilation: An attempt at a theoretical approach*. Warsaw Collegium Civitas. Retrieved from http://migracje.civitas.edu.pl/migracje/images/pdf_eng/chapter%203.pdf

Chen, Y., & Ross, H. (2015). "Creating a home away from home": Chinese undergraduate student enclaves in US higher education. *Journal of Current Chinese Affairs*, *44*(3), 155–181.

Church, A. T. (1982). Sojourner adjustment. *Psychological Bulletin*, *91*(3), 540.

Coles, R., & Swami, V. (2012). The sociocultural adjustment trajectory of international university students and the role of university structures: A qualitative investigation. *Journal of Research in International Education*, *11*(1), 87–100.

Cortazzi, M., & Jin, L. (1997). Communication for learning across culture. In D. McNamara & R. Harris (Eds.), *Overseas students in higher education: Issues in teaching and learning* (pp. 76–90). London: Routledge.

Duanmu, J., Li, G., & Chen, W. (2009). Determinants of international students' academic performance: A comparison between chinese and other international students. *Journal of Studies in International Education*, *14*(4), 389–405.

Durkin, K. (2008). The middle way: East Asian master's students' perceptions of critical argumentation in UK universities. *Journal of Studies in International Education*, *12*(1), 38–55.

Furnham, A., & Alibhai, N. (1985). The friendship networks of foreign students: A replication and extension of the functional model. *International Journal of Psychology*, *20*(3–4), 709–722.

Gu, Q., & Schweisfurth, M. (2006). Who adapts? beyond cultural models of 'the' Chinese learner. *Language, Culture and Curriculum*, *19*(1), 74–89.

Guan, H. (2007). *Anpassung und Integration der chinesischen Studierenden in Deutschland-eine Untersuchung anhand des Beispiels an der Universität Bremen* (Doctoral Dissertation).

Hendrickson, B., Rosen, D., & Aune, R. K. (2011). An analysis of friendship networks, social connectedness, homesickness, and satisfaction levels of international students. *International Journal of Intercultural Relations, 35*(3), 281–295.

Kajanus, A. (2016). *Chinese student migration, gender and family*. Springer.

Kennedy, P. (2002). Learning cultures and learning styles: Myth-understandings about adult (Hong Kong) Chinese learners. *International Journal of Lifelong Education, 21*(5), 430–445.

Kim, Y. Y. (2000). *Becoming intercultural: An integrative theory of communication and cross-cultural adaptation*. London: Sage Publications.

Li, A., & Gasser, M. B. (2005). Predicting Asian international students' sociocultural adjustment: A test of two mediation models. *International Journal of Intercultural Relations, 29*(5), 561–576.

Luo, X., & Kück, S. (2011). Gibt es Lernstile, die kulturspezifisch sind? Eine interkulturelle Annährung an das Lernstilkonzept anhand einer vergleichenden Untersuchung am Beispiel deutscher und chinesischer Studenten. *Interculture Journal: Online-Zeitschrift Für Interkulturelle Studien, 10*(15), 37–62.

Mannan, M. A. (2007). Student attrition and academic and social integration: Application of Tinto's model at the university of Papua New Guinea. *Higher Education, 53*(2), 147–165.

Mao, X. (2011). *Die soziale und wirtschaftliche Llage der chinesischen Studierenden in Berlin 2010*. GRIN Verlag.

Maundeni, T. (2001). The role of social networks in the adjustment of African students to British society: Students' perceptions. *Race, Ethnicity and Education, 4*(3), 253–276.

Ministry of Education of P. R. of China. (2016). Trend of Chinese students studying abroad in 2015. Retrieved from http://www.moe.gov.cn/jyb_xwfb/gzdt_gzdt/s5987/201603/t20160316_233837.html

Nield, K. (2009). The problems of applying labels of learning style to national cultures. *International Journal of Learning, 16*(7), 425–434.

Rienties, B., Beausaert, S., Grohnert, T., Niemantsverdriet, S., & Kommers, P. (2012). Understanding academic performance of international students: The role of ethnicity, academic and social integration. *Higher Education, 63*(6), 685–700.

Sayers, J., & Franklin, T. (2008). Culture shock! Cultural issues in a tertiary course using reflective techniques. *Reflective Practice, 9*(1), 79–88.

Severiens, S. E., & Schmidt, H. G. (2009). Academic and social integration and study progress in problem based learning. *Higher Education, 58*(1), 59–69.

Smith, C. S. (2017). Canada beckons international students with a path to citizenship. *The New York Times*.

Strohschneider, S., & Guss, D. (1999). The fate of the moros: A cross-cultural exploration of strategies in complex and dynamic decision making. *International Journal of Psychology, 34*(4), 235–252.

Süssmuth, R. (2009). The future of migration and integration policy in Germany. *Migration Policy Institute*, 1–23.

Terenzini, P. T., & Pascarella, E. T. (1977). Voluntary freshman attrition and patterns of social and academic integration in a university: A test of a conceptual model. *Research in Higher Education, 6*(1), 25–43.

Tinto, V. (1975). Dropout from higher education: A theoretical synthesis of recent research. *Review of Educational Research, 45*(1), 89–125.

Tinto, V. (1997). Classrooms as communities: Exploring the educational character of student persistence. *Journal of Higher Education*, 599–623.

Tremblay, K. (2005). Academic mobility and immigration. *Journal of Studies in International Education, 9*(3), 196–228.

UNESCO Institute for Statistics. (2016). Global flow of tertiary-level students. Retrieved from http://uis.unesco.org/en/uis-student-flow

Vita, G. D. (2001). Learning styles, culture and inclusive instruction in the multicultural classroom: A business and management perspective. *Innovation in Education and Teaching International, 38*(2), 165–174.

Wissenschaft Weltoffen. (2016). *Wissenschaft weltoffen kompakt: Facts and figures on the international nature of studies and research in Germany*. Deutsche Akademische Austauschdienst (DAAD) und Deutsche Zentrum für Hochschul- und Wissenschaftsforschung (DZHW GmbH). Retrieved from http://www.wissenschaftweltoffen.de/publikation/wiwe_2016_verlinkt.pdf

Wu, Q. (2015). Re-examining the "Chinese learner": A case study of mainland chinese students' learning experiences at british universities. *Higher Education, 70*(4), 753–766.

Yuen, C., & Lee, S. N. (1994). Applicability of the learning style inventory in an Asian context and its predictive value. *Educational and Psychological Measurement, 54*(2), 541–549.

Zhang, H. (2013). *Academic adaptation and cross-cultural learning experiences of chinese students at American universities: A narrative inquiry* (Doctoral Dissertation).

Zhou, J. (2009). *Zwischen "elite von Morgen" und liu-xue-laji ("Müllstudenten"): Chinesische studenten in Deutschland* (Doctoral Dissertation). Retrieved from https://portal.dnb.de/opac.htm?method=simpleSearch&cqlMode=true&query=idn%3D1000848345

Zhu, J. (2012). *Academic adjustment of Chinese students at German universities* (Doctoral Dissertation).

Zhu, J. (2016). Approaching the end: Appreciating the German learning environment. In *Chinese overseas students and intercultural learning environments* (pp. 175–186) Springer.

About the Author

Hanwei Li is a Marie Curie PhD researcher working on a European Commission funded project entitled Transnational Migration, Citizenship and the Circulation of Rights and Responsibilities (TRANSMIC). She is currently pursuing a joint degree of PhD in Education at the University of Tampere and PhD in Sociology at the University of Bielefeld. Her research interests include: Asia-Europe student mobility, academic integration, socio-cultural integration, internationalization of higher education transnationalism, investment migration, and citizenship.

Permissions

All chapters in this book were first published in Social Inclusion, by Cogitatio Press; hereby published with permission under the Creative Commons Attribution License or equivalent. Every chapter published in this book has been scrutinized by our experts. Their significance has been extensively debated. The topics covered herein carry significant findings which will fuel the growth of the discipline. They may even be implemented as practical applications or may be referred to as a beginning point for another development.

The contributors of this book come from diverse backgrounds, making this book a truly international effort. This book will bring forth new frontiers with its revolutionizing research information and detailed analysis of the nascent developments around the world.

We would like to thank all the contributing authors for lending their expertise to make the book truly unique. They have played a crucial role in the development of this book. Without their invaluable contributions this book wouldn't have been possible. They have made vital efforts to compile up to date information on the varied aspects of this subject to make this book a valuable addition to the collection of many professionals and students.

This book was conceptualized with the vision of imparting up-to-date information and advanced data in this field. To ensure the same, a matchless editorial board was set up. Every individual on the board went through rigorous rounds of assessment to prove their worth. After which they invested a large part of their time researching and compiling the most relevant data for our readers.

The editorial board has been involved in producing this book since its inception. They have spent rigorous hours researching and exploring the diverse topics which have resulted in the successful publishing of this book. They have passed on their knowledge of decades through this book. To expedite this challenging task, the publisher supported the team at every step. A small team of assistant editors was also appointed to further simplify the editing procedure and attain best results for the readers.

Apart from the editorial board, the designing team has also invested a significant amount of their time in understanding the subject and creating the most relevant covers. They scrutinized every image to scout for the most suitable representation of the subject and create an appropriate cover for the book.

The publishing team has been an ardent support to the editorial, designing and production team. Their endless efforts to recruit the best for this project, has resulted in the accomplishment of this book. They are a veteran in the field of academics and their pool of knowledge is as vast as their experience in printing. Their expertise and guidance has proved useful at every step. Their uncompromising quality standards have made this book an exceptional effort. Their encouragement from time to time has been an inspiration for everyone.

The publisher and the editorial board hope that this book will prove to be a valuable piece of knowledge for researchers, students, practitioners and scholars across the globe.

List of Contributors

Ines Stolpe
Mongolian Studies, Bonn University, 53113 Bonn, Germany

Astrid Mattes
Department of Political Science, University of Vienna, 1010 Vienna, Austria

Edgar Zavala-Pelayo and Manuel Góngora-Mera
Lateinamerika-Institut, Freie Universität Berlin, 14197 Berlin, Germany

Amyn B. Sajoo
Simon Fraser University, Faculty of Arts & Social Sciences, Vancouver, BC V6B 5K3, Canada

Marit Ursin
Norwegian Centre for Child Research, Norwegian University of Science and Technology, 7491 Trondheim, Norway

Maggie Walter
School of Social Sciences, University of Tasmania, Hobart, TAS 7001, Australia

Laurence Lessard-Phillips
Institute for Research into Superdiversity, School of Social Policy, University of Birmingham, Birmingham, B15 2TT, UK

Yaojun Li
Department of Sociology, University of Manchester, Manchester, M13 9PL, UK
Cathie Marsh Institute for Social Research, University of Manchester, Manchester, M13 9PL, UK

Anna Clarke
Cambridge Centre for Housing & Planning Research, Department of Land Economy, University of Cambridge, Cambridge

Neli Demireva
Department of Sociology, University of Essex, Colchester, CO4 3SQ, UK

Anthony Heath
Nuffield College, University of Oxford, Oxford, OX1 3UQ, UK

Michael Nollert and Amir Sheikhzadegan
Department of Social Sciences, University of Fribourg, 1700 Fribourg, Switzerland

Michelle Pidgeon
Faculty of Education, Simon Fraser University, Surrey, BC V3T 0A3, Canada

Yaojun Li
Department of Sociology, University of Manchester, Manchester, M13 9PL, UK
Cathie Marsh Institute for Social Research, University of Manchester, Manchester, M13 9PL, UK

Yizhang Zhao
Department of Social Statistics, University of Manchester, Manchester, M13 9PL, UK

Julie Clark and Angela Curl
Urban Studies, University of Glasgow, Glasgow, G12 8RS, UK

Colin Pooley
Lancaster Environment Centre, Lancaster University, Lancaster, LA1 4YQ, UK

Isobel Anderson
Faculty of Social Sciences, University of Stirling, Stirling, FK9 4LA, UK

Evelyn Dyb
Urban and Regional Research Institute, Oslo and Akershus University College, 0130 Oslo, Norway

Joe Finnerty
School of Applied Social Studies, University College Cork, Cork, Ireland

Douglas Pratt
School of Social Sciences, Faculty of Arts and Social Sciences, University of Waikato, Hamilton 3240, New Zealand
Faculty of Theology, University of Bern, 3012 Bern, Switzerland

Hanwei Li
Faculty of Education, University of Tampere, 33100 Tampere, Finland
Bielefeld Graduate School in History and Sociology, University of Bielefeld, 33615 Bielefeld, Germany

Index